CLYMER®

YAMAHA

XT600 & TT600 • 1983-1989

The world's finest publisher of mechanical how-to manuals

INTERTEC PUBLISHING
P.O. Box 12901, Overland Park, Kansas 66282-2901

FIRST EDITION
First Printing April, 1991
Second Printing December, 1992
Third Printing April, 1995
Fourth Printing August, 1997
Fifth Printing August, 1999
Sixth Printing August, 2001

Printed in U.S.A.

ISBN: 0-89287-546-1

Library of Congress: 91-55145

Technical photography by Ed Scott..

Technical and photographic assistance by Curt Jordan, Jordan Engineering, Santa Ana, California.

Technical illustrations by Mitzi McCarthy.

PRODUCTION: Elizabeth Couzens.

CLYMER PUBLICATIONS

Intertec Directory & Book Division

Chief Executive Officer Timothy M. Andrews
President Ron Wall
Vice President, Directory & Book Division Rich Hathaway

The following books and guides are published by Intertec Publishing.

CLYMER SHOP MANUALS

Boat Motors and Drives
Motorcycles and ATVs
Snowmobiles
Personal Watercraft

ABOS/INTERTEC/CLYMER BLUE BOOKS AND TRADE-IN GUIDES

Recreational Vehicles
Outdoor Power Equipment
Agricultural Tractors
Lawn and Garden Tractors
Motorcycles and ATVs
Snowmobiles and Personal Watercraft
Boats and Motors

AIRCRAFT BLUEBOOK-PRICE DIGEST

Airplanes
Helicopters

AC-U-KWIK DIRECTORIES

The Corporate Pilot's Airport/FBO Directory
International Manager's Edition
Jet Book

I&T SHOP SERVICE MANUALS

Tractors

INTERTEC SERVICE MANUALS

Snowmobiles
Outdoor Power Equipment
Personal Watercraft
Gasoline and Diesel Engines
Recreational Vehicles
Boat Motors and Drives
Motorcycles
Lawn and Garden Tractors

CONTENTS

QUICK REFERENCE DATA

TIRE INFLATION PRESSURE

	Front tire	Rear tire
XT600		
Size	3.00-S21-4PR	4.60-S18-4PR
Tire pressure		
0-198 lb. (0-90 kg)	22 psi (147 kPa)	22 psi (147 kPa)
Maximum load	22 psi (147 kPa)	26 psi (177 kPa)
High speed riding	22 psi (147 kPa)	22 psi (147 kPa)
Off-road riding	14 psi (98.1 kPa)	14 psi (98.1 kPa)
TT600		
Size	100/80-21-4PR	140/80-18-4PR
Tire pressure	14 psi (98.1 kPa)	14 psi (98.1 kPa)

RECOMMENDED LUBRICANTS AND FUEL

Engine oil	Yamalube 4-cycle oil, SAE 20W/40 or 10W/30 SE motor oil
Front fork oil	10 wt. fork oil
Air filter	Foam air filter oil
Drive chain	Chain lube recommended for O-ring drive chains
Control cables	Cable lube
Control lever pivots	10W/30 motor oil
Swing arm pivot shaft	Lithium base waterproof wheel bearing grease
Suspension pivot shaft	Molybdenum disulfide grease
Steering head bearings	Lithium base waterproof wheel bearing grease
Fuel	Regular grade—research octane 87 or higher
Brake fluid	DOT 3

APPROXIMATE REFILL CAPACITIES

Engine oil	
Periodic oil change	2,000 cc (2.1 US qt.)
With filter change	2,100 cc (2.2 US qt.)
Engine rebuild	2,400 cc (2.5 US qt.)
Front fork (each)	
XT600	481-485 cc (16.2-16.38 US oz.)
TT600	589 cc (19.9 US oz.)
Front fork oil level	
XT600	*
TT600	125 cc (4.92 oz.)
Fuel tank	
XT600	
Total	11.0 liters (2.9 US gal.)
Reserve	2 liters (0.5 US gal.)
TT600	
Total	11.0 liters (2.9 US gal.)
Reserve	3 liters (0.8 US gal.)

* Not specified by Yamaha.

MAINTENANCE AND TUNE-UP TORQUE SPECIFICATIONS

Item	N•m	ft.-lb.
Oil drain bolt		
Crankcase	30	22
Oil tank	18	13
Oil filter cover screws	10	7.2
Oil filter cover screw	7	5.1
Oil filter cover bleed screw	5	3.6
Spark plug	18	13
Front axle nut		
XT600	100	72
TT600	58	42
Rear axle nut		
XT600	100	72
TT600	105	75
Front fork cap	23	17
Front fork pinch bolts	23	17
Handlebar clamp bolts	23	17
Valve stem nut	14	10

TUNE-UP SPECIFICATIONS

Valve clearance (cold)	
XT600	
Intake	0.07-0.12 mm (0.0028-0.0047 in.)
Exhaust	0.12-0.17 mm (0.0047-0.0067 in.)
TT600	
Intake	0.05-0.10 mm (0.002-0.004 in.)
Exhaust	0.12-0.17 mm (0.0047-0.0067 in.)
Engine compression pressure	
Standard	1,079 kPa (156 psi)
Minimum	883 kPa (128 psi)
Maximum	1,177 kPa (171 psi)
Spark plugs	
Type	
XT600	NGK DP8EA-9 or ND X24EP-U9
TT600	NGK DP7EA-9
Gap	0.8-0.9 mm (0.031-0.035 in.)
Ignition timing	Fixed
Idle speed	
XT600	1,300 rpm
TT600	1,300-1,400 rpm
Drive chain free play	
XT600	30-40 mm (1.2-1.6 in.)
TT600	20-30 mm (0.8-1.2 in.)

REPLACEMENT BULBS

	XT600	TT600
Headlight	60W/55W (12V)	55W (12V)
Taillight	—	8W (12V)
Taillight/brake light	27W/8W (12V)	—
Flasher light	27W (12V)	—
License plate light	8W (12V)	—
Meter lights	3.4W (12V)	—

CLYMER®

YAMAHA

XT600 & TT600 • 1983-1989

CHAPTER ONE

GENERAL INFORMATION

This detailed, comprehensive manual covers the 1984-1989 Yamaha XT600 and the 1983-1986 TT600 single.

Troubleshooting, tune-up, maintenance and repair are not difficult, if you know what tools and equipment to use and what to do. Step-by-step instructions guide you through jobs ranging from simple maintenance to complete engine and suspension overhaul.

This manual can be used by anyone from a first time do-it-yourselfer to a professional mechanic. Detailed drawings and clear photographs give you all the information you need to do the work right.

Some of the procedures in this manual require the use of special tools. The resourceful mechanic can, in many cases, think of acceptable substitutes for special tools—there is always another way. This can be as simple as using a few pieces of threaded rod, washers and nuts to remove or install a bearing or fabricating a tool from scrap material. However, using a substitute for a special tool is not recommended as it can be dangerous and may damage the part. If you find that a tool can be designed and safely made, but will require some type of machine work, you may want to search out a local community college or high school that has a machine shop curriculum. Shop teachers sometimes welcome outside work that can be used as practical shop applications for advanced students.

Table 1 lists model coverage with engine serial numbers.

Metric and U.S. standards are used throughout this manual. U.S. to metric conversion is given in **Table 2**.

Tables 1-5 are found at the end of the chapter.

MANUAL ORGANIZATION

This chapter provides general information and discusses equipment and tools useful both for preventive maintenance and troubleshooting.

Chapter Two provides methods and suggestions for quick and accurate diagnosis and repair of problems. Troubleshooting procedures discuss typical symptoms and logical methods to pinpoint the trouble.

Chapter Three explains all periodic lubrication and routine maintenance necessary to keep your Yamaha operating well and competitive. Chapter Three also includes recommended tune-up procedures, eliminating the need to constantly consult other chapters on the various assemblies.

Subsequent chapters describe specific systems such as the engine top end, engine bottom end, clutch, transmission, fuel, exhaust, electrical, suspension, steering and brakes. Each chapter provides disassembly, repair, and assembly procedures in simple step-by-step form. If a repair is impractical for a home mechanic, it is so indicated. It is usually faster and less expensive to take such repairs to a Yamaha dealer or competent repair shop. Specifications concerning a particular system are included at the end of the appropriate chapter.

NOTES, CAUTIONS AND WARNINGS

The terms NOTE, CAUTION and WARNING have specific meanings in this manual. A NOTE provides additional information to make a step or procedure easier or clearer. Disregarding a NOTE could cause inconvenience, but would not cause damage or personal injury.

A CAUTION emphasizes areas where equipment damage could occur. Disregarding a CAUTION could cause permanent mechanical damage; however, personal injury is unlikely.

A WARNING emphasizes areas where personal injury or even death could result from negligence. Mechanical damage may also occur. WARNINGS *are to be taken seriously.* In some cases, serious injury and death has resulted from disregarding similar warnings.

SAFETY FIRST

Professional mechanics can work for years and never sustain a serious injury. If you observe a few rules of common sense and safety, you can enjoy many safe hours servicing your own machine. If you ignore these rules you can hurt yourself or damage the equipment.

1. *Never* use gasoline as a cleaning solvent.
2. *Never* smoke or use a torch in the vicinity of flammable liquids, such as cleaning solvent, in open containers.
3. If welding or brazing is required on the machine, remove the fuel tank and rear shock to a safe distance, at least 50 feet away.
4. Use the proper sized wrenches to avoid damage to fasteners and injury to yourself.
5. When loosening a tight or stuck nut, be guided by what would happen if the wrench should slip. Be careful; protect yourself accordingly.
6. When replacing a fastener, make sure to use one with the same measurements and strength as the old one. Incorrect or mismatched fasteners can result in damage to the vehicle and possible personal injury. Beware of fastener kits that are filled with cheap and poorly made nuts, bolts, washers and cotter pins. Refer to *Fasteners* in this chapter for additional information.
7. Keep all hand and power tools in good condition. Wipe greasy and oily tools after using them. They are difficult to hold and can cause injury. Replace or repair worn or damaged tools.
8. Keep your work area clean and uncluttered.
9. Wear safety goggles during all operations involving drilling, grinding, the use of a cold chisel or anytime you feel unsure about the safety of your eyes. Safety goggles should also be worn anytime solvent and compressed air is used to clean a part.
10. Keep an approved fire extinguisher (**Figure 1**) nearby. Be sure it is rated for gasoline (Class B) and electrical (Class C) fires.
11. When drying bearings or other rotating parts with compressed air, never allow the air jet to rotate the bearing or part. The air jet is capable of rotating them at speeds far in excess of those for which they were designed. The bearing or rotating part is very likely to disintegrate and cause serious injury and damage. To prevent bearing damage when using compressed air, hold the inner bearing race by hand (**Figure 2**).

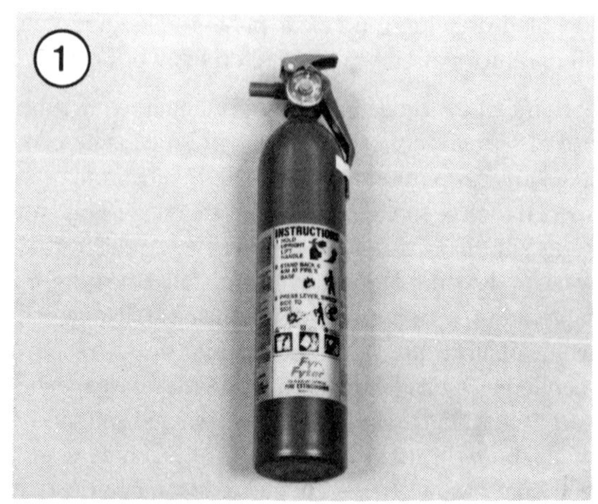

SERVICE HINTS

Most of the service procedures covered are straightforward and can be performed by anyone reasonably handy with tools. It is suggested, however, that you consider your own capabilities carefully before attempting any operation involving major disassembly of the engine or transmission.

Take your time and do the job right. Do not forget that a newly rebuilt engine must be broken in the same way as a new one. Keep the rpm's within the limits given in your Yamaha owner's manual when you get back on the road or out in the dirt.

1. "Front," as used in this manual, refers to the front of the motorcycle; the front of any component is the end closest to the front of the motorcycle. The "left-" and "right-hand" sides refer to the position of the parts as viewed by a rider sitting on the seat facing forward. For example, the throttle control is on the right-hand side. These rules are simple, but confusion can cause a major inconvenience during service.

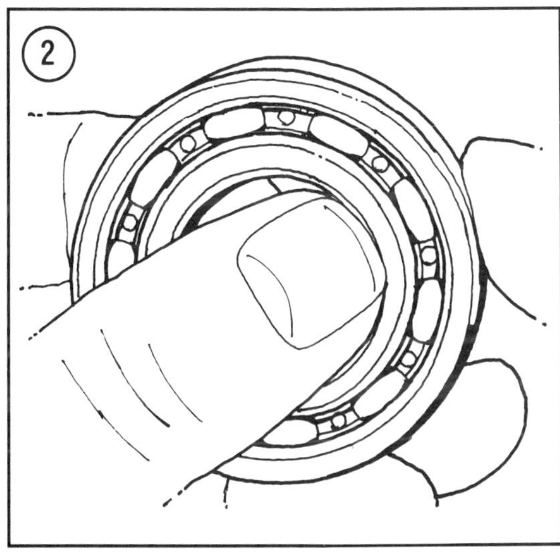

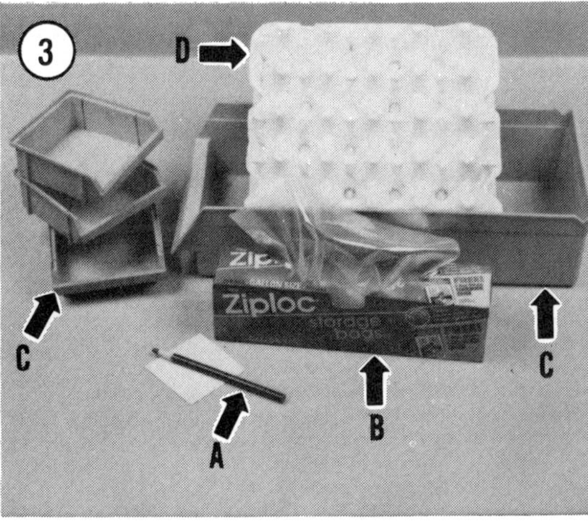

2. Whenever servicing the engine or clutch, or when removing a suspension component, the bike should be secured in a safe manner. An excellent support for Yamaha is a wooden box or stand. A sturdy box can be made with 3/4 in. plywood that will last a long time if constructed well.

WARNING

Never disconnect the positive (+) battery cable unless the negative (–) cable has first been disconnected. Disconnecting the positive cable while the negative cable is still connected may cause a spark. This could ignite hydrogen gas given off by the battery, causing an explosion.

3. Disconnect the negative battery cable when working on or near the electrical, clutch, or starter systems and before disconnecting any electrical wires. On most batteries, the negative terminal will be marked with a minus (–) sign and the positive terminal with a plus (+) sign.

4. Tag all similar internal parts for location and mark all mating parts for position (A, **Figure 3**). Record number and thickness of any shims as they are removed. Small parts such as bolts can be identified by placing them in plastic sandwich bags (B, **Figure 3**). Seal and label them with masking tape.

5. Place parts from a specific area of the engine (e.g., cylinder head, cylinder, clutch, shift mechanism, etc.) into plastic boxes (C, **Figure 3**) to keep them separated.

6. When disassembling transmission shaft assemblies, use an egg flat (the type that restaurants get their eggs in) (D, **Figure 3**) and set the parts from the shaft in one of the depressions in the same order in which they were removed.

7. Wiring should be tagged with masking tape and marked as each wire is removed. Again, do not rely on memory alone.

8. Finished surfaces should be protected from physical damage or corrosion. Keep gasoline and brake fluid off painted surfaces.

9. Use penetrating oil on frozen or tight bolts, then strike the bolt head a few times with a hammer and

punch (use a screwdriver on screws). Avoid the use of heat where possible, as it can warp, melt or affect the temper of parts. Heat also ruins finishes, especially paint and plastics.

10. No parts removed or installed (other than bushings and bearings) in the procedures given in this manual should require unusual force during disassembly or assembly. If a part is difficult to remove or install, find out why before proceeding.

11. Cover all openings after removing parts or components to prevent dirt, small tools, etc. from falling in.

12. Read each procedure *completely* while looking at the actual parts before starting a job. Make sure you *thoroughly* understand what is to be done and then carefully follow the procedure, step by step.

13. Recommendations are occasionally made to refer service or maintenance to a Yamaha dealer or a specialist in a particular field. In these cases, the work will be done more quickly and economically than if you performed the job yourself.

14. In procedural steps, the term "replace" means to discard a defective part and replace it with a new or exchange unit. "Overhaul" means to remove, disassemble, inspect, measure, repair or replace defective parts, reassemble and install major systems or parts.

15. Some operations require the use of a hydraulic press. It would be wiser to have these operations performed by a shop equipped for such work, rather than to try to do the job yourself with makeshift equipment that may damage your machine.

16. Repairs go much faster and easier if your machine is clean before you begin work. There are many special cleaners on the market, like Bel-Ray Degreaser, for washing the engine and related parts. Follow the manufacturer's directions on the container for the best results. Clean all oily or greasy parts with cleaning solvent as you remove them. See *Washing the Bike* in this chapter.

WARNING

***Never** use gasoline as a cleaning agent. It presents an extreme fire hazard. Be sure to work in a well-ventilated area when using cleaning solvent. Keep a fire extinguisher, rated for gasoline fires, handy just in case.*

CAUTION

If you use a car wash to clean your bike, don't direct the high pressure water hose at fork seals, steering bearings, carburetor hoses, suspension linkage components, wheel bearings and electrical components (e.g., instrument cluster). The water will flush grease out of the bearings or damage the seals. After washing your bike, remove the wheels and clean the wheel drums (if so equipped) of all water and dirt.

17. Much of the labor charges for repairs made by dealers are for the time involved in the removal, disassembly, assembly, and reinstallation of other parts in order to reach the defective part. It is frequently possible to perform the preliminary operations yourself and then take the defective unit to the dealer for repair at considerable savings.

18. If special tools are required, make arrangements to get them before you start. It is frustrating and time-consuming to get partly into a job and then be unable to complete it.

19. Make diagrams (or take a Polaroid picture) wherever similar-appearing parts are found. For instance, crankcase bolts are often not the same length. You may think you can remember where everything came from—but mistakes are costly. There is also the possibility that you may be sidetracked and not return to work for days or even weeks—in which time carefully laid out parts may have become disturbed.

20. When assembling parts, be sure all shims and washers are replaced exactly as they came out.

21. Whenever a rotating part butts against a stationary part, look for a shim or washer. Use new gaskets if there is any doubt about the condition of the old

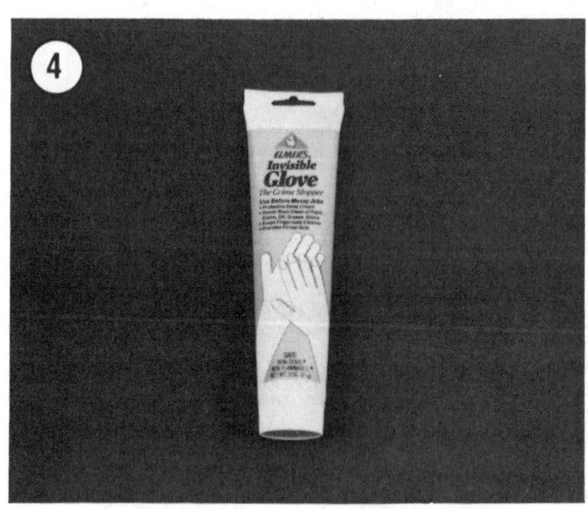

ones. A thin coat of oil on non-pressure type gaskets may help them seal more effectively.

22. High spots may be sanded off a piston with sandpaper, but fine emery cloth and oil will do a much more professional job.

23. Carbon can be removed from the head, the piston crowns and the exhaust ports with a dull screwdriver. Do *not* scratch machined surfaces. Wipe off the surface with a clean cloth when finished.

24. A baby bottle makes a good measuring device for adding oil to the front forks. Get one that is graduated in fluid ounces and cubic centimeters. After it has been used for this purpose, do *not* let a small child drink out of it as there will always be an oil residue in it.

25. If it is necessary to make a clutch cover or ignition cover gasket and you do not have a suitable old gasket to use as a guide, you can use the outline of the cover and gasket material to make a new gasket. Apply engine oil to the cover gasket surface. Then place the cover on the new gasket material and apply pressure with your hands. The oil will leave a very accurate outline on the gasket material that can be cut around.

CAUTION

When purchasing gasket material to make a gasket, measure the thickness of the old gasket and purchase gasket material with the same approximate thickness.

26. Heavy grease can be used to hold small parts in place if they tend to fall out during assembly. However, keep grease and oil away from electrical and brake components.

27. A carburetor is best cleaned by disassembling it and soaking the parts in a commercial carburetor cleaner. Never soak gaskets and rubber parts in these cleaners. Never use wire to clean out jets and air passages. They are easily damaged. Use compressed air to blow out the carburetor only if the float has been removed first.

28. There are many items available that can be used on your hands before and after working on your bike. A little preparation prior to getting "all greased up" will help when cleaning up later. Before starting out, work Vaseline, soap or a product such as Invisible Glove (**Figure 4**) onto your forearms, into your hands and under your fingernails and cuticles. This will make cleanup a lot easier. For cleanup, use a waterless hand soap such as Sta-Lube and then finish up with powdered Boraxo and a fingernail brush (**Figure 5**).

WASHING THE BIKE

The Yamaha TT600 is an off-road motorcycle and if you are riding it often and maintaining it properly, you will spend a good deal of time cleaning it. The Yamaha XT600 is a dual-purpose motorcycle that is meant to be ridden on the highway as well as off road. If you are doing a lot of off-road riding and maintaining it properly, you will spend a good deal of time cleaning it. After riding your Yamaha off-road, wash the bike. It will make maintenance and service procedures quick and easy. More important, proper cleaning will prevent dirt from falling into critical areas undetected. Failing to clean the bike or cleaning it incorrectly will add to your maintenance costs and shop time because dirty parts wear out prematurely. It's unthinkable that your bike could break because of improper cleaning, but it can happen.

When cleaning your Yamaha, you will need a few tools, shop rags, scrub brush, bucket, liquid cleaner and access to water. Many riders use a coin-operated car wash. Coin-operated car washes are convenient and quick, but with improper use, the high water pressures can do more damage than good to your bike.

NOTE

A safe biodegradable, non-toxic and non-flammable liquid cleaner that works well for washing your bike as well as for removing grease and oil from engine and suspension parts is Simple Green. Simple Green can be purchased through some supermarkets, hardware, garden and discount supply houses. Follow the directions on the container for recommended dilution ratios.

When cleaning your bike, and especially when using a spray type degreaser, remember that what goes on the bike will rinse off and drip onto your driveway or into your yard. If you can, use a degreaser at a coin-operated car wash. If you are cleaning your bike at home, place thick cardboard or newspapers underneath the bike to catch the oil and grease deposits that are rinsed off.

CAUTION

*The factory installed drive chain on all XT600 and TT600 models has O-rings installed between the chain plates. Lubrication for the chain pins is sealed by the O-rings (**Figure 6**). However, the chain rollers require external oiling. For the O-ring chain to work properly, it requires proper cleaning and lubrication practices. Do not clean the O-ring drive chain with a high-pressure water hose, such as those found in coin-operated car washes. The high pressure can damage the O-rings and cause premature chain failure. If you are using a degreaser to clean your bike, note that the degreaser may damage the chain's rubber or neoprene O-rings. Always check that the degreaser is specified for use on O-ring type chains. See **Chain Cleaning** in Chapter Three for additional information on drive chain cleaning and lubrication. If possible, remove the drive chain before cleaning the bike.*

1. Place the bike on a stand.

2. Check the following before washing the bike:

   a. Make sure the gas cap is screwed on tightly.

   b. Make sure the oil fill cap is tight.

   c. Plug the silencer opening with a large cork or rag.

3. Wash the bike from top to bottom with soapy water. Use the scrub brush to get excess dirt out of the wheel rims and engine crannies. Concentrate on the upper controls, engine, side panels and gas tank during this wash cycle. Don't forget to wash dirt and mud from underneath the fenders and engine crankcase.

4. Remove the gas tank, side panels and seat. Wrap a plastic bag around the ignition coil and CDI unit. Concentrate the second wash cycle on the frame tube

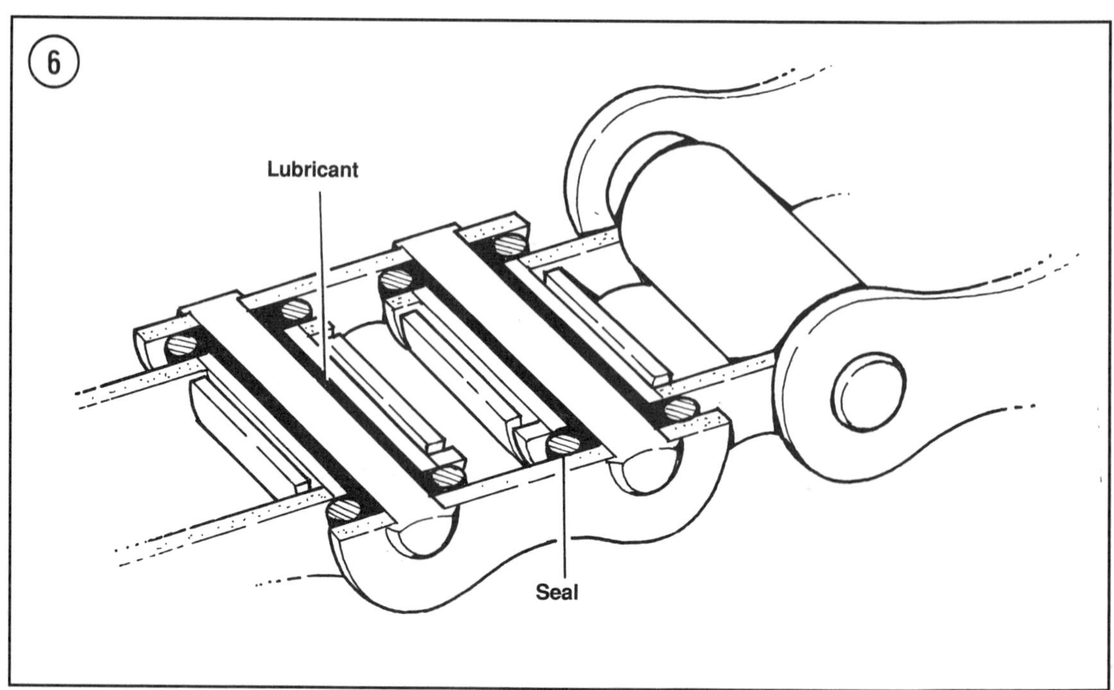

members, outer airbox areas, suspension linkage, rear shock and swing arm.

5. Direct the hose underneath the engine and swing arm. Wash this area thoroughly. If this area is extremely dirty, you may want to lay the bike on its side. Protect the finish when laying the bike down.

6. The final wash is the rinse. Use cold water without soap and spray the entire motorcycle again. Use as much time and care when rinsing the bike as when washing it. Built up soap deposits will quickly corrode electrical connections and remove the natural oils from tires, causing premature cracks and wear. Make sure you thoroughly rinse the bike off.

7. Tip the bike from side-to-side to allow any water that has collected on horizontal surfaces to drain off.

8. If you are washing the bike at home, start the engine. Idle the engine to burn off any internal moisture. Idle the bike long enough to use the gas remaining in the float bowl. This will prevent fuel leakage problems when cleaning the carburetor later.

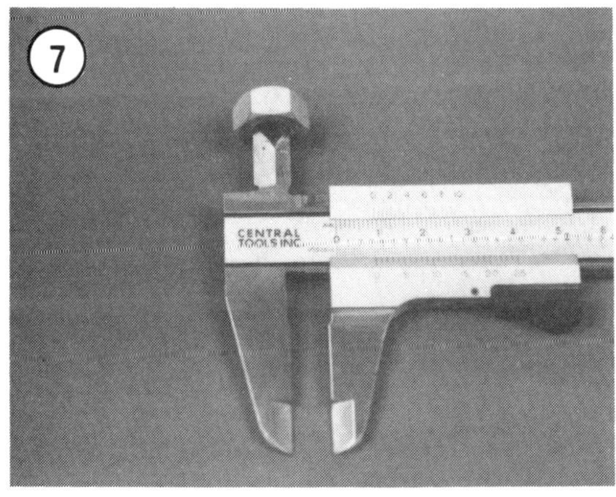

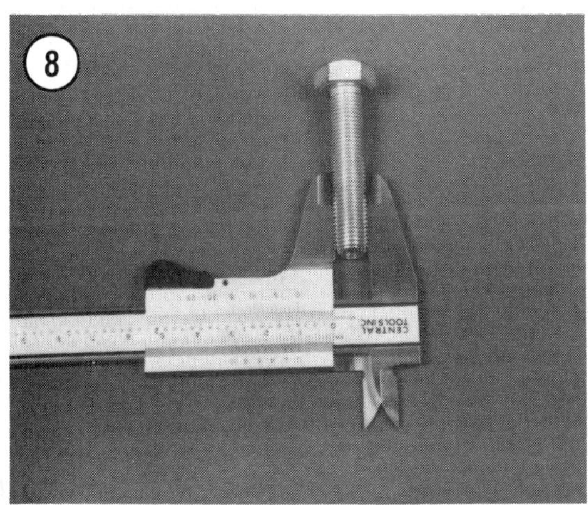

9. Before taking the bike into the garage, wipe it dry with a shop rag. Inspect the machine as you dry it for further signs of dirt and grime. Make a quick visual inspection of the frame and other painted pieces. Spray any worn-down spots with WD-40 or Bel-Ray 6-in-1 to prevent rust from building on the bare metal. When the bike is back at your work area, you can repaint the bare areas with touch-up paint after wiping off the WD-40. A quick shot from a touch-up paint can each time you work on the bike will keep it looking sharp and stop rust from building and weakening parts.

10. Lubricate the drive chain with a specially approved drive chain lubricant specified for O-ring use. See Chapter Three.

TORQUE SPECIFICATIONS

Torque specifications throughout this manual are given in Newton-meters (N•m) and foot-pounds (ft.-lb.).

Existing torque wrenches calibrated in meter kilograms can be used by performing a simple conversion. All you have to do is move the decimal point one place to the right; for example, 3.5 mkg = 35 N•m. This conversion is accurate enough for mechanical work even though the exact mathematical conversion is 3.5 mkg = 34.3 N•m.

Refer to **Table 3** for standard torque specifications for various size screws, bolts and nuts that may not be listed in the respective chapters. To use the table, first determine the size of the bolt or nut. Use a vernier caliper and measure the inside dimension of the threads of the nut (**Figure 7**) and across the threads for a bolt (**Figure 8**).

FASTENERS

The materials and designs of the various fasteners used on your Yamaha are not arrived at by chance or accident. Fastener design determines the type of tool required to work the fastener. Fastener material is carefully selected to decrease the possibility of physical failure.

Nuts, bolts and screws are manufactured in a wide range of thread patterns. To join a nut and bolt, the diameter of the bolt and the diameter of the hole in the nut must be the same. It is just as important that the threads on both be properly matched.

The best way to tell if the threads on 2 fasteners are matched is to turn the nut on the bolt (or the bolt into the threaded hole in a piece of equipment) with fingers only. Be sure both pieces are clean. If much force is required, check the thread condition on each fastener. If the thread condition is good but the fasteners jam, the threads are not compatible. A thread pitch gauge (**Figure 9**) can also be used to determine pitch. Yamaha motorcycles are manufactured with ISO (International Organization for Standardization) metric fasteners. The threads are cut differently than that of American fasteners (**Figure 10**).

Most threads are cut so that the fastener must be turned clockwise to tighten it. These are called right-hand threads. Some fasteners have left-hand threads; they must be turned counterclockwise to be tightened. Left-hand threads are used in locations where normal rotation of the equipment would tend to loosen a right-hand threaded fastener.

ISO Metric Screw Threads

ISO (International Organization for Standardization) metric threads come in 3 standard thread sizes: coarse, fine and constant pitch. The ISO coarse pitch is used for most all common fastener applications. The fine pitch thread is used on certain precision tools and instruments. The constant pitch thread is used mainly on machine parts and not for fasteners. The constant pitch thread, however, is used on all metric thread spark plugs.

ISO metric threads are specified by the capital letter M followed by the diameter in millimeters and the pitch (or the distance between each thread) in millimeters. For example, a M8 - 1.25 bolt is one that has a diameter of 8 millimeters with a distance of 1.25 millimeters between each thread. The measurement across 2 flats on the head of the bolt (**Figure 11**) indicates the proper wrench size to be used. **Figure 12** shows how to determine bolt diameter.

NOTE
*When purchasing a bolt from a dealer or parts store, it is important to know how to specify bolt length. The correct way to measure bolt length is by measuring the length starting from underneath the bolt head to the end of the bolt (**Figure 13**). Always measure bolt*

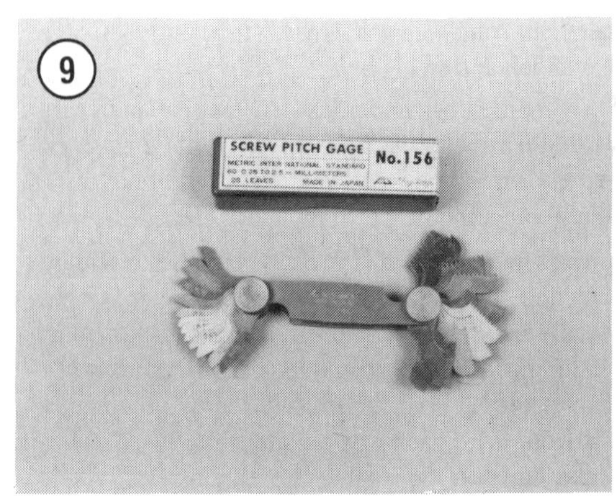

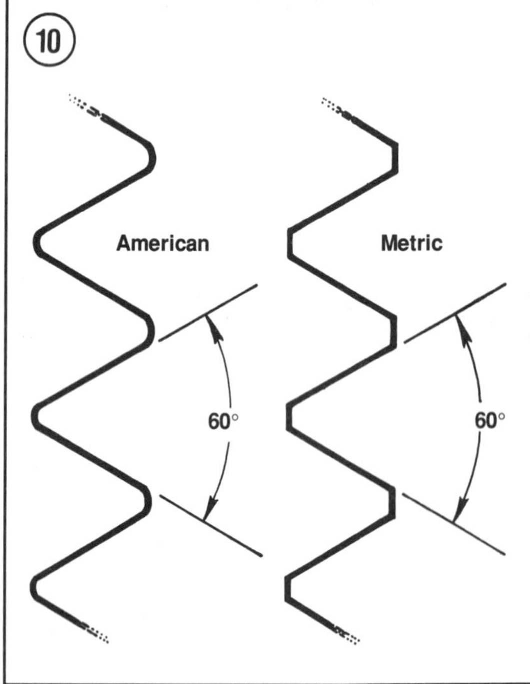

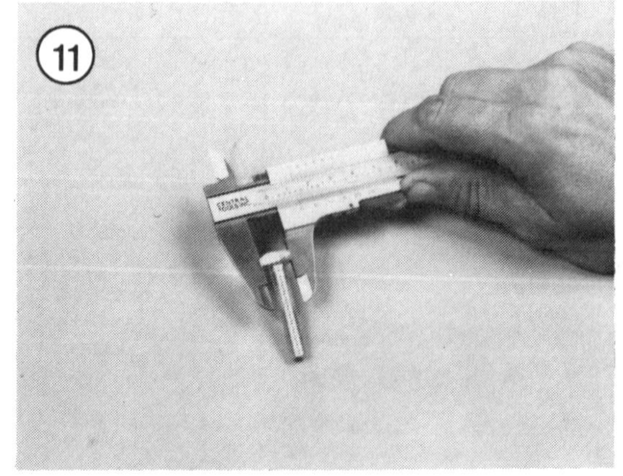

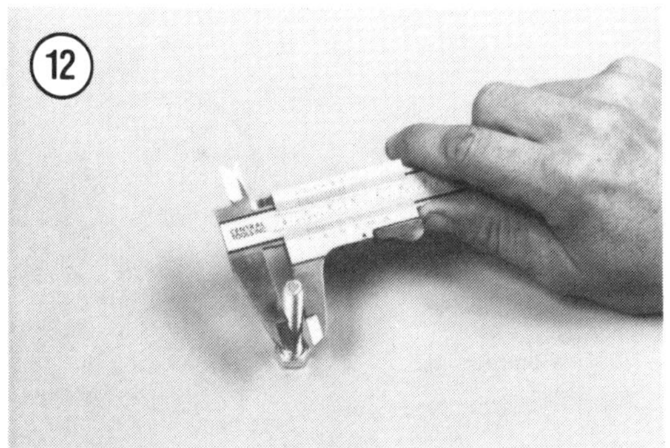

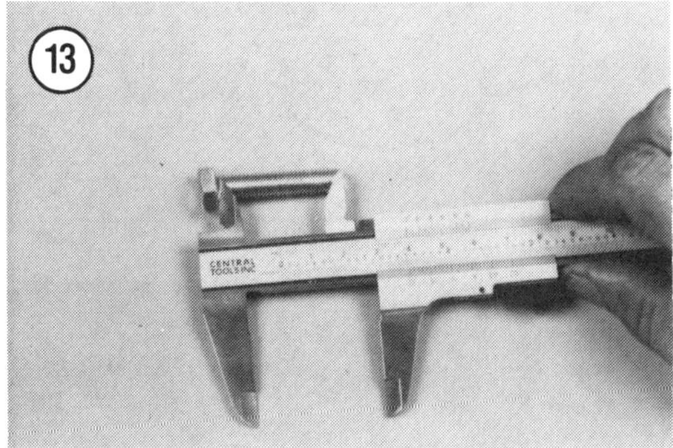

length in this manner to prevent from purchasing bolts that are too long.

Machine Screws

There are many different types of machine screws. **Figure 14** shows a number of screw heads requiring different types of turning tools. Heads are also designed to protrude above the metal (round) or to be slightly recessed in the metal (flat). See **Figure 15**.

Bolts

Commonly called bolts, the technical name for these fasteners is cap screws. Metric bolts are described by the diameter and pitch (or the distance between each thread). For example, a M8 - 1.25 bolt is one that has a diameter of 8 millimeters and a distance of 1.25 millimeters between each thread. The measurement across 2 flats on the head of the bolt (**Figure 11**) indicates the proper wrench size to be used. Use a vernier caliper and measure across

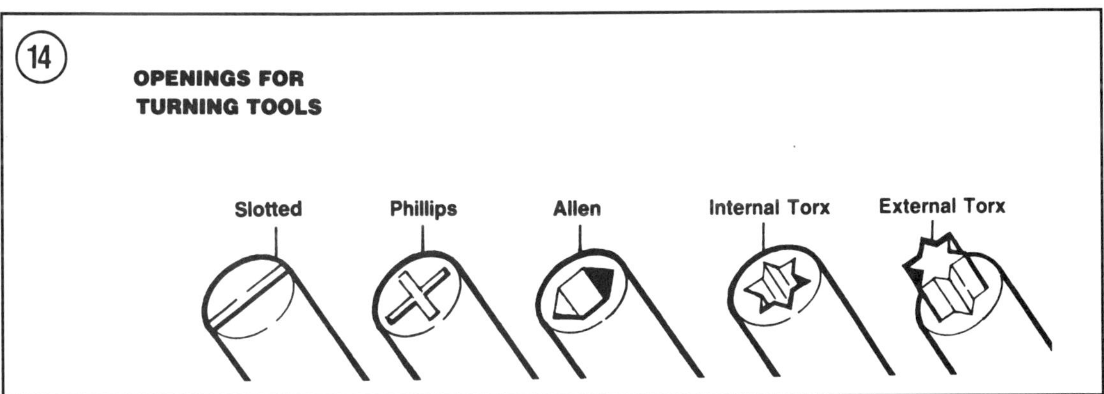

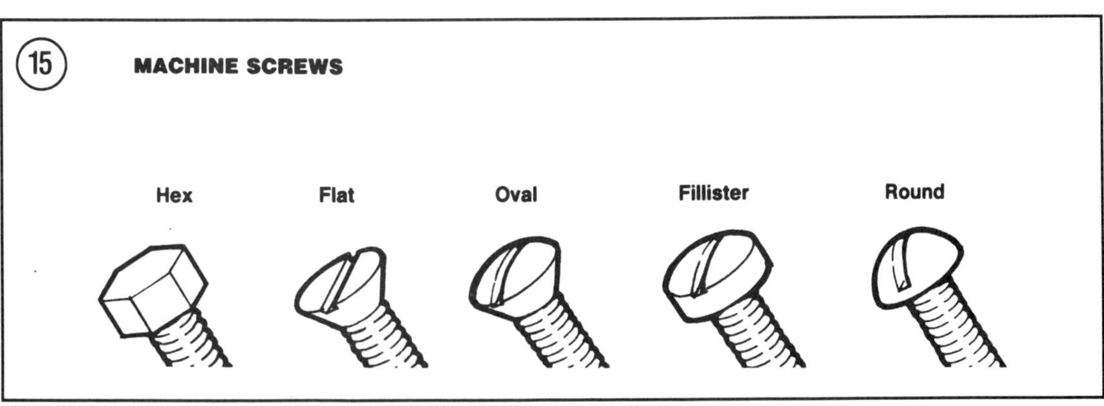

the threads (**Figure 12**) to determine the bolt diameter and to measure the length (**Figure 13**).

Nuts

Nuts are manufactured in a variety of types and sizes. Most are hexagonal (6-sided) and fit on bolts, screws and studs with the same diameter and pitch.

Figure 16 shows several types of nuts. The common nut is generally used with a lockwasher. Self-locking nuts have a nylon insert which prevents the nut from loosening; no lockwasher is required. Wing nuts are designed for fast removal by hand. Wing nuts are used for convenience in non-critical locations.

To indicate the size of a metric nut, manufacturers specify the diameter of the opening and the thread pitch. This is similar to bolt specifications, but without the length dimension. The measurement across 2 flats on the nut indicates the proper wrench size to be used (**Figure 17**).

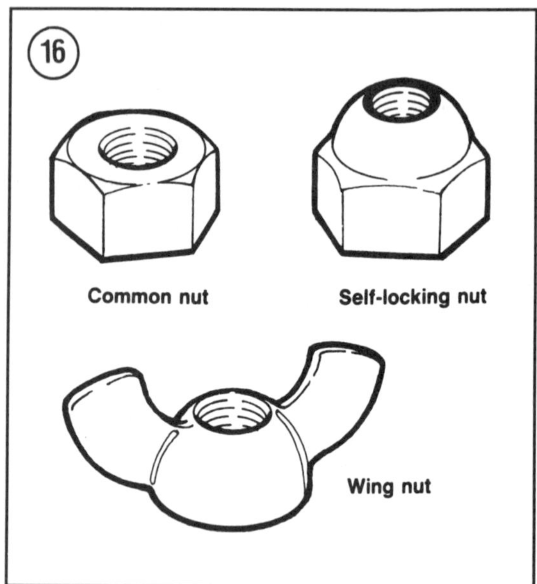

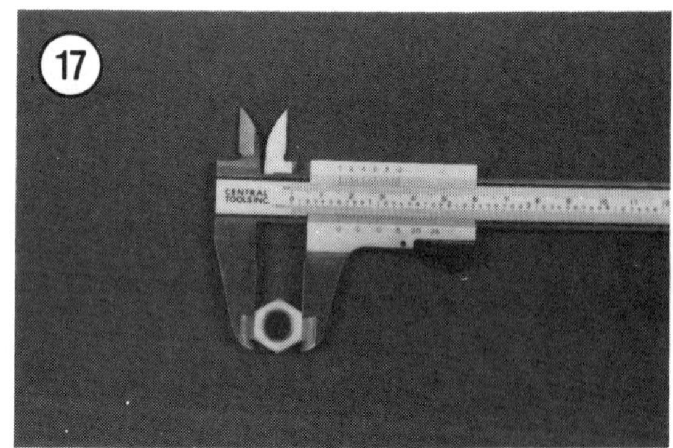

Self-locking Fasteners

Several types of bolts, screws and nuts incorporate a system that develops an interference between the bolt, screw, nut or tapped hole threads. Interference is achieved in various ways: by distorting threads, coating threads with dry adhesive or nylon, distorting the top of an all-metal nut, using a nylon insert in the center or at the top of a nut, etc.

Self-locking fasteners offer greater holding strength and better vibration resistance. Some self-locking fasteners can be reused if in good condition. Others, like the nylon insert nut, form an initial locking condition when the nut is first installed; the nylon forms closely to the bolt thread pattern, thus reducing any tendency for the nut to loosen. When the nut is removed, the locking efficiency is greatly reduced. For greatest safety, it is recommended that you install new self-locking fasteners whenever they are removed.

Washers

There are 2 basic types of washers: flat washers and lockwashers. Flat washers are simple discs with a hole to fit a screw or bolt. Lockwashers are designed to prevent a fastener from working loose due

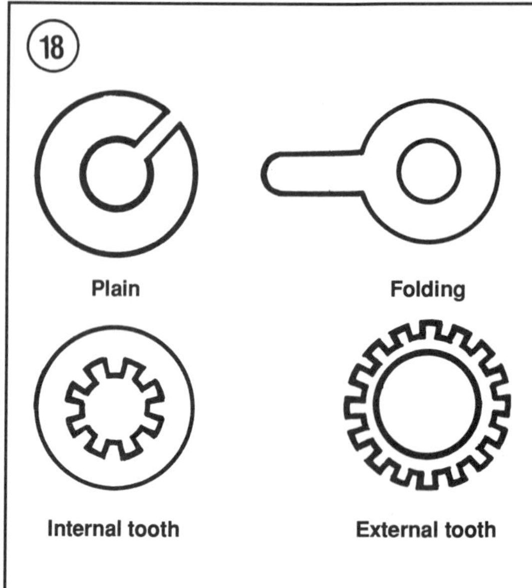

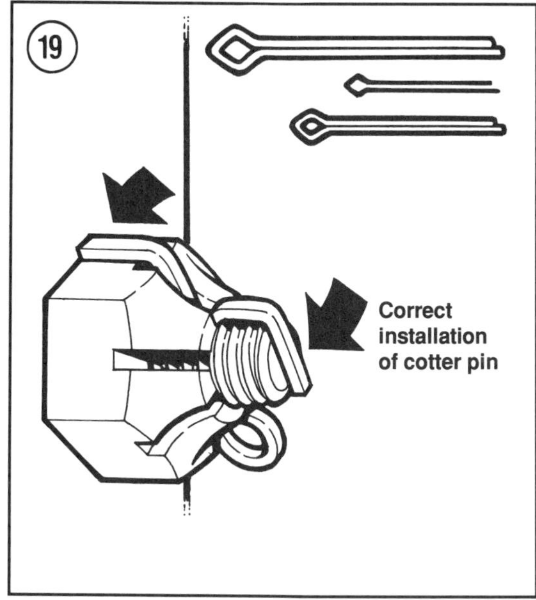

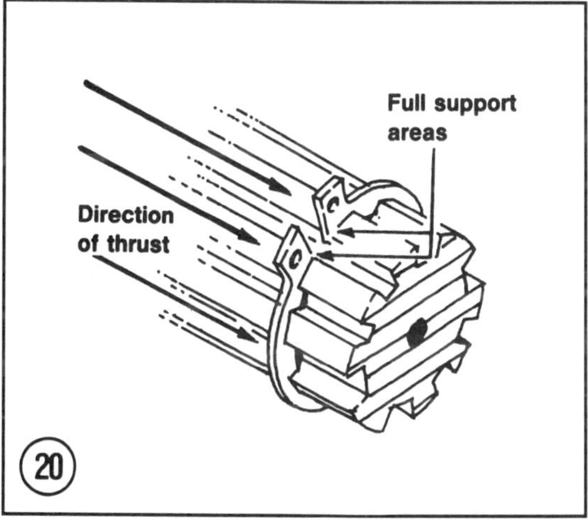

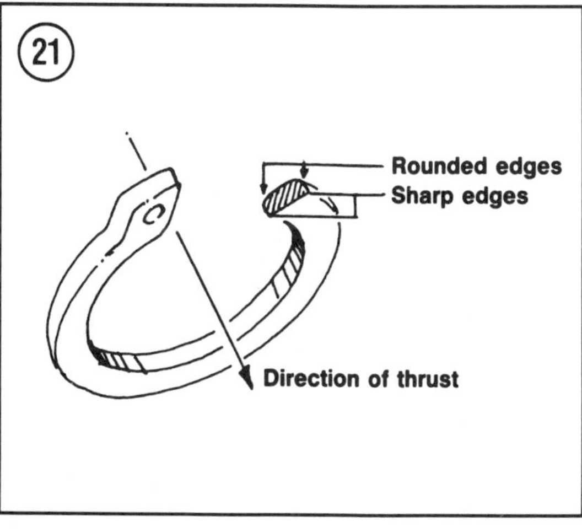

to vibration, expansion and contraction. **Figure 18** shows several types of washers. Washers are also used in the following functions:

a. As spacers.

b. To prevent galling or damage of the equipment by the fastener.

c. To help distribute fastener load during torquing.

d. As seals.

Note that flat washers are often used between a lockwasher and a fastener to provide a smooth bearing surface. This allows the fastener to be turned easily with a tool.

Cotter Pins

Cotter pins (**Figure 19**) are used to secure special kinds of fasteners. The threaded stud must have a hole in it; the nut or nut lock piece has castellations around which the cotter pin ends wrap. Cotter pins should not be reused after removal.

Circlips

Circlips or snap rings can be internal or external design. They are used to retain items on shafts (external type) or within tubes (internal type). In some applications, circlips of varying thicknesses are used to control the end play of parts assemblies. These are often called selective circlips. Circlips should be replaced during installation, as removal weakens and deforms them.

Two basic styles of circlips are available: machined and stamped circlips. Machined circlips (**Figure 20**) can be installed in either direction (shaft or housing) because both faces are machined, thus creating two sharp edges. Stamped circlips (**Figure 21**) are manufactured with one sharp edge and one rounded edge. When installing stamped circlips in a thrust situation (transmission shafts, fork tubes, etc.), the sharp edge must face away from the part producing the thrust. When installing circlips, observe the following:

a. Compress or expand circlips only enough to install them.

b. After the circlip is installed, make sure it is completely seated in its groove.

Transmission circlips become worn with use and increase side play. For this reason, always use new circlips whenever a transmission is be reassembled.

LUBRICANTS

Periodic lubrication assures long life for any type of equipment. The *type* of lubricant used is just as important as the lubrication service itself, although in an emergency the wrong type of lubricant is better than none at all. The following paragraphs describe the types of lubricants most often used on motorcycle equipment. Be sure to follow the manufacturer's recommendations for lubricant types.

Generally, all liquid lubricants are called "oil." They may be mineral-based (including petroleum bases), natural-based (vegetable and animal bases), synthetic-based or emulsions (mixtures). "Grease" is an oil to which a thickening base has been added so that the end product is semi-solid. Grease is often classified by the type of thickener added; lithium soap is commonly used.

Engine Oil

Four-stroke oil for motorcycle and automotive engines is classified by the American Petroleum Institute (API) and the Society of Automotive Engineers (SAE) in several categories. Oil containers display these classifications on the top or label.

API oil classification is indicated by letters; oils for gasoline engines are identified by an "S". Yamaha models described in this manual require SE or SF classified oil.

Viscosity is an indication of the oil's thickness. The SAE uses numbers to indicate viscosity; thin oils have low numbers while thick oils have high numbers. A "W" after the number indicates that the viscosity testing was done at low temperature to simulate cold-weather operation. Engine oils fall into the 5W-30 and 20W-50 range.

Multi-grade oils (for example 10W-40) are less viscous (thinner) at low temperatures and more viscous (thicker) at high temperatures. This allows the oil to perform efficiently across a wide range of engine operating conditions. The lower the number, the better the engine will start in cold climates. Higher numbers are usually recommended for engines running in hot weather conditions.

Grease

Greases are graded by the National Lubricating Grease Institute (NLGI). Greases are graded by number according to the consistency of the grease; these range from No. 000 to No. 6, with No. 6 being the most solid. A typical multipurpose grease is

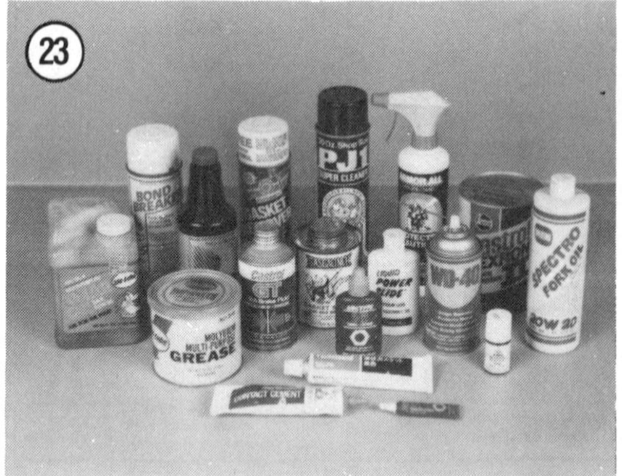

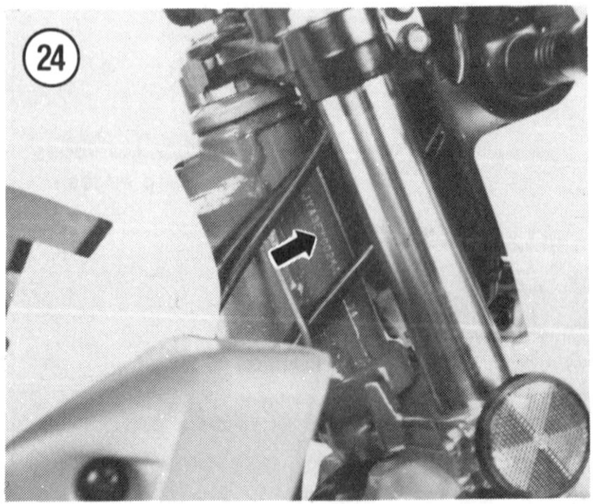

NLGI No. 2. For specific applications, equipment manufacturers may require grease with an additive such as molybdenum disulfide (MOS2) (**Figure 22**).

EXPENDABLE SUPPLIES

Certain expendable supplies are required during maintenance and repair work. These include grease, oil, gasket cement, wiping rags and cleaning solvent. Ask your dealer for the special locking compounds, silicone lubricants and other products (**Figure 23**) which make vehicle maintenance simpler and easier. Cleaning solvent or kerosene is available at some service stations or hardware stores.

WARNING
Having a stack of clean shop rags on hand is important when performing engine and suspension service work. However, to prevent the possibility of fire damage from spontaneous combustion from a pile of solvent soaked rags, store them in a lid sealed metal container until they can be washed or discarded.

NOTE
To prevent from absorbing solvent and other chemicals into your skin while cleaning parts, wear a pair of petroleum-resistant rubber gloves. These can be purchased through industrial supply houses or well-equipped hardware stores.

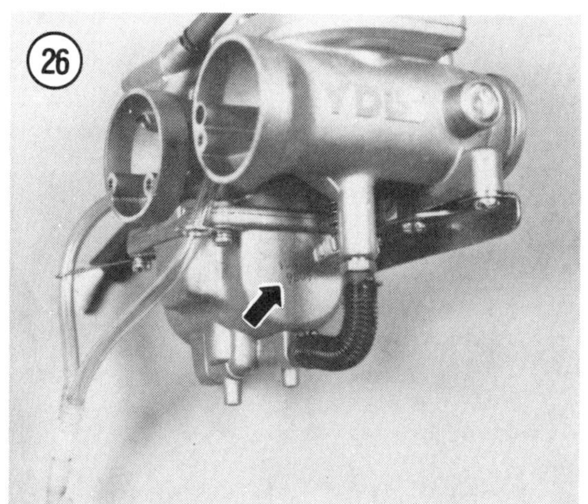

PARTS REPLACEMENT

Yamaha makes frequent changes during a model year, some minor, some relatively major. When you order parts from the dealer or other parts distributor, always order by frame and engine numbers. The frame number and the vehicle identification number are stamped on the right-hand side of the steering head pipe (**Figure 24**). The engine number is stamped on a raised pad on the right-hand crankcase (**Figure 25**). The carburetor number (**Figure 26**) is on the right-hand side of the float bowl.

Write the numbers down and carry them with you. Compare new parts to old before purchasing them. If they are not alike, have the parts manager explain the difference to you. **Table 1** lists engine and frame serial numbers for the XT600 and TT600 models covered in this manual.

NOTE
*If your Yamaha was purchased second-hand and you are not sure of its model year, use the bike's engine serial number and the information listed in **Table 1**. Read your bike's engine serial number. Then compare the number with the engine and serial numbers listed in **Table 1**. If your bike's serial number is listed in **Table 1**, cross-reference the number with the adjacent model number and year.*

EMISSION CONTROL AND BATTERY DECALS (XT600)

On models so equipped, a vehicle emission control information decal (A, **Figure 27**) is fixed to the backside of the frame's right-hand side cover. This decal lists all emission control related tune-up information.

On California models, an emission hose routing label (B, **Figure 27**) is also fixed to the back of the side cover.

A battery breather hose diagram (C, **Figure 27**) and a battery caution label (D, **Figure 27**) are fixed to the backside of the side cover. Refer to these whenever servicing or removing the battery for service.

BASIC HAND TOOLS

Many of the procedures in this manual can be carried out with simple hand tools and test equipment familiar to the average home mechanic. Keep your tools clean and in a tool box. Keep them organized with the sockets and related drives together, the open-end combination wrenches together, etc. After using a tool, wipe off dirt and grease with a clean cloth and return the tool to its correct place.

Top-quality tools are essential; they are also more economical in the long run. If you are now starting to build your tool collection, stay away from the "advertised specials" featured at some parts houses, discount stores and chain drug stores. These are usually a poor grade tool that can be sold cheaply and that is exactly what they are—*cheap*. They are usually made of inferior material, and are thick, heavy and clumsy. Their rough finish makes them difficult to clean and they usually don't last very long. If it is ever your misfortune to use such tools, you will probably find out that the wrenches do not fit the heads of bolts and nuts correctly and damage the fastener.

Quality tools are made of alloy steel and are heat treated for greater strength. They are lighter and better balanced than cheap ones. Their surface is smooth, making them a pleasure to work with and easy to clean. The initial cost of good-quality tools may be more but they are cheaper in the long run. Don't try to buy everything in all sizes in the beginning; do it a little at a time until you have the necessary tools.

The following tools are required to perform virtually any repair job on a bike. Each tool is described and the recommended size given for starting a tool collection. **Table 4** includes the tools that should be on hand for simple home repairs and/or major overhaul as shown in **Figure 28**. Additional tools and

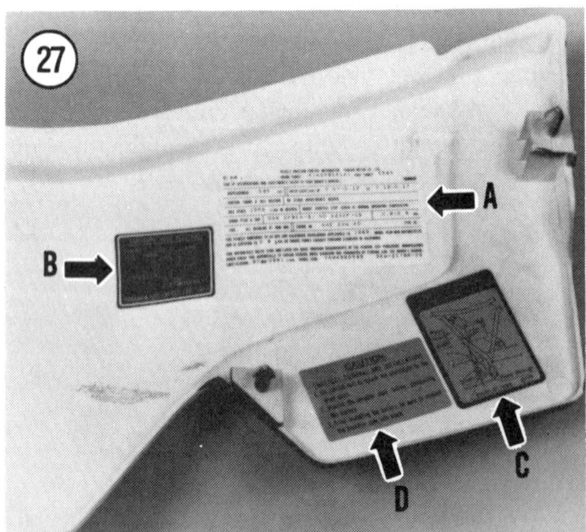

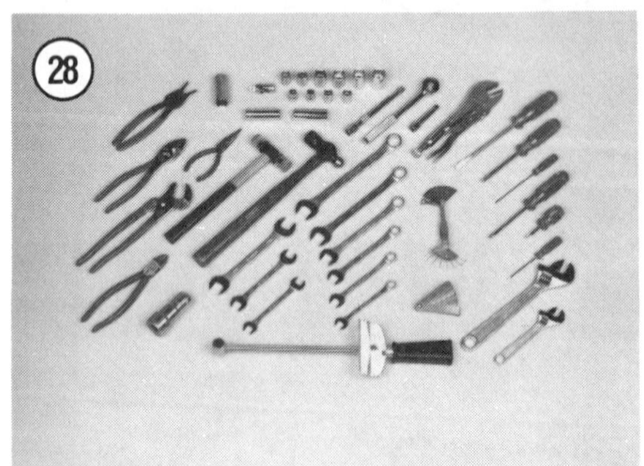

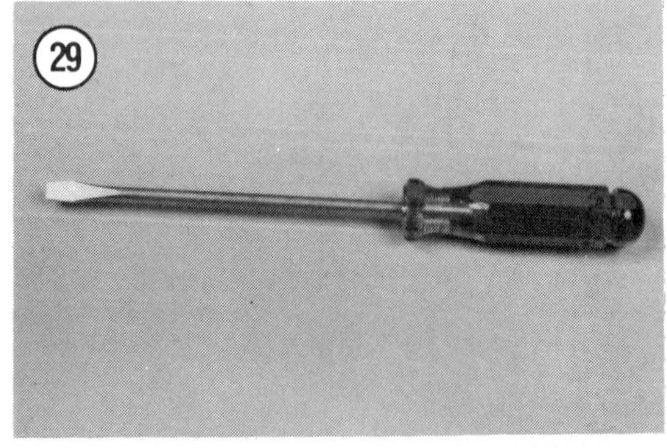

some duplicates may be added as you become more familiar with the bike. Almost all motorcycles and bikes (with the exception of the U.S. built Harley and some English bikes) use metric size bolts and nuts. If you are starting your collection now, buy metric sizes.

Screwdrivers

The screwdriver is a very basic tool, but if used improperly it will do more damage than good. The slot on a screw has a definite dimension and shape. A screwdriver must be selected to conform with that shape. Use a small screwdriver for small screws and a large one for large screws or the screw head will be damaged.

Two basic types of screwdriver are required: common (flat-blade) screwdrivers (**Figure 29**) and Phillips screwdrivers (**Figure 30**).

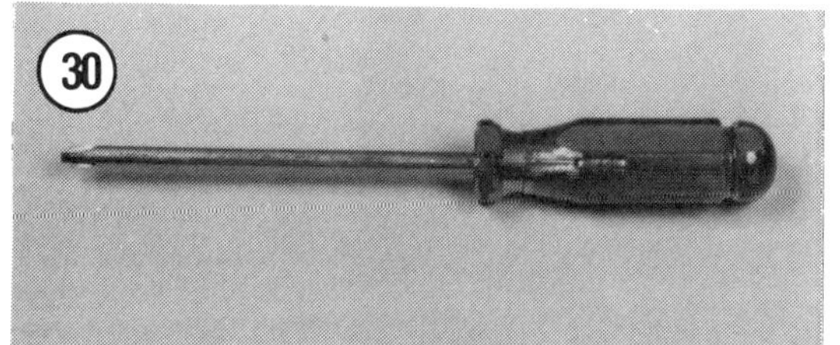

Screwdrivers are available in sets which often include an assortment of common and Phillips blades. If you buy them individually, buy at least the following:

a. Common screwdriver—5/16 × 6 in. blade.

b. Common screwdriver—3/8 × 12 in. blade.

c. Phillips screwdriver—size 2 tip, 6 in. blade.

Use screwdrivers only for driving screws. Never use a screwdriver for prying or chiseling metal. Do not try to remove a Phillips or Allen head screw with a common screwdriver (unless the screw has a combination head that will accept either type); you can damage the head so that the proper tool will be unable to remove it.

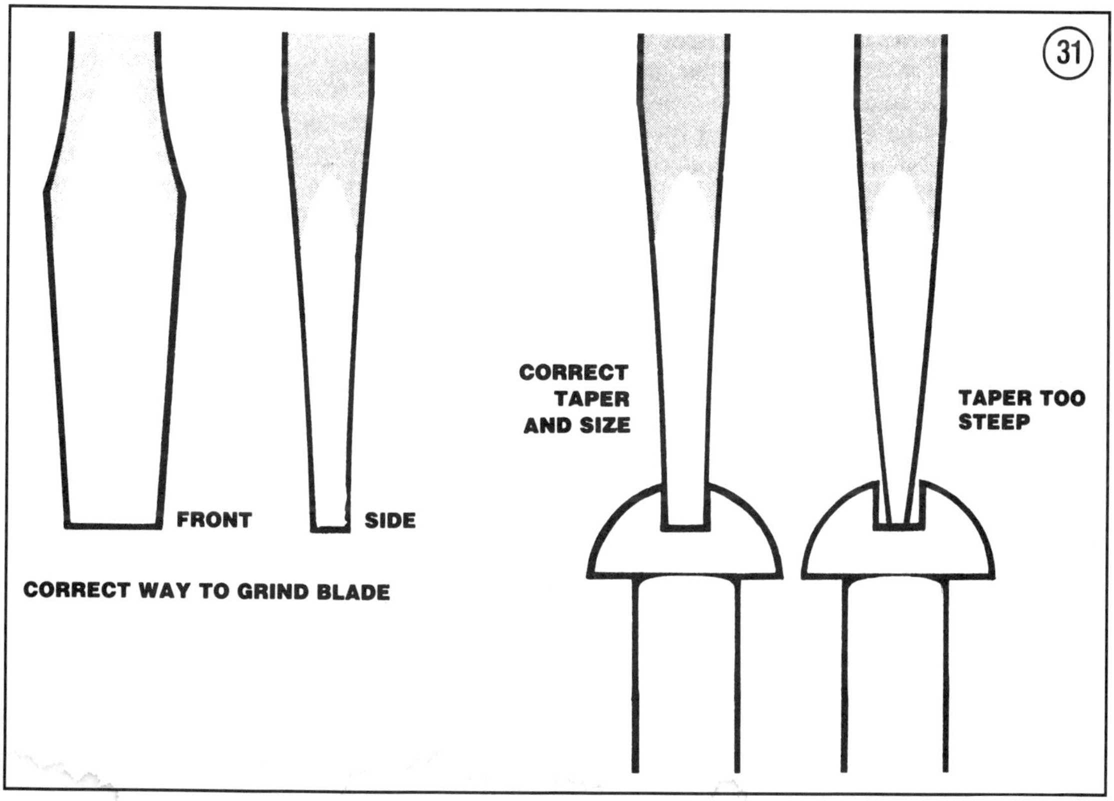

Keep screwdrivers in the proper condition and they will last longer and perform better. Always keep the tip of a common screwdriver in good condition. **Figure 31** shows how to grind the tip to the proper shape if it becomes damaged. Note the symmetrical sides of the tip.

Pliers

Pliers come in a wide range of types and sizes. Pliers are useful for cutting, bending and crimping. They should never be used to cut hardened objects or to turn bolts or nuts. **Figure 32** shows several pliers useful in motorcycle repairs.

Each type of pliers has a specialized function. Slip-joint pliers are general purpose pliers and are used mainly for holding things and for bending.

Needlenose pliers are used to hold or bend small objects. Channel-lock pliers can be adjusted to hold various sizes of objects; the jaws remain parallel to grip around objects such as pipe or tubing. There are many more types of pliers. The ones described here are most suitable for bike repairs.

Vise-grip Pliers

Vise-grip pliers (**Figure 33**) are used to hold objects very tightly like a vise. But avoid using them unless absolutely necessary since their sharp jaws will permanently scar any objects which are held. Vise-grip pliers are available in many types for more specific tasks.

Circlip Pliers

Circlip pliers (**Figure 34**) are special in that they are only used to remove circlips from shafts or within engine or suspension housings. When purchasing circlip pliers, there are two kinds to distinguish from. External pliers (spreading) are used to remove circlips that fit on the outside of a shaft. Internal pliers (squeezing) are used to remove circlips which fit inside a gear or housing.

WARNING
Because circlips can sometimes slip and "fly off" during removal and installation, always wear safety glasses.

Box-end, Open-end and Combination Wrenches

Box-end, open-end and combination wrenches are available in sets or separately in a variety of sizes. On open-end and box-end wrenches, the number stamped near the end refers to the distance between 2 parallel flats on the hex head bolt or nut. On combination wrenches, the number is stamped near the center.

Open-end wrenches are speedy and work best in areas with limited overhead access. Their wide flat jaws make them unstable for situations where the bolt or nut is sunken in a well or close to the edge of a casting. These wrenches grip only two flats of a

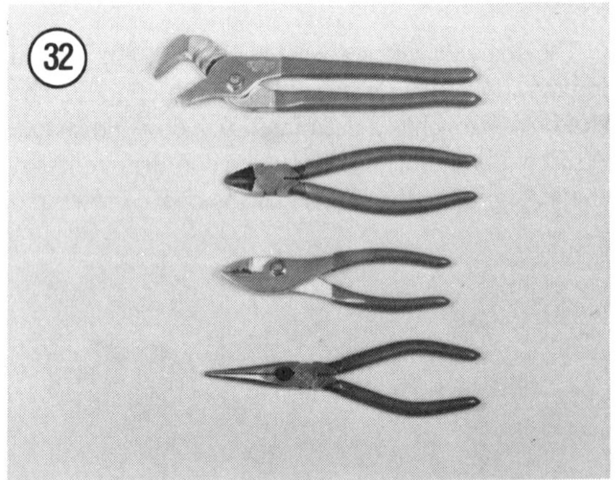

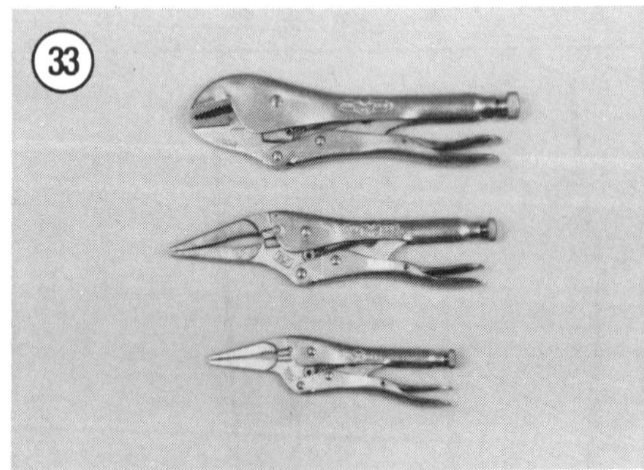

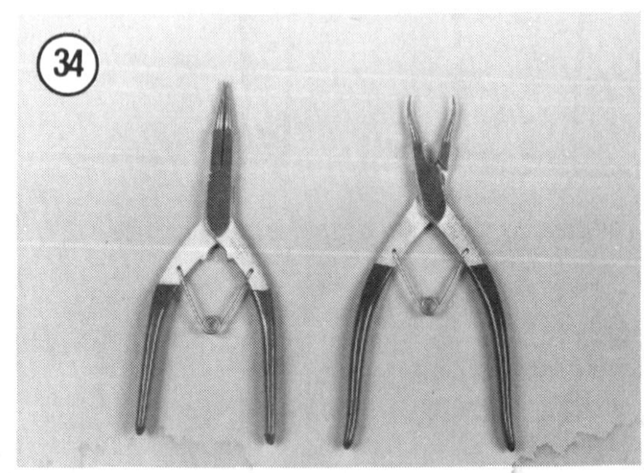

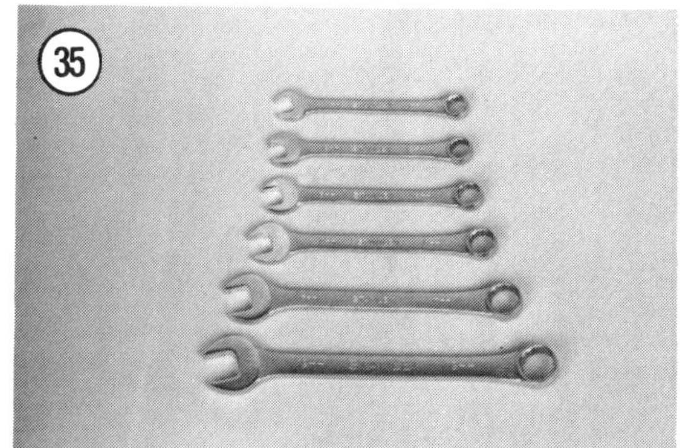
35

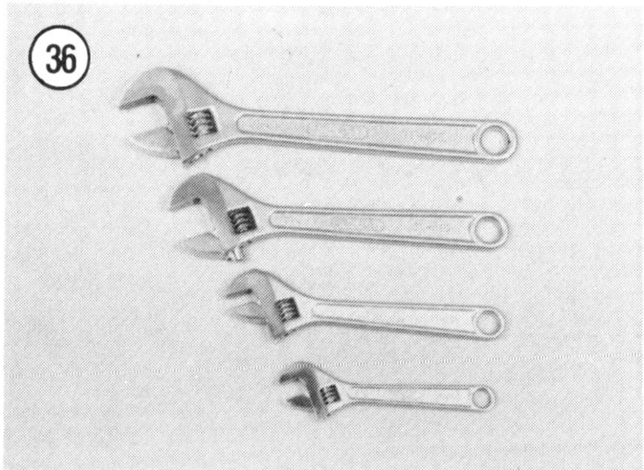
36

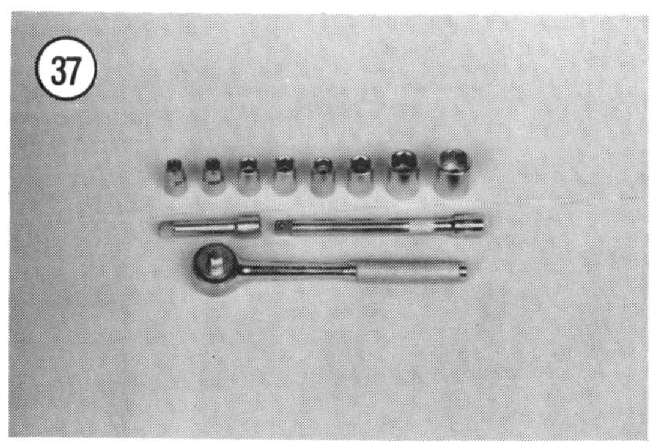
37

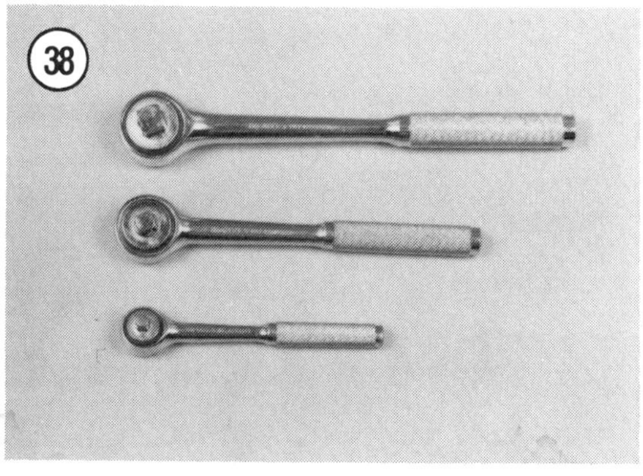
38

fastener so if either the fastener head or the wrench jaws are worn, the wrench may slip off.

Box-end wrenches require clear overhead access to the fastener but can work well in situations where the fastener head is close to another part. They grip on all six edges of a fastener for a very secure grip. They are available in either 6-point or 12-point. The 6-point gives superior holding power and durability but requires a greater swinging radius. The 12-point works better in situations with limited swinging radius.

Combination wrenches (**Figure 35**) have open-end on one side and box-end on the other with both ends being the same size. These wrenches are favored by professionals because of their versatility.

Adjustable (Crescent) Wrenches

An adjustable wrench (sometimes called crescent wrench) can be adjusted to fit nearly any nut or bolt head which has clear access around its entire perimeter. Adjustable wrenches (**Figure 36**) are best used as a backup wrench to keep a large nut or bolt from turning while the other end is being loosened or tightened with a proper wrench.

Adjustable wrenches have only two gripping surfaces which make them more subject to slipping off the fastener and damaging the part and possibly injuring your hand. The fact that one jaw is adjustable only aggravates this shortcoming.

These wrenches are directional; the solid jaw must be the one transmitting the force. If you use the adjustable jaw to transmit the force, it will loosen and possibly slip off.

Adjustable wrenches come in all sizes but something in the 6 to 8 in. range is recommended as an all-purpose wrench.

Socket Wrenches

This type is undoubtedly the fastest, safest and most convenient to use. Sockets which attach to a ratchet handle (**Figure 37**) are available with 6-point or 12-point openings and 1/4, 3/8, 1/2 and 3/4 in. drives. The drive size indicates the size of the square hole which mates with the ratchet handle (**Figure 38**).

Several large sockets are required for the disassembly of the engine. These large sockets are not usually included in standard socket sets. These sizes are a must and are as follows:

a. Balancer gear nut and clutch nut: 30 mm.
b. Primary gear nut: 36 mm.

Allen Wrenches

Allen wrenches (**Figure 39**) are available in sets or separately in a variety of sizes. These sets come in SAE and metric size, so be sure to buy a metric set. Allen bolts are sometimes called socket bolts. Sometimes the bolts are difficult to reach and it is suggested that a variety of Allen wrenches be purchased (e.g., socket driven, T-handle and extension type) as shown in **Figure 40**. The majority of the Allen bolts used on the XT600 and TT600 is the No. 5.

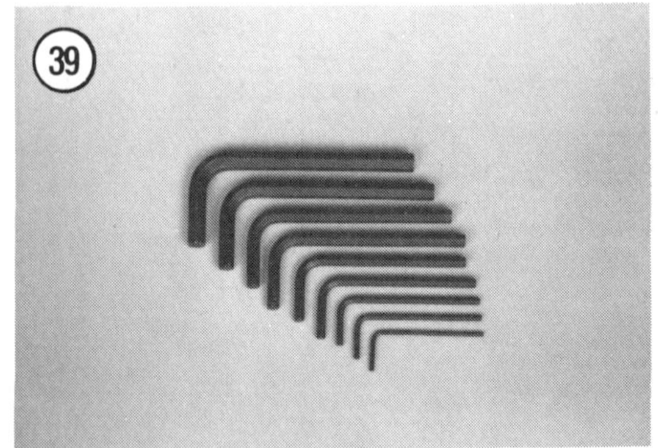

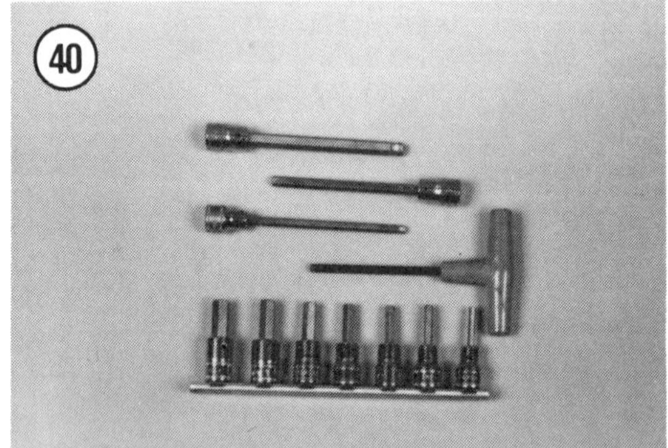

Torque Wrench

A torque wrench is used with a socket to measure how tightly a nut or bolt is installed. They come in a wide price range and with either 3/8 or 1/2 in. square drive (**Figure 41**). The drive size indicates the size of the square drive which mates with the socket. Purchase one that measures 0-280 N•m (0-200 ft.-lb.).

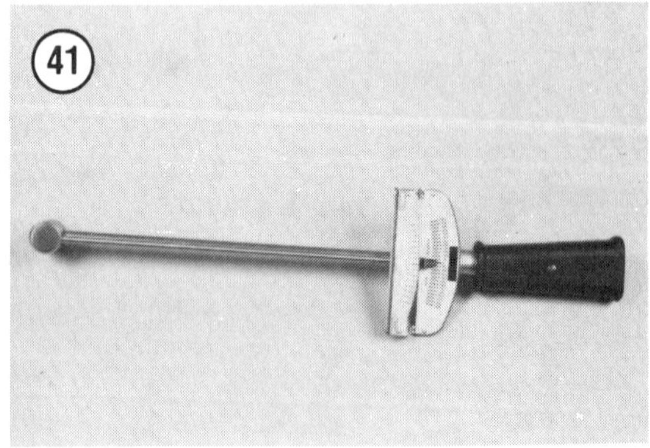

Impact Driver

This tool might have been designed with the bike in mind. This tool makes removal of fasteners easy and eliminates damage to bolts and screw slots. Impact drivers and interchangeable bits (**Figure 42**) are available at most large hardware, motorcycle or auto parts stores. Don't purchase a cheap one as they do not work as well and require more force (the "use a larger hammer" syndrome) than a moderately priced one. Sockets can also be used with a hand impact driver. However, make sure that the socket is designed for use with an impact driver or air tool. Do not use regular hand sockets, as they may shatter during use.

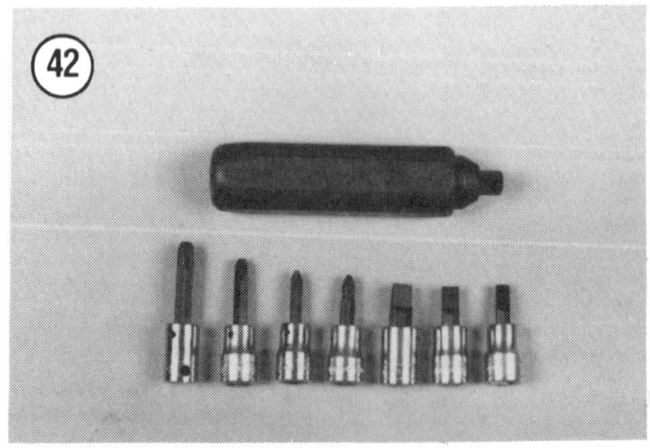

Hammers

The correct hammer (**Figure 43**) is necessary for repairs. Use only a hammer with a face (or head) of rubber or plastic or the soft-faced type that is filled with buckshot. These are sometimes necessary in engine teardowns. *Never* use a metal-faced hammer on engine or suspension parts, as severe damage will result in most cases. You can always produce the same amount of force with a soft-faced hammer. A metal-faced hammer, however, will be required when using a hand impact driver.

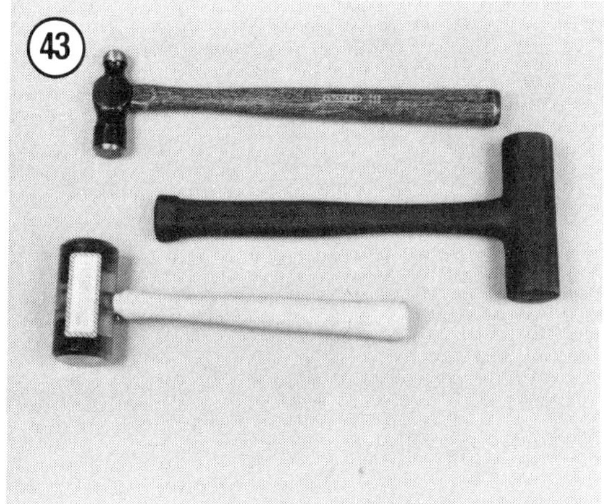
43

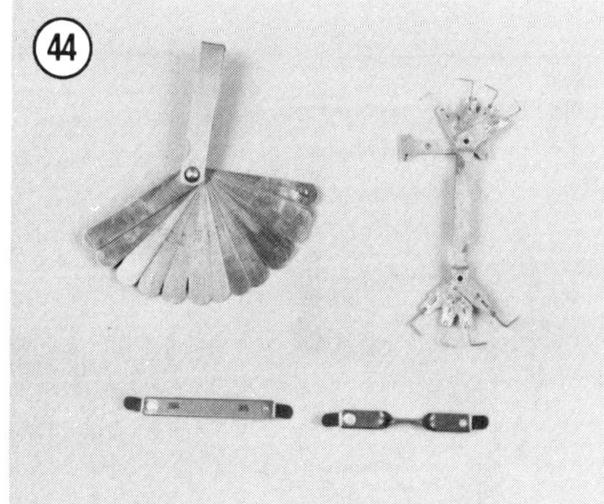
44

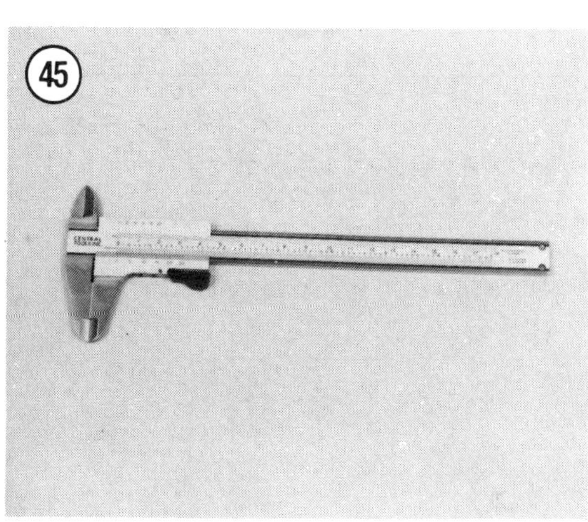
45

PRECISION MEASURING TOOLS

Measurement is an important part of motorcycle service. When performing many of the service procedures in this manual, you will be required to make a number of measurements. These include basic checks such as valve clearance, engine compression and spark plug gap. As you get deeper into engine disassembly and service, measurements will be required to determine the size and condition of the piston and cylinder bore, valve and guide wear, camshaft wear, crankshaft runout and so on. When making these measurements, the degree of accuracy will dictate which tool is required. Precision measuring tools are expensive. If this is your first experience at engine or suspension service, it may be more worthwhile to have the checks made at a Yamaha dealer or machine shop. However, as your skills and enthusiasm increase for doing your own service work, you may want to begin purchasing some of these specialized tools. The following is a description of the measuring tools required during engine and suspension overhaul.

Feeler Gauge

Feeler gauges come in assorted sets and types (**Figure 44**). The feeler gauge is made of either a piece of flat or round hardened steel of a specified thickness. Wire gauges are used to measure spark plug gap. Flat gauges are used for all other measurements. Feeler gauges are also designed for specialized uses, such as for measuring valve clearances. On these gauges, the gauge end is usually small enough and angled so as to make checking valve clearances easier.

Vernier Caliper

This tool (**Figure 45**) is invaluable when reading inside, outside and depth measurements to within close precision. It can be used to measure clutch spring length and the thickness of clutch plates, shims and thrust washers.

Outside Micrometers

One of the most reliable tools used for precision measurement is the outside micrometer (**Figure 46**). Outside micrometers will be required to measure valve shim thickness, piston diameter and valve stem diameter. Outside micrometers are also used with other tools to measure the cylinder bore and the valve guide inside diameters. Micrometers can be purchased individually or as a set.

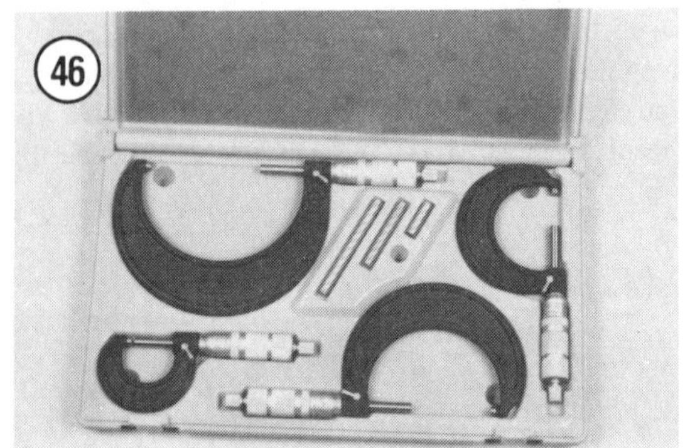
46

Dial Indicator

Dial indicators (**Figure 47**) are precision tools used to check dimension variations on machined parts such as transmission shafts and axles and to check crankshaft and axle shaft end play. Dial indicators are available with various dial types for different measuring requirements. For motorcycle repair, select a dial indicator with a continuous dial (**Figure 48**).

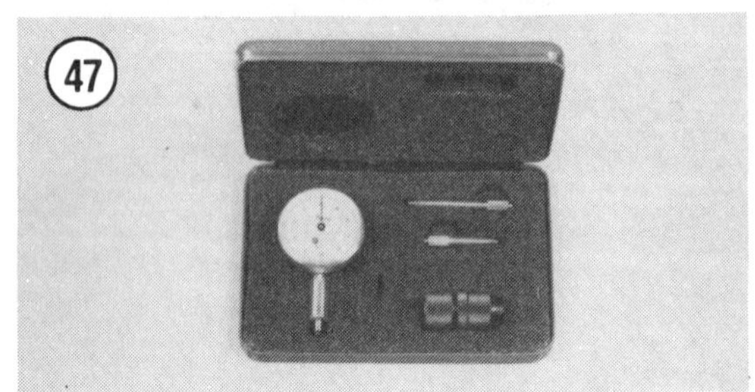
47

48

Cylinder Bore Gauge

The cylinder bore gauge is a very specialized precision tool. The gauge set shown in **Figure 49** is comprised of a dial indicator, handle and a number of length adapters to adapt the gauge to different bore sizes. The bore gauge can be used to make cylinder bore measurements such as bore size, taper and out-of-round. Depending on the bore gauge, it can sometimes be used to measure brake caliper and master cylinder bore sizes. An outside micrometer must be used together with the bore gauge to determine bore dimensions.

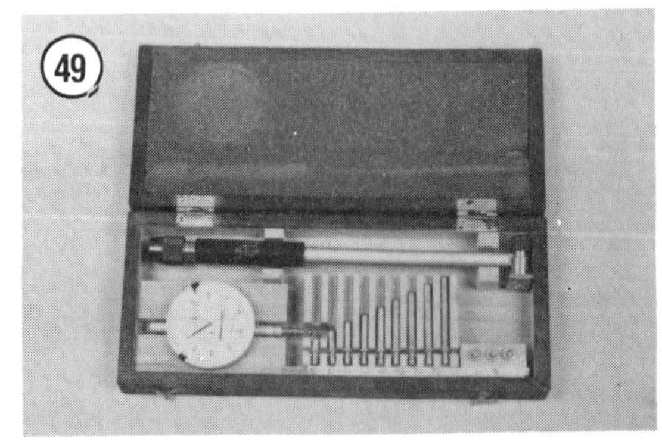
49

Small Hole Gauges

A set of small hole gauges allow you to measure a hole, groove or slot ranging in size up to 13 mm (0.500 in.). A small hole gauge will be required to measure valve guide, brake caliper and brake master cylinder bore diameters. An outside micrometer must be used together with the small hole gauge to determine bore dimensions.

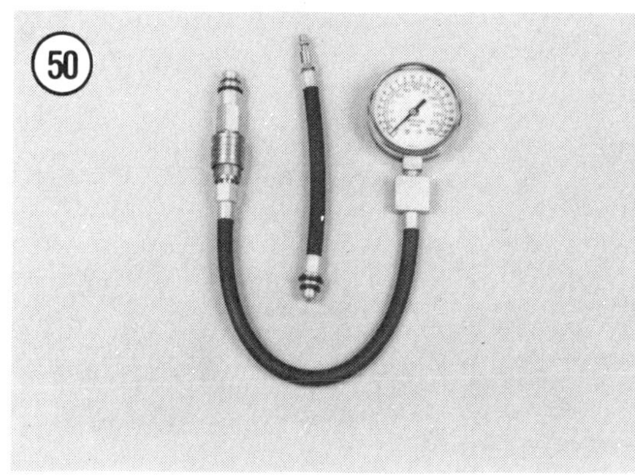

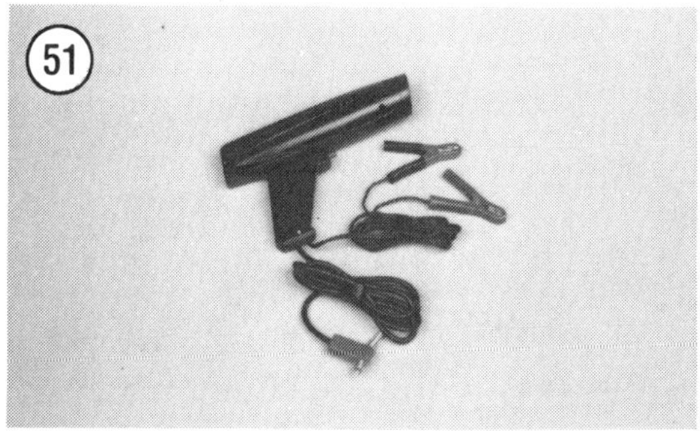

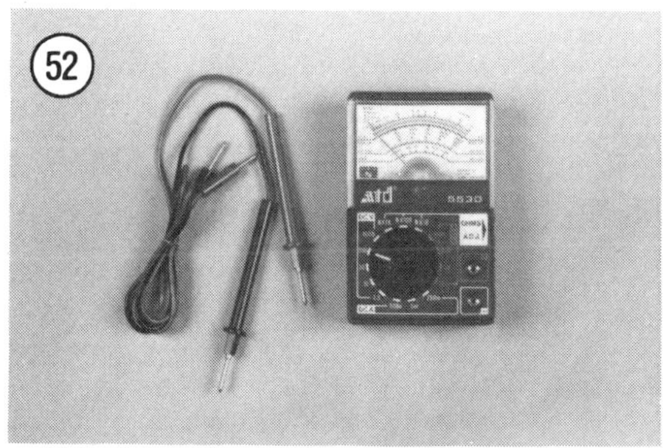

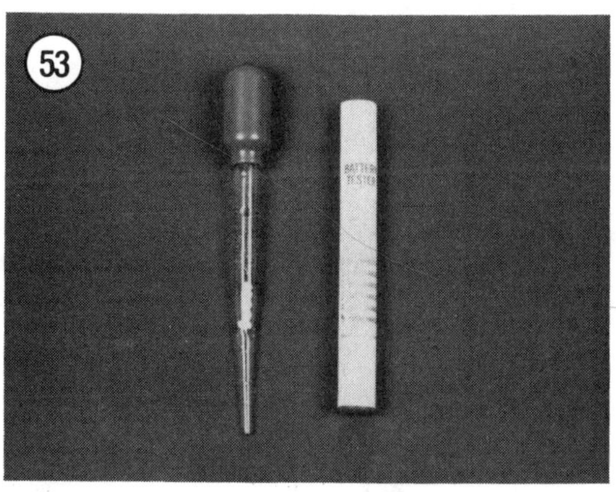

Compression Gauge

An engine with low compression cannot be properly tuned and will not develop full power. A compression gauge (**Figure 50**) measures engine compression. The one shown has a flexible stem with an extension that can allow you to hold it while kicking the engine over. Open the throttle all the way when checking engine compression. See Chapter Three.

Strobe Timing Light

This instrument is useful for checking ignition timing. By flashing a light at the precise instant the spark plug fires, the position of the timing mark can be seen. The flashing light makes a moving mark appear to stand still opposite a stationary mark.

Suitable lights range from inexpensive neon bulb types to powerful xenon strobe lights (**Figure 51**). A light with an inductive pickup is recommended to eliminate any possible damage to ignition wiring. Use according to manufacturer's instructions.

Multimeter or VOM

This instrument (**Figure 52**) is invaluable for electrical system troubleshooting. See *Electrical Troubleshooting* in Chapter Nine for its use.

Battery Hydrometer

A hydrometer (**Figure 53**) is the best way to check a battery's state of charged. A hydrometer measures the weight or density of the sulfuric acid in the battery's electrolyte in specific gravity.

Screw Pitch Gauge

A screw pitch gauge (**Figure 54**) determines the thread pitch of bolts, screws, studs, etc. The gauge is made up of a number of thin plates. Each plate has a thread shape cut on one edge to match one thread pitch. When using a screw pitch gauge to determine a thread pitch size, try to fit different blade sizes onto the bolt thread until both threads match (**Figure 55**).

Magnetic Stand

A magnetic stand (**Figure 56**) is used to securely hold a dial indicator when checking the runout of a round object or when checking the end play of a shaft.

V-Blocks

V-blocks (**Figure 57**) are precision ground blocks used to hold a round object when checking its runout or condition. In motorcycle repair, V-blocks can be used when checking the runout of such items as valve stems, camshaft, balancer shaft, crankshaft, wheel axles and fork tubes.

SPECIAL TOOLS

This section describes special tools unique to motorcycle service and repair.

Spoke Wrench

This special wrench is used to tighten wheel spokes (**Figure 58**). Always use the correct size wrench to prevent from rounding out and damaging the spoke nipple.

The Grabbit

The Grabbit (**Figure 59**) is a special tool used to hold the clutch boss when removing the clutch nut and to secure the drive sprocket when removing the sprocket nut.

Tire Levers

When riding and maintaining a dual-purpose motorcycle, get use to changing tires. To prevent from pinching tubes during tire changing, purchase a good set of tire levers (**Figure 60**). Never use a screwdriver in place of a tire lever; refer to Chapter Ten for its use. Before using a tire lever, check the working end of the tool and remove any burrs. Don't use a tire lever for prying anything but tires.

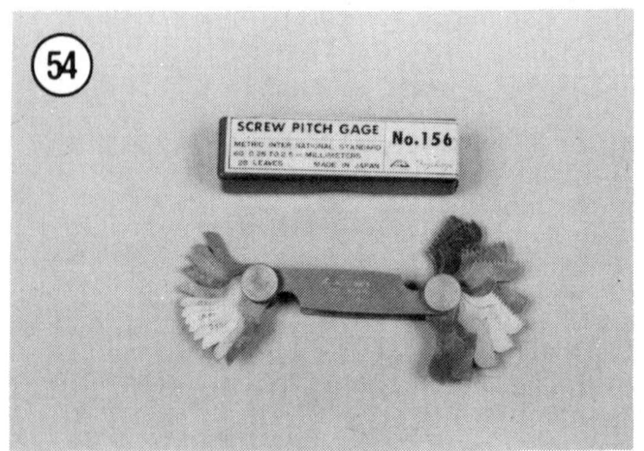

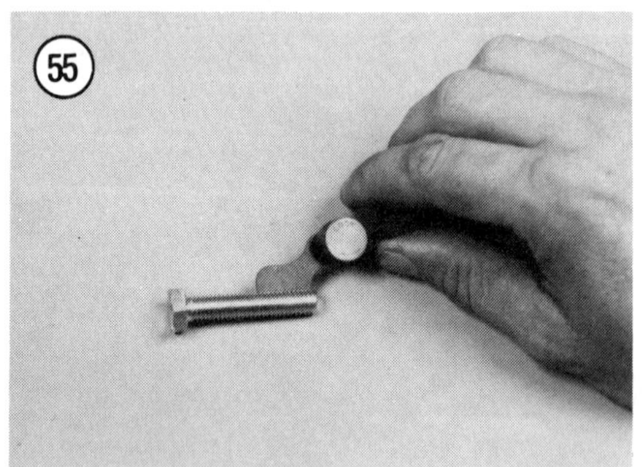

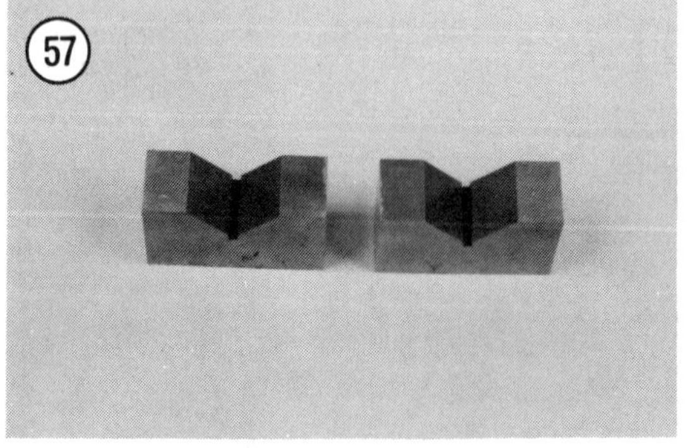

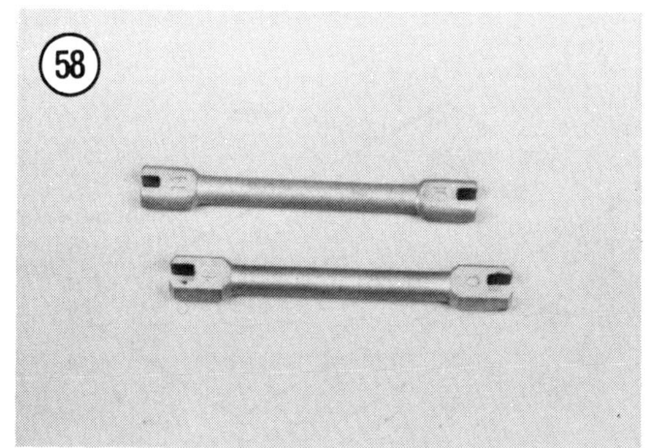
58

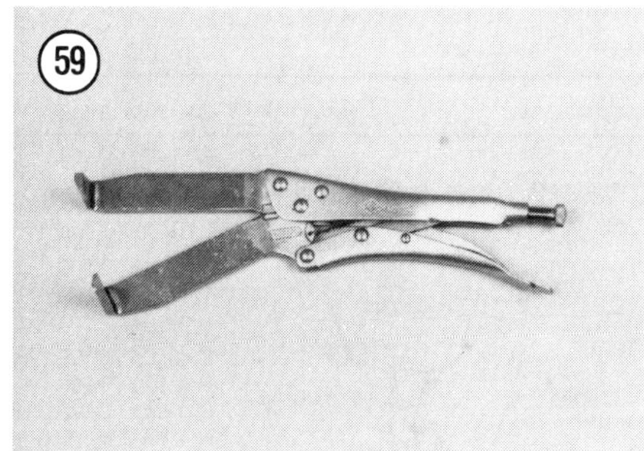
59

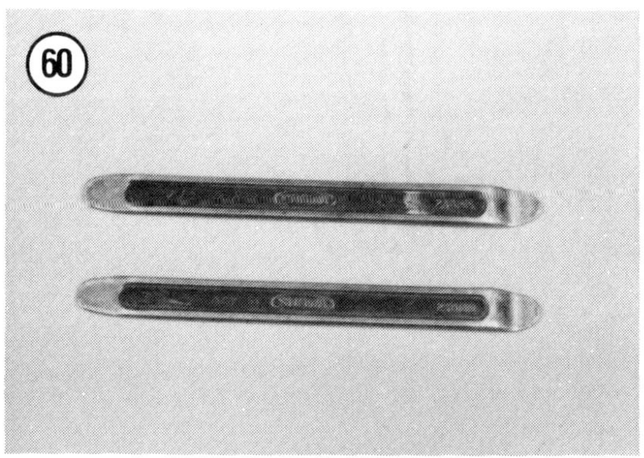
60

61

Flywheel Puller

A flywheel puller will be required whenever it is necessary to remove the rotor and service the stator plate assembly. In addition, when disassembling the engine, the rotor must be removed before the crankcases can be split. There is no satisfactory substitute for this tool. Because the rotor is a taper fit on the crankshaft, makeshift removal often results in crankshaft and rotor damage. Don't think about removing the rotor without this tool.

Chain Breaker

A chain breaker (**Figure 61**) is a useful tool for cutting a drive chain to size. Attempting to cut a drive chain using improper methods or tools may cause chain damage.

Special Tools

A few special tools may be required for major service. These are described in the appropriate chapters and are available either from a Yamaha dealer or other manufacturers as indicated.

MECHANIC'S TIPS

Removing Frozen Nuts and Screws

When a fastener rusts and cannot be removed, several methods may be used to loosen it. First, apply penetrating oil such as Liquid Wrench or WD-40 (available at hardware or auto supply stores). Apply it liberally and let it penetrate for 10-15 minutes. Rap the fastener several times with a small hammer; do not hit it hard enough to cause damage. Reapply the penetrating oil if necessary.

For frozen screws, apply penetrating oil as described, then insert a screwdriver in the slot and rap the top of the screwdriver with a hammer. This loosens the rust so the screw can be removed in the normal way. If the screw head is too chewed up to use this method, grip the head with Vise-grip pliers and twist the screw out.

Avoid applying heat unless specifically instructed, as it may melt, warp or remove the temper from parts.

Removing Broken Screws or Bolts

When the head breaks off a screw or bolt, several methods are available for removing the remaining portion.

If a large portion of the remainder projects out, try gripping it with Vise-grip pliers. If the projecting portion is too small, file it to fit a wrench or cut a slot in it to fit a screwdriver. See **Figure 62**.

If the head breaks off flush, use a screw extractor. To do this, centerpunch the exact center of the remaining portion of the screw or bolt. Drill a small hole in the screw and tap the extractor into the hole. Back the screw out with a wrench on the extractor. See **Figure 63**.

62

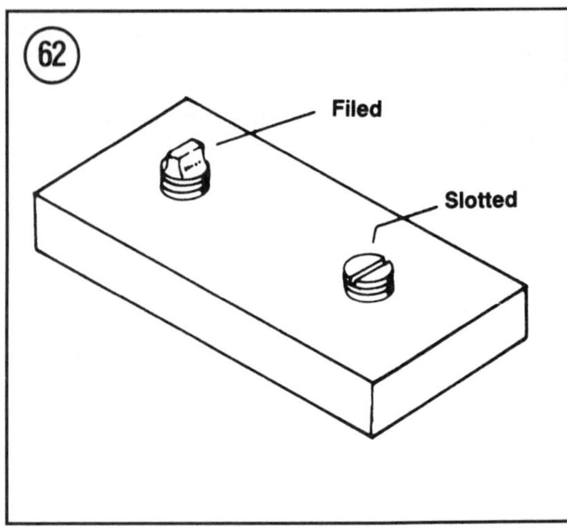

63

REMOVING BROKEN SCREWS AND BOLTS

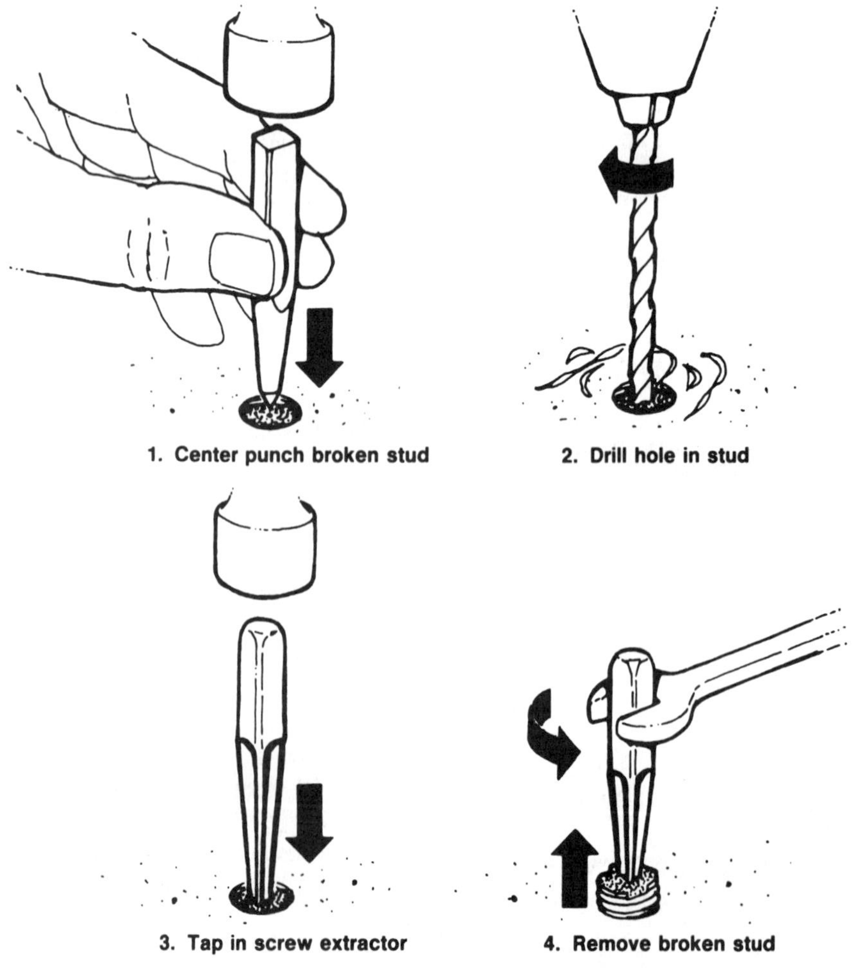

1. Center punch broken stud
2. Drill hole in stud
3. Tap in screw extractor
4. Remove broken stud

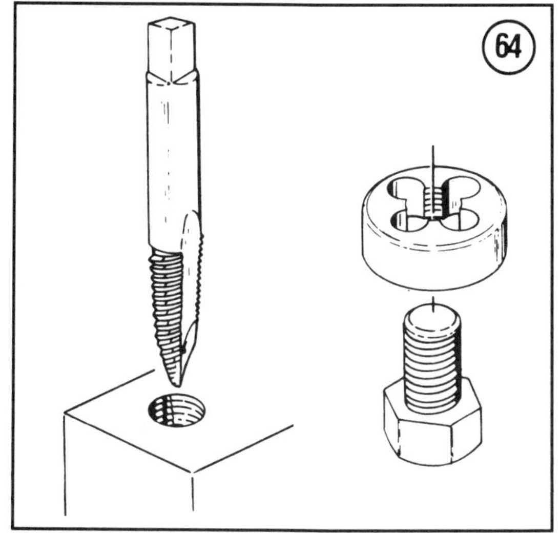

64

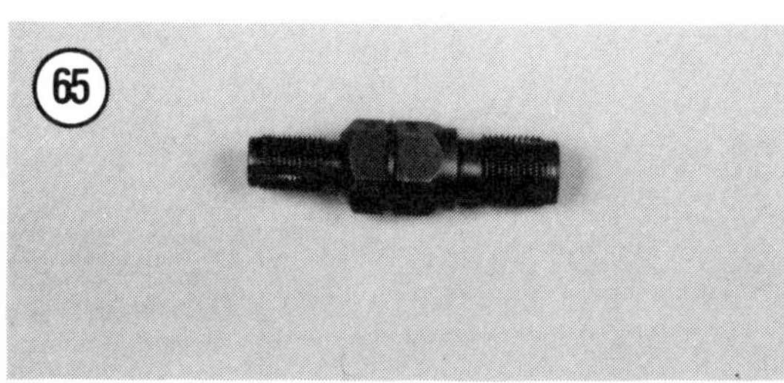

65

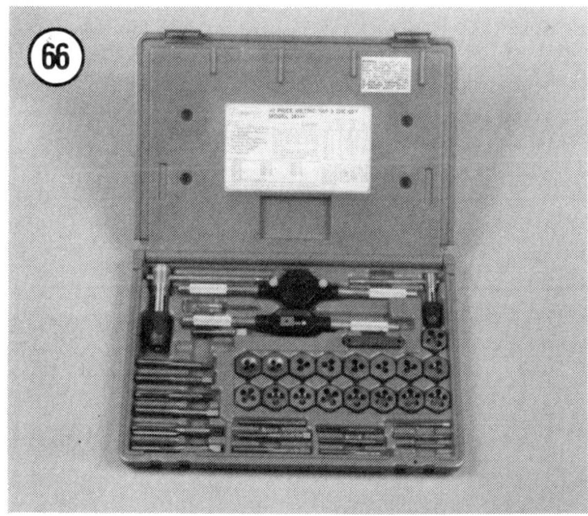

66

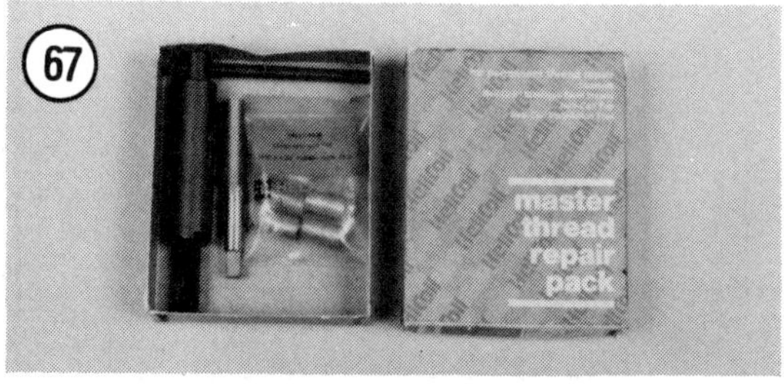

67

Remedying Stripped Threads

Occasionally, threads are stripped through carelessness or impact damage. Often the threads can be cleaned up by running a tap (for internal threads on nuts) or die (for external threads on bolts) through the threads. See **Figure 64**. To clean or repair spark plug threads, a spark plug tap can be used (**Figure 65**).

NOTE
*Tap and dies can be purchased individually or in a set as shown in **Figure 66**.*

If an internal thread is damaged, it may be necessary to install a Helicoil (**Figure 67**) or some other type of thread insert. Follow the manufacturer's instructions when installing their insert.

RIDING SAFETY

General Tips

1. Read your owner's manual and know your machine.
2. Check the throttle and brake controls before starting the engine.
3. Know how to make an emergency stop.
4. Never add fuel while anyone is smoking in the area or when the engine is running.
5. Never wear loose scarves, belts or boot laces that could catch on moving parts.
6. Always wear eye and head protection and protective clothing to protect your *entire* body. Today's riding apparel is very stylish and you will be ready for action as well as being well protected.
7. Riding in the winter months requires a good set of clothes to keep your body dry and warm, otherwise your entire trip may be miserable. If you dress properly, moisture will evaporate from your body. If you become too hot and if your clothes trap the moisture, you will become cold. Even mild temperatures can be very uncomfortable and dangerous when combined with a strong wind or traveling at high speed. See **Table 5** for wind chill factors. Always dress according to what the wind chill factor is, not the ambient temperature.
8. Never allow anyone to operate the bike without proper instruction. This is for their bodily protection

and to keep your machine from damage or destruction.

9. Use the "buddy system" for long trips, just in case you have a problem or run out of gas.

10. Never attempt to repair your machine with the engine running except when necessary for certain tune-up procedures.

11. Check all of the machine components and hardware frequently, especially the wheels and the steering.

Operating Tips

1. Avoid dangerous terrain.

2. Keep the headlight, turn signal lights and taillight free of dirt.

3. Always steer with both hands.

4. Be aware of the terrain and avoid operating the bike at excessive speed.

5. Do not panic if the throttle sticks. Turn the engine stop switch to the OFF position.

6. Do not tailgate. Rear end collisions can cause injury and machine damage.

7. Do not mix alcoholic beverages or drugs with riding—*ride straight.*

8. Check your fuel supply regularly. Be sure you have enough to reach the next fuel stop.

Table 1 ENGINE AND CHASSIS NUMBERS

Model number	Year	Engine/frame serial no. start to end
XT600L	1984	49N-000101-on
XT600LC	1984	49R-000101-on
XT600N	1985	49N-002101-on
XT600NC	1985	49R-002101-on
XT600S	1986	49N-003101-on
XT600SC	1986	49R-003101-on
XT600T	1987	49N-010101-on
XT600TC	1987	49R-010101-on
XT600U	1988	3EW-000101-on
XT600UC	1988	3EW-002101-on
XT600W	1989	3EW-004101-on
XT600WC	1989	3EW-007101-on
TT600K	1983	34K-000101-on
TT600L	1984	34K-020101-on
TT600N	1985	55U-000101-on
TT600S	1986*	55U-005101-on

* Last year of production for the TT600 model.

Table 2 DECIMAL AND METRIC EQUIVALENTS

Fractions	Decimal in.	Metric mm	Fractions	Decimal in.	Metric mm
1/64	0.015625	0.39688	33/64	0.515625	13.09687
1/32	0.03125	0.79375	17/32	0.53125	13.49375
3/64	0.046875	1.19062	35/64	0.546875	13.89062
1/16	0.0625	1.58750	9/16	0.5625	14.28750
5/64	0.078125	1.98437	37/64	0.578125	14.68437
3/32	0.09375	2.38125	19/32	0.59375	15.08125
7/64	0.109375	2.77812	39/64	0.609375	15.47812
1/8	0.125	3.1750	5/8	0.625	15.87500
9/64	0.140625	3.57187	41/64	0.640625	16.27187
5/32	0.15625	3.96875	21/32	0.65625	16.66875
11/64	0.171875	4.36562	43/64	0.671875	17.06562
3/16	0.1875	4.76250	11/16	0.6875	17.46250
13/64	0.203125	5.15937	45/64	0.703125	17.85937
7/32	0.21875	5.55625	23/32	0.71875	18.25625
15/64	0.234375	5.95312	47/64	0.734375	18.65312
1/4	0.250	6.35000	3/4	0.750	19.05000
17/64	0.265625	6.74687	49/64	0.765625	19.44687
9/32	0.28125	7.14375	25/32	0.78125	19.84375
19/64	0.296875	7.54062	51/64	0.796875	20.24062
5/16	0.3125	7.93750	13/16	0.8125	20.63750
21/64	0.328125	8.33437	53/64	0.828125	21.03437
11/32	0.34375	8.73125	27/32	0.84375	21.43125
23/64	0.390625	9.92187	57/64	0.890625	22.62187
13/32	0.40625	10.31875	29/32	0.90625	23.01875
27/64	0.421875	10.71562	59/64	0.921875	23.41562
7/16	0.4375	11.11250	15/16	0.9375	23.81250
29/64	0.453125	11.50937	61/64	0.953125	24.20937
15/32	0.46875	11.90625	31/32	0.96875	24.60625
31/64	0.484375	12.30312	63/64	0.984375	25.00312
1/2	0.500	12.70000	1	1.00	25.40000

Table 3 GENERAL TORQUE SPECIFICATIONS*

Thread size	N•m	ft.-lb.
Bolt		
6 mm	6	4.5
8 mm	15	11
10 mm	30	22
12 mm	55	40
14 mm	85	61
16 mm	130	94
Nut		
10 mm	6	4.5
12 mm	15	11
14 mm	30	22
17 mm	55	40
19 mm	85	61
22 mm	130	94

* Use these torque figures for all fasteners not individually listed.

Table 4 WORKSHOP TOOLS

Tool	Size or specification
Screwdriver	
Common	1/8 × 4 in. blade
Common	5/16 × 8 in. blade
Common	3/8 × 12 in. blade
Phillips	Size 2 tip, 6 in. overall
Pliers	
Slip joint	6 in. overall
Vise Grips	10 in. overall
Needlenose	6 in. overall
Channel lock	12 in. overall
Snap ring	Assorted
Wrenches	
Box-end set	Assorted
Open-end set	Assorted
Crescent	6 in. and 12 in. overall
Socket set	1/2 in. drive ratchet with assorted metric sockets
Socket drive extensions	1/2 in. drive, 2 in., 4 in. and 6 in.
Socket universal joint	1/2 in. drive
Allen	Socket driven (long and short), T-handle driven and 90°
Hammers	
Soft faced	—
Plastic faced	—
Metal faced	—
Other special tools	
Impact driver	1/2 in. drive with assorted bits
Torque wrench	1/2 in. driver (ft.-lb.)
Flat feeler gauge	Metric set

Table 5 WINDCHILL FACTOR

Estimated Wind Speed in MPH	Actual Thermometer Reading (° F)											
	50	40	30	20	10	0	−10	−20	−30	−40	−50	−60
	Equivalent Temperature (° F)											
Calm	50	40	30	20	10	0	−10	−20	−30	−40	−50	−60
5	48	37	27	16	6	−5	−15	−26	−36	−47	−57	−68
10	40	28	16	4	−9	−21	−33	−46	−58	−70	−83	−95
15	36	22	9	−5	−18	−36	−45	−58	−72	−85	−99	−112
20	32	18	4	−10	−25	−39	−53	−67	−82	−96	−110	−124
25	30	16	0	−15	−29	−44	−59	−74	−88	−104	−118	−133
30	28	13	−2	−18	−33	−48	−63	−79	−94	−109	−125	−140
35	27	11	−4	−20	−35	−49	−67	−82	−98	−113	−129	−145
40	26	10	−6	−21	−37	−53	−69	−85	−100	−116	−132	−148
*												
	Little Danger (for properly clothed person)				**Increasing Danger**			**Great Danger**				
					• Danger from freezing of exposed flesh •							

* Wind speeds greater than 40 mph have little additional effect

CHAPTER TWO

TROUBLESHOOTING

Diagnosing mechanical problems is relatively simple if you use orderly procedures and keep a few basic principles in mind. The first step in any troubleshooting procedure is to define the symptoms as closely as possible and then localize the problem. Subsequent steps involve testing and analyzing those areas which could cause the symptoms. A haphazard approach may eventually solve the problem, but it can be very costly in terms of wasted time and unnecessary parts replacement.

Proper lubrication, maintenance and periodic tune-ups as described in Chapter Three will reduce the necessity for troubleshooting. Even with the best of care, however, a dirt and dual-purpose motorcycle is prone to problems which will require troubleshooting.

Never assume anything. Do not overlook the obvious. If you are riding along and the engine suddenly quits, check the easiest, most accessible problem spots first. Is there gasoline in the tank? Is the fuel shutoff valve in the ON position? Has the spark plug wire fallen off?

If nothing obvious turns up in a quick check, look a little further. Learning to recognize and describe symptoms will make repairs easier for you or a mechanic at the shop. Describe problems accurately and fully. Saying that "it won't run" isn't the same thing as saying "it quit climbing a hill and won't start," or that "it sat in my garage for 3 months and then wouldn't start."

Gather as many symptoms as possible to aid in diagnosis. Note whether the engine lost power gradually or all at once, what color smoke came from the exhaust and so on. Remember that the more complicated a machine is, the easier it is to troubleshoot because symptoms point to specific problems.

After the symptoms are defined, areas which could cause problems are tested and analyzed. Guessing at the cause of a problem may provide the solution, but it can easily lead to frustration, wasted time and a series of expensive, unnecessary parts replacements.

You do not need fancy equipment or complicated test gear to determine whether repairs can be attempted at home. A few simple checks could save a large repair bill and lost time while the bike sits in a dealer's service department. On the other hand, be realistic and do not attempt repairs beyond your abilities. Service departments tend to charge heavily for putting together a disassembled engine that may have been abused. Some won't even take on such a job—so use common sense, don't get in over your head.

OPERATING REQUIREMENTS

An engine needs 3 basics to run properly: correct fuel/air mixture, compression and a spark at the right time. If one basic requirement is missing, the engine will not run. Four-stroke engine operating principles are described in Chapter Four under *Engine Principles*. The ignition system is the weakest link of the 3 basics. More problems result from ignition breakdowns than from any other source. Keep that in mind before you begin tampering with carburetor adjustments and the like.

If a bike has been sitting for any length of time and refuses to start, check and clean the spark plug. Check the condition of the battery to make sure it has an adequate charge. If these are okay, then look to the gasoline delivery system. This includes the tank, fuel shutoff valve and fuel line to the carburetor. If your bike has a steel tank, rust may have formed in the tank, obstructing fuel flow. Gasoline deposits may have gummed up carburetor jets and air passages. Gasoline tends to lose its potency after standing for long periods. Condensation may contaminate it with water. Drain the old gas and try starting with a fresh tankful.

TROUBLESHOOTING INSTRUMENTS

Chapter One lists the instruments needed and detailed instruction on their use.

STARTING THE ENGINE

When your engine refuses to start, frustration can cause you to forget basic starting principles and procedures. The following outline will guide you through basic starting procedures.

NOTE
The TT600 models are not equipped with the sidestand switch nor the neutral switches.

An ignition control system is installed on all XT600 models that consists of an ignition control unit, neutral indicator light, neutral switch and a sidestand switch. When the ignition switch and the engine stop switch are ON, the ignition will produce a spark for starting only if the following conditions exist:

a. The sidestand is up (the sidestand switch is ON). The engine will start if the transmission is in gear and the clutch lever is pulled in.

b. The transmission is in neutral (the neutral switch is ON).

Always allow the engine to sufficiently warm up before riding off. Do not rev or accelerate hard with a cold engine as this may cause premature engine wear.

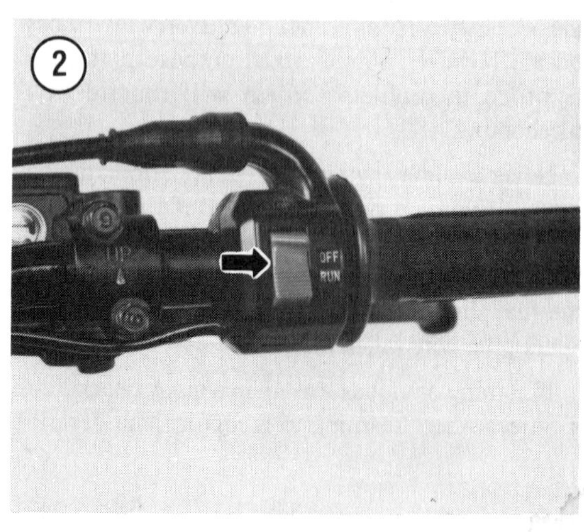

Starting a Cold Engine

1. Shift the transmission into NEUTRAL.
2. Turn the fuel valve to ON.

3A. On XT600 models, perform the following:

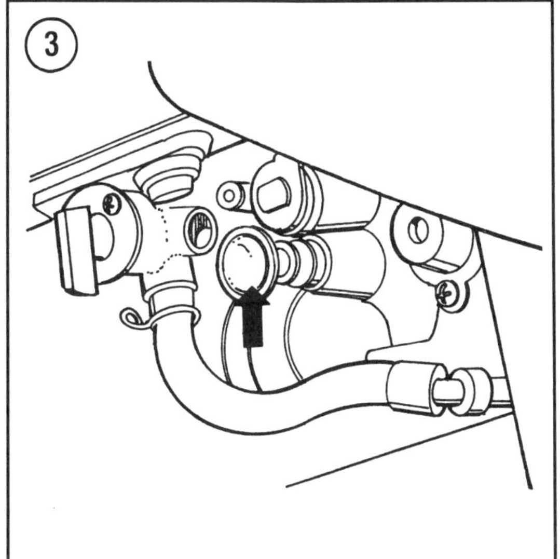

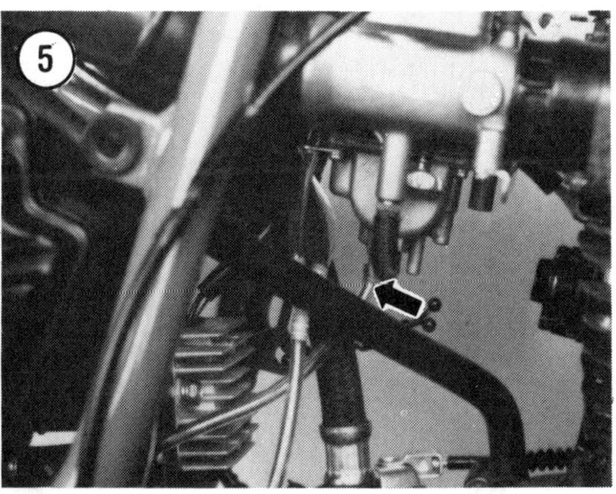

a. Open the choke. Pull the choke lever back toward the handgrip (**Figure 1**).
b. Turn the ignition key to ON.
c. Turn the engine stop switch to the RUN position (**Figure 2**). Position the sidestand up.

3B. On TT600 models, pull the choke knob (**Figure 3**) out.

4. With the throttle completely *closed*, kick the engine over.
5. When the engine starts, work the throttle slightly to keep it running.
6. Idle the engine approximately for a minute or until the throttle responds cleanly and the choke can be closed.

Starting a Warm or Hot Engine

1. Shift the transmission into NEUTRAL.
2. Turn the fuel valve to ON.

3A. On XT600 models, perform the following:

a. Make sure the choke is closed. The choke lever should be pushed toward the front of the bike (**Figure 4**) for a warm engine.
b. Turn the ignition key to ON and the engine stop switch to the RUN position. Position the sidestand up.

3B. On TT600 models, make sure the choke is closed. The choke knob should be pushed in toward the carburetor (**Figure 3**) for a warm engine.

4. Open the throttle slightly and kick the engine over. If the engine does not start, try again with the throttle opened approximately 1/4 to 1/2.

Starting a Flooded Engine

If the engine is flooded, open the throttle all the way and kick the engine over until it starts.

NOTE

*If the engine refuses to start, check the carburetor overflow hose attached to the fitting at the bottom of the float bowl (**Figure 5**). If fuel is running out of the hose, the float may be stuck open.*

STARTING DIFFICULTIES

When the bike is difficult to start, or won't start at all, it does not help to kick away at the kickstarter. Check for obvious problems even before getting out your tools. Go down the following list step by step. Do each one. If the bike still will not start, refer to the appropriate troubleshooting procedures which follow in this chapter.

1. Is there fuel in the tank? Remove the filler cap (**Figure 6**) and rock the bike from side-to-side. Listen for fuel sloshing around.

WARNING
Do not use an open flame to check in the tank. A serious explosion is certain to result.

2. On TT600 models, make sure the fuel tank cap vent line is not kinked or pinched.

3. If there is fuel in the tank, pull off the fuel line at the carburetor. Turn the fuel valve to RES (**Figure 7**) and see if fuel flows freely. If none comes out and there is a fuel filter installed in the fuel line, remove the filter and turn the fuel valve to RES again. If fuel flows, the filter is clogged and should be replaced. If no fuel comes out, the fuel valve may be shut off, blocked by foreign matter, or the fuel cap vent may be plugged. If the carburetor is getting usable fuel, turn to the compression next.

NOTE
*All XT600 models sold in California are equipped with an evaporative emission control system. On these models, the fuel cap is unvented. Instead of checking the fuel cap, check the carbon canister hoses for bending, kinks or other damage. Refer to **Emission Control** in Chapter Eight.*

4. If the engine is getting fuel, kick the kickstarter normally and observe its operation. If the kickstarter feels normal (adequate engine compression), proceed to Step 4. However, if the kickstarter operation feels unusually light or heavy, perform the *Compression Test* under *Tune-Up* in Chapter Three.

5A. On XT600 models, check that the engine stop switch (**Figure 2**) is in the RUN position. If necessary, test the switch as described under *Switches* in Chapter Nine.

5B. On TT600 models, make sure the engine kill switch (**Figure 8**) is not stuck or working improperly. If necessary, test the switch as described under *Switches* in Chapter Nine.

6. Is the spark plug wire on tight (**Figure 9**). Push it on and slightly rotate it to clean the electrical connection between the plug and the connector.

7. Is the choke lever in the correct position? Refer to *Starting the Engine* in this chapter.

ENGINE STARTING TROUBLESHOOTING

An engine that refuses to start or is difficult to start is very frustrating. More often than not, the problem is very minor and can be found with a simple and logical troubleshooting approach.

The following items show a beginning point from which to isolate engine starting problems.

Engine Fails to Start

Perform the following spark test to determine if the ignition system is operating properly.

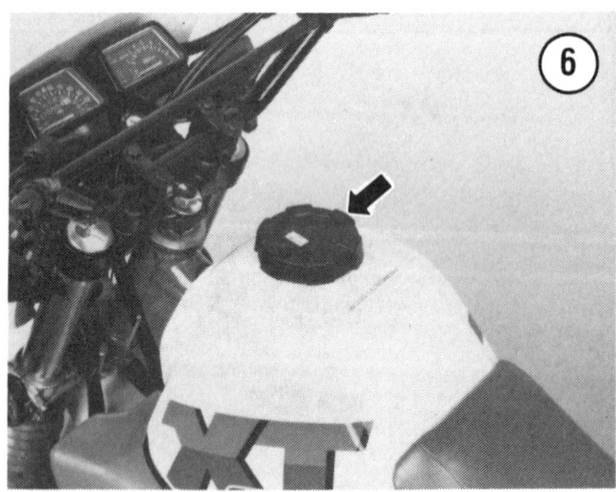

CAUTION
Before removing the spark plug in Step 1, clean all dirt and debris from the plug base. Dirt that falls into the cylinder will cause rapid piston, piston ring and cylinder wear.

NOTE
If you are checking the spark plug while on the trail, more than likely there is dirt clogged underneath the fuel tank. When the spark plug is removed, dirt could fall from the tank and into the cylinder. If you do not have time to remove the fuel tank, wrap a large clean cloth or riding jacket around the fuel tank. Then remove the spark plug and check or replace it as required. Remove the cloth after reinstalling the spark plug.

1. Remove the spark plug.
2. Connect the spark plug wire and connector to the spark plug and touch the spark plug base to the cylinder head to ground it. Position the spark plug so you can see the electrode.
3. On XT600 models, turn the ignition key to ON and the engine stop switch to RUN. Position the sidestand up.
4. Kick the engine over with the kickstarter. A fat blue spark should be evident across the spark plug electrode.

WARNING
Do not hold the spark plug, wire or connector or a serious electrical shock may result. If it is necessary to hold the high voltage lead, do so with an insulated pair of pliers. The high voltage generated by the ignition system could produce serious or fatal shocks.

5. If the spark is good, check for one or more of the following possible malfunctions:
   a. Obstructed fuel line or fuel filter.
   b. Leaking head or cylinder base gasket.
6. If spark is not good, check for one or more of the following:
   a. Weak ignition coil.
   b. Weak CDI unit.
   c. Loose electrical connections.
   d. Dirty electrical connections.
   e. Loose or broken ignition coil ground wire.

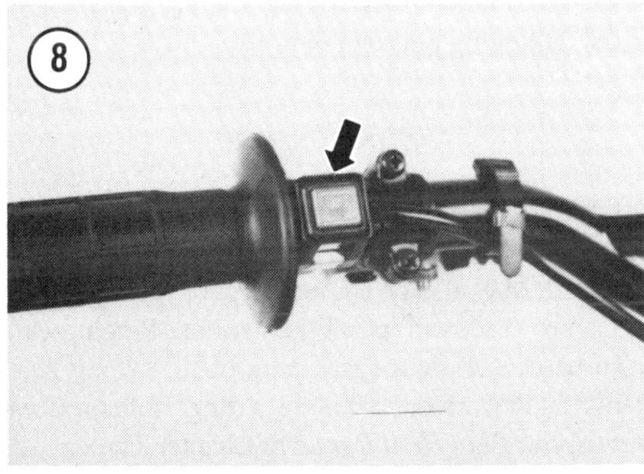

8

9

Engine is Difficult to Start

Check for one or more of the following possible malfunctions:

a. Fouled spark plug.
b. Improperly operating choke.
c. Contaminated fuel system.
d. Improperly adjusted carburetor.
e. Loose electrical connections.
f. Dirty electrical connections.
g. Weak CDI unit.
h. Weak ignition coil.
i. Poor compression.

Engine Will Not Crank

If the engine will not crank because of a mechanical problem, check for one or more of the following possible malfunctions:

a. Defective kickstarter and/or gear.
b. Seized piston.

c. Seized crankshaft bearings.
d. Broken connecting rod.

ENGINE PERFORMANCE

In the following check list, it is assumed that the engine runs, but is not operating at peak performance. This will serve as a starting point from which to isolate a performance malfunction.

The possible causes for each malfunction are listed in a logical sequence and in order of probability.

Engine Will Not Idle

a. Carburetor incorrectly adjusted.
b. Pilot jet clogged.
c. Obstructed fuel line or fuel shutoff valve.
d. Fouled or improperly gapped spark plug.

Engine Misses at High Speed

a. Fouled or improperly gapped spark plug.
b. Improper carburetor main jet selection.
c. Carburetor main jet and/or needle jet clogged.
d. Obstructed fuel line or fuel shutoff valve.
e. Ignition timing incorrect due to ignition system malfunction.

Engine Overheating

a. Incorrect carburetor jetting or fuel/oil ratio mixture.
b. Ignition timing incorrect due to ignition system malfunction.
c. Improper spark plug heat range.
d. Intake system air leak.
e. Damaged or blocked cooling fins on cylinder and/or cylinder head.
f. Dragging brake(s).

Excessive Exhaust Smoke and Engine Runs Roughly

a. Clogged air filter element.
b. Carburetor adjustment incorrect—mixture too rich.
c. Carburetor floats damaged or incorrectly adjusted.
d. Choke not operating correctly.
e. Water or other contaminants in fuel.
f. Clogged fuel line.
g. Excessive piston-to-cylinder clearance.
h. Valve component wear.

Engine Loses Power

a. Carburetor incorrectly adjusted.
b. Engine overheating.
c. Ignition timing incorrect due to ignition system malfunction.
d. Incorrectly gapped spark plug.
e. Obstructed muffler.
f. Dragging brake(s).

Engine Lacks Acceleration

a. Carburetor adjustment incorrect.
b. Clogged fuel line.
c. Ignition timing incorrect due to ignition system malfunction.
d. Dragging brake(s).

ENGINE NOISES

1. *Knocking or pinging during acceleration*—Caused by using a lower octane fuel than recommended. May also be caused by poor fuel available at some "discount" gasoline stations. Pinging can also be caused by a spark plug of the wrong heat range and incorrect carburetor jetting. Refer to *Correct Spark Plug Heat Range* in Chapter Three.
2. *Slapping or rattling noises at low speed or during acceleration*—May be caused by piston slap, i.e., excessive piston-to-cylinder wall clearance.
3. *Knocking or rapping while decelerating*—Usually caused by excessive rod bearing clearance.
4. *Persistent knocking and vibration*—Usually caused by worn main bearings.
5. *Rapid on-off squeal*—Compression leak around cylinder head gasket or spark plug.

EXCESSIVE VIBRATION

This can be difficult to find without disassembling the engine. Usually this is caused by loose engine or suspension mounting hardware.

CLUTCH

The three basic clutch troubles are:

a. Clutch noise.

b. Clutch slipping.

c. Improper clutch disengagement.

All clutch troubles, except adjustments, require partial engine disassembly to identify and cure the problem. Refer to Chapter Six for procedures.

The troubleshooting procedures outlined in **Figure 10** will help you solve the majority of clutch troubles in a systematic manner.

TRANSMISSION

The basic transmission troubles are:

a. Excessive gear noise.

b. Difficult shifting.

c. Gears pop out of mesh.

d. Incorrect shift lever operation.

Transmission symptoms are sometimes hard to distinguish from clutch symptoms. Be sure that the clutch is not causing the trouble before working on the transmission.

The troubleshooting procedures outlined in **Figure 11** will help you solve the majority of transmission troubles.

IGNITION SYSTEM

All XT600 and TT600 models are equipped with a capacitor discharge ignition (CDI) system. This solid state system uses no contact breaker point or other moving parts. Because of the solid state design, problems with the capacitor discharge system

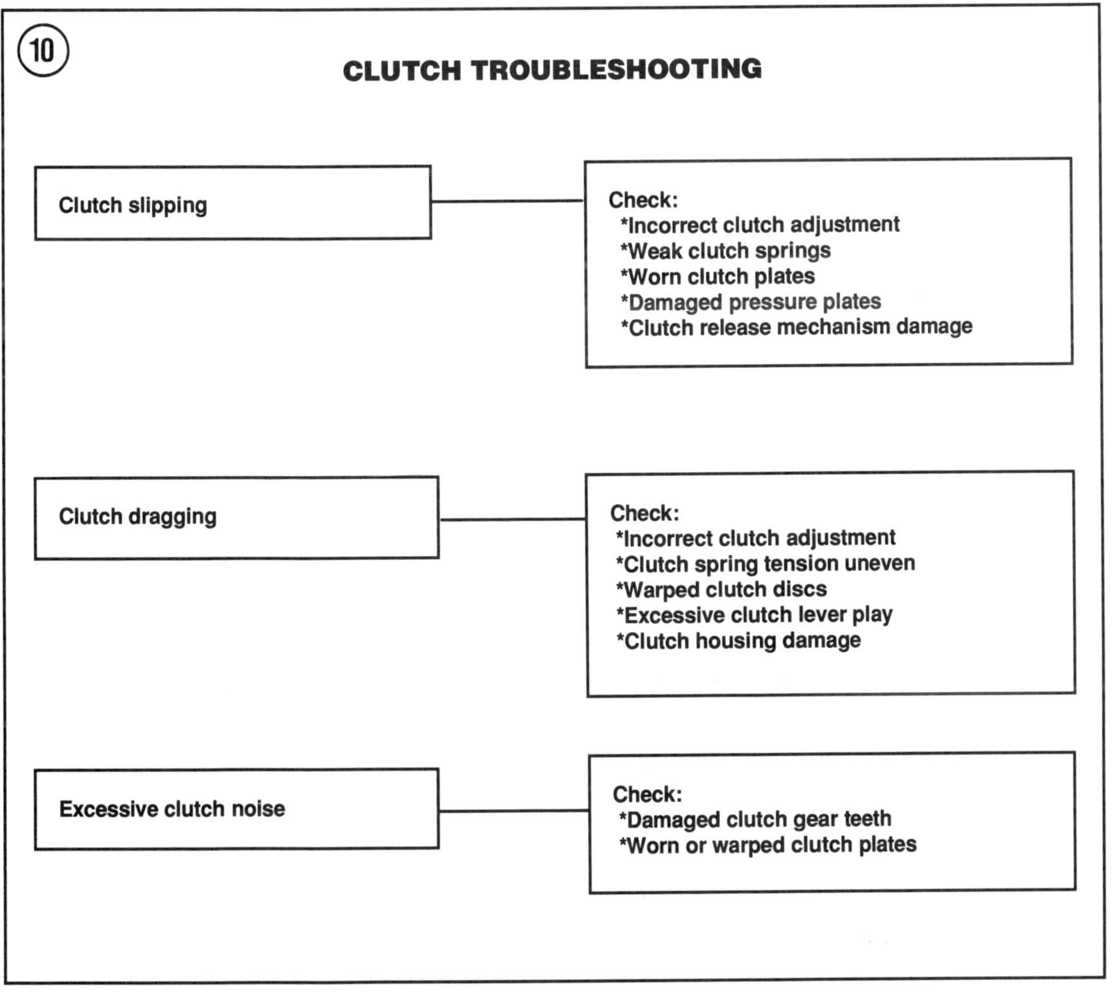

are relatively few. However, when problems arise they stem from one of the following:

a. Weak spark.

b. No spark.

It is possible to check CDI systems that:

a. Do not spark.

b. Have broken or damaged wires.

c. Have a weak spark.

It is difficult to check CDI systems that malfunction due to:

a. Vibration problems.

b. Components that malfunction only when the engine is hot or under a load.

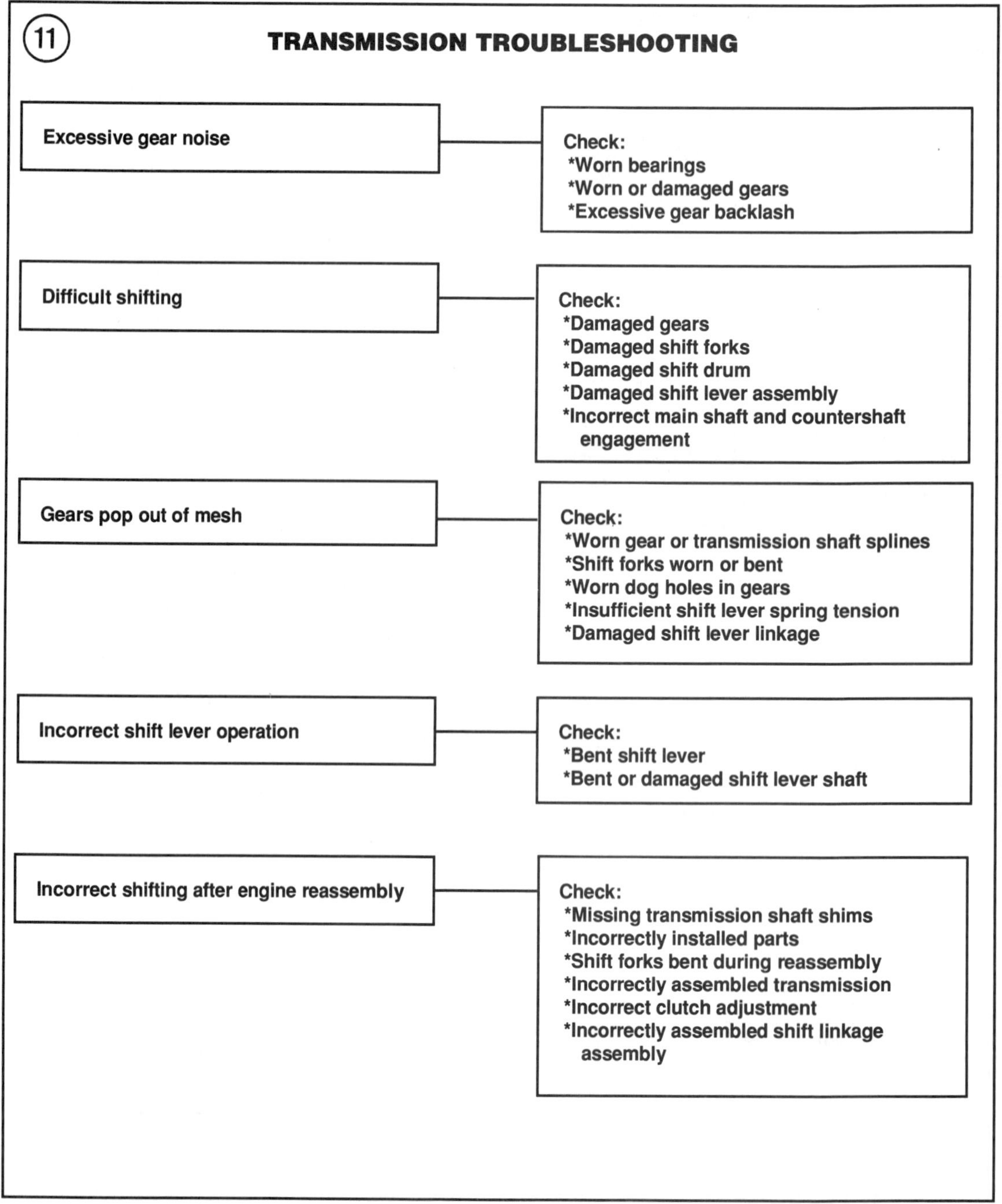

1. Disconnect the engine stop switch (XT600) or kill switch (TT600) and see if the problem still exists.

2. Make sure that the stator plate screws are tight. If the screws are loose, recheck the ignition timing as described in Chapter Three.

3. Remove the fuel tank and un tape all electrical connectors. Make sure the connectors are connected properly. If necessary, clean the connectors with electrical contact cleaner.

4. Check the stator plate for cracks or damage that would cause the coils to be out of alignment.

5. If you cannot locate the problem, refer to *Ignition System Troubleshooting* in Chapter Nine.

FRONT SUSPENSION AND STEERING

Poor handling may be caused by improper front or rear tire pressure, a damaged or bent frame or front steering components, worn swing arm bushings, worn wheel bearings or dragging brakes.

BRAKES

Front Disc Brake

The front disc brake is critical to riding performance and safety. It should be inspected frequently and any problems located and repaired immediately. When replacing or refilling the brake fluid, use only DOT 3 brake fluid from a closed and sealed container. See Chapter Twelve for additional information on brake fluid and disc brake service. The troubleshooting procedures in **Figure 12** will help you isolate the majority of front disc brake troubles.

Drum Brake

The drum brake is relatively simple in design and operation. Yet, many riders do not get full stopping power because the shoes and drum are covered with residue. This residue buildup is due mainly from lack of maintenance. To work properly, the drum brakes must be cleaned and serviced weekly. Periodic maintenance will also allow inspection of parts so that they can be replaced before a part fails.

Refer to the troubleshooting chart in **Figure 13** for drum brake problems and checks to make.

Figures 12 and 13 are on the following pages.

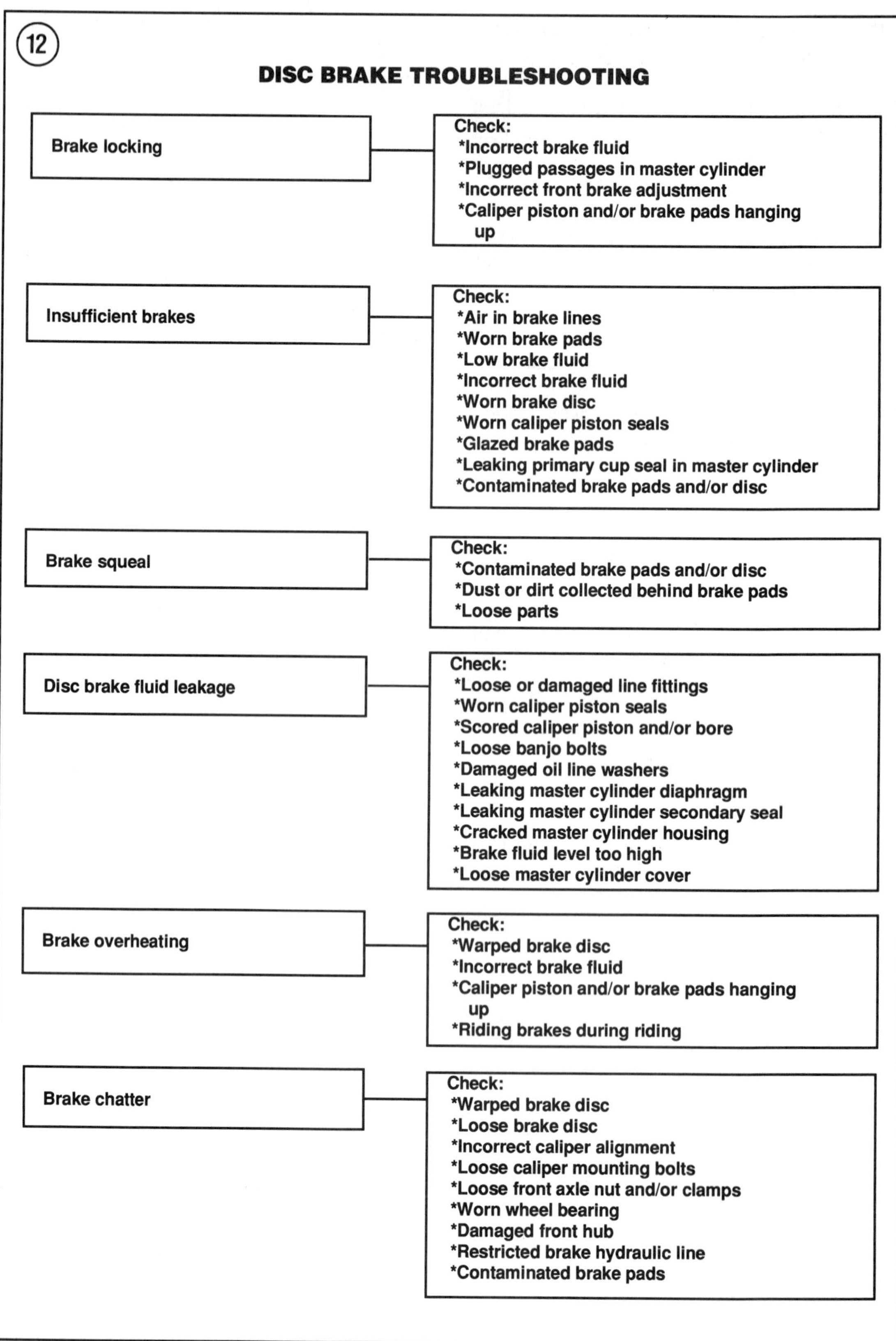
12
DISC BRAKE TROUBLESHOOTING
Brake locking
Check:
*Incorrect brake fluid
*Plugged passages in master cylinder
*Incorrect front brake adjustment
*Caliper piston and/or brake pads hanging up
Insufficient brakes
Check:
*Air in brake lines
*Worn brake pads
*Low brake fluid
*Incorrect brake fluid
*Worn brake disc
*Worn caliper piston seals
*Glazed brake pads
*Leaking primary cup seal in master cylinder
*Contaminated brake pads and/or disc
Brake squeal
Check:
*Contaminated brake pads and/or disc
*Dust or dirt collected behind brake pads
*Loose parts
Disc brake fluid leakage
Check:
*Loose or damaged line fittings
*Worn caliper piston seals
*Scored caliper piston and/or bore
*Loose banjo bolts
*Damaged oil line washers
*Leaking master cylinder diaphragm
*Leaking master cylinder secondary seal
*Cracked master cylinder housing
*Brake fluid level too high
*Loose master cylinder cover
Brake overheating
Check:
*Warped brake disc
*Incorrect brake fluid
*Caliper piston and/or brake pads hanging up
*Riding brakes during riding
Brake chatter
Check:
*Warped brake disc
*Loose brake disc
*Incorrect caliper alignment
*Loose caliper mounting bolts
*Loose front axle nut and/or clamps
*Worn wheel bearing
*Damaged front hub
*Restricted brake hydraulic line
*Contaminated brake pads

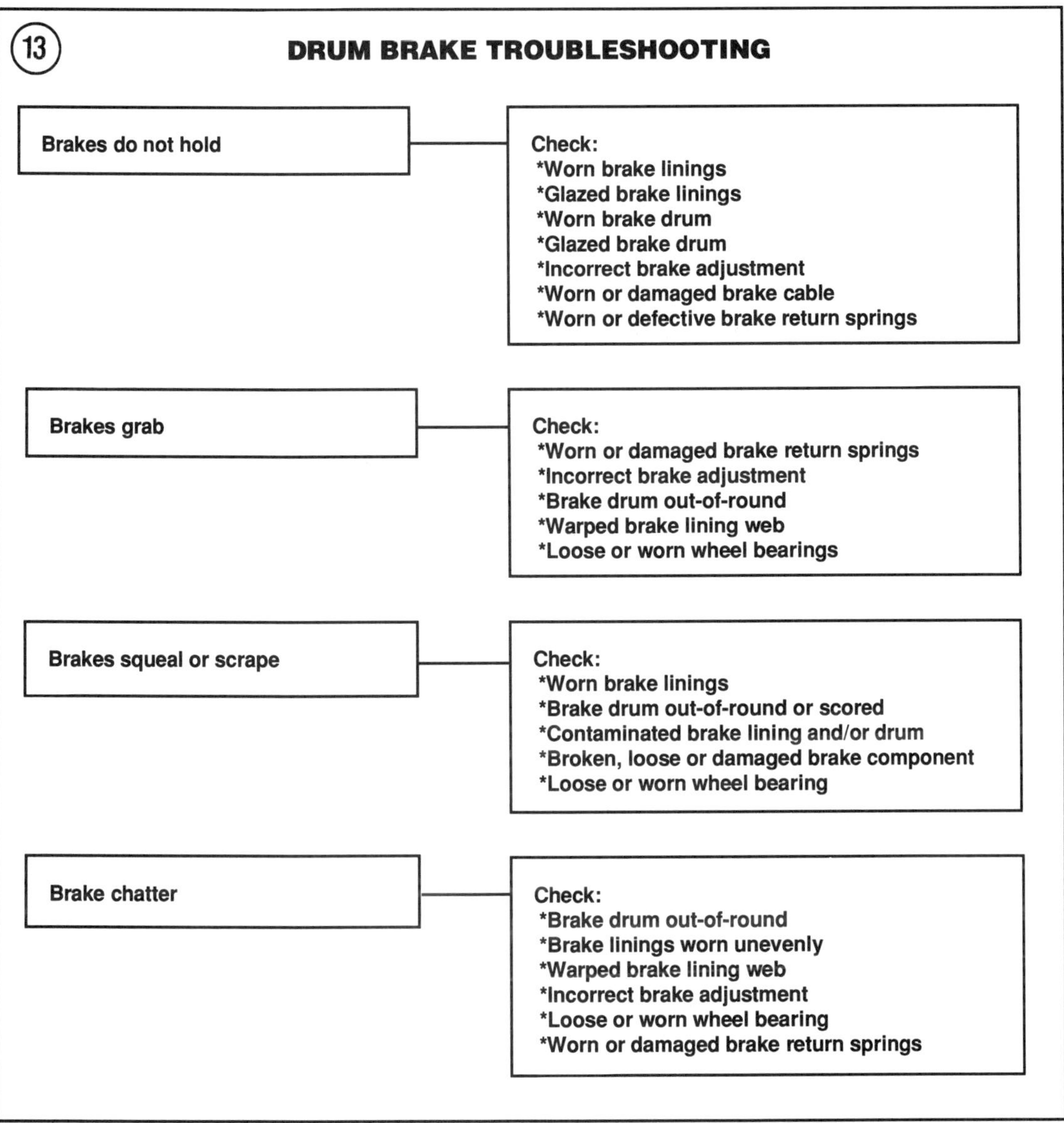
13
DRUM BRAKE TROUBLESHOOTING
Brakes do not hold
Check:
*Worn brake linings
*Glazed brake linings
*Worn brake drum
*Glazed brake drum
*Incorrect brake adjustment
*Worn or damaged brake cable
*Worn or defective brake return springs
Brakes grab
Check:
*Worn or damaged brake return springs
*Incorrect brake adjustment
*Brake drum out-of-round
*Warped brake lining web
*Loose or worn wheel bearings
Brakes squeal or scrape
Check:
*Worn brake linings
*Brake drum out-of-round or scored
*Contaminated brake lining and/or drum
*Broken, loose or damaged brake component
*Loose or worn wheel bearing
Brake chatter
Check:
*Brake drum out-of-round
*Brake linings worn unevenly
*Warped brake lining web
*Incorrect brake adjustment
*Loose or worn wheel bearing
*Worn or damaged brake return springs

CHAPTER THREE

LUBRICATION, MAINTENANCE AND TUNE-UP

Your bike should be cared for by two methods: preventive and corrective maintenance. Because a motorcycle is subjected to tremendous heat, stress and vibration—even in normal use—preventive maintenance prevents costly and unexpected corrective maintenance. When neglected, any bike becomes unreliable and actually dangerous to ride. When properly maintained, your Yamaha is one of the most reliable bikes available and will give many miles and years of dependable and safe riding. By maintaining a routine service schedule as described in this chapter, costly mechanical problems and unexpected breakdowns can be prevented.

The procedures presented in this chapter can be easily performed by anyone with average mechanical skills. **Table 1** is a suggested factory maintenance schedule. **Tables 1-7** are located at the end of this chapter.

PRE-CHECKS

The following checks should be performed prior to the first ride of the day.

1. Inspect the fuel line and fittings for wetness.
2. Make sure the fuel tank is full of fresh gasoline.
3. Make sure the air filter element is clean and that the cover is securely in place.
4. Check the engine oil level in the oil tank.
5. Check the operation of the clutch and adjust if necessary.
6. Check that the clutch and brake levers operate properly with no binding.
7. On XT600 models, check the hydraulic fluid level in the front master cylinder. Add fluid if necessary.
8. Inspect the condition of the front and rear suspension. Make sure it has a good solid feel with no looseness.
9. Check the drive chain for wear and correct tension.
10. Check tire pressure, refer to **Table 2**.

NOTE

*While checking tire pressure, also check the position of the valve stem. If the valve stem is cocked sideways like that shown in **Figure 1**, your riding time could end quickly because of a flat tire. Refer to **Tires and Wheels** in this chapter.*

11. Check the exhaust system for leakage or damage.
12. Check the tightness of all fasteners, especially engine and suspension mounting hardware.
13. Check the rear driven sprocket and bolts as follows:
   a. Check the sprocket holes for signs of egg-shaping. If the sprocket is found in this condition, the sprocket bolts have loosened during riding. If wear is severe, it is suggested that you replace the sprocket before the hub is destroyed.
   b. Check the sprocket nuts for tightness and make sure the lockwasher tabs are against the nuts.
   c. Replace nuts that have started to round at their corners.

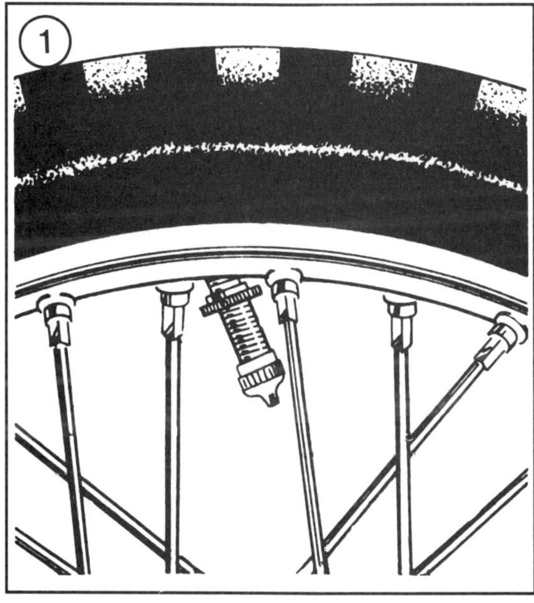

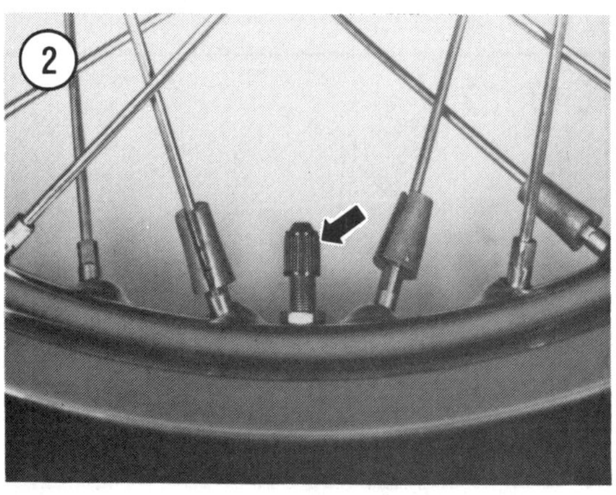

14. On XT600 models, pull the front brake lever and check that the brake light comes on.
15. On XT600 models, apply the rear brake pedal and check that the brake light comes on soon after you have begun depressing the pedal.
16. On XT600 models, with the engine running, check to see that the headlight and taillight are on.
17A. On XT600 models, move the dimmer switch up and down between the high and low positions, and check to see that both headlight elements are working.
17B. On TT600 models, pull the light switch up to the ON position and check to see that both the headlight and taillight are working.
18. On XT600 models, push the turn signal switch to the left position and then to the right position and check that all 4 turn signal lights work properly.
19. On XT600 models, push the horn button and note if the horn blows loudly.
20. If the horn or any light failed to work properly, refer to Chapter Nine.

TIRES AND WHEELS

Tire Pressure

Tire pressure should be checked and adjusted to maintain good traction and handling. An accurate gauge should be carried in your tool box. The approximate tire inflation pressure specifications are listed in **Table 2**.

NOTE
*After checking and adjusting the air pressure, make sure to install the air valve cap (**Figure 2**). The cap prevents small pebbles and dirt from collecting in the valve stem; this could allow air leakage or result in incorrect tire pressure readings.*

Tire Inspection

The tires take a lot of punishment due to the variety of terrain they are subject to. Inspect them periodically for excessive wear, cuts, abrasions, etc. Sidewall tears are the most common cause of tire failure. This type of damaged is usually caused by sharp rocks or other trail conditions when riding off-road. Often times, sidewall tears cannot be seen from the outside. If necessary, remove the tire from the rim as described in Chapter Ten. Run your hand around the inside tire casing to feel for tears or sharp objects imbedded in the casing. The outside of the tire can be inspected visually.

While checking the tires, also check the position of the valve stem. If the valve stem is cocked sideways like that shown in **Figure 1**, your riding day could end because of a flat tire. Refer to *Valve Stem Alignment* in this chapter.

Wheel Spoke Tension

Tap each spoke with a wrench. The higher the pitch of sound it makes, the tighter the spoke. The lower the sound frequency, the looser the spoke. A "ping" is good, a "klunk" says the spoke is too loose.

If one or more spokes are loose, tighten them as described in Chapter Ten.

NOTE
Most spokes loosen as a group rather than individually. Extra-loose spokes should be tightened carefully. Bringing just a few spokes tight into the rim will put improper pressure across the wheel. Refer to Chapter Ten.

Rim Inspection

Frequently inspect the condition of the wheel rims. If a rim has been damaged it may be enough to cause excessive side-to-side play. Refer to in Chapter Ten.

Valve Stem Alignment

Before each riding day, check each tube valve stem for alignment. **Figure 1** shows a valve stem that has slipped. If the tube is not repositioned, the valve stem will eventually pull away from the tube, causing a flat. However, don't get your tire irons out yet. The tube can be aligned without removing the tire.

1. Thoroughly wash the tire (especially the sides) if it is dirty or caked with mud.
2. Remove the valve stem core and release all air pressure from the tube.
3. Loosen the rim locknut (**Figure 3**) if so equipped.
4. With an assistant steadying the bike and holding the front brake on, squeeze the tire and break the tire-to-wheel seal all the way around the perimeter of the wheel. If the tire seal is very tight, it may be necessary to lay the bike on its side and break the tire seal with your foot or a rubber mallet. Use care though; have an assistant steady the bike so that it doesn't rock and damage the handlebars or a control lever.
5. After the tire seal is broken, put the bike on a stand so that the wheel clears the ground.
6. Apply a mixture of soap and water from a spray container (like that used when changing a tire) along the tire bead on both sides of the tire.
7. Have an assistant apply the brake "hard." If necessary, tighten the front or rear brake adjuster.
8. Using both of your hands, grab hold of the tire and turn it and the tube until the valve stem is straight up at 90° to the rim as shown in **Figure 2**.
9. When the valve stem is straight up, install the valve stem core and inflate the tire. If the soap and water solution has dried, reapply it to help the tire seat on the rim. Check the tire to make sure it seats all the way around the rim.

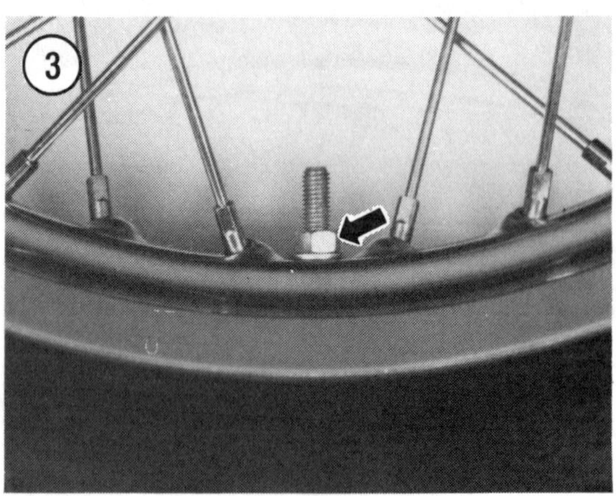

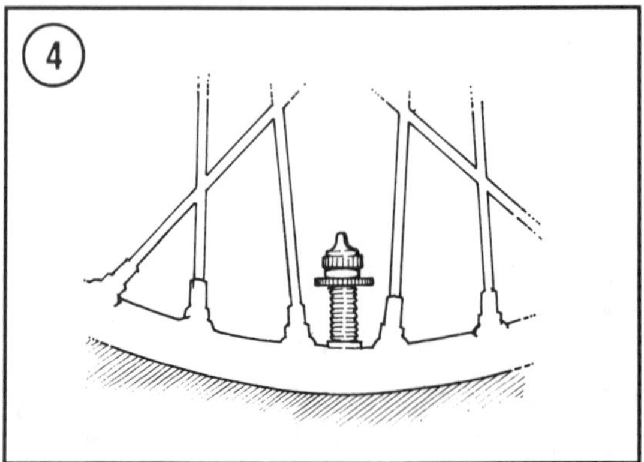

WARNING
Do not overinflate the tire and tube. If the tire will not seat properly, remove the valve stem core and re-lubricate the tire.

10. Tighten the rim locknut (**Figure 3**) securely.
11. Adjust the tire pressure as listed in **Table 2**.
12. Install the valve stem nut but do not tighten it against the rim. If the tire and tube slip again, the valve stem will pull away from the tube and cause a flat. Instead, tighten the nut against the valve cap as shown in **Figure 4**. This will allow the valve stem to slip without damage until you can reposition the tire and tube.

LUBRICANTS

Engine Oil

Oil is classified according to its viscosity, which is an indication of how thick it is. The Society of Automotive Engineers (SAE) system distinguishes oil viscosity by numbers, called "weights." Thick (heavy) oils have higher viscosity numbers than thin (light) oils. For example, a 5 weight (SAE 5) oil is a light oil while a 90 weight (SAE 90) oil is relatively heavy. The viscosity of the oil has nothing to do with its lubricating properties.

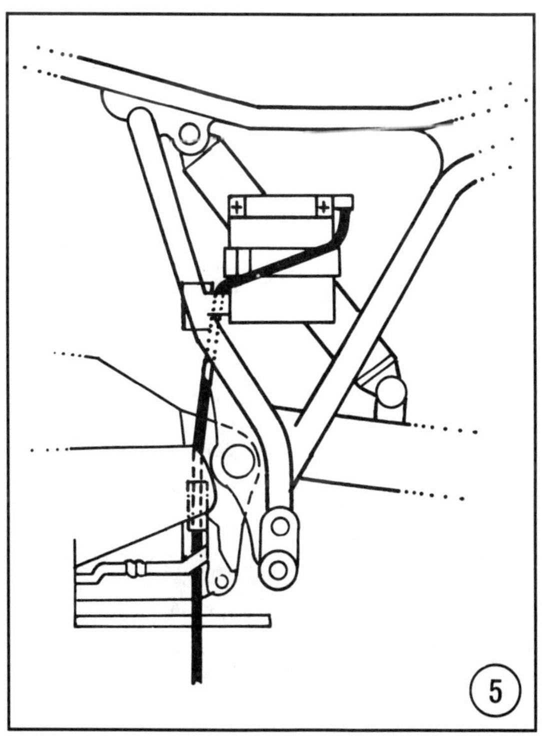

Grease

A good-quality grease—preferably waterproof—should be used for many of the parts on your Yamaha. Water does not wash grease off parts as easily as it washes off oil. In addition, grease maintains its lubricating qualities better than oil on long and strenuous events.

In some cases in this book a special grease called molybdenum disulfide grease is specified. It is used on some parts during engine assembly and on some suspension components. Whenever this type of grease is specified, it should be used as it has special lubricating qualities. Be sure to use this special type of grease, even though it may be more expensive than ordinary multipurpose grease.

BATTERY (XT600)

The battery is an important component in your Yamaha's electrical system. It is also the one most frequently neglected. In addition to checking and correcting the battery electrolyte level on a weekly basis, the battery should be cleaned and inspected at periodic intervals.

The battery used on your Yamaha should be checked periodically for electrolyte level, state of charge and corrosion. During hot weather periods, frequent checks are recommended. If the electrolyte level is below the fill line, add distilled water as required. To assure proper mixing of the water and acid, operate the engine immediately after adding water. *Never* add battery acid instead of water; this will shorten the battery's life.

CAUTION
*If it becomes necessary to remove the battery vent tube when performing any of the following procedures, make sure to route the tube correctly during installation to prevent acid from spilling onto surrounding parts. A battery vent tube routing diagram is shown in **Figure 5**.*

NOTE
***Recycle your old battery**. When you replace the old battery, be sure to turn in the old battery at that time. The lead*

*plates and the plastic case can be recycled. Most motorcycle dealers will accept your old battery in trade when you purchase a new one, but if they will not, many automotive supply stores certainly will. **Never** place an old battery in your household trash since it is illegal, in most states, to place any acid or lead (heavy metal) contents in landfills. There is also the danger of the battery being crushed in the trash truck and spraying acid on the truck operator.*

Removal/Electrolyte Level Check/Installation

The battery is the heart of the electrical system. It should be checked and serviced as indicated in **Table 1**. Most electrical system troubles can be attributed to neglect of this vital component.

In order to correctly service the electrolyte level, it is necessary to remove the battery from the frame. The electrolyte level should be maintained between the two marks on the battery case (**Figure 6**). If the electrolyte level is low, it's a good idea to completely remove the battery so that it can be thoroughly cleaned, serviced and checked.

1. Make sure the ignition switch is turned OFF.
2. Remove the seat.
3. Remove the frame left-hand side cover (**Figure 7**).
4. Disconnect the battery negative (–) cable electrical connector (A, **Figure 8**) from the terminal on the battery.
5. Disconnect the battery positive (+) cable electrical connector (B, **Figure 8**).
6. Disconnect the battery hold-down strap (**Figure 9**).
7. Pull the battery out slightly and disconnect the battery vent tube (**Figure 10**) from the right-hand side of the battery. Leave the breather tube routed through the frame.
8. Lay several thick layers of old newspapers or disposable shop cloths on top of your workbench where you intend to place the battery. This will protect the work bench surface if there is electrolyte residue on the sides and bottom of the battery.
9. Carefully slide the battery out of the battery box in the frame and remove it.
10. Set the battery on the newspapers or disposable shop cloths (**Figure 11**).

WARNING
Protect your eyes, skin and clothing. If electrolyte gets into your eyes, flush your eyes thoroughly with clean water and get prompt medical attention.

CAUTION
Be careful not to spill battery electrolyte on painted or polished surfaces. The

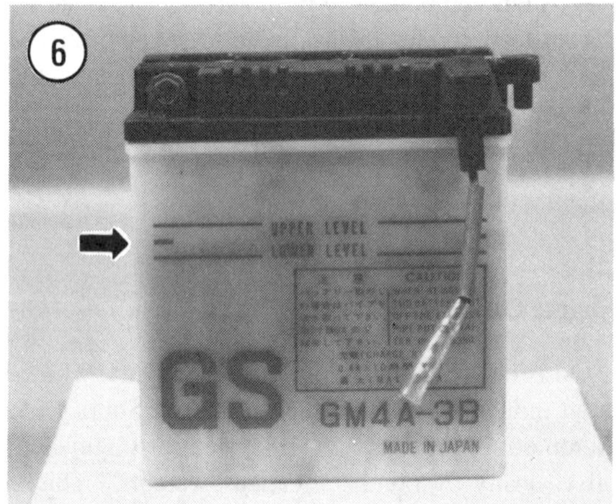

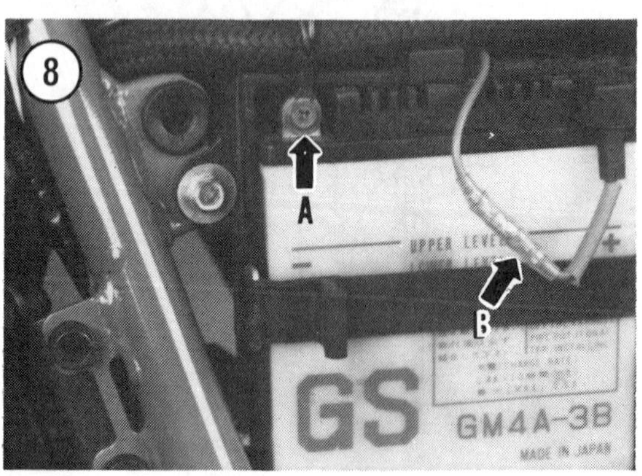

9

10

11

12

liquid is highly corrosive and will damage the finish. If it is spilled, wash it off immediately with soapy water and thoroughly rinse with clean water.

11. If the electrolyte level is low, remove the caps (**Figure 12**) from the battery cells and add distilled water. Never add electrolyte (acid) to correct the level. Fill only to the upper battery level mark (**Figure 6**).

12. Install the battery filler caps (**Figure 12**) and tighten securely.

NOTE

If distilled water has been added, reinstall the battery caps and gently shake the battery for several minutes to help mix the new water with the existing electrolyte.

CAUTION

If distilled water has been added to a battery in freezing or near freezing weather, add it to the battery, dress warmly and then ride the bike for a ***minimum of 30 minutes****. This will help mix the water thoroughly into the electrolyte. Distilled water is lighter than electrolyte and will float on top of the electrolyte if it is not mixed in properly. If the water stays on the top, it may freeze and fracture the battery case, ruining the battery.*

13. After the fluid level has been corrected and the battery allowed to stand for a few minutes, remove the battery caps and check the specific gravity of the electrolyte with a hydrometer following the manufacturer's instructions for reading the instrument. See *Battery Testing* in this chapter.

14. After the battery has been refilled, recharged or replaced, install it by reversing these removal steps. Note the following.

15. Be sure to attach the battery vent tube (**Figure 10**) onto the right-hand side of the battery. Make sure the breather tube is routed correctly through the frame.

16. Clean the battery negative (–) terminal (A, **Figure 13**), the positive cable electrical connector (B, **Figure 13**) and the battery positive (+) terminal (C, **Figure 13**). Also clean the surrounding case (D, **Figure 13**).

17. Carefully clean the interior of the battery box (**Figure 14**) with solvent and a disposable rag or towel. Clean out all loose corrosive powder that may have fallen off of a corroded battery.
18. Reinstall the battery in the frame.
19. Coat the battery terminals with Vaseline or protective spray (**Figure 15**) to retard corrosion and decomposition of the terminals.

CAUTION
If the breather tube was removed from the frame, be sure to route it so that residue will not drain onto any part of the bike's frame or drive chain. The tube must be free of bends or twists as any restrictions may pressurize the battery and damage it.

CAUTION
The battery must be installed in the frame correctly so that the battery cables will be attached to the correct terminals (positive-to-positive and negative-to-negative).

20. Position the battery so the battery cable terminals are facing toward the outside (**Figure 16**).

CAUTION
*Make sure to reconnect the battery hold down strap (**Figure 9**) to prevent the battery from vibrating during riding. Vibration can damage the battery plates and short out the battery internally.*

NOTE
*When reconnecting the battery electrical leads, always reconnect the battery positive (+) electrical connector (**B, Figure 8**) first, then reconnect the negative lead to the negative terminal on the battery (**A, Figure 8**).*

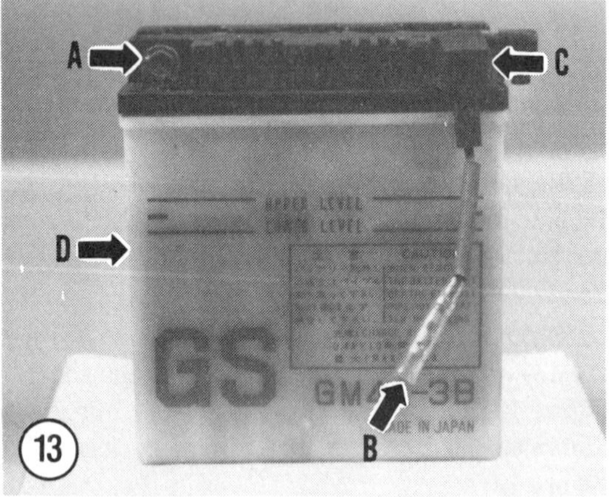

Testing

Hydrometer testing is the best way to check battery condition. Use a hydrometer with numbered graduations from 1.100 to 1.300 rather than one with just color-coded bands. To use the hydrometer, perform the following.

1. Remove the battery as described in this chapter.

2. Remove the battery filler caps (**Figure 12**) from each cell.

3. Squeeze the rubber ball, insert the tip into the cell and release the pressure on the ball.

NOTE
It is important to note that specific gravity varies with temperature. If a temperature-compensated hydrometer is not used, add 0.004 to the specific gravity reading for every 10° above 80° F (25° C). For every 10° below 80° F (25° C), subtract 0.004.

4. Draw enough electrolyte to float the weighted float inside the hydrometer. Note the number in line with the surface of the electrolyte (**Figure 17**), this is the specific gravity for this cell.

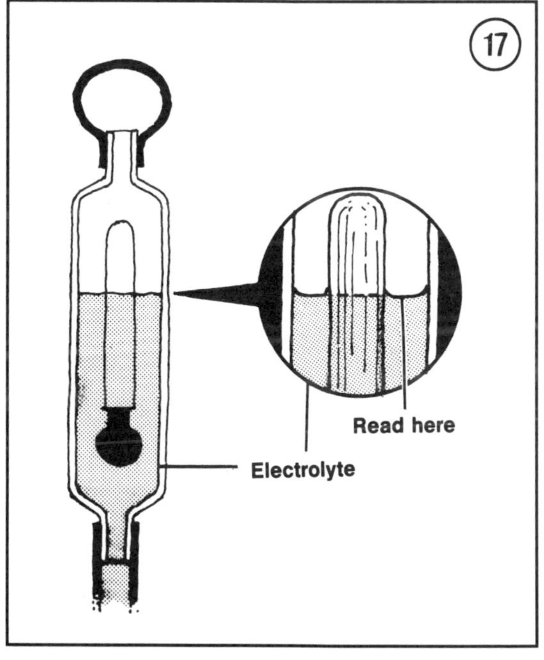

a. The specific gravity of the electrolyte in each battery cell is an excellent indication of that cell's condition. A fully charged cell will read from 1.265-1.280, while a cell in good condition reads from 1.225-1.265 and anything below 1.125 is practically dead. Refer to **Figure 18**.

b. If the cells test in the poor range, the battery requires recharging. The hydrometer is useful for checking the progress of the charging operation. **Table 3** shows approximate state of charge.

5. Squeeze the rubber ball again and return the electrolyte to the cell from which it came.

6. Install the caps onto each battery cell and tighten securely.

7. Install the battery as described in this chapter.

Charging

CAUTION
Always remove the battery from the bike's frame before connecting the battery charger. Never recharge a battery in the bike's frame; the corrosive mist that is emitted during the charging process will corrode all surrounding surfaces.

WARNING
During the charging process, highly explosive hydrogen gas is released from the battery. The battery should be charged only in a well-ventilated area away from any open flames (including pilot lights on home gas appliances). Do not allow any smoking in the area. Never check the charge by arcing (connecting pliers or other metal objects)

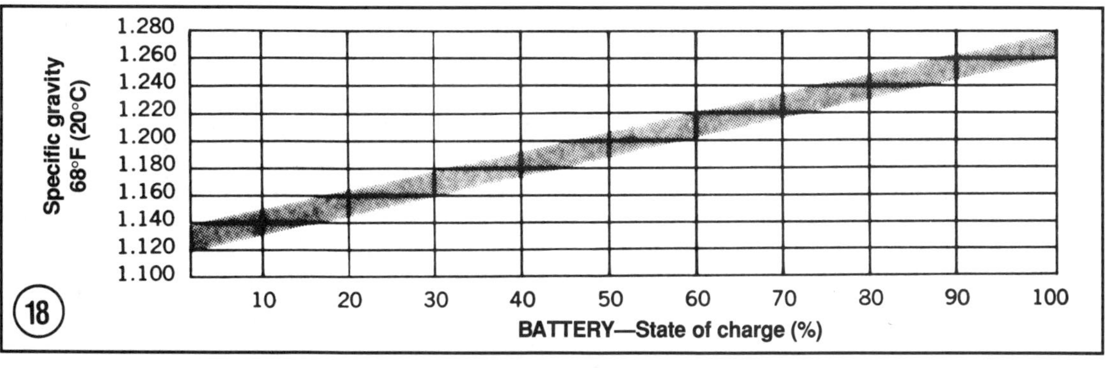

across the terminals; the resulting spark can ignite the hydrogen gas.

1. Remove the battery as described in this chapter.

2. Pull back the rubber boot (A, **Figure 19**) and disconnect the electrical wire (B, **Figure 19**) from the battery positive terminal.

3. Connect the positive (+) charger lead to the positive battery terminal and the negative (–) charger lead to the negative battery terminal.

4. Remove all vent caps (**Figure 12**) from the battery.

5. Set the charger at 12 volts and switch it ON. Normally, a battery should be charged at a slow charge rate of 1/10 its given capacity. The recommended charging rate for batteries in models covered in this manual is 0.3 amps.

CAUTION
*The electrolyte level must be maintained at the upper level (**Figure 6**) during the charging cycle; check and refill as necessary.*

6. The charging time depends on the discharged condition of the battery. For example, if the specific gravity of your battery is 1.180, the approximate charging time would be 6 hours.

Battery Electrical Cable Connectors

To ensure good electrical contact between the battery and the electrical cables, the cables must be clean and free of corrosion.

1. If the electrical cable terminals are badly corroded, disconnect them from the bike's electrical system.

2. Thoroughly clean each connector with a wire brush and then with a baking soda solution. Wipe dry with a clean cloth.

3. After cleaning, apply a very thin coat of petroleum jelly, such as Vaseline or a light mineral grease, to the battery terminals before reattaching the cables.

4. If disconnected, connect the electrical cables to the bike's electrical system.

5. After connecting the electrical cables, apply a light coating of Vaseline or protective spray (**Figure 15**) to the electrical terminals of the battery to retard corrosion and decomposition of the terminals.

New Battery Installation

When replacing the old battery with a new one, be sure to charge it completely (specific gravity, 1.260-1.280) before installing it in the bike. Failure to do so, or using the battery with a low electrolyte level will permanently damage the battery. When purchasing a new battery, the correct battery capacity is 12 volts/4 amp hours.

PERIODIC LUBRICATION

Engine Oil Level Check

The engine in the XT600 and TT600 models is a dry-sump type where the engine oil is stored in the oil tank rather than in the engine crankcase. The oil tank is located on the left-hand side of the bike under the frame's left-hand side cover.

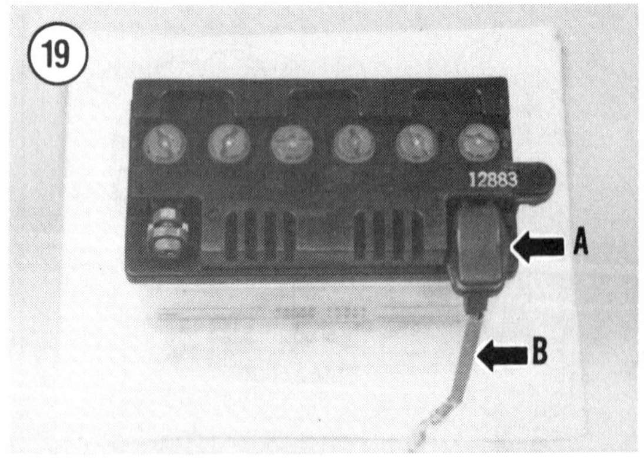

WARNING
*Do **not** unscrew the filler cap/dipstick after a high-speed ride. The oil tank is slightly pressurized from the heated oil and the heated oil may spurt out of the tank and burn your skin. Wait 2-3 minutes until the oil cools down to approximately 60° C (140° F). Protect yourself accordingly.*

1. If the engine is cold, start the engine and let it reach normal operating temperature. Usually 10-15 minutes of stop-and-go riding is sufficient.

2. Allow the engine to idle for more than 10 seconds and then shut it off.

3. Stop the engine and allow the oil to settle for 1-2 minutes.

4. Park the bike on level ground and rest it on the sidestand.

5. Remove the frame left-hand side cover (**Figure 7**).

6. Have an assistant hold the bike in the upright position.

7. Unscrew the oil tank filler cap/dipstick and wipe it clean with a lint-free cloth. Refer to **Figure 20** for XT600 models or **Figure 21** for TT600 models.

8. Reinsert it onto the threads in the hole; do *not* screw it in.

9. Remove the filler cap/dipstick and check the oil level. The bike must be on level ground and upright for a correct reading.

10. The oil level should be between the upper (MAX) and lower (MIN) lines (**Figure 22**). The oil level should never be above the upper line nor below the lower line.

11. If there is *no oil* on the filler cap/dipstick, perform the following:
   a. Insert a small funnel into the filler hole in the oil tank.
   b. Add the recommended weight and type of engine oil as indicated in **Table 4** until the oil level is at the MIN line on filler cap/dipstick.
   c. Install the filler cap/dipstick and screw it on all the way.
   d. Start the engine and let it reach normal operating temperature. Usually 10-15 minutes of stop-and-go riding is sufficient.
   e. Allow the engine to idle for more than 10 seconds and then shut it off.
   f. Allow the oil to settle for 1-2 minutes.
   g. Recheck the oil level and adjust if necessary.

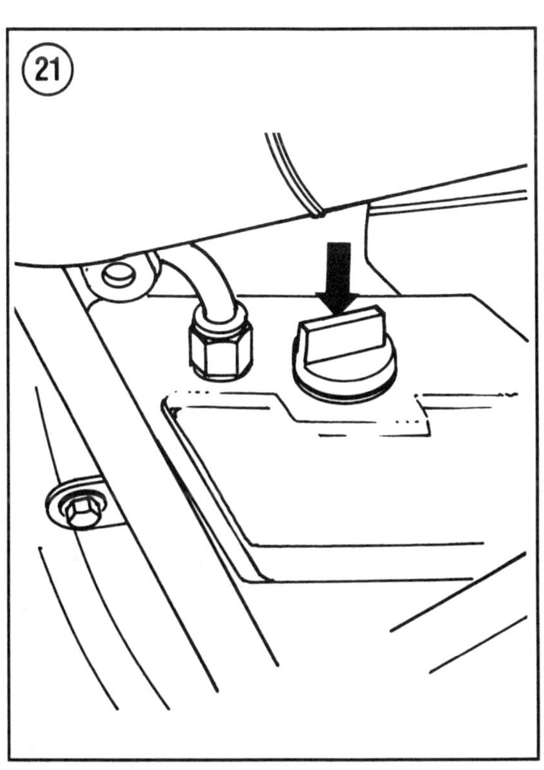

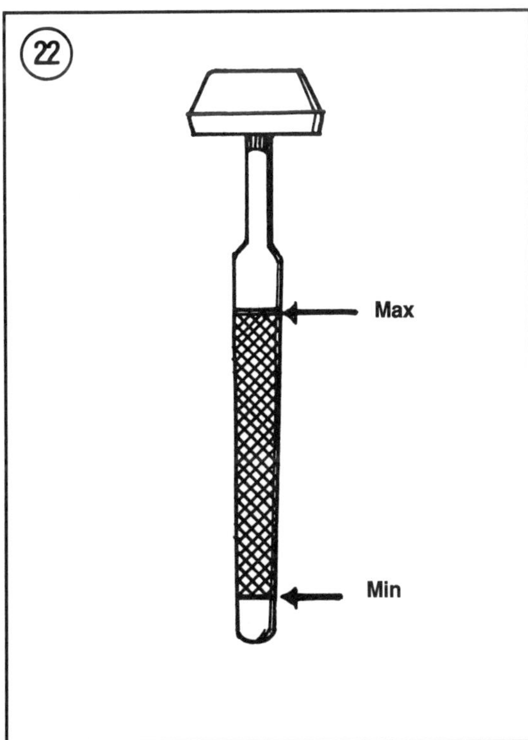

12. If additional oil is necessary, perform the following:

   a. Insert a small funnel into the filler hole in the oil tank.
   b. Add the recommended weight and type of engine oil indicated in **Table 4** to correct the level. Do not overfill.

13. Install the filler cap/dipstick and screw it on securely.
14. Install the frame left-hand side cover.

Engine Oil and Filter Change

The factory-recommended oil and filter change interval is specified in **Table 1**. This assumes that the motorcycle is operated in moderate climates. The time interval is more important than the mileage interval because combustion acids, formed by gasoline and water vapor, will contaminate the oil even if the motorcycle is not run for several months. If a motorcycle is operated under dusty conditions, the oil will get dirty more quickly and should be changed more frequently than recommended.

Use only a high-quality detergent oil with an API classification of SE or SF. The classification is stamped on top of the can or on the bottle label (**Figure 23**). Always try to use the same brand of oil at each oil change. Use of oil additives is not recommended. Refer to **Table 4** for recommended weight of oil to use.

To change the engine oil and filter you will need the following:

   a. Drain pan.
   b. Funnel.
   c. Can opener or pour spout (oil in cans).
   d. Allen wrench.
   e. 19 mm wrench or socket to remove drain plug.
   f. 3 quarts of oil. Refer to **Table 5** for specified quantities.
   g. New oil filter element.

There are a number of ways to discard the used oil safely. The easiest way is to pour it from the drain pan into a gallon plastic bleach, juice or milk container for disposal.

NOTE

Never dispose of motor oil in the trash, on the ground, or down a storm drain. Many service stations accept used motor oil and waste haulers provide curbside used motor oil collection. Do not combine other fluids with motor oil to be recycled. To locate a recycler, contact the American Petroleum Institute (API) at ***www.recycleoil.org****.*

NOTE

Warming the engine allows the oil to heat up; thus it flows freely and carries contamination and any sludge buildup out with it.

1. If the engine is cold, start the engine and let it reach normal operating temperature. Usually 10-15 minutes of stop-and-go riding is sufficient. Shut the engine off.

NOTE

Skid plate removal is not necessary, but it will keep some of the oil from draining onto it in the next step.

2. On XT600 models, remove the bolts securing the skid plate (A, **Figure 24**) and remove the skid plate.

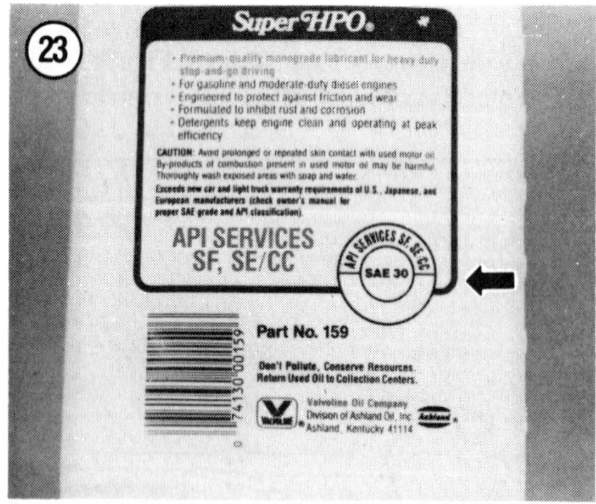

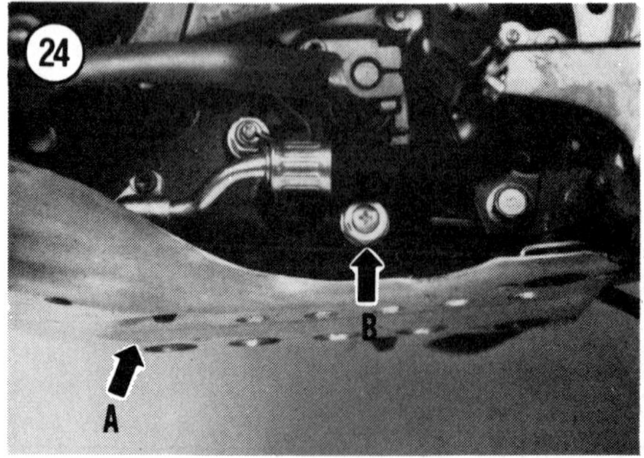

This will allow the oil to drain directly into the drain pan and not onto the skid plate.

WARNING
During the next step, hot oil will spurt from the drain plug hole. Be ready to move your hand away quickly once the drain plug is removed so hot oil will not run on your hand and down your arm.

25

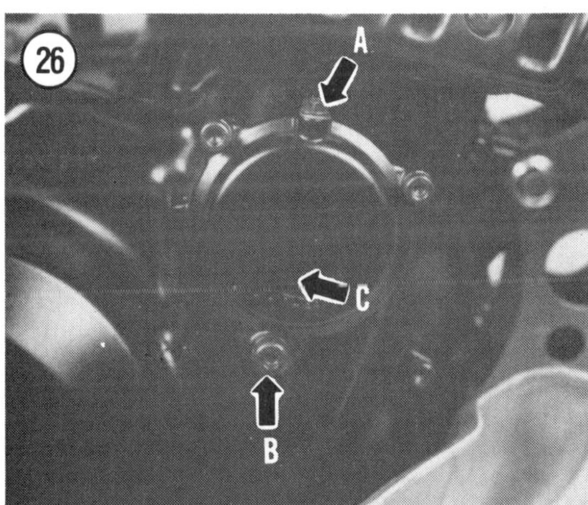

26

27

3. Remove the frame's left-hand side cover (**Figure 7**).
4. To drain the oil tank, perform the following:
   a. Unscrew the oil tank filler cap/dipstick from the oil tank. Refer to **Figure 20** for XT600 models or **Figure 21** for TT600 models.
   b. Place a drip pan under the drain bolt location on the oil tank and have an assistant hold the drain pan in this position.
   c. Remove the oil tank drain bolt and gasket (**Figure 25**) from the base of the oil tank.
   d. Allow the oil to drain for a minimum of 5 minutes.
   e. Inspect the gasket on the drain bolt for wear or damage, replace if necessary.
   f. Reinstall the drain bolt and gasket. Tighten the bolt to the torque specification listed in **Table 6**.
5. To drain the residual oil from the crankcase, perform the following:
   a. Move the drain pan under the crankcase on the left-hand side and remove the engine drain bolt and gasket (B, **Figure 24**).
   b. Allow the oil to drain for a minimum of 5 minutes.
   c. Inspect the gasket on the drain bolt for wear or damage, replace if necessary.
   d. Thoroughly clean out the drain plug area in the crankcase with a shop rag and solvent.
   e. Reinstall the drain bolt and gasket. Tighten the bolt to the torque specification listed in **Table 6**.
6. To drain the residual oil from the oil filter cavity, perform the following:
   a. Move the drain pan under the crankcase on the left-hand side and remove the air bleed screw and gasket (A, **Figure 26**) on the oil filter cover.
   b. Remove the lower screw (B, **Figure 26**) securing the cover. This screw also doubles as the drain screw.
   c. Allow the oil to drain for a minimum of 5 minutes.
   d. Remove the remaining screws and remove the oil filter cover (C, **Figure 26**).
   e. Withdraw the oil filter (A, **Figure 27**) from the receptacle in the crankcase.
   f. Place the used oil filter in a heavy plastic bag to contain any residual oil. Close off the end of the bag to prevent oil from draining out.

3

g. Clean off the inner surface of the oil filter cover and the filter receptacle (**Figure 28**) in the crankcase with a shop rag and cleaning solvent. Remove any oil sludge if necessary. Wipe it dry with a clean, lint-free cloth.
h. Remove the O-ring seal from the oil filter cover (**Figure 29**) and from the drain bolt hole in the crankcase (**Figure 30**). Inspect the O-rings for hardness or deterioration, replace if necessary. Reinstall the O-ring seals.
i. Install a new oil filter element with the rubber O-ring (B, **Figure 27**) facing out toward the cover.
j. Install the oil filter cover and install the screws securing the cover. Tighten the screws to the torque specification listed in **Table 6**.
k. Inspect the gasket on the air bleed screw for wear or damage, replace if necessary.
l. Reinstall the air bleed screw and gasket. Tighten the screw to the torque specification listed in **Table 6**.

7. To remove and clean the oil strainer in the oil tank, perform the following:
a. Remove the screws securing the lower oil line fitting (**Figure 31**) to the oil tank.
b. Carefully lower the oil line down and away from the oil tank.
c. Remove the oil strainer.
d. Remove the O-ring seals from the lower oil line fitting. Inspect the O-rings for hardness or deterioration, replace if necessary. Reinstall the O-ring seals.
e. Thoroughly clean the oil strainer with solvent and a soft-tooth brush and thoroughly dry with compressed air. Inspect the filter screen for holes or defects. If the oil strainer is damaged in any way, replace it.
f. Install the O-ring seals into the lower oil line fitting.
g. Install the oil strainer and move the lower oil line into position on the base of the oil tank.
h. Install the screws and tighten securely.

8. Insert a funnel into the oil fill hole in the oil tank and fill the engine with the correct type (**Table 4**) and quantity (**Table 5**) of oil.

9. Screw in the oil filler cap/dipstick into the oil tank and tighten securely. Refer to **Figure 20** for XT600 models or **Figure 21** for TT600 models.

10. Start the engine and check for oil leaks. If necessary, tighten any drain bolts or screws.

11. Turn the engine off and check the oil level, correct if necessary.

12. Install the skid plate underneath the engine and install the bolts. Tighten the bolts securely.

13. Install the frame's left-hand side cover.

28

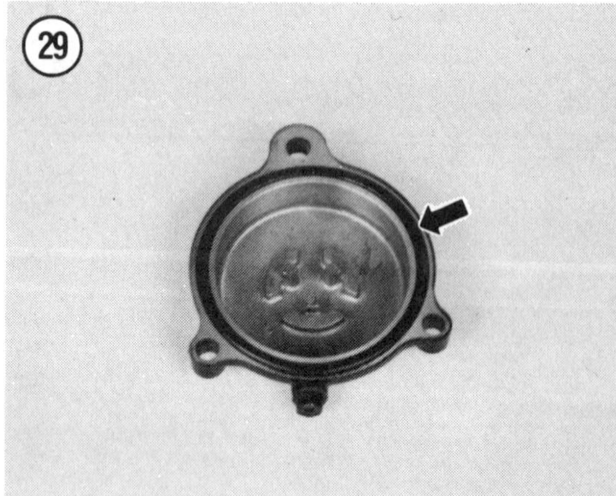
29

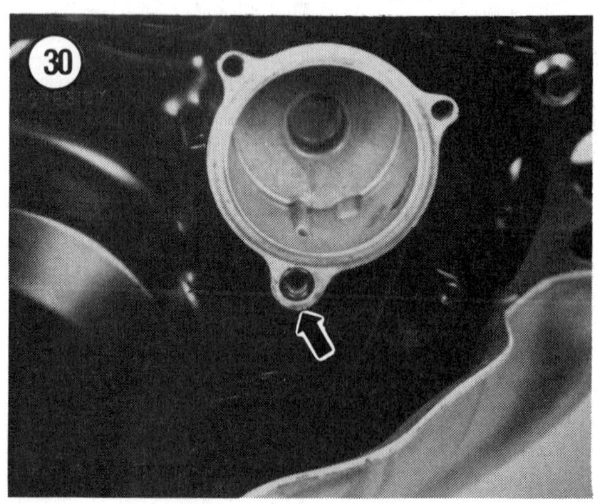
30

Oil Pressure Check

If you feel the oil pressure is not up to specification, perform the following.

NOTE

This is also a good check to perform after disassembling or rebuilding the engine. After the initial start-up of the engine, perform this test to make sure the oil is circulating correctly.

1. Start the engine and let it idle for 2-3 minutes. Turn the engine off.

2. Remove the air bleed screw and gasket (A, **Figure 32**) from the oil filter cover.

3. Remove the screws securing the exhaust pipe protector (B, **Figure 32**) and remove the protector.

4. Install an oil pressure gauge adaptor (Yamaha part No. YU-08030) into the air bleed screw opening in the oil filter cover.

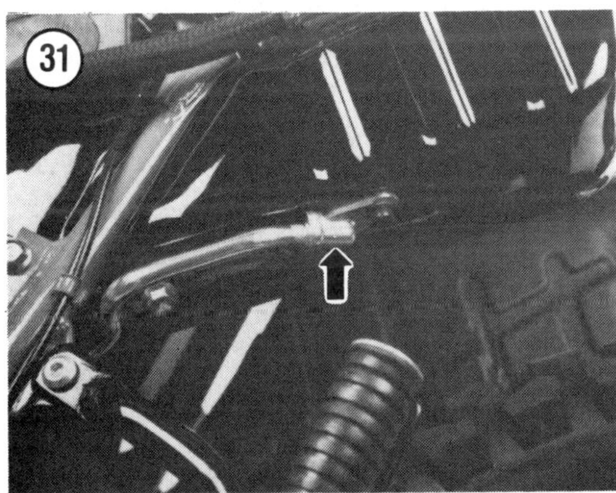
31

32

5A. If using an oil pressure gauge, perform the following:

a. Attach the oil pressure gauge to the gauge adaptor.
b. Start the engine and allow it to idle; do not increase engine rpm.
c. The specified oil pressure is 9.81-19.6 kPa (1.42-2.84 psi). If the oil pressure is below that specified, immediately stop the engine and determine and correct the problem.
d. Turn the engine off and disconnect the oil pressure gauge from the gauge adaptor.

5B. If an oil pressure gauge is not available, you can at least check to see that the oil is traveling from the engine to the oil tank as follows:

a. Attach a length of clear vinyl hose that fits snugly onto the oil pressure gauge adaptor installed in Step 4.
b. Remove the frame's left-hand side cover.
c. Remove the oil filler cap/dipstick from the oil tank. Refer to **Figure 20** for XT600 models or **Figure 21** for TT600 models.
d. Place the other end of the clear vinyl hose into the dipstick opening in the oil tank.
e. Start the engine and allow it to idle; do not increase engine rpm.
f. Oil should flow through the vinyl hose and into the oil tank. If not, immediately stop the engine and locate the problem.
g. Turn the engine off and disconnect the vinyl hose from oil pressure gauge adaptor and remove the hose from the oil tank.
h. Install the oil filler cap/dipstick into the oil tank and tighten securely. Refer to **Figure 20** for XT600 models or **Figure 21** for TT600 models.
i. Install the frame's left-hand side cover.

6. Unscrew the oil pressure gauge adaptor from the oil filter cover.

7. Install the air bleed screw and gasket (A, **Figure 32**) and tighten to the torque specification listed in **Table 6**.

8. Install the exhaust pipe protector (B, **Figure 32**) and screws. Tighten the screws securely.

9. Recheck the engine oil level after the oil has settled and fill if necessary until the correct level is obtained.

Front Fork Oil Change

The fork oil should be changed at the interval listed in **Table 1** or once a year. If it becomes contaminated with dirt or water, change it immediately.

NOTE
If you recycle your old engine oil, ***never*** *add used fork oil to the old engine oil. Most oil retailers that accept old oil for recycling may not accept the oil if other fluids (fork oil, brake fluid or any other type of petroleum based fluids) have been combined with it.*

1. Place the motorcycle on a stand so that the front wheel clears the ground.
2. Remove the handlebar assembly as described in Chapter Ten.

CAUTION
Release the air pressure gradually. If released too fast, oil may spurt out with the air. Protect your eyes accordingly.

3. Remove the fork tube air valve cap. Refer to **Figure 33** for XT600 models or **Figure 34** for TT600 models.
4. Use a small screwdriver or punch and release all air pressure in the fork.
5. Place a drip pan underneath the drain screw. Remove the drain screw and allow the oil to drain. Refer to **Figure 35** for XT600 models or **Figure 36** for TT600 models. Never reuse the oil.

CAUTION
Do not allow the fork oil to contact any of the brake components or to run onto the front tire.

6. Repeat Step 5 for the opposite fork.
7. Remove the stand from underneath the bike. With both of the bike's wheels on the ground, apply the front brake and push down on the handlebar. Repeat this action until all the oil is released from the fork tube.
8. Check the drain screw O-ring seal. Replace it if worn, hardened or damaged.
9. Apply Loctite 242 (blue) onto the screw threads and reinstall the drain screw. Tighten it securely.
10. Place the motorcycle back on the stand so that the front wheel clears the ground.

33

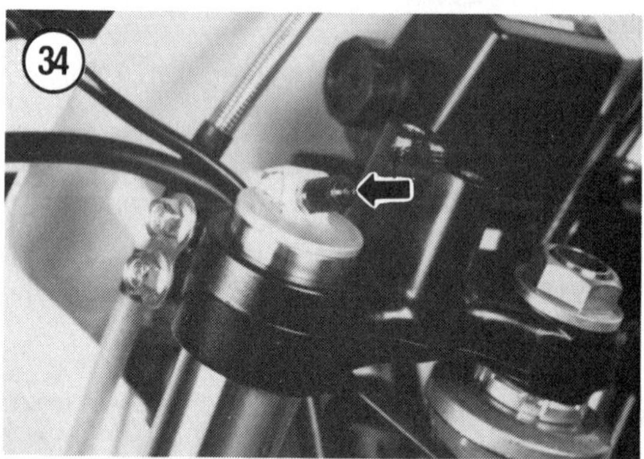
34

35

36

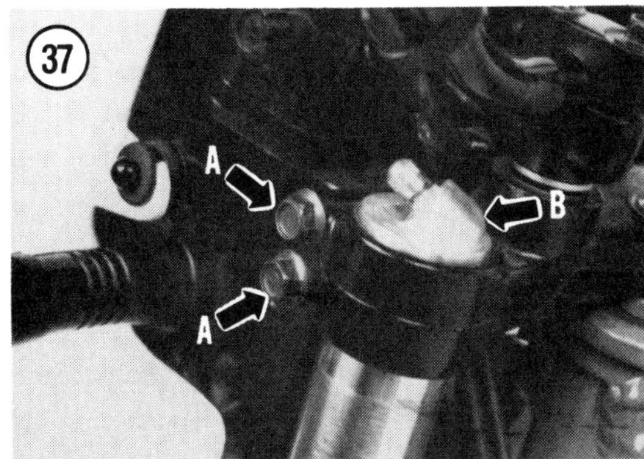

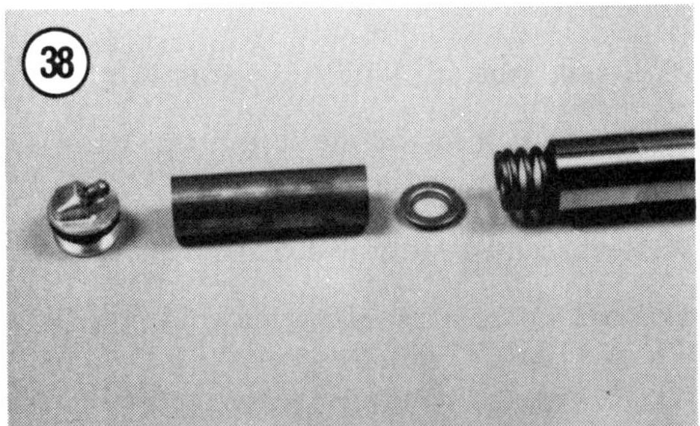

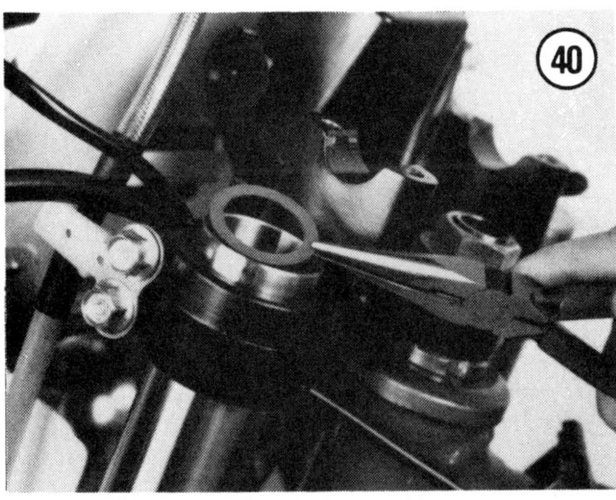

11A. On XT600 models, perform the following:

a. Loosen the top fork tube pinch bolts (A, **Figure 37**).

b. Loosen and remove the fork cap (B, **Figure 37**).

NOTE
Figure 38 *is shown with the fork assembly removed for clarity. It is not necessary to remove the fork assembly for this procedure.*

c. Remove the spacer and the spring seat (**Figure 38**).

d. Place a clean shop cloth around the upper fork bridge to catch any residual fork oil as the fork spring is withdrawn in the next step.

e. Remove the fork spring.

11B. On TT600 models, perform the following:

a. Loosen the top fork tube pinch bolts (A, **Figure 39**).

b. Loosen and remove the fork cap (B, **Figure 39**).

c. Remove the spacer.

d. Remove the spring seat (**Figure 40**).

e. Place a clean shop cloth around the upper fork bridge to catch any residual fork oil as the fork spring is withdrawn in the next step.

f. Remove the fork spring (**Figure 41**).

12. Fill the fork with the specified weight (see **Table 4**) and quantity (see **Table 5**) of fork oil.

13. Repeat Step 11 and Step 12 for the opposite fork.

14. Push down on the front wheel so that both forks are completely extended.

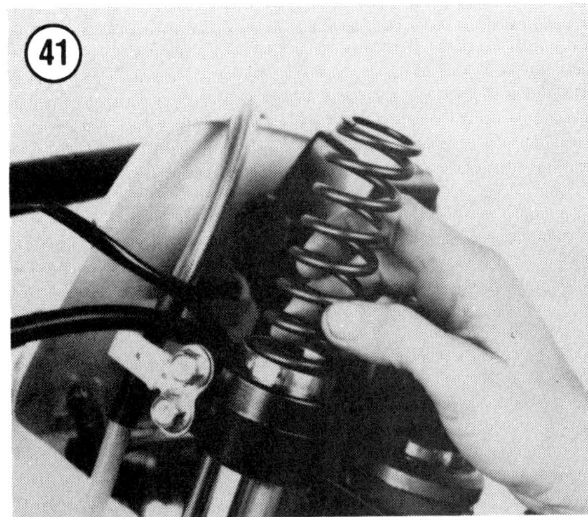

15. Check the O-ring (**Figure 42**) on the fork cap. Replace it if worn or damaged.

16. Position the fork spring with the closer wound coils toward the top of the fork and install the fork spring, spring seat and spacer.

17. Place the fork cap on the spring seat and push it down. Install the fork cap by carefully threading it into the fork. Don't cross thread it. Tighten the fork cap to the tightening torque in **Table 6**.

18A. On XT600 models, after the fork cap bolt is tightened, check that the air valve is pointing toward the front of the bike or to a maximum of 45° from straight ahead (**Figure 43**). If the air valve does not locate in this area, perform the following:

a. Loosen the lower fork bridge bolts (**Figure 44**).
b. Rotate the fork tube until the air valve is located as indicated.
c. Tighten the lower fork bridge bolt to the torque specification in **Table 6**.

18B. On TT600 models, after the fork cap bolt is tightened, check that the air valve is pointing toward the front of the bike (**Figure 45**). If the air valve does not locate in this area, perform the following:

a. Loosen the lower fork bridge bolts.
b. Rotate the fork tube until the air valve is located as indicated.
c. Tighten the lower fork bridge bolt to the torque specification in **Table 6**.

19. Tighten the fork tube pinch bolts to the torque specification in **Table 6**.

20. Repeat Steps 15-19 for the opposite fork.

21. Inflate each fork to the correct amount of air pressure as described in this chapter.

22. Remove the stand from underneath the bike.

23. Road test the bike and check for oil leaks.

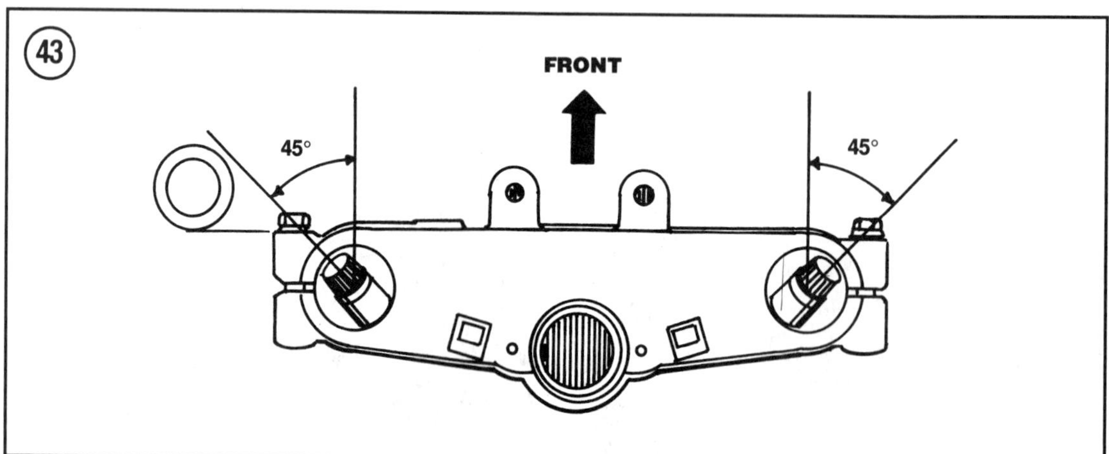

Drive Chain

The factory installed drive chain on all models is an O-ring type that has O-rings installed between the chain plates. Lubrication for the chain pins is permanently sealed by the O-rings (**Figure 46**). However, the chain rollers require external oiling. For the O-ring chain to work properly, it requires proper cleaning and lubrication practices. Do not clean the O-ring drive chain with a high-pressure water hose, such as those found in coin-operated car washes. The high pressure can damage the chains O-rings, resulting in the loss of the internal lubrication which will lead to pre-mature chain failure.

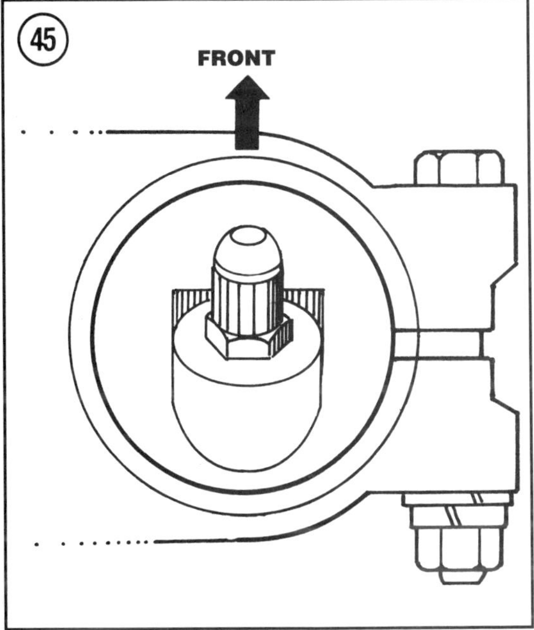

A properly maintained drive chain will provide maximum service life and reliability. The drive chain should be lubricated before each ride and during the day as required. Models that are ridden off-road will require more frequent drive chain lubrication and cleaning because they are subjected to dirt, water and mud not normally encountered in street riding.

Periodic lubrication

1. Place wood block(s) under the engine to support the bike securely.

2. Shift the transmission to NEUTRAL.

3. Oil the bottom run of the drive chain with a commercial chain lubricant formulated for use on O-ring drive chains. If this is not available, SAE 30-50 engine oil can be used.

4. Rotate the rear wheel until the entire drive chain run is lubricated.

5. Moisten a shop cloth in solvent or with soap and water and wipe off any chain lubrication residue from the rear tire and rim.

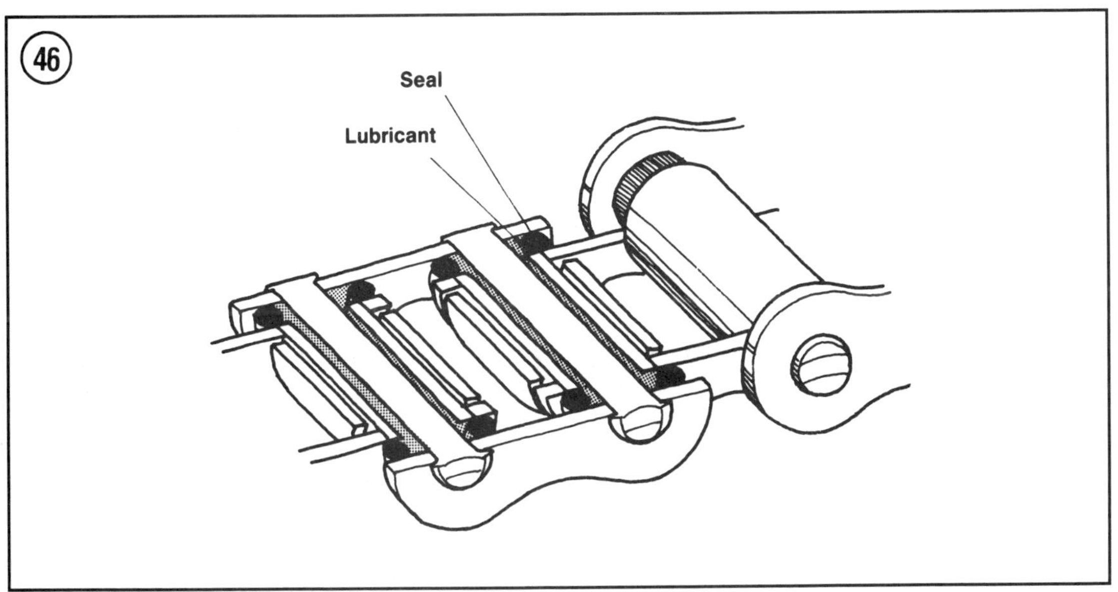

Chain cleaning

1. Disconnect the master link (**Figure 47**) and remove the chain from the motorcycle.

CAUTION
Use only kerosene for cleaning an O-ring equipped drive chain. Do not use gasoline or other solvents since they will cause the O-rings to swell or deteriorate.

2. Immerse the chain in a pan of kerosene and allow it to soak for about a half hour. Move it around and flex it during this period so that the dirt around the rollers may work its way out.

3. Hang up the drive chain and allow it to thoroughly dry. Place an empty container underneath the chain to catch all kerosene runoff.

4. While the drive chain is still hanging up, lubricate it with a good grade of chain lubricant formulated for use on O-ring drive chains. Carefully following the manufacturer's instructions.

5. Reinstall the chain on the motorcycle. Use a new master link clip and install it so that the closed end of the clip is facing the direction of chain travel (**Figure 48**). Store the old master link in your bike's tool bag so that it can be used in case of an emergency.

WARNING
Always check the master link clip after the bike has been rolled backwards such as unloading from a truck or trailer. The master link clip may have snagged on the chain guide or tensioner and become disengaged. Obviously, losing a chain while riding can cause a serious spill not to mention the chain and engine damage which may occur.

Control Cables

The control cables should be lubricated at intervals as described in **Table 1**. Also they should be inspected at this time for fraying and the cable sheath should be checked for chafing. The cables are relatively inexpensive and should be replaced when found to be faulty.

A can of cable lube and a cable lubricator will be required for this procedure.

NOTE
If you are having trouble with the stock cables, you may want to install Teflon-lined cables. These cables are smoother than the stock cables and can be washed

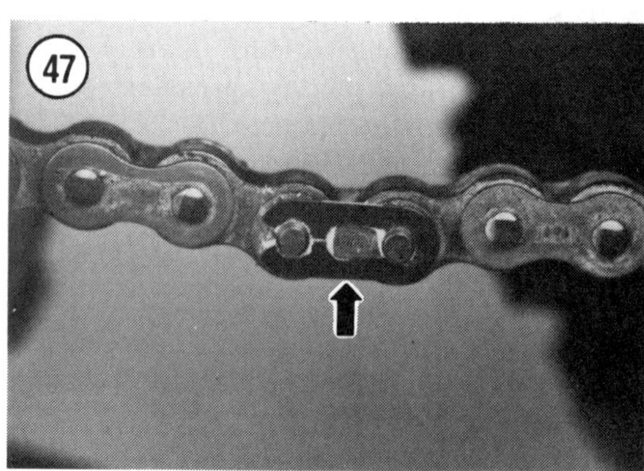

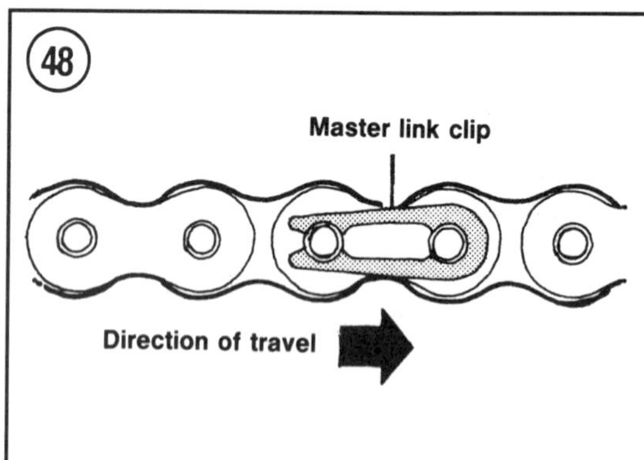

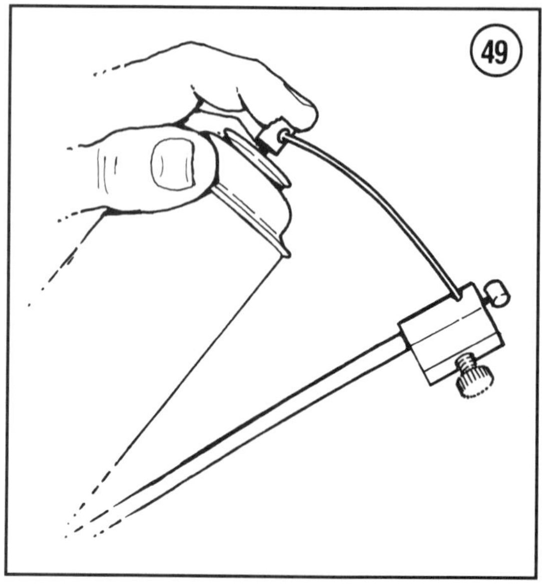

in warm soapy water. They don't require any oiling and will last longer than steel-lined cables.

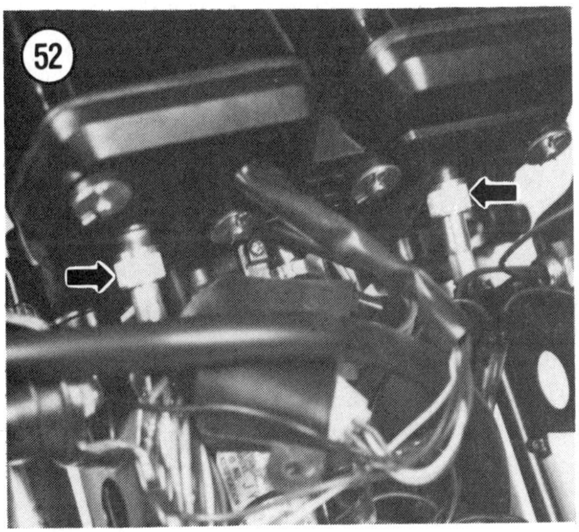

This procedure should be performed on steel-lined cables only. *Do not* oil Teflon-lined cables.

1. Disconnect the cables from the clutch lever and the throttle grip assembly and from where they attach to the carburetor and clutch mechanism.

2. Attach a cable lubricator following the manufacturer's instructions (**Figure 49**).

3. Insert the nozzle of the lubricant can into the lubricator, press the button on the can and hold down until the lubricant begins to flow out the cable's other end.

NOTE

Place a shop cloth at the end of the cable to catch the oil as it runs out the end or place the end in an empty container. Discard this oil as it is dirty.

4. Remove the lubricator, reconnect the cable(s) and adjust the cable(s) as described in this chapter.

Swing Arm and Relay Arm Lubrication

Grease nipples are fitted to the swing arm (**Figure 50**) and relay arm pivot shafts (**Figure 51**) for periodic lubrication. At the intervals specified in **Table 1**, use a grease gun filled with a lithium soap base grease and lubricate each of the pivot shafts.

CAUTION

Make sure to wipe off the grease nipple with a shop cloth before using the grease gun. This prevents dirt from being mixed with the grease and contaminating the pivot shaft and bearing area.

Wipe off the grease nipples after applying the grease. This will lessen the amount of dirt that will collect at these points.

Speedometer/Tachometer Cable Lubrication

Lubricate the speedometer and tachometer (XT600 only) cables every year or whenever needle operation become erratic.

1. Remove the headlight faring as described under *Headlight Bulb Replacement* in Chapter Nine.

2A. On XT600 models, unscrew the retaining collar (**Figure 52**) and remove the cables from each instrument or from the front wheel or the cylinder head.

2B. On TT600 models, unscrew the retaining collar (**Figure 53**) and remove the cable from the speedometer instrument or from the front wheel.

3. Pull the cable(s) from the cable sheath.

4. If the grease on the cable is contaminated, thoroughly clean off all old grease.

5. Thoroughly coat the cable with a good grade of multipurpose grease and reinstall into the sheath.

6. Make sure the cable is correctly seated into the drive unit. If the cable is hard to seat, perform the following:

   a. *Speedometer cable*: Unscrew the cable collar (**Figure 54**) at the front wheel and disconnect the cable from the speedometer drive unit.
   b. *Tachometer cable (XT600 only)*: Remove the small Phillips screw (A, **Figure 55**) on the cylinder head drive unit and pull the tachometer cable (B, **Figure 55**) out of the drive unit.
   c. Reassemble the cable into the drive units and attach the cables at the instrument panel. Tighten all cable collars or screw securely.

7. Install the headlight faring as described under *Headlight Bulb Replacement* in Chapter Nine.

53

54

55

56

Miscellaneous Lubrication Points

Use SAE 10W/30 motor oil and lubricate the clutch lever, front brake lever, rear brake pedal pivot point and the sidestand pivot point.

PERIODIC MAINTENANCE

Drive Chain Free Play Inspection

The drive chain must have adequate free play so that the chain is not strung tight when the swing arm is horizontal. On the other hand, too much play may cause the chain to jump off the sprockets with potentially disastrous results. When riding in mud and sand, dirt buildup will make the chain tighter. Recheck chain play and readjust as required. Set free play within the specifications listed in **Table 7**.

1. Shift the transmission to NEUTRAL.

2. Place the bike on a stand so that the rear wheel clears the ground. Spin the rear wheel and check the chain for tightness at several spots. Check and adjust the chain at its tightest point.

3. Lower the bike so that both wheels are on the ground and the bike is in a vertical position. Have an

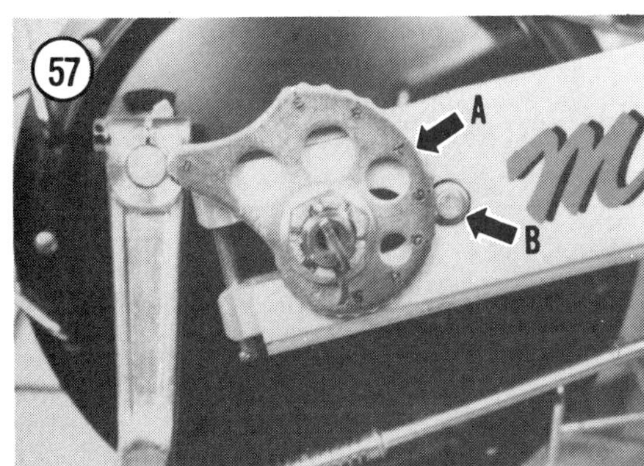

57

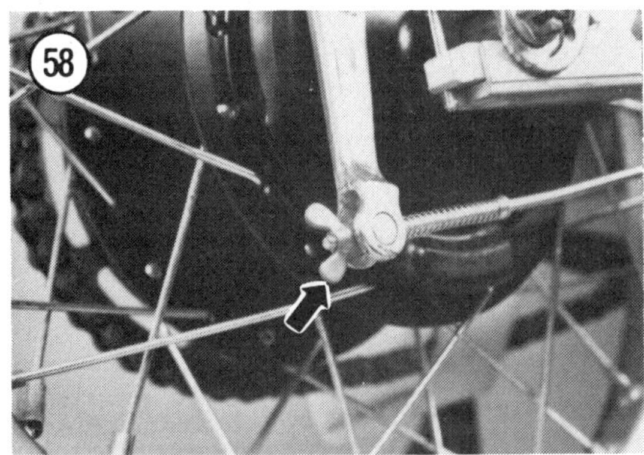
58

59

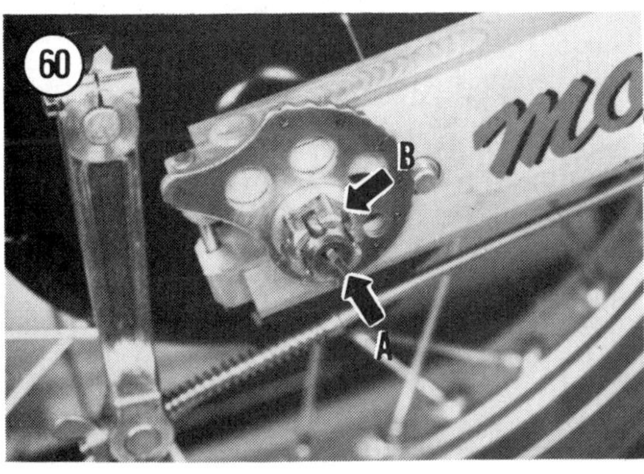

60

assistant sit on the seat when performing the following step.

4. Push the middle of the lower chain run up and down (**Figure 56**). The play should be within the specifications in **Table 7**.

Drive Chain Adjustment

When adjusting the drive chain, you must also maintain rear wheel alignment. A misaligned rear wheel can cause poor handling and pulling to one side, as well as increased sprocket and chain wear.

Cam type chain adjusters are used on all models. Slots (A, **Figure 57**) are cut into the outside of the adjuster that align with a series of numbers and index marks. The slots engage a hardened pin (B, **Figure 57**) installed in each side of the swing arm. When both adjusters are set at the same mark, the rear wheel should be aligned correctly.

1. Loosen the rear brake adjuster wing nut. Refer to **Figure 58** for XT600 models or **Figure 59** for TT600 models.

2A. On XT600 models, remove the cotter pin (A, **Figure 60**) and loosen the rear axle nut (B, **Figure 60**). Discard the cotter pin.

2B. On TT600 models, loosen the rear axle nut (A, **Figure 61**).

3. Turn each chain adjuster (B, **Figure 61**) back an equal amount until the chain play is within specification. The left- and right-hand adjusters should be set to the same alignment mark. Do not overtighten the drive chain as it will result in premature drive chain, drive sprocket and driven sprocket wear.

4. When the chain play is correct, check wheel alignment. Sight along the top of the drive chain

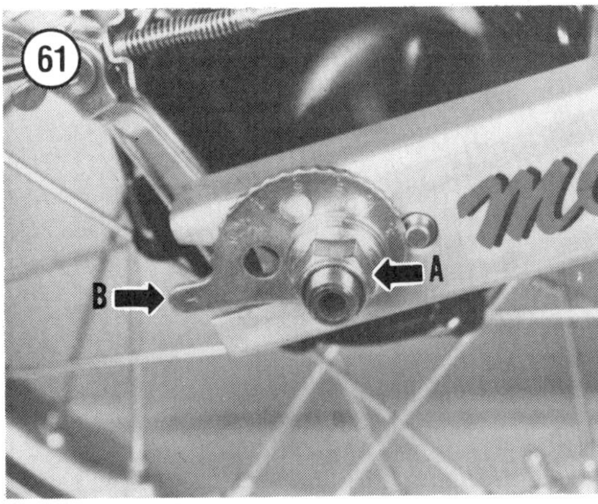

61

from the rear sprocket to see that it is correctly aligned. It should leave the top of the rear sprocket in a straight line (A, **Figure 62**). If it is cocked to one side or the other (B and C, **Figure 62**), the wheel is incorrectly aligned and must be corrected.

NOTE
*If the chain alignment is incorrect, check the chain adjusters (**A, Figure 57**) for damage. If the adjusters are okay, check the hardened pin (**B, Figure 57**) installed in each side of the swing arm.*

NOTE
*To prevent a spongy-feeling brake, **partially** tighten the axle nut, spin the wheel, stop it forcefully with the brake pedal, then tighten the axle nut. This centers the brake backing plate in the brake drum.*

5. Tighten the axle nut to the torque specification in **Table 6**.

NOTE
When tightening the axle nut, check the position of the chain adjusters. Typically, one adjuster will slip or rotate out of its adjustment slot (usually the one on the opposite side of the axle nut) as the axle nut is tightened. If an adjuster moves, check the hardened pins and the adjuster(s) for damage. Because the adjuster engagement area is small, any damage to the adjuster or pin will allow the adjuster to slip when the axle nut is tightened. When tightening the axle nut, make sure the adjuster slots engage the hardened pin completely. If an adjuster does not register with the hardened pin correctly, it will become damaged. This is something you will have to check whenever the rear axle nut is tightened.

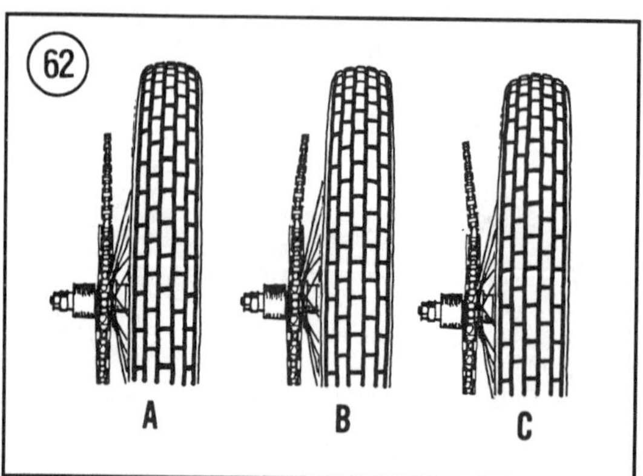

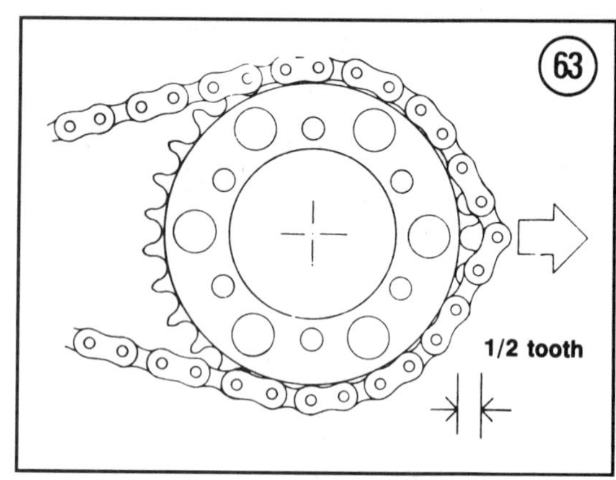

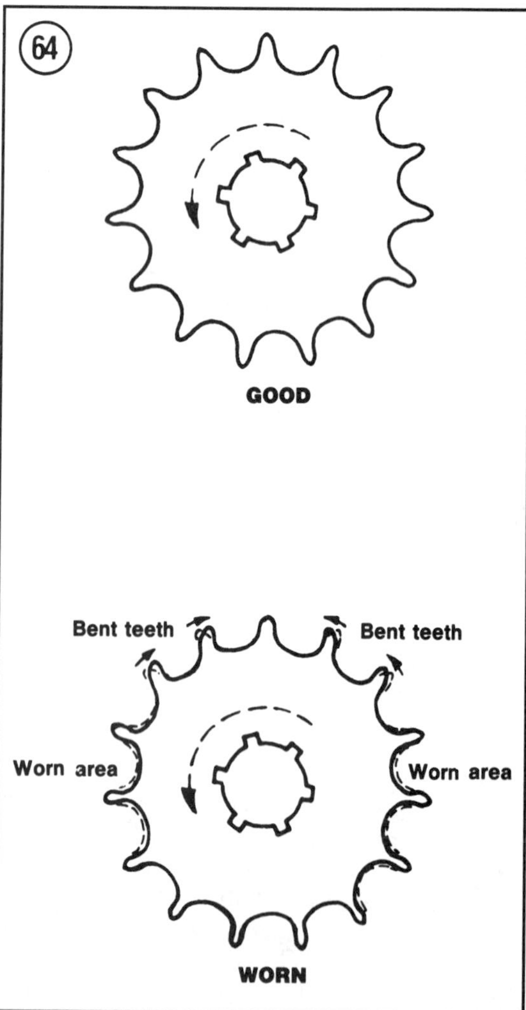

6. Recheck drive chain play and alignment.

7. On XT600 models, install a new cotter pin through the end of the axle. Bend the pin over to lock the nut.

8. Adjust the rear brake as described under *Rear Brake Adjustment* in this chapter.

Drive Chain Inspection

Even with proper lubrication, cleaning and periodic adjustment, the drive chain and both sprockets will wear out. Wear to the pins and bushings results in chain stretch or lengthening of the chain.

To get an indication of chain stretch, pull one of the links away from the rear driven sprocket (**Figure 63**). If the link pulls away more than 1/2 the height of a sprocket tooth, the chain should be replaced.

If the drive chain is worn, inspect the rear driven sprocket and the engine drive sprocket for undercutting or sharp teeth (**Figure 64**). If wear is evident, replace the sprockets too, or you'll soon wear out a new drive chain.

NOTE

*Check the inner faces of the inner plates (**Figure 65**). They should be lightly polished on both sides. If they show considerable wear on both sides, the sprockets are not aligned. Adjust alignment as described under **Drive Chain Adjustment** in this chapter.*

Drive Chain Rollers, Guide and Slider Inspection and Replacement

The drive chain guard (**Figure 66**), the chain guide (**Figure 67**) and the swing arm chain slider (**Figure 68**) should be inspected and replaced as necessary. A worn or damaged chain guard, guide or slider will allow the drive chain to damage the swing arm.

3

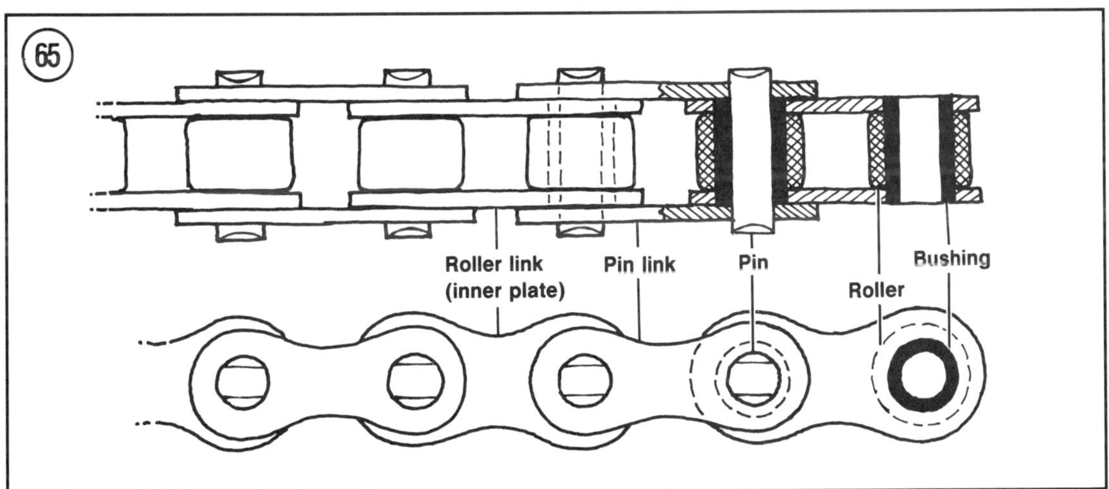

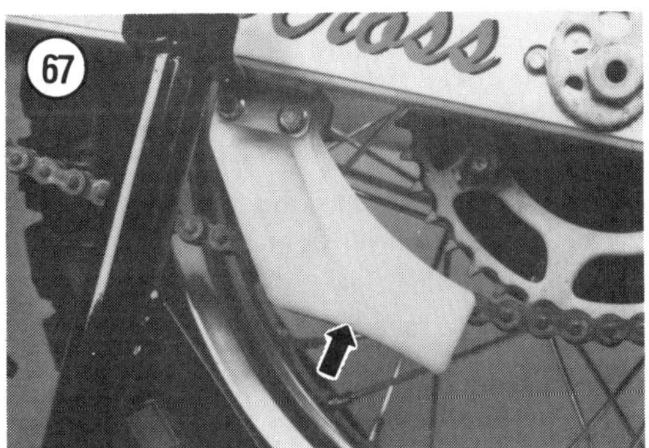

1. To replace a drive chain guard, perform the following:
   a. Remove the swing arm as described under *Swing Arm Removal/Installation* in Chapter Eleven.
   b. Slide the guard off of the left-hand side of the swing arm pivot point.
   c. Install a new guard and reinstall the swing arm.
2. To replace a swing arm chain guide, perform the following:
   a. Remove the drive chain as described under *Drive Chain Removal/Installation* in Chapter Eleven.
   b. Remove the bolts securing the guide (**Figure 67**) to the swing arm and remove the guide.
   c. Install a new guide and bolts. Tighten the bolts securely.
3. To replace a swing arm chain slider, perform the following:
   a. Remove the swing arm as described under *Swing Arm Removal/Installation* in Chapter Eleven.
   b. Remove the bolts securing the slider (**Figure 69**) and remove the slider.
   c. Install a new slider and bolts. Tighten the bolts securely.
   d. Reinstall the swing arm.

Front Disc Brake Lever Adjustment

Brake pad wear in the caliper is automatically adjusted as the piston moves forward in the caliper. However, the front brake lever free play must be maintained to prevent excessive brake drag. This would cause premature brake pad wear. Adjust the brake lever so there is approximately 5-8 mm (3/16-5/16 in.) free play.

1. Slide the rubber cover (**Figure 70**) away from the front brake lever.
2. Loosen the adjust screw locknut (A, **Figure 71**) and turn the adjust screw (B, **Figure 71**) in or out to obtain the correct amount of brake lever free play.
3. Tighten the locknut and recheck the free play.
4. Reposition the rubber cover back over the brake lever.
5. Operate the brake lever and make sure it moves freely.

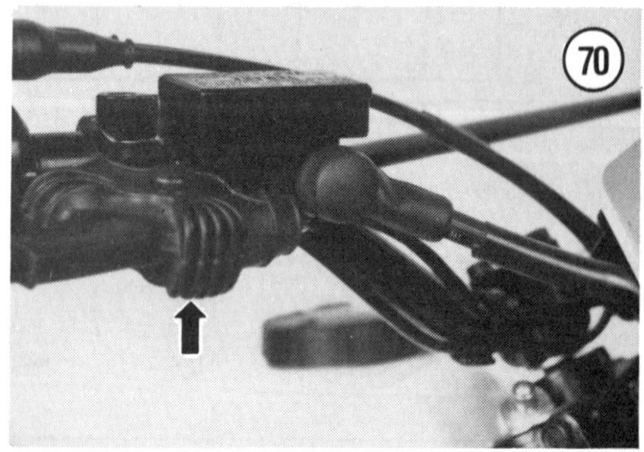

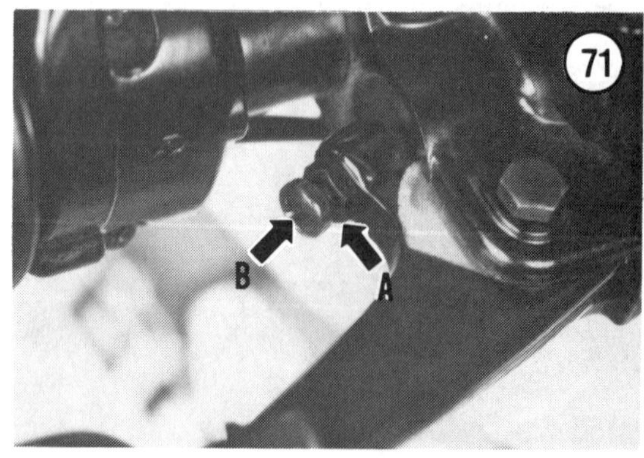

Front Drum Brake Lever Free Play Adjustment

The front brake lever free play is the movement (**Figure 72**) required to actuate the brake; it must not be adjusted so closely that the brake shoes contact the drum with the lever in the relaxed position.

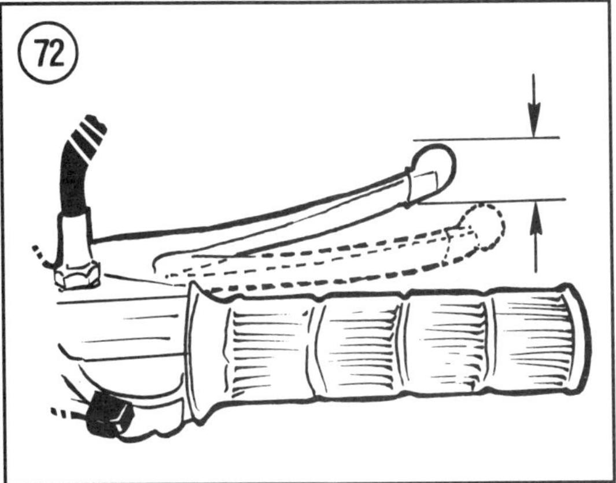

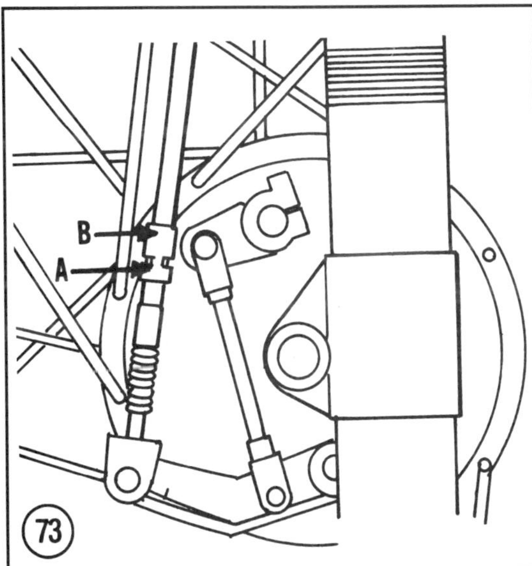

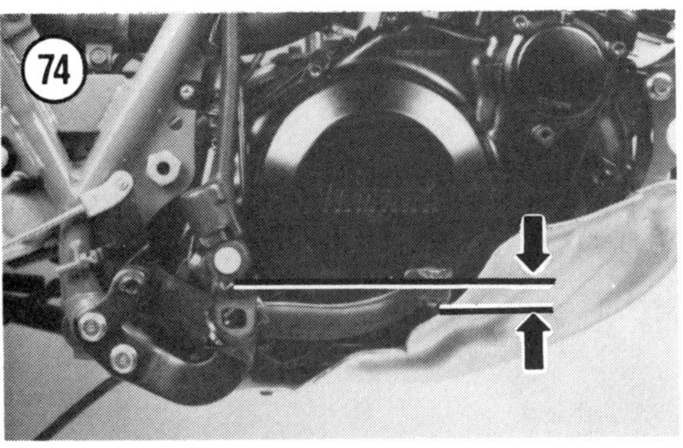

The front brake cable should be adjusted so there is 5-8 mm (3/16-5/16 in.) of front brake lever free play.

Minor adjustments should be made at the brake lever and major adjustments should be made at the brake panel on the front wheel.

1. Slide the rubber cover away from the front brake lever.
2. Loosen the locknut and turn the adjuster barrel in or out to obtain the correct amount of brake lever free play.
3. Tighten the locknut and recheck the free play.
4. Because of normal brake wear, this adjustment will eventually be used up. It is then necessary to loosen the locknut and turn the adjuster barrel all the way toward the hand grip. Tighten the locknut.
5. At the front brake panel, loosen the locknut (A, **Figure 73**) and turn the adjust nut (B, **Figure 73**) until the brake lever can be used once again for minor adjustments. Tighten the locknut.
6. At the front brake lever, loosen the locknut and turn the adjuster barrel in or out to obtain the correct amount of brake lever free play.
7. Reposition the rubber cover over the brake lever.
8. Operate the brake lever and make sure it moves freely.

NOTE
If the correct amount of free play cannot be obtained, replace the brake cable as described in Chapter Twelve.

Rear Brake Pedal Adjustment

Two adjustments are required for proper rear brake adjustment:

a. Rear brake pedal height.
b. Rear brake free play.

Rear brake pedal height

1. Measure the height position from the top of the right-hand footpeg to the top of the rear brake pedal (**Figure 74**). The specified distance is 5-10 mm (0.2-0.4 in.).
2. To adjust the pedal height, loosen the pedal adjust screw locknut (A, **Figure 75**) and turn the adjust screw (B, **Figure 75**) as required.

3. Tighten the locknut securely and recheck the pedal height position.

Rear brake free play

Rear brake pedal free play must be checked and maintained due to brake shoe wear. This adjustment must also be performed after the rear wheel is removed or the drive chain is adjusted.

1. With your hand, move the rear brake pedal from its at-rest position to the point where the shoes contact the brake drum. The specified distance is 20-30 mm (0.8-1.2 in.).

2. Check the rear brake pedal height position as described in this chapter and adjust if necessary.

3. To adjust the pedal free play, turn the rear brake adjuster wing nut in either direction to obtain the correct amount of free play. Refer to **Figure 58** for XT600 models or **Figure 59** for TT600 models.

4. Rotate the rear wheel and check for brake drag. Also operate the pedal several times to make sure it returns to the at-rest position immediately after release.

NOTE
Brake drag can sometimes be difficult to check because of the drag induced by the drive chain. If you are having brake problems and you want to be sure you have removed all brake drag, remove the master link and slip the drive chain off of the rear driven sprocket. Spin the rear wheel and check the rear brake. Adjust the rear brake as required and reconnect the drive chain.

WARNING
Do not ride your bike until you are sure the rear brake is operating correctly.

Rear Brake Light Switch Adjustment (XT600)

1. Turn the ignition switch to ON.

2. Depress the brake pedal. The light should come on just as the rear brake begins to work.

3. To make the light come on earlier, hold the switch body (A, **Figure 76**) and turn the adjusting nut (B, **Figure 76**) as required.

Front Brake Fluid Level Check

The brake fluid in the front brake reservoir should always be kept above the lower level line marked on the master cylinder window (**Figure 77**) with DOT 3 brake fluid.

NOTE
If the brake fluid level lowers rapidly, check the disc brake line and all line fittings for leakage.

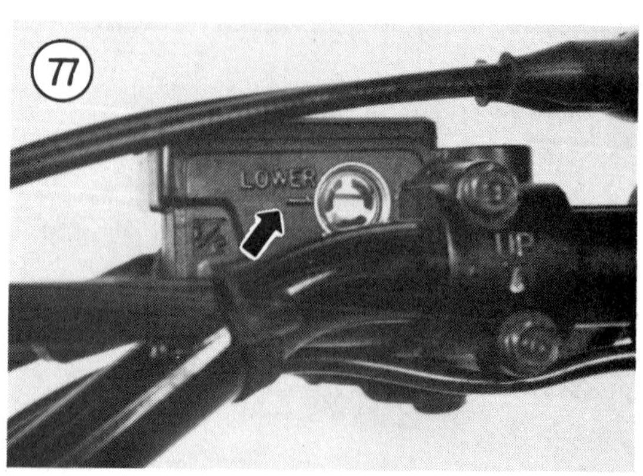

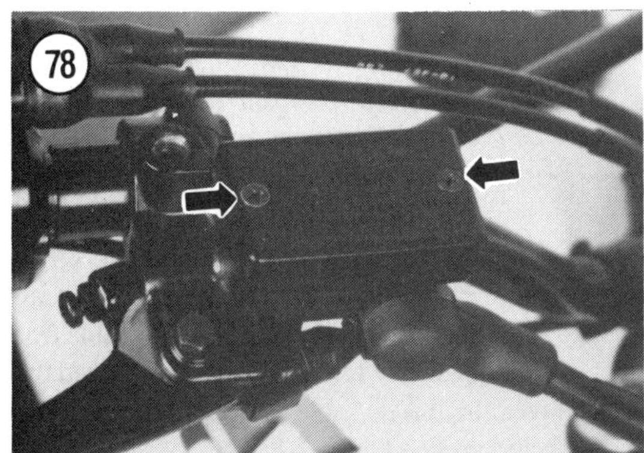

1. Place the bike on level ground and position the handlebar so the master cylinder reservoir is level.
2. Clean any dirt from the top cover prior to removing the cover.
3. Remove the top cover screws (**Figure 78**) and remove the cover and diaphragm.

WARNING
Use brake fluid clearly marked DOT 3 and specified for disc brakes. Others may vaporize and cause brake failure. Do not intermix different brands or types of brake fluid as they may not be compatible. Do not intermix a silicone based (DOT 5) brake fluid as it can cause brake component damage leading to brake system failure.

CAUTION
Be careful when handling brake fluid. Do not spill it on painted or plastic surfaces as it will destroy the surface. Wash the area immediately with soap and water and thoroughly rinse it off.

4. Add fresh DOT 3 brake fluid from a sealed container.
5. Reinstall the diaphragm and top cover. Install the screws and tighten securely.

Disc Brake Hose

Check the brake hose (**Figure 79**) between the master cylinder and the brake caliper. If there is any leakage, tighten the union bolts and bleed the brake as described under *Bleeding the System* in Chapter Twelve. If this does not stop the leak or if a brake hose is obviously damaged, cracked or chafed, replace the brake line and bleed the system.

Disc Brake Pad Wear

The brake pads can be inspected for wear without disassembling the caliper assembly or removing the brake pads.

On XT600 models, from the front of the bike, look up into the lower portion of the caliper assembly. Inspect the lower edge of the brake pads (**Figure 80**).

On TT600 models, from the front of the bike, look into the inspection window (**Figure 81**) in the front of the caliper assembly. Inspect the edge of the brake pads.

3

Replace the brake pads if they are worn to a thickness of 0.8 mm (0.031 in.) or less. Refer to Chapter Twelve for brake pad replacement.

Disc Brake Fluid Change

Every time the reservoir cover is removed, a small amount of dirt and moisture enters the brake fluid. The same thing happens if a leak occurs or any part of the hydraulic system is loosened or disconnected. Dirt can clog the system and cause unnecessary wear. Water in the brake fluid will vaporize at a high temperature, impairing the hydraulic action and reducing the brake's stopping ability.

To maintain peak performance, change the brake fluid once a year. To change brake fluid, follow the *Brake Bleeding* procedure in Chapter Twelve.

WARNING
Use brake fluid clearly marked DOT 3 and specified for disc brakes. Others may vaporize and cause brake failure. Do not intermix different brands or types of brake fluid as they may not be compatible. Do not intermix a silicone based (DOT 5) brake fluid as it can cause brake component damage leading to brake system failure.

Rear Brake Shoe Wear Check

To check rear brake shoe wear, depress the rear brake pedal. Then check the pointed wear indicator (A, **Figure 82**) fixed to the brake arm. If the indicator points to the wear limit line (B, **Figure 82**) cast into the brake panel plate, replace the brake shoes. Refer to Chapter Twelve for brake shoe replacement.

Clutch Adjustment

Continuous use of the clutch lever causes the clutch cable to stretch. For the clutch to operate correctly, the clutch cable free play must be maintained at 2-3 mm (3/32-1/8 in.). If there is no clutch cable free play, the clutch cannot disengage completely. This would cause clutch slippage and rapid clutch plate wear.

The clutch cable has two adjustment points, one at the clutch hand lever and one on the engine's left-hand crankcase cover.

NOTE
When rebuilding or reassembling the clutch assembly, perform the ***Clutch Mechanism Adjustment*** *in Chapter Six before adjusting the clutch cable.*

1. Pull the clutch lever toward the handlebar. When cable resistance is felt, hold the lever and measure the gap shown in **Figure 83**. This is clutch cable free play. If resistance was felt as soon as you pulled the clutch lever, there is no cable free play. If adjustment is necessary, proceed to Step 2.

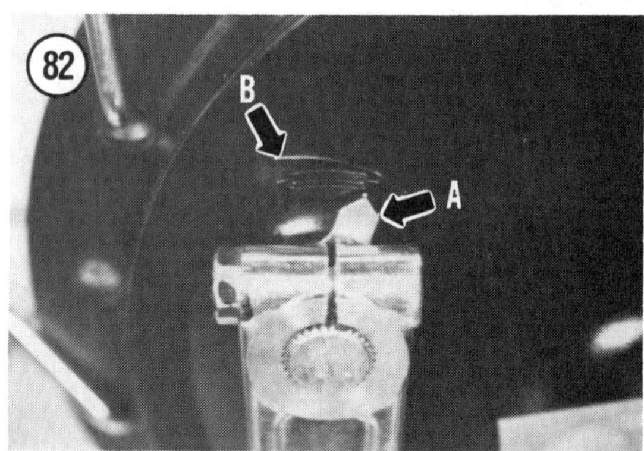

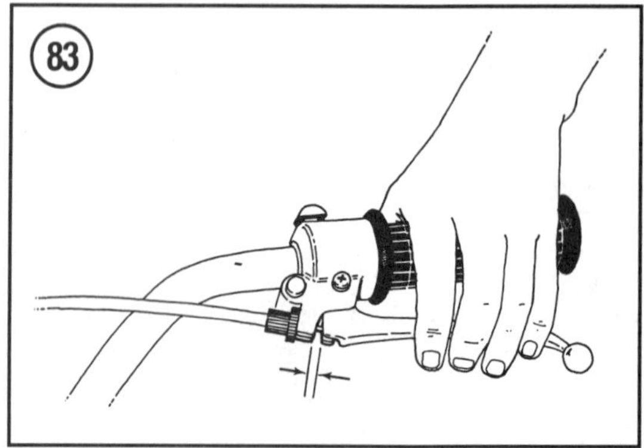

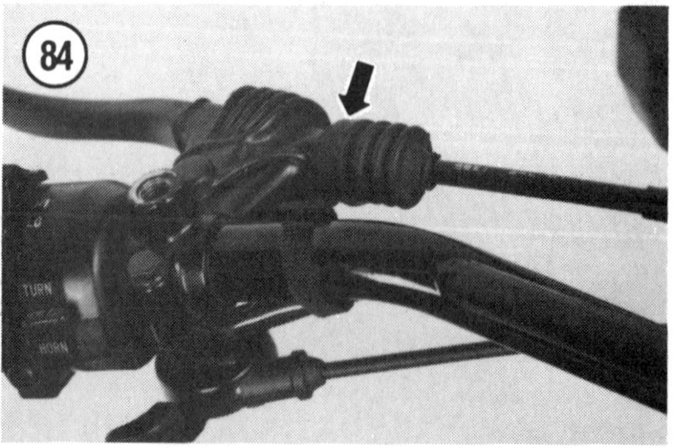

2. Slide back the rubber boot (**Figure 84**) from the clutch lever.

3. At the clutch hand lever, loosen the locknut (A, **Figure 85**) and turn the adjusting barrel (B, **Figure 85**) in or out to obtain the correct amount of free play. Tighten the locknut.

4. If the proper amount of free play cannot be achieved at the handlebar adjuster, perform the following:

   a. At the clutch hand lever adjuster, loosen the locknut (A, **Figure 85**) and turn the adjuster (B, **Figure 85**) all the way in toward the clutch lever.
   b. At the left-hand crankcase cover on the engine, loosen the clutch cable adjuster locknuts (A, **Figure 86**). Turn the adjusting barrel (B, **Figure 86**) and move the cable to take up as much clutch cable slack as possible. Tighten the locknuts (A, **Figure 86**).
   c. At the hand lever, loosen the locknut (A, **Figure 85**) and turn the adjusting barrel (B, **Figure 85**) in or out to obtain the correct amount of free play. Tighten the locknut.

5. If the clutch cable free play cannot be achieved using these adjustment points, the clutch cable has stretched excessively and must be replaced.

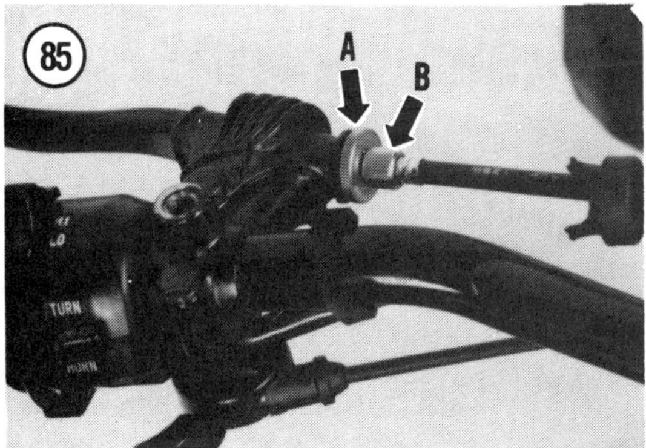

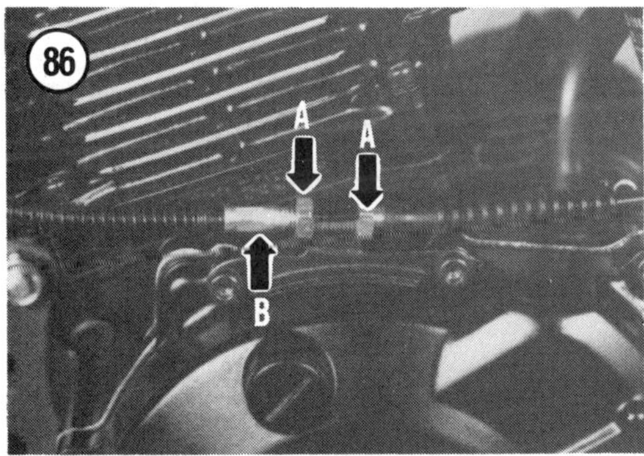

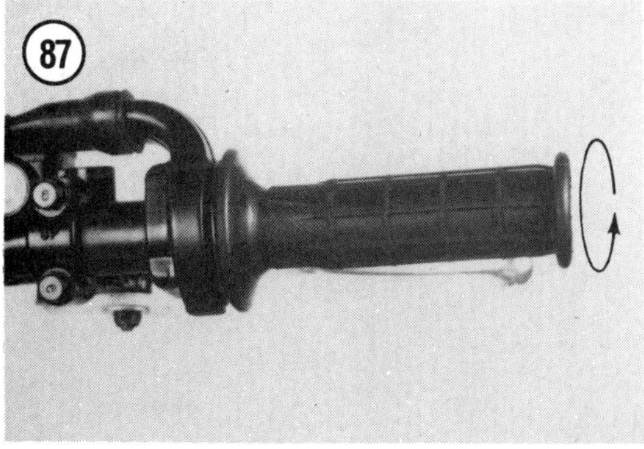

Throttle Cable Adjustment and Operation

All models use a dual throttle cable setup. One cable is a "pull" cable and the other is a "push" cable. For correct operation, the throttle should have 2-5 mm (3/32-3/16 in.) free play. In time, the throttle cable free play will become excessive from cable stretch. This will delay throttle response and affect low speed operation. On the other hand, if there is no throttle cable free play, an excessively high idle can result.

1. Start the engine and allow it to reach normal operating temperature. Usually 10-15 minutes of stop-and-go riding is sufficient.
2. Adjust the engine idle speed as described in this chapter.
3. With the engine at idle, twist the throttle (**Figure 87**) to increase engine speed.
4. Determine the amount of movement (free play) required to raise the engine speed from idle. If the free play is incorrect, perform the following.
5. Shut the engine off.
6. Remove the fuel tank as described under *Fuel Tank Removal/Installation* in Chapter Eight.
7. Locate the 2 throttle cables at the point where they attach to the carburetor assembly. Some of the throttle cables are labeled with a number 1 and 2. The No. 1 is the "pull" cable and is attached to the top portion of the throttle cable bracket on the carburetor assembly. The No. 2 is the "push" cable and is attached to the lower portion of the throttle cable bracket on the carburetor assembly.

8. Loosen the No. 1 "pull" throttle cable adjuster locknuts (A, **Figure 88**) and turn the adjuster (B, **Figure 88**) until the free play is correct. Tighten the locknuts. If the free play is still not correct, proceed to Step 9.

9. If the free play was not corrected by turning the No. 1 "pull" cable, adjust the No. 2 throttle cable. Loosen the No. 2 throttle "push" cable adjuster locknuts (A, **Figure 89**) and turn the adjuster (B, **Figure 89**) until the free play is correct. Tighten the locknuts and recheck the free play adjustment.

NOTE
If the throttle cable free play cannot be adjusted correctly, the throttle cables have stretched excessively and must be replaced as a set as described in Chapter Eight.

10. Make sure the throttle grip rotates freely from a fully closed to fully open position.

11. Reinstall the fuel tank.

12. Start the engine and allow it to idle. Turn the handlebar from side-to-side. If the idle increases, the throttle cables are routed incorrectly or there is not enough cable free play. Reroute or readjust the cables.

Throttle Grip

Periodically, the throttle grip and throttle housing should be cleaned and serviced.

1. Remove the Phillips screws (A, **Figure 90**) securing the throttle housing.

2. Separate the throttle housings (B, **Figure 90**).

3. Disconnect the throttle cables (C, **Figure 90**) at the twist grip.

4. Clean the inner twist grip bore with electrical contact cleaner.

5. Clean the throttle housings thoroughly.

6. Check the end of the handlebar for burrs or other damage that would cause the twist grip to stick or operate sluggishly. If necessary, smooth the end of the handlebar with a fine-cut file.

7. Lubricate the handlebar portion where the throttle grip rides and the metal surface of the throttle assembly with a good-quality multipurpose grease.

8. Install by reversing these steps. Make sure the throttle grip rotates freely from a fully closed to fully open position.

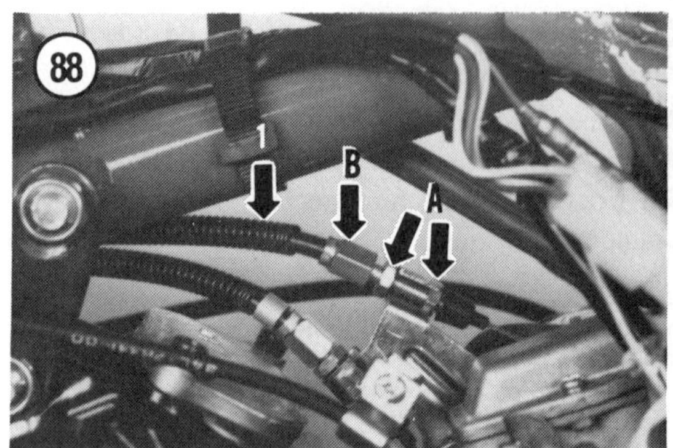

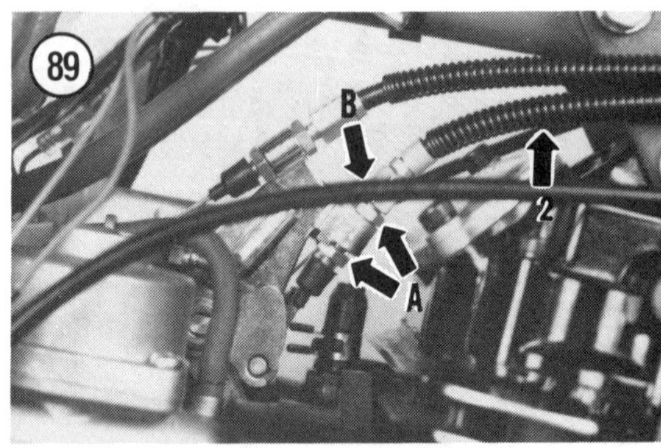

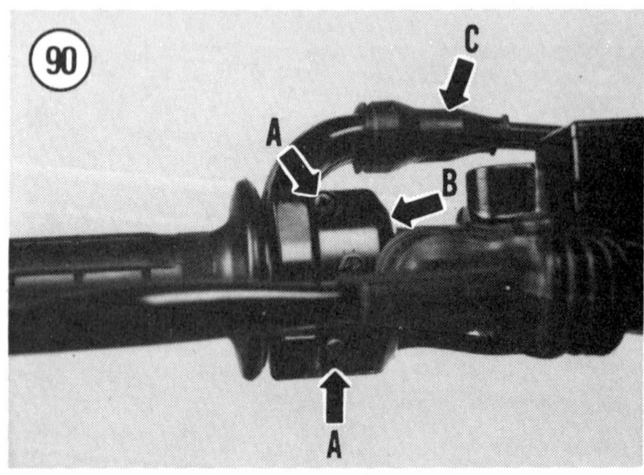

Decompression Cable Adjustment

The decompression cable should always be checked and adjusted after *adjusting the valves* and/or after the cable is removed or replaced. The specified free play is 0.5 mm (0.02 in.).

1. Place the bike on its sidestand.
2. Remove the fuel tank as described under *Fuel Tank Removal/Installation* in Chapter Eight.

CAUTION
To prevent expensive engine damage, refer to ***CAUTIONS*** *under* ***Spark Plug Removal*** *in this chapter.*

3. Disconnect the spark plug lead (A, **Figure 91**) and remove the spark plug as described in this chapter. This will make it easier to rotate the engine by hand.
4. Remove the exhaust valve adjuster covers (B, **Figure 91**) and the intake valve adjuster cover (C, **Figure 91**) from the cylinder head cover.
5. Remove the 2 covers (**Figure 92**) from the timing holes on the left-hand crankcase cover.

NOTE
A cylinder at top dead center (TDC) of its compression stroke will have free play in both of its rocker arms, indicating that both the intake and exhaust valves are closed.

6. Using a 19 mm socket and wrench (**Figure 93**) on the alternator nut, rotate the rotor *counterclockwise* until the cylinder is at top dead center (TDC) on the compression stroke. To determine TDC for the cylinder, perform the following:
   a. Align the "T" mark on the rotor (**Figure 94**) with the crankcase timing mark (**Figure 95**).

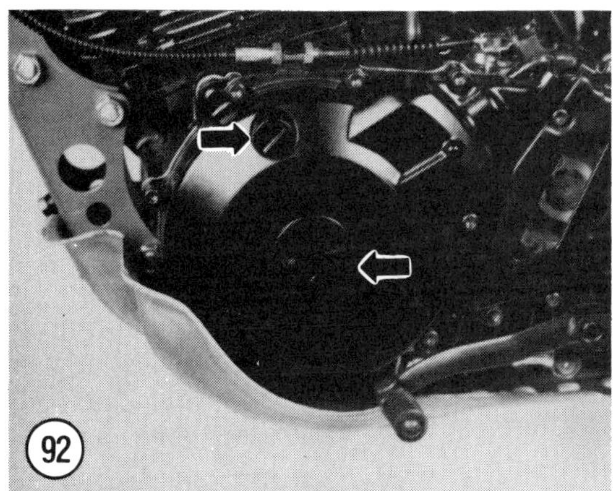
92

93

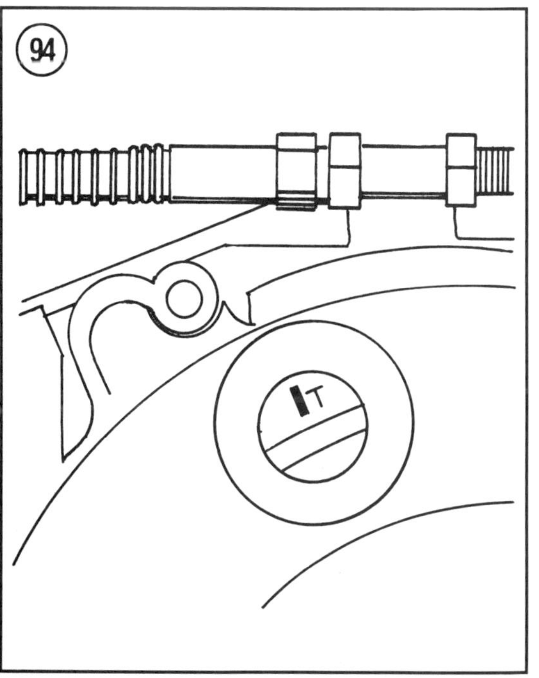

94

95

b. Wiggle both sets of rocker arms. There should be free play in all 4 rocker arms, indicating that both the intake and exhaust valve sets are closed.

c. If either the intake or exhaust rocker arms *do not* have free play, rotate the rotor *counter-clockwise* an additional 360° and again align the "T" mark on the rotor with the crankcase timing mark (**Figure 95**).

d. Again wiggle both sets of rocker arms. There should be free play in all 4 rocker arms, indicating that both sets of intake and exhaust valves are closed. The cylinder is now at top dead center (TDC) on the compression stroke.

7. Measure the free play at the tip (**Figure 96**) of the decompression cam lever (A, **Figure 97**). The correct amount of free play, "Dimension A" (**Figure 97**) is 0.5 mm (0.02 in.).

8. To adjust the free play, loosen the cable adjuster locknut (B, **Figure 97**) and turn the adjuster (C, **Figure 97**) until the correct amount of free play is achieved. Tighten the locknut (B, **Figure 97**) securely.

CAUTION
If the free play is not adjusted correctly, it will result in hard starting (excessive free play) or cause erratic engine idle and possibly a burned exhaust valve (insufficient free play).

9. Inspect the O-ring seal (**Figure 98**) on both timing hole covers for hardness or deterioration. Replace if necessary.

10. Install the 2 covers (**Figure 92**) into the timing holes on the left-hand crankcase cover.

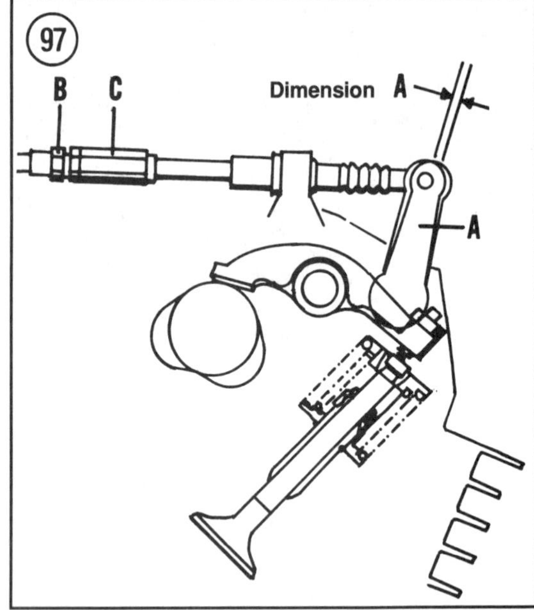

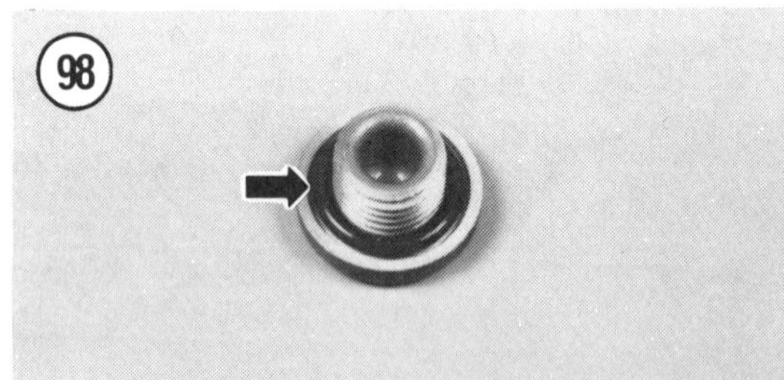

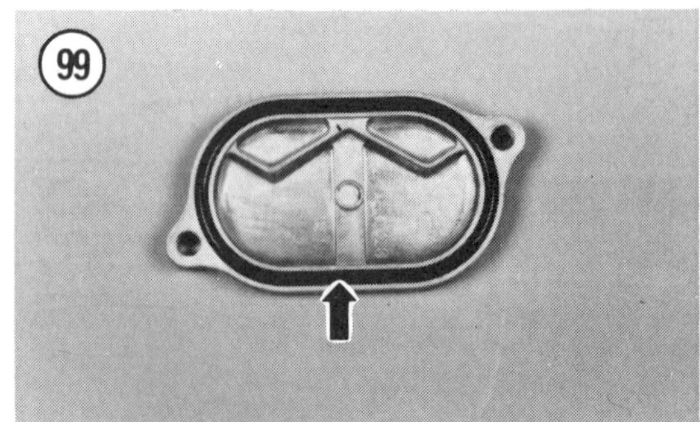

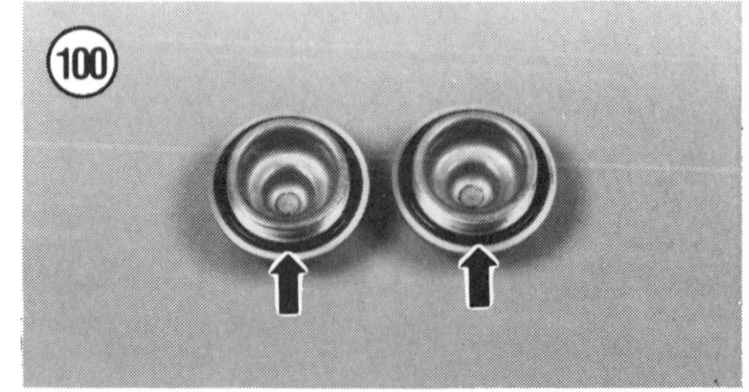

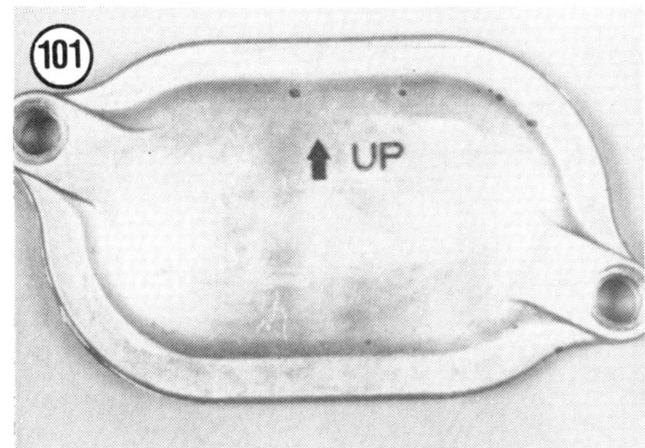

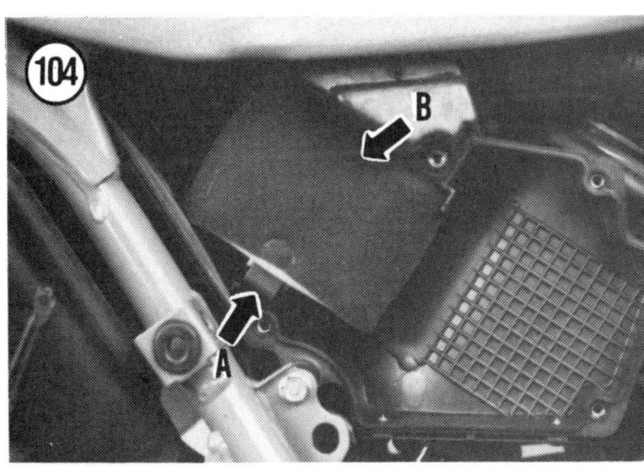

11. Inspect the O-ring seals on the valve adjuster covers for hardness or deterioration. Refer to **Figure 99** and **Figure 100**. Replace if necessary.

NOTE
*Position the intake valve adjuster cover with the arrow and UP mark (**Figure 101**) facing up.*

12. Install the exhaust valve adjuster covers (B, **Figure 91**) and the intake valve adjuster cover (C, **Figure 91**) onto the cylinder head cover.
13. Install the spark plug and the fuel tank and reconnect the spark plug lead.

Air Filter Removal/Cleaning/Installation

The air filter element should be removed, cleaned, and re-oiled at intervals indicated in **Table 1**.

The air filter removes dust and abrasive particles from the air before it enters the carburetors and engine. Very fine particles that may enter into the engine will cause rapid wear to the piston rings, cylinder and bearings and may clog small passages in the carburetors. Never run your Yamaha without the air filter element installed.

Proper air filter servicing can do more to insure long service from your engine than any other single item.

NOTE
This cleaning procedure covers the Yamaha factory installed air filter element. If you are using an accessory air filter, refer to the manufacturer's instructions for cleaning. Some accessory air filter elements cannot be cleaned—they must be replaced when they become dirty.

All models are equipped with a foam air filter element. To work properly, the filter element must be properly cleaned and oiled with a *foam* air filter oil.

1. Remove the frame right-hand side cover (**Figure 102**).
2A. On XT600 models, perform the following:
   a. Remove the screws securing the air filter cover and remove the cover (**Figure 103**).
   b. Carefully remove the air filter element set plate (A, **Figure 104**).

c. Carefully pull the air filter element assembly (B, **Figure 104**) out of the air box.

2B. On TT600 models, perform the following:

NOTE
There was a running change on the attachment methods of the air filter cover. The cover is either held in place with a rubber strap or by screws. Follow the procedure that relates to your model.

a. Either remove the screws securing the air filter cover (**Figure 105**) or unhook the rubber strap (**Figure 106**) securing the air filter cover and remove the cover.

b. Unscrew the wing nut (A, **Figure 107**) and carefully pull the air filter element assembly (B, **Figure 107**) out of the air box.

3. Examine the inside of the air box (**Figure 108**). There should be no signs of dust or dirt on the inside of the air box cover or sides. If dirt is noticeable, the air filter may be damaged or it was improperly serviced or installed.

4. Clean the inside of the air box with a clean shop rag soaked in solvent or soap and water.

5. After the air box has dried, coat the inside of the air box with a thin layer of wheel bearing grease. Apply the grease with your hands so that it covers all of the air box inside surfaces. The grease works like an additional filter and will help to absorb any dirt in the air box.

CAUTION
Do not clean the air filter element with gasoline. Besides being an extreme fire hazard, gasoline will break down the seam glue used to hold the filter together. This will cause filter damage and allow unfiltered air to enter the engine.

6A. On XT600 models, perform the following:

a. Separate the air filter element (A, **Figure 109**) from the inner plastic guide (B, **Figure 109**).

b. Separate the air filter elements from each other (**Figure 110**).

6B. On TT600 models, perform the following:

a. Separate the air filter element from the outer plastic guide.

b. Separate the air filter element from the inner plastic guide.

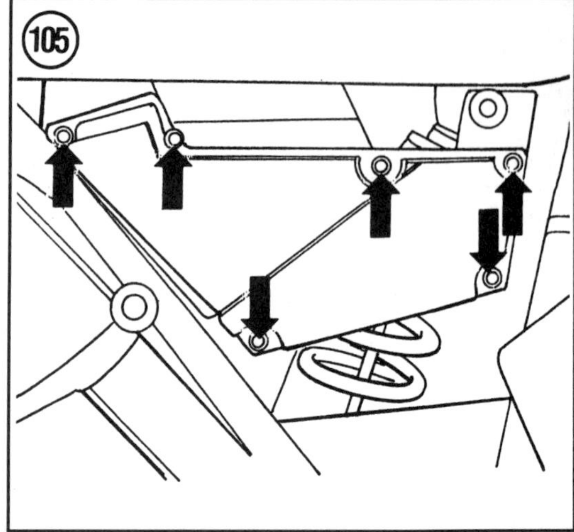

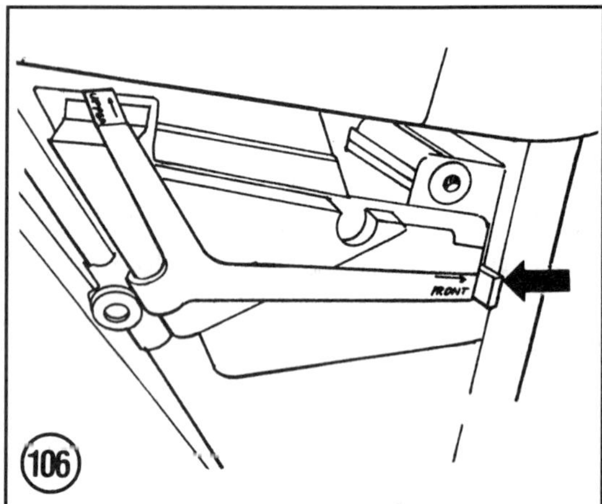

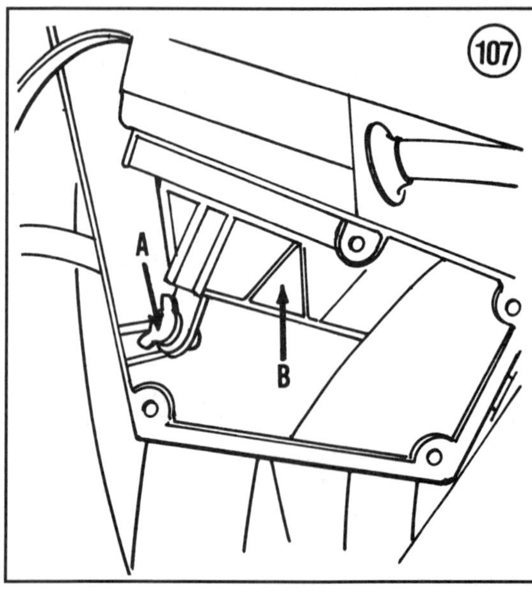

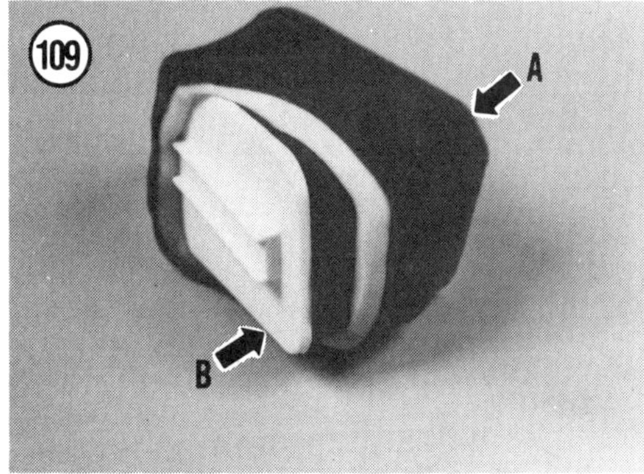

7. Fill a clean pan with liquid cleaner and warm water. If you are using an accessory air filter, the manufacturer may also sell a special air filter cleaner. Check with your dealer.

8. Submerge the air filter elements into the cleaning solution and gently work the cleaner into the filter pores. Soak and squeeze (gently) the elements to clean them.

CAUTION
Do not wring or twist the elements when cleaning them. This harsh action could damage a filter pore or tear the filter loose at a seam. This would allow unfiltered air to enter the engine and cause severe and rapid engine wear.

9. Rinse the filter under warm water while soaking and gently squeezing it.

10. Repeat Step 8 and Step 9 two or three times or until there are no signs of dirt being rinsed from the filter.

11. After cleaning the filter element, inspect it (them) (**Figure 110**). If torn or broken in any area, it should be replaced. Do not run the engine with a damaged filter as it may allow dirt to enter the engine and cause severe engine wear.

12. Set the filter element(s) aside and allow them to dry thoroughly.

CAUTION
A damp filter will not trap fine dust. Make sure the filter is completely dry before oiling it.

13. Properly oiling an air filter element is a messy job. You may want to wear a pair of disposable latex gloves when performing this procedure. Oil the filter as follows:

a. Purchase a box of gallon size reclosable storage bags. These bags can be used when cleaning the filter as well as for storing engine and carburetor parts during disassembly.
b. Place the cleaned filter element into a storage bag (**Figure 111**).
c. Pour foam air filter oil onto the filter to soak it.
d. Gently squeeze and release the outside of the bag to soak the filter oil into the filter's pores. Repeat until all of the filter's pores are discolored evenly with the oil.

   e. Remove the filter from the bag and check the pores for uneven oiling. This is indicated by light or dark areas. If necessary, re-soak the filter and squeeze it again.
   f. When the filter oiling is even, squeeze the filter a final time.

14. Remove the filter element from the bag.

15. On XT600 models, perform the following:
   a. Repeat Step 13 and Step 14 for the other filter element.
   b. Reassemble the 2 elements (**Figure 110**).

16. Inspect the inner guide (**Figure 112**) for wear or damage, replace if necessary.

17A. On XT600 models, install the air filter elements onto the inner plastic guide (**Figure 113**). Make sure it fits on properly all the way around the perimeter (**Figure 114**).

17B. On TT600 models, perform the following:
   a. Install the air filter element onto the inner plastic guide. Make sure it fits on properly all the way around the perimeter.
   b. Install the outer plastic guide onto the outer surface of the air filter element.

18. Apply a coat of light weight grease to the filter's sealing surface (**Figure 115**).

19. Check the seal on the air filter cover for wear or damage. The seal is a weak area as it is easily deformed and damaged. Replace the seal if necessary.

20A. On XT600 models, perform the following:
   a. Carefully push the air filter element assembly (A, **Figure 116**) into the air box housing.
   b. Install the air filter element set plate (B, **Figure 116**). Make sure it is properly seated in the air box and against the air filter element.
   c. Install the air filter cover and screws (**Figure 103**). Tighten the screws in a crisscross pattern and tighten securely. Do not overtighten as the plastic cover and case may be distorted or fractured.

20B. On TT600 models, perform the following:
   a. Carefully push the air filter element assembly (**Figure 117**) into the air box housing.
   b. Install and tighten the wing nut (A, **Figure 107**) securing the air filter element.
   c. Align the tab on the backside of the cover with the air filter element assembly (**Figure 118**) and install the cover.

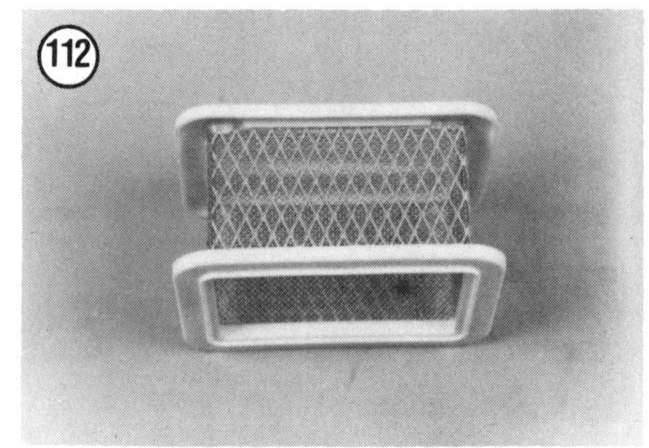
112

113

114

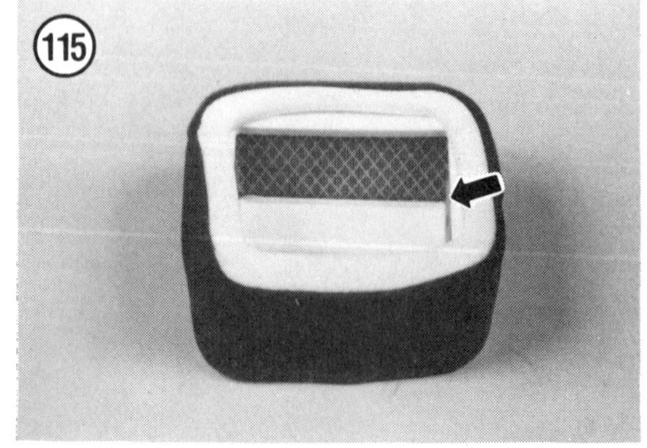
115

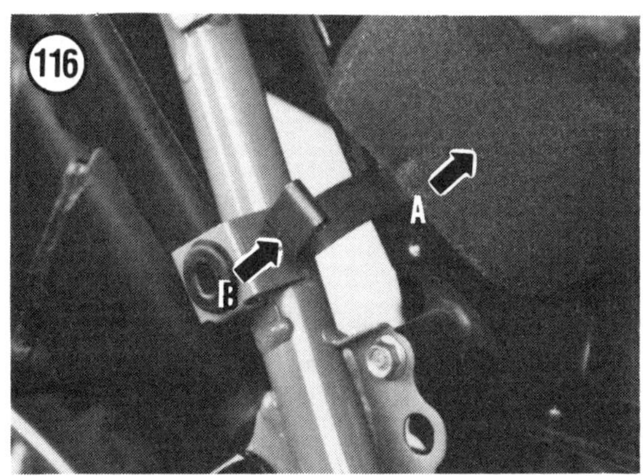

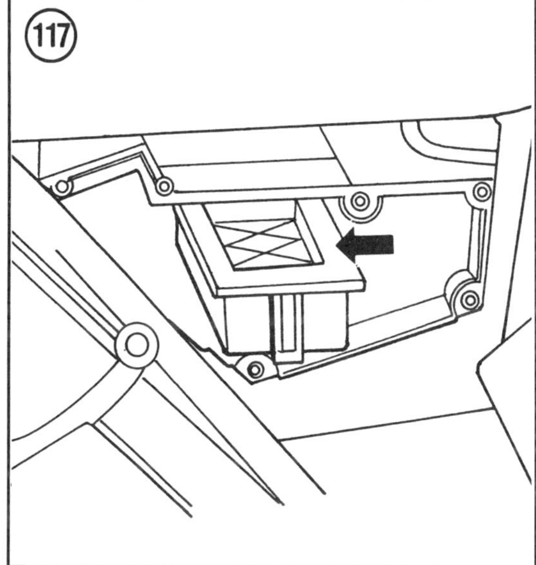

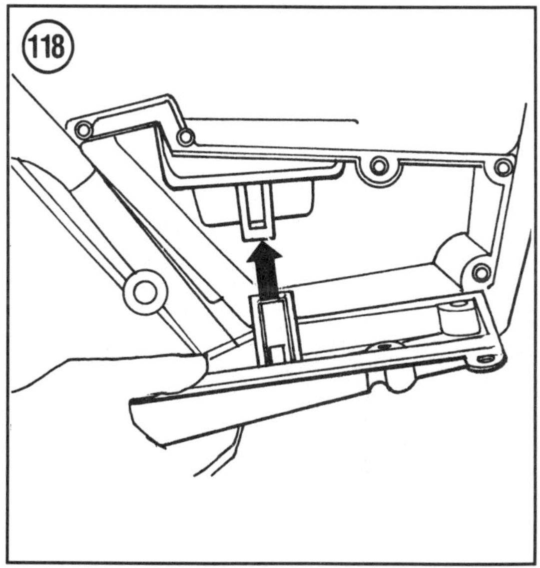

NOTE

On models where the cover is attached with screws, tighten the screws in a crisscross pattern and tighten securely. Do not overtighten the screws as the plastic cover and the case may be distorted or fractured.

d. Either install the screws securing the air filter cover (**Figure 105**) or hook the rubber strap (**Figure 106**) securing the air filter cover.

21. Install the frame's right-hand side cover.
22. Pour the left-over filter oil from the bag back into the bottle for reuse.
23. Dispose of the plastic bag safely.

Fuel Line Inspection

Inspect the fuel line from the fuel tank to the carburetor assembly (**Figure 119**). If it is cracked or starting to deteriorate, it must be replaced. Make sure the small hose clamps are in place and holding securely. Also make sure that the overflow and vent tubes are in place and are not kinked.

WARNING

A damaged or deteriorated fuel line presents a very dangerous fire hazard to both the rider and the machine if fuel should spill onto a hot engine or exhaust pipe.

NOTE

If you have been experiencing fuel contamination that is plugging up carburetors jets (especially the pilot jet), install a fuel filter in the fuel line between the fuel tank and the carburetor. Use the stock Yamaha fasteners to hold the line

to the filter. If the contamination problem is severe, you may want to flush the fuel tank before installing the filter.

Emission Control Hoses (California Models)

All XT600 models originally sold in California are equipped with an evaporative emission control system. Refer to *Emission Control* in Chapter Eight for inspection procedures and additional information.

Wheel Bearings

The wheel bearings should be periodically checked for roughness or other damage. Factory equipped sealed bearings do not require periodic lubrication. However, if non-sealed bearings have been installed by a previous owner, they should be cleaned and repacked every six months or more often if the vehicle is operated often in water (especially salt water). Service procedures are covered in Chapter Ten (front) and Chapter Eleven (rear).

Steering Head Adjustment Check

Tapered roller bearings are installed in the upper and lower bearing mounting areas. A loose bearing adjustment will hamper steering and cause premature bearing and race wear. In severe conditions, a loose bearing adjustment can cause loss of control. Steering head play should be checked often, especially after riding the bike off-road.

1. Place the bike on a stand so that the front wheel clears the ground.
2. Center the front wheel. Push lightly against the left handlebar grip to start the wheel turning to the right, then let go. The wheel should continue turning under its own momentum until the forks hit their stop. Try the same in the other direction.
3. If, with a light push in either direction, the front wheel will turn all the way to the stop, the steering adjustment is not too tight.
4. Center the front wheel and kneel in front of it. Grasp the bottoms of the fork legs. Try to pull the forks toward you, and then try to push them toward the engine. If no play is felt, the steering adjustment is not too loose.
5. If the steering adjustment is too tight or too loose, readjust it as described under *Steering Adjustment* in Chapter Ten.

Handlebars

Inspect the handlebars weekly for any signs of damage. A bent or damaged handlebar should be replaced. The knurled section of your bars should be kept very rough. Keep the clamps clean with a wire brush. Any time that the bars slip in the clamps (like when you land flat and they move forward slightly) they should be removed and wire brushed clean to prevent small balls of aluminum from gathering in the clamps and reducing the grip surface area.

Spark Arrester Cleaning

Periodically remove the screw holding the spark arrester (**Figure 120**) and pull it out of the end of the muffler housing. Clean the pipe of all exhaust residue with a wire brush and solvent. Reverse to install.

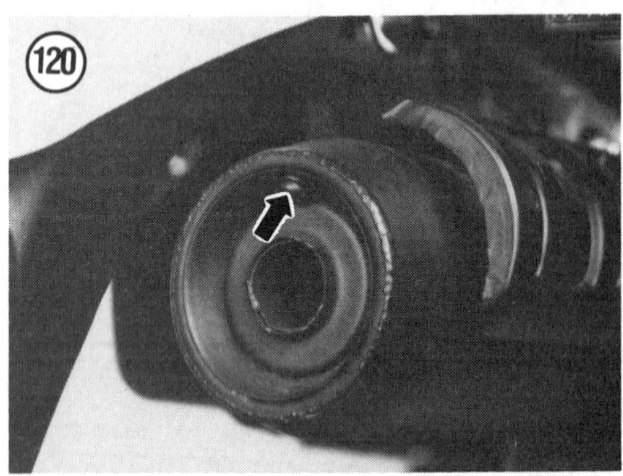

Nuts, Bolts, and Other Fasteners

Constant vibration can loosen many of the fasteners on the motorcycle. Check the tightness of all fasteners, especially those on:

a. Engine mounting hardware.
b. Engine crankcase covers.
c. Handlebar and front forks.
d. Gearshift lever.
e. Kickstarter lever.
f. Brake pedal and lever.
g. Clutch lever.
h. Exhaust system.

FRONT FORK AIR PRESSURE

For proper fork operation, the air pressure must be maintained at the correct pressure and both forks must have the same pressure.

1. Support the bike so that the front wheel clears the ground.
2. Remove the air valve caps. Refer to **Figure 121** for XT600 models or **Figure 122** for TT600 models.

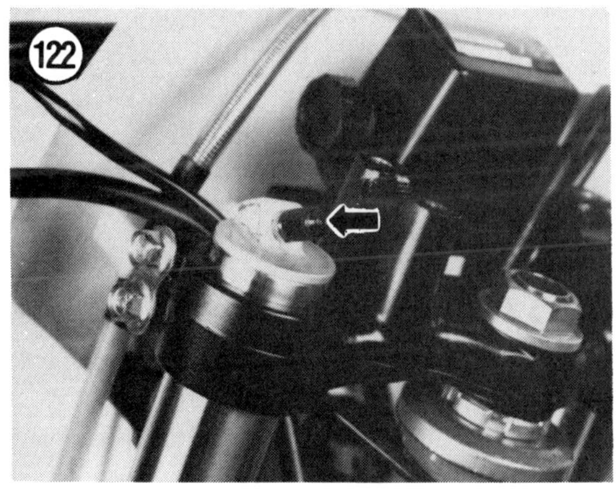

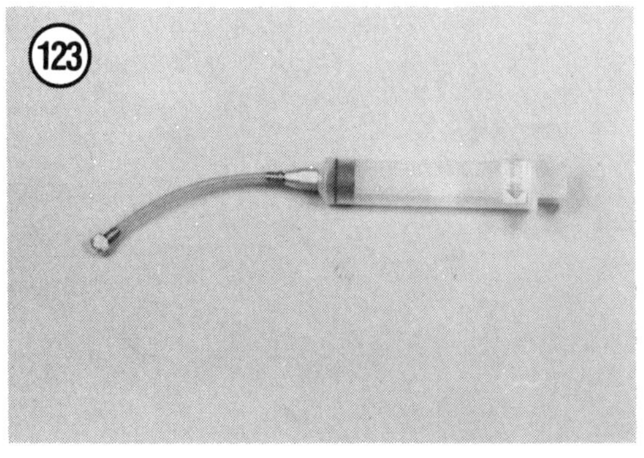

CAUTION

Never use a high pressure air supply to pressurize the forks. Never exceed the recommended maximum allowable air pressure or the oil seal will be damaged. The air pressure difference between the 2 forks should be 1.4 psi (9.81 kPa).

WARNING

*Use only compressed air—**do not** use any other type of compressed gas as an explosion may result. Never heat the front forks with a torch or place them near an open flame or extreme heat.*

3. Attach a small manual air pump (**Figure 123**) to the air valve fitting on one of the fork tubes.

4A. On XT600 models, inflate to the desired inflation pressure, making sure to keep within the following pressure range:

a. Standard: 5.7 psi (39.2 kPa).
b. Maximum: 14.2 psi (98.1 kPa).

4B. On TT600 models, inflate to the desired inflation pressure, making sure to keep within the following pressure range:

a. Standard: 0 psi (0 kPa).
b. Maximum: 17 psi (118 kPa).

5. Repeat for the opposite fork.

NOTE

The difference in air pressure between the right- and left-hand fork should be 1.4 psi (9.81 kPa) or less.

6. Reinstall the air valve cap.

ENGINE TUNE-UP

A tune-up consists of a series of inspections, adjustments and parts replacements to compensate for normal wear and deterioration of engine components. Regular tune-ups are especially important to a dual-purpose motorcycle.

Since proper engine operation depends upon a number of interrelated system functions, a tune-up consisting of only one or 2 corrections will seldom give lasting results. For improved power, performance and operating economy, a thorough and systematic procedure of analysis and correction is necessary.

The following paragraphs discuss each facet of a proper tune-up —which should be performed in the order given. Unless otherwise specified, the engine should be completely cool before starting any tune-up procedure.

NOTE
It is a good idea to start the engine after each one of the tune-up procedures is completed and make sure it runs okay. If for some reason, the procedure was not done correctly or a faulty new part(s) was installed, you can then concentrate on that specific procedure and part(s) and correct the problem. If you wait until all of the tune-up procedures are completed and then the bike runs worse or does not start at all, then you have to narrow it down to which one of the procedures or parts is causing the problem.

A tune-up consists of the following:

a. Valve clearance check and adjustment.
b. Engine compression check.
c. Ignition system inspection.
d. Carburetor check and adjustment.

To perform a tune-up on your Yamaha, you will need the following tools and equipment:

a. Spark plug wrench.
b. Ratchet and assorted sockets.
c. Allen wrenches.
d. Flat feeler gauge.
e. Compression gauge.
f. Spark plug feeler gauge and gap adjusting tool.
g. Ignition timing light.
h. Tachometer.

Valve Clearance Measurement

Valve clearance measurement must be made with the engine cool, at room temperature. Preferably, let the bike sit overnight and check the valve clearance the first thing in the morning.

The intake valves are located at the rear of the cylinder head and the exhaust valves are located at the front. The correct valve clearances are listed in **Table 7**.

1. Place the bike on its sidestand.

2. Remove the fuel tank as described under *Fuel Tank Removal/Installation* in Chapter Eight.

CAUTION
To prevent expensive engine damage, refer to ***CAUTIONS*** *under* ***Spark Plug Removal*** *in this chapter.*

3. Disconnect the spark plug lead (A, **Figure 124**) and remove the spark plug as described in this chapter. This will make it easier to rotate the engine by hand.

124

125

126

4. Remove the exhaust valve adjuster covers (B, **Figure 124**) and the intake valve adjuster cover (C, **Figure 124**) from the cylinder head cover.

5. Remove the 2 covers (**Figure 125**) from the timing holes on the left-hand crankcase cover.

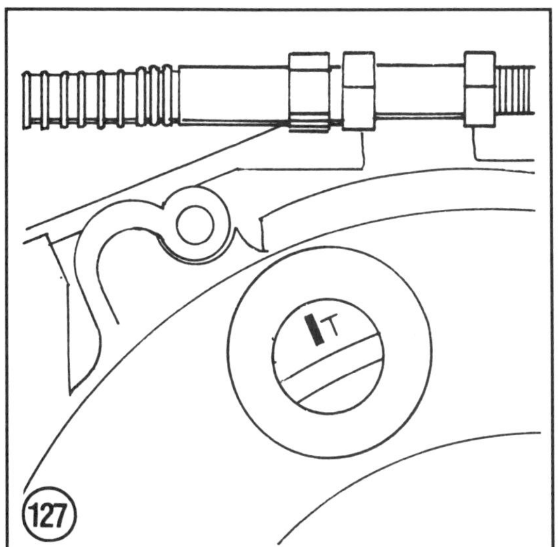

NOTE
A cylinder at top dead center (TDC) of its compression stroke will have free play in all of its rocker arms, indicating that all the intake and exhaust valves are closed.

6. Using a 19 mm socket and wrench (**Figure 126**) on the alternator nut, rotate the rotor *counterclockwise* until the cylinder is at top dead center (TDC) on the compression stroke. To determine TDC for the cylinder, perform the following:

a. Align the "T" mark on the rotor (**Figure 127**) with the crankcase timing mark (**Figure 128**).
b. Wiggle both sets of rocker arms. There should be free play in all 4 rocker arms, indicating that both the intake and exhaust valve sets are closed.
c. If either the intake or exhaust rocker arms *do not* have free play, rotate the rotor *counterclockwise* an additional 360° and again align the "T" mark on the rotor with the crankcase timing mark (**Figure 128**).
d. Again wiggle both sets of rocker arms. There should be free play in all 4 rocker arms, indicating that both sets of intake and exhaust valves are closed. The cylinder is now at top dead center (TDC) on the compression stroke.

7. With the engine in this position, check the clearance of all of the intake and exhaust valves.

8. Check the clearance by inserting a flat feeler gauge between the rocker arm and the valve stem (A, **Figure 129**). When the clearance is correct, there will be a slight drag on the feeler gauge when it is inserted and withdrawn. Measure the valve clearance for both the intake and exhaust valves.

9. To adjust the valve clearance, perform the following:

a. Loosen the valve adjuster locknut with a wrench (B, **Figure 129**) and turn the adjuster either in or out until there is a slight drag on the feeler gauge.
b. Hold the adjuster with the wrench and tighten the locknut to the torque specification listed in **Table 6**.
c. Recheck the clearance to make sure the adjuster did not turn while tightening the locknut. Readjust if necessary.

10. Repeat Step 9 for all 4 valves.

3

11. After all valve clearances have been adjusted, using the alternator rotor nut, rotate the engine several complete revolutions to seat all components.

12. Reinspect all valve clearances as described in this procedure. If any of the clearances are still not within specification, repeat this procedure until all clearances are correct.

13. Adjust the decompression cable as described under *Decompression Cable Adjustment* in this chapter.

14. Inspect the O-ring seal (**Figure 130**) on both timing hole covers for hardness or deterioration. Replace if necessary.

15. Install the 2 covers (**Figure 125**) into the timing holes on the left-hand crankcase cover.

16. Inspect the O-ring seals on the valve adjuster covers for hardness or deterioration. Refer to **Figure 131** and **Figure 132**. Replace if necessary.

NOTE
*Position the intake valve adjuster cover with the arrow and UP mark (**Figure 133**) facing up.*

17. Install the exhaust valve adjuster covers (B, **Figure 124**) and the intake valve adjuster cover (C, **Figure 124**) onto the cylinder head cover.

18. Install the spark plug and reconnect the spark plug lead.

19. Install the fuel tank as described under *Fuel Tank Removal/Installation* in Chapter Eight.

20. Start the bike and make sure it runs correctly.

Compression Test

An engine with low compression cannot be properly tuned. A compression test measures the compression built up in the cylinder. At every tune-up, check cylinder compression. Record the results and compare them at the next check. A running record will show trends in deterioration so that corrective action can be taken before complete failure. The results, when properly interpreted, can indicate general cylinder, piston ring and valve condition.

NOTE
The valves must be properly adjusted to correctly interpret the results of this test.

1. Ensure that the choke valve is completely open. Make sure the engine stop switch is in the OFF position.

CAUTION
*To prevent expensive engine damage, refer to **CAUTIONS** under **Spark Plug Removal** in this chapter.*

2. Remove the spark plug as described in this chapter.

NOTE
*A screw-in type compression gauge with a flexible adapter will be required for this procedure. See **Compression Gauge** in Chapter One. Before using the gauge, check that the rubber gasket on the end of the adapter is not cracked or damaged; the gasket seals the cylinder to ensure accurate compression readings.*

3. Connect the compression gauge to the cylinder following manufacturer's instructions. Lubricate the adapter threads with engine oil to prevent damaging the spark plug threads.

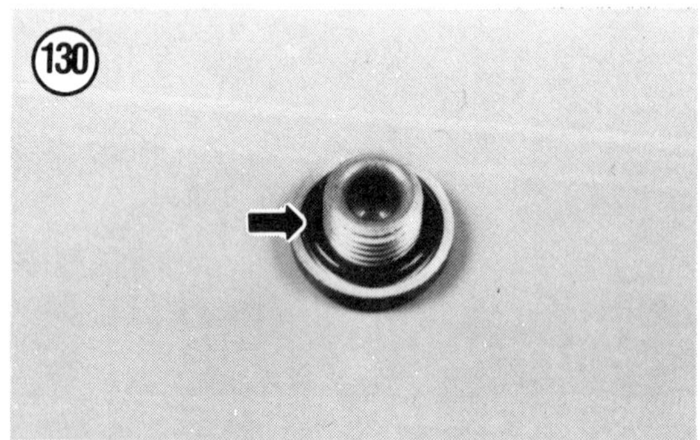

130

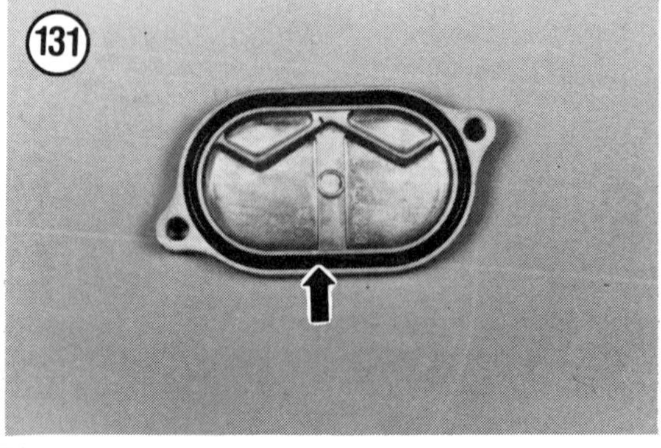

131

4. *Open the throttle completely* and using the kick-starter, kick the engine over until there is no further rise in pressure. Maximum pressure is usually reached with 4-7 kicks.

5. Record the reading and then relieve the gauge pressure valve. Remove the compression gauge.

6. Standard compression pressure is specified in **Table 7**. Greater differences indicate worn or broken rings, leaky or sticky valves, blown head gasket or a combination of all. If a low reading (10% or more below specified compression pressure) is obtained, it indicates valve or ring trouble. To determine which, pour about a teaspoon of engine oil through the spark plug hole onto the top of the piston. Turn the engine over once to distribute the oil, then take another compression test and record the reading. If the compression increases significantly, the valves are good but the rings are defective. If compression does not increase, the valves require servicing.

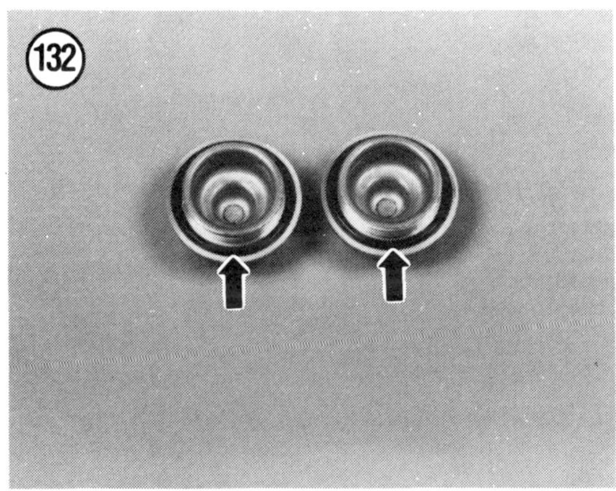

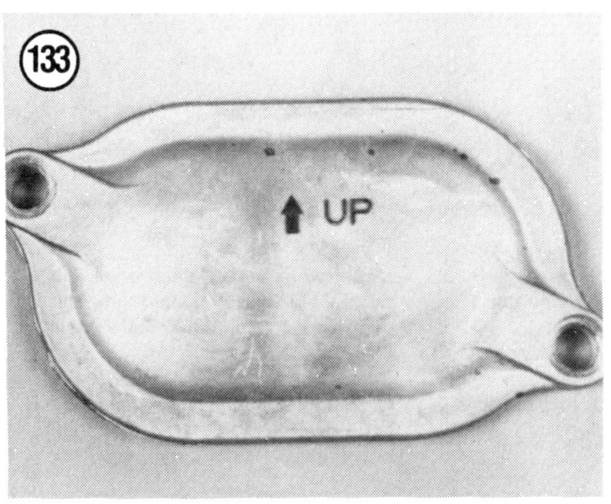

NOTE
If the compression is low, the engine cannot be tuned to maximum performance. The worn parts must be replaced and the engine rebuilt.

7. Disconnect the compression gauge and install the spark plug.

3

Correct Spark Plug Heat Range

The proper spark plug is important in obtaining maximum performance and reliability. The condition of a used spark plug can tell a trained mechanic a lot about engine condition and carburetion.

Select a plug of the heat range designed for the loads and conditions under which the bike will be run. Use of incorrect heat ranges can cause a seized piston, scored cylinder wall, or damaged piston crown.

In general, use a hot plug for low speeds and low temperatures. Use a cold plug for high speeds, high engine loads and high temperatures. The plug should operate hot enough to burn off unwanted deposits, but not so hot that they burn themselves or cause preignition. A spark plug of the correct heat range will show a light tan color on the portion of the insulator within the cylinder after the plug has been in service. See **Figure 134**.

The reach (length) of a plug is also important. A longer than normal plug could interfere with the piston, causing permanent and severe damage. Refer to **Figure 135**.

The standard heat range spark plug for the various models is listed in **Table 7**.

Spark Plug Removal

1. On XT600 models, remove the screws (A, **Figure 136**) and washers securing the left-hand air scoop (B, **Figure 136**) and remove the air scoop and inner guide. This is necessary to gain access to the spark plug.
2. Grasp the spark plug lead (**Figure 137**) as near the plug as possible and pull it off the plug. If it is stuck to the plug, rotate it slightly to break it loose.

CAUTION
When the spark plug is removed, dirt surrounding the plug can fall into the spark plug hole. This can cause expen-

SPARK PLUG CONDITION

NORMAL

- Identified by light tan or gray deposits on the firing tip.
- Can be cleaned.

GAP BRIDGED

- Identified by deposit buildup closing gap between electrodes.
- Caused by oil or carbon fouling. If deposits are not excessive, the plug can be cleaned.

OIL FOULED

- Identified by wet black deposits on the insulator shell bore and electrodes.
- Caused by excessive oil entering combustion chamber through worn rings and pistons, excessive clearance between valve guides and stems, or worn or loose bearings. Can be cleaned. If engine is not repaired, use a hotter plug.

CARBON FOULED

- Identified by black, dry fluffy carbon deposits on insulator tips, exposed shell surfaces and electrodes.
- Caused by too cold a plug, weak ignition, dirty air cleaner, too rich a fuel mixture, or excessive idling. Can be cleaned.

LEAD FOULED

- Identified by dark gray, black, yellow, or tan deposits or a fused glazed coating on the insulator tip.
- Caused by highly leaded gasoline. Can be cleaned.

WORN

- Identified by severely eroded or worn electrodes.
- Caused by normal wear. Should be replaced.

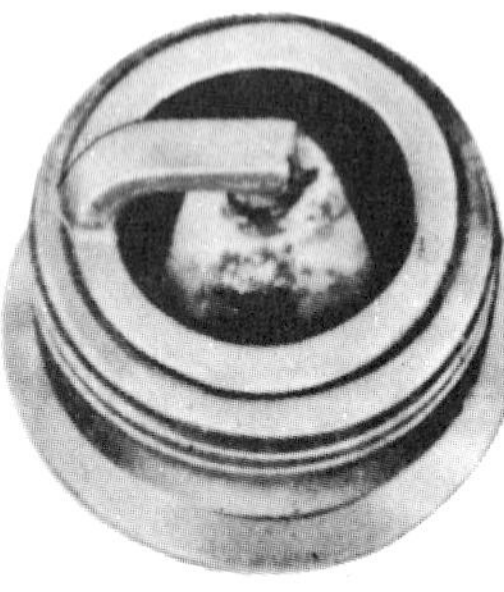

FUSED SPOT DEPOSIT

- Identified by melted or spotty deposits resembling bubbles or blisters.
- Caused by sudden acceleration. Can be cleaned.

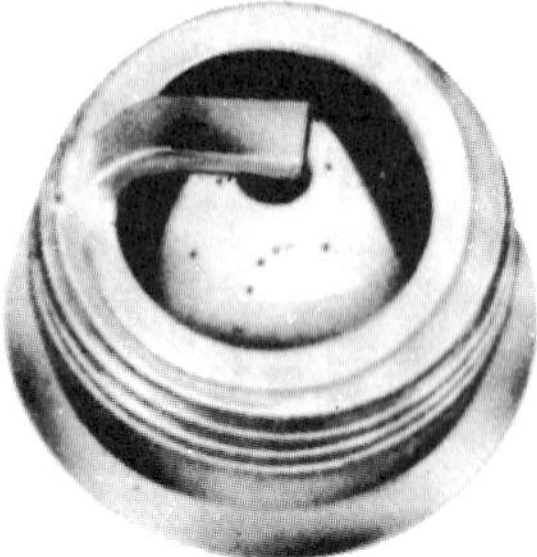

OVERHEATING

- Identified by a white or light gray insulator with small black or gray brown spots and with bluish-burnt appearance of electrodes.
- Caused by engine overheating, wrong type of fuel, loose spark plugs, too hot a plug, or incorrect ignition timing. Replace the plug.

PREIGNITION

- Identified by melted electrodes and possibly blistered insulator. Metallic deposits on insulator indicate engine damage.
- Caused by wrong type of fuel, incorrect ignition timing or advance, too hot a plug, burned valves, or engine overheating. Replace the plug.

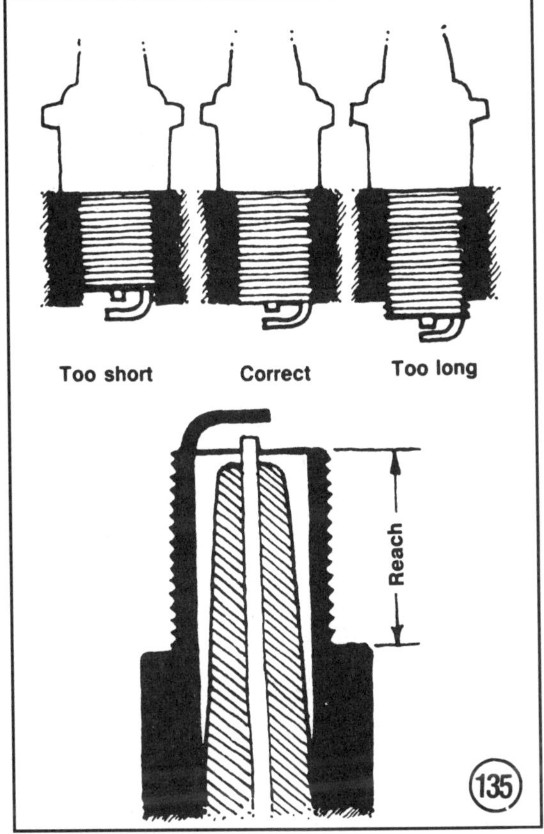

sive engine damage. In addition, dirt built-up underneath the fuel tank can also break loose and fall into the spark plug hole. If necessary, wrap a large cloth around the fuel tank before removing the spark plug.

3. Blow away any dirt that has accumulated next to the spark plug base with compressed air. If you don't have an air compressor, you can purchase cans of compressed inert gas from a photo supply store.

CAUTION

The spark plug is buried down in the cylinder head cavity and difficult to reach. Use the spark plug wrench supplied in the factory tool kit to avoid damaging the spark plug with a deep socket and socket extension during removal.

4. Remove the spark plug with a 14 mm spark plug wrench.

NOTE

If the plug is difficult to remove, apply penetrating oil, like WD-40 or Liquid Wrench, around the base of the plug and let it soak in about 10-20 minutes.

5. Inspect the plug carefully. Look for a broken center porcelain, excessively eroded electrodes, and excessive carbon or oil fouling.

Gapping and Installing the Plug

A new spark plug should be carefully gapped to ensure a reliable, consistent spark. You must use a special spark plug tool with a round gauge.

1. Remove the new spark plug from the box. Screw in the small piece (**Figure 138**) that may be loose in the box.

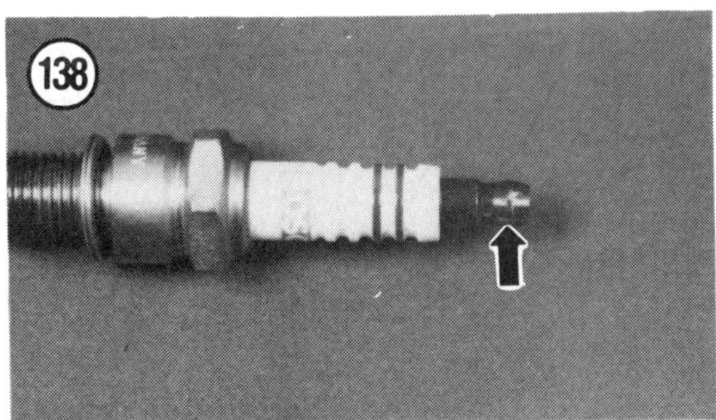

2. Insert a feeler gauge between the center and side electrode (**Figure 139**). The correct gap is listed in **Table 7**. If the gap is correct, you will feel a slight drag as you pull the gauge through. If there is no drag, or the gauge won't pass through, bend the side electrode with the gapping tool (**Figure 140**) to set the proper gap. Remeasure with the wire gauge.

CAUTION
Never try to close the electrode gap by tapping the spark plug on a solid surface. This can damage the plug internally. Always use the special tool to open or close the gap.

3. Check the spark plug hole threads and clean with an appropriate size spark plug chaser, if necessary, before installing the plug. This will remove any corrosion, carbon build-up or minor flaws from the threads. Coat the chaser threads with grease to catch chips or foreign matter. Use care to avoid cross-threading.
4. Apply a thin film of anti-seize compound (**Figure 141**) to the spark plug threads.

NOTE
The spark plug well is too deep and narrow to hand-hold the spark plug and get it started by hand. The piece of vinyl tube used in Step 5 will still give you "the feel" of starting the plug by hand to avoid cross-threading it.

5. Attach a section of vinyl tubing (A, **Figure 142**) onto the end of the spark plug (B, **Figure 142**) and use this tubing to install the spark plug into the cylinder head. Screw the plug in by hand until it seats. Very little effort is required. If force is necessary, you have the plug cross-threaded. Unscrew it and try again.
6. Use a spark plug wrench and tighten the plug an additional 1/4 to 1/2 turn after the gasket has made contact with the head or tighten it to the torque specification in **Table 6**. If you are installing an old, regaped plug and reusing the old gasket, only tighten an additional 1/4 turn.

NOTE
Do not overtighten. This will only squash the gasket and destroy its sealing ability.

7. Install the spark plug wire. Make sure it is on tight.

Reading Spark Plugs

Much information about engine and spark plug performance can be determined by careful examination of the spark plug. This information is more valid after performing the following steps.

1. Ride the bike a short distance at full throttle in any gear.
2. Push the engine stop switch to the OFF position before closing the throttle and simultaneously pull in the clutch or shift to neutral; coast and brake to a stop.

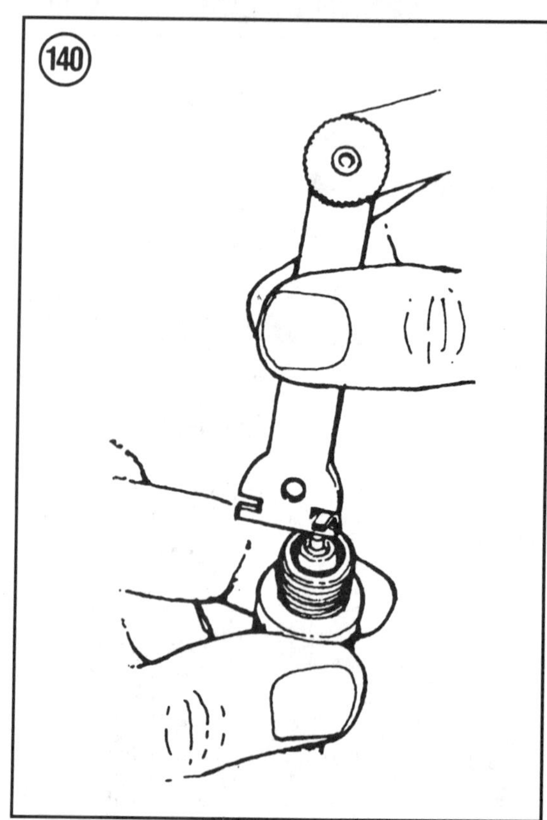

3. Remove the spark plug and examine it. Compare it to **Figure 134**.

If the insulator is white or burned, the engine is running hot. If you changed the spark plug, make sure the new plug has the correct heat range.

A too-cold plug will have sooty or oily deposits.

If the plug has a light tan or gray colored deposit and no abnormal gap wear or electrode erosion is evident, the plug and the engine are running properly.

If the plug exhibits a black insulator tip, damp oily film over the firing end, and a carbon layer over the entire nose, it is oil fouled. An oil fouled plug can be cleaned, but it is better to replace it.

NOTE
A too-hot or too-cold plug reading is also an indication that the engine is not operating correctly. If the correct spark plug is installed for the altitude that you are riding in, one of the engine systems is malfunctioning or the system is tuned incorrectly. Refer to Chapter Two.

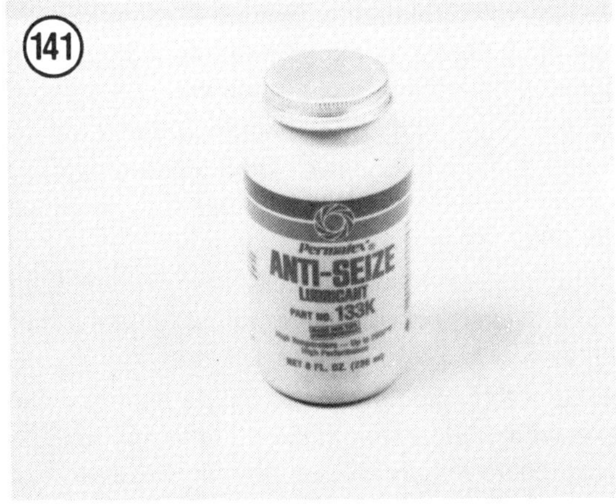

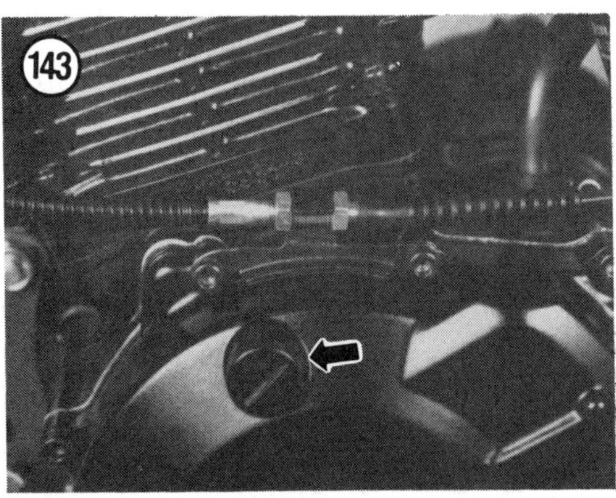

Ignition Timing

The models covered in this manual are equipped with a capacitor discharge ignition (CDI) system. This system uses no breaker points and is non-adjustable. The timing should be checked to make sure all ignition components are operating correctly.

Incorrect ignition timing can cause a drastic loss of engine performance and efficiency. It may also cause overheating.

Before starting on this procedure, check all electrical connections related to the ignition system. Make sure all connections are tight and free of corrosion and that all ground connections are tight. Refer to *Ignition System* in Chapter Nine.

1. Place the bike on the sidestand.
2. On XT600 models, remove the screws (A, **Figure 136**) and washers securing the left-hand air scoop (B, **Figure 136**) and remove the air scoop and inner guide. This is necessary to gain access to the spark plug.
3. Remove the upper cover (**Figure 143**) from the timing hole on the left-hand crankcase cover.
4. Connect a portable tachometer following the manufacturer's instructions. The bike's tachometer is not accurate enough in the low rpm range for this adjustment.
5. Connect a timing light to the spark plug following the manufacturer's instructions.
6. Start the engine and let it idle at 1,200 rpm. This idle speed is 100 rpm lower than the normal idle speed. Adjust accordingly.

7. Aim the timing light at the timing hole in the left-hand crankcase cover and pull the trigger. If the "T" timing mark aligns with the timing mark on the crankcase (**Figure 128**), the timing is correct.
8. Shut off the engine and disconnect the timing light and portable tachometer.
9. If the timing is incorrect, refer to *Ignition System* in Chapter Nine. There is no method of adjusting ignition timing and if the timing is incorrect, one of the components in the ignition system is faulty and must be replaced.
10. Inspect the O-ring seal on the upper cover for hardness or deterioration. Replace if necessary.
11. Install the upper cover (**Figure 143**) into the timing hole in the left-hand crankcase cover.
12. On XT600 models, install the left-hand air scoop and inner guide. Install and tighten the screws (A, **Figure 136**) securely.

Carburetor Idle Speed Adjustment

Proper idle speed is a balance between a low enough idle to give adequate compression braking and a high enough idle to prevent engine stalling (if desired). The idle air/fuel mixture affects transition from idle to part throttle openings.

1. Make sure that the throttle cable free play is adjusted correctly as described in this chapter.
2. Start the engine and allow it to warm up for 2-3 minutes.
3. Turn the throttle stop screw (**Figure 144**) to set the idle speed.

WARNING
With the engine idling, move the handlebar from side-to-side. If idle speed increases during this movement, the throttle cable needs adjusting or it may be incorrectly routed through the frame. Correct this problem immediately. Do not ride the bike in this unsafe condition.

STORAGE

Several months of inactivity can cause serious problems and a general deterioration of your Yamaha. This is especially true in areas of weather extremes. During the winter months it is advisable to specially prepare the bike for lay-up.

Selecting a Storage Area

Most riders store their bikes in their home garages. If you do not have a home garage, facilities suitable for long-term motorcycle storage are readily available for rent or lease in most areas. In selecting a building, consider the following points.

1. The storage area must be dry, free from dampness and excessive humidity. Heating is not necessary, but the building should be well insulated to minimize extreme temperature variations.
2. Buildings with large window areas should be avoided, or such windows should be masked (also a good security measure) if direct sunlight can fall on the bike.
3. Buildings in industrial areas, where factories are liable to emit corrosive fumes, are not desirable, nor are facilities near bodies of salt water.
4. The area should be selected to minimize the possibility of loss from fire, theft or vandalism. The area should be fully insured, perhaps with a package covering fire, theft, vandalism, weather and liability. Talk this over with your insurance agent and get approval on these matters. The building should be fireproof and items such as the security of doors and windows, alarm facility, and proximity of police should be considered.

Preparing Bike for Storage

Careful preparation will minimize deterioration and make it easier to restore the bike to service later. Use the following procedure.

1. Wash the bike completely. Make certain to remove all dirt in all the hard to reach parts like the cooling

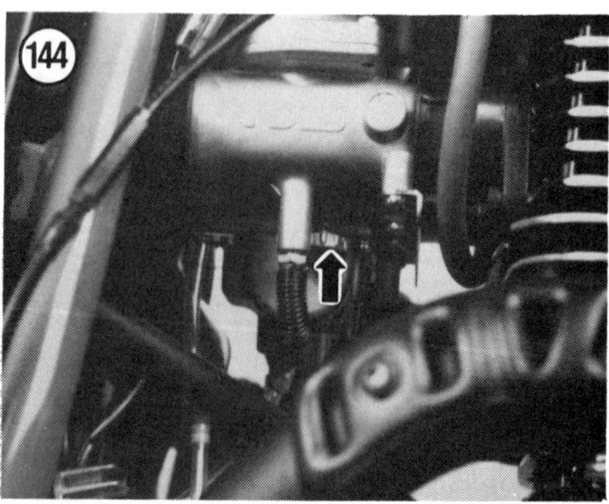
144

fins on the cylinder head and cylinder. Tip the bike from side-to-side to drain off any water that may be trapped on horizontal surfaces.

2. Completely dry all parts of the bike to remove all moisture. Wax all painted and polished surfaces, including any chromed areas.
3. Run the bike for about 20-30 minutes to warm up the oil. Drain the oil, as described in this chapter, regardless of the time since the last oil change. Refill with the normal quantity and type of engine oil.
4. Drain all gasoline from the fuel tank, interconnecting hose, and the carburetor. Leave the fuel shutoff valve in the ON position.
5. Lubricate the drive chain and control cables; refer to specific procedures in this chapter.
6. Remove the spark plug and add about one teaspoon of engine oil into the cylinder. Reinstall the spark plug and turn the engine with the kickstarter to distribute the oil to the cylinder walls and piston. Depress the engine kill switch while doing this to prevent it from starting.
7. Tape or tie a plastic bag over the end of the silencer to prevent the entry of moisture.
8. Check the tire pressure, inflate to the correct pressure and move the bike to the storage area. Place it securely on a stand or wood blocks with both wheels off the ground.
9. Remove the battery as described in this chapter. Coat the battery cables with a petroleum jelly such as Vaseline or a light mineral grease. Store the battery in a warm an accessible area so that it can be checked monthly.
10. Cover the bike with a tarp, blanket or heavy plastic drop cloth. Place this cover over the bike mainly as a dust cover—do not wrap it tightly, especially any plastic material, as it may trap moisture causing condensation. Leave room for air to circulate around the bike.

Inspection During Storage

Try to inspect the bike weekly while in storage. Any deterioration should be corrected as soon as possible. For example, if corrosion of bright metal parts is observed, cover them with a light coat of grease or silicone spray after a thorough polishing.

Turn the engine over a couple of times. Don't start it; use the kickstarter and hold the kill switch ON. Pump the front forks to keep the seals lubricated.

Once a month, check the battery as described in this chapter. Service as required.

Restoring Bike to Service

A bike that has been properly prepared and stored in a suitable area requires only light maintenance to restore to service. It is advisable, however, to perform a spring tune-up.

1. Before removing the bike from the storage area, reinflate the tires to the correct pressures. Air loss during storage may have nearly flattened the tires, and moving the bike can cause damage to tires, tubes and rims.
2. When the bike is brought to the work area, turn the fuel shutoff valve to the OFF position, and refill the fuel tank with recommended fuel. Remove the main jet cover on the base of the carburetor, turn the fuel shutoff valve to the ON position, and allow several cups of fuel to pass through the fuel system. Turn the fuel shutoff valve to the OFF position and install the main jet cover.

WARNING

Place a metal container under the carburetor to catch all expelled fuel—this presents a real fire danger if allowed to drain onto the bike and the floor. Dispose of the fuel properly.

3. Remove the spark plug and squirt a small amount of fuel into the cylinder to help remove the oil coating.
4. Reinstall the battery as described in this chapter. Service or charge battery as required.
5. Install a fresh spark plug and start up the engine.
6. Perform the standard tune-up as described earlier in this chapter.
7. Check the operation of the engine stop switch. Oxidation of the switch contacts during storage may make it inoperative.
8. Clean and test ride the motorcycle.

Tables are on the following pages.

Table 1 MAINTENANCE SCHEDULE*

Every 300 miles (500 km)	Lubricate drive chain. Check and adjust drive chain slack. Check drive chain for excessive wear.
Initial 600 miles (1,000 km)	Check and adjust valve clearance. Check and adjust carburetor idle speed (TT600). Check spark plug gap and condition (TT600). Change engine oil and filter. Clean oil strainer. Check and adjust rear brake pedal free play. Check and adjust clutch cable free play. Check rear suspension mounting hardware for tightness (TT600). Lubricate control cables. Check sidestand switch operation (XT600).
Every 4,000 miles (6,000 km) or 6 months	Check and adjust valve clearance. Check spark plug gap and condition. Check crankcase ventilation system (XT600). Check fuel line. Replace if necessary. Check exhaust system and gaskets. Check and adjust carburetor idle speed. Check and adjust carburetor throttle cable. Check and adjust decompression cable free play. Change engine oil and filter. Clean oil strainer. Clean and re-oil air filter element. Check and adjust rear brake pedal free play. Check brake pad wear (front disc brake). Check brake shoe wear (front and rear). Check and adjust clutch cable free play. Lubricate control cables. Lubricate swing arm pivot shaft. Lubricate suspension link pivot shafts. Lubricate brake and clutch lever pivot bolts. Lubricate sidestand pivot shaft. Lubricate kickstarter crank boss. Change front fork oil. Check front steering bearing play. Check wheel bearing condition. Check shock absorber operation and for leakage. Check battery specific gravity and fluid level (XT600). Check sidestand switch operation (XT600).
Every 8000 miles (12,000 km) or 12 months	Replace spark plug.
Every 15,200 miles (24,000 km) or 24 months	Repack front steering bearings.

* This Yamaha factory maintenance schedule should be considered as a guide to general maintenance and lubrication intervals. Harder than normal use and exposure to mud, water, sand, high humidity, etc. will dictate more frequent attention to most maintenance items.

Table 2 TIRE INFLATION PRESSURE

	Front tire	Rear tire
XT600		
Size	3.00-S21-4PR	4.60-S18-4PR
Tire pressure		
0-198 lb. (0-90 kg)	22 psi (147 kPa)	22 psi (147 kPa)
Maximum load	22 psi (147 kPa)	26 psi (177 kPa)
High speed riding	22 psi (147 kPa)	22 psi (147 kPa)
Off-road riding	14 psi (98.1 kPa)	14 psi (98.1 kPa)
TT600		
Size	100/80-21-4PR	140/80-18-4PR
Tire pressure	14 psi (98.1 kPa)	14 psi (98.1 kPa)

Table 3 BATTERY STATE OF CHARGE

Specific gravity	State of charge
1.110-1.130	Discharged
1.140-1.160	Almost discharged
1.170-1.190	One-quarter charged
1.200-1.220	One-half charged
1.230-1.250	Three-quarters charged
1.260-1.280	Fully charged

Table 4 RECOMMENDED LUBRICANTS AND FUEL

Engine oil	Yamalube 4-cycle oil, SAE 20W/40 or 10W/30 SE or SF motor oil
Front fork oil	10 wt. fork oil
Air filter	Foam air filter oil
Drive chain	Chain lube recommended for O-ring drive chains
Control cables	Cable lube
Control lever pivots	10W/30 motor oil
Swing arm pivot shaft	Lithium base waterproof wheel bearing grease
Suspension pivot shaft	Molybdenum disulfide grease
Steering head bearings	Lithium base waterproof wheel bearing grease
Fuel	Regular grade—research octane 87 or higher
Brake fluid	DOT 3

Table 5 APPROXIMATE REFILL CAPACITIES

Engine oil	
Periodic oil change	2,000 cc (2.1 US qt.)
With filter change	2,100 cc (2.2 US qt.)
Engine rebuild	2,400 cc (2.5 US qt.)
Front fork (each)	
XT600	481-485 cc (16.2-16.38 US oz.)
TT600	589 cc (19.9 US oz.)
Front fork oil level	
XT600	*
TT600	125 cc (4.92 oz.)
Fuel tank	
XT600	
Total	11.0 liters (2.9 US gal.)
Reserve	2 liters (0.5 US gal.)
TT600	
Total	11.0 liters (2.9 US gal.)
Reserve	3 liters (0.8 US gal.)

* Not specified by Yamaha.

Table 6 MAINTENANCE AND TUNE-UP TORQUE SPECIFICATIONS

Item	N•m	ft.-lb.
Oil drain bolt		
Crankcase	30	22
Oil tank	18	13
Oil filter cover screws	10	7.2
Oil filter cover screw	7	5.1
Oil filter cover bleed screw	5	3.6
Spark plug	18	13
Front axle nut		
XT600	100	72
TT600	58	42
Rear axle nut		
XT600	100	72
TT600	105	75
Front fork cap	23	17
Front fork pinch bolts	23	17
Handlebar clamp bolts	23	17
Valve stem nut	14	10

Table 7 TUNE-UP SPECIFICATIONS

Valve clearance (cold)	
XT600	
Intake	0.07-0.12 mm (0.0028-0.0047 in.)
Exhaust	0.12-0.17 mm (0.0047-0.0067 in.)
TT600	
Intake	0.05-0.10 mm (0.002-0.004 in.)
Exhaust	0.12-0.17 mm (0.0047-0.0067 in.)
Engine compression pressure	
Standard	1,079 kPa (156 psi)
Minimum	883 kPa (128 psi)
Maximum	1,177 kPa (171 psi)
Spark plugs	
Type	
XT600	NGK DP8EA-9 or ND X24EP-U9
TT600	NGK DP7EA-9
Gap	0.8-0.9 mm (0.031-0.035 in.)
Ignition timing	Fixed
Idle speed	
XT600	1,300 rpm
TT600	1,300-1,400 rpm
Drive chain free play	
XT600	30-40 mm (1.2-1.6 in.)
TT600	20-30 mm (0.8-1.2 in.)

CHAPTER FOUR

ENGINE TOP END

The engine is an air-cooled, single overhead cam, four-valve, single. Valves are operated by a single chain-driven camshaft.

This chapter provides complete service and overhaul procedures, including information for disassembly, removal, inspection, service and reassembly of the engine top end components. These include the camshaft, valves, cylinder head, piston, piston rings and cylinder subassemblies.

Before starting any work, read the service hints in Chapter One. You will do a better job with this information fresh in your mind.

Throughout the text, there is frequent mention of the right-hand and left-hand side of the engine. This refers to the engine as it sits in the bike's frame, *not* as it sits on your workbench. "Right-" and "left-hand" refers to a rider sitting on the seat facing forward.

Table 1 lists general engine specifications and **Table 2** lists engine service specifications. **Tables 1-3** are at the end of the chapter.

ENGINE PRINCIPLES

Figure 1 explains basic four-stroke engine operation. This will be helpful when troubleshooting or repairing your engine.

SERVICING ENGINE IN FRAME

Many components can be serviced while the engine is mounted in the frame:

a. Cylinder head cover and rocker arms.
b. Cylinder head and cylinder.
c. Piston rings and piston.
d. External gearshift mechanism.
e. Clutch.
f. Kickstarter.
g. Oil pump.
h. Carburetor assembly.
i. Alternator assembly and electrical systems.

LOWERING ENGINE IN FRAME

This procedure is necessary in order to remove the top end components covered in this chapter. The engine must be lowered in the frame to allow additional room for cylinder head cover removal.

If the entire engine is going to be removed, refer to *Engine Removal/Installation* in Chapter Five.

1. Drain the engine oil as described under *Engine Oil and Filter Change* in Chapter Three.

2A. On XT600 models, remove the bolts securing the engine skid plate (**Figure 2**) and remove the skid plate.

2B. On TT600 models, remove the bolts securing the engine guard and remove the guard.

3. Support the bike on a stand and raise the rear wheel off the ground with a suitable wheel stand.

1 4-STROKE ENGINE PRINCIPLES

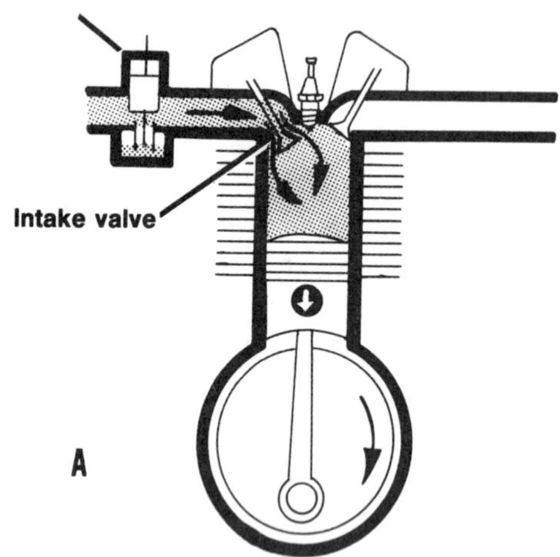

As the piston travels downward, the exhaust valve is closed and the intake valve opens, allowing the new air-fuel mixture from the carburetor to be drawn into the cylinder. When the piston reaches the bottom of its travel (BDC), the intake valve closes and remains closed for the next 1 1/2 revolutions of the crankshaft.

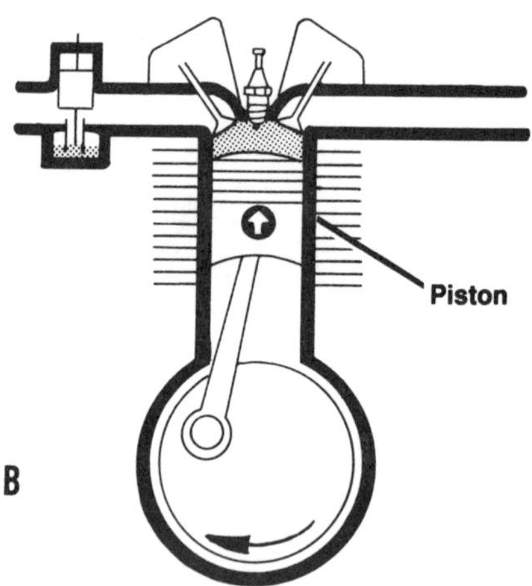

While the crankshaft continues to rotate, the piston moves upward, compressing the air-fuel mixture.

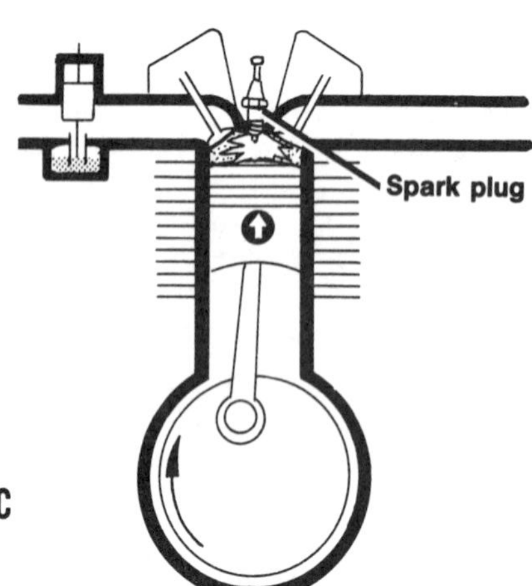

As the piston almost reaches the top of its travel, the spark plug fires, igniting the compressed air-fuel mixture. The piston continues to top dead center (TDC) and is pushed downward by the expanding gases.

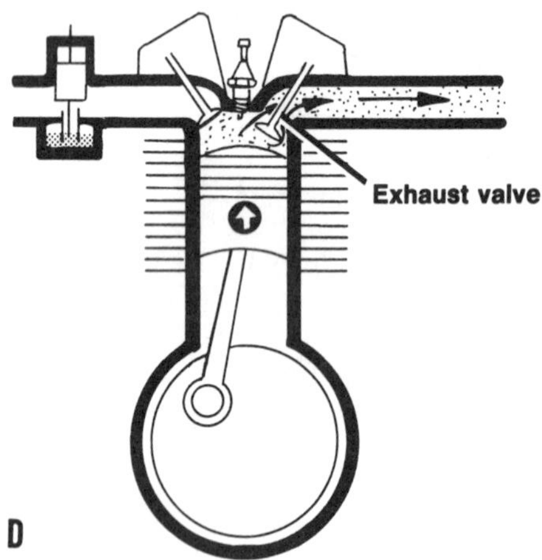

When the piston almost reaches BDC, the exhaust valve opens and remains open until the piston is near TDC. The upward travel of the piston forces the exhaust gases out of the cylinder. After the piston has reached TDC, the exhaust valve closes and the cycle starts all over again.

2

4. Remove the left- and right-hand side covers.

5. Remove the seat as described under *Seat Removal/Installation* in Chapter Thirteen.

6. Disconnect the battery negative (–) electrical terminal connector (**Figure 3**).

7. Remove the fuel tank as described under *Fuel Tank Removal/Installation* in Chapter Eight.

8. Remove the exhaust pipe and muffler assembly as described under *Exhaust System Removal/Installation* in Chapter Eight.

9. Disconnect the spark plug cap (**Figure 4**) from the spark plug and tie it up out of the way. Do *not* remove the spark plug.

10. Disconnect the crankcase breather pipe (**Figure 5**) from the cylinder head cover.

11. Remove the carburetor assembly as described under *Carburetor Removal/Installation* in Chapter Eight.

12. Place a hydraulic jack underneath the engine. Raise the jack so that the pad just rests against the bottom of the engine. Place a block of wood on the jack pad to protect the engine case. If you do not have access to a jack, place wood blocks underneath the engine. The idea is to have a support available when the engine mount bolts are loosened.

13. Remove the bolts, lockwashers and nuts securing the cylinder head-to-frame mount plates (**Figure 6**) and remove the plates.

14. Remove the bolts and locknuts securing the engine front mounting bracket (**Figure 7**) and remove the mounting bracket.

15. Loosen the engine-to-swing arm pivot shaft nut (A, **Figure 8**). Do *not* remove the nut nor the pivot shaft—they are to remain in place.

16. Wrap the backside of the frame front down tube with duct tape to prevent scratching the paint.

17. Remove the lower engine mount locknut and bolt (B, **Figure 8**).

3

4

5

6

18. Gradually release the jack pressure and allow the engine to pivot down in the front and rest against the frame down tube.

19. Reposition the engine in the frame by reversing these steps. Note the following.

20. Tighten all mounting bolts and nuts to the torque specifications listed in **Table 3**.

21. Refill the engine with the correct type and amount of engine oil as described under *Engine Oil and Filter Change* in Chapter Three.

CYLINDER HEAD COVER AND ROCKER ARMS

The cylinder head cover and rocker arms can be removed with the engine in the frame but the engine must be lowered in the frame to allow room for cylinder head cover removal.

Cylinder Head Cover Removal/Installation

Refer to **Figure 9** for this procedure.

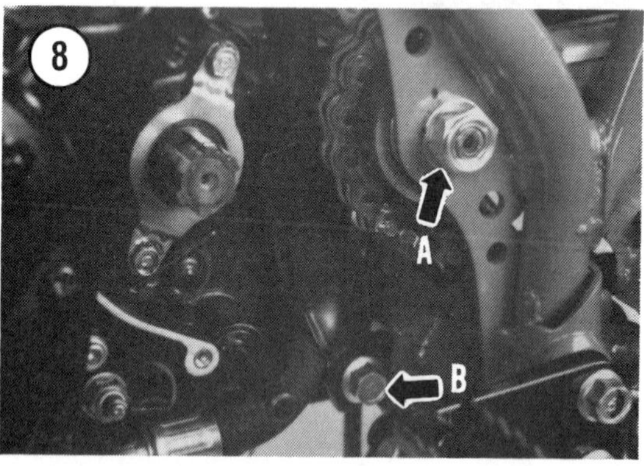

CYLINDER HEAD AND COVER

1. Decompression cable
2. Decompression lever
3. Spring
4. Oil seal
5. Washer
6. Bolt
7. O-ring seal
8. Intake valve adjuster cover
9. Cylinder head cover
10. O-ring seal
11. Plug
12. Valve guide
13. Clip
14. Locating dowel
15. Cylinder head
16. Threaded stud
17. Absorber
18. Oil seal
19. O-ring seal
20. Tachometer drive unit (XT600 only)
21. Oil seal
22. Exhaust valve adjust cover
23. O-ring

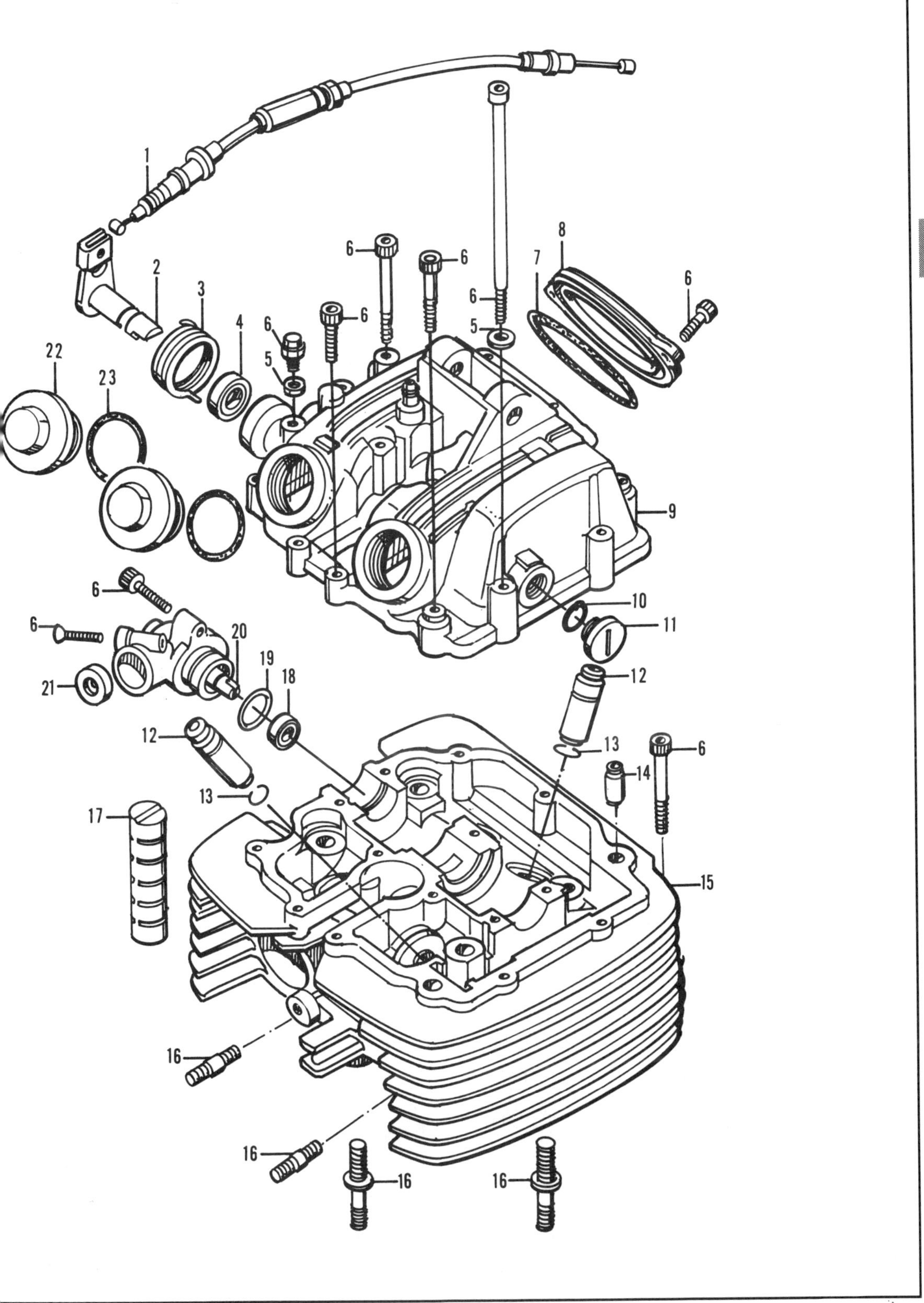
1
2
3
4
5
6
7
8
9
10
11
12
13
14
15
16
17
18
19
20
21
22
23

1. Disconnect the spark plug lead (A, **Figure 10**) and remove the spark plug as described under *Spark Plugs* in Chapter Three. This will make it easier to rotate the engine by hand.

2. Remove the exhaust valve adjuster covers (B, **Figure 10**) and the intake valve adjuster cover (C, **Figure 10**) from the cylinder head cover.

3. Remove the 2 covers (**Figure 11**) from the timing holes on the left-hand crankcase cover.

NOTE
A cylinder at top dead center (TDC) of its compression stroke will have free play in both of its rocker arms, indicating that all of the intake and exhaust valves are closed.

NOTE
Step 4 is necessary to relieve any strain on the rocker arms during cylinder head cover removal.

4. Using a 19 mm socket and wrench (**Figure 12**) on the alternator nut, rotate the rotor *counterclockwise* until the cylinder is at top dead center (TDC) on the compression stroke. To determine TDC for the cylinder, perform the following:

a. Align the "T" mark on the rotor (**Figure 13**) with the crankcase timing mark (**Figure 14**).

b. Wiggle both sets of rocker arms. There should be free play in all 4 rocker arms, indicating that both the intake and exhaust valve sets are closed.

c. If either the intake or exhaust rocker arms *do not* have free play, rotate the rotor *counter-*

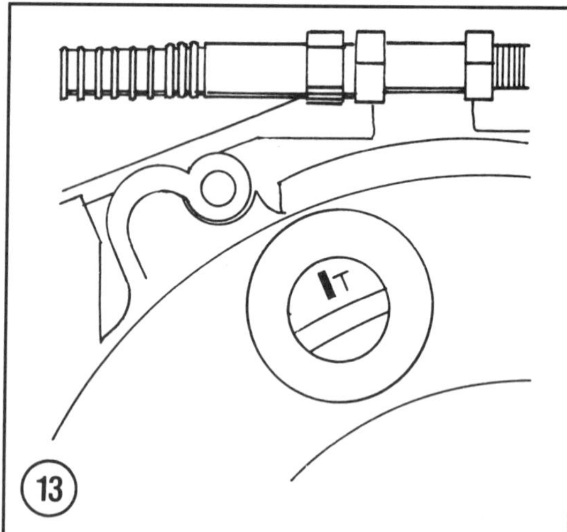

clockwise an additional 360° and again align the "T" mark on the rotor with the crankcase timing mark (**Figure 14**).

d. Again wiggle both sets of rocker arms. There should be free play in all 4 rocker arms, indicating that both sets of intake and exhaust valves are closed. The cylinder is now at top dead center (TDC) on the compression stroke.

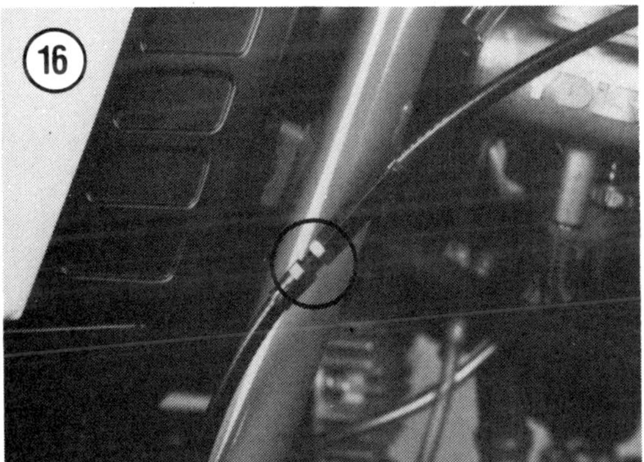

5. On XT600 models, remove the screw (A, **Figure 15**) securing the tachometer drive cable and disengage the drive cable (B, **Figure 15**) from the unit.
6. Lower the engine in the frame as described in this chapter.
7. Loosen the locknut and turn the adjuster (**Figure 16**) on the decompression cable at the mid-point in the cable.
8. Disconnect the decompression cable from the lever (A, **Figure 17**).
9. Remove the cylinder head cover bolt securing the decompression lever cable mounting bracket (B, **Figure 17**) and move the bracket and cable out of the way.

10A. On XT600 models, remove the bolts securing the tachometer drive unit (A, **Figure 18**) and remove the drive unit.

10B. On TT600 models, remove the bolts securing the cap and remove the cap.

11. Remove the bolt (B, **Figure 18**) securing the decompression relief lever and remove the lever (C, **Figure 18**) and spring.
12. Using a crisscross pattern, loosen the bolts securing the cylinder head cover (**Figure 19**) in 2-3 stages. Remove all bolts—don't forget the single

4

bolt (A, **Figure 20**) within the intake valve adjuster cavity and the one located between the mounting bosses (B, **Figure 20**). Don't lose the copper washer under the 2 center bolts (**Figure 21**).

13. Lift the cylinder head cover up and remove it. Don't lose the locating dowels.
14. Inspect the cylinder head cover and rocker arms as described in this chapter.
15. Install by reversing these removal steps, note the following.
16. Make sure the engine is still at TDC on the compression stroke.

NOTE
Make sure both cylinder head cover and cylinder head mating surfaces are clean and free of all old gasket material. This is to make sure you get a leak free seal.

17. Apply a light coat of a black *non-hardening liquid gasket* such as Three Bond (**Figure 22**) or equivalent to the mating surfaces of both cylinder head cover and cylinder head mating surfaces.
18. Make sure the locating dowels (**Figure 23**) are in place in the cylinder head.
19. Install the single 50 mm bolt located between the mounting bosses (B, **Figure 20**) prior to moving the cylinder head into position on the cylinder head. The bolt is too long to be installed after the cylinder head cover in installed due to interference with the frame tube directly above it.
20. Set the cylinder head cover onto the cylinder head. Push it down squarely into place until it engages the dowel pins and then seats completely against the cylinder head.
21. Install all of the cylinder head cover bolts. Don't forget the single bolt (A, **Figure 20**) within the intake valve adjuster cavity. Be sure to install the copper washer under the 2 center bolts (**Figure 21**). There is a "W" cast into the cylinder head cover directly next to each bolt hole.

22. Tighten the cylinder head cover bolts in a crisscross pattern and to the torque specification in **Table 3.**

23A. On XT600 models, inspect the O-ring seal (**Figure 24**) on the tachometer drive unit and drive

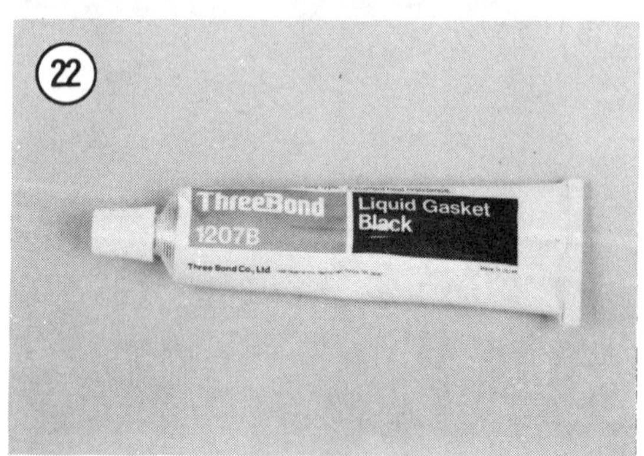

cable (**Figure 25**) for hardness or deterioration, replace if necessary.

23B. On TT600 models, inspect the O-ring seal on the cap for hardness or deterioration, replace if necessary.

24. Install the decompression lever assembly as follows:

a. Slide the spring onto the lever.
b. Lightly oil the lever shaft and install it into the cylinder head (C, **Figure 18**). Engage the spring with the cylinder head.
c. A groove is machined in the middle of the decompression lever (**Figure 26**). Install the lever bolt (B, **Figure 18**) so that the end of the bolt engages the lever groove. Tighten the bolt securely.

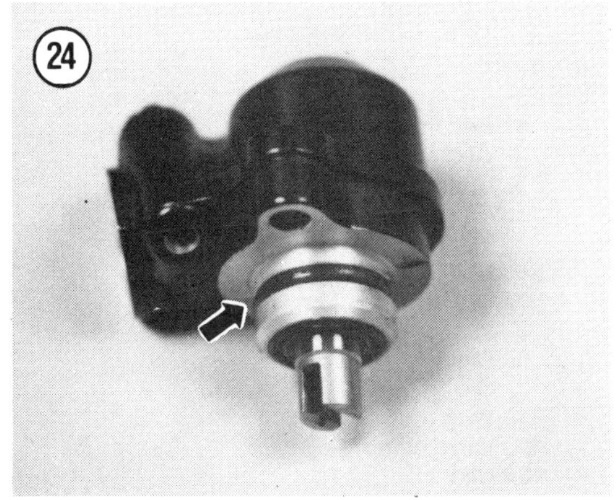

Cylinder Head Cover Inspection

1. Inspect the cylinder head cover for cracks or damage (**Figure 27**). Replace if necessary.
2. Inspect the cylinder head mounting bosses (**Figure 28**) for cracks or damage. If any cracks are visible, replace the cylinder head cover since it helps to stabilize the upper end of the engine in the frame.
3. Check the decompression lever oil seal (**Figure 29**) for wear, damage or signs of oil leakage. Replace the seal as follows:

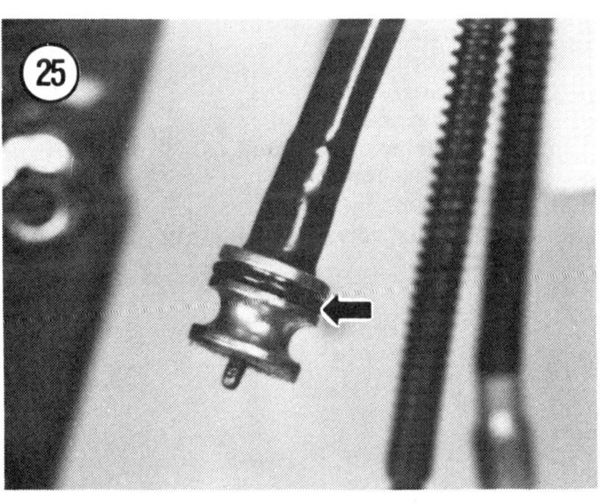

a. Carefully pry the oil seal out of the cylinder head with a straight-tipped screwdriver. Place a rag underneath the screwdriver to prevent from damaging the cylinder head.
b. Clean the oil seal mounting area with solvent and dry thoroughly. Check the mounting area for cracks or other damage before installing the new seal.
c. Tap the new seal into position with a suitable size socket placed on the outside of the seal. Tap the seal until it is flush with the bore surface.

4. Check the decompression lever (**Figure 30**) for excessive wear or damage.

Rocker Arm Disassembly/Assembly

Refer to **Figure 31** and **Figure 32** for this procedure.

Keep the rocker arm assemblies separated in their respective sets. Do not intermix the parts as they have taken on their own unique wear pattern. Both

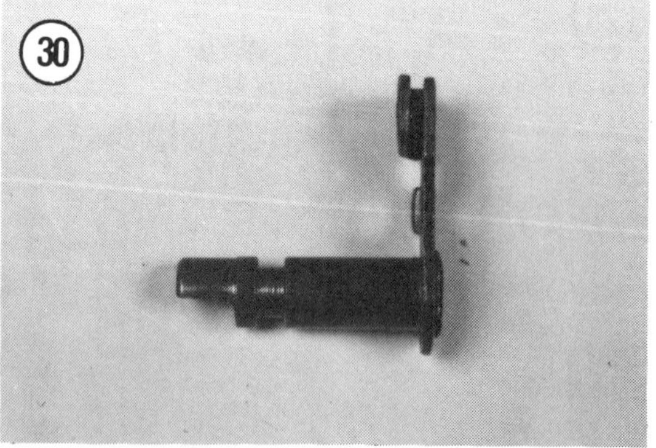

CYLINDER HEAD AND COVER

1. Decompression cable
2. Decompression lever
3. Spring
4. Oil seal
5. Washer
6. Bolt
7. O-ring seal
8. Intake valve adjuster cover
9. Cylinder head cover
10. O-ring seal
11. Plug
12. Valve guide
13. Clip
14. Locating dowel
15. Cylinder head
16. Threaded stud
17. Absorber
18. Oil seal
19. O-ring seal
20. Tachometer drive unit (XT600 only)
21. Oil seal
22. Exhaust valve adjuster cover
23. O-ring

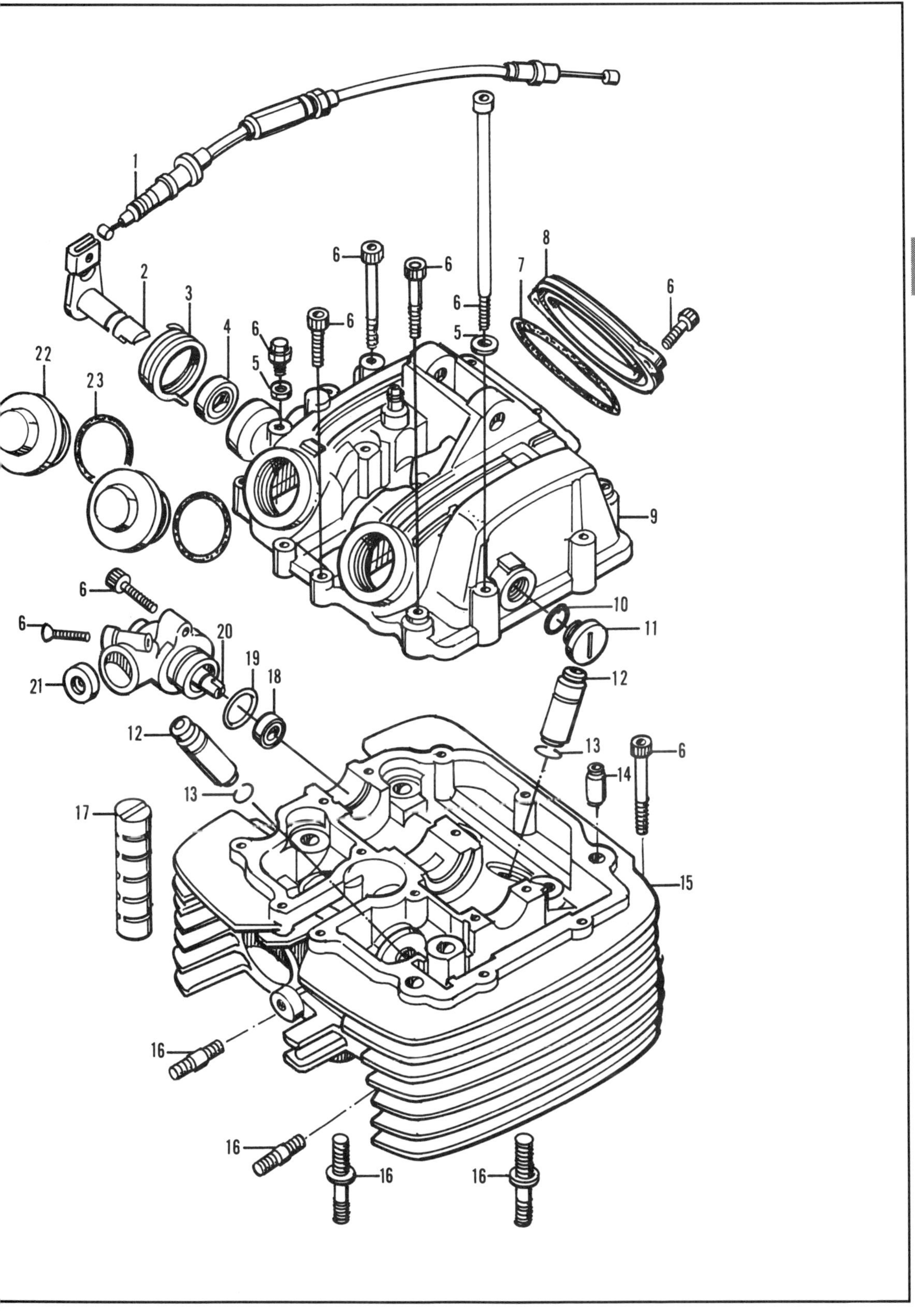
1
2
3
4
5
6
7
8
9
10
11
12
13
14
15
16
17
18
19
20
21
22
23

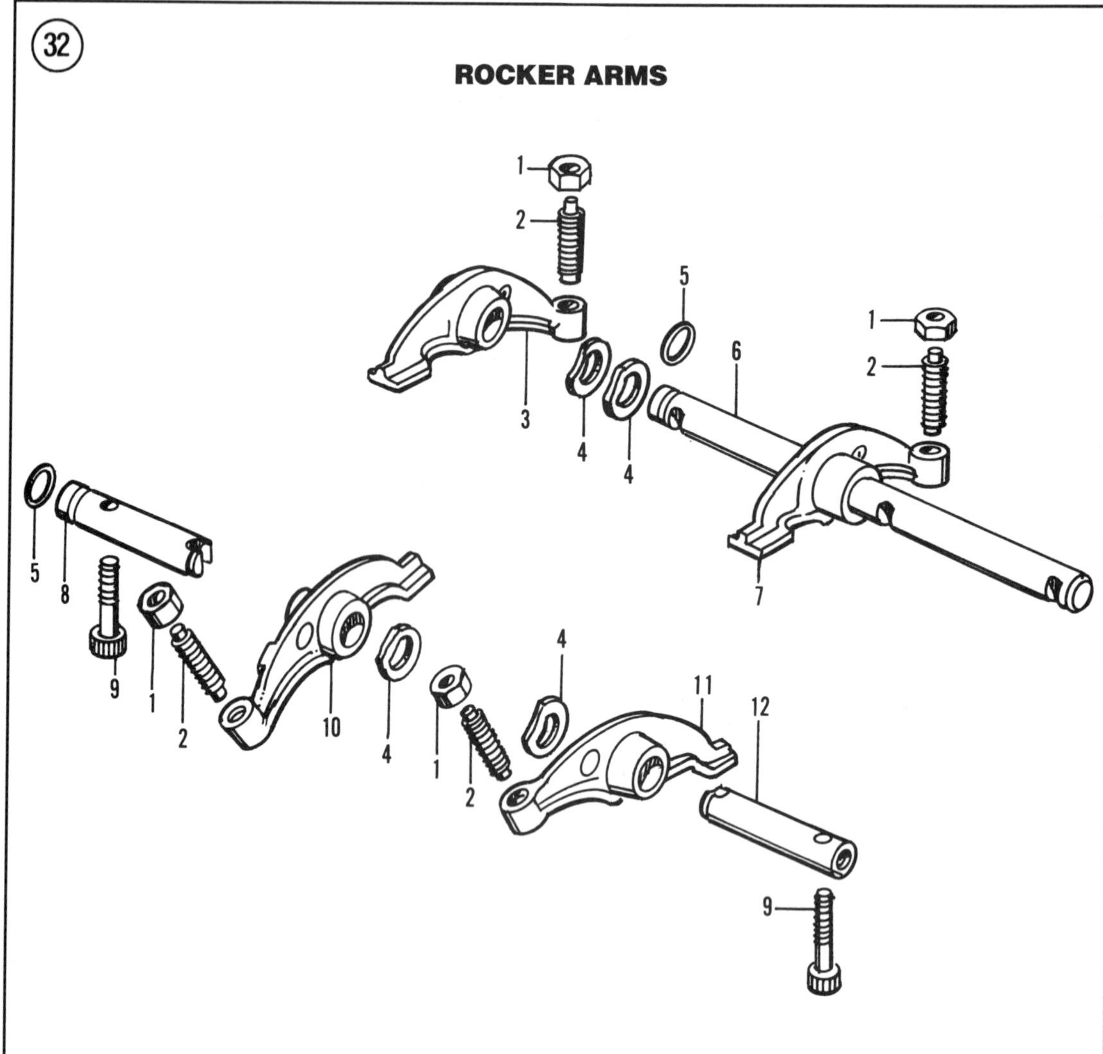

1. Locknut
2. Adjuster
3. Intake rocker arm (right-hand)
4. Spring washer
5. O-ring seal
6. Intake rocker arm shaft
7. Intake rocker arm (left-hand)
8. Exhaust rocker arm shaft (right-hand)
9. Bolt
10. Exhaust rocker arm (right-hand)
11. Exhaust rocker arm (left-hand)
12. Exhaust rocker arm shaft (left-hand)

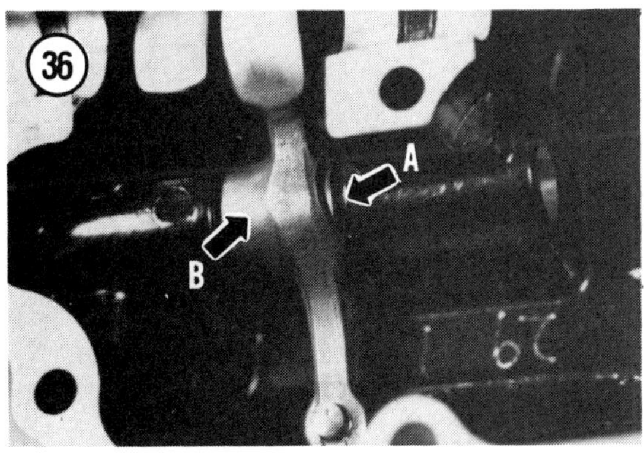

intake rocker arms ride on one long rocker arm shaft while each exhaust rocker arm rides on its own individual short rocker arm shaft.

1. Remove the rocker shaft cover and O-ring seal (**Figure 33**).

2. Screw a 6 mm bolt (**Figure 34**) into the threaded receptacle in the end of the long intake rocker arm shaft.

3. Partially withdraw the intake rocker arms shaft and remove the left-hand rocker arm and wave washer (**Figure 35**).

4. Continue to withdraw the intake rocker arm shaft and remove the wave washer (A, **Figure 36**) and the right-hand rocker arm (B, **Figure 36**).

5. Completely remove the rocker arm shaft (**Figure 37**) and unscrew the 6 mm bolt from it. Refer to **Figure 38** for the order of parts removed.

6. Screw in a 6 mm bolt (**Figure 39**) into the threaded receptacle in the end of the left-hand short exhaust rocker arm shaft.

7. Remove the Allen bolt (A, **Figure 40**) securing the rocker arm in place.

8. Partially withdraw the exhaust rocker arm shaft and remove the left-hand rocker arm (B, **Figure 40**) and wave washer (C, **Figure 40**).

9. Completely remove the rocker arm shaft and unscrew the 6 mm bolt from it.

10. Screw in a 6 mm bolt into the threaded receptacle in the end of the right-hand short exhaust rocker arm shaft.

11. Remove the Allen bolt (D, **Figure 40**) securing the rocker arm in place.

12. Partially withdraw the exhaust rocker arm shaft and remove the right-hand rocker arm (E, **Figure 40**) and wave washer (F, **Figure 40**).

13. Completely remove the rocker arm shaft and unscrew the 6 mm bolt from it.

14. Install the rocker arms and shaft into the cylinder head by reversing these steps. Note the following.

15. Refer to **Figure 41** for correct placement of exhaust valve rocker arms and to **Figure 42** for the intake rocker arms. They must be installed as shown in order to align properly with the camshaft lobes.

16. Be sure to install the wave washers in their correct location as noted during removal.

17. Prior to pushing the long intake rocker arm shaft all the way in, align the relief (A, **Figure 43**) in the shaft with the bolt hole (B, **Figure 43**) in the cylinder head cover.

18. Prior to pushing the short exhaust rocker arm shaft all the way in, align the relief in the shaft with the Allen bolt hole (C, **Figure 43**) in the cylinder head cover.

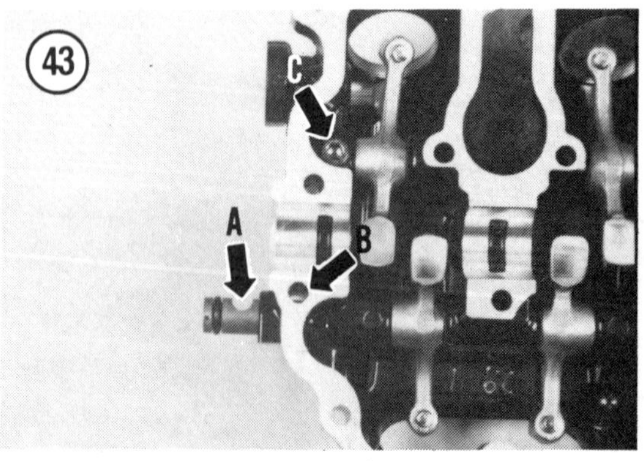

Rocker Arm

Inspection

Refer to **Figure 44** for this procedure.

Do not intermix the parts as they have taken on their own unique wear pattern.

1. Clean all parts of one set in solvent and thoroughly dry with compressed air.
2. Inspect the rocker arm bore for signs of wear or scoring.
3. Inspect the rocker arm for cracks or damage.
4. Check the rocker arm pad (A, **Figure 45**) where it rides on the camshaft and where it rides on the valve stem (B, **Figure 45**). Each place must be smooth with no gouges or wear points. Replace the rocker arm if necessary.

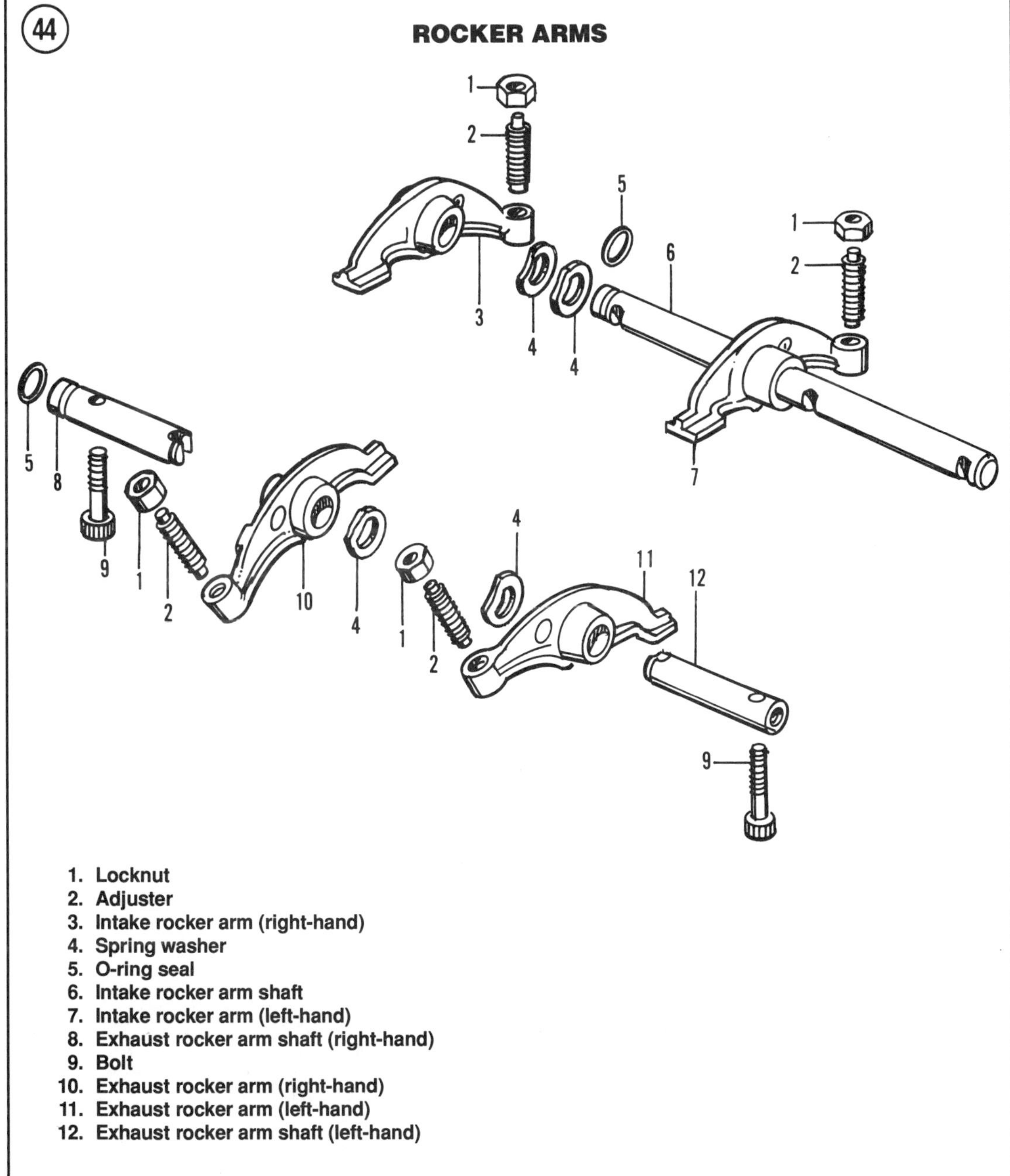

(44) **ROCKER ARMS**

1. Locknut
2. Adjuster
3. Intake rocker arm (right-hand)
4. Spring washer
5. O-ring seal
6. Intake rocker arm shaft
7. Intake rocker arm (left-hand)
8. Exhaust rocker arm shaft (right-hand)
9. Bolt
10. Exhaust rocker arm (right-hand)
11. Exhaust rocker arm (left-hand)
12. Exhaust rocker arm shaft (left-hand)

5. Check the rocker arm adjust screw and locknut (**Figure 46**) for wear or damage. Replace the adjust screw and locknut if necessary.
6. Inspect the rocker arm shaft where the rocker arms ride (**Figure 47**) for signs of wear or scoring.
7. Inspect the O-ring seal (**Figure 48**) on each rocker arm shaft for wear, deterioration or hardness, replace if necessary.
8. Measure the inside diameter of the rocker arm (**Figure 49**) with a micrometer. Compare to the dimension listed in **Table 2**.
9. Measure the outside diameter of the rocker arm shaft (**Figure 50**) with a micrometer. Compare to the dimension listed in **Table 2**.
10. Subtract the rocker arm shaft outer diameter from the rocker arm inner diameter. This will give the oil clearance between the 2 parts. Compare to the dimension listed in **Table 2**. If the clearance is greater than specified, replace the rocker arm and the rocker arm shaft as a set.
11. Roll the rocker arm shafts on a flat surface like a piece of plate glass. Check for signs of bending or damage. Replace the rocker arm shafts if any bending is evident.

CAMSHAFT AND TENSIONER

This section describes removal, inspection and installation procedures for the camshaft components. Refer to **Figure 51** for this procedure.

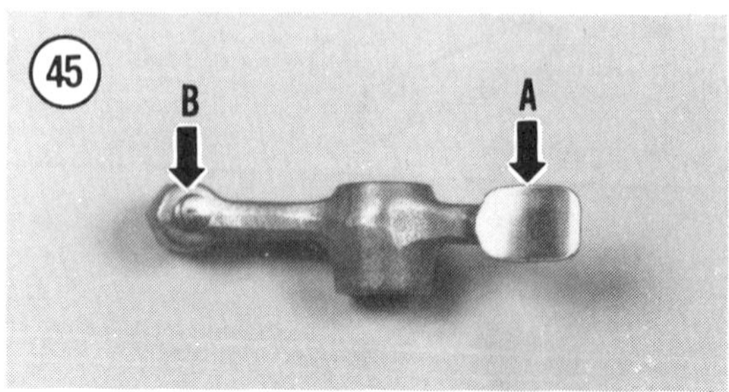

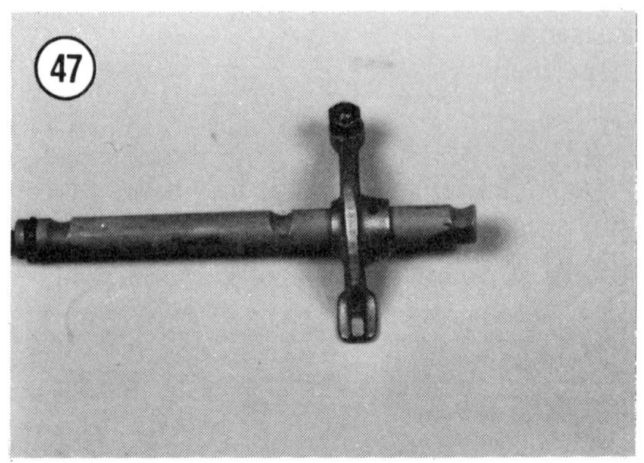

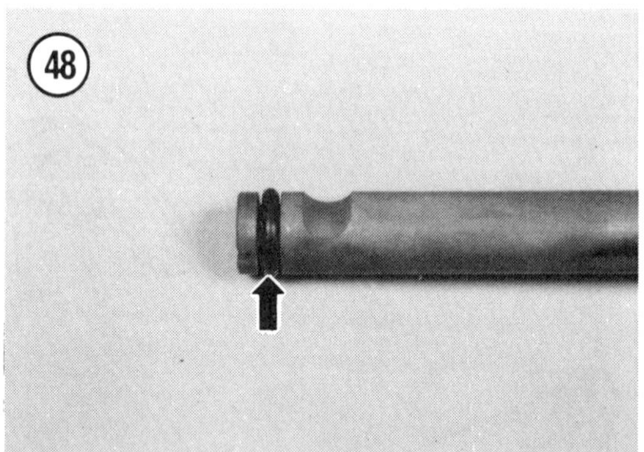

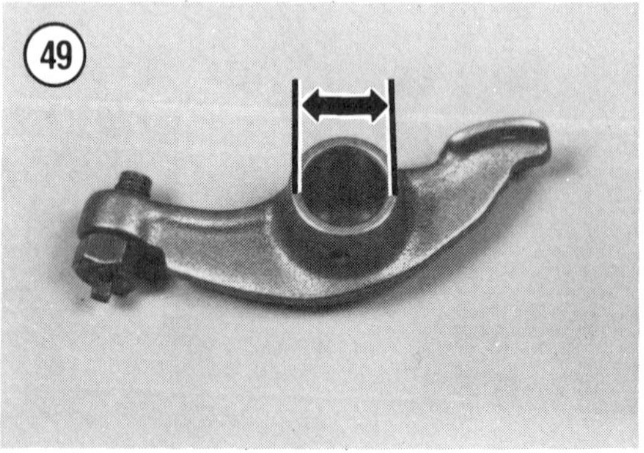

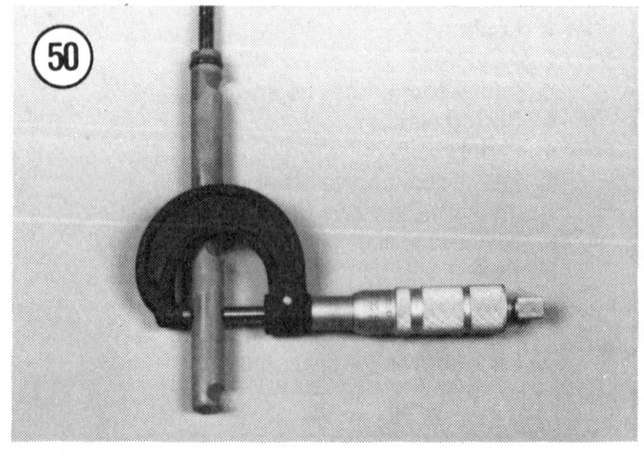

(51)

CAMSHAFT, DRIVE CHAIN AND TENSIONER

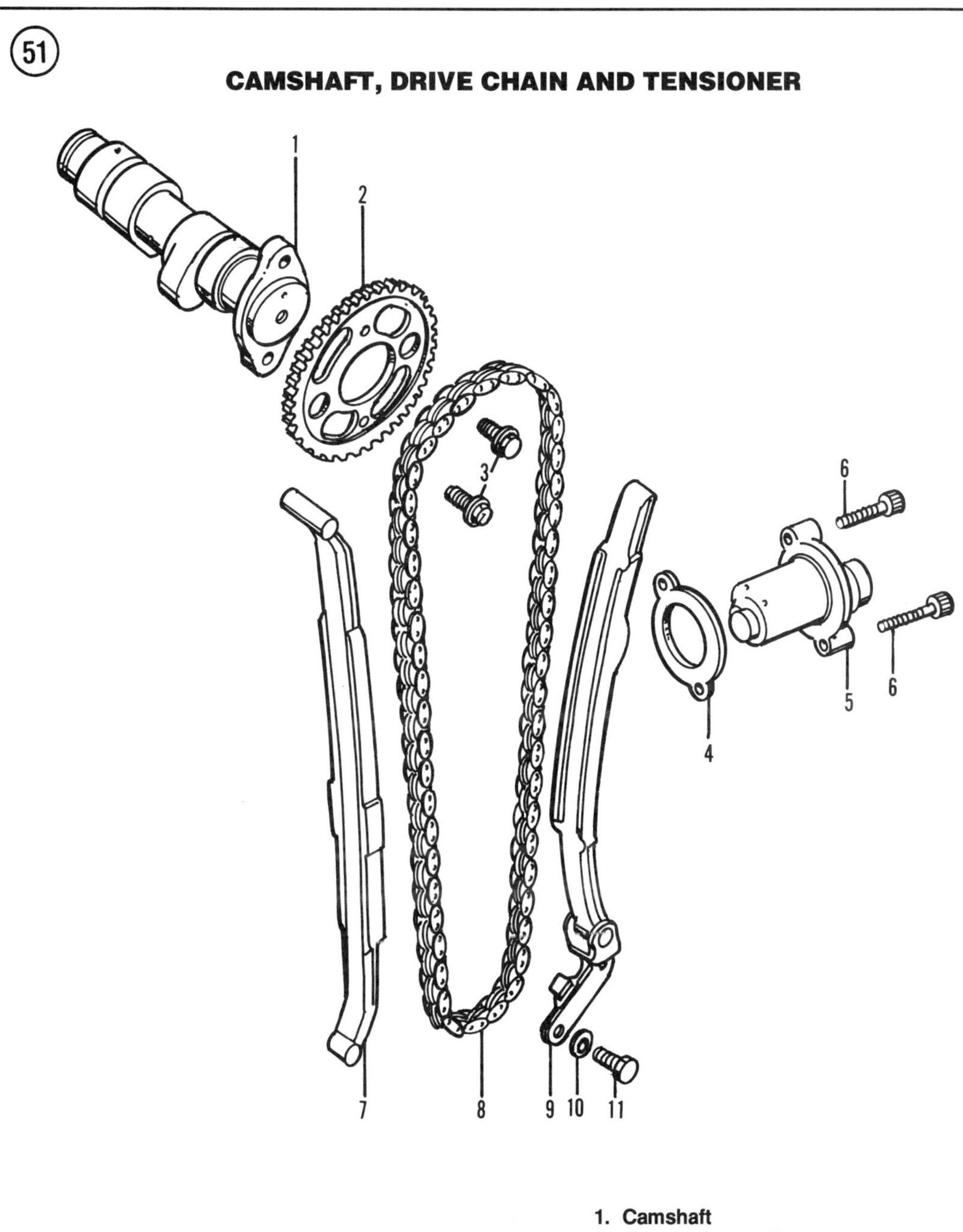

1. Camshaft
2. Camshaft sprocket
3. Bolts
4. Gasket
5. Camshaft chain tensioner assembly
6. Bolt
7. Camshaft chain front guide
8. Camshaft drive chain
9. Camshaft chain rear guide
10. Washer
11. Bolt

Removal

1. Remove the cylinder head cover and rocker arm assembly as described in this chapter.
2. Remove the bolts securing the camshaft drive chain tensioner assembly (**Figure 52**) and remove the assembly and gasket. This will relieve camshaft drive chain tension.
3. Remove the exposed bolt (**Figure 53**) securing the sprocket to the camshaft.
4. Using a 19 mm socket and wrench (**Figure 54**) on the alternator rotor nut, rotate the engine *counter-clockwise* until the other sprocket bolt is visible.
5. Remove the remaining exposed bolt securing the sprocket to the camshaft.
6. Disengage the camshaft chain from the camshaft sprocket and remove the sprocket.
7. Rest the chain on the camshaft sprocket mounting flange (**Figure 55**) at the end of the camshaft.
8. Tie a piece of wire to the camshaft drive chain.
9. Carefully remove the camshaft slowly to prevent damaging any camshaft lobe or bearing surface in the cylinder head.
10. Remove the camshaft front chain guide (A, **Figure 56**) from the chain tunnel in the cylinder head and cylinder.
11. Pull up on the drive chain (**Figure 57**) and tie the loose end of the wire, attached in Step 8, to the frame (B, **Figure 56**). This will prevent the chain from falling down into the crankcase.

CAUTION
The crankshaft can be turned with the camshaft removed. However, pull the camshaft chain up tight and make sure it is properly meshed with the crank-shaft drive sprocket. This will prevent the chain from bunching up on the

57

crankshaft sprocket and damaging the crankshaft and crankcase.

Camshaft Inspection

1. Check cam lobes (A, **Figure 58**) for wear. The lobes should not be scored and the edges should be square.
2. Even though the cam lobe surface appears to be satisfactory, with no visible signs of wear, each lobe must be measured with a micrometer. Measure the lobe height (**Figure 59**) and replace the camshaft if worn to or beyond the service specifications listed in **Table 2**.
3. Check the camshaft bearing journals (B, **Figure 58**) for wear and scoring.
4. Even though the camshaft bearing journal surface appears satisfactory, with no visible signs of wear, the camshaft bearing journal outside diameter must be measured with a micrometer (**Figure 60**). Replace the shaft if worn to or beyond the service specifications listed in **Table 2**.
5. Place the camshaft on a set of V-blocks and check its runout with a dial indicator at the bearing surface locations. Replace the camshaft if runout exceeds the service limit in **Table 2**.
6. Make sure the oil holes (**Figure 61**) are clear. If necessary, clean out with a piece of wire and blow out with compressed air.
7. Inspect the camshaft sprocket (**Figure 62**). Check the sprocket for worn or damaged gear teeth. Also

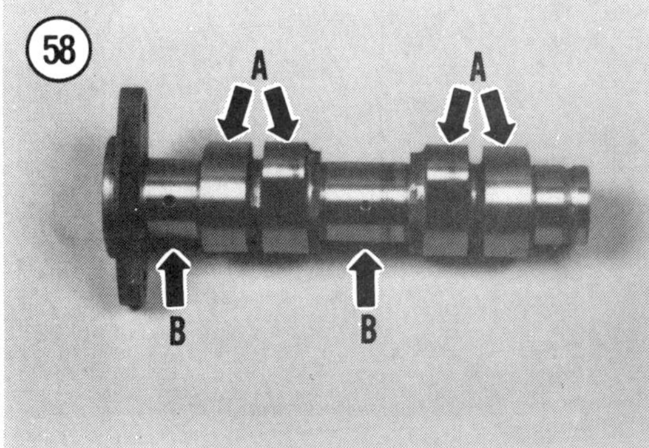

58

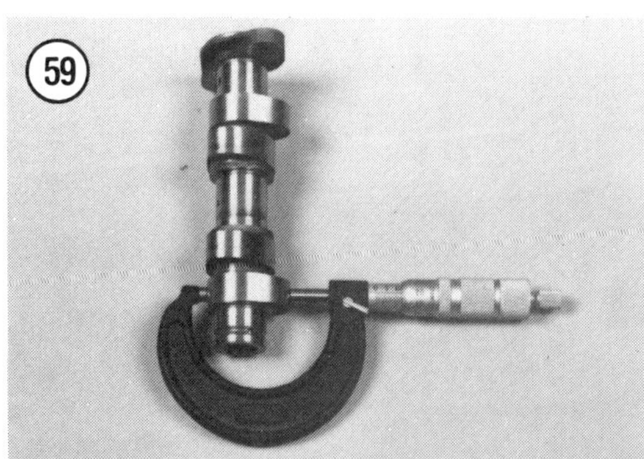
59

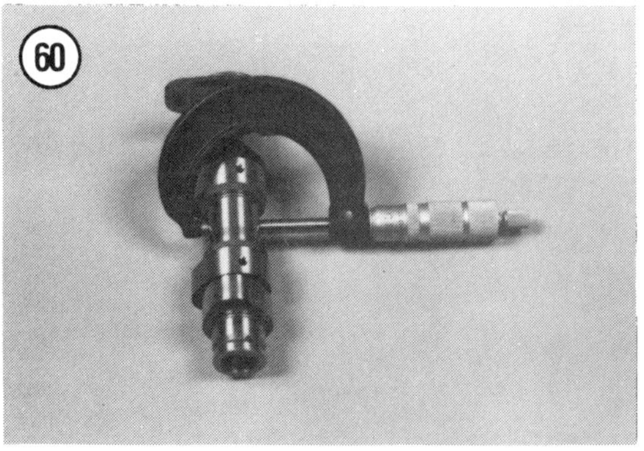
60

61

62

4

check the teeth for cracking or rounding, replace if necessary.

NOTE
If the camshaft sprocket is worn, also check the camshaft chain, the drive sprocket on the crankshaft, chain guides and chain tensioner.

8. Check the camshaft bearing journals in the cylinder head (**Figure 63**) and cylinder head cover (**Figure 64**) for wear and scoring. They should not be scored or excessively worn. If necessary, replace the cylinder head and cylinder head cover as a matched pair.
9. Check the cam chain guides as described in this chapter.

Camshaft Bearing Clearance Measurement

1. Wipe all oil residue from each camshaft bearing surface in the cylinder head and cylinder head cover.

NOTE
*The camshaft is **not** installed for this procedure.*

2. Make sure the locating dowels are installed in the cylinder head.
3. Install the cylinder head cover and bolts. Tighten the bolts in a crisscross pattern to the torque specification listed in **Table 3**.

NOTE
***Figure 64** is shown with the cylinder head cover removed in order to show the measurement locations.*

4. Use a bore gauge and measure the camshaft bearing surfaces in the cylinder head and cylinder head cover in 3 locations (**Figure 64**).
5. Remove the bolts securing the cylinder head cover and remove the cover.
6. Subtract the camshaft bearing surface outer diameter from the cylinder head cover and cylinder head bearing surface inner diameter. This will give the oil clearance between the 2 parts. Compare to the dimension listed in **Table 2**.
7. If the clearance exceeds the wear limit in **Table 2**, determine which parts must be replaced. If the camshaft bearing journal is less than specified, replace the camshaft. If the camshaft is within specifications, the cylinder head cover and cylinder head must be replaced as a matched set.

Camshaft Chain Tensioner Inspection

The camshaft chain tensioner automatically takes up the tension on the drive chain. There are no provisions for any form of adjustment.

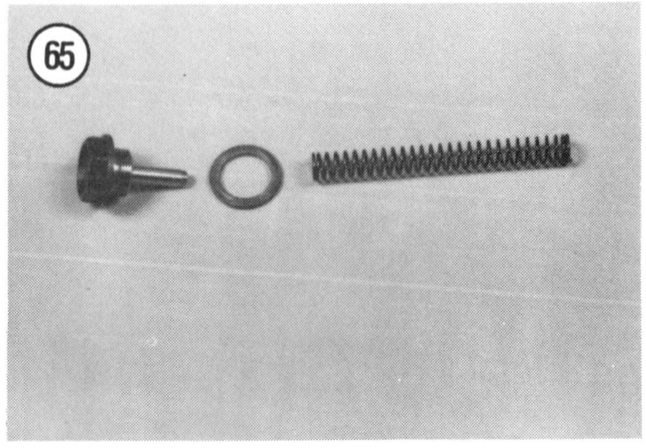

If any part of the tensioner is damaged, replace the entire assembly as replacement parts are not available.

1. Inspect the bolt, washer and spring (**Figure 65**) for wear or damage.
2. Check the tensioner body for cracks, wear or damage. Refer to **Figure 66** and **Figure 67**.

Camshaft Installation

Refer to **Figure 68** for this procedure.

1. If still installed, remove the alternator rotor as described under *Alternator Rotor Removal/Installation* in Chapter Nine.
2. Coat all camshaft lobes and bearing journals and the camshaft bearing surfaces in the cylinder head cover and cylinder head with molybdenum disulfide grease or assembly oil.
3. Rotate the crankshaft *counterclockwise* until the timing mark on the crankshaft aligns with the timing mark pointer on the crankcase (**Figure 68**).

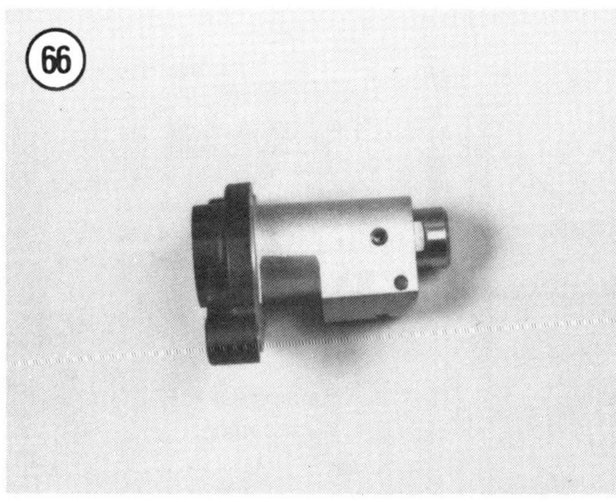
66

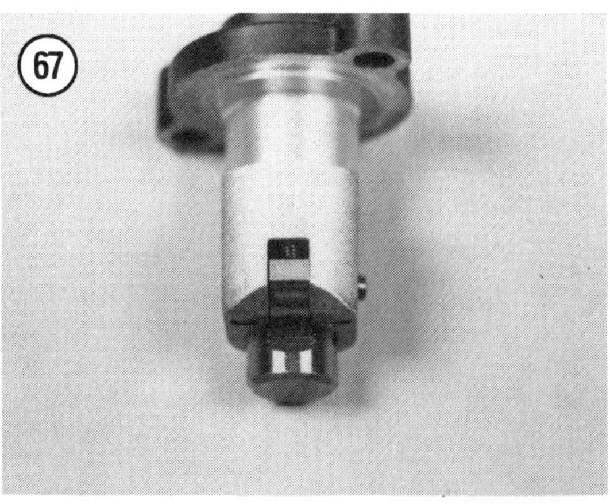
67

4. Install the camshaft front chain guide (A, **Figure 56**) into the chain tunnel in the cylinder head and cylinder. Make sure it is properly located in the receptacle in the crankcase.
5. Carefully install the camshaft slowly to prevent damaging any camshaft lobe or bearing surface in the cylinder head. Set the camshaft in the cylinder head bearing surfaces and position it with the camshaft lobes facing down.
6. Rest the chain on the camshaft sprocket mounting flange (**Figure 55**) at the end of the camshaft.
7. Install the camshaft sprocket partially into position within the drive chain cavity in the cylinder head.
8. Position the camshaft sprocket with the upper position mark on the sprocket facing up and with the sprocket timing marks horizontal in line with the cylinder head surface and mesh the sprocket with the drive chain. Remove the wire from the drive chain.
9. Install the camshaft sprocket and drive chain onto the shoulder on the end of the camshaft.
10. Temporarily align the timing marks on the sprocket with the top surface of the cylinder head.

CAUTION

Very expensive damage could result from improper camshaft and chain alignment. Make sure alignment is correct. If alignment is incorrect, it must be corrected at this time.

11. Pull up on the *front* section of the drive chain until all slack is removed from the drive chain. At this point the following timing marks must align as shown in **Figure 68**:
    a. The timing mark on the crankshaft must still be aligned with the timing mark pointer on the crankcase.
    b. The upper position mark (A, **Figure 69**) on the sprocket must be facing up.
    c. The timing marks on the sprocket (B, **Figure 69**) must be aligned with the top surface of the cylinder head.
12. If any of the timing marks are not aligned, realign them at this time.

CAUTION

The camshaft sprocket bolts are made of a hardened material. When replacing these bolts, use only Yamaha replacement bolts specified for this application. Do not substitute with another type of

4

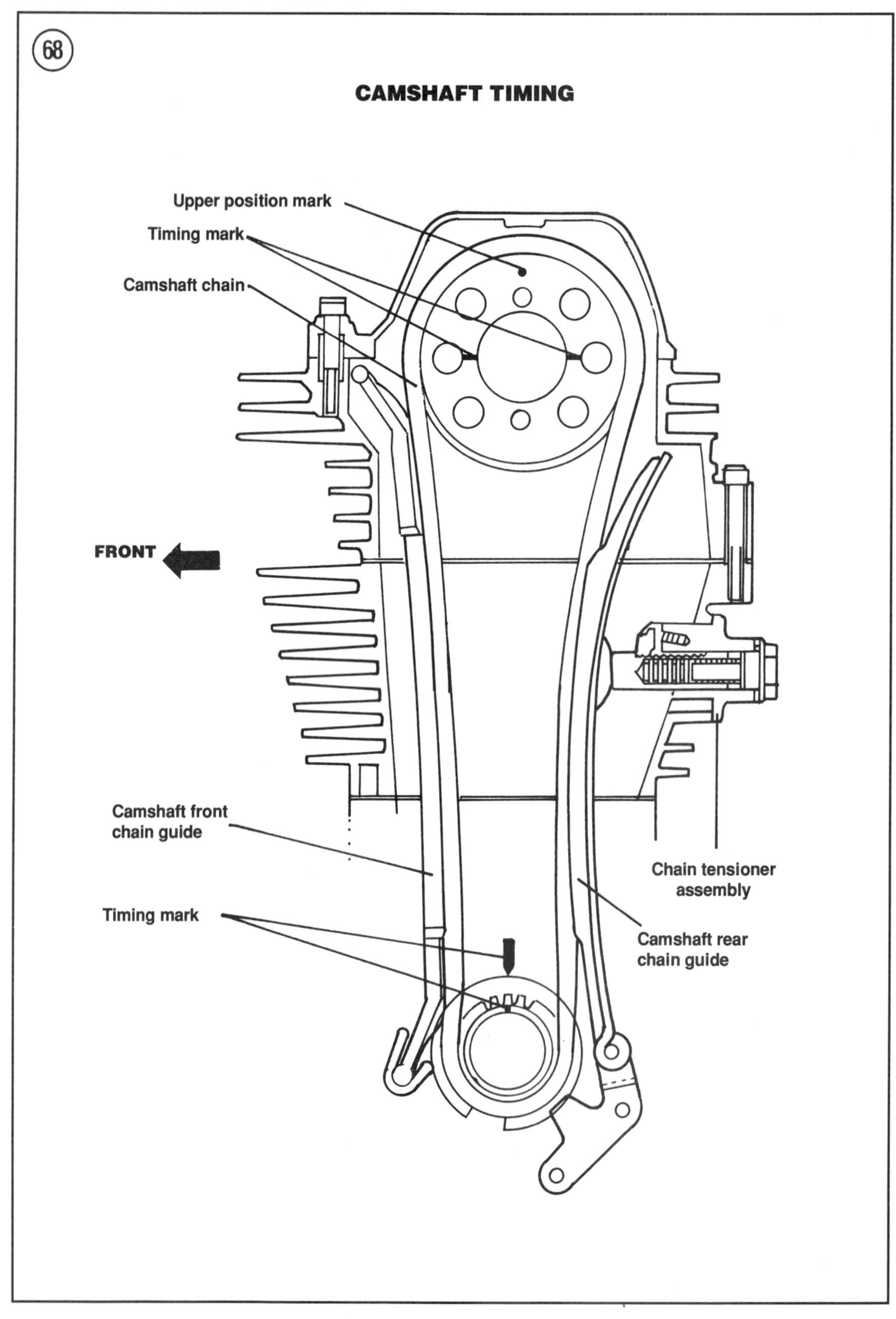
68
CAMSHAFT TIMING
Upper position mark
Timing mark
Camshaft chain
FRONT
Camshaft front chain guide
Timing mark
Chain tensioner assembly
Camshaft rear chain guide

bolt as severe engine damage could result from bolt breakage.

13. Install the bolt into the exposed bolt hole (C, **Figure 69**) to secure the sprocket to the camshaft. Tighten the bolt to a good finger-tight at this time.

14. Install the alternator rotor as described under *Alternator Rotor Removal/Installation* in Chapter Nine.

CAUTION
If there is any binding while turning the crankshaft in Step 15, "stop." Recheck the camshaft timing marks. Improper timing can cause valve and piston damage.

15. Using a 19 mm socket and wrench (**Figure 54**) on the alternator rotor nut, rotate the engine *counterclockwise* until the other sprocket bolt hole is visible.

16. Apply Loctite 271 (red) to the sprocket bolt, then install the remaining bolt securing the sprocket to the camshaft. Tighten the bolt to the torque specification listed in **Table 3**.

17. Using a 19 mm socket and wrench (**Figure 54**) on the alternator rotor nut, rotate the engine *counterclockwise* until the other sprocket bolt installed in Step 13 is visible. Remove the bolt (C, **Figure 69**).

18. Apply Loctite 271 (red) to the sprocket bolt, then install the bolt and tighten to the torque specification listed in **Table 3**.

19. Remove the end plug from the camshaft drive chain tensioner body and remove the spring and gasket.

20. Push the tensioner plunger back into the tensioner body.

21. Install a new gasket and camshaft drive chain tensioner body (A, **Figure 70**) into the cylinder. Tighten the bolts to the torque specification listed in **Table 3**.

22. Install the spring (B, **Figure 70**), gasket (A, **Figure 71**) and end plug (B, **Figure 71**). Tighten the end plug to the torque specification listed in **Table 3**.

NOTE
When turning the crankshaft in the following steps, turn it ***counterclockwise****.*

CAUTION
If there is any binding while turning the crankshaft in Step 23, "stop." Recheck the camshaft timing marks. Improper timing can cause valve and piston damage.

23. Rotate the engine *counterclockwise* 720° (2 full turns).

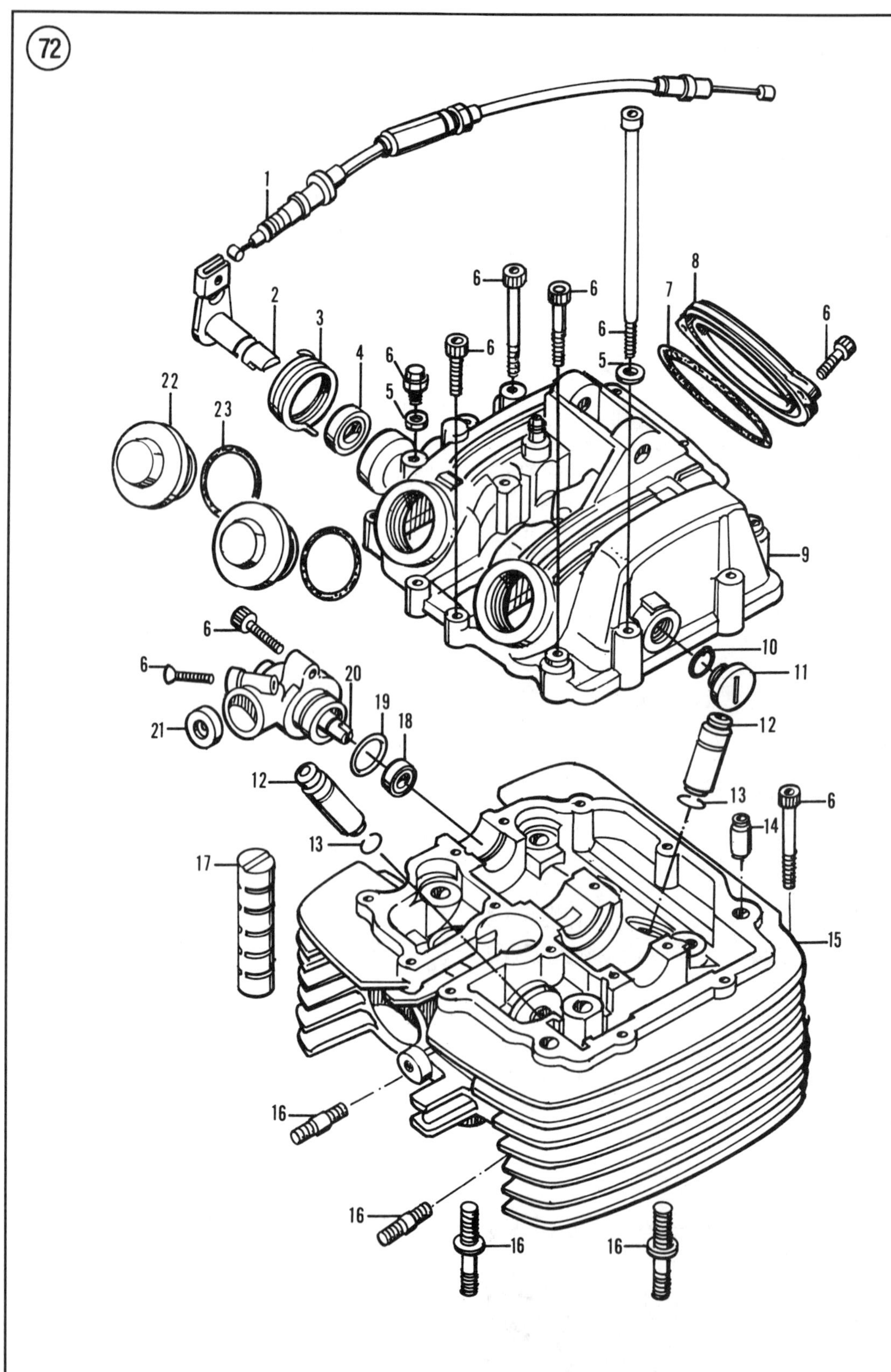
72
1
2
3
4
5
6
7
8
9
10
11
12
13
14
15
16
17
18
19
20
21
22
23

CYLINDER HEAD AND COVER

1. Decompression cable
2. Decompression lever
3. Spring
4. Oil seal
5. Washer
6. Bolt
7. O-ring seal
8. Intake valve adjsuter cover
9. Cylinder head cover
10. O-ring seal
11. Plug
12. Valve guide
13. Clip
14. Locating dowel
15. Cylinder head
16. Threaded stud
17. Absorber
18. Oil seal
19. O-ring seal
20. Tachometer drive unit (XT600 only)
21. Oil seal
22. Exhaust valve adjuster cover
23. O-ring

CAUTION

Very expensive damage could result from improper camshaft and drive chain alignment. Make this final check to be sure alignment is correct. If alignment is incorrect, it must be corrected at this time.

24. Make sure the following timing marks are still aligned as shown in **Figure 68**:
    a. The timing mark on the crankshaft must still be aligned with the timing mark pointer on the crankcase.
    b. The upper position mark on the sprocket must be facing up.
    c. The timing marks on the sprocket must be aligned with the top surface of the cylinder head.
25. If the alignment is incorrect, correct by removing the camshaft and sprocket bolts and repositioning the sprocket on the drive chain.
26. Install the cylinder head cover and rocker arm assembly as described in this chapter.
27. Check valve adjustment and the decompression lever as described in Chapter Three.

CYLINDER HEAD

Removal

Refer to **Figure 72** for this procedure.

1. Remove the cylinder head cover and camshaft as described in this chapter.
2. Remove the Allen bolt (**Figure 73**) on the left-hand rear corner of the cylinder head.

3. Using a crisscross pattern, loosen in 2-3 stages the bolts (**Figure 74**) securing the cylinder head to the cylinder.

4. Remove the front cylinder head-to-cylinder Acorn nut and washer (**Figure 75**).

5. Remove the rear cylinder head-to-cylinder Acorn nut and washer (**Figure 76**).

6. Loosen the cylinder head by tapping around the perimeter with a soft-faced rubber or plastic mallet.

7. Untie the wire securing the camshaft drive chain to the exterior of the engine.

8. Lift the cylinder head (A, **Figure 77**) off of the cylinder and feed the wire (B, **Figure 77**) through the chain cavity in the cylinder.

9. Place the cylinder head on a soft surface upside down to prevent scratching or otherwise damaging the cylinder head-to-cylinder block mating surface. Remove and discard the cylinder head gasket.

10. Retie the camshaft drive chain wire to the exterior of the crankcase.

11. Remove the cylinder head gasket and discard it.

12. Don't lose the 2 dowel pins. It is not necessary to remove the dowel pins if they are not loose; if they are loose, remove them so they will not get misplaced.

13. Place a clean shop rag into the cam chain tunnel in the cylinder to prevent the entry of foreign matter.

NOTE

After removing the cylinder head, check the top and bottom mating surfaces for any indications of leakage. Also check the head and cylinder gasket for signs of leakage. A blown cylinder head gasket could indicate possible cylinder head warpage or other damage.

74

75

76

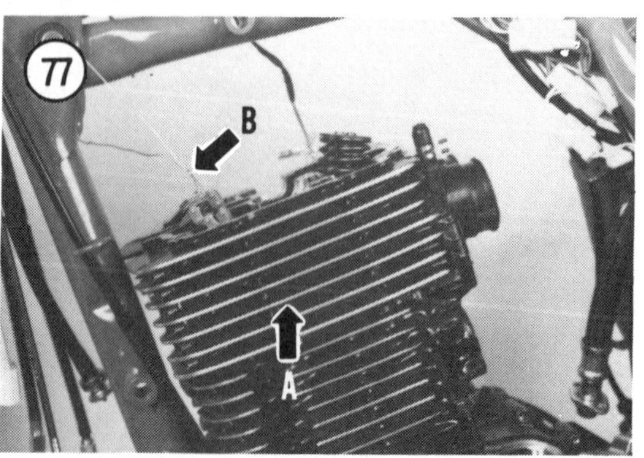

77

Cylinder Head Inspection

1. Thoroughly clean the outside of the cylinder head. Use a stiff brush, soap and water and clean out all road dirt and mud from the cooling fins (**Figure 78**). If necessary, use a piece of wood and scrape away any lodged dirt and mud. Clogged cooling fins can cause overheating leading to possible engine damage.

2. Remove all traces of gasket residue from the cylinder head and cylinder mating surfaces. Do not scratch the gasket surface.

CAUTION
If the combustion chamber is cleaned while the valves are removed, you will damage the valve seat surfaces. A damaged or even slightly scratched valve seat will cause poor valve seating.

3. Without removing the valves, remove all carbon deposits from the combustion chamber (A, **Figure 79**). Use a fine wire brush dipped in solvent or make a scraper from hardwood. Take care not to damage the cylinder head, valves or spark plug threads.

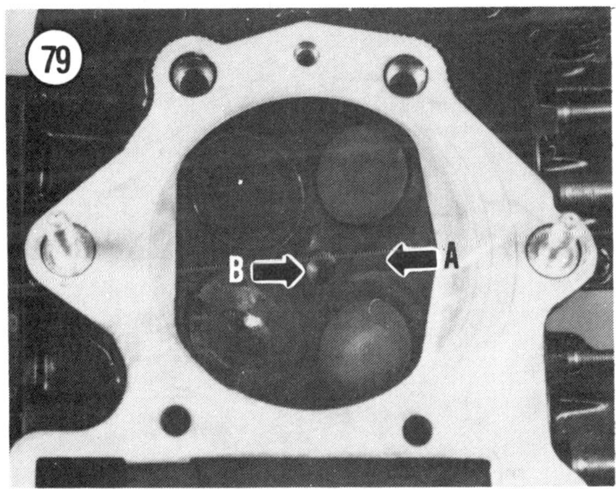

NOTE
When using a tap to clean spark plug threads, coat the tap with an aluminum tap cutting fluid or kerosene.

NOTE
Aluminum spark plug threads are commonly damaged due to galling, cross-threading and overtightening. To prevent galling, apply an anti-seize compound on the plug threads before installation and do not overtighten.

4. Examine the spark plug threads (B, **Figure 79**) in the cylinder head for damage. If damage is minor or if the threads are dirty or clogged with carbon, use a spark plug thread tap (**Figure 80**) to clean the threads following the manufacturer's instructions. If thread damage is severe, the threads can be restored by installing a steel thread insert. Thread insert kits can be purchased at automotive supply stores or you can have the inserts installed by a Yamaha dealer or machine shop.

5. After all carbon is removed from combustion chambers, and valve ports and the spark plug thread holes are repaired, clean the entire head in solvent and dry with compressed air.

NOTE
If the cylinder head was bead-blasted, make sure to clean the head thoroughly with solvent and then with hot water and soap. Then rinse with a high-pressure garden hose and plenty of water. Bead-blasting residue grit seats in small crevices and other areas and can be hard to get out. Also chase each exposed thread with a tap to remove grit between the threads or you may damage a thread later. Residual grit left in the engine will wind up in the oil and cause premature piston, ring and bearing wear.

6. Examine the crown of the piston. The crown should show no signs of wear or damage. If the crown appears pecked or spongy-looking, also check the spark plug, valves and combustion chamber for aluminum deposits. If these deposits are found, the cylinder is suffering from excessive heat caused by a lean fuel mixture or preignition.

CAUTION
Do not clean the piston crown with the cylinder assembled on the crankcase.

Carbon scraped from the top of the piston could fall between the cylinder wall and piston and onto the piston rings. Because carbon grit is very abrasive, premature cylinder, piston and ring wear will occur. If the piston crown is heavily coated with carbon, remove the piston as described in this chapter and clean it. Excessive carbon build-up on the piston crown reduces piston cooling which raises engine compression and causes overheating.

7. Check for cracks in the combustion chamber and exhaust ports (**Figure 81**). A cracked cylinder head must be replaced if it cannot be repaired by welding.

8. After the cylinder head has been thoroughly cleaned, place a straightedge across the gasket surface at several points. Measure warp by attempting to insert a feeler gauge between the straightedge and cylinder head at each location. Maximum allowable warpage is listed in **Table 2**. Warpage or nicks in the cylinder head surface could cause an air leak and result in overheating. If warpage exceeds this limit, the cylinder head must be resurfaced or replaced. Consult a Yamaha dealer or machine shop experienced in this type of work.

9. Inspect the carburetor intake boots (**Figure 82**) for cracks or other damage that would allow unfiltered air to enter the engine. Also check the hose clamps for breakage or fatigue. When installing boots, install a new O-ring between the boot and cylinder head. Be sure to reinstall them with the boot marked "L" on the left-hand side and the boot marked "R" on the right-hand side.

10. Check the 2 cylinder head lower studs (**Figure 83**) for looseness or thread damage. Slight thread damage can be repaired with a thread file or die. If thread damage is severe, replace the damaged stud(s) as follows:

NOTE

Stud replacement will require two wrenches, two nuts, a new stud and a tube of Loctite 271 (red).

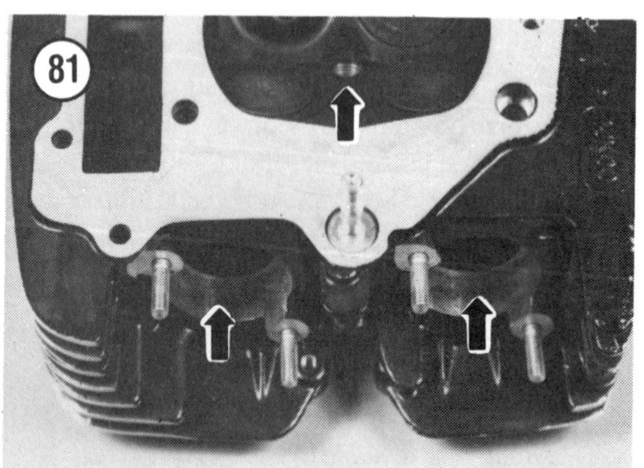

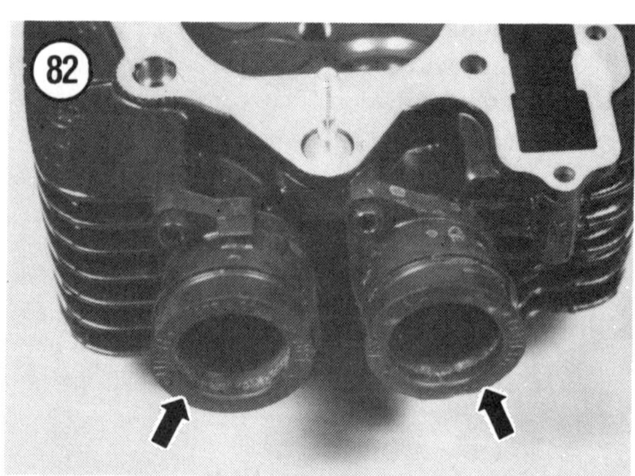

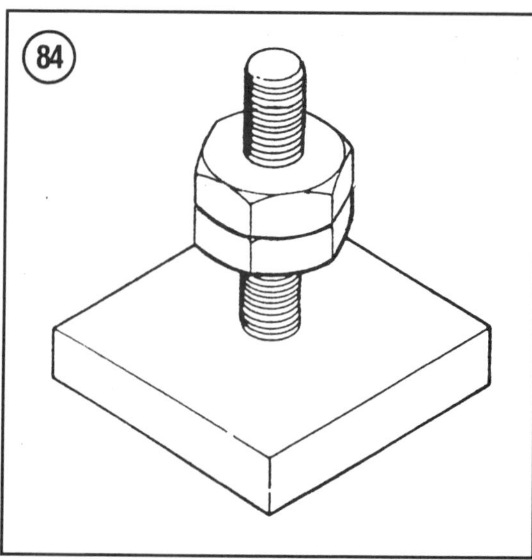

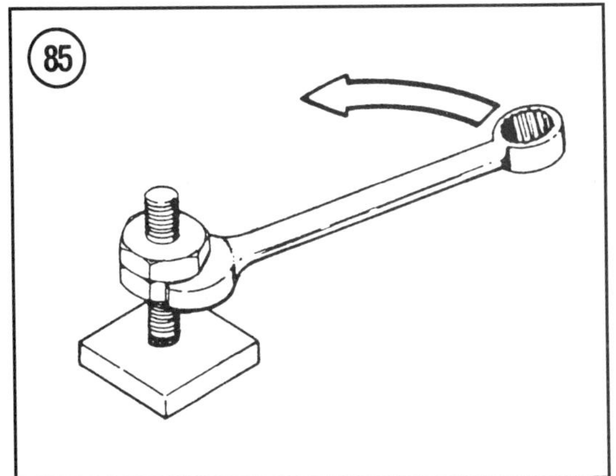

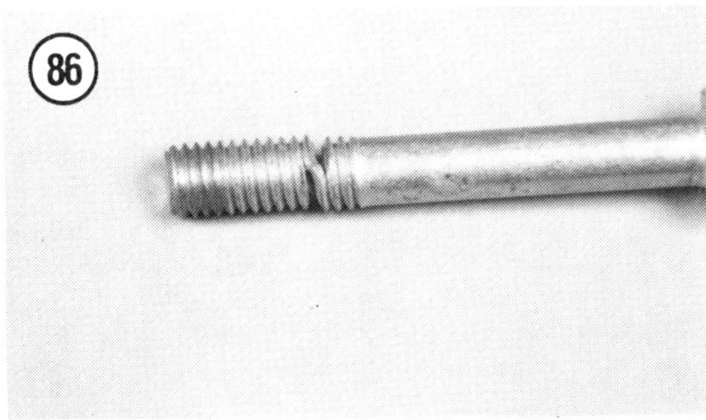

a. Screw two nuts onto the end of the damaged stud as shown in **Figure 84**. If the stud threads are too severely damaged, you may have to remove the stud with a pair of Vise-grip pliers.
b. With 2 wrenches, tighten the nuts against each other.
c. Unscrew the stud with a wrench on the lower nut (**Figure 85**).
d. Clean the tapped hole with solvent and check for thread damage and carbon build-up. If necessary, clean the threads with the correct size metric tap.
e. Remove the nuts from the old stud and install them on the end of a new stud.
f. Tighten the nuts against each other.
g. Apply Loctite 271 (red) to the threads of the new stud.
h. Screw the stud into the cylinder head with a wrench on the upper nut. Tighten the stud securely.
i. Remove the nuts from the new stud.

11. Check the valves and valve guides as described under *Valves and Valve Components* in this chapter.
12. Check the cylinder head bolts (**Figure 86**) for thread damage, cracks and twisting. Also check the washers for cracks and other damage.

Installation

1. Clean the cylinder head (**Figure 87**) and cylinder mating surfaces of all gasket residue.
2. Remove the shop rag from the camshaft chain tunnel in the cylinder.
3. If removed, install the 2 locating dowels (A, **Figure 88**) on the right-hand side of the cylinder.
4. Install a new gasket (**Figure 89**) onto the center locating dowel and install the dowel (B, **Figure 88**).

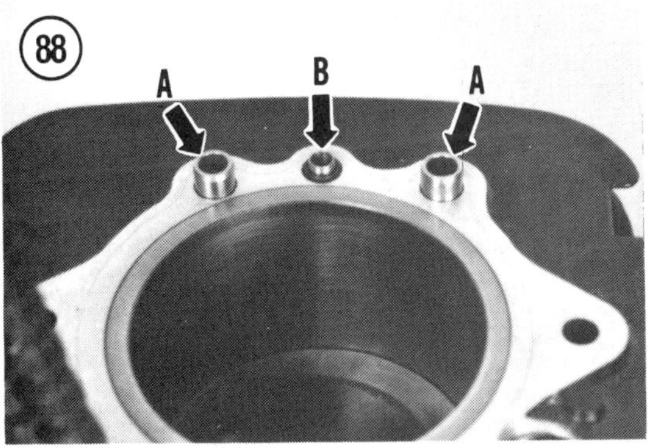

5. Install a new cylinder head gasket (A, **Figure 90**).
6. Untie the camshaft chain wire and guide the cam chain (B, **Figure 90**) and wire through the cylinder head tunnel and install the cylinder head (A, **Figure 77**).
7. Make sure the cylinder head seats squarely against the cylinder. Tie the loose end of the wire to the frame (B, **Figure 77**).
8. Lubricate the cylinder head bolt threads with engine oil.
9. Install the cylinder head bolts and washers finger-tight (**Figure 74**).
10. Install the front (**Figure 75**) and rear (**Figure 76**) Acorn nuts and washers finger-tight.
11. Tighten the cylinder head bolts in a crisscross pattern in 2-3 steps to the torque specifications in **Table 3**.
12. Tighten the front (**Figure 75**) and rear (**Figure 76**) Acorn nuts to the torque specifications in **Table 3**.
13. Install and tighten the Allen bolt (**Figure 73**) on the left-hand rear corner of the cylinder head. Tighten the bolt securely.
14. Install the camshaft and cylinder head cover as described in this chapter.

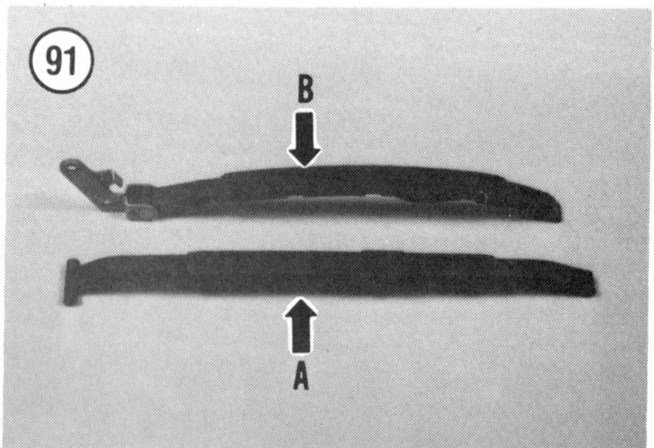

CAMSHAFT CHAIN GUIDES

Check the front (A, **Figure 91**) and rear (B, **Figure 91**) camshaft chain guides for wear, damage or cracks. Inspect the pivot point (**Figure 92**) of the rear guide for wear or damage, replace if necessary.

The front camshaft chain guide can be removed after removing the cylinder head cover. The camshaft chain rear guide removal is described under *Camshaft Chain and Rear Guide* in Chapter Five.

If the chain guides are worn or damaged, also check the camshaft chain tensioner and the camshaft drive chain.

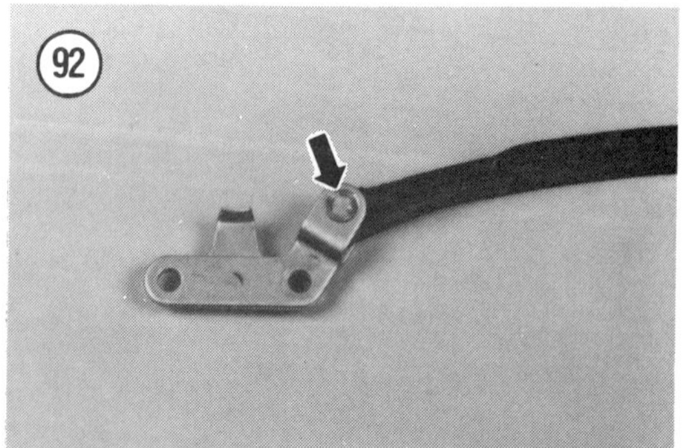

VALVES AND VALVE COMPONENTS

Correct valve service requires a number of special tools. The following procedures describe how to check for valve component wear and to determine what type of service is required. In most cases, valve troubles are caused by poor valve seating, worn valve guides and burned valves. A valve spring compressor (**Figure 93**) will be required to remove the valves.

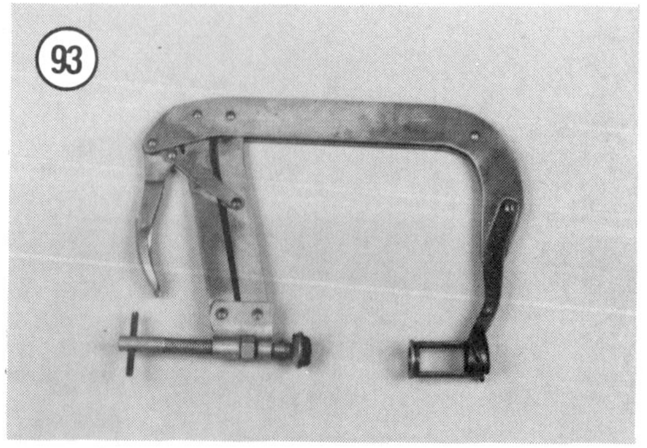

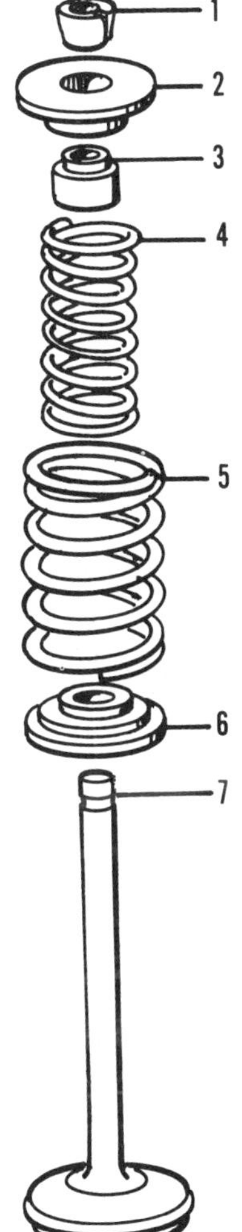

1. Keepers
2. Spring retainer
3. Oil seal
4. Inner valve spring
5. Outer valve spring
6. Lower spring seat
7. Valve

A general practice among those who do their own service is to remove the cylinder head and take it to a machine shop or dealer for inspection and service. Since the cost is low relative to the required effort and equipment, this is the best approach, even for the experienced mechanics.

This procedure is included for those who choose to do their own valve service. Refer to **Figure 94** for this procedure.

4

Valve Removal

1. Remove the cylinder head as described in this chapter.

2. Install a valve spring compressor squarely over the valve retainer with the other end of the tool placed against the valve head (**Figure 95**).

3. Tighten the valve spring compressor until the valve keepers separate. Lift the valve keepers out through the valve spring compressor (**Figure 96**) with needlenose pliers.

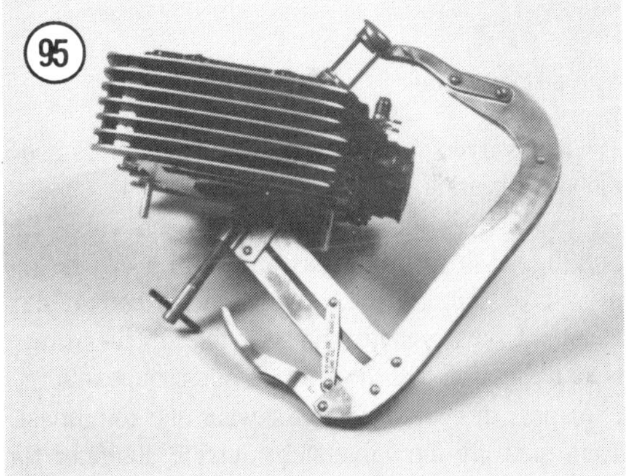

4. Gradually loosen the valve spring compressor and remove it from the head. Remove the spring retainer (**Figure 97**).
5. Remove the outer (**Figure 98**) and inner (**Figure 99**) valve springs.

CAUTION
*Remove any burrs from the valve stem grooves before removing the valve (**Figure 100**). Otherwise the valve guides will be damaged.*

6. Turn the cylinder head over and remove the valve (**Figure 101**).
7. Turn the cylinder head over and pull the oil seal (A, **Figure 102**) off of the valve guide.
8. Remove the spring lower seat (B, **Figure 102**).

CAUTION
*All component parts of each valve assembly (**Figure 103**) must be kept together. Do not mix with like components from other valves or excessive wear may result.*

9. Repeat Steps 2-8 and remove remaining valve(s).

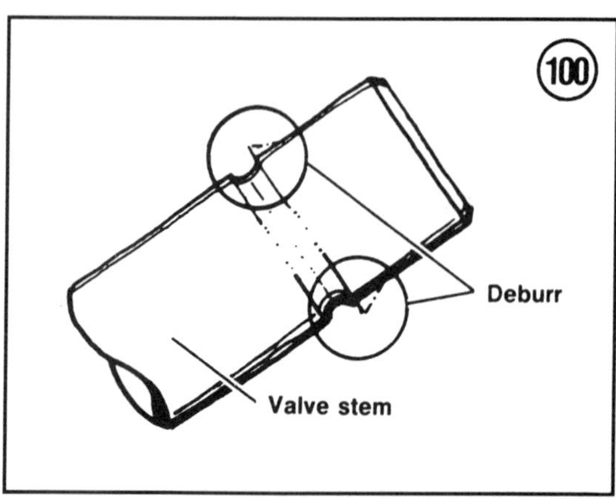

Valve Inspection

1. Clean valves in solvent. Do not gouge or damage the valve seating surface.
2. Inspect the contact surface of each valve for burning. Minor roughness and pitting can be removed by lapping the valve as described in this chapter. Excessive unevenness to the contact surface is an indication that the valve is not serviceable.
3. Inspect the valve stems for wear and roughness. Then measure the valve stem outside diameter for wear using a micrometer (**Figure 104**). Compare with specifications in **Table 2**.
4. Measure the thickness of the valve head (**Figure 105**) "Dimension A," the beveled end thickness "Dimension B" and stem length to the cotter groove "Dimension C." Compare to dimensions listed in **Table 2**.
5. Remove all carbon and varnish from the valve guides with a stiff spiral wire brush before checking wear.

NOTE
If you do not have the required measuring devices, proceed to Step 7.

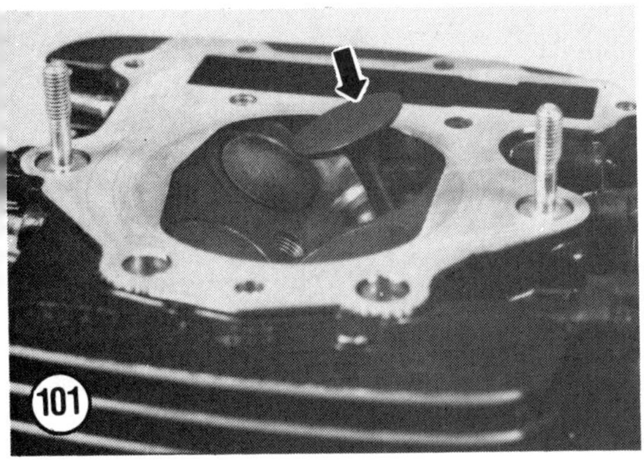

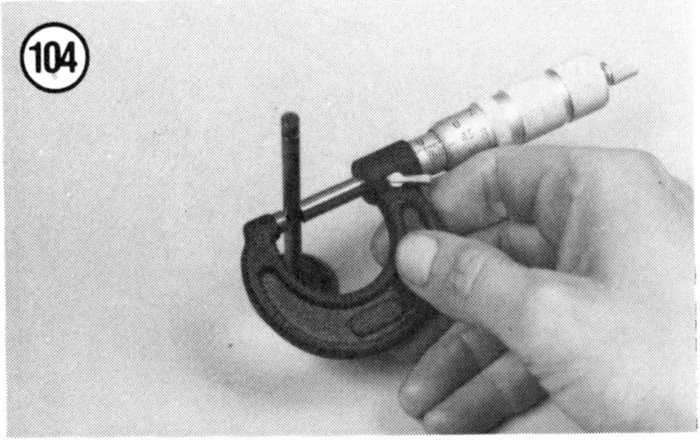

6. Measure each valve guide (A, **Figure 106**) at top, center and bottom inside diameter with a small hole gauge (B, **Figure 106**). Then measure the small hole gauge with a micrometer to determine the valve guide inside diameter. Compare measurements with specification in **Table 2**.

7. Subtract the measurement made in Step 3 from the measurement made in Step 6. The difference is the valve guide-to-valve stem clearance. See **Table 2** for correct clearance. Replace any guide or valve that is not within tolerance. Valve guide replacement is described later in this chapter.

8. If a small hole gauge is not available, insert each valve in its guide. Hold the valve just slightly off its

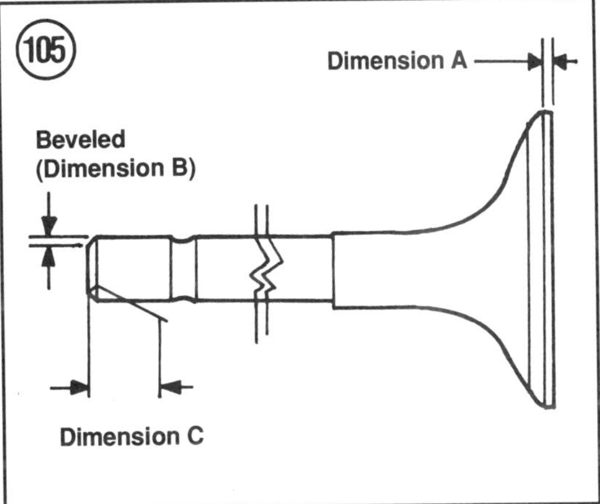

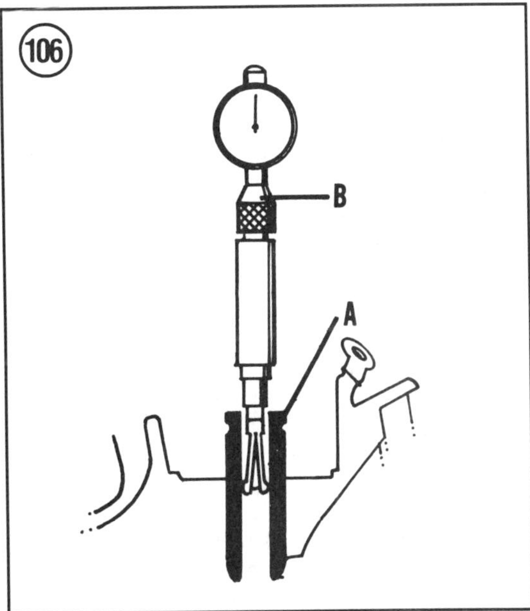

4

seat and rock it sideways. If the valve rocks more than slightly, the guide is probably worn and should be replaced. As a final check, take the cylinder head to a dealer or machine shop and have the valve guides measured.

9. Check the inner and outer valve springs (**Figure 103**) as follows:

   a. Check each of the valve springs for visual damage.
   b. Use a square and check each spring for distortion or tilt (**Figure 107**). Compare to specifications in **Table 2**.
   c. Measure the valve spring length with a vernier caliper (**Figure 108**). All should be of length specified in **Table 2** with no bends or other distortion.
   d. Replace defective springs as a set.

10. Check the valve spring retainer and valve keepers. If they are in good condition, they may be reused.

11. Inspect valve seats (**Figure 109**). If worn or burned, they may be reconditioned as described in this chapter. Seats and valves in near-perfect condition can be reconditioned by lapping with fine carborundum paste. Lapping, however, is always inferior to precision grinding. Check as follows:

   a. Clean the valve seat and valve mating areas with aerosol electrical contact cleaner.
   b. Coat the valve seat with machinist's blue.
   c. Install the valve into its guide (**Figure 101**) and rotate it against its seat with a valve lapping tool (**Figure 110**). See *Valve Lapping* in this chapter.
   d. Lift the valve out of the guide and measure the seat width with vernier calipers (**Figure 111**).
   e. The seat width for intake and exhaust valves should measure within the specifications listed in **Table 2** all the way around the seat. If the seat width exceeds the service limit (**Table 2**), regrind the seats as described in this chapter.
   f. Remove all machinist's blue residue from the seats and valves.

12. Check the valve stem runout with a V-block and dial indicator as shown in **Figure 112**. Compare runout to specifications in **Table 2**.

13. Measure the head diameter of each valve with a vernier caliper or micrometer (**Figure 113**). Compare to specifications in **Table 2**.

107

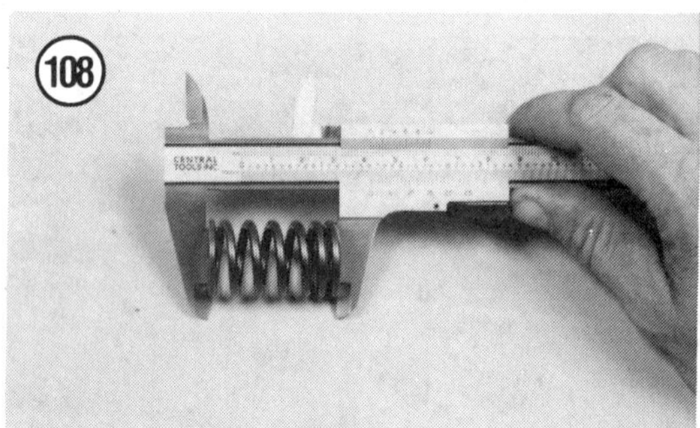
108

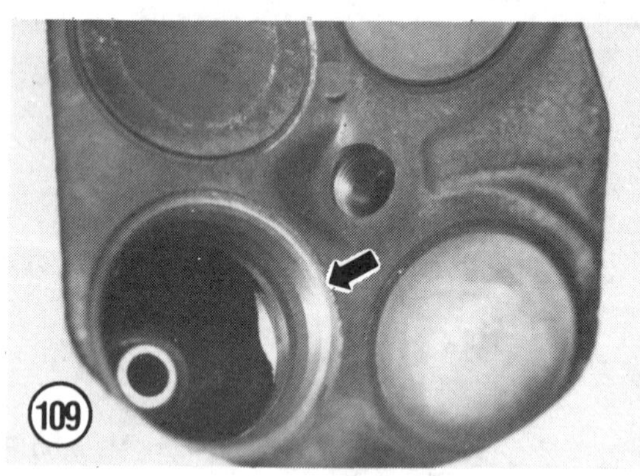
109

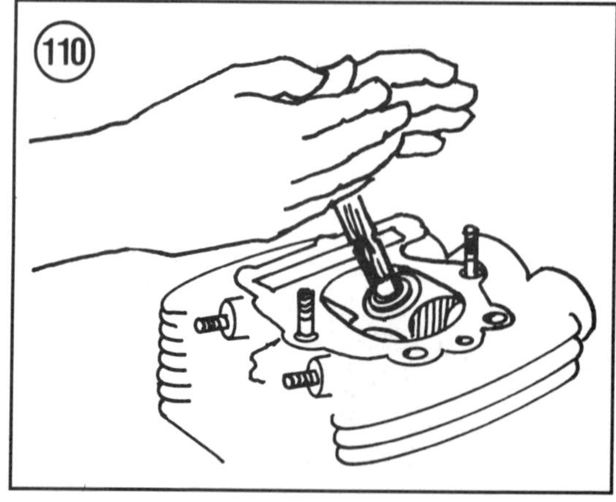
110

Valve Guide Replacement

The valve guides must be removed and installed with special tools that can be ordered from a Yamaha dealer or motorcycle accessory store. The required special tools are listed as follows:

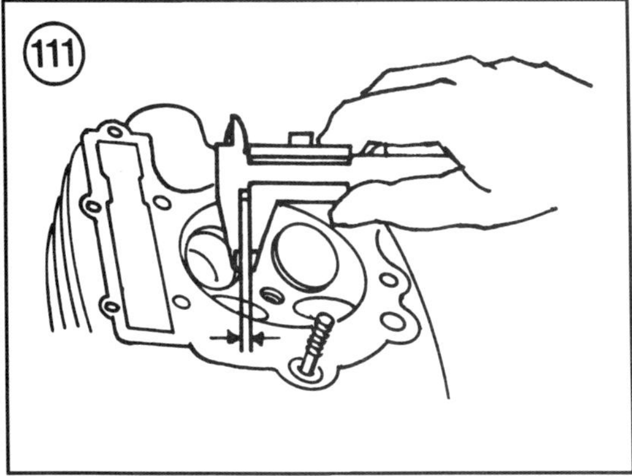
111

112

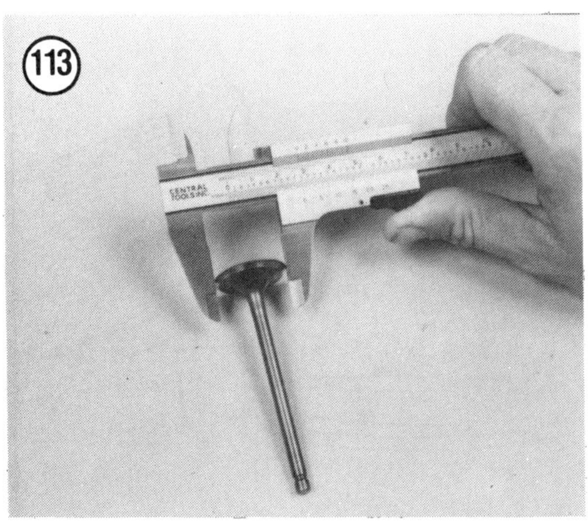

113

a. 7 mm valve guide remover, Yamaha part No. YM-01125.

b. Valve guide installer, Yamaha part No. YM-04017.

c. 7 mm valve guide reamer, Yamaha part No. 90890-01227.

NOTE

Before driving the valve guides out of the cylinder head, place the new valve guides in the freezer. The freezing temperature will reduce the outer diameter of the new guides slightly and make installation easier.

1. Measure the distance from the top of the valve guide to the cylinder head. Record this distance so that the new guide can be installed to the correct height.

CAUTION

Before heating the cylinder head in this procedure to remove the valve guide(s), wash the cylinder head thoroughly with detergent and water. Rinse and rewash the cylinder head as required to remove all traces of oil and other debris.

CAUTION

Even though the cylinder head has been washed there ***may*** *be a residual oil or solvent odor left in the oven after heating the cylinder head. If you use a household oven, first check with the person who uses the oven for food preparation to avoid getting into trouble.*

2. The valve guides are installed with a slight interference fit. The cylinder head must be heated to a temperature of approximately 212-300° F (100-150° C) in a shop oven or on a hot plate.

CAUTION

Do not heat the cylinder head with a torch (propane or acetylene)—never bring a flame into contact with the cylinder head. The direct heat may cause warpage of the cylinder head.

WARNING

Heavy gloves must be worn when performing this procedure—the cylinder head will be very hot.

3. Remove the cylinder head from the oven or hot plate and place onto wood blocks with the combustion chamber facing *up*.

4. Drive the old valve guide (**Figure 114**) out from the combustion chamber side of the cylinder head (**Figure 115**) with the valve guide remover.

5. After the cylinder head cools, check the guide bore for carbon or other contamination. Clean the bore thoroughly.

6. Reheat the cylinder head to approximately 212-300° F (100-150° C).

7. Remove the cylinder head from the oven or hot plate and place it on wood blocks with the combustion chamber facing *down*.

8. Using the valve guide installer, install the new valve guide (**Figure 116**) so that distance from the cylinder head to the top of the valve guide is the same as that recorded in Step 1.

9. After the cylinder head has cooled to room temperature, ream the new valve guides as follows:

   a. Coat the valve guide and valve guide reamer with cutting oil.
   b. See **Figure 117**. Ream the valve guide by rotating the reamer *clockwise* only. Do not turn the reamer counterclockwise.
   c. Measure the valve guide inside diameter with a small hole gauge (**Figure 106**). Then measure the small hole gauge with a micrometer to determine the valve guide inside diameter. The valve guide should be within the service specifications listed in **Table 2**.

10. The valve seats must be refaced with a 45° cutter after replacing valve guides. Reface the valve seats as described under *Valve Seat Reconditioning* in this chapter.

11. Clean the cylinder head thoroughly in solvent. Lightly oil the valve guides to prevent rust.

Valve Seat Reconditioning

The valve seats must be cut with special tools that are available from a Yamaha dealer or motorcycle accessory dealer. The following tools will be required:

a. Valve seat cutters (see Yamaha dealer for part numbers).
b. Vernier caliper.
c. Machinist's blue.
d. Valve lapping tool (**Figure 118**).

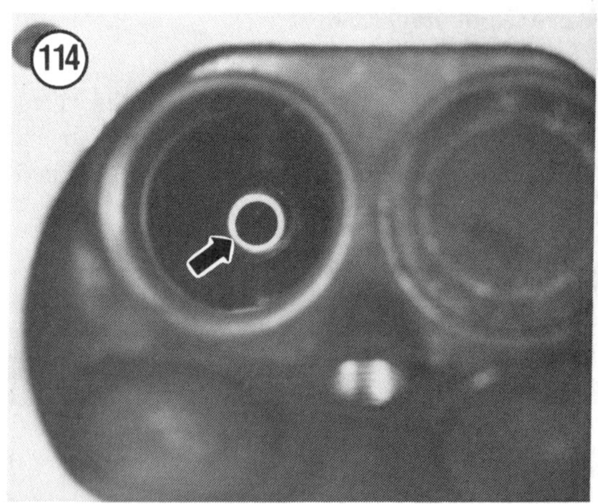

114

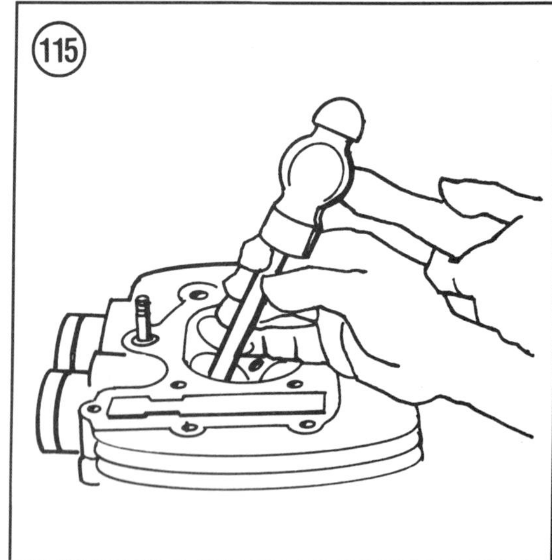

115

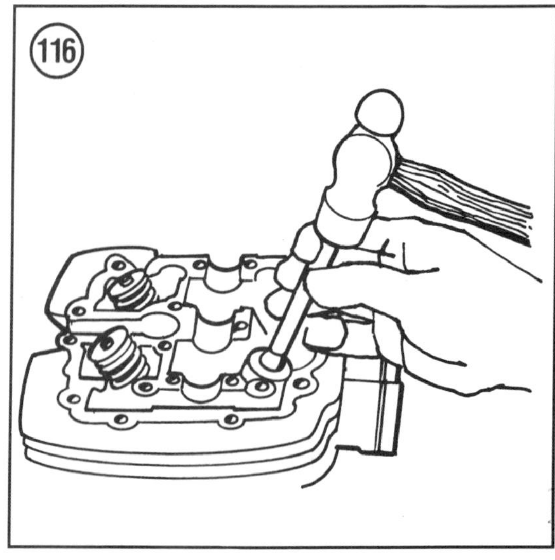

116

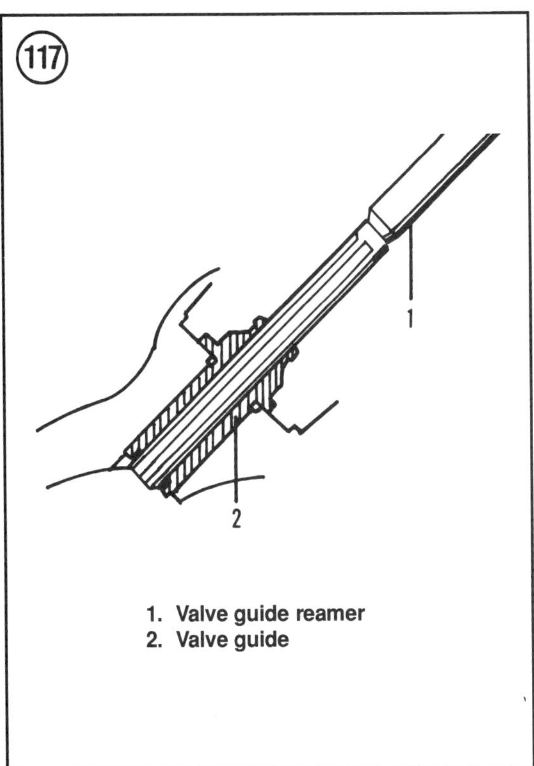

1. Valve guide reamer
2. Valve guide

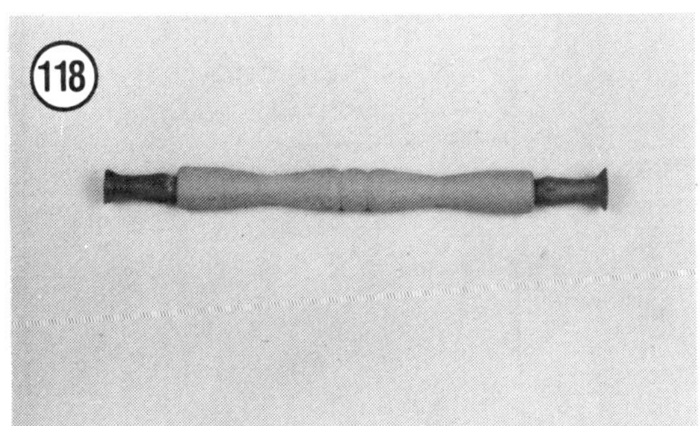

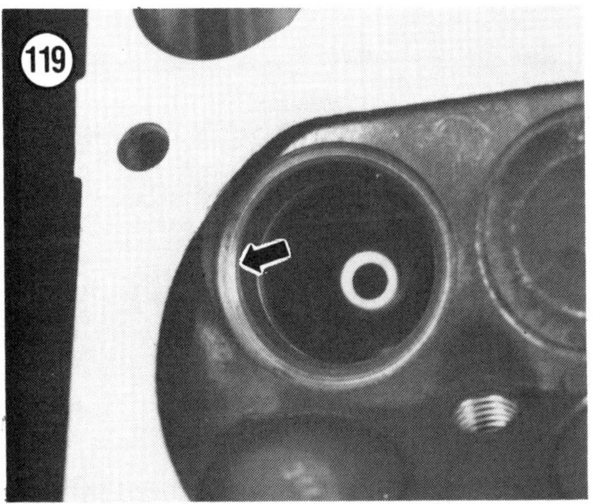

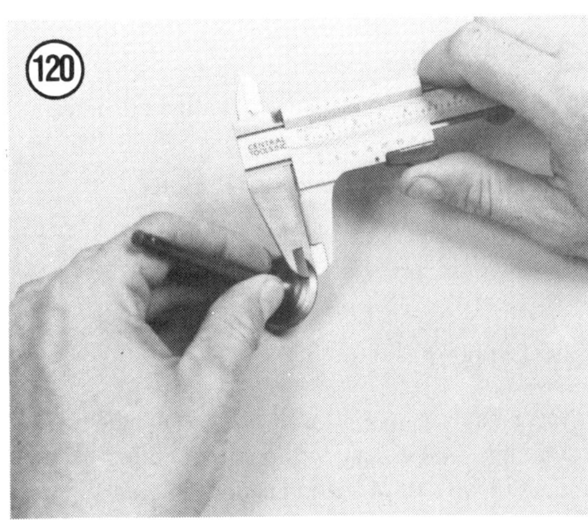

NOTE

Follow the manufacturer's instructions with using valve seat facing equipment.

1. Inspect valve seats (**Figure 119**). If worn or burned, they may be reconditioned. Seats and valves in near-perfect condition can be reconditioned by lapping with fine carborundum paste. Lapping, however, is always inferior to precision grinding. Check as follows:

   a. Clean the valve seat and valve mating areas with an aerosol electrical contact cleaner.

   b. Coat the valve seat with machinist's blue.

   c. Install the valve into its guide and rotate it against its seat with a valve lapping tool (**Figure 110**). See *Valve Lapping* in this chapter.

   d. Lift the valve out of the guide and measure the seat width with vernier calipers (**Figure 120**).

   e. The seat width for intake and exhaust valves should measure within the specifications listed in **Table 2** all the way around the seat. If the seat width exceeds the service limit in **Table 2**, regrind the seats as follows.

CAUTION

When grinding valve seats, work ***slowly*** *to prevent from grinding the seats too much. Overgrinding the valve seats will sink the valves too far into the cylinder head. Sinking the valves too far may reduce valve clearance and make it impossible to adjust valve clearance. If overgrinding occurs, the cylinder head will have to be replaced.*

4

2. Install a 45° cutter onto the valve tool and lightly cut the valve seat to remove roughness.

3. Measure the valve seat with a vernier caliper (**Figure 111**). Record the measurement to use as a reference point when performing the following.

CAUTION
The 30° cutter removes material quickly. Work carefully and slowly and check your progress often.

4. Install a 30° cutter onto the valve tool and lightly cut the seat to remove 1/4 of the existing valve seat.

5. Install a 60° cutter onto the valve tool and lightly cut the seat to remove the lower 1/4 of the existing valve seat.

6. Measure the valve seat with a vernier caliper. Then fit a 45° cutter onto the valve tool and cut the valve seat to the specified seat width listed in **Table 2**.

7. When the valve seat width is correct, check valve seating as follows.

8. Clean the valve seat and valve mating areas with an aerosol electrical contact cleaner.

9. Coat the valve seat with machinist's blue.

10. Install the valve into its guide and rotate it against its seat with a valve lapping tool (**Figure 110**). See *Valve Lapping* in this chapter.

11. Remove the valve and check the contact area on the valve (A, **Figure 121**). Interpret results as follows:

a. The valve contact area should be approximately in the center of the valve seat area (B, **Figure 121**).

b. If the contact area is too high on the valve (C, **Figure 121**), lower the seat with a 30° flat cutter.

c. If the contact area is too low on the valve (D, **Figure 121**), raise the seat with a 60° interior cutter.

d. Refinish the seat using a 45° cutter.

12. When the contact area is correct, lap the valve as described in this chapter.

Valve Lapping

Valve lapping is a simple operation which can restore the valve seal without machining if the amount of wear or distortion is not too great.

This procedure should only be performed after determining that valve seat width and outside diameter are within specifications.

1. Smear a light coating of fine grade valve lapping compound on seating surface of valve.

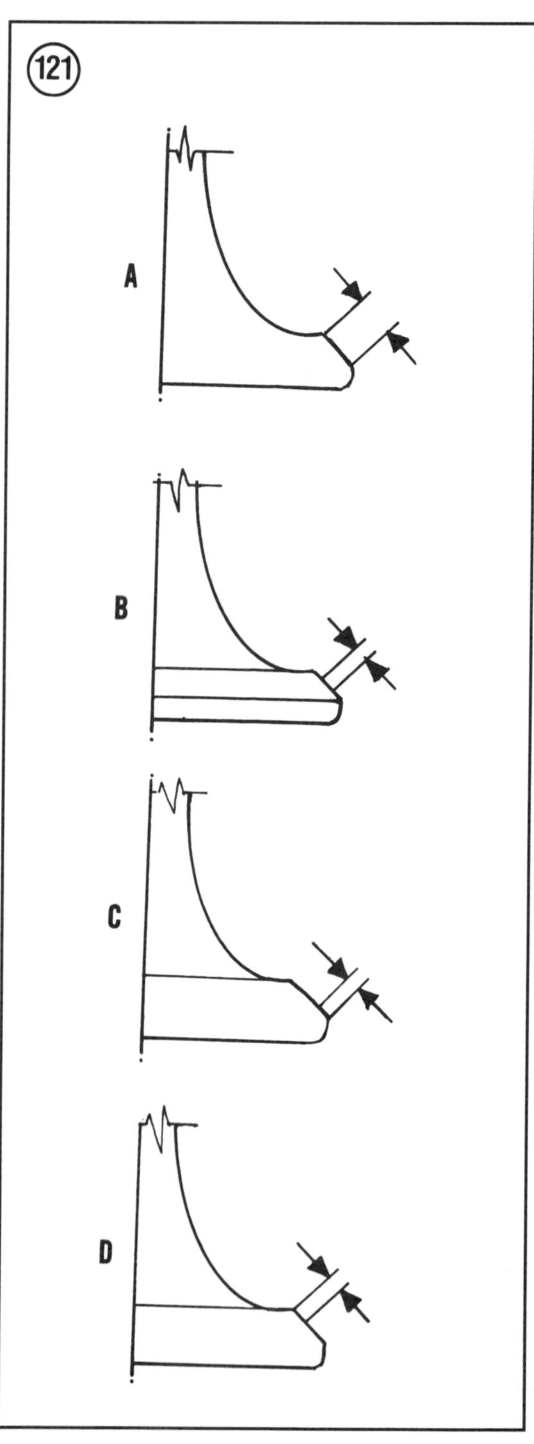

2. Insert the valve into the head.

3. Wet the suction cup of the lapping stick (**Figure 118**) and stick it onto the head of the valve. Lap the valve to the seat by spinning the lapping stick in both directions. Every 5 to 10 seconds, rotate the valve 180° in the valve seat. Continue this action until the mating surfaces on the valve and seat are smooth and equal in size.

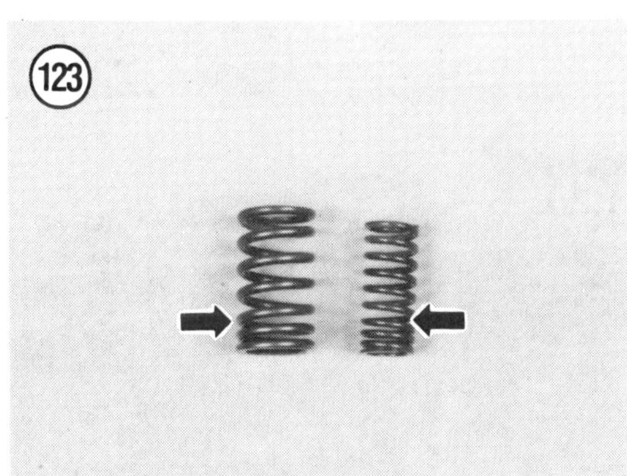

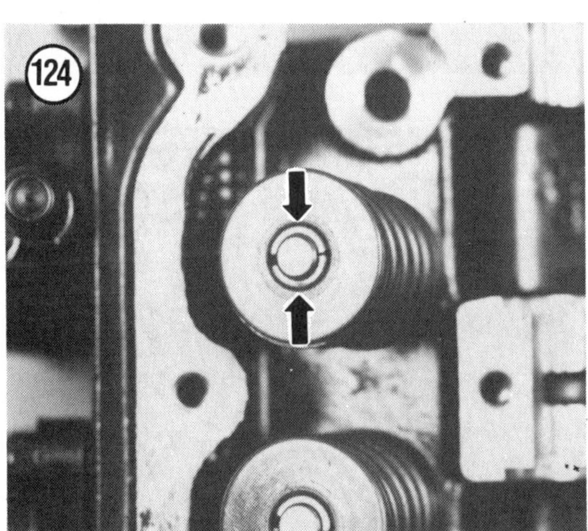

4. Closely examine valve seat in cylinder head. It should be smooth and even with a smooth, polished seating "ring."

5. Thoroughly clean the valves and cylinder head in solvent to remove all grinding compound. Any compound left on the valves or the cylinder head will end up in the engine and cause excessive wear and damage.

6. After the lapping has been completed and the valve assemblies have been reinstalled into the head, the valve seal should be tested. Check the seal of each valve by pouring solvent into each of the intake and exhaust ports. There should be no leakage past the seat. If leakage occurs, combustion chamber will appear wet. If fluid leaks past any of the seats, disassemble that valve assembly and repeat the lapping procedure until there is no leakage.

Valve Installation

1. Coat a valve stem with molybdenum disulfide paste and install the valve into its correct guide. Refer to **Figure 101** and **Figure 122**.

2. Install the spring lower seat (B, **Figure 102**).

NOTE
Oil seals should be replaced whenever a valve is removed.

3. Carefully slide a new oil seal (A, **Figure 102**) over the valve and seat it onto the end of the valve guide.

NOTE
Install valve springs with the narrow pitch end (end with coils closest together) facing the cylinder head. See ***Figure 123****.*

4. Install the inner (**Figure 99**) and outer valve springs (**Figure 98**).

5. Install the upper valve spring seat (**Figure 97**).

6. Push down on the spring retainer with the valve spring compressor (**Figure 95**) and install the valve keepers (**Figure 96**).

7. After releasing tension from the compressor, examine valve keepers and make sure they are seated correctly (**Figure 124**).

8. After the springs have been installed, gently tap on the end of the valve stem (**Figure 125**) with a soft aluminum or brass drift and hammer. This will ensure that the keepers are properly installed and seated.
9. Repeat Steps 1-8 for remaining valve(s).
10. Check valve clearance and adjust as necessary as described in Chapter Three.

CYLINDER BLOCK

The alloy cylinder block has a pressed-in cast iron cylinder sleeve.

On XT600 models, if the cylinder is out of specification, the cylinder can be bored to 0.5 mm (0.020 in.) oversize and an additional 0.5 mm (0.020 in.) to a final 1.0 mm (0.040 in.) oversize.

On TT600 models, if the cylinder is out of specification, the cylinder sleeve must be removed and a new sleeve installed.

Removal

Refer to **Figure 126** for this procedure.

1. Remove the cylinder head as described under *Cylinder Head Removal/Installation* in this chapter.
2. Remove the following fasteners securing the cylinder block to the crankcase:
   a. Left-hand side Allen bolts (**Figure 127**).

NOTE
*Only the rear special long nut is visible in **Figure 128**. There is also a front special long nut on the same side of the cylinder block. Be sure to remove **both** special long nuts.*

   b. Left-hand side special long nuts and washers (**Figure 128**).
   c. Right-hand side nuts and washers (**Figure 129**).
3. Loosen the cylinder block by tapping around the perimeter with a rubber or plastic mallet.
4. Untie the wire (A, **Figure 130**) securing the camshaft drive chain to the frame.
5. Pull the cylinder block (B, **Figure 130**) straight up and off the crankcase. Feed the camshaft drive chain and wire through the chain channel in the cylinder block. Retie the wire to the crankcase.
6. If necessary, remove the piston as described under *Piston Removal/Installation* in this chapter.

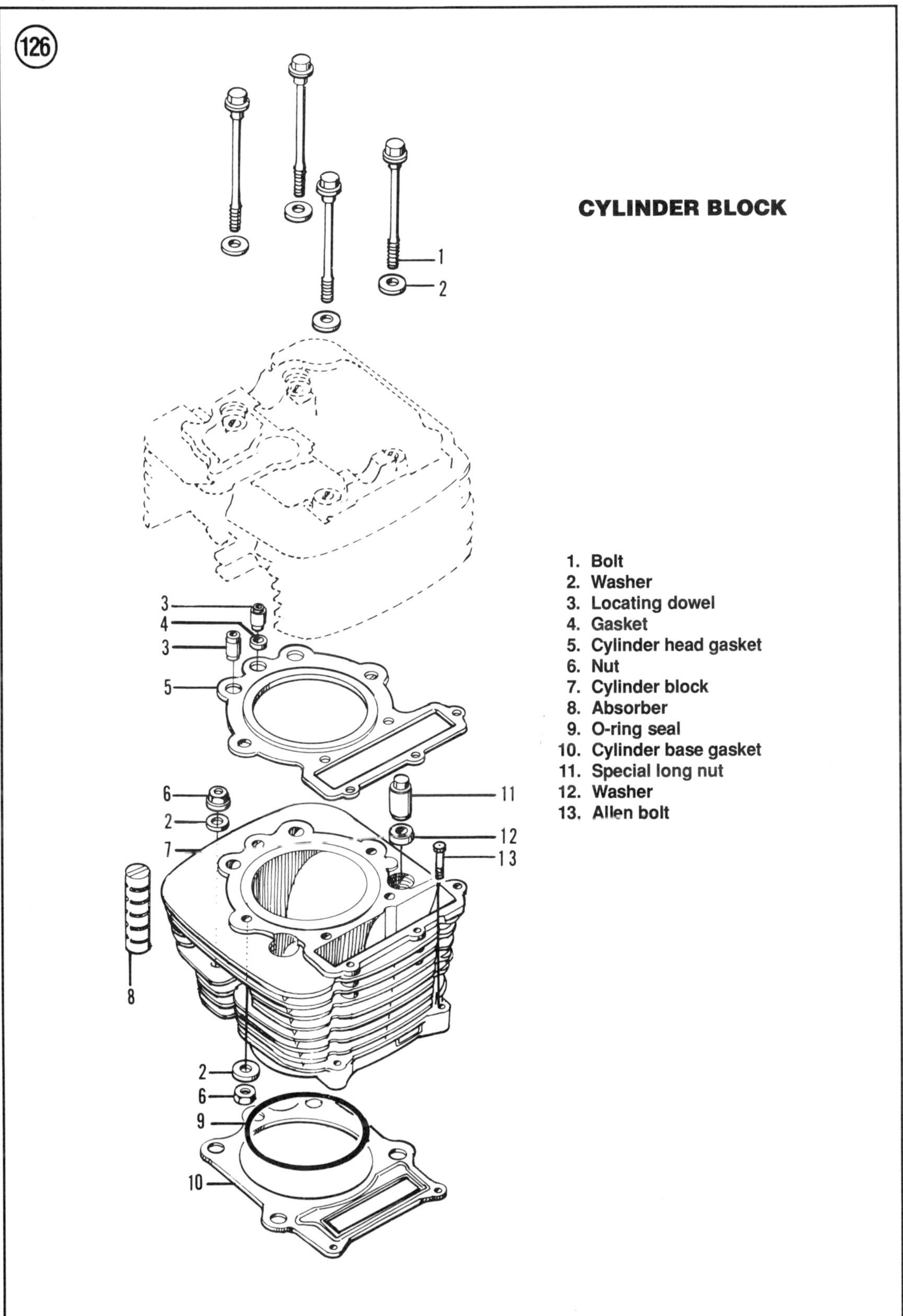

4

CYLINDER BLOCK

1. Bolt
2. Washer
3. Locating dowel
4. Gasket
5. Cylinder head gasket
6. Nut
7. Cylinder block
8. Absorber
9. O-ring seal
10. Cylinder base gasket
11. Special long nut
12. Washer
13. Allen bolt

7. Don't lose the locating dowel on the right-hand side.
8. Remove the cylinder base gasket and discard it.
9. Stuff clean shop rags into the crankcase opening to prevent foreign objects from falling into the crankcase.
10. If necessary, remove the piston as described in this chapter.

Inspection

1. Thoroughly clean the outside of the cylinder block. Use a stiff brush, soap and water and clean out all road dirt and mud from the cooling fins (**Figure 131**). If necessary, use a piece of wood and scrape away all lodged dirt and mud. Clogged cooling fins can cause overheating leading to possible engine damage.
2. Wash the cylinder block in solvent to remove any oil and carbon particles. The cylinder bore must be cleaned thoroughly before attempting any measurement as incorrect readings may be obtained.
3. Remove all gasket residue from the top (A, **Figure 132**) and bottom (A, **Figure 133**) gasket surfaces.
4. Check the locating dowel pin holes (B, **Figure 132** and B, **Figure 133**) for cracks or other damage.
5. Check the cylinder O-ring (**Figure 134**) for wear or deterioration; replace if necessary.
6. Measure the cylinder bore with a bore gauge or inside micrometer (**Figure 135**). Then measure the bore gauge with a micrometer to determine the bore diameter. Measure the cylinder bore at the points shown in **Figure 136**. Measure in 2 axes—in line with the piston pin and at 90° to the pin. If the taper or out-of-round is greater than specifications listed in **Table 2**, on XT600 models, the cylinder must be rebored to the next oversize and new piston and rings installed. On TT600 models, the cylinder sleeve must be replaced.

NOTE

*On XT600 models, the new piston should be obtained first before the cylinder is bored so that the piston can be measured. The cylinder must be bored to match the piston. Piston-to-cylinder clearance is specified in **Table 2**.*

7. If the cylinder is not worn past the service limit, check the bore (**Figure 137**) carefully for scratches or gouges. The bore still may require boring and

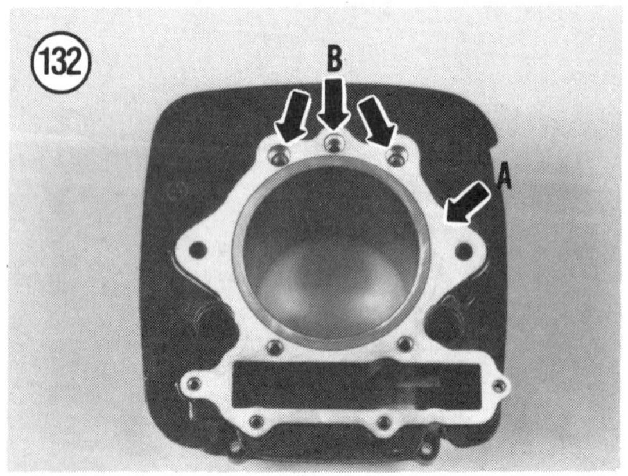

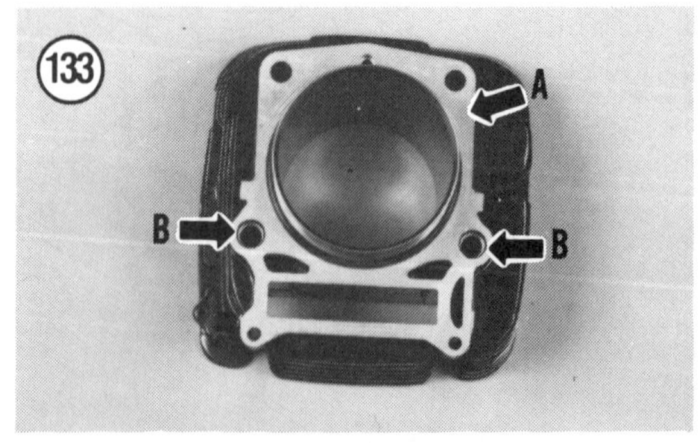

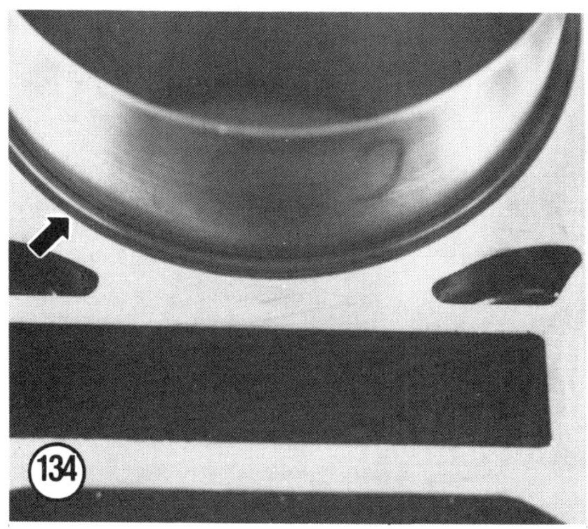

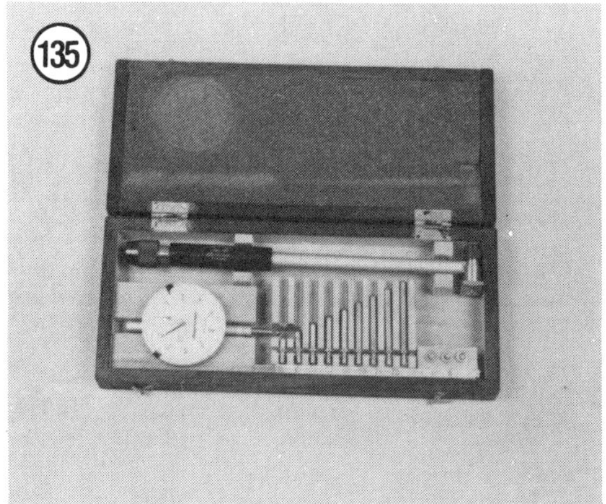

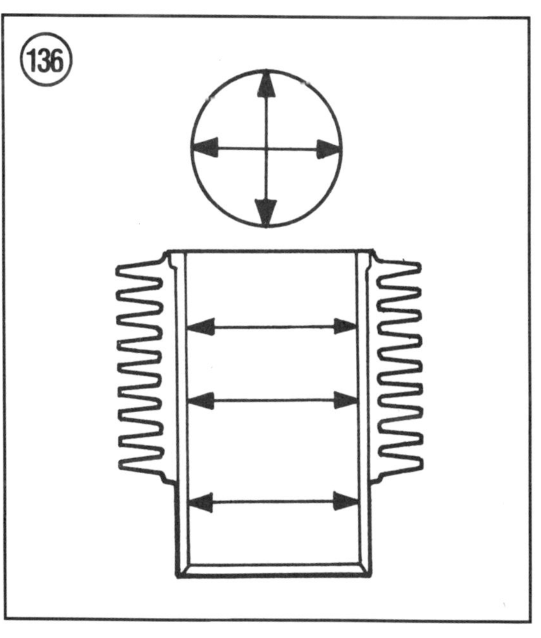

reconditioning on XT600 models or the sleeve may have to be replaced on TT600 models.

8. If the cylinder requires boring (XT600 models) or the sleeve replaced (TT600 models); remove all dowel pins from the cylinder before taking it to a dealer or machine shop for service.

9. After the cylinder has been serviced, wash the bore in hot soapy water. This is the only way to clean the cylinder wall of the fine grit material left from the boring or honing job on XT600 models or manufacturing processes on TT600 models. After washing the cylinder wall, run a clean white cloth through it. The cylinder wall should show no traces of grit or other debris. If the rag is dirty, the cylinder wall is not clean and must be rewashed. After the cylinder is cleaned, lubricate the cylinder wall with clean engine oil to prevent the cylinder liner from rusting.

CAUTION

A combination of soap and water is the only solution that will completely clean the cylinder wall. Solvent and kerosene cannot wash fine grit out of cylinder crevices. Grit left in the cylinder will act as a grinding compound and cause premature wear to the new rings.

10. Wipe the cylinder bore dry with lint-free cloths and compressed air. Apply a light coat of fresh engine oil to keep the cylinder wall from rusting.

4

Installation

1. Check that the top (A, **Figure 132**) and bottom (A, **Figure 133**) cylinder mating surfaces are clean of all old gasket residue.

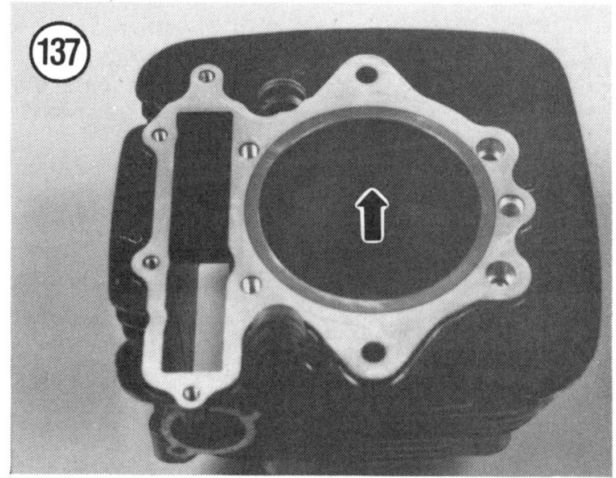

2. Check that the top surface of the crankcase is clean of all gasket residue.

3. If removed, install the 2 locating dowels (A, **Figure 138**) on the left-hand side of the cylinder.

4. Install a new cylinder base gasket (B, **Figure 138**). Make sure all holes align.

5. Install a new gasket (**Figure 139**) onto the center locating dowel on the right-hand side and install the dowel (**Figure 140**).

6. If removed, install the piston, as described in this chapter.

CAUTION
Make sure the piston pin circlips are installed and seated correctly.

7. Lubricate the cylinder wall and piston liberally with engine oil prior to installation.

8. Untie the wire securing the camshaft drive chain to the crankcase.

9. Feed the wire through the chain channel in the cylinder block.

CAUTION
If using a hose clamp, don't tighten the clamp any more than necessary to compress the rings. If the rings can't slip through easily, the clamp may gouge the rings.

10. Carefully align the cylinder with the piston and install the cylinder (**Figure 141**). Compress each ring as it enters the cylinder with your fingers or by using an aircraft type hose clamp.

NOTE
Once the cylinder is installed, pull the camshaft chain and wire up through the cylinder block.

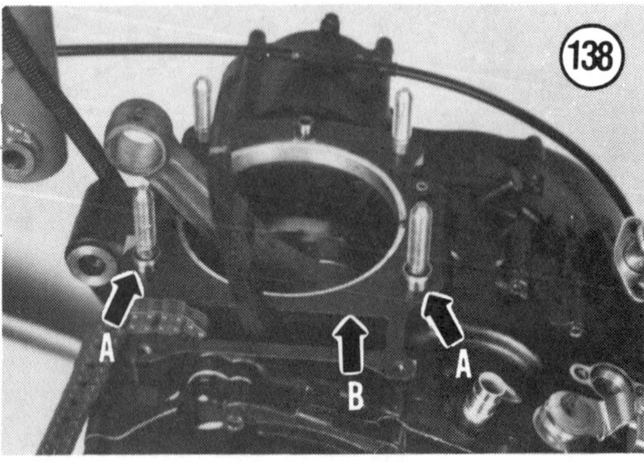

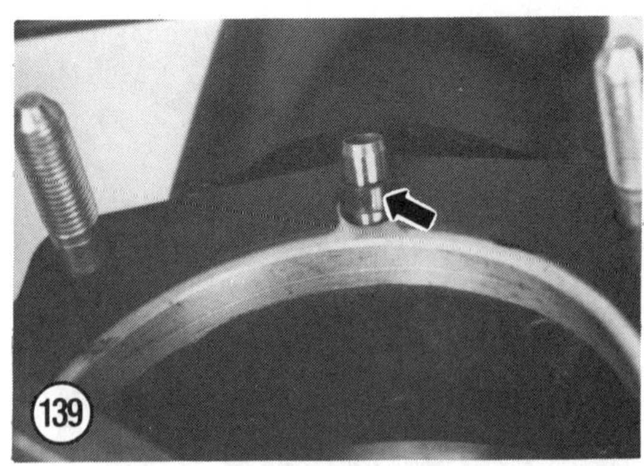

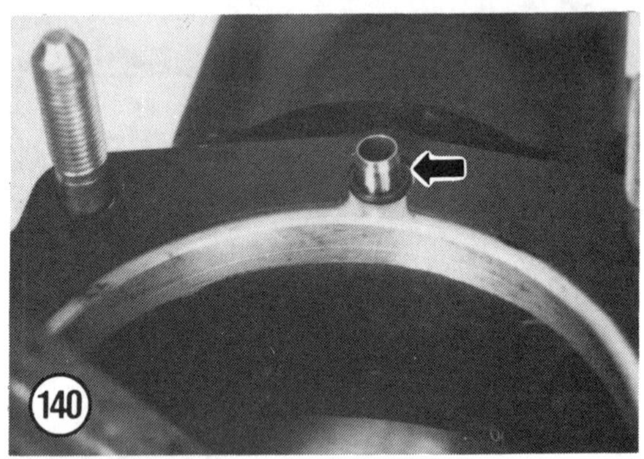

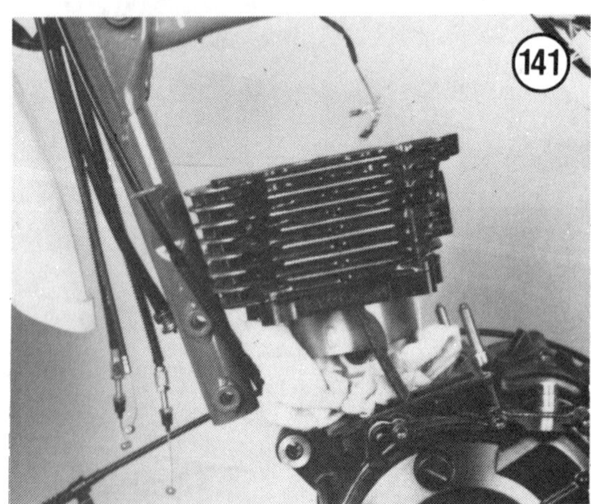

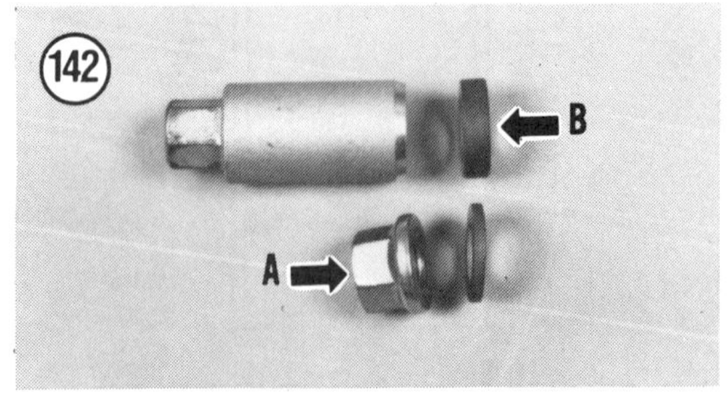

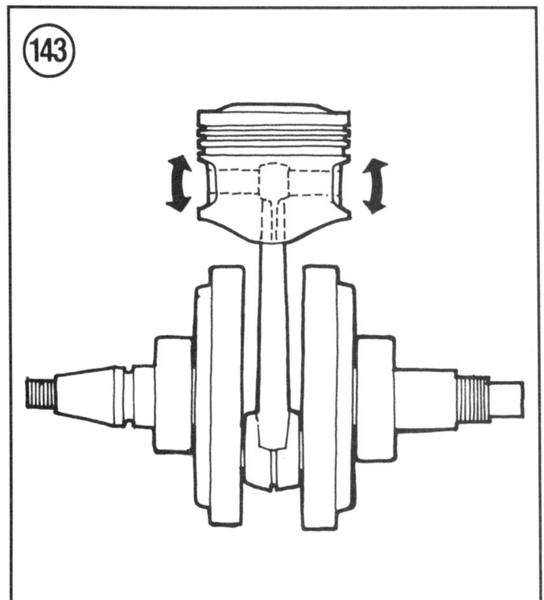

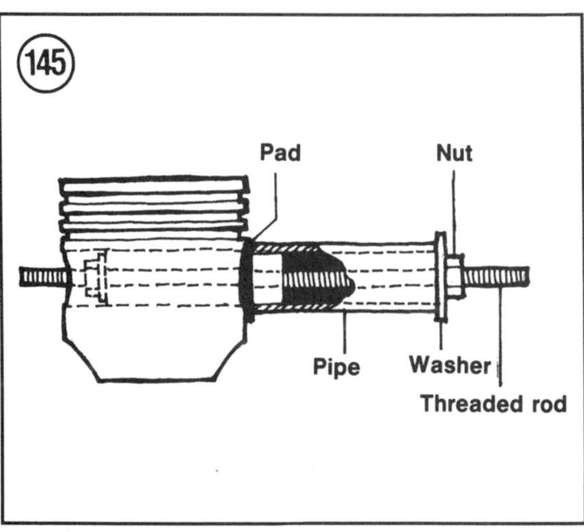

11. Retie the wire to the frame (A, **Figure 130**).
12. Push the cylinder (B, **Figure 130**) all the way down.
13. While holding the cylinder down with one hand, operate the kickstarter lever with your other hand. The piston should move smoothly and quietly up and down in the bore. If it doesn't—stop and correct the problem.
14. Install the following fasteners securing the cylinder block to the crankcase:
   a. Right-hand side nuts and washers. Refer to A, **Figure 142** and **Figure 129**.

NOTE
*Only the rear special long nut is visible in **Figure 128**. Be sure to install the front special long nut on the same side of the cylinder block. Be sure to install **both** special long nuts.*

   b. Left-hand side special long nuts and washers. Refer to B, **Figure 142** and **Figure 128**.
   c. Left-hand side Allen bolts (**Figure 127**).
15. After all bolts and nuts have been installed, tighten them in a crisscross pattern to the torque specifications listed in **Table 3**.
16. Install the cylinder head as described in this chapter.

PISTON

Piston Removal/Installation

1. Remove the cylinder as described in this chapter.
2. Stuff the crankcase with clean shop rags to prevent objects from falling into the crankcase.
3. Before removing the piston, hold the rod tightly and rock the piston (**Figure 143**). Any rocking motion (do not confuse with the normal sliding motion) indicates wear on the piston pin, rod bushing, pin bore, or more likely, a combination of all three.
4. Remove the circlips from the piston pin bores (**Figure 144**).

NOTE
Discard the piston circlips. New circlips must be installed during reassembly.

5. Push the piston pin out of the piston by hand. If the pin is tight, use a homemade tool (**Figure 145**) to remove it. Do not drive the piston pin out as this

action may damage the piston pin, connecting rod or piston.

6. Lift the piston (**Figure 146**) off the connecting rod.

7. Inspect the piston as described in this chapter.

NOTE
New piston circlips should be installed.

8. Coat the connecting rod bushing, piston pin and piston with assembly oil.

9. Insert the piston pin through one side of the piston until its end extends slightly beyond the inside of the boss (**Figure 147**).

10. Place the piston over the connecting rod so that the arrow on the piston crown (**Figure 148**) faces forward.

11. Push the piston pin in farther until it starts to enter the connecting rod. Then it may be necessary to move the piston around until the pin enters the connecting rod. Do not force installation or damage may occur. If the pin does not slide easily, use the homemade tool (**Figure 145**) but eliminate the piece of pipe. Push the pin in until it is centered in the piston.

12. Install the piston circlips (**Figure 144**) into the circlip groove on each side of the piston. Make sure the circlips seat all the way in the circlip grooves.

Piston Inspection

1. Remove the piston rings as described in this chapter.

CAUTION
Large carbon accumulations reduce piston cooling and results in detonation and piston damage.

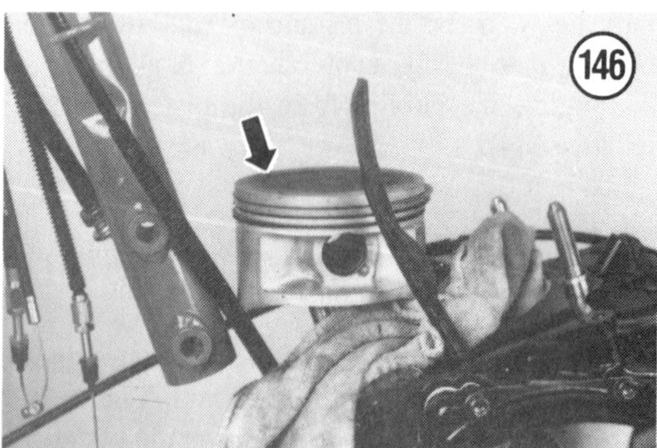

2. Carefully clean the piston as follows:
   a. Clean the carbon from the piston crown (A, **Figure 149**) with a soft scraper or wire wheel.
   b. Be sure to remove all deposits from the valve reliefs (B, **Figure 149**) in the piston crown.

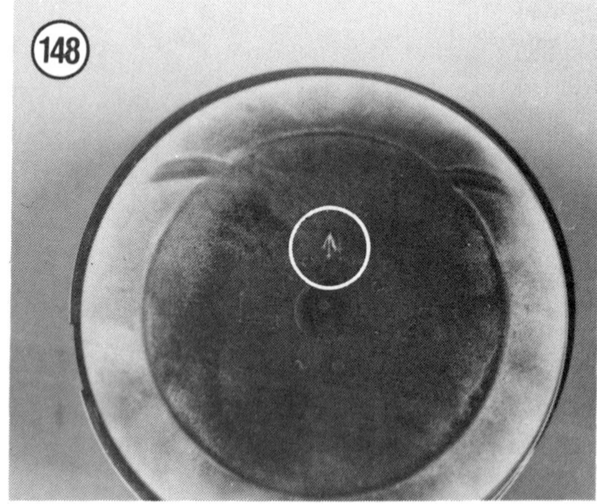

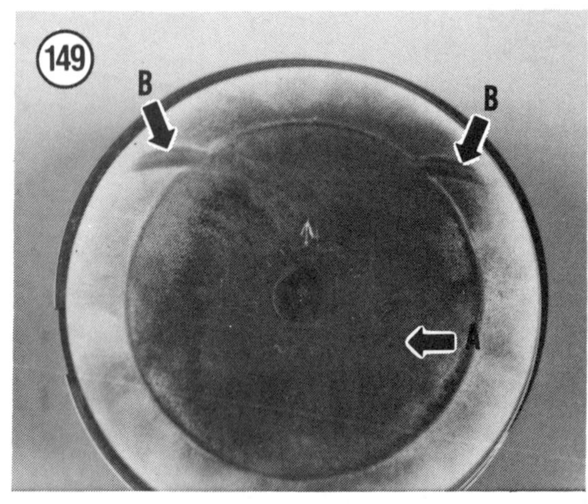

c. Do not remove or damage the carbon ridge around the circumference of the piston above the top ring (**Figure 150**).

d. If the piston, rings and cylinder are found to be dimensionally correct and can be reused, removal of the carbon ring from the top of the piston or the carbon ridges from the cylinders will promote excessive oil consumption.

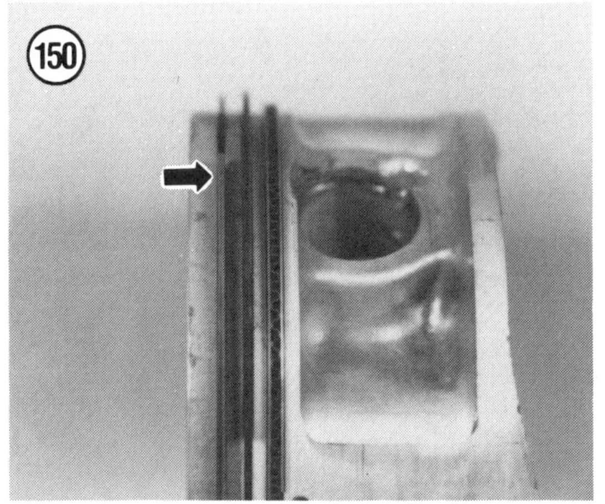

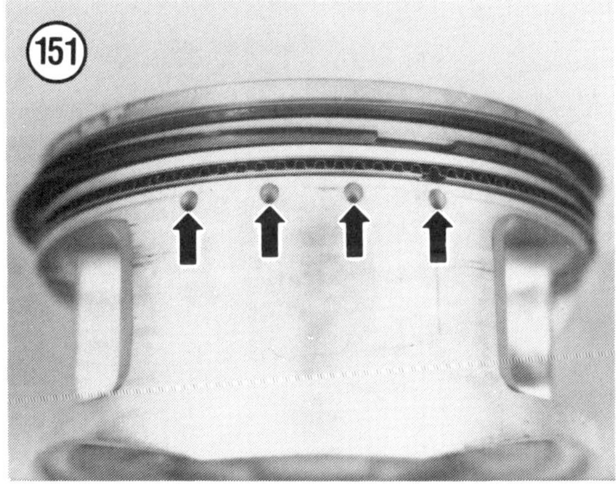

CAUTION
Do not wire brush the sides of the piston as the brush will leave scratches on the ring grooves and piston skirt.

3. After cleaning the piston, examine the crown. The crown should show no signs of wear or damage. If the crown appears pecked or spongy-looking, also check the spark plug, valves and combustion chamber for aluminum deposits. If these deposits are found, the cylinder is suffering from excessive heat caused by a lean fuel mixture or preignition.

4. Examine each ring groove for burrs, dented edges and wide wear. Pay particular attention to the top compression ring groove, as it usually wears more than the others. Because the oil rings are constantly bathed in oil, these rings and grooves wear little compared to compression rings and their grooves. If there is evidence of oil ring groove wear or if the oil ring assembly is tight and difficult to remove, the piston skirt may have collapsed due to excessive heat and is permanently deformed. Replace the piston.

5. Check the oil control holes in the piston for carbon or oil sludge buildup. Refer to **Figure 151**, **Figure 152** and **Figure 153**. Clean the holes with a small diameter drill bit of the correct size.

6. Check the piston skirt for cracks or other damage. If a piston shows signs of partial seizure (bits of aluminum buildup on the piston skirt), the piston should be replaced and the cylinder bored (if neces-

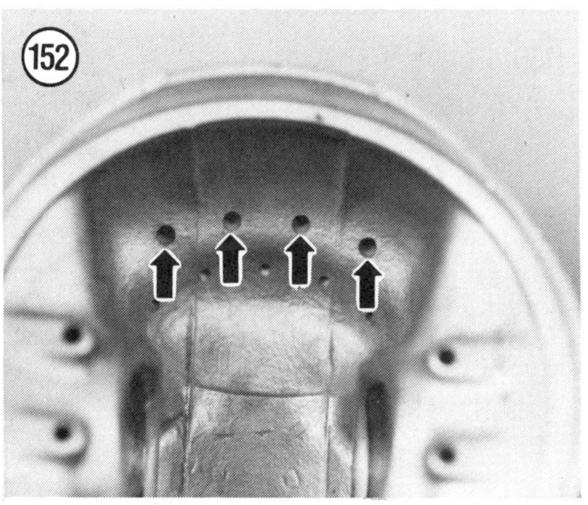

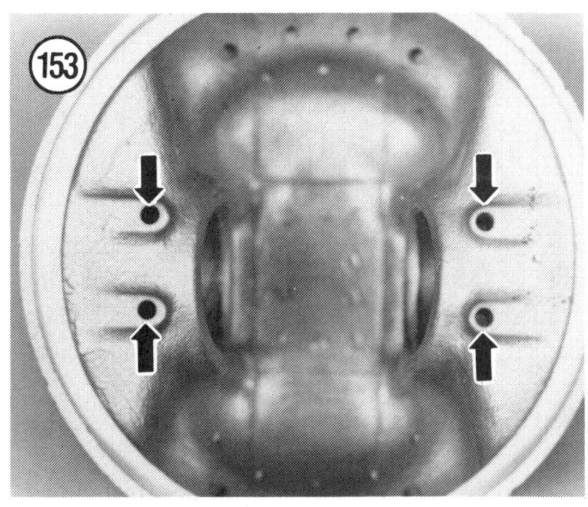

4

sary) to reduce the possibility of engine noise and further piston seizure.

NOTE
If the piston skirt is worn or scuffed unevenly from side-to-side, the connecting rod may be bent or twisted.

7. Inspect the piston pin for chrome flaking or cracks. Replace if necessary. Yamaha does not provide specifications for the outer diameter of the piston pin.
8. Oil the piston pin and install it in the piston (**Figure 154**). Slowly rotate the piston pin and check for radial play. If any radial play exists, the piston pin and piston should be replaced as a set.
9. Install a new piston pin circlip in each piston circlip groove and check the groove for wear or circlip looseness by pulling the circlip from side-to-side. If the circlip has any side play, the groove is worn and the piston must be replaced.
10. Measure piston-to-cylinder clearance as described under *Piston Clearance* in this chapter.
11. If damage or wear indicate that piston replacement is required, select a new piston as described under *Piston Clearance* in this chapter.

Piston Clearance

1. Make sure the piston and cylinder walls are clean and dry.
2. Measure the cylinder bore with a bore gauge or inside micrometer. Then measure the bore gauge with a micrometer to determine the bore diameter. Measure the cylinder bore at the points shown in **Figure 136**. Measure in 2 axes—in line with the piston pin and at 90° to the pin.

NOTE
When measuring the piston diameter in Step 3, measure the piston diameter at a point 5 mm (0.197 in.) from the lower edge of the piston skirt.

3. Measure the piston diameter with a micrometer (**Figure 155**) at a right angle to the piston pin bore.
4. Subtract the piston diameter from the largest bore diameter; the difference is piston-to-cylinder clearance.
5A. On XT600 models, if clearance exceeds specifications, the piston should be replaced and the cylinder bored oversize. Purchase the new piston first. Measure its diameter and add the specified clearance to determine the proper cylinder bore diameter.
5B. On TT600 models, if clearance exceeds specifications, the piston should be replaced and the cylinder sleeve replaced by a Yamaha dealer or machine shop.

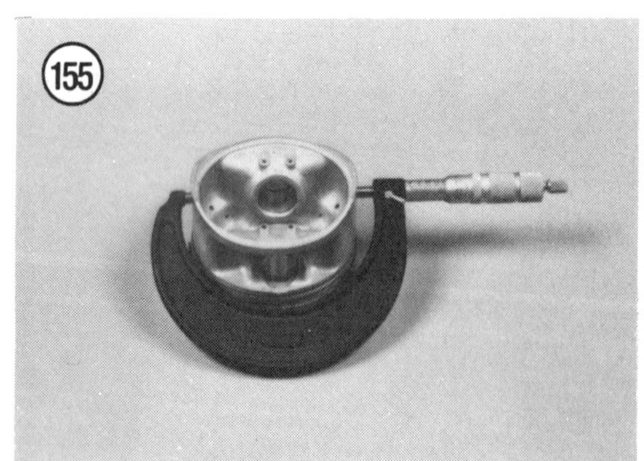

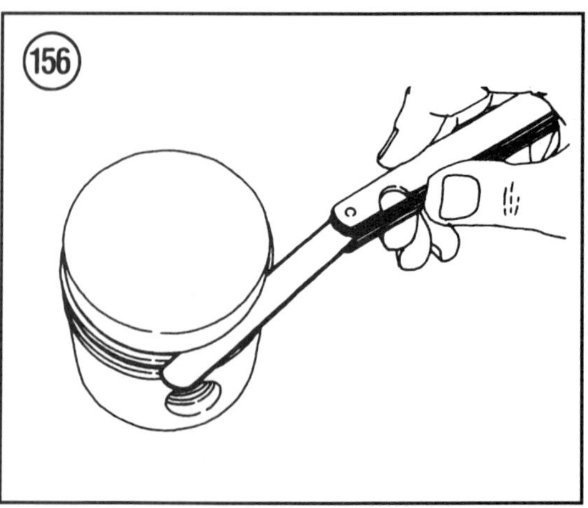

PISTON RINGS

Inspection/Removal/Installation

1. Measure the side clearance of each ring in its groove with a flat feeler gauge (**Figure 156**) and compare with the specifications in **Table 2**. If the clearance is greater than specified, the rings must be replaced. If the clearance is still excessive with the new rings, the piston must be replaced.

WARNING
The edges of all piston rings are very sharp. Be careful when handling them to avoid cut fingers.

NOTE
*Store the rings in order of removal (**Figure 157**).*

2. Remove the old rings with a ring expander tool (**Figure 158**) or by spreading the ring ends with your thumbs and lifting the rings up evenly (**Figure 159**).
3. Using a broken piston ring, remove all carbon from the piston ring grooves (**Figure 160**).
4. Inspect grooves carefully for burrs, nicks or broken or cracked lands. Replace piston if necessary.
5. Check end gap of each ring. To check, insert the ring into the top of the cylinder bore approximately 20 mm (25/32 in.) and square it with the cylinder wall by tapping it with the piston.
6. Measure the end gap with a feeler gauge. Compare gap with **Table 2**. Replace ring if gap is too large. If the gap on the new ring is smaller than specified, hold a small file in a vise, grip the ends of the ring with your fingers and enlarge the gap.
7. Roll each ring around its piston groove as shown in **Figure 161** to check for binding. Minor binding may be cleaned up with a fine-cut file.

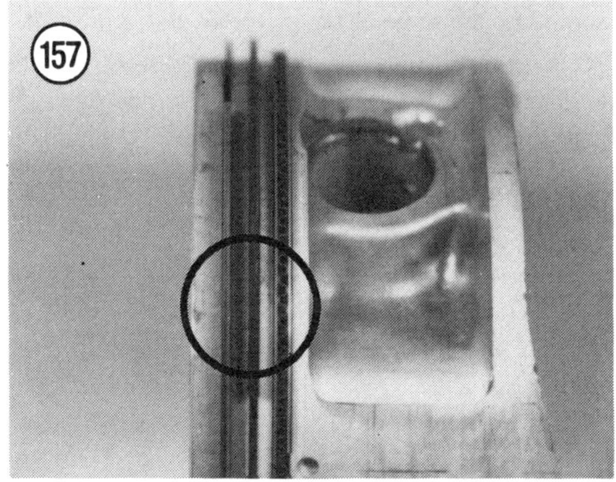
157

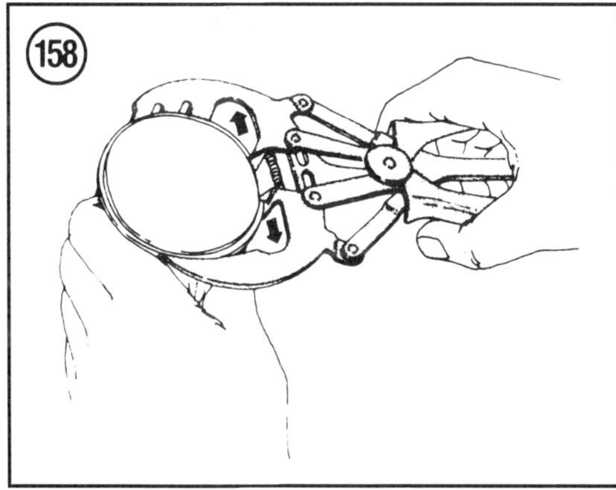
158

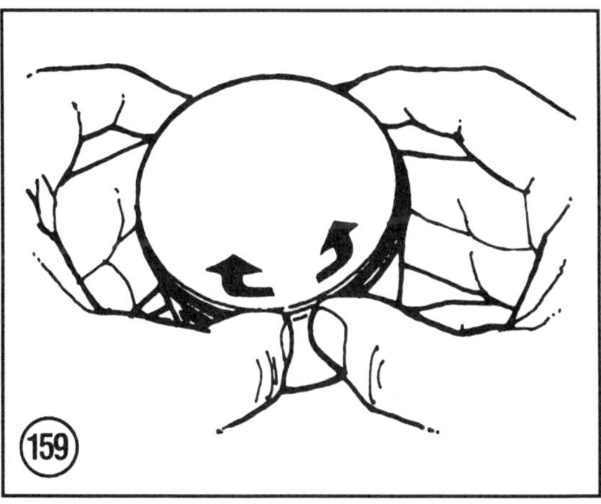
159

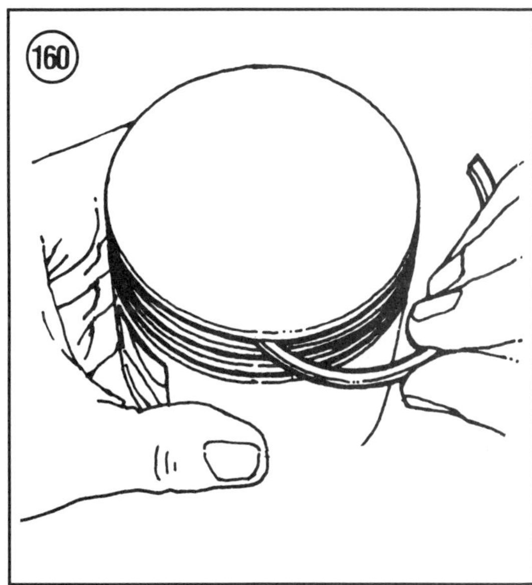
160

4

NOTE
Install all rings with the manufacturer's markings facing up.

8. Install the piston rings—first the bottom, then the middle, then the top ring—by carefully spreading the ends with your thumbs and slipping the rings over the top of the piston. Remember that the piston rings must be installed with the marks on them facing up toward the top of the piston or there is the possibility of oil pumping past the rings.
9. Install the oil ring assembly into the bottom ring groove. The assembly is comprised of 2 steel rails and 1 expander. The expander is installed in the middle of the steel rails.
10A. On XT600 models, the top and middle piston rings are slightly different. The middle ring's outer surface is square and must be installed in the middle groove. The top ring is slightly tapered at the outer surface and must be installed in the top groove.
10B. On TT600 models, the top and middle piston rings are different. The middle ring is slightly tapered and must be installed in the middle groove. The top ring's outer surface edges are slightly rounded and must be installed in the top groove.
11. Make sure the rings are seated completely in their grooves all the way around the piston.
12. Apply clean engine oil to the piston rings and grooves.

WARNING
The edges of all piston rings are very sharp. Wear cotton gloves or use a shop rag in the next step. Be careful when handling the rings to avoid cutting fingers.

13. Carefully and slowly rotate each piston ring around in its groove in the piston. Make sure the ring rotates freely with no binding or dragging. The ring must be free and move easily so that when the engine is running each ring can rotate in its groove freely.
14. Distribute the ring ends at 120° apart from each other around the piston. The important thing is that the ring gaps are not aligned with each other when installed to prevent compression pressure from escaping past them on the initial start up.
15. On XT600 models, if installing oversize compression rings, check the number to make sure the correct rings are being installed. The ring numbers should be the same as the piston oversize number.
16. If new rings are installed, the cylinder must be deglazed or honed. This will help to seat the new rings. If necessary, refer honing service to a Yamaha dealer or motorcycle repair shop. After honing, measure the end gap of each ring and compare to dimensions in **Table 2**.

NOTE
*If the cylinder was deglazed or honed, clean the cylinder bore as described under **Cylinder Block Inspection** in this chapter.*

17. Follow the *Break-in Procedure* in Chapter Five if new pistons or new piston rings have been installed.

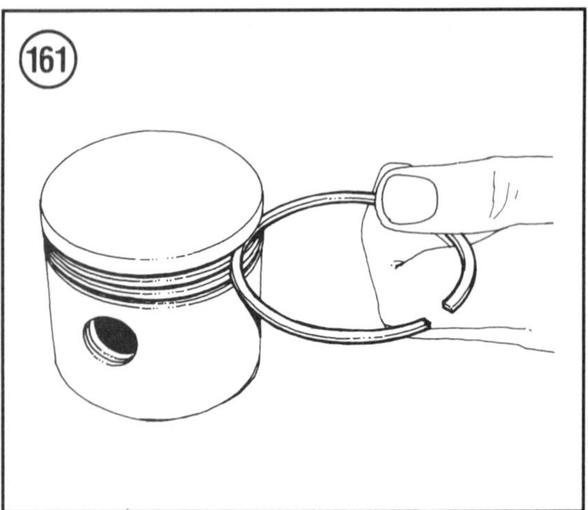

Table 1 GENERAL ENGINE SPECIFICATIONS

Engine type	4-stroke, SOHC, 4-valve single cylinder
Bore × stroke	95.0 × 84.0 mm (3.740 × 3.307 in.)
Compression ratio	8.5:1
Displacement	595 cc (36.3 cu. in.)
Lubrication system	Dry sump

Table 2 ENGINE TOP END SERVICE SPECIFICATIONS

Item	Specifications mm (in.)	Wear limit mm (in.)
Rocker arm bore ID	12.000-12.018	12.05
	(0.4724-0.4731)	(0.4744)
Rocker arm shaft OD	11.976-12.009	11.95
	(0.4715-0.4720)	(0.4705)
Rocker arm-to-shaft		
oil clearance	0.009-0.042	—
	(0.0004-0.0017)	—
Camshaft—XT600		
Lobe (intake)		
Height	36.52-36.62	36.42
	(1.438-1.442)	(1.433)
Base circle	30.01-30.11	28.91
	(1.182-1.185)	(1.138)
Lobe (exhaust)		
Height	36.70-36.80	36.60
	(1.445-1.449)	(1.441)
Base circle	30.07-30.17	28.97
	(1.184-1.188)	(1.141)
Bearing journal OD	22.967-22.980	—
	(0.9043-0.9047)	—
Bearing surface in	23.000-23.021	—
cylinder head ID	(0.9055-0.9063)	—
Bearing oil clearance	—	0.020-0.054
	—	(0.0008-0.0021)
Runout limit	—	0.03
	—	(0.001)
Camshaft—TT600		
Lobe (intake)		
Height	36.50-36.60	36.40
	(1.437-1.440)	(1.433)
Base circle	30.07-30.17	28.97
	(1.1838-1.1878)	(1.1405)
Lobe (exhaust)		
Height	36.69-36.79	36.57
	(1.445-1.448)	(1.4398)
Base circle	30.12-30.22	28.99
	(1.186-1.189)	(1.1413)
Bearing journal OD	22.967-22.980	—
	(0.9043-0.9047)	—
Bearing surface in	23.000-23.021	—
cylinder head ID	(0.9055-0.9063)	—
Bearing oil clearance	—	0.020-0.054
	—	(0.0008-0.0021)
Runout limit	—	0.03
	—	(0.001)

(continued)

Table 2 ENGINE TOP END SERVICE SPECIFICATIONS (continued)

Item	Specifications mm (in.)	Wear limit mm (in.)
Cylinder head		
Warp limit	—	0.03
	—	(0.0012)
Cylinder		
Bore	94.97-95.02	—
	(3.739-3.741)	
Taper limit	—	0.05
	—	(0.002)
Out of round	—	0.01
	—	(0.0004)
Piston (XT600)		
Diameter		
Standard	94.945-95.035	—
	(3.738-3.742)	—
2nd over	95.50	—
	(3.760)	—
4th over	96.00	—
	(3.780)	—
Piston-to-cylinder	0.045-0.065	—
clearance	(0.0018-0.0026)	—
Piston (TT600)		
Diameter	94.935-94.985	—
	(3.737-3.739)	—
Piston-to-cylinder	0.045-0.065	—
clearance	(0.0018-0.0026)	—
Piston rings		
End gap		
Top and 2nd	0.30-0.45	—
	(0.012-0.018)	—
Oil	0.20-0.70	—
	(0.008-0.028)	—
Side clearance		
Top	0.04-0.08	—
	(0.002-0.003)	—
2nd	0.03-0.07	—
	(0.001-0.003)	—
Oil	0.02-0.06	—
	(0.0008-0.0024)	—
Valve		
Stem runout limit	—	0.01
	—	(0.0004)
Valve stem outside diameter		
Intake	6.975-6.990	—
	(0.2746-0.2752)	—
Exhaust	6.955-6.970	—
	(0.2738-0.2744)	—
Head diameter		
Intake	35.90-36.10	—
	(1.413-1.421)	—
Exhaust	29.90-30.10	—
	(1.216-1.224)	—
Face width	2.26	—
	(0.089)	—
Seat width	1.0-1.2	—
	(0.039-0.047)	—

(continued)

Table 2 ENGINE TOP END SERVICE SPECIFICATIONS (continued)

Item	Specifications mm (in.)	Wear limit mm (in.)
Head thickness		
Intake	1.0-1.4	—
	(0.039-0.055)	—
Exhaust	0.8-1.2	—
	(0.031-0.047)	—
Valve guide inside diameter		
Intake and	7.000-7.012	7.10
exhaust	(0.2756-0.2761)	(0.28)
Valve stem-to-guide clearance		
Intake	0.010-0.037	—
	(0.0004-0.0015)	—
Exhaust	0.030-0.057	—
	(0.0012-0.0022)	—
Valve springs		
Inner (all)	40.1	—
	(1.58)	—
Outer (all)	43.8	—
	(1.72)	—
Spring tilt limit	—	1.7
inner and outer	—	(0.067)

4

Table 3 ENGINE TOP END TIGHTENING TORQUES

Item	N•m	ft.-lb.
Cylinder head cover bolts	10	7.2
Camshaft sprocket bolts*	10	7.2
Camshaft chain tensioner		
Body bolts	10	7.2
End plug	20	14
Cylinder head		
Bolts	25	18
Acorn nuts	20	14
Cylinder block-to-crankcase		
8 mm nuts	22	16
10 mm nuts	38	28
Bolts	10	7.2
Engine mounting bolts		
Front mounting bracket bolts	58	43
Cylinder head-to-frame mounting bolts	58	43
Swing arm pivot bolt nut	100	73

* Apply Loctite 271 (red) before tightening screw.

CHAPTER FIVE

ENGINE LOWER END

This chapter describes service procedures for the following lower end components:

a. Crankcases.
b. Crankshaft.
c. Connecting rod.
d. Transmission (removal and installation).
e. Internal shift mechanism (removal and installation).

Prior to removing and disassembling the crankcase, clean the entire engine and frame with a good-grade commercial degreaser, like Gunk or Bel-Ray engine degreaser or equivalent. It is easier to work on a clean engine and you will do a better job.

Make certain that you have all the necessary tools available, especially any special tool(s), and purchase replacement parts prior to disassembly. Also make sure you have a clean place to work.

One of the more important aspects of engine overhaul is preparation. Improper preparation before and failing to identify and store parts during removal will cause a headache when it comes time to reinstall and assemble the engine. Before removing the first bolt and to prevent frustration during installation, get a number of boxes, plastic bags and containers and store the parts as they are removed (**Figure 1**). Also have on hand a roll of masking tape and a permanent, waterproof marking pen to label each part or assembly as required. If your bike was purchased second hand and it appears that some of the wiring may have been changed or replaced, it will be to your advantage to label each electrical connection before disconnecting it.

Throughout the text there is frequent mention of the right-hand and left-hand side of the engine. This refers to the engine as it sits in the bikes frame, *not* as it sits on your workbench. "Right-" and "left-hand" refers to a rider sitting on the seat facing forward.

Crankshaft service specifications are listed in **Table 1**. **Tables 1 and 2** are found at the end of the chapter.

SERVICING ENGINE IN FRAME

Some of the components can be serviced while the engine is mounted in the frame (the bike's frame is

a great holding fixture—especially for breaking loose stubborn bolts and nuts):

a. External gearshift mechanism.
b. Clutch.
c. Kickstarter.
d. Oil pump.
e. Carburetor.
f. Alternator and electrical systems.

ENGINE

Removal/Installation

If service work requires only the removal of top end component(s), the engine can remain in the frame, but the engine must be lowered in the frame to allow additional room for cylinder head cover removal. This procedure is described under *Lowering Engine in Frame* in Chapter Four.

If the engine requires crankcase disassembly, the engine must be removed from the frame. It will be easier to remove as many of the sub-assemblies from the exterior of the engine before removing the crankcase from the frame since the frame can be used as a holding fixture as the engine is disassembled. Attempting to disassemble the complete engine on top of a workbench is more time consuming and will require an assistant to help hold the engine while you loosen many of the *very tight* larger nuts and bolts.

1. Drain the engine oil as described under *Engine Oil and Filter Change* in Chapter Three.

2A. On XT600 models, remove the bolts securing the engine skid plate (**Figure 2**) and remove the skid plate.

2B. On TT600 models, remove the bolts securing the engine guard and remove the guard.

3. Support the bike on a stand and raise the rear wheel off the ground with a suitable wheel stand.

4. Remove the left- and right-hand side covers.

5. Remove the seat as described under *Seat Removal/Installation* in Chapter Thirteen.

6. Disconnect the battery negative (–) electrical terminal connector (**Figure 3**).

7. Remove the fuel tank (A, **Figure 4**) as described under *Fuel Tank Removal/Installation* in Chapter Eight.

8. Disconnect the carbon canister hose at the carburetor. Then remove the canister mounting bolts and remove the canister (B, **Figure 4**).

9. Remove the exhaust pipe and muffler assembly as described under *Exhaust System Removal/Installation* in Chapter Eight.

10. Remove the right-hand footpeg/brake pedal bracket assembly as described under *Rear Brake Pedal Removal/Installation* in Chapter Twelve.

11. Remove the horn as described under *Horn Removal/Installation* in Chapter Nine.

12. Disconnect the spark plug cap (**Figure 5**) from the spark plug and tie it up out of the way. Do *not* remove the spark plug.

13. Disconnect the crankcase breather pipe (**Figure 6**) from the cylinder head cover.

14. Remove the pinch bolt securing the shift lever (A, **Figure 7**) and pull the shift lever off the shaft. If the splined boss is tight on the shaft, spread the slot open with a screwdriver.

15. Remove the screws securing the drive sprocket cover (B, **Figure 7**) and remove the cover.

16. Remove the bolts securing the inlet oil hose fitting (**Figure 8**) to the side of the crankcase. Move the hose out of the way and remove the O-ring from the fitting.

17. Place the loose end of the hose in a sealable plastic bag. Close the end of the bag around the hose to prevent the entry of foreign matter and to catch any residual oil that may drain out of the hose.

18. Disconnect the crankcase ventilation hose at the crankcase (A, **Figure 9**) and remove the hose from the engine and frame.

19. Remove the bolts securing the outlet oil hose (B, **Figure 9**) to the top of the crankcase. Move the hose out of the way and remove the O-ring from the fitting.

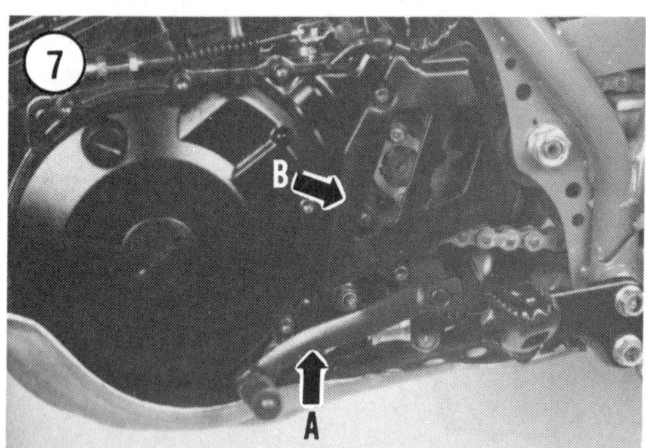

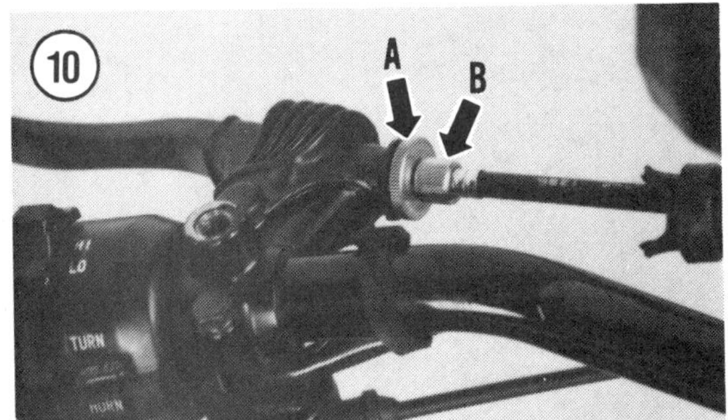

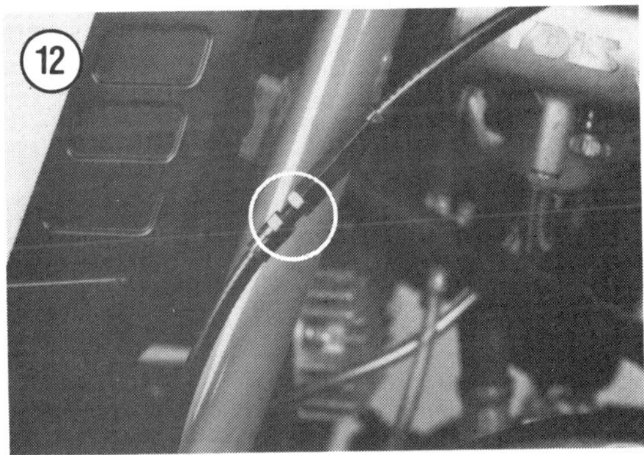

20. Place the loose end of the hose in a sealable plastic bag. Close the end of the bag around the hose to prevent the entry of foreign matter and to catch any residual oil that may drain out of the hose.

21. Slide back the rubber boot on the clutch lever.

22. Loosen the clutch cable adjuster locknut (A, **Figure 10**) and turn the adjuster (B, **Figure 10**) toward the clutch lever.

23. Disconnect the clutch cable at the crankcase release lever (C, **Figure 9**) and move the cable out of the way.

24A. On XT600 models, remove the bolts securing the tachometer drive unit (A, **Figure 11**) and remove the drive unit.

24B. On TT600 models, remove the bolts securing the cap and remove the cap.

25. Disconnect the decompression cable as follows:

a. Loosen the adjuster locknut and turn the adjuster (**Figure 12**) to obtain as much cable slack as possible.

b. Remove the bolt (B, **Figure 11**) securing the decompression relief lever and remove the lever (C, **Figure 11**) and spring.

c. Remove the screws securing the decompression cable lower lever cover (**Figure 13**) and remove the cover.

d. Remove the nut (A, **Figure 14**) securing the lever and disconnect the cable (B, **Figure 14**) from the lever. Remove the cable.

NOTE

If the drive chain is tight, loosen the rear axle nut, loosen the chain adjusters and push the rear wheel forward to allow drive chain slack.

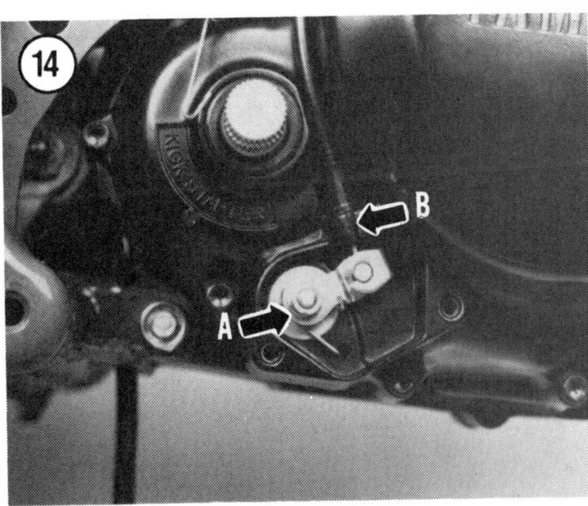

26. Remove the drive sprocket as follows:
   a. Remove the sprocket lockplate mounting bolts (**Figure 15**).
   b. Turn the sprocket lockplate (**Figure 16**) in either direction to clear the raised splines and slide it off of the transmission countershaft.
   c. Slide the drive sprocket and drive chain (**Figure 17**) off of the transmission countershaft.

27A. On XT600 models, disconnect the following electrical connectors (A, **Figure 18**):
   a. Charge coil/lighting coil connector.
   b. Source coil/pickup coil connector.
   c. Disconnect the electrical wire clamp(s) (B, **Figure 18**) from the wires and route the wiring harness away from the frame.

27B. On TT600 models, disconnect the following electrical connectors:
   a. Charge coil/lighting coil connector.
   b. Source coil/pickup coil connector.
   c. Disconnect the electrical wire clamp(s) from the wires and route the wiring harness away from the frame.

28. Remove the carburetor assembly as described under *Carburetor Removal/Installation* in Chapter Eight.

29. If the engine requires disassembly, remove the following sub-assemblies:
   a. Alternator stator and rotor assembly (Chapter Nine).
   b. Clutch (Chapter Six).
   c. Primary drive gear and balancer driven gear assemblies (this chapter).
   d. Kickstarter (Chapter Six).
   e. Oil pump (this chapter).

30. Remove the engine assembly from the frame as follows:

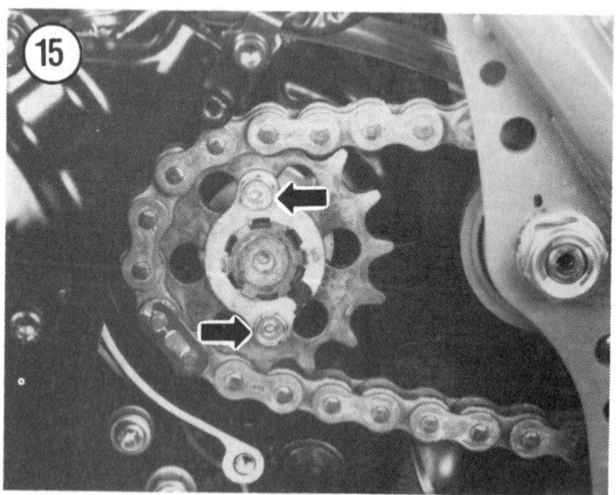

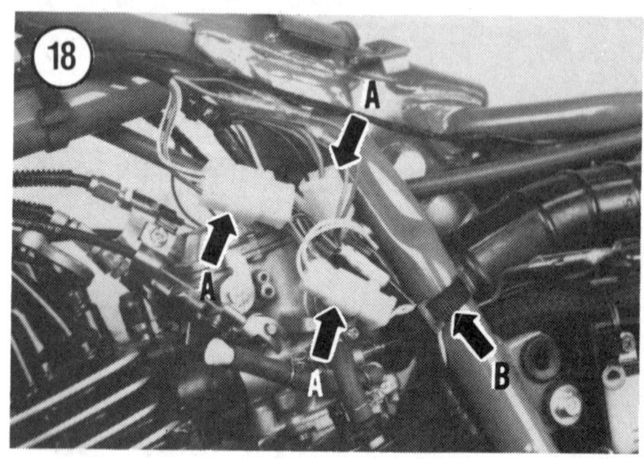

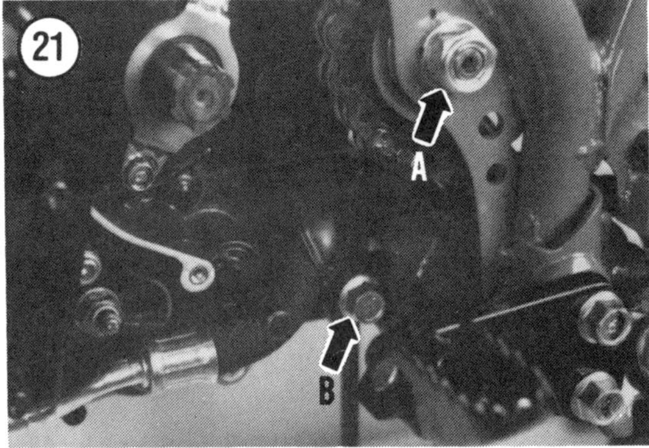

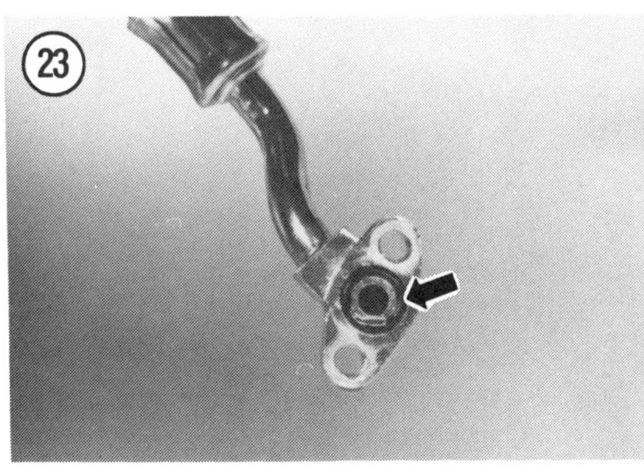

a. Place a hydraulic jack underneath the engine. Raise the jack so that the pad just rests against the bottom of the engine. Place a block of wood on the jack pad to protect the engine case. If you do not have access to a jack, place wood blocks underneath the engine. The idea is to have a support available when the engine mount bolts are loosened.

b. Remove the bolts, lockwashers and nuts securing the cylinder head-to-frame mount plates (**Figure 19**) and remove the plates.

c. Remove the bolts and locknuts securing the engine front mounting bracket (**Figure 20**) and remove the mounting bracket.

d. Loosen the engine-to-swing arm pivot shaft nut (A, **Figure 21**).

e. Remove the lower engine mount locknut and bolt (B, **Figure 21**).

f. Remove the engine-to-swing arm pivot shaft nut (A, **Figure 21**) and partially withdraw the pivot shaft (A, **Figure 22**) from the right-hand side. Only withdraw the pivot shaft enough to clear the engine crankcase mounting area.

g. Lift the engine (B, **Figure 22**) out of the right-hand side of the frame.

h. Push the pivot shaft back through the swing arm to hold it securely in place. Install the pivot bolt nut and hand tighten.

31. While the engine is removed, check the engine frame mounts for cracks or other damage.

32. Install by reversing these removal steps. Note the following.

33. Install all engine mounting bolts in from the left-hand side.

34. Tighten the engine mounting bolts to the torque specifications in **Table 2**. Tighten the pivot shaft nut to the torque specification in **Table 2**.

35. To minimize the chance of an oil leak, install *new* O-ring seals on the oil tank fittings. Refer to **Figure 23** for the inlet hose and **Figure 24** for the outlet hose.

36. Refill the engine oil as described in Chapter Three.

37. Adjust the following as described in Chapter Three:

a. Decompression cable.
b. Clutch cable.
c. Drive chain.
d. Rear brake pedal.

38. Start the engine and check for leaks.

CRANKCASE AND CRANKSHAFT

Disassembly of the crankcase—splitting the cases—and removal of the crankshaft assembly requires engine removal from the frame. However, the cylinder head, cylinder and all other attached assemblies should be removed with the engine in the frame as described in Chapter Four and this chapter.

The crankcase is made in 2 halves of precision diecast aluminum alloy and is of the "thin-walled" type. To avoid damage to them, do not hammer or pry on any of the interior or exterior projected walls. These areas are easily damaged if stressed beyond what they are designed for. They are assembled without a gasket; only gasket sealer is used while dowel pins align the crankcase halves when they are bolted together. The crankcase halves are sold as a matched set only. If one crankcase halve is severely damaged, both must be replaced.

The crankshaft assembly is made up of 2 full-circle flywheels pressed together on a hollow crankpin. The connecting rod big end bearing on the crankpin is a needle bearing assembly (**Figure 25**). The crankshaft assembly is supported by 2 ball bearings in the crankcase.

The procedure which follows is presented as a complete, step-by-step major lower end overhaul that should be followed if the engine is to be completely reconditioned.

Remember that the right- and left-hand side of the engine relates to the engine as it sits in the bike's frame, not as it sits on your workbench.

Special Tools

When installing the crankshaft into the left-hand crankcase, a special tool is required to pull the crankshaft back into the crankcase. Yamaha crankshaft installing set (part No. YU-90050) and the Yamaha adapter (part No. YU-91044) (**Figure 26**). These tools are used together to pull the crankshaft back into the crankcase assembly. Remember, the crankshaft and crankcase halves can be easily damaged by improper reassembly techniques.

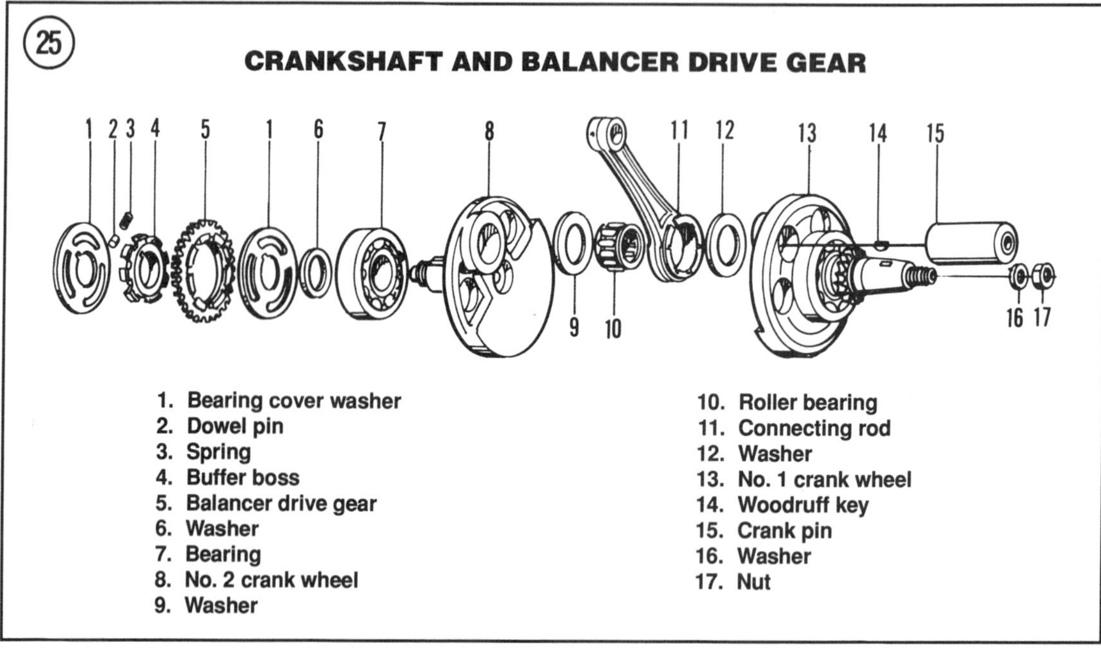

CRANKSHAFT AND BALANCER DRIVE GEAR

1. Bearing cover washer
2. Dowel pin
3. Spring
4. Buffer boss
5. Balancer drive gear
6. Washer
7. Bearing
8. No. 2 crank wheel
9. Washer
10. Roller bearing
11. Connecting rod
12. Washer
13. No. 1 crank wheel
14. Woodruff key
15. Crank pin
16. Washer
17. Nut

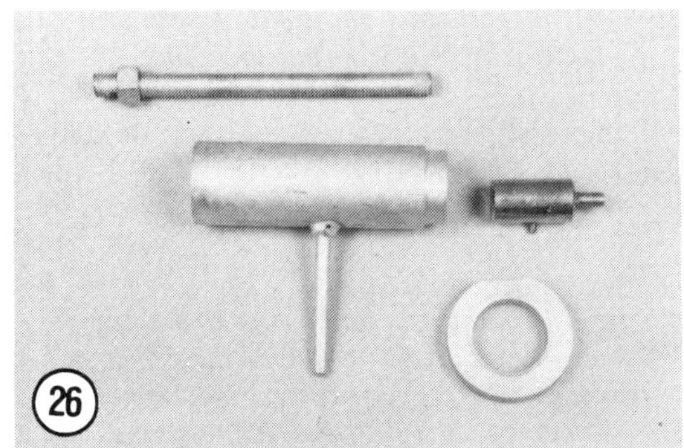

26

27

Crankcase Disassembly

This procedure describes disassembly of the crankcase halves and removal of the crankshaft, transmission shaft assemblies and the internal shift mechanism. Disassembly and reassembly of the transmission and the internal shift mechanism assemblies are described in Chapter Seven.

1. Remove all exterior engine assemblies from the crankcase assembly as described in this chapter and other related chapters.

2. Note the position of any hose clamps attached to the crankcase bolts. They must be reinstalled in the same location.

3. To prevent from damaging the countershaft oil seal when the countershaft is removed, install an O-ring in the drive sprocket lockplate groove in the end of the transmission countershaft.

4. Place the engine assembly on a couple of wood blocks with the left-hand side facing up (**Figure 27**).

5. Loosen all bolts on the left-hand side securing the crankcase halves together one-quarter turn. To prevent warpage, loosen them in the crisscross torque pattern shown in **Figure 28**.

28

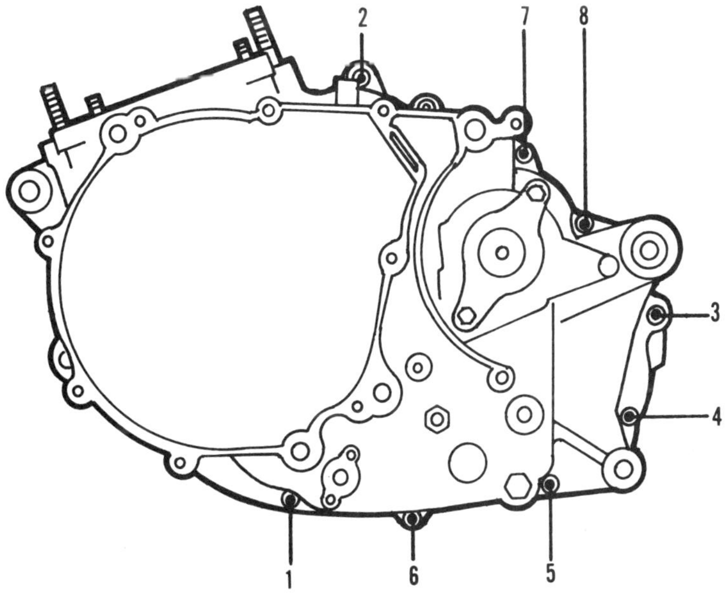

NOTE
To prevent losing the bolts and to ensure proper location during assembly, draw the left-hand crankcase outline on cardboard, then punch holes to correspond with bolt locations. Insert the bolts in their appropriate locations.

6. Remove all bolts loosened in Step 5. Be sure to remove all of them.
7. Turn the engine assembly over on a couple of wood blocks with the right-hand side facing up.
8. Loosen all bolts on the right-hand side securing the crankcase halves together one-quarter turn. To prevent warpage, loosen them in the circular torque pattern shown in **Figure 29**.

NOTE
To prevent losing the bolts and to ensure proper location during assembly, draw the right-hand crankcase outline on cardboard, then punch holes to correspond with bolt locations. Insert the bolts in their appropriate locations.

9. Remove all bolts loosened in Step 8. Be sure to remove all of them.

CAUTION
Perform this operation over and close down to the work bench as the crankcase halves may easily separate. ***Do not*** *hammer on the crankcase halves as they will be damaged.*

CAUTION
Pry points have been cast into the 2 crankcase halves. When prying the crankcase halves apart in Step 9, only pry between the pry points. ***Do not*** *pry between the crankcase mating surfaces. Doing so will result in oil leaks, requiring replacement of both case halves.*

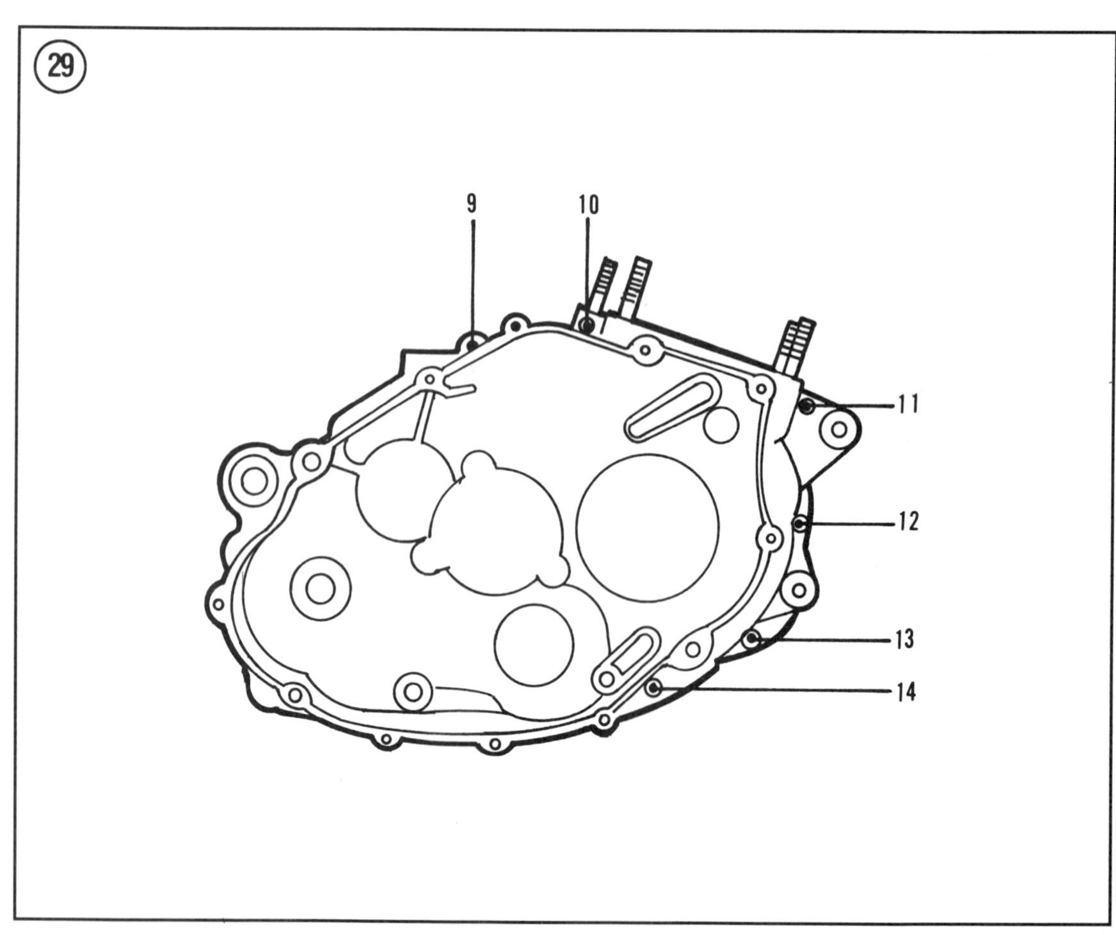

10. Use 2 large flat-tipped screwdrivers at the crankcase pry points and carefully pry the crankcase halves apart. Use a plastic, soft-faced or rubber mallet and tap the transmission shafts to help during crankcase separation.

11. Carefully lift the right-hand crankcase assembly off of the engine. The transmission, balancer shaft, crankshaft and internal shift mechanism will stay in the left-hand crankcase half.

NOTE
Check the crankshaft shafts and the right-hand crankcase half for shims that may have been installed by a previous owner. There are no factory installed shims on the outer portion of the transmission shafts, balancer shaft or crankshaft.

30

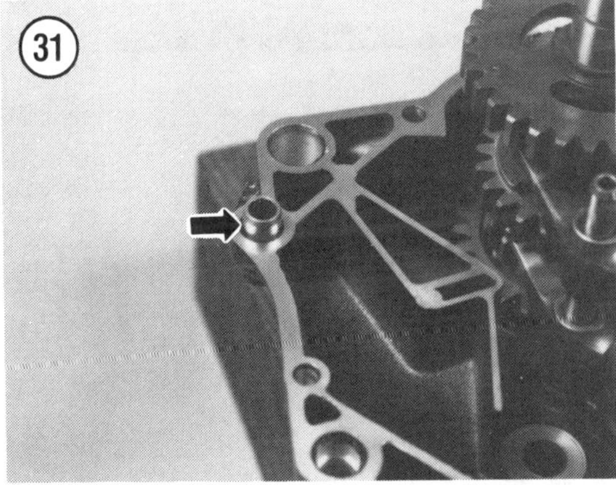
31

12. Remove the front dowel pin (**Figure 30**), the rear dowel pin (**Figure 31**) and the dowel pin and O-ring seal (**Figure 32**) from the left-hand crankcase half.

13. Remove the balancer shaft (**Figure 33**).

NOTE
The gearshift lever is subject to a lot of abuse on a dual-purpose bike that is ridden off-road. If the motorcycle has been in a hard spill, the gearshift lever may have been hit and the change shaft may have been bent. If the change shaft is bent, it is very hard to straighten without subjecting the crankcase to abnormal stress where the shaft enters the case. If the change shaft is bent enough to prevent it from being withdrawn from the crankcase, there is little recourse but to cut the change shaft off with a hacksaw very close to the crankcase. It is much cheaper in the long run to replace the change shaft than risk damaging a set of expensive crankcases. After cutting off the end of the shaft, use a file or rotary grinder to remove all burrs from the shaft before removing it.

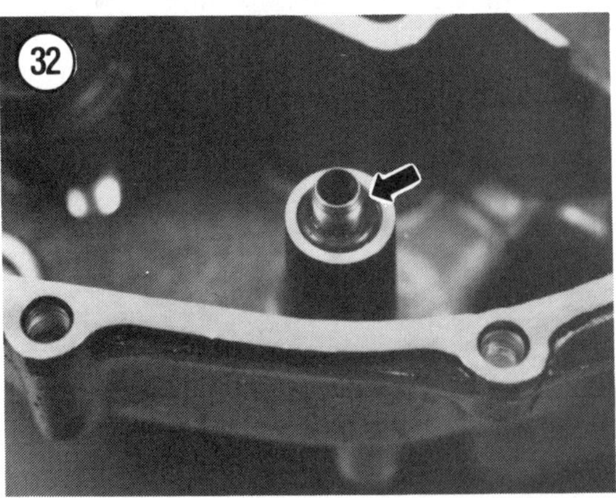
32

33

5

14. Remove the transmission and internal shift mechanism assembly as follows:

a. Remove the change shaft (A, **Figure 34**) and shift shaft (B, **Figure 34**).
b. Remove the No. 1 shift fork shaft (A, **Figure 35**).
c. Remove the No. 2 shift fork shaft (B, **Figure 35**).
d. Remove all 3 shift forks.
e. Remove the shift drum (C, **Figure 35**).

NOTE
It may be necessary to use a plastic, soft-faced or rubber mallet and tap the end of the transmission shafts in order to remove them from the crankcase.

f. Remove the 2 transmission shafts (**Figure 36**) as an assembly.

15. Remove the crankshaft (**Figure 37**) from the left-hand crankcase half. If the crankshaft will not separate from the crankcase easily, perform Step 16.

16. If the crankshaft will not separate easily from the crankcase, perform the following:

a. Thread the rotor holding bolt into the end of the crankshaft.
b. Install the crankcase separating tool into the threaded holes on the left-hand crankcase. Center the pressure bolt on the end of the crankshaft. Tighten the long separating bolts into the crankcase, making sure the tool body is parallel with the crankcase. If necessary, back out one of the long bolts.
c. Screw the puller *clockwise* and push the crankshaft out of the crankcase.
d. When the crankshaft is free of the crankcase bearing, remove it.

17. If necessary, remove the screws securing the oil pump strainer (A, **Figure 38**) and cap (B, **Figure 38**). Remove the strainer, cap and gasket (C, **Figure 38**).

18. On XT600 models, if necessary, remove the neutral indicator switch (**Figure 39**).

Crankcase Inspection

1. Remove the crankcase oil seals as described under *Bearing and Oil Seal Replacement* in this chapter.

CAUTION
When drying the crankcase bearings in Step 2, do not allow the inner bearing

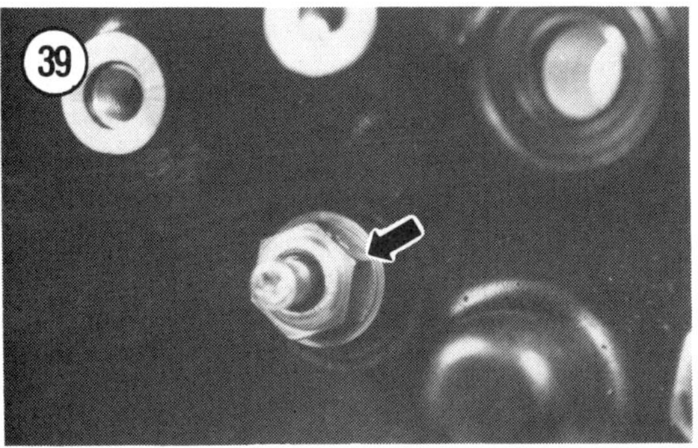

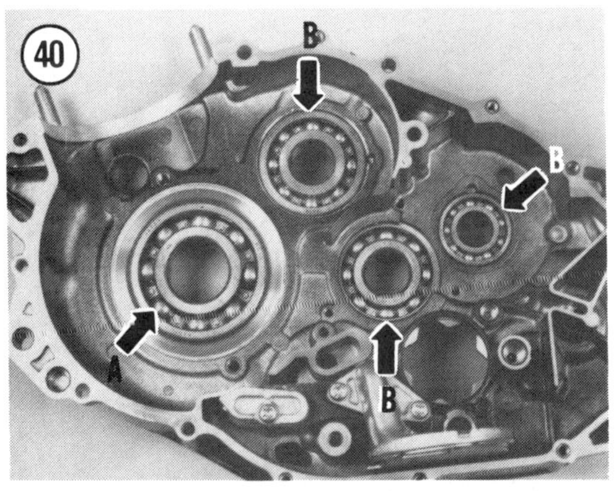

race to spin. The bearing will be dry of all lubrication and damage will result. When drying the bearings, hold the inner race with your hand.

CAUTION

In addition, when drying bearings with compressed air, never allow the air jet to rotate the bearing. The air jet is capable of rotating the bearing at speeds far in excess of those for which they were designed. The likelihood of a bearing disintegrating and causing serious injury and damage is very great.

2. Clean both crankcase halves inside and out and all crankcase bearings with cleaning solvent. Thoroughly dry with compressed air and wipe off with a clean shop cloth. Be sure to remove all traces of old gasket sealer from all mating surfaces.
3. Oil the crankshaft main bearings with engine oil before checking the bearings in Steps 4 and 5.
4. Check the crankshaft main bearings (A, **Figure 40**) for roughness, pitting, galling, and play by rotating them slowly by hand. If any roughness or play can be felt in the bearing, it must be replaced.

NOTE

Always replace both crankcase main bearings as a set.

5. Inspect all remaining bearings as described in the previous step. Refer to **Figure 41** and B, **Figure 40**.
6. Replace any worn or damaged bearings as described under *Bearing and Oil Seal Replacement* in this chapter.
7. Carefully inspect the crankcase halves for cracks and fractures, especially in the lower areas (**Figure 42**) where they are vulnerable to rock damage. Also,

check the areas around the stiffening ribs, around bearing bosses and threaded holes. If any are found, have them repaired by a shop specializing in the repair of precision aluminum castings or replace the crankcase halves.

8. Check the crankcase bolt threaded holes in both crankcase halves for thread damage or dirt or oil buildup. If necessary, clean or repair the threads with a suitable size metric tap. Coat the tap threads with kerosene or an aluminum tap fluid before use.

9. Check the crankcase studs (**Figure 43**) for tightness. Tighten securely if necessary. Inspect the threads for damage or dirt or oil buildup. If necessary, clean or repair the threads with a suitable size metric tap. Coat the tap threads with kerosene or an aluminum tap fluid before using tap.

10. Check the kickstarter stop for damage. Also check the stop bolts for tightness.

11. Inspect the oil pump receptacle in the right-hand crankcase half. Inspect the O-ring seal areas (A, **Figure 44**) and oil pump mounting bolt holes (B, **Figure 44**) for damage.

12. Make sure the oil tank oil line inlet opening (**Figure 45**) and outlet opening (**Figure 46**) are clear. If necessary, clean them out with a piece of wire and solvent, then blow out with compressed air.

Bearing and Oil Seal Replacement

1. Pry out the oil seals with a screwdriver. Refer to **Figure 47** and **Figure 48**. Place a rag or wood block underneath the screwdriver to prevent from damaging the crankcase. If the seals are old and difficult to remove, heat the cases as described later and use an awl to punch a small hole in the steel backing of the seal. Install a small sheet metal screw into the seal and pull the seal out with a pair of pliers.

CAUTION

Do not install the screw too deep or it may contact and damage the bearing behind it.

NOTE

An impact driver with a Phillips bit (described in Chapter One) will be required to loosen the bearing retainer plate screws described in Step 2. Attempting to loosen the screws with a Phillips screwdriver may ruin the screw heads, thus preventing them from being removed.

2. Some bearings and/or oil seals are held in position by a retainer plate (A, **Figure 49**). Remove the screws (B, **Figure 49**) securing the retainers before removing the bearings and/or oil seals. If it is not necessary to remove the bearings and/or oil seals, check the retainer plate screws for tightness, tighten if necessary.

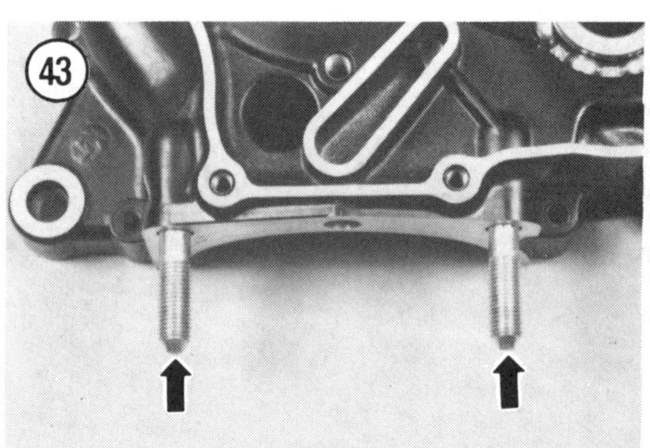

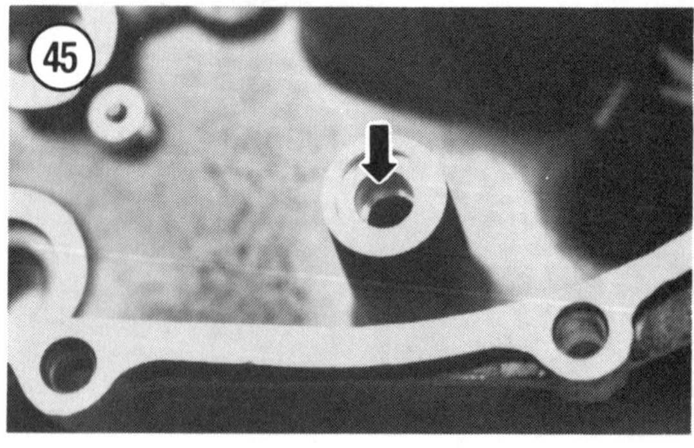

CAUTION
Before heating the crankcases in this procedure to remove the bearings, wash the cases thoroughly with detergent and water. Rinse and rewash the cases as required to remove all traces of oil and other debris.

CAUTION
Even though the crankcase has been washed, there **may** *be residual oil or a solvent odor left in the oven after heating the crankcase. If you use a household oven, first check with the person who uses the over for food preparation to avoid getting into trouble.*

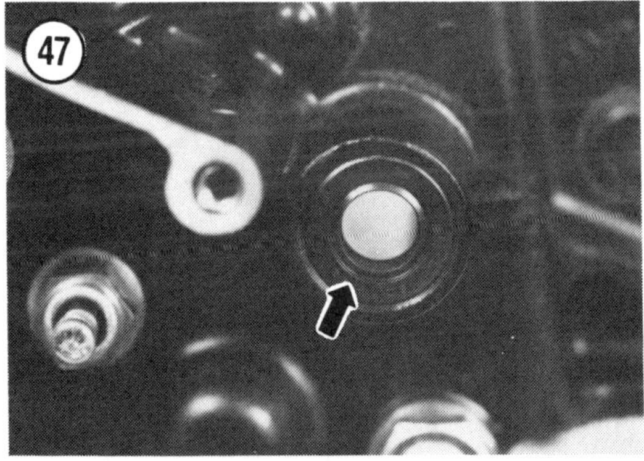

3. While heating up the crankcase halves, place the new bearings in a freezer for about one-half hour if possible. Chilling them will slightly reduce their overall diameter while the hot crankcase is slightly larger due to heat expansion. This will make installation much easier.

4. The bearings are installed with a slight interference fit. The crankcase must be heated to a temperature of about 212° F (100° C) in a shop oven or on a hot plate. An easy way to check to see that it is at the proper temperature is to drop tiny drops of water on the crankcase; if they sizzle and evaporate immediately, the temperature is correct. Heat only one crankcase half at a time.

CAUTION
Do not heat the cases with a torch (propane or acetylene)—never bring a flame into contact with the bearing or case. The direct heat will destroy the case hardening of the bearing and will likely warp the case half.

5. Remove the crankcase from the oven or hot plate and hold onto the 2 crankcase studs with a kitchen pot holder, heavy gloves, or heavy shop cloths—*it is hot.*

NOTE
A suitable size socket and extension works well for removing and installing bearings.

6. Hold the crankcase with the bearing side down and tap the bearing out. Repeat for all bearings in that case half.

NOTE
Prior to installing new bearing(s) or oil seal(s), apply a light coat of lithium based grease to the inside and outside to aid in installation. Be sure to apply the same grease to the lips of new oil seals.

7. While the crankcase is still hot, press the new bearing(s) into place in the crankcase by hand until it seats completely. If necessary, tap the bearings into the case with a suitable size socket placed on the outer bearing race. Do not drive the bearing in by tapping on the inner bearing race as the bearing will be damaged.

NOTE
Always install bearings with the manufacturer's mark or number facing outward or so that after the crankcase is assembled you can still see these marks.

NOTE
Pack all crankcase oil seals with a heat durable grease before installation.

8. Oil seals can be installed with a suitable size socket and extension. When installing oil seals, it is important to drive the seal in squarely. Drive the seals in until they are flush with the surrounding surface area of the crankcase.
9. Align the bearing and/or oil seal retainers with the crankcase. Apply Loctite 242 (blue) to the retainer screws and tighten them securely.

Crankshaft Inspection

1. Clean the crankshaft thoroughly with solvent. Dry the crankshaft thoroughly. Then lubricate all bearing surfaces with a light coat of engine oil to prevent rusting.
2. Check the crankshaft journals (A, **Figure 50**) and crankpin for scratches, heat discoloration or other defects.
3. Check the flywheel taper, threads and keyway (B, **Figure 50**) for damage. If necessary, clean or repair the threads with a suitable size metric tap. Coat the tap threads with kerosene or an aluminum tap fluid

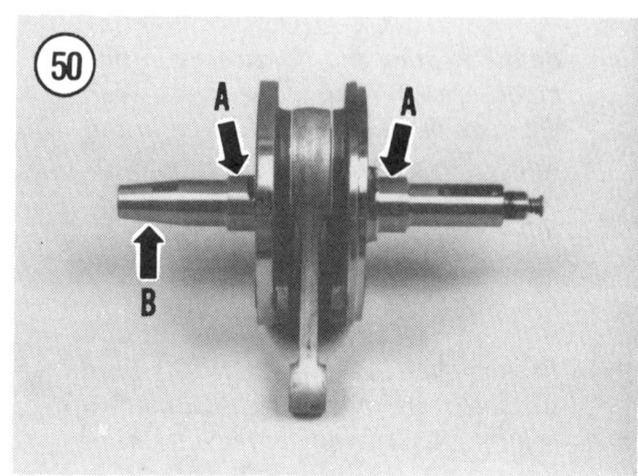

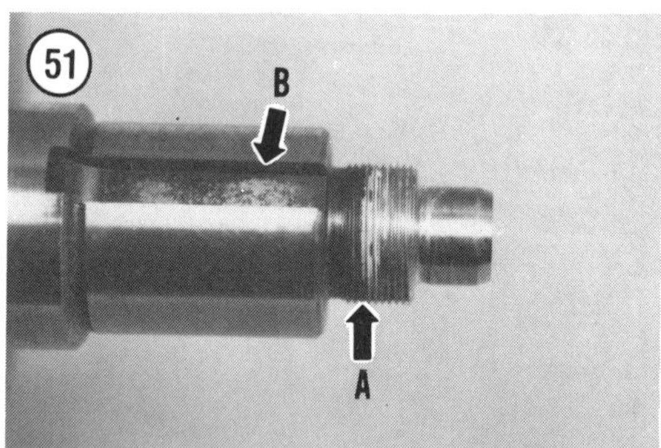

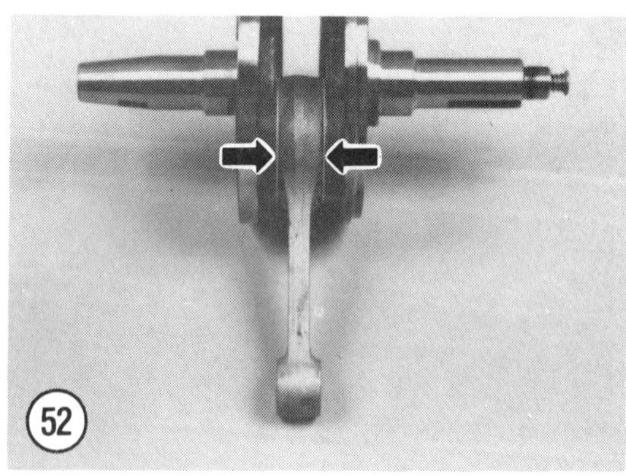

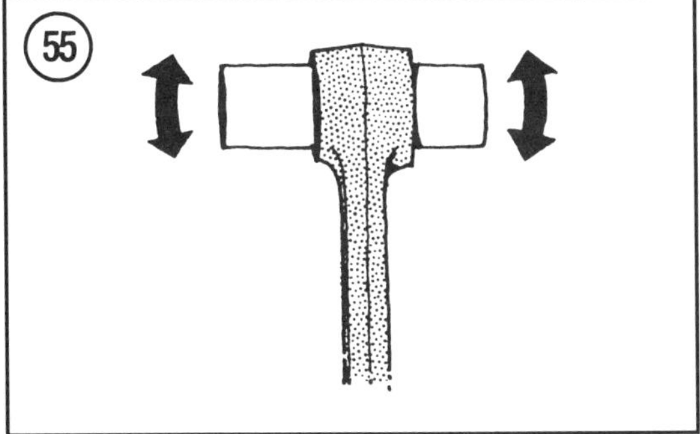

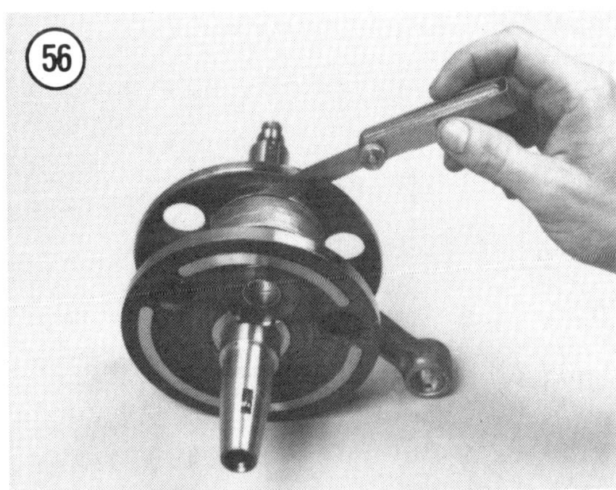

before using tap. If one crankshaft half is damaged, the crankshaft can be disassembled and the damaged part replaced as described in this chapter.

4. Check the balancer drive gear retaining nut threads (A, **Figure 51**) and keyway (B, **Figure 51**) for wear or damage. If one crankshaft half is damaged, the crankshaft can be disassembled and the damaged part replaced as described in this chapter.

5. Check the crankshaft oil seal surfaces for grooving, pitting or scratches.

6. Check the crankshaft bearing surfaces for chatter marks and excessive or uneven wear. Minor cases of chatter marks may be cleaned up with 320 grit carborundum cloth. If 320 cloth is used, clean crankshaft in solvent and check surfaces. If they did not clean up properly, disassemble the crankshaft and replace the damaged part.

7. Check the crankshaft lower end area (**Figure 52**) for signs of seizure, bearing or thrust washer damage or connecting rod damage.

8. Check the connecting rod small end (**Figure 53**) for signs of excessive heat (blue coloration) or other damage.

9. Apply engine oil to the piston pin and install the pin into the connecting rod (**Figure 54**). Slowly rotate the piston pin and check for radial play (**Figure 55**). If any play exists, the piston pin should be replaced, providing the rod bore is in good condition.

10. Slide the connecting rod to one side and check the connecting rod-to-crankshaft side clearance with a flat feeler gauge (**Figure 56**). Compare to dimensions given in **Table 1**. If the clearance is greater than specified, the crankshaft assembly must be disassembled and the connecting rod replaced.

11. Inspect the camshaft drive chain sprocket (**Figure 57**). Check the sprocket for worn or damaged gear teeth. Also check the teeth for cracking or rounding, replace if necessary.

NOTE
If the camshaft drive sprocket is worn, also check the camshaft sprocket, drive chain, chain guides and chain tensioner.

12. Check crankshaft runout with a dial indicator and V-blocks as shown in **Figure 58**. Retrue the crankshaft if the runout exceeds the service limit in **Table 1**.

13. If necessary, overhaul the crankshaft as described in this chapter.

Crankshaft Overhaul

Crankshaft overhaul requires a hydraulic press of 30 ton capacity, holding jigs, crankshaft alignment jig, dial indicators and a micrometer or vernier caliper. The crankshaft assembly is shown in **Figure 59**.

1. Measure the crank wheel width with a micrometer or vernier caliper (**Figure 60**). Record the measurement so that it can be used during crankshaft reassembly.
2. Mark the side of the crank wheels with machinist blue. When the fluid has dried, scribe alignment marks across both crankwheels with a square and a scribe (**Figure 61**). These marks can be used to help align the crank wheels during its initial assembly.
3. Place the crankshaft assembly in a suitable jig so that it is perfectly flat. Then press out the crankpin. Use an adapter between the press and crankpin. See

(58)

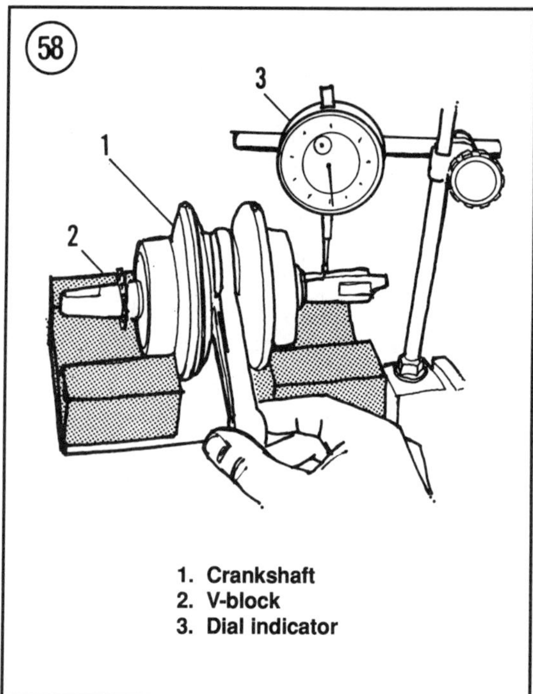

1. Crankshaft
2. V-block
3. Dial indicator

(59)

CRANKSHAFT

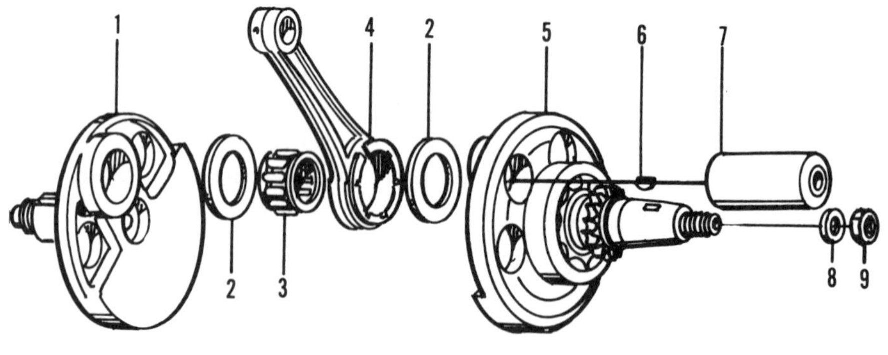

1 4 2 5 6 7
2 3 8 9

1. No. 2 crank wheel
2. Washer
3. Roller bearing
4. Connecting rod
5. No. 1 crank wheel
6. Woodruff key
7. Crank pin
8. Washer
9. Nut

Figure 62. Make sure to catch the lower crank half and crankpin assembly.

WARNING

When pressing the crankpin out, check that the crankshaft assembly remains flat. Because of the amount of force required to disassembly the crankshaft, the jig may bend slightly and side load the pin. This is dangerous and must be avoided. If the jig starts to bend, you will have to use stiffer material to support the crankshaft.

4. Remove the spacers, connecting rod and lower end bearing (**Figure 63**).

60

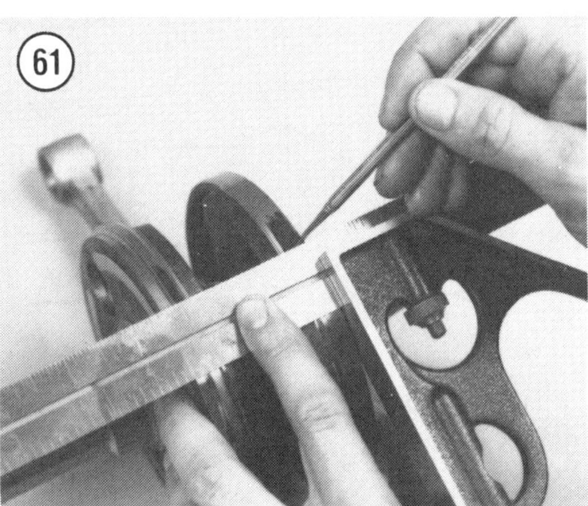

61

62

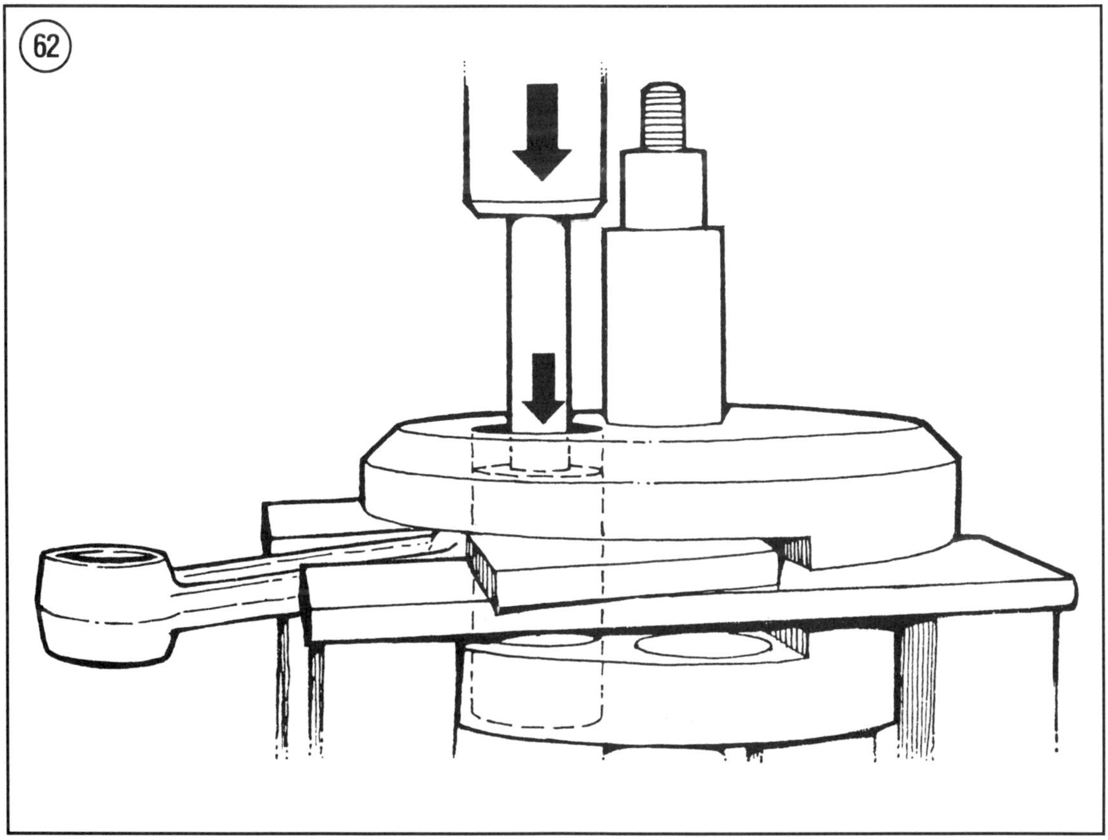

63

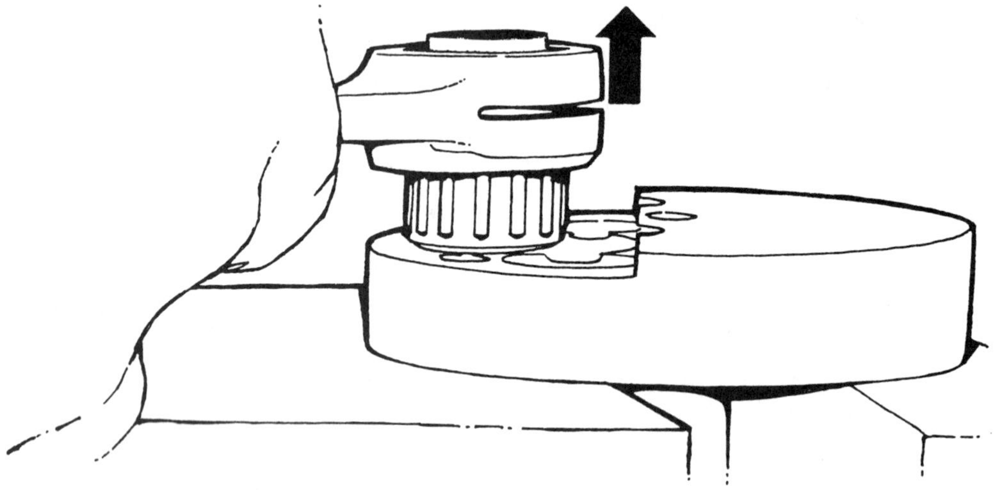

64

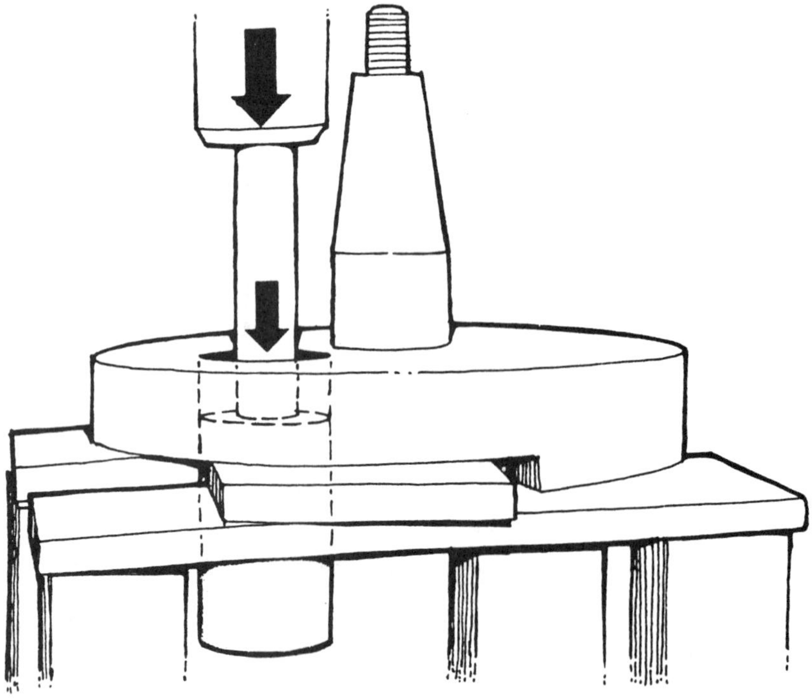

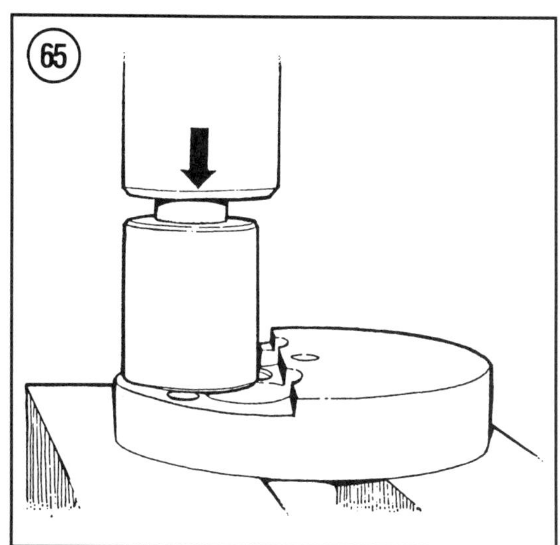

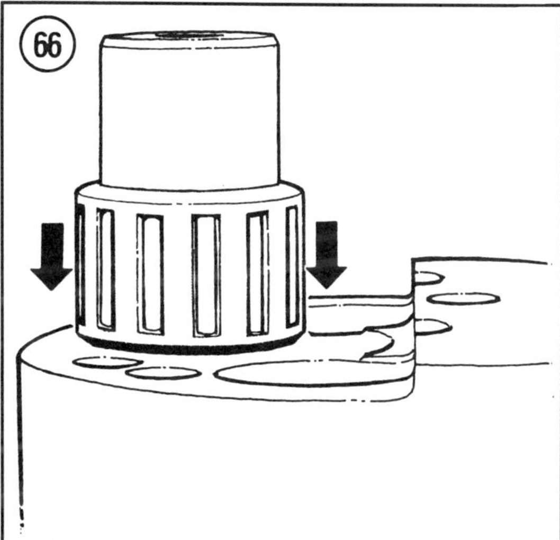

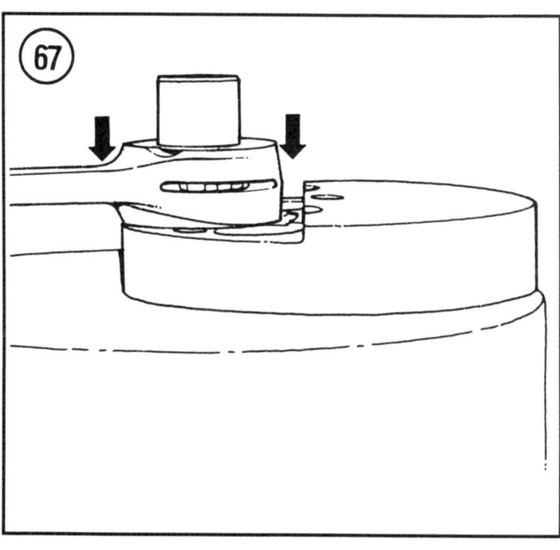

5. Press out the crankpin (**Figure 64**).

6. Wash the crankshaft assembly components thoroughly in solvent and dry.

CAUTION
When assembling the crankshaft assembly, the oil passages in the crank pin and the crank half must be aligned within 1 mm (0.04 in.).

NOTE
When reassembling the crankshaft, apply white assembly grease to all bearing surfaces.

5

7. Using a suitable alignment fixture, press the replacement crankpin into one crank half (**Figure 65**) until the crankpin is flush with the outside of the crank half.

8. Install a spacer and the needle bearing over the crankpin (**Figure 66**).

9. Install the connecting rod (**Figure 67**) and the remaining spacer. There is no front or back to the connecting rod; it fits either way.

10. Using a small square and the marks made during disassembly (**Figure 68**), start pressing the crank half onto the crankpin.

11. Insert a suitable size feeler gauge between the upper thrust washer and the crank half (**Figure 69**). Then continue pressing the crank half onto the crankpin until the feeler gauge fits tightly. Refer to connecting rod side clearance in **Table 1** for clearance.

12. Release all pressure from the press. The feeler gauge will then slip out easily.

13. Measure crank wheel width (**Figure 60**) and compare to the specifications recorded in Step 1. Use this measurement as a guide only. The connecting rod side clearance should be the determining factor when assembling the crankshaft assembly.

14. Check and adjust crankshaft alignment as described in this chapter.

Crankshaft Alignment

After overhauling the crankshaft or when disassembling the engine, it is important to check crankshaft alignment and adjust as required so that both crank halves and the shafts extending from them all rotate on a common center. The crankshaft should

68

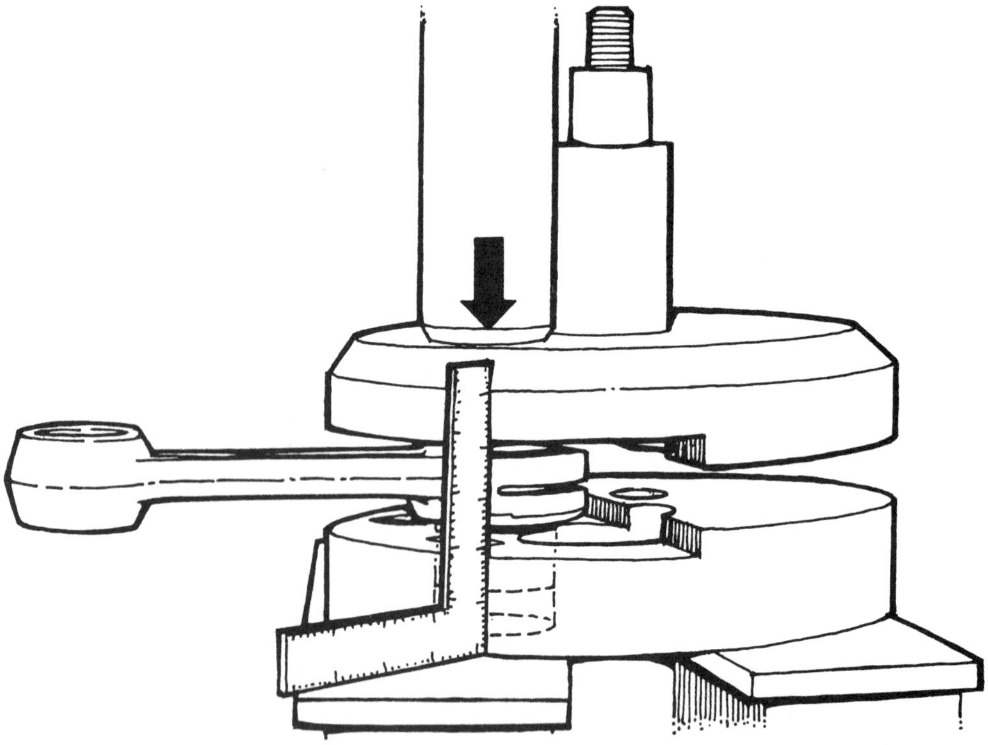

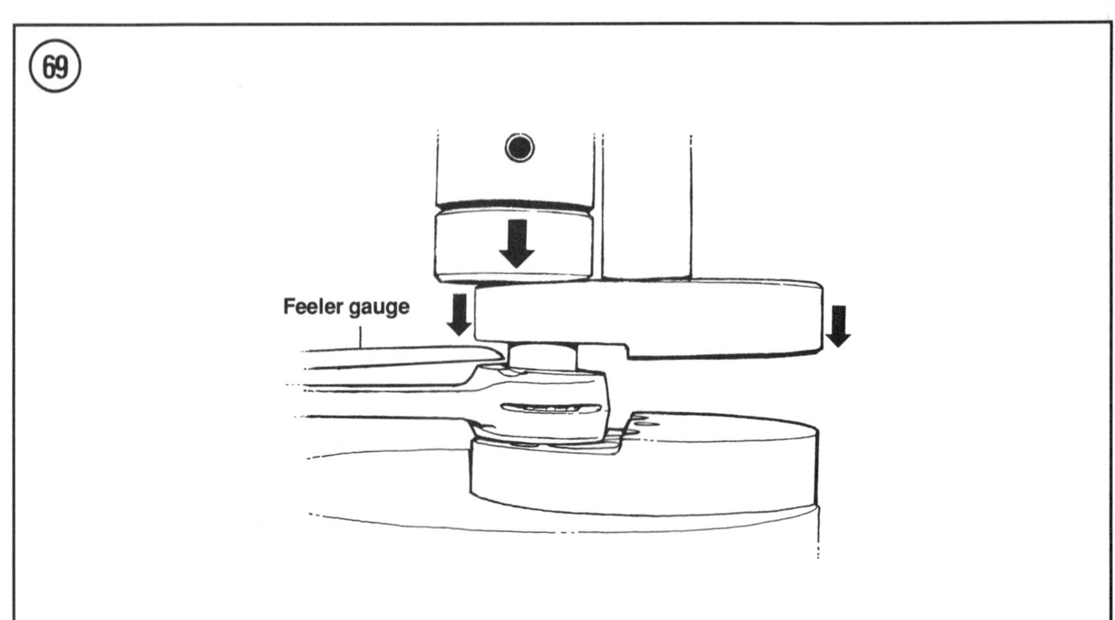

be checked for runout and wheel deflection as follows.

Mount the assembled crankshaft in a suitable fixture or on V-blocks using 2 dial indicators (**Figure 70**). Slowly rotate the crankshaft through one or more complete turns and observe both dial indicators. One of several conditions will be observed:

1. *Runout*: Neither dial indicator needle begins its swing at the same time, and the needles will move in opposite directions during part of the crankshaft rotation cycle. Each needle will probably indicate a different amount of total travel. This condition is caused by eccentricity (both crank wheels not being on the same center). To correct, slowly rotate the crankshaft assembly until the drive side dial gauge indicates its maximum. Mark the rim of the drive side crank wheel at the point in line with the plungers on both dial indicators.

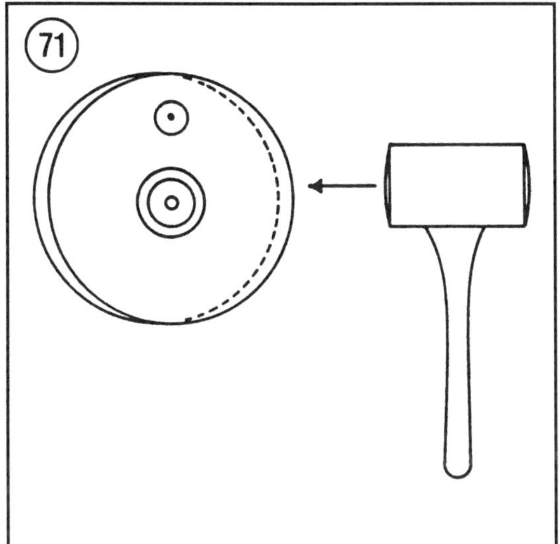

Remove the crankshaft assembly. Then, while holding one side of the crankshaft, strike the chalk mark a sharp blow with a brass hammer (**Figure 71**). Recheck alignment after each blow, and continue this procedure until both dial gauges begin and end their swings at the same time.

CAUTION

Make sure that only a brass-faced hammer is used to strike the crankshaft wheels. A lead hammer will damage the crankshaft wheels, requiring replacement.

2. *Wheel deflection*: The crank wheels can become pinched or spread. This condition can be checked by measuring crank wheel width (**Figure 60**) at various spots or by checking runout with 2 dial indicators (**Figure 72** and **Figure 73**). When checking in an

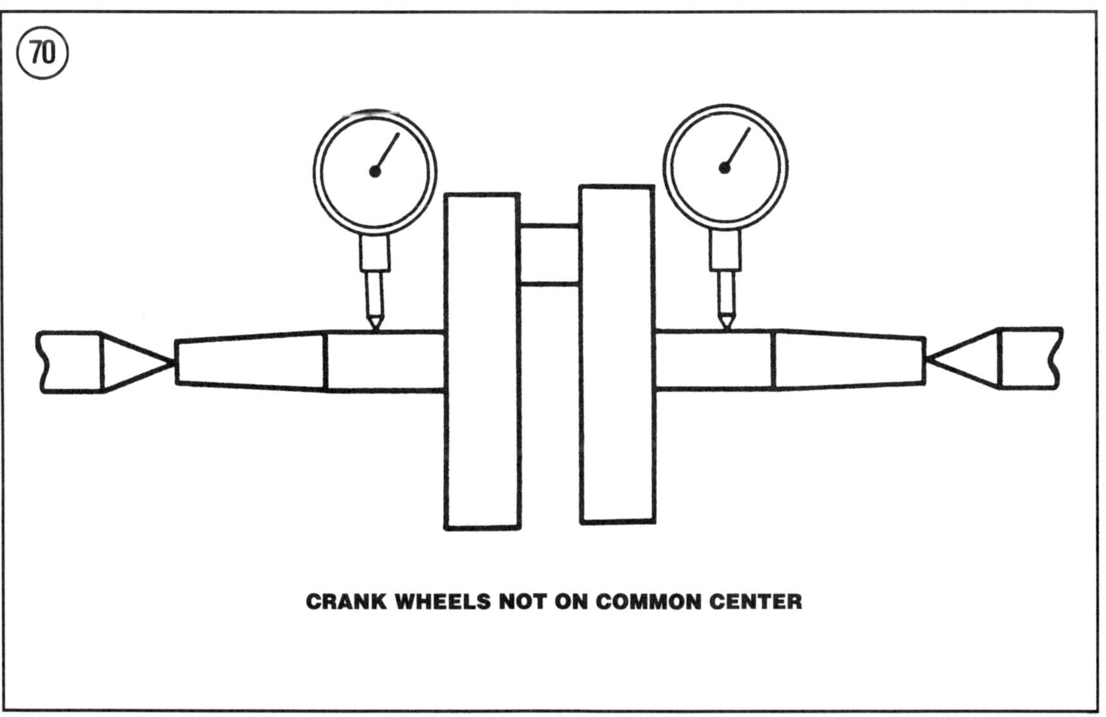

5

(72)

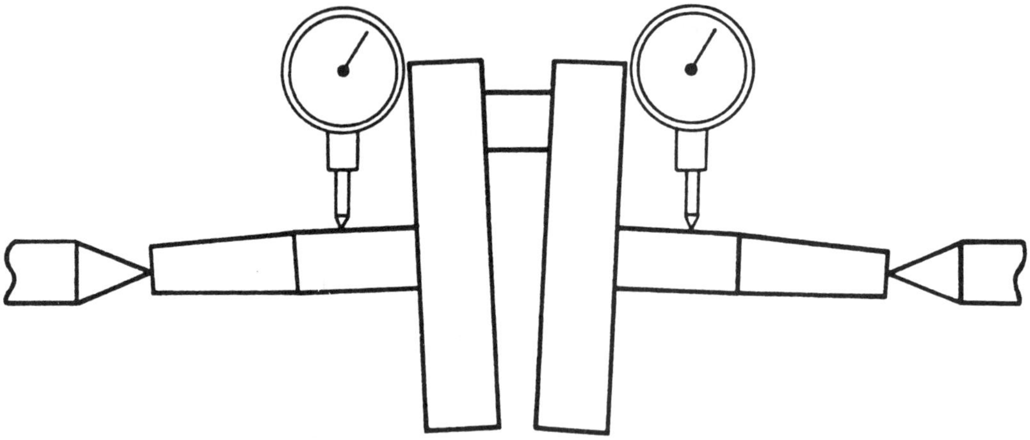

CRANK WHEELS PINCHED TOGETHER

(73)

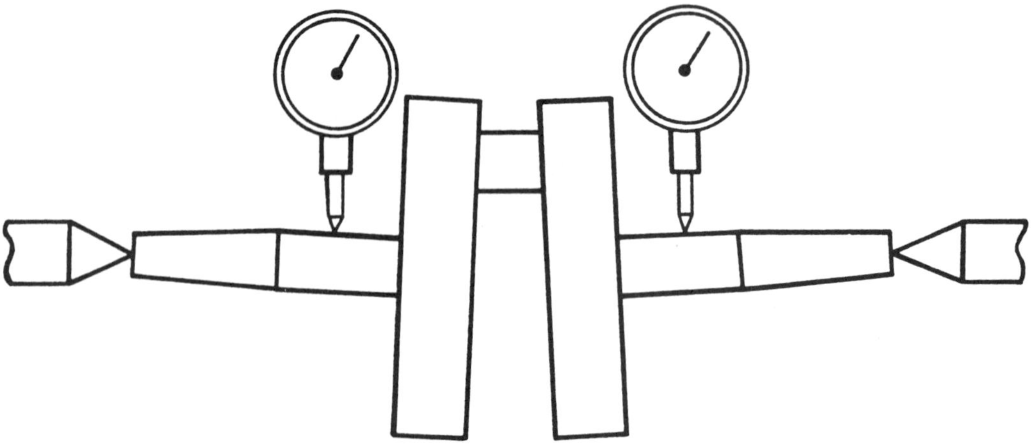

CRANK WHEELS SPREAD APART

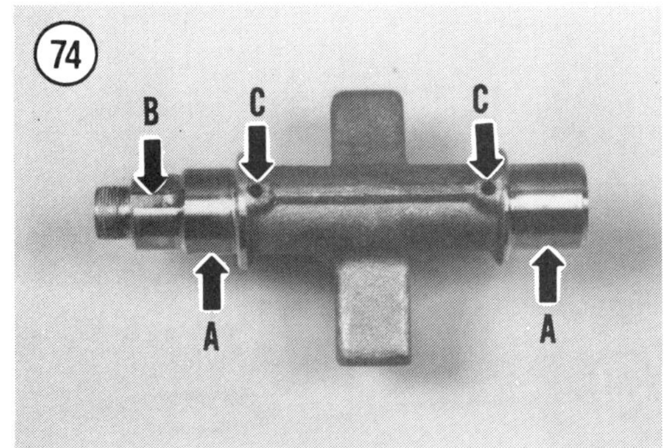

alignment jig, both dial indicators will indicate maximum travel when the crankpin is toward the dial gauges if the crank wheels are pinched. Correct the condition by removing the crankshaft assembly from the fixture. Then drive a wedge or chisel between the two crank wheels at a point opposite maximum dial gauge indication. Recheck alignment after each adjustment. Continue until the dial gauges indicate no more than 0.03 mm (0.0010 in.) runout.

If the dial gauges indicated their maximum when the crankpin was on the side of the alignment jig away from the dial gauges, the crank wheels are spread. Correct this condition by tapping the outside of one of the wheels toward the other with a brass hammer. Recheck alignment after each blow. Continue adjustment until runout is within 0.03 mm (0.0010 in.) runout.

NOTE

When adjusting wheel deflection, it will be necessary to check and adjust runout as required.

Balancer Shaft Inspection

1. Check the balancer shaft bearing journals (A, **Figure 74**) for deep scoring, excessive wear, heat discoloration or cracks.
2. Check the keyway (B, **Figure 74**) in the end of the balancer shaft for cracks or excessive wear.
3. Make sure the oil holes (C, **Figure 74**) are clear. Clean out with a piece of wire and solvent, then blow out with compressed air.
4. Check the balancer driven gear retaining nut threads (**Figure 75**) for wear or damage. If necessary, clean or repair the threads with a suitable size metric tap. Coat the tap threads with kerosene or an aluminum tap fluid before using tap.
5. Replace the balancer shaft if necessary.

Crankcase Assembly

1. On XT600 models, if removed, install the neutral indicator switch (**Figure 76**) and tighten securely.
2. If removed, install a new gasket (A, **Figure 77**), the cap (B, **Figure 77**) and the oil pump strainer (C, **Figure 77**). Install the screws and tighten securely.
3. Pack all of the crankcase oil seals with a heat durable grease.

4. Apply engine oil to both crankshaft main bearings.
5. If using the Yamaha special tool set, you will need the following: the installing set (part No. YU-90050/XT600) or (part No. YU-90069/TT600), the pot spacer (part No. YM-91044/XT600) or (part No. YU-90069/TT600). Also needed for the TT600 model is the No. 10 adapter (part No. YU-90069). Install the crankshaft into the left-hand crankcase as follows:

NOTE
*If you do not have access to the Yamaha crankshaft installing set shown in **Figure 78**, a tool can be fabricated using the parts shown in **Figure 79**. It is important to note that the long threaded bolts must have a metric thread size of M10 × 1.25. If you cannot find a metric bolt of this size, purchase a 5/8 in. threaded rod and have one end rethreaded to the metric size M10 × 1.25. This can be done by a machine shop. The long nut used to connect the 2 bolts can be made by drilling and tapping a piece of hex stock.*

CAUTION
If you do not have access to a tool, have the crankshaft installed by a dealer or machine shop. Do not drive the crankshaft into the bearing. Do not drive the crankshaft into the crankcase with a hammer.

a. Apply a light coat of engine oil to the left-hand crankshaft bearing journal.
b. Place the left-hand crankcase assembly on wood blocks. Then insert the crankshaft into the main bearing so that the crankshaft assembly is square with the crankcase mating surface. Using hand pressure only, push the crankshaft into the bearing until it stops.
c. Tilt the crankcase assembly up and install the crankshaft installing set.

CAUTION
*When installing the crankshaft, make sure to position the connecting rod at top dead center (TDC) (**Figure 80**). If the connecting rod turns sideways it could catch onto the side of the crankcase; this would damage the connecting rod and the crankcase.*

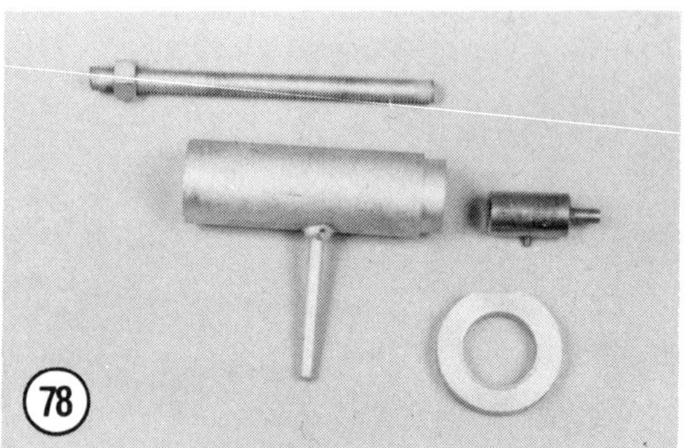
78

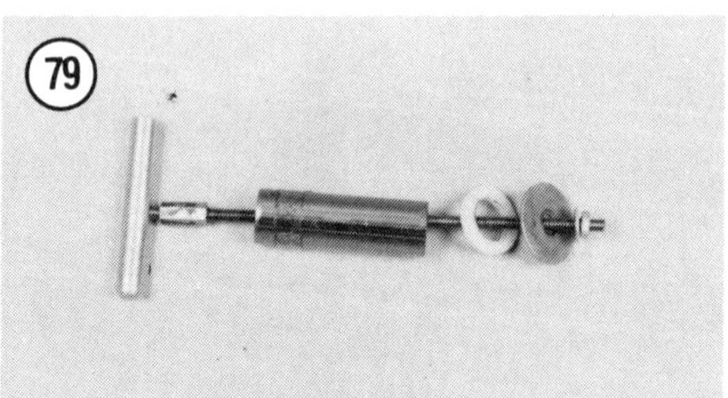
79

80

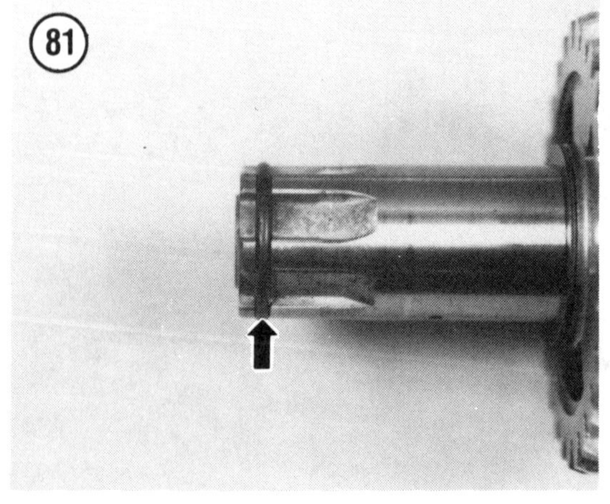
81

82

83

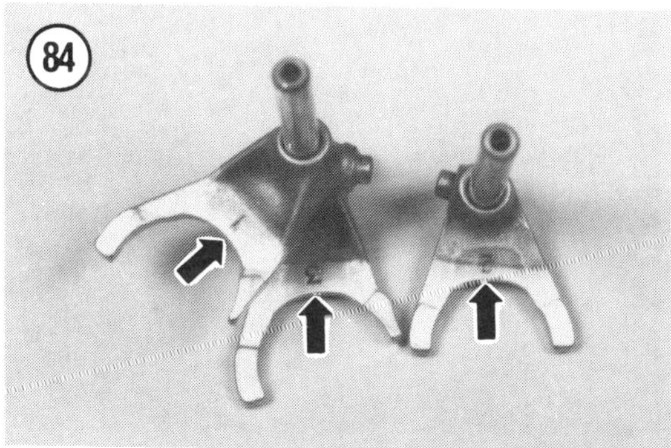
84

85

d. Using the crankshaft installing set, pull the crankshaft into the crankcase. Check the crankshaft often to make sure it is being pulled straight in with no side load. Pull the crankshaft until it is completely seated in the crankcase.

e. After installing the crankshaft, remove the crankshaft tool. Then spin the crankshaft. It should turn freely without any signs of roughness or noise.

6. Place the left-hand crankcase and crankshaft assembly onto wood blocks.

7. Apply engine oil to the inner race of all bearings in the left-hand crankcase half.

8. Install the transmission and internal shift mechanism as follows:

a. If removed, install an O-ring onto the end of the countershaft as shown in **Figure 81**. The O-ring will prevent the possibility of damaging the countershaft oil seal when the shaft is installed.

NOTE

There are no factory-installed shims on the outside of the gears that are not secured by a circlip. However, a previous owner may have re-shimmed the transmission and there may be shims placed on the outside of the circlips or gear. If this is the case, make sure you do not drop a shim into the case when installing the transmission shafts.

b. Mesh the transmission shafts together (**Figure 82**) and install the transmission assembly into the left-hand crankcase bearings. After the transmission shafts have been installed, use a soft-faced or plastic mallet and tap on the end of both shafts (**Figure 83**) to make sure the shafts are completely seated.

NOTE

*The shift forks are labeled with an embossed number (**Figure 84**) on one side. Install the shift forks so that the number faces down (facing toward the left-hand side).*

c. To avoid confusion relating to the correct placement of the shift forks (**Figure 85**), refer to **Figure 86**. This shows the shift forks and the shift fork shafts in place without the transmission shafts and shift drum blocking the view.

d. Engage the No. 1 shift fork (A, **Figure 87**) and the No. 2 shift fork (B, **Figure 87**) countershaft gears.
e. Engage the No. 3 shift fork with the main shaft gear (**Figure 88**).
f. Pivot each of the shift forks away from the center of the area where the shift drum will be located.
g. Insert the shift drum into the blind hole in the case (**Figure 89**).
h. Engage the pin on the No. 1 shift fork with the bottom shift drum groove (A, **Figure 90**).
i. Engage the pin on the No. 3 shift fork with the top shift drum groove (B, **Figure 90**).
j. Engage the pin on the No. 2 shift fork with the middle shift drum groove (**Figure 91**).
k. Install the No. 1 shift fork shaft (A, **Figure 92**) through the No. 2 shift fork.
l. Install the No. 2 shift fork shaft (B, **Figure 92**) through the No. 3 and No. 1 shift forks.
m. Make sure both shift forks are seated completely in the crankcase.

92

93

94

95

NOTE

Step 9 is best done with the aid of a helper as the assemblies are loose and don't want to spin very easily. Have the helper spin the transmission shaft while you turn the shift drum through all the gears.

9. Spin the transmission shafts and shift through the gears using the shift drum. Make sure you can shift into all gears. This is the time to find that something may be installed incorrectly—not after the crankcase is completely assembled.

10. After making sure the transmission shifts into all of the gears correctly, shift the transmission assembly into NEUTRAL. On XT600 models, the shift drum tab will align with the neutral switch (**Figure 93**) in the crankcase.

11. Install the balancer shaft (**Figure 94**).

12. Install the front dowel pin (**Figure 95**) and the rear dowel pin (**Figure 96**) into the left-hand crankcase half.

13. Install a new O-ring seal (**Figure 97**) on the dowel pin and install the dowel pin and O-ring seal

96

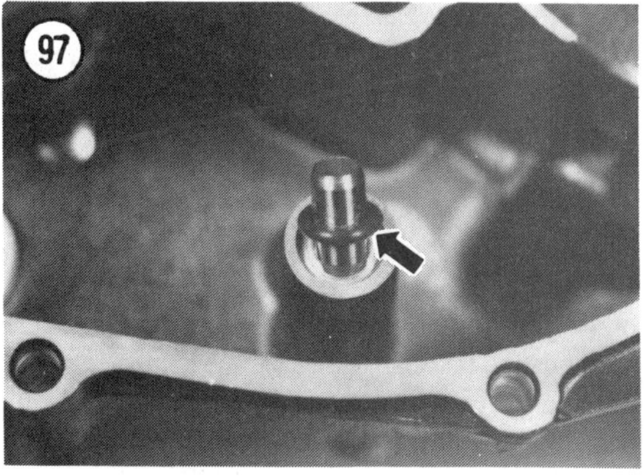

97

(**Figure 98**) into the oil tank oil line inlet opening in the left-hand crankcase half.

14. Install the change shaft (**Figure 99**).

15. Install the shift shaft (A, **Figure 100**) and align the index marks (B, **Figure 100**) on the two shafts. These marks must align otherwise the transmission will not shift properly.

NOTE

Make sure both crankcase mating surfaces are clean and free of all old gasket material. This is to make sure you get a leak free seal.

16. Apply a light coat of a black *non-hardening liquid gasket* such as Three Bond (**Figure 101**) or equivalent to the mating surfaces of both crankcase halves.

17. Set the right-hand crankcase half over the left-hand crankcase half on the blocks. Push it down squarely into place until it engages the dowel pins and then seats completely against the left-hand crankcase half.

CAUTION

Crankcase halves should fit together without force. If the crankcase halves do not fit together completely, do not attempt to pull them together with the crankcase screws. Separate the crankcase halves and investigate the cause of the interference. If the transmission shafts were disassembled, recheck to make sure that a gear is not installed backwards. Crankcase halves are a matched set and are very expensive. Do not risk damage by trying to force the cases together.

18. Install the crankcase bolts in the right-hand crankcase and tighten only finger-tight at this time.

19. Turn the crankcase assembly over and install the bolts in the left-hand crankcase. Tighten only finger-tight at this time.

20. Tighten the bolts in the left-hand crankcase in 2 stages in the order shown in **Figure 102**. Tighten to the torque specification listed in **Table 2**.

21. Turn the crankcase assembly over and tighten the bolts in the right-hand crankcase in 2 stages in the order shown in **Figure 103**. Tighten to the torque specification listed in **Table 2**.

22. After the crankcase halves are completely assembled, rotate the crankshaft and transmission shafts to

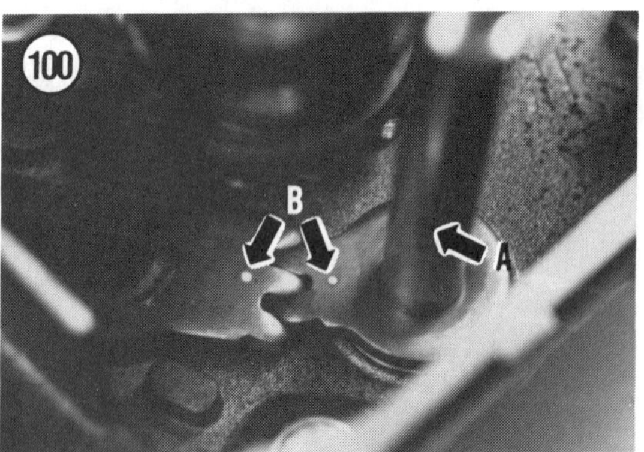

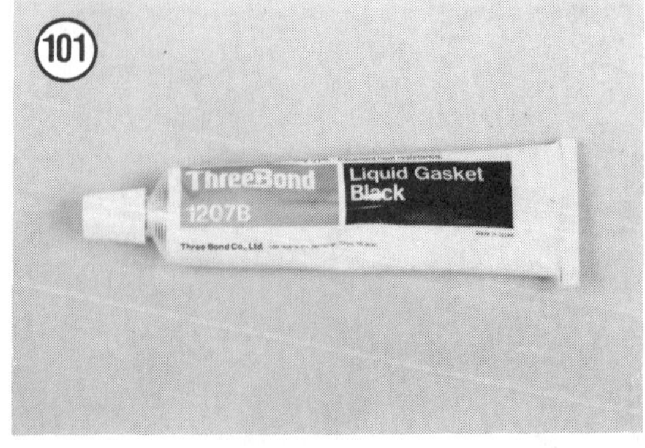

102

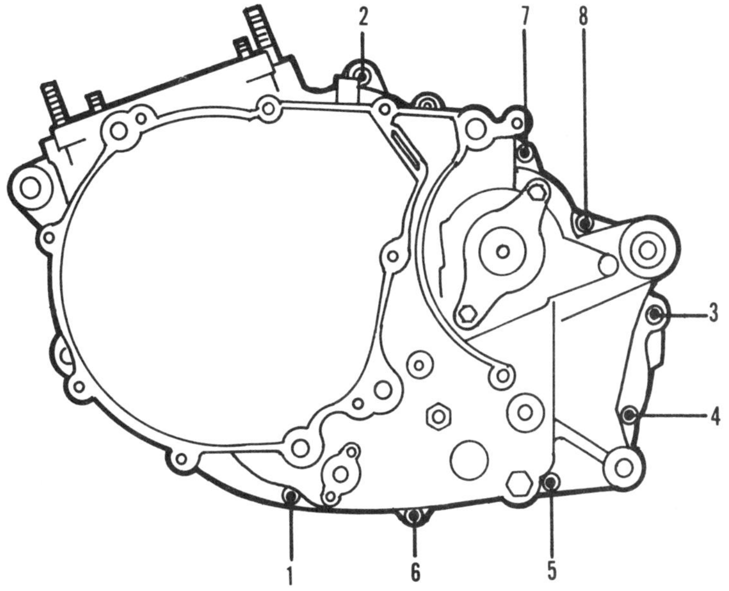

103

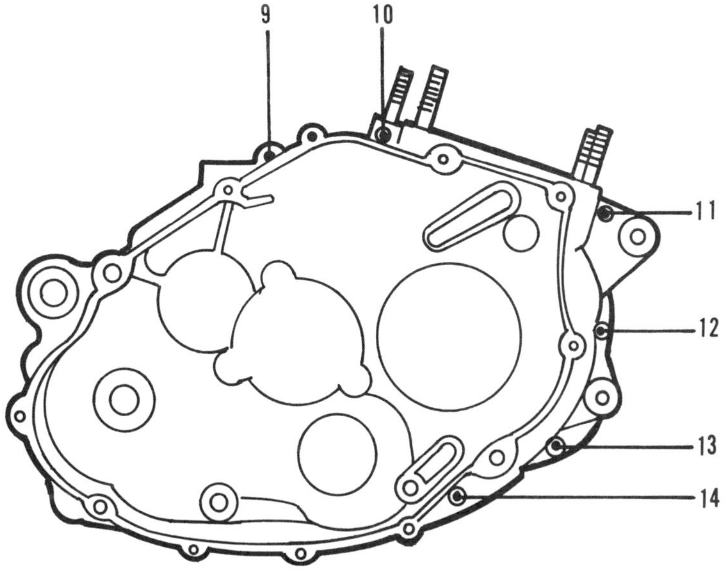

make sure there is no binding. If any is present, disassemble the crankcase and correct the problem.

23. Remove the O-ring from the end of the countershaft.

24. Install all exterior engine assemblies as described in this chapter and other related chapters.

BREAK-IN PROCEDURE

If the piston rings were replaced, a new piston installed, the cylinder rebored or honed (XT600 models) or new liner installed (TT600 models) or major lower end work performed, the engine should be broken in just as though it were new. The performance and service life of the engine depends greatly on a careful and sensible break-in.

During break-in, oil consumption will be higher than normal. It is therefore important to frequently check and correct the oil level (Chapter Three). At no time during the break-in or later should the oil level be allowed to drop below the minimum level. If the oil level is low, the oil will become overheated resulting in insufficient lubrication and increased wear.

For the first 300 miles (500 km), do not operate the engine above 4,000 rpm. Yamaha recommends to stop the engine and allow it to cool for approximately 5 to 10 minutes after each one hour of operation. Prolonged steady running at one speed, no matter how moderate, is to be avoided as well as hard acceleration.

Between 300-600 miles (500-1,000 km), do not operate the engine above 5,000 rpm or use full throttle at any time.

After 600 miles (1,000 km), change the engine oil and filter as described in Chapter Three. It is essential to perform this service to ensure that all of the particles produced during break-in are removed from the lubrication system. The small added expense may be considered a smart investment that will pay off in increase engine life.

After 600 miles (1,000 km), the engine may be operated at full throttle.

Table 1 CRANKSHAFT SERVICE SPECIFICATIONS

Item	Specifications mm (in.)	Wear limit mm (in.)
Crankshaft		
Width	74.95-75.00	—
	(2.321-2.323)	—
Runout limit	—	0.03
	—	(0.001)
Connecting rod-to-crankshaft		
side clearance	0.25-0.75	—
	(0.0098-0.0295)	—
Small end	0.8	—
free play limit	(0.031)	—

Table 2 ENGINE LOWER END TIGHTENING TORQUES

	N•m	ft.-lb.
Engine mounting bolts		
Front mounting bracket bolts	58	43
Cylinder head-to-frame		
mounting bolts	58	43
Swing arm pivot bolt nut	100	73
Crankcase bolts	14	7.2

CHAPTER SIX

CLUTCH, KICKSTARTER AND EXTERNAL SHIFT MECHANISM

This chapter describes service procedures for the following sub-assemblies:

a. Clutch.
b. Clutch release mechanism.
c. Primary drive gear and balancer driven gear.
d. Lower cam chain sprocket and chain.
e. Kickstarter.
f. External shift mechanism.
g. Oil pump.
h. Oil tank and hoses.

These sub-assemblies can be removed with the engine in the frame. General clutch specifications are listed in **Table 1**. **Tables 1-5** are found at the end of the chapter.

CLUTCH COVER AND DECOMPRESSION LEVER

Removal/Installation

1. Drain the engine oil as described under *Engine Oil and Filter Change* in Chapter Three.
2A. On XT600 models, remove the bolts securing the engine skid plate (**Figure 1**) and remove the skid plate.
2B. On TT600 models, remove the bolts securing the engine guard and remove the guard.

3. Remove the right-hand footpeg/brake pedal bracket assembly as described under *Rear Brake Pedal Removal/Installation* in Chapter Twelve.

4. Remove the pinch bolt securing the shift lever (A, **Figure 2**) and pull the shift lever off the shaft. If the splined boss is tight on the shaft, spread the slot open with a screwdriver.

5. Remove the screws securing the drive sprocket cover (B, **Figure 2**) and remove the cover.

6. Disconnect the decompression cable as follows:

a. Loosen the adjuster locknut and turn the adjuster (**Figure 3**) to obtain as much cable slack as possible.

b. Remove the screws (A, **Figure 4**) securing the decompression cable lower lever cover (B, **Figure 4**) and remove the cover.

c. Remove the nut (A, **Figure 5**) securing the lever and disconnect the cable from the lever (B, **Figure 5**) and move the cable out of the way.

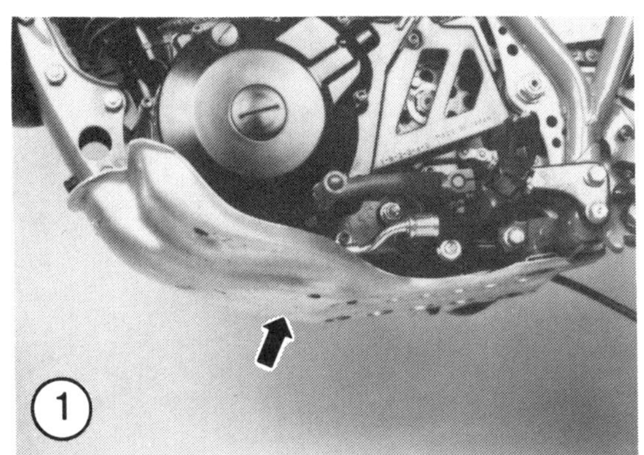

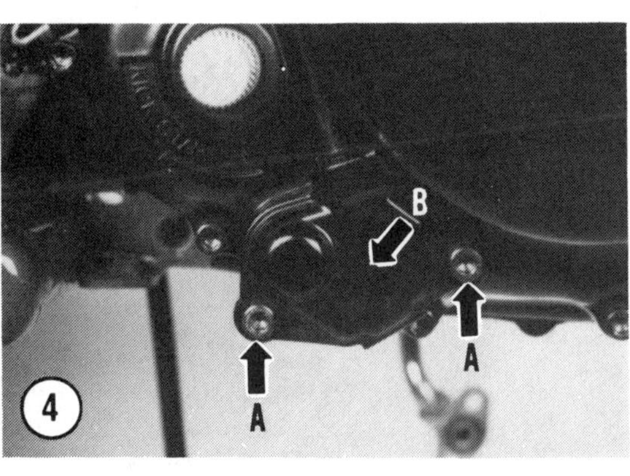

NOTE
The following steps are shown with the engine partially disassembled for clarity. It is not necessary to remove any assemblies other than those specified in this procedure.

7. Remove the bolts securing the clutch cover and remove the cover (**Figure 6**).

8. Remove the gasket (**Figure 7**) and both locating dowel pins (**Figure 8**). Discard the gasket.

6

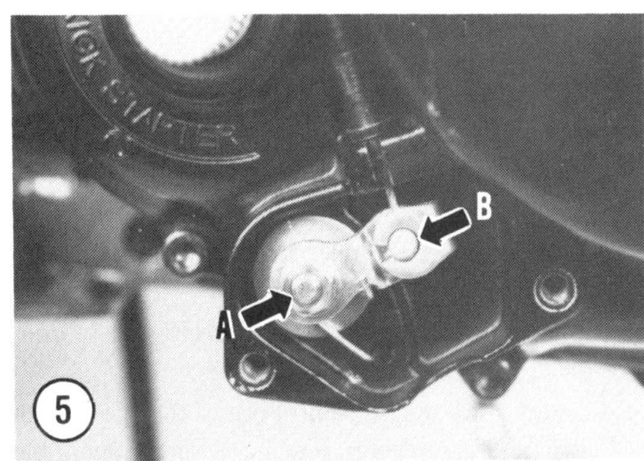

9. Install by reversing these removal steps. Note the following.
10. Make sure to install the 2 dowel pins and a new cover gasket.
11. Refill the engine with oil as described in Chapter Three.
12. Adjust the decompression lever as described under *Decompression Cable Adjustment* in Chapter Three.

8

Clutch Cover Oil Seal Replacement

Replace the kickstarter shaft and decompression lever oil seals if worn or damaged.

1. Remove the clutch cover as described in this chapter.
2. Remove the decompression lever from the clutch cover as described in this chapter.
3. Remove the kickstarter shaft shim (**Figure 9**) from the inner surface of the clutch cover.
4. Carefully pry the oil seal(s) out of the cover with a flat-tipped screwdriver. Place a rag underneath the screwdriver to prevent from damaging the clutch cover.
5. Remove all oil residue from the seal area and clean the cover thoroughly in solvent. Dry with compressed air.
6. Check the seal mounting area for any signs of damage. Repair with fine-grit sandpaper or a fine-cut file. Thoroughly clean the area with solvent to remove any sandpaper or filing residue.
7. Install the new seal(s) by tapping it into the cover with a suitable size socket placed on the outer seal surface. Tap the seal(s) in squarely until it is flush with the case.

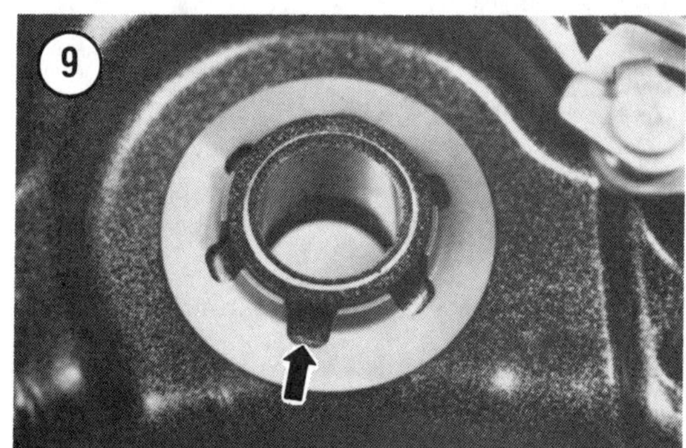
9

11

Decompression Lever Removal/Installation

Refer to **Figure 10** for this procedure.

1. Remove the clutch cover as described in this chapter.
2. Remove the circlip (A, **Figure 11**) and washer (B, **Figure 11**) from the shaft.
3. Withdraw the decompression lever (**Figure 12**) out of the clutch cover.
4. Check the lever assembly for worn or damaged parts.

12

5. Install by reversing these removal steps. Note the following.
6. Position the decompression lever in the clutch cover within the plate as shown in **Figure 12**.
7. After installation is complete, move the lever up and down to make sure it moves correctly with no binding.

CLUTCH

The clutch is a wet multi-plate type which operates immersed in the oil supply it shares with the transmission. The clutch boss is splined to the transmission mainshaft and the clutch housing can rotate freely on the mainshaft. The clutch housing is geared to the primary drive gear that is attached to the crankshaft.

The clutch release mechanism is mounted within the left-hand crankcase cover on the opposite side of the clutch mechanism.

The clutch can be removed with the engine in the frame.

Removal

Refer to **Figure 13** for this procedure.

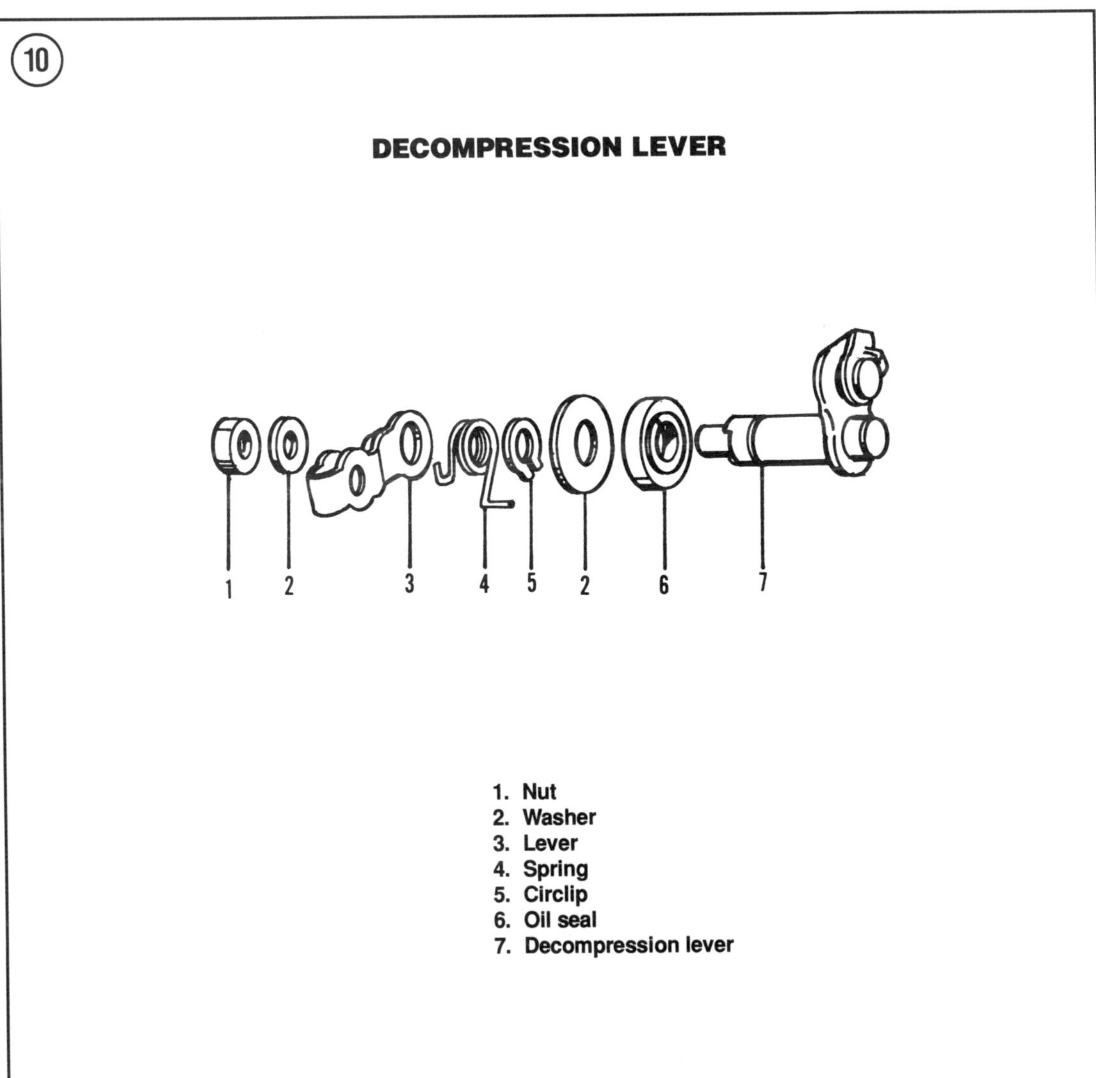

(13)

CLUTCH, CLUTCH RELEASE MECHANISM AND PRIMARY DRIVE GEAR

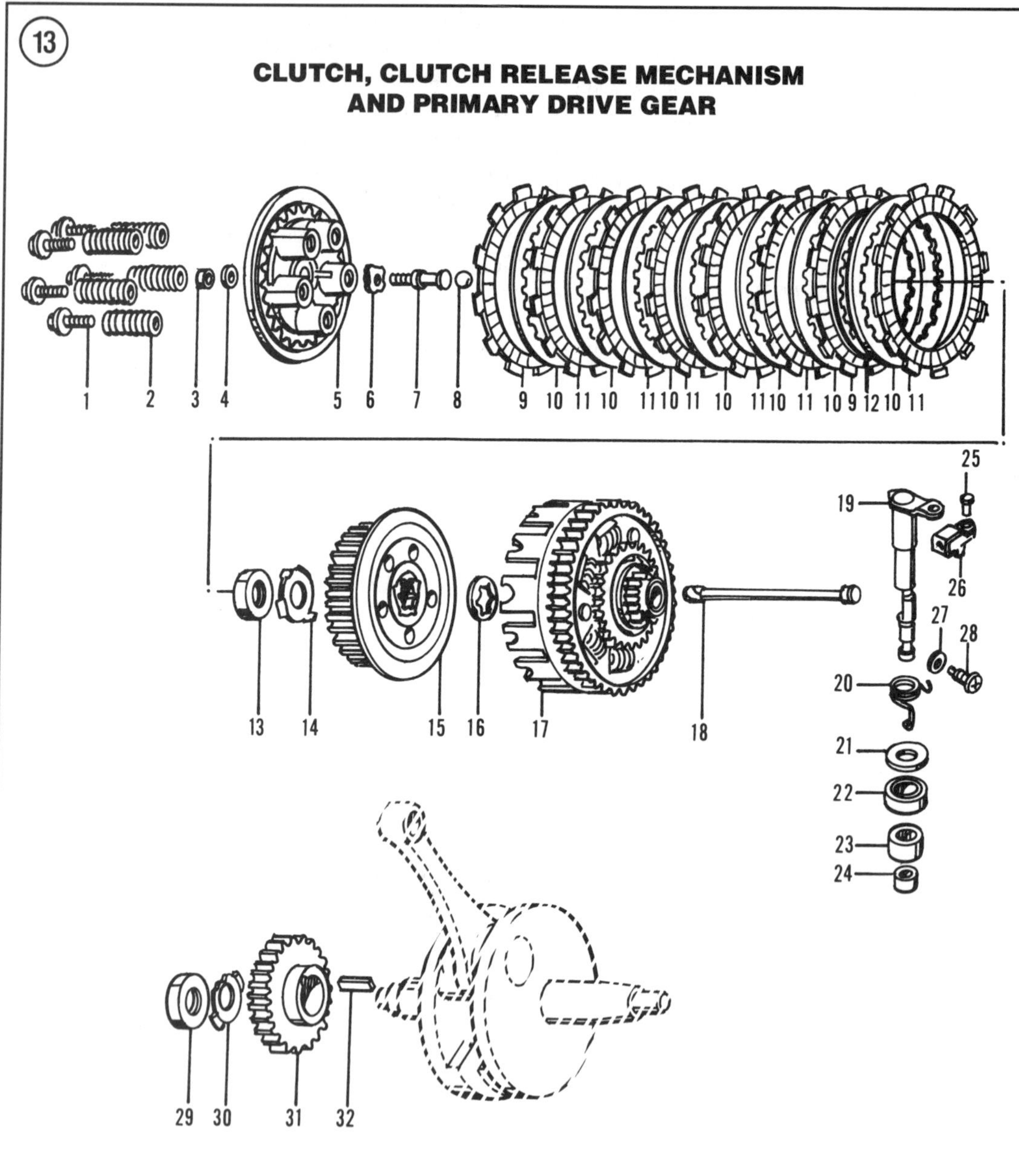

1. Bolt
2. Spring
3. Locknut
4. Washer
5. Pressure plate
6. Push plate
7. Pushrod No. 1
8. Steel ball
9. Friction plate
10. Clutch plate
11. Friction plate
12. Clutch boss spring
13. Nut
14. Lockwasher
15. Clutch boss
16. Splined thrust washer
17. Clutch housing
18. Pushrod No. 2
19. Lever
20. Spring
21. Washer
22. Oil seal
23. Roller bearing
24. Cylindrical bearing
25. Pin
26. Joint
27. Washer
28. Screw
29. Nut
30. Lockwasher
31. Primary drive gear
32. Pin

1. Remove the clutch cover as described in this chapter.
2. Loosen the clutch spring bolts in a crisscross pattern. Then remove the bolts (**Figure 14**).
3. Remove the clutch springs (**Figure 15**).
4. Remove the pressure plate (**Figure 16**).

NOTE
The first and the second to last friction plate have a larger inner diameter. Also there is a clutch boss spring used in conjunction with the last friction plate. Note their location during removal since they must be reinstalled in the exact same location during installation.

5. Remove all friction plates and steel clutch plates. Remove all plates in order.
6. Remove the clutch ball (**Figure 17**).
7. Remove the pushrod No. 2 (**Figure 18**) with a pencil magnet.
8. Straighten the clutch nut lockwasher tab away from the clutch nut.

CAUTION
*In Step 9, do **not** insert a screwdriver or pry bar between the clutch housing and the clutch boss to try to keep the clutch boss from rotating. The fingers on the clutch housing are fragile and can be easily broken.*

NOTE
The "Grabbit" (part No. 969103) is available from Joe Bolger Products Inc., Summer Street, Barre MA 01005.

6

CAUTION
Do not clamp the "Grabbit" on too tight as it may gall or damage the grooves in the clutch hub.

9. Secure the clutch boss with a holding tool such as the "Grabbit" (**Figure 19**). Turn the clutch nut (**Figure 20**) *counterclockwise* and remove it.
10. Remove the lockwasher (**Figure 21**).
11. Remove the clutch boss (**Figure 22**).
12. Remove the splined thrust washer (**Figure 23**).
13. Remove the clutch housing (**Figure 24**).
14. If necessary, remove the locknut and washer (**Figure 25**), then remove the push plate and the pushrod No. 1 (**Figure 26**) from the pressure plate.

Inspection

Clutch service specifications and wear limits are listed in **Table 2**.
1. Clean all parts in solvent and thoroughly dry with compressed air.

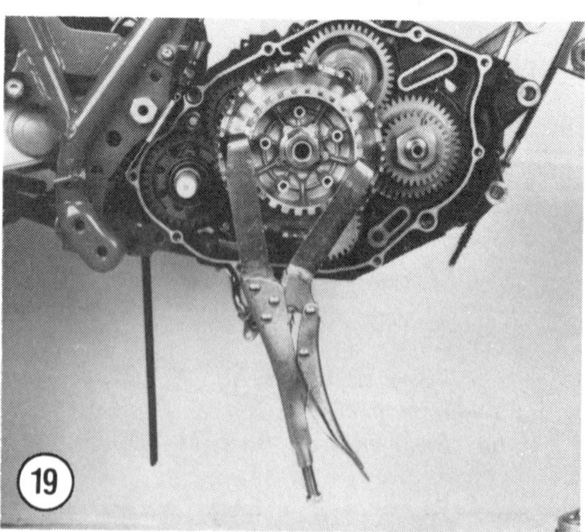
19

20

21

22

23

24

2. Measure the free length of each clutch spring (**Figure 27**) with a vernier caliper. Compare to specification listed in **Table 2** and replace the springs as a set if any one spring has sagged to become too short.

NOTE
*The first and the second to last friction plate have a **larger inner diameter** (**A**, **Figure 28**) and are thicker than all other friction plates. Keep this in mind when measuring the friction plates in the next step.*

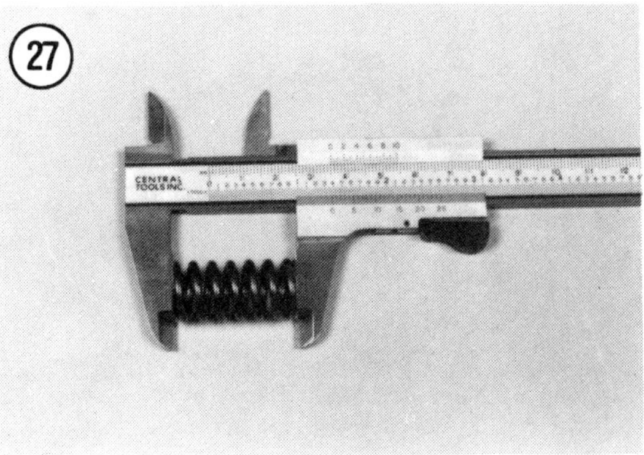

3. **Table 1** lists the number of stock friction plates. The friction material is made of cork that is bonded onto an aluminum plate for warp resistance and durability. Measure the thickness of each friction plate at several places around the disc (**Figure 29**) with a micrometer or vernier caliper. Replace all friction plates if any one is found worn to the service limit listed in **Table 2**. Do not replace only 1 or 2 plates.

4. **Table 1** lists the number of stock clutch metal plates. Place each clutch metal plate on a surface plate or a thick piece of glass and check for warpage with a feeler gauge (**Figure 30**). If any plate is

6

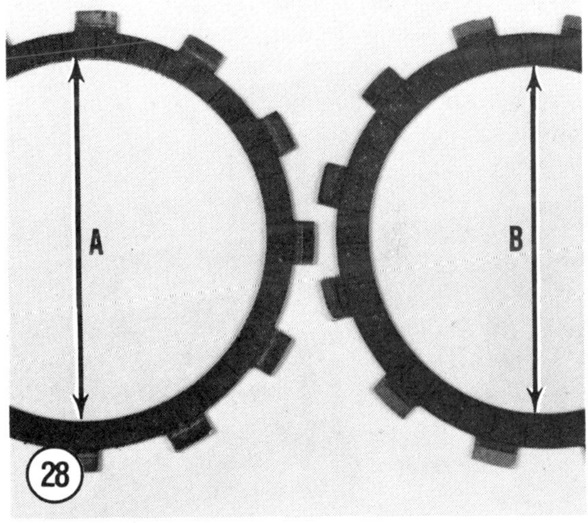

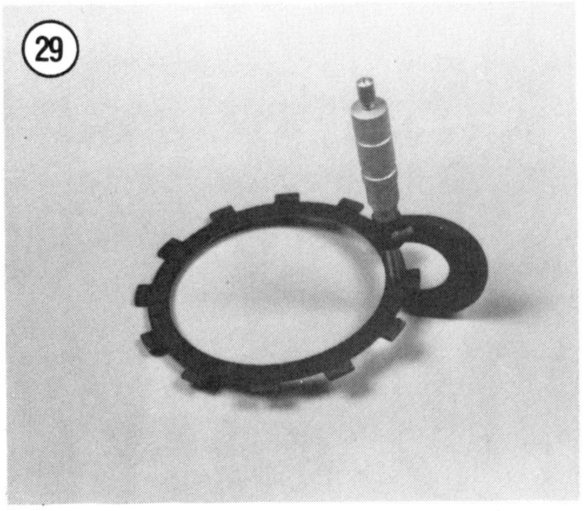

warped more than specified in **Table 2**, replace the entire set of plates. Do not replace only 1 or 2 plates.

5. The clutch metal plate inner teeth (**Figure 31**) mesh with the clutch boss splines (**Figure 32**). Check the splines for cracks or galling. They must be smooth for chatter-free clutch operation. If the clutch boss splines (**Figure 32**) are worn, check the clutch metal plate teeth for wear or damage.

6. Inspect the shaft splines (**Figure 33**) in the clutch boss assembly. If damage is only a slight amount, remove any small burrs with a fine-cut file. If damage is severe, replace the clutch boss assembly.

7. Inspect the clutch boss bolt studs (**Figure 34**) for thread damage or cracks at the base of the studs. Thread damage may be repaired with the correct size metric tap. Use kerosene on the tap threads. If a bolt stud is cracked, the clutch boss must be replaced.

8. The friction plates have tabs (**Figure 35**) that slide in the clutch housing grooves (**Figure 36**). Inspect the tabs for cracks or galling in the grooves. The tabs (**Figure 35**) must be smooth for chatter-free clutch operation. Light damage can be repaired with an oilstone. Replace the clutch housing if damage is severe.

32

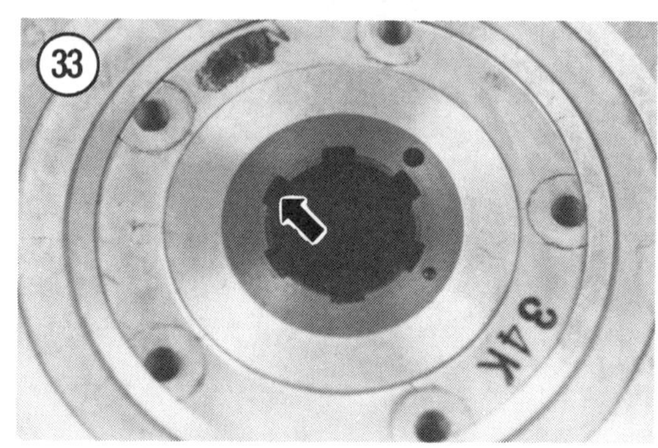

33

30

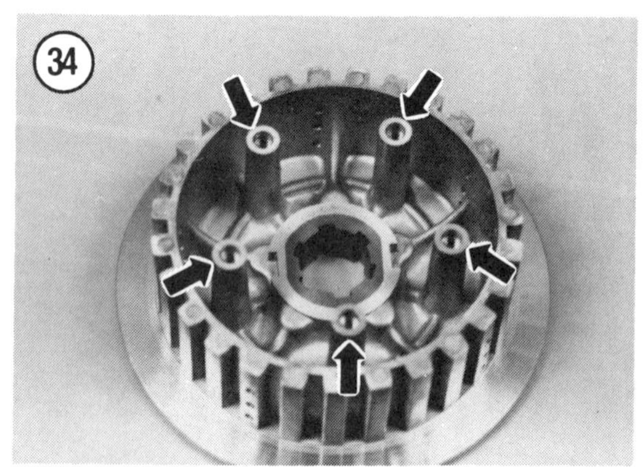
34

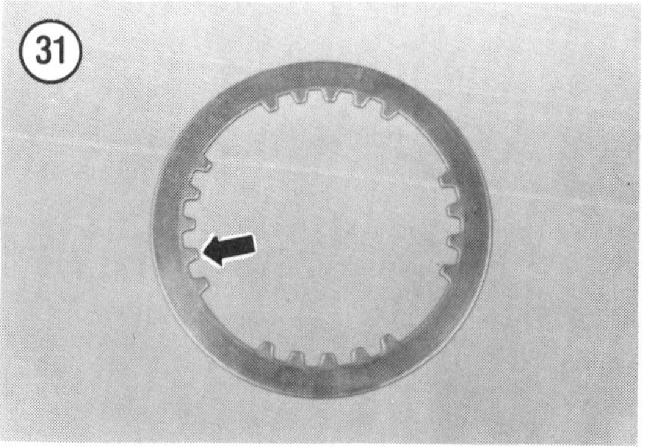
31

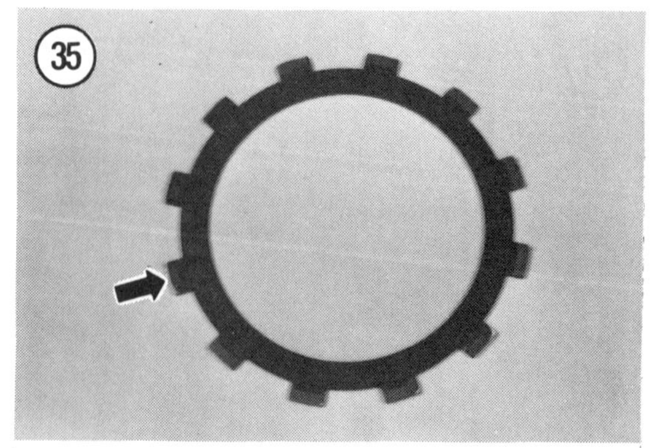
35

36

37

38

39

9. Check the clutch housing bearing bore (**Figure 37**) for cracks, deep scoring, excessive wear or heat discoloration. If the bearing bore is damaged, also check the mainshaft for damage. Replace worn or damaged parts.

10. Check the clutch housing gear teeth (**Figure 38**) for tooth wear, damage or cracks. Replace the clutch housing if necessary.

NOTE

If the clutch housing gear teeth are damaged, the gear teeth on the primary drive gear and the kickstarter idler gear may also be damaged; inspect them also.

11. Check the clutch housing oil pump gear teeth (A, **Figure 39**) and kickstarter gear teeth (B, **Figure 39**) for tooth wear, damage or cracks. Replace the clutch housing if necessary.

12. Check the damper springs (**Figure 40**) in the clutch housing for damage or breakage. If any of the springs are damaged or have sagged, replace the clutch housing.

13. Check the pushrod (**Figure 41**) for straightness with a set of V-blocks and a dial indicator or roll the

6

40

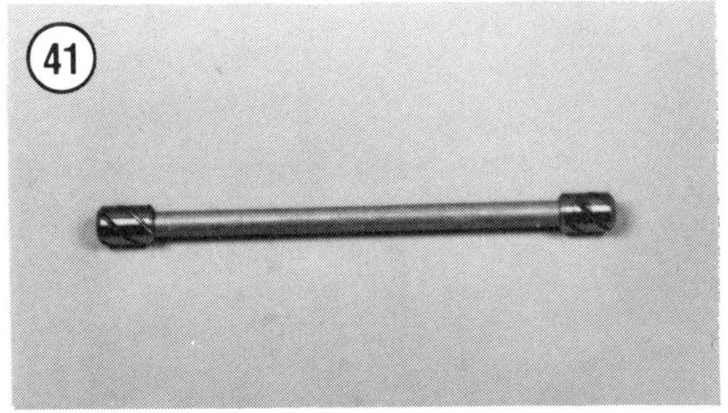
41

pushrod on a flat surface such as a surface plate or a piece of thick glass. Replace the pushrod if it exceeds the bend limit in **Table 2**.

14. Check the steel ball (A, **Figure 42**) and the end of the pushrod (B, **Figure 42**) where the steel ball rides for wear or damage. Replace the damaged part(s).

15. Check the pressure plate spring towers (**Figure 43**) and splines (**Figure 44**) for cracks at the base of the tower.

16. If there is any doubt as to the condition of any clutch part, replace it with a new one.

17. Check the clutch boss spring (**Figure 45**) for distortion or damage, replace if necessary.

Assembly

1. Coat all clutch parts with clean engine oil before reassembly.

2. Install the clutch housing (**Figure 24**). Turn the kickstarter idle gear, oil pump gear and primary drive gear while installing the clutch housing. Make sure all gears are properly meshed before pushing the clutch housing on all the way.

3. Install the splined thrust washer (**Figure 23**).

4. Install the clutch boss (**Figure 22**).

NOTE
Install a new lockwasher if the old one has been removed 2 times.

5. Align the 2 tabs on the lockwasher with the 2 flat notches in the clutch boss and install the lockwasher (**Figure 21**).

6. Install the clutch nut and secure the clutch boss with the same tool used during removal. Tighten the clutch nut (**Figure 20**) to the torque specification in **Table 3**.

7. Apply a light coat of grease to the pushrod prior to installation. Install the clutch pushrod (**Figure 18**).

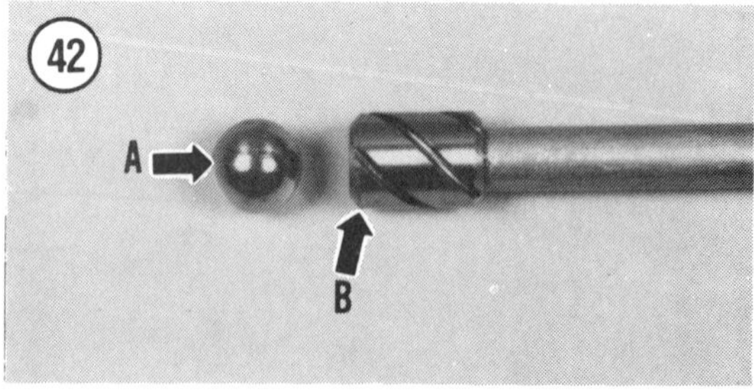

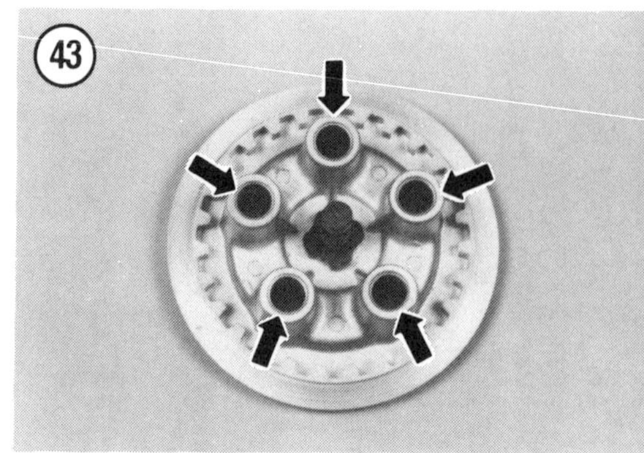

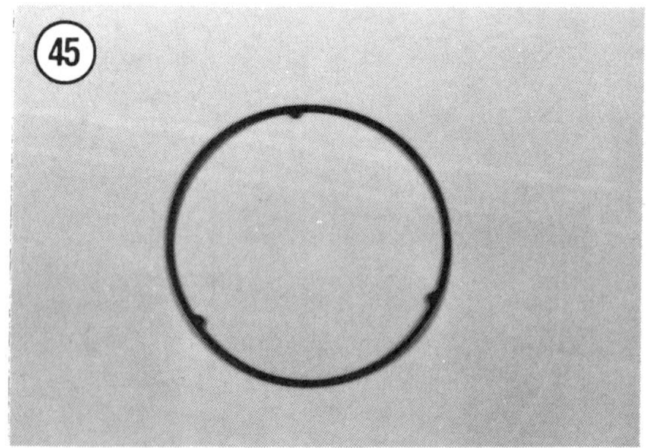

8. Apply a light coat of grease to the ball and install it (**Figure 17**). Make sure it does not roll out.

9. Install the friction plates and clutch plates onto the clutch boss as follows:

   a. First install one of the 6 friction plates (**Figure 46**) with the smaller inner diameter (B, **Figure 28**).
   b. Install a clutch plate (**Figure 47**).
   c. Install the clutch guide spring (**Figure 48**) and then one of the 2 friction plates (**Figure 49**) with the *larger inner diameter* (A, **Figure 28**). The friction plate must fit over the spring guide. If it doesn't, you have installed the wrong friction plate—remove it and install the correct one.
   d. Continue to install the clutch plate (**Figure 50**) and then a friction plate, alternating them until all are installed. The last item installed is the other friction plate (**Figure 51**) with the *larger inner diameter* (A, **Figure 28**).

CAUTION

If either or both friction discs and/or clutch plates have been replaced with new ones or if they were cleaned, apply new engine oil to all surfaces to avoid damaging the plates or having the clutch lock up when used for the first time.

10. If the No.1 pushrod was removed, perform the following:

   a. Install the push plate onto the pushrod No. 1 and install this assembly into the backside of the pressure plate (**Figure 26**).
   b. On the front side of the pressure plate, install the washer and locknut.

c. Tighten the locknut (**Figure 25**) only finger-tight at this time since it must be adjusted after the clutch is completely assembled.

11. Align the arrow (A, **Figure 52**) on the pressure plate with the punch mark (B, **Figure 52**) on the clutch boss and install the pressure plate (**Figure 16**).
12. Install the clutch springs (**Figure 15**) and bolts (**Figure 14**). Securely tighten the bolts in a crisscross pattern.
13. Perform the *Clutch Mechanism Adjustment* as described in this chapter.
14. Install the clutch cover as described in this chapter.

Clutch Mechanism Adjustment

This procedure should be performed whenever the clutch assembly is disassembled or when major clutch adjustment is required.

1. Remove the clutch cover (A, **Figure 53**) as described in this chapter.
2. Slide back the rubber boot (**Figure 54**) on the clutch lever.
3. Loosen the clutch cable adjuster locknut (A, **Figure 55**) at the handlebar. Then turn the adjuster (B, **Figure 55**) counterclockwise to obtain as much clutch cable slack as possible.
4. Disconnect the clutch cable (B, **Figure 53**) at the push lever (C, **Figure 53**) on the left-hand side of the engine.

NOTE

***Figure 56** is shown with the clutch pressure plate removed from the engine for clarity. Do not remove it for this adjustment.*

5. Loosen the clutch mechanism adjuster locknut (A, **Figure 56**).
6. Push the clutch push lever (C, **Figure 53**) toward the front of the engine until the point (D, **Figure 53**) on the end of the lever aligns with the embossed mark on the crankcase. Hold the lever in this position.
7. Using a flat-bladed screwdriver, turn the end of push rod No. 1 (B, **Figure 56**) in or out until the end of it lightly touches the clutch pushrod ball. Tighten the locknut (A, **Figure 56**) to the torque specification listed in **Table 3**.
8. Release the push lever on the left-hand side of the engine.
9. Reconnect the clutch cable (B, **Figure 53**) to the push lever (C, **Figure 53**).
10. Adjust the clutch as described under *Clutch Adjustment* in Chapter Three.
11. Reinstall the clutch cover as described in this chapter.

CLUTCH RELEASE MECHANISM

Removal/Installation

Refer to **Figure 57** for this procedure.

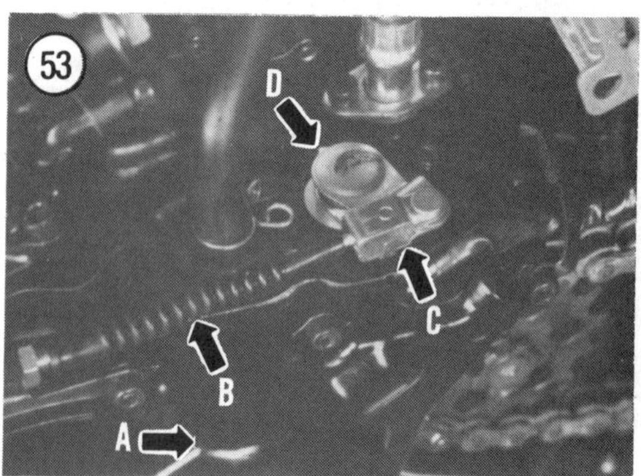

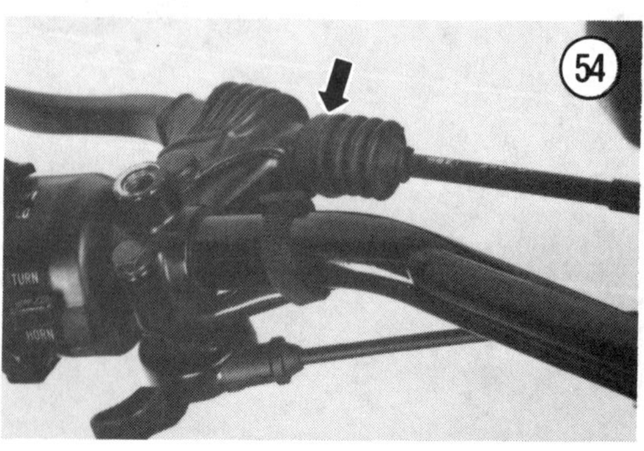

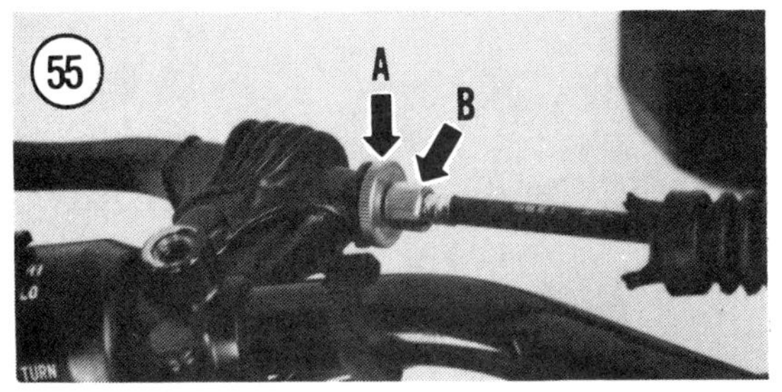

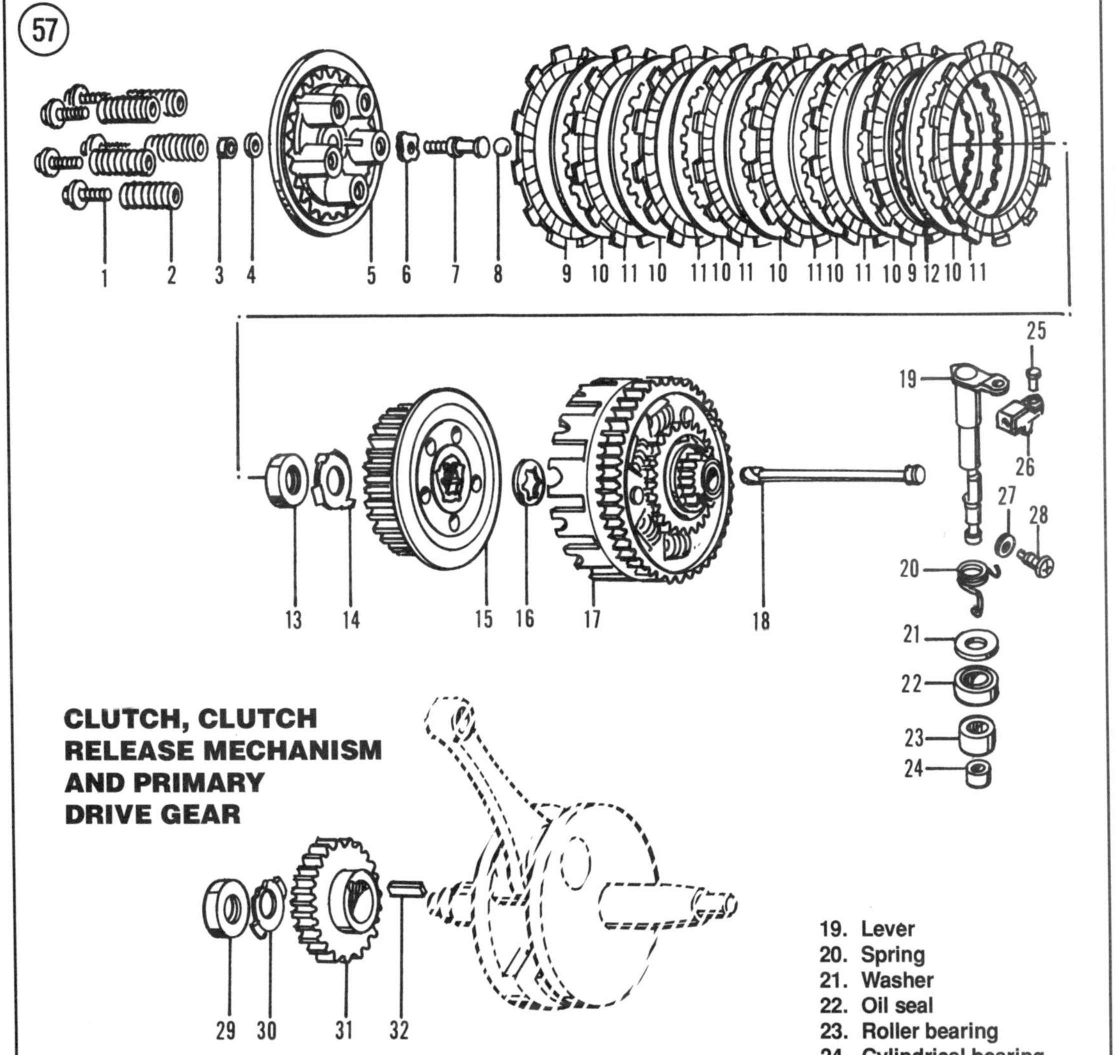

57

CLUTCH, CLUTCH RELEASE MECHANISM AND PRIMARY DRIVE GEAR

1. Bolt
2. Spring
3. Locknut
4. Washer
5. Pressure plate
6. Push plate
7. Pushrod No. 1
8. Steel ball
9. Friction plate
10. Clutch plate
11. Friction plate
12. Clutch boss spring
13. Nut
14. Lockwasher
15. Clutch boss
16. Splined thrust washer
17. Clutch housing
18. Pushrod No. 2
19. Lever
20. Spring
21. Washer
22. Oil seal
23. Roller bearing
24. Cylindrical bearing
25. Pin
26. Joint
27. Washer
28. Screw
29. Nut
30. Lockwasher
31. Primary drive gear
32. Pin

1. Slide back the rubber boot (A, **Figure 58**) on the clutch lever.

2. Loosen the clutch cable adjuster locknut (B, **Figure 58**) at the handlebar. Then turn the adjuster (C, **Figure 58**) *counterclockwise* to obtain as much clutch cable slack as possible.

3. Disconnect the clutch cable (A, **Figure 59**) at the push lever (B, **Figure 59**) on the left-hand side of the engine.

4. Remove the alternator stator assembly as described under *Stator Assembly Removal/Installation* in Chapter Nine.

5. Remove the Phillips screw and washer (A, **Figure 60**) securing the push lever.

6. Lift the push lever, spring and washer (B, **Figure 60**) up and out of the crankcase.

7. Check the push lever (A, **Figure 61**) for any signs of wear, cracks or breakage. Check the spring (A, **Figure 62**) and the pivot joint (B, **Figure 62**) for wear or damage. Replace the spring or the push lever assembly if worn or damaged.

8. Install the push lever and spring into the crankcase. Install the Phillips screw and washer (A, **Fig-**

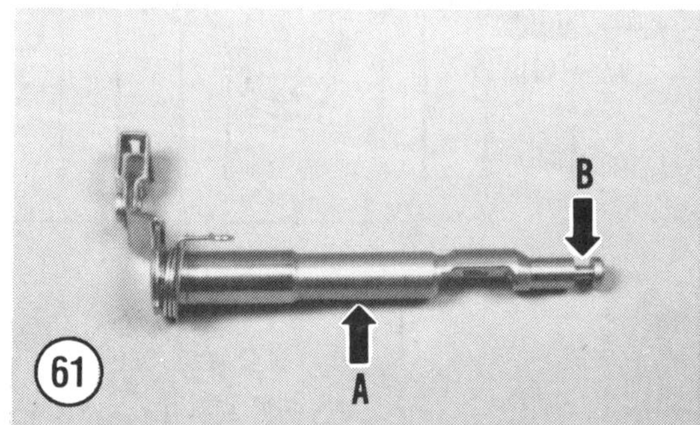

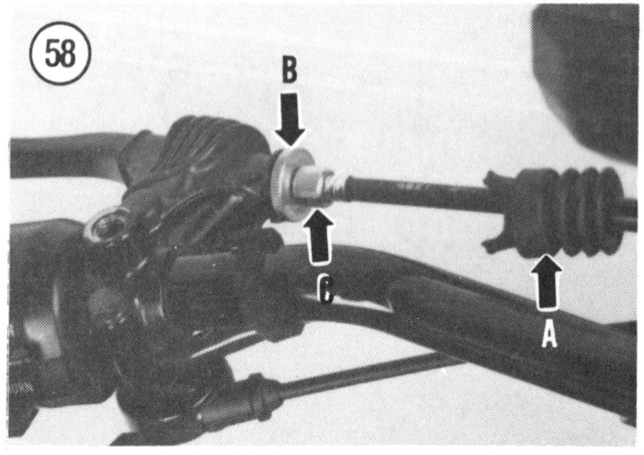

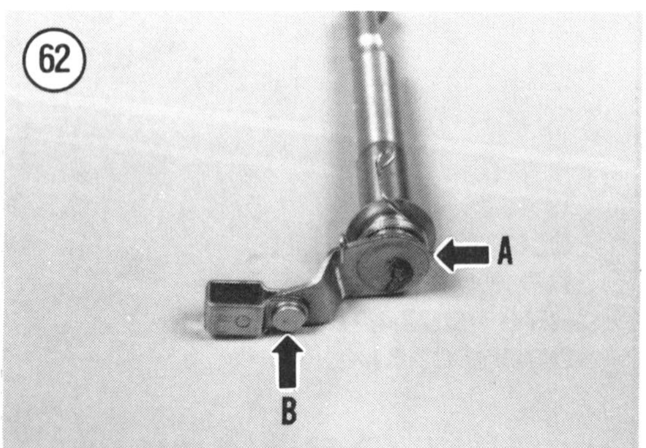

ure 60) so that it engages the push lever bottom groove (B, **Figure 61**). Tighten the screw securely.

9. Be sure to properly index the spring into the groove (**Figure 63**). This is necessary for proper clutch operation.

10. Connect the clutch cable (A, **Figure 59**) onto the push lever (B, **Figure 59**) on the left-hand side of the engine.

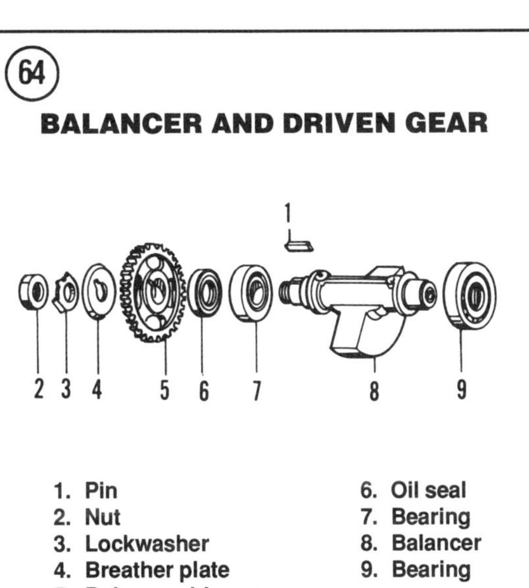

1. Pin
2. Nut
3. Lockwasher
4. Breather plate
5. Balancer driven gear
6. Oil seal
7. Bearing
8. Balancer
9. Bearing

11. Perform the *Clutch Mechanism Adjustment* described in this chapter.

12. Install the alternator stator assembly as described under *Stator Assembly Removal/Installation* in Chapter Nine.

PRIMARY DRIVE GEAR, BALANCER DRIVE AND DRIVEN GEARS

This procedure describes service to the primary drive gear and the balancer drive and driven gears. Removal of the balancer shaft requires crankcase disassembly as described in Chapter Five.

The balancer system eliminates the vibration normally associated with a large displacement single cylinder engine. The engine and frame are designed for use with this balancer system. If the balancer is disconnected or eliminated, excessive engine vibration will occur.

CAUTION

Any applicable manufacturer's warranty will be voided if the balancer system is modified, disconnected or removed.

Refer to **Figure 64** and **Figure 65** for this procedure.

6

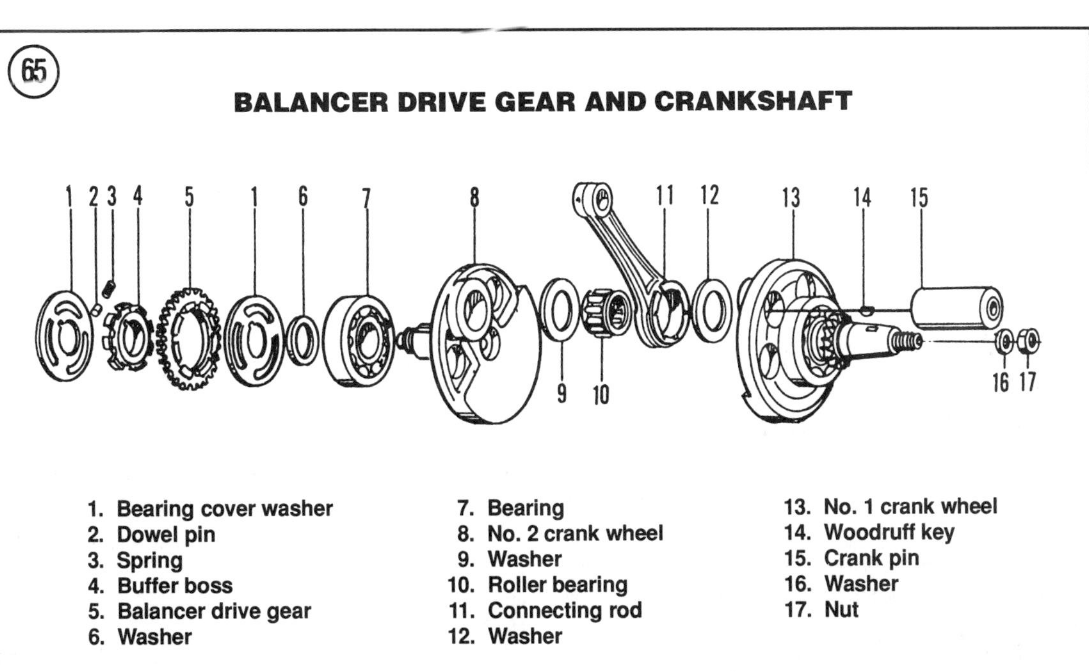

1. Bearing cover washer
2. Dowel pin
3. Spring
4. Buffer boss
5. Balancer drive gear
6. Washer
7. Bearing
8. No. 2 crank wheel
9. Washer
10. Roller bearing
11. Connecting rod
12. Washer
13. No. 1 crank wheel
14. Woodruff key
15. Crank pin
16. Washer
17. Nut

Removal

1. Remove the clutch cover as described in this chapter.
2. Place a soft copper or brass washer (A, **Figure 66**) between the gear teeth of the primary drive gear and the clutch outer housing gear.
3. Straighten the lockwasher tabs away from the primary drive gear nut.
4. Loosen the nut (B, **Figure 66**) securing the primary drive gear to the crankshaft. Remove the copper or brass washer.
5. Remove the clutch as described in this chapter.
6. Place a soft copper or brass washer (A, **Figure 67**) between the gear teeth of the primary drive gear and the balancer gear.
7. Straighten the lockwasher tabs away from the balancer driven gear nut.
8. Loosen the nut (B, **Figure 67**) securing the balancer driven gear to the balancer shaft assembly. Remove the copper or brass washer.
9. Remove the primary drive gear nut (**Figure 68**) and the lockwasher (A, **Figure 69**).
10. Remove the balancer driven gear nut (**Figure 70**).

72

73

74

75

11. From the balancer shaft, remove the following:
    a. The lockwasher (A, **Figure 71**).
    b. The breather plate (B, **Figure 71**).
    c. The balancer driven gear (**Figure 72**) and the key.
12. From the crankshaft, remove the following:
    a. The primary drive gear (**Figure 73**).
    b. The bearing cover washer (**Figure 74**).
    c. The balancer drive gear assembly (**Figure 75**).
    d. The bearing cover washer (**Figure 76**).
    e. The key (**Figure 77**) and the washer (**Figure 78**).
13. Inspect all parts as described in this chapter.

76

77

78

Inspection

1. Clean all of the parts in solvent and thoroughly dry.
2. When the parts have been cleaned and are dry, visually inspect them for any signs of wear, cracks, breakage or other damage.
3. The balancer drive gear (**Figure 79**) can be disassembled and if necessary, worn or damaged parts can be replaced.
4. Check the gear teeth on the balancer drive gear (**Figure 80**), the primary drive gear (**Figure 81**) and the balancer driven gear (A, **Figure 82**) for wear or damage. Replace the gear if necessary.
5. Inspect the keyway in the primary drive gear (**Figure 83**) and the balancer driven gear (B, **Figure 82**) for wear or damage. Replace the gear if necessary.
6. Check the bearing cover washers (**Figure 84**) for wear or damage. Replace as a set if one is damaged.

Installation

NOTE
Nearly all of the following components are machined with a keyway for alignment purposes. Make sure to install the parts correctly onto their respective shafts.

1. Onto the crankshaft, install the following:
   a. Install the washer (**Figure 78**).
   b. Install the key (**Figure 77**) into the groove.
   c. Align the slot in the bearing cover washer with the keyway in the crankshaft and install the bearing cover washer (**Figure 76**).
   d. Install the balancer drive gear assembly (**Figure 75**).
   e. Align the slot in the bearing cover washer with the keyway in the crankshaft and install the bearing cover washer (**Figure 74**).
   f. Install the primary drive gear (**Figure 73**).
2. Onto the balancer shaft, install the following parts:

NOTE
Do not install the key into the slot in the balancer shaft at this time. It will be installed after the 2 gears are properly aligned. This way is easier since you don't have to try to hold the crankshaft and piston in any certain position.

79

80

81

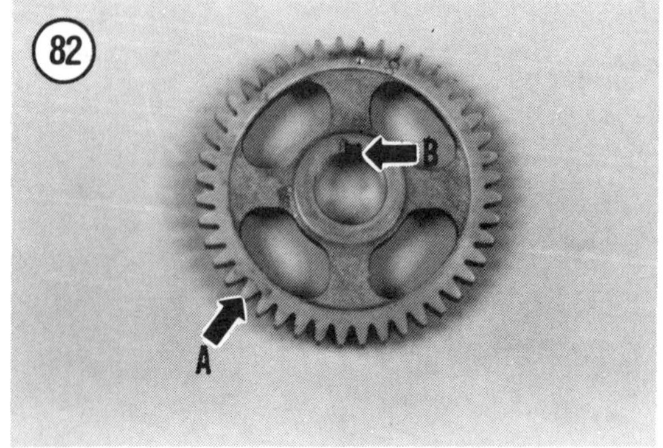

82

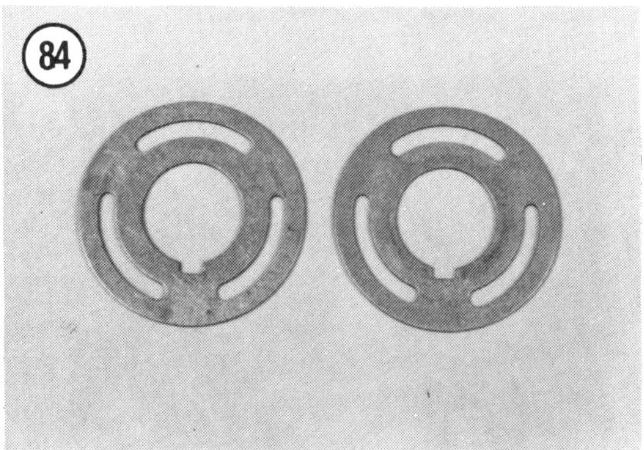

a. Partially install the balancer driven gear (**Figure 72**) onto the balancer shaft.

CAUTION
The index marks on both gears must be exactly aligned as indicated in the following step, otherwise, there will be excessive engine vibration. This vibration will result in major fatigue to engine and frame components.

b. Position the balancer driven gear with the index mark facing toward the outside and partially install the balancer driven gear so that it is aligned with the index mark on the balancer drive gear (**Figure 85**). Push the driven gear all the way on.

c. Rotate the balancer driven gear until the gear keyway aligns with the keyway on the balancer shaft. Install the key (**Figure 86**) into the keyway in both the gear and shaft.

d. After the key has been installed, recheck and make sure both index marks are still aligned (**Figure 85**). Realign if necessary.

e. Install the breather plate (B, **Figure 71**).

f. Align the tab of the *new* lockwasher (C, **Figure 71**) with the balancer shaft keyway and install the lockwasher.

g. Install the nut (**Figure 70**). Do *not* tighten it at this time.

3. Align the tab on a *new* lockwasher (B, **Figure 69**) with the primary drive keyway and install the lockwasher (A, **Figure 69**).

4. Install the nut (**Figure 68**). Do *not* tighten the nut at this time.

5. Use the same tool used during removal to tighten the balancer driven gear nut (A, **Figure 87**) and primary drive gear nut (B, **Figure 87**). Refer to the torque specifications in **Table 3**.

6. Bend the lockwasher tabs up against both nuts to lock them in place.

7. Install the clutch as described in this chapter.

CAMSHAFT CHAIN AND REAR GUIDE

This procedure describes service to the camshaft chain and the rear camshaft chain guide.

Removal

1. Remove the balancer drive gear as described under *Primary Drive Gear and Balancer Drive and Driven Gears* in this chapter.
2. If the camshaft is still installed, remove it as described under *Camshaft Removal* in Chapter Four.
3. If the alternator rotor is still installed, remove the rotor as described under *Alternator Rotor Removal/Installation* in Chapter Nine.
4. Remove the bolts (A, **Figure 88**) securing the camshaft chain rear guide.
5. Remove the rear guide (A, **Figure 89**) and baffle plate (B, **Figure 88**).
6. Remove the camshaft chain (B, **Figure 89**) from the camshaft sprocket on the crankshaft.
7. Inspect the parts as described in this chapter.

Inspection

1. Clean all parts in solvent and thoroughly dry.
2. If the camshaft chain (**Figure 90**) is worn, the sprockets (upper and lower) as well as the camshaft chain guides are probably worn also. Inspect all parts closely. Running the engine with new and used parts will cause rapid wear to the new parts. Always replace these parts as a set.
3. Check the front (A, **Figure 91**) and rear (B, **Figure 91**) camshaft chain guides for wear, damage or cracks.
4. Inspect the pivot point (**Figure 92**) of the rear guide for wear or damage, replace if necessary.

Installation

1. Install the camshaft chain onto the camshaft sprocket on the crankshaft (**Figure 93**). Make sure it is properly meshed with the sprocket.
2. Install the rear guide (A, **Figure 89**).
3. Install the baffle plate (B, **Figure 88**) and index it within the locating tabs (**Figure 94**) in the crankcase.
4. Apply Loctite 242 (blue) to the rear guide bolts (A, **Figure 88**). Tighten the bolts to the torque specification listed in **Table 3**.
5. Install the alternator rotor as described under *Alternator Rotor Removal/Installation* in Chapter Nine.
6. Install the camshaft as described under *Camshaft Installation* in Chapter Four.

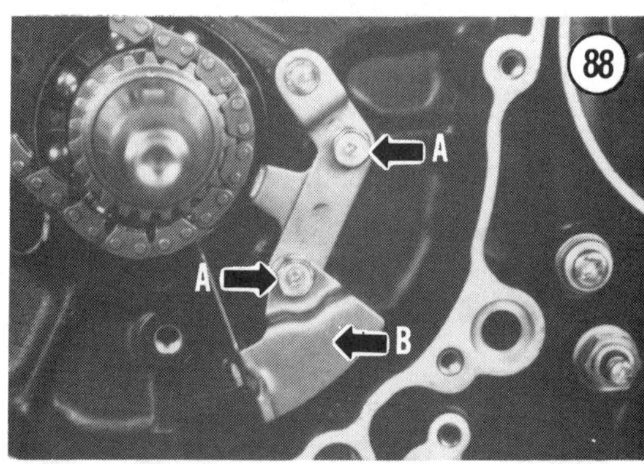

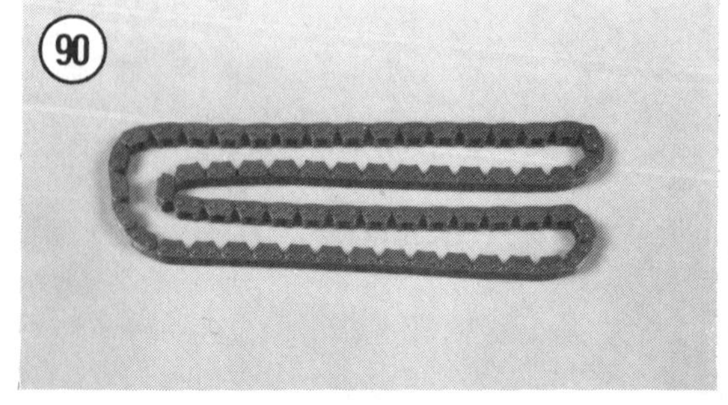

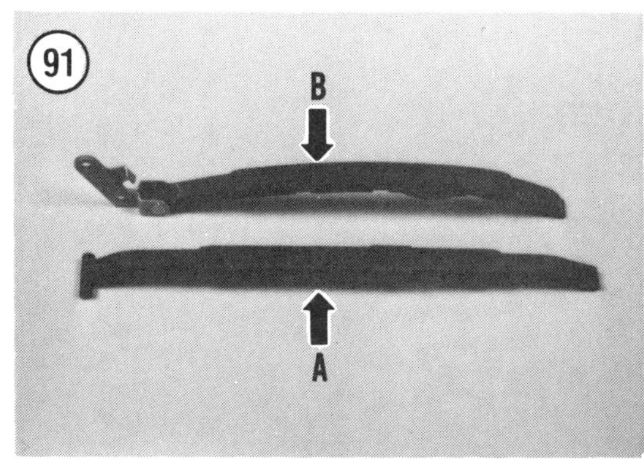

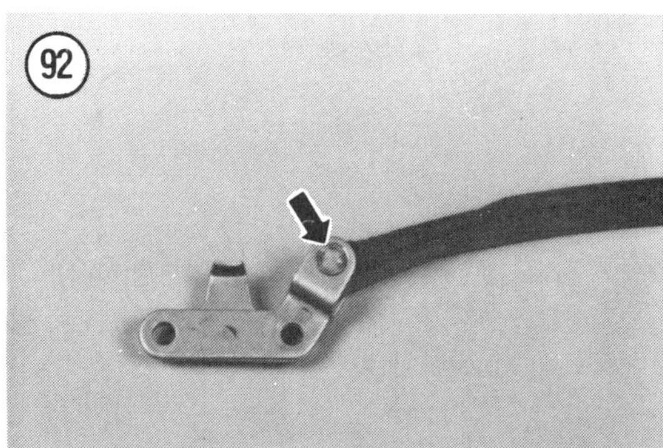

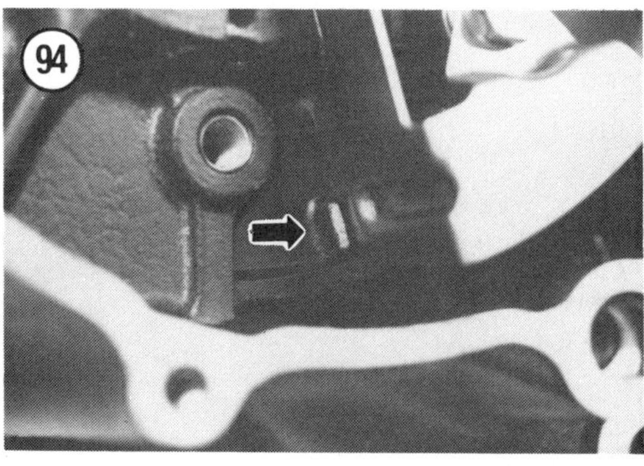

7. Install the balancer drive gear as described under *Primary Drive Gear, Balancer Drive and Driven Gears* in this chapter.

KICKSTARTER

Removal

Refer to **Figure 95** for this procedure.

1. Remove the clutch as described in this chapter.
2. Remove the kickstarter idle gear as follows:
   a. Remove the circlip (**Figure 96**).
   b. Remove the washer (A, **Figure 97**).
   c. Remove the kickstarter idle gear (B, **Figure 97**).
   d. Remove the washer (**Figure 98**).
   e. Remove the circlip (**Figure 99**).
3. Using a pair of needlenose or vise grip pliers, remove the kickstarter return spring from its post position in the crankcase (**Figure 100**).
4. Release the spring and allow it to relax. Then rotate the kickstarter assembly *counterclockwise* by hand and remove it from the crankcase.

NOTE
*There is a washer (**Figure 101**) on the end of the kickstarter shaft, don't lose it during removal.*

5. If neccssary, disassemble the kickstarter shaft assembly and service it as described in this chapter.

Installation

1. Apply a small amount of cold grease to the washer and install it onto the end of the kickstarter shaft (**Figure 101**).
2. With the kickstarter stopper positioned at the top, insert the kickstarter into the crankcase (**Figure 102**).
3. Using needlenose or vise grip pliers, rotate the return spring *clockwise* (**Figure 103**) and hook the return spring onto the spring post in the crankcase (**Figure 100**). Make sure it is correctly positioned in the spring post groove.
4. Install the kickstarter idle gear as follows:
   a. Install the circlip (**Figure 99**).
   b. Install the washer (**Figure 98**).
   c. Position the kickstarter idle gear with the raised boss (**Figure 104**) side going on first

(95)

KICKSTARTER

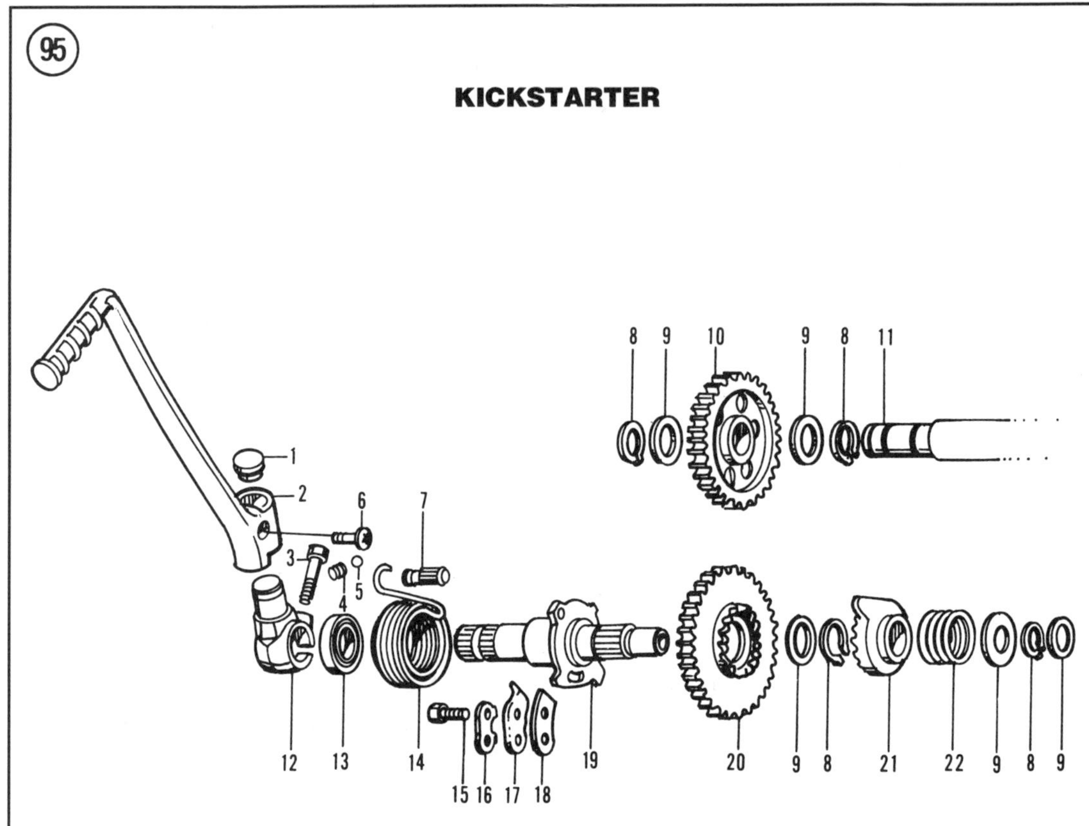

1. Cap
2. Kickstarter lever
3. Bolt
4. Spring
5. Steel ball
6. Bolt
7. Boss
8. Circlip
9. Washer
10. Kickstarter idle gear
11. Transmission countershaft
12. Kick boss
13. Oil seal
14. Return spring
15. Bolt
16. Lockwasher
17. Guide plate
18. Stopper plate
19. Kickstarter shaft
20. Kickstarter gear
21. Kickstarter ratchet wheel
22. Spring

96
97
A
B
98
99
100
101
102
103

and install the kickstarter idle gear (B, **Figure 97**).

d. Install the washer (A, **Figure 97**).

e. Install the circlip (**Figure 96**). Make sure the circlip is properly seated in the shaft groove.

5. Install the clutch as described in this chapter.

Disassembly

Refer to **Figure 95** for this procedure.

NOTE
*A helpful "tool" that should be used for kickstarter disassembly is a large egg flat (the type restaurants get their eggs in). See **Figure 105**. As you remove a part from the shaft, set it in one of the depressions in the same position from which it was removed. This is an easy way to remember the correct relationship of all parts.*

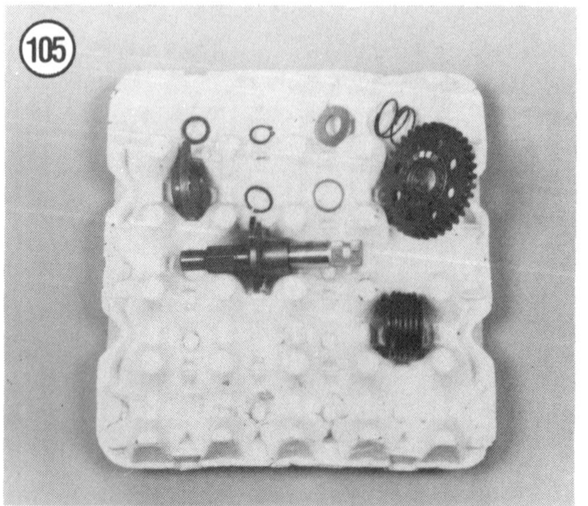

1. Remove the return spring (**Figure 106**) from the shaft.
2. Remove the washer (**Figure 107**).
3. Remove the circlip (**Figure 108**) and slide off the spring cover (**Figure 109**), the ratchet spring (A, **Figure 110**) and kickstarter ratchet wheel (B, **Figure 110**).
4. Remove the circlip (**Figure 111**) and slide off the washer (**Figure 112**) and the kickstarter gear (A, **Figure 113**).

Inspection

1. Wash all parts thoroughly in solvent and dry with compressed air.
2. Check for broken, chipped, or missing teeth on the kickstarter gear and ratchet wheel (**Figure 114**). If either part is damaged, replace the kickstarter gear and ratchet wheel as a set.
3. Check for broken, chipped, or missing teeth on the kickstarter idle gear (**Figure 115**). Replace the gear if necessary.

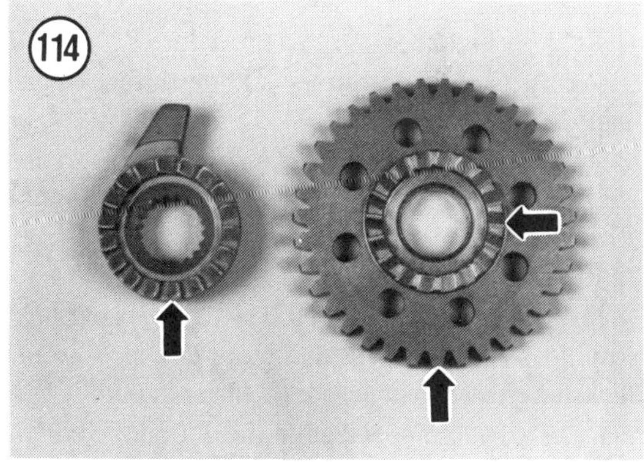

6

4. Inspect the kickstarter shaft as follows:
   a. Check the kickstarter lever splines (A, **Figure 116**) for damage that would allow the lever to slip when the kickstarter is used.
   b. Check the shaft surface (B, **Figure 116**) for cracks, deep scoring or other damage.
   c. Check the return spring hole in the shaft for cracks, wallowing or other conditions that would allow the spring to slip out when using the kickstarter.
   d. Install the kick gear onto the shaft and check that the gear operates smoothly on the shaft. Check the shaft splines (C, **Figure 116**) for cracks or other damage.
   e. Replace the kickstarter shaft if necessary.
5. Check the return spring for cracks, breakage or other damage. Replace if necessary.
6. Measure the ratchet spring free length with a vernier caliper (**Figure 117**). Replace the spring if the free length has sagged to the limit listed in **Table 4**.

Assembly

Refer to **Figure 95** for this procedure.

1. Apply assembly oil to the sliding surfaces of all parts.
2. Install the kickstarter gear (A, **Figure 113**) so that the ratchet teeth go on last as shown in B, **Figure 113**.
3. Install the washer (**Figure 112**).
4. Install the circlip (**Figure 111**) into the groove next to the washer. After installing the circlip, spin the kickstarter gear to make sure it turns smoothly.

5A. On XT600 models, align the dot on the end of the kickstarter shaft (A, **Figure 118**) with the dot on the ratchet wheel (B, **Figure 118**) and install the ratchet wheel. Make sure this alignment is correct.

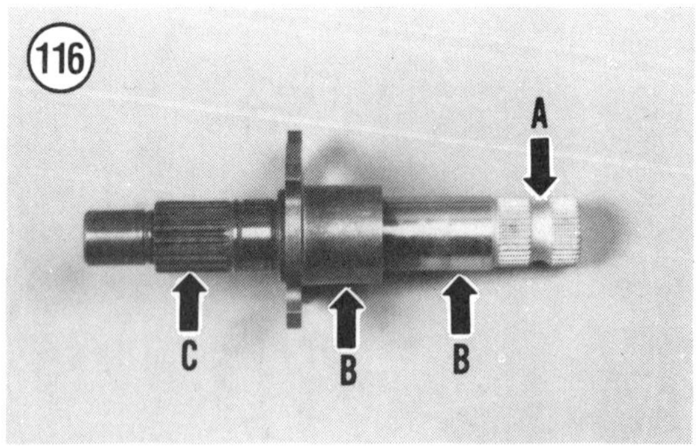

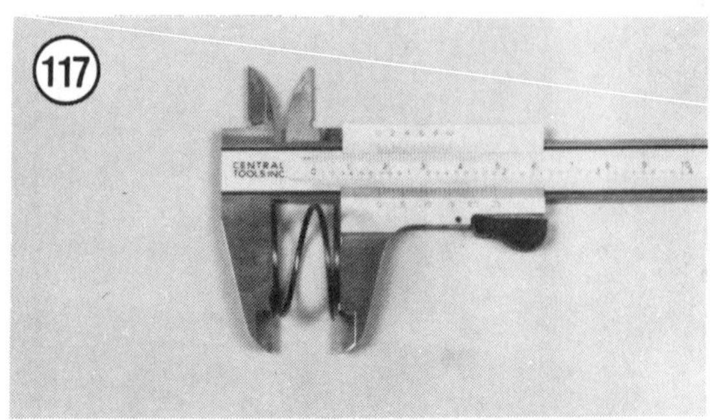

121

122

123

124

5B. On TT600 models, align the dot on the end of the kickstarter shaft (A, **Figure 119**) with the straight surface on the ratchet wheel (B, **Figure 119**) and install the ratchet wheel. Make sure this alignment is correct.

6. Install the ratchet wheel spring (A, **Figure 110**).
7. Install the spring cover (**Figure 109**).
8. Compress the spring and install the circlip (**Figure 108**). Make sure the circlip seats in the groove completely.
9. Apply a light coat of cold grease to the washer to keep the washer in place on the shaft and install the washer (**Figure 107**).
10. Install the return spring (A, **Figure 120**) and hook the end of the return spring (B, **Figure 120**) into the notch in the kickstarter shaft.
11. After assembly is complete, refer to **Figure 121** and make sure all parts are installed correctly.

OIL PUMP

Removal/Installation

1. Remove the clutch as described in this chapter.
2. Remove the circlip (**Figure 122**) securing the idle gear.
3. Remove the idle gear (**Figure 123**).
4. Remove the oil pump mounting screws and remove the oil pump (**Figure 124**).
5. Remove the O-rings (**Figure 125**) from the crankcase cavity and discard them.
6. Install by reversing these removal steps. Note the following.
7. If the oil pump was disassembled or cleaned in solvent, pour clean engine oil into the 2 openings in the backside of the oil pump. This will prime the pump for the first start up.

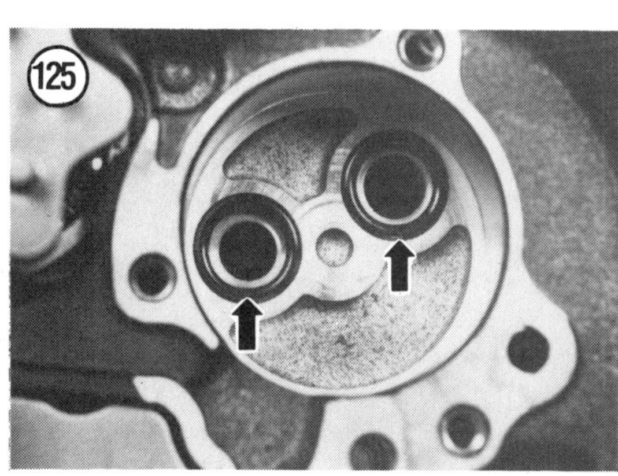
125

8. Install new O-ring seals (**Figure 125**) in the crankcase cavity and make sure they are in place.
9. Tighten the oil pump mounting bolts securely.
10. Make sure the idle gear circlip seats in the shaft groove completely.

Disassembly

Replacement parts for the oil pump are not available. If any part of the oil pump is faulty, the entire oil pump must be replaced.

The oil pump has 2 chambers with 2 sets of rotors of different thickness. The thin set of rotors are for the "feed" side of the oil pump while the thick set of rotors are for the "scavenger" side of the oil pump.

NOTE
*A helpful "tool" that should be used for oil pump disassembly is a large egg flat (the type restaurants get their eggs in). See **Figure 126**. As you remove a part from the shaft, set it in one of the depressions in the same position from which it*

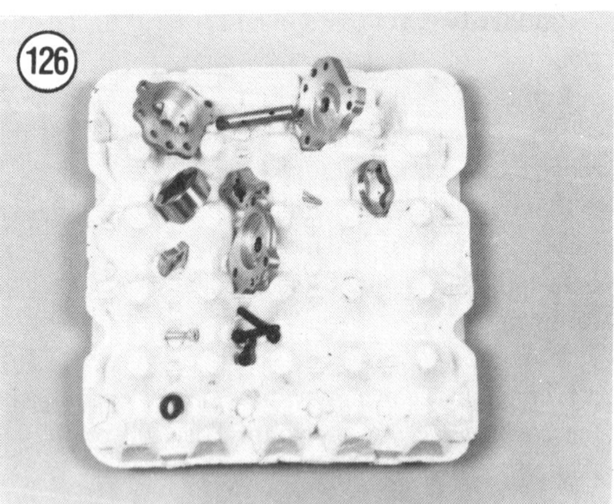
126

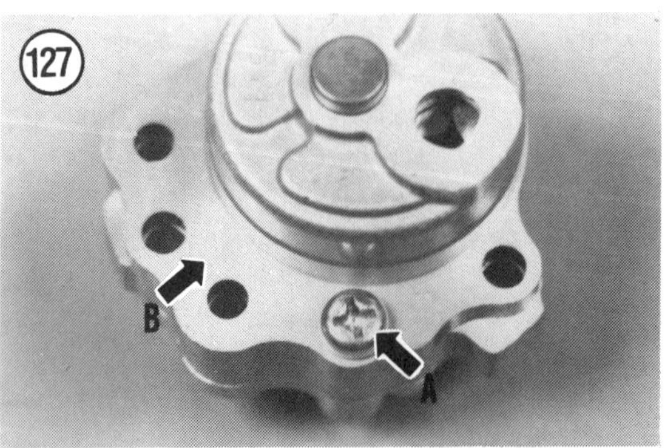
127

128

129

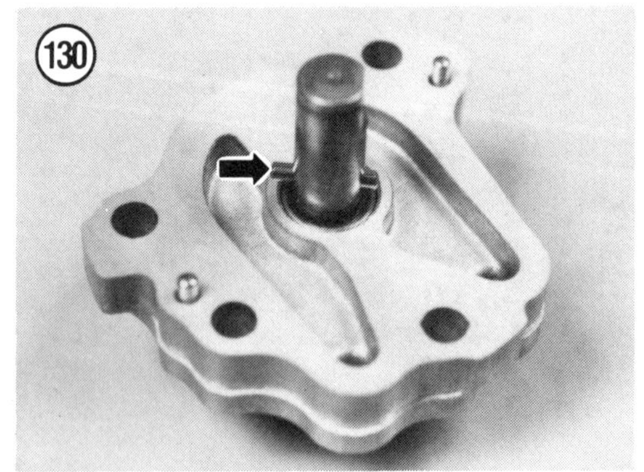
130

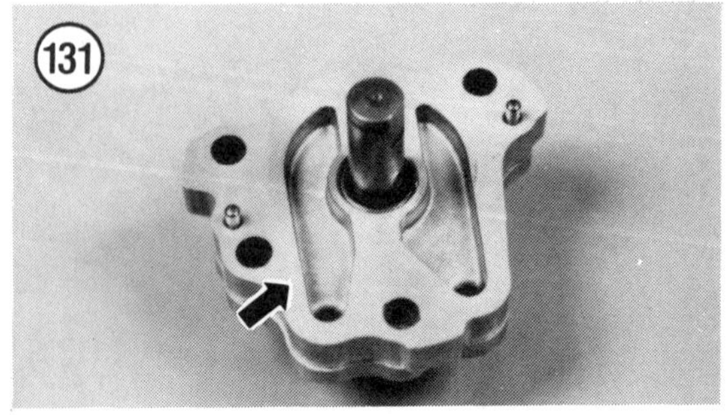
131

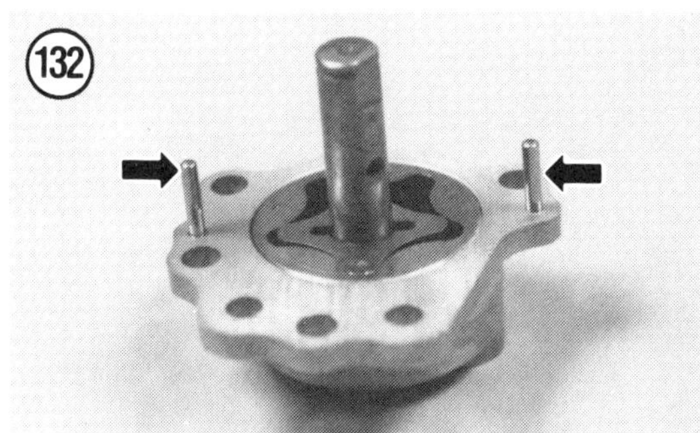

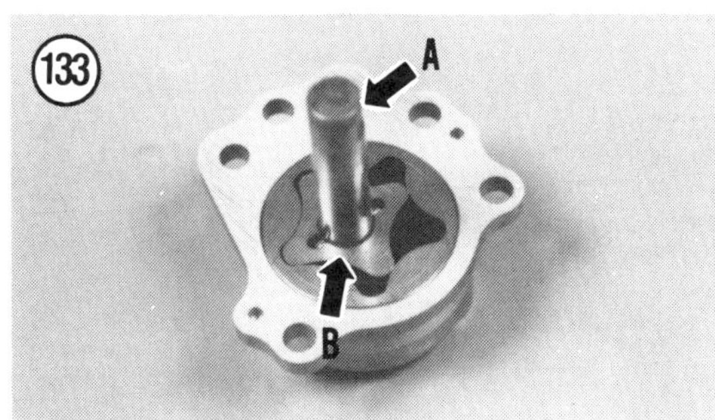

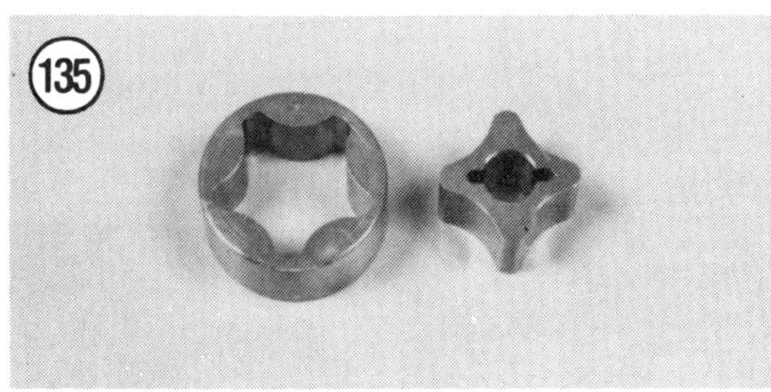

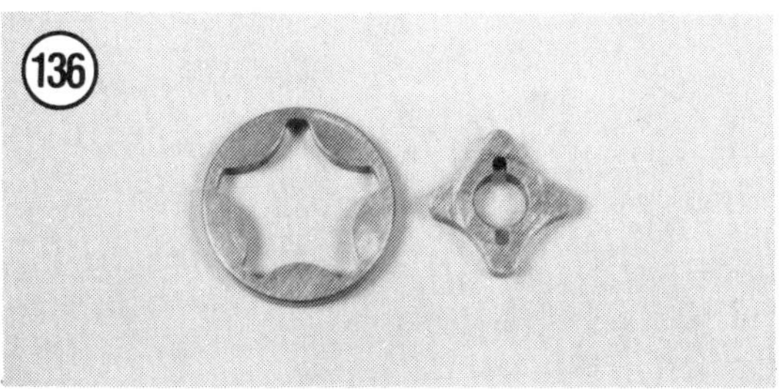

was removed. This is an easy way to remember the correct relationship of all parts.

1. Remove the Phillips screw (A, **Figure 127**) holding the assembly together.
2. Turn the oil pump assembly over and remove the "feed" rotor cover.
3. Remove the outer (**Figure 128**) and inner (**Figure 129**) "feed" rotors.
4. Remove the dowel pin (**Figure 130**).
5. Remove the separator panel (**Figure 131**).
6. Remove the 2 alignment pins (**Figure 132**).
7. Remove the pump shaft (A, **Figure 133**) and inner "scavenger" rotor (B, **Figure 133**).
8. Remove the outer "scavenger" rotor (**Figure 134**).
9. Inspect all parts as described in this chapter.

Inspection

1. Clean all parts in solvent and dry thoroughly.
2. Inspect the inner and outer rotors for scoring, cracks or other damage. Refer to **Figure 135** and **Figure 136**. Check the inner rotor pin slot for damage.
3. Check both oil pump covers (**Figure 137** and **Figure 138**) and separator panel (**Figure 139**) for

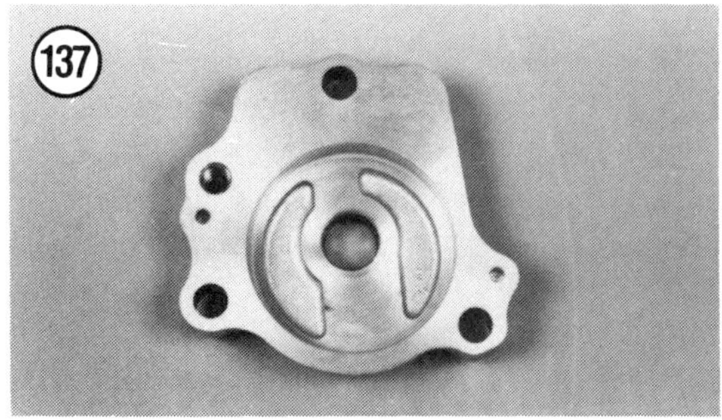

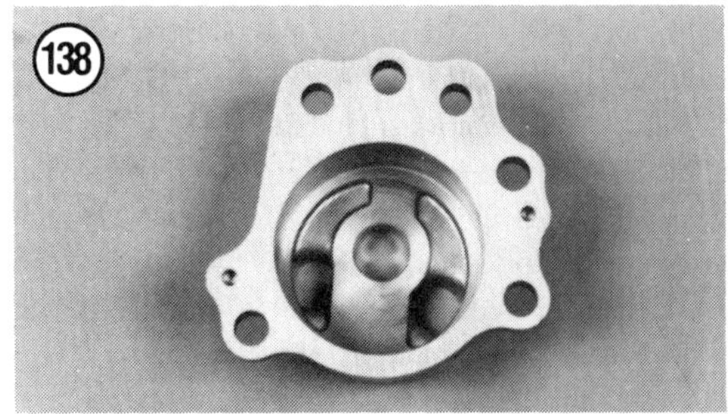

cracks or other damage. Check the shaft rotating area in each part for wear or damage.

4. Check the gear (**Figure 140**) for cracks, wear, breakage or other damage.

5. Check the pin holes (**Figure 141**) in the oil pump driven gear shaft. Check the hole for cracks or other damage.

6A. Inspect the thick "feed" rotors as follows:

a. Install the outer and inner "feed" rotors into the housing. Make sure the inner rotor pin slot faces up.

b. Check the clearance between the inner tip and the outer rotor with a flat feeler gauge (**Figure 142**). If the clearance is greater than the service limit in **Table 5**, the oil pump must be replaced.

6B. Inspect the thin "scavenger" rotors as follows:

a. Install the outer and inner "scavenger" rotors into the housing. Make sure the inner rotor pin slot faces up.

b. Check the clearance between the inner tip and the outer rotor with a flat feeler gauge (**Figure 143**). If the clearance is greater than the service limit in **Table 5**, the oil pump must be replaced.

7. Remove the rotors after performing the tests in Step 6.

Assembly

1. Apply clean engine oil to all components.

2. Install the "scavenger" outer rotor into the cover (**Figure 134**).

3. Install the pin (A, **Figure 144**) into the hole in the shaft that is away from the end with the circlip groove (B, **Figure 144**).

4. Install the shaft into the inner "scavenger" rotor and make sure the pin is indexed correctly (**Figure 145**).

5. Install shaft (A, **Figure 133**) and the inner rotor (B, **Figure 133**) into the cover and outer rotor.

6. Install the 2 alignment pins (**Figure 132**).

7. Install the separator panel (**Figure 131**).

8. Install the pin (**Figure 130**) into the shaft hole.

9. Install the "feed" inner rotor (**Figure 129**) and make sure the pin is indexed correctly.

10. Install the "feed" outer rotor (**Figure 128**) and make sure the pin is indexed correctly

11. Install the "feed" rotor cover (B, **Figure 127**).

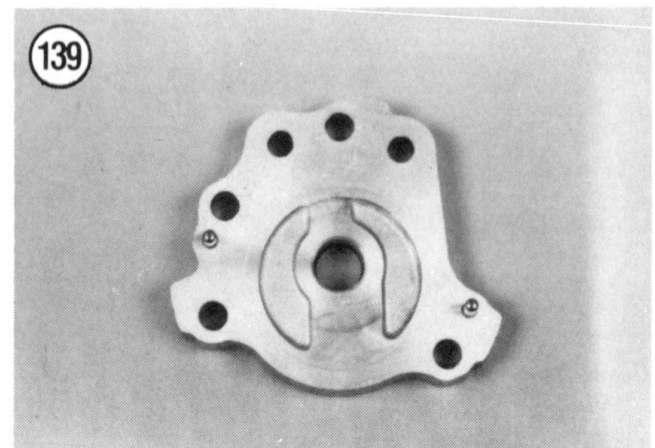
139

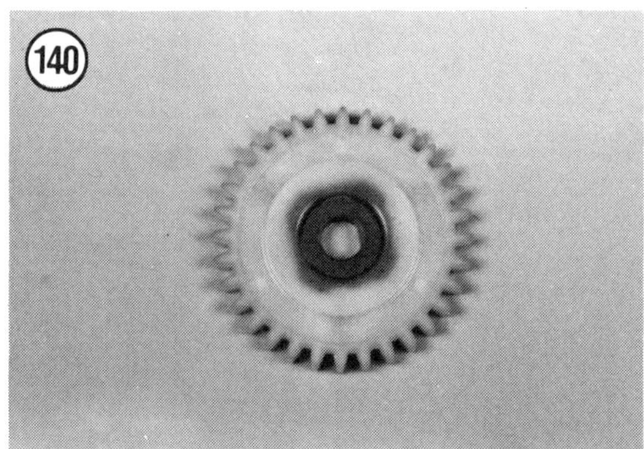
140

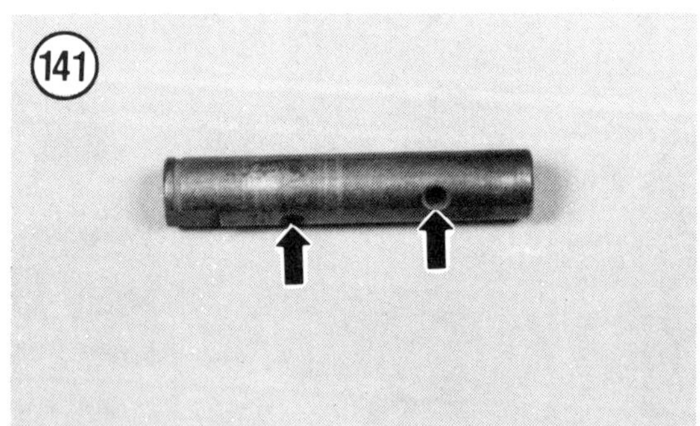
141

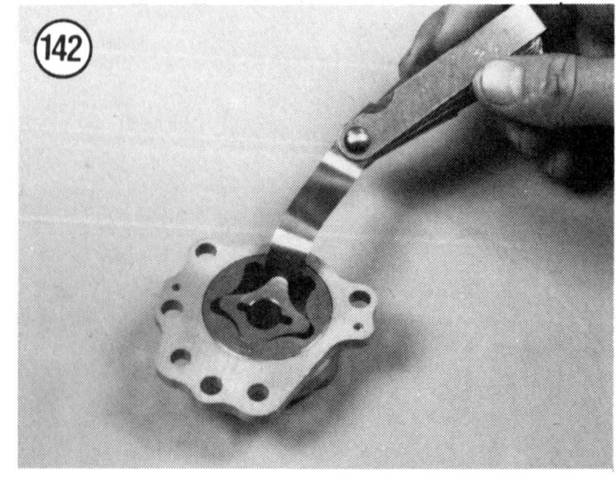
142

12. Apply Loctite 242 (blue) to the Phillips screw threads and install the screw (A, **Figure 127**) and tighten it securely.

13. Turn the pump shaft and make sure it turns smoothly. If the pump shaft is tight, something is wrong. Disassemble the pump and check the parts.

143

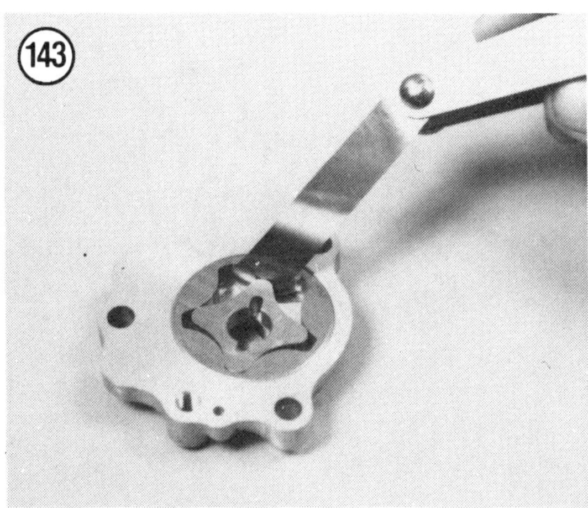

144

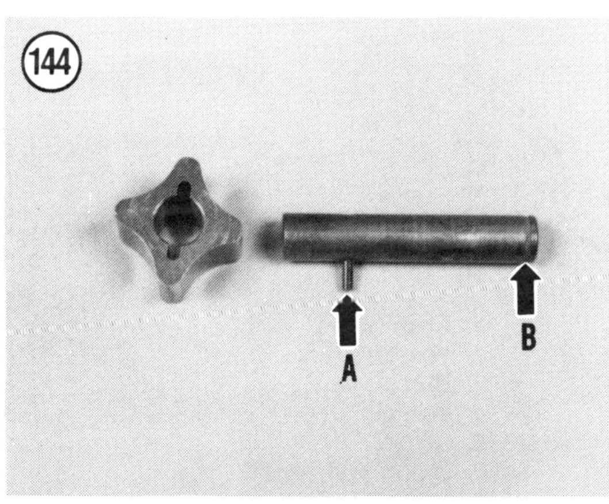

145

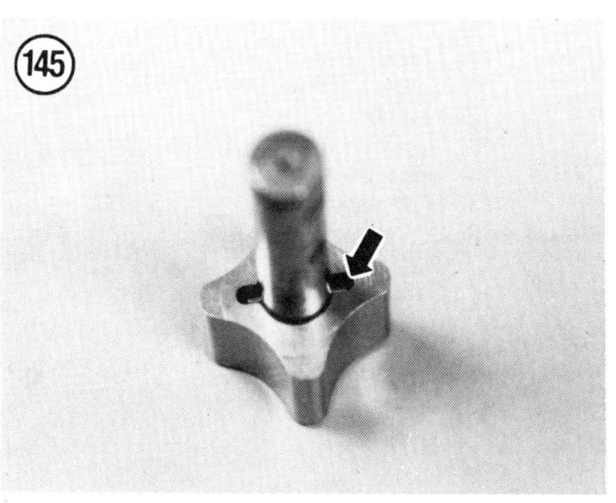

OIL TANK AND OIL HOSES

Oil Tank Removal/Installation

Refer to **Figure 146** for XT600 models or **Figure 147** for TT600 models for this procedure.

NOTE
This procedure is shown on a XT600 model. Where differences occur between the 2 models they are identified.

1. Place the motorcycle on a stand to support the bike securely.
2. Remove the left-hand side cover (**Figure 148**).
3. Remove the seat (A, **Figure 149**) as described in Chapter Thirteen.
4. To drain the oil tank, perform the following:
   a. Remove the filler cap/dipstick from the oil tank. Refer to B, **Figure 149** for XT600 models or A, **Figure 150** for TT600 models.
   b. Place a drip pan under the drain bolt location on the oil tank and have an assistant hold the drain pan in this position.
   c. Remove the oil tank drain bolt and gasket from the base of the oil tank. Refer to (**Figure 151**) for XT600 or B, **Figure 150** for TT600 models.
   d. Allow the oil to drain for a minimum of 5 minutes.
   e. Inspect the gasket on the drain bolt for wear or damage, replace if necessary.
   f. Reinstall the drain bolt and gasket. Tighten the drain bolt to the torque specification listed in **Table 3**.

5A. On XT600 models, to remove the lower oil hose from the oil tank, perform the following:
   a. Remove the screws securing the lower oil hose fitting (A, **Figure 152**) to the oil tank.
   b. Carefully lower the oil hose down and away from the oil tank.
   c. Remove the oil strainer.
   d. Place the loose end of the hose in a re-closable plastic bag. Close the end of the bag around the hose to prevent the entry of foreign matter and to catch any residual oil that may drain out of the hose.

5B. On TT600 models, to remove the lower oil hose from the oil tank, perform the following:

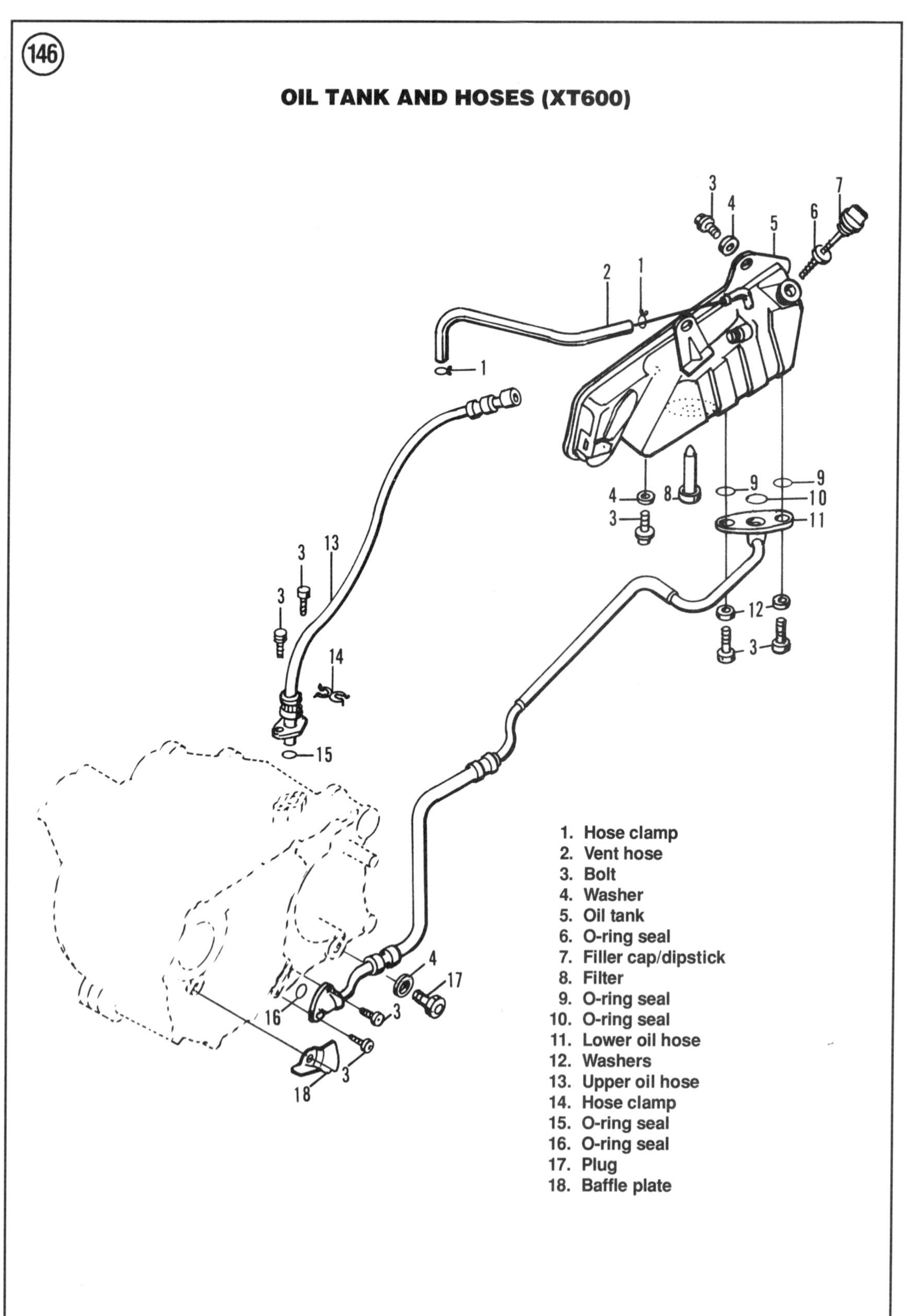
146
OIL TANK AND HOSES (XT600)
1. Hose clamp
2. Vent hose
3. Bolt
4. Washer
5. Oil tank
6. O-ring seal
7. Filler cap/dipstick
8. Filter
9. O-ring seal
10. O-ring seal
11. Lower oil hose
12. Washers
13. Upper oil hose
14. Hose clamp
15. O-ring seal
16. O-ring seal
17. Plug
18. Baffle plate

OIL TANK AND HOSES (TT600)

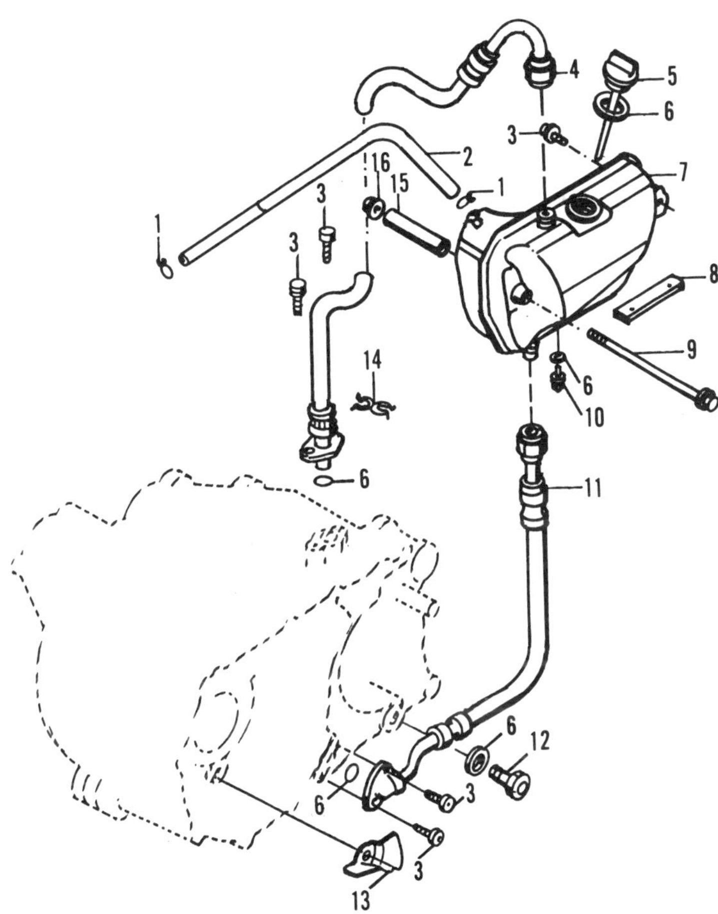

1. Hose clamp
2. Vent hose
3. Bolt
4. Upper oil hose
5. Filler cap/dipstick
6. O-ring seal
7. Oil tank
8. Rubber damper strip
9. Bolt
10. Drain bolt
11. Lower oil hose
12. Plug
13. Baffle plate
14. Hose clamp

a. Unscrew the fitting securing the upper oil hose fitting (C, **Figure 150**) to the oil tank.
b. Carefully lower the oil hose down and away from the oil tank.
c. Place the loose end of the hose in a re-closable plastic bag. Close the end of the bag around the hose to prevent the entry of foreign matter and to catch any residual oil that may drain out of the hose.

6. To remove the upper oil hose from the oil tank, perform the following:
   a. Unscrew the fitting securing the upper oil hose fitting to the oil tank. Refer to B, **Figure 152** for XT600 models or C, **Figure 150** for TT600 models.
   b. Carefully pull the oil hose off and away from the oil tank.
   c. Place the loose end of the hose in a re-closable plastic bag. Close the end of the bag around the hose to prevent the entry of foreign matter and to catch any residual oil that may drain out of the hose.
7. Disconnect the vent hose (C, **Figure 152**) from the top of the oil tank.

NOTE
There may still be some residual oil in the oil tank. Place your fingers over the oil hose openings to prevent the oil from draining out after the tank is removed from the frame.

8. Remove the bolts and washers securing the oil tank to the frame and remove the oil tank.
9. Install by reversing these removal steps. Note the following.
10. Tighten the oil tank mounting bolts securely.
11. On XT600 models, perform the following:
    a. Remove the O-ring seals (**Figure 153**) from the lower oil hose fitting.
    b. Inspect the O-rings for hardness or deterioration, replace if necessary. Reinstall the O-ring seals.
    c. Thoroughly clean the oil strainer with solvent and a soft-tooth brush and thoroughly dry with compressed air.
    d. Inspect the filter screen for holes or defects. If the oil strainer is damaged in any way, replace it.
    e. Install the O-ring seals into the lower oil hose fitting.

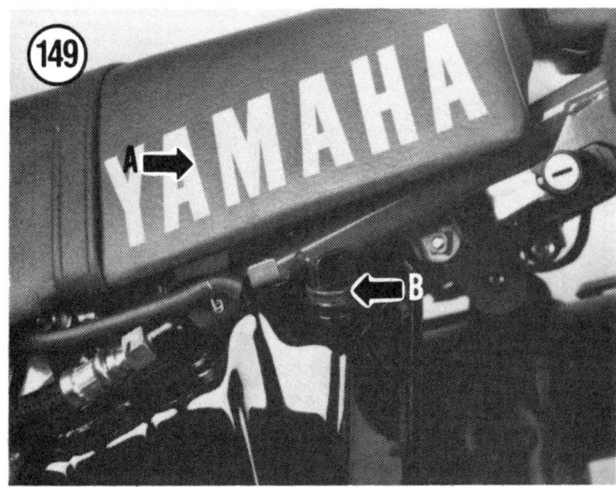

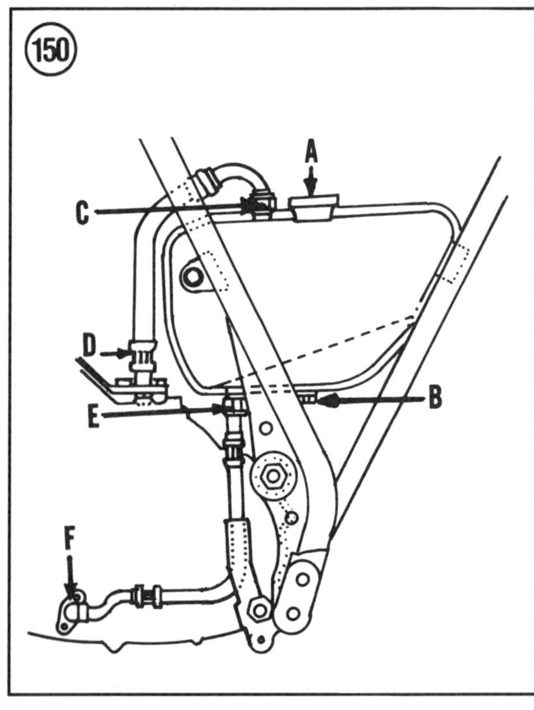

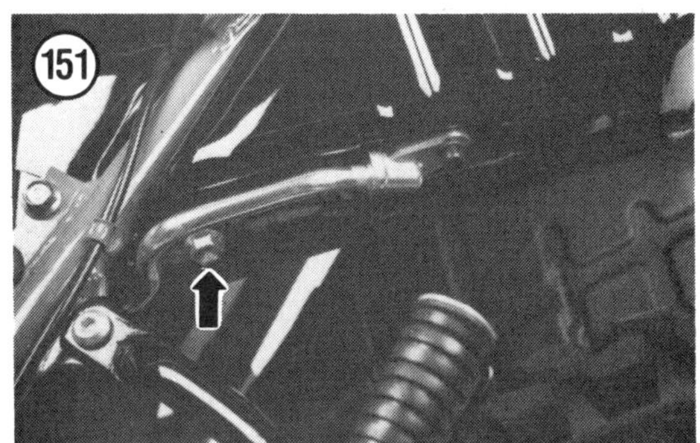

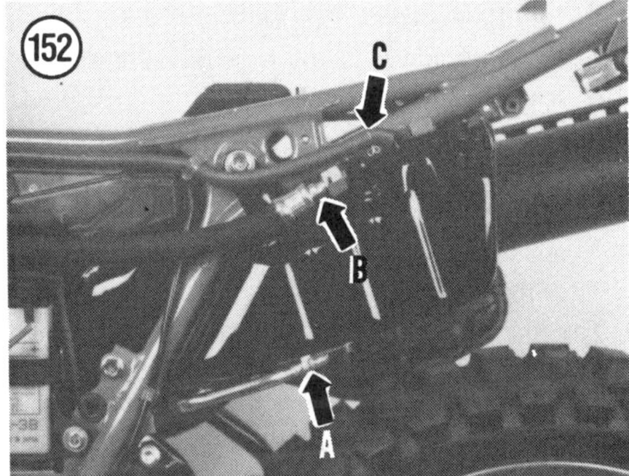

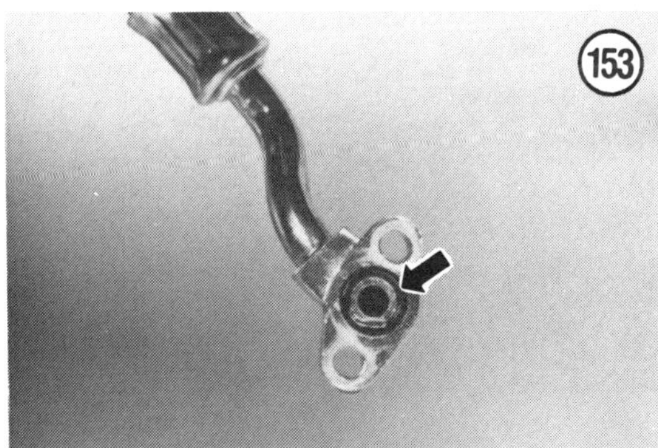

f. Install the oil strainer and move the lower oil hose into position on the base of the oil tank.
g. Install the screws and tighten securely.

12. Refill the oil tank with the correct type and quantity of oil as described under *Engine Oil and Filter Change* in Chapter Three.
13. Start the engine and check for oil leaks. If necessary, tighten any drain bolts or screws.
14. Turn the engine off and check the oil level, correct if necessary.

Upper Oil Hose Removal/Installation

Refer to **Figure 146** for XT600 models or **Figure 147** for TT600 models for this procedure.

NOTE
This procedure is shown on a XT600 model. Where differences occur between the 2 models, they are identified.

1. Place the motorcycle on a stand to support the bike securely.
2. Remove the left-hand side cover (**Figure 148**).
3. Remove the seat (A, **Figure 149**) as described in Chapter Thirteen.
4. Unscrew the fitting securing the upper oil hose fitting to the oil tank. Refer to B, **Figure 152** for XT600 models or C, **Figure 150** for TT600 models.
5. Carefully pull the oil hose off and away from the oil tank.
6. Place the loose end of the hose in a re-closable plastic bag. Close the end of the bag around the hose to prevent the entry of foreign matter and to catch any residual oil that may drain out of the hose.

7A. On XT600 models, remove the bolts (A, **Figure 154**) securing the upper oil hose (B, **Figure 154**) to the top of the crankcase.

7B. On TT600 models, remove the bolts securing the upper oil hose (D, **Figure 150**) to the top of the crankcase.

8. The oil hose will be filled with oil. Either place a small container under the fitting or a disposable rag to catch the oil when the fitting is removed.
9. Move the hose out of the way and drain out the residual oil.
10. Place the end of the hose in a re-closable plastic bag. Close the end of the bag around the hose to prevent the entry of foreign matter and to catch any residual oil that may drain out of the hose.

6

11. Remove the upper oil hose from the frame.
12. Install by reversing these removal steps. Note the following.
13. Inspect the O-ring (**Figure 155**) on the lower fitting for hardness or deterioration, replace if necessary. Reinstall the O-ring seal into the lower fitting.
14. Install the lower fitting onto the top surface of the crankcase and tighten the bolts securely.
15. Refill the oil tank with the correct type and quantity of oil as described under *Engine Oil and Filter Change* in Chapter Three.
16. Start the engine and check for oil leaks. If necessary, tighten the bolts or fitting.
17. Turn the engine off and check the oil level, correct if necessary.

Lower Oil Hose Removal/Installation

Refer to **Figure 146** for XT600 models or **Figure 150** for TT600 models for this procedure.

NOTE
This procedure is shown on a XT600 model. Where differences occur between the 2 models they are identified.

1. Drain the engine oil as described under *Engine Oil and Filter Change* in Chapter Three.
2. Remove the left-hand side cover (**Figure 148**).
3. Remove the seat (A, **Figure 149**) as described in Chapter Thirteen.
4A. On XT600 models, remove the bolts securing the engine skid plate (**Figure 156**) and remove the skid plate.
4B. On TT600 models, remove the bolts securing the engine guard and remove the guard.
5. Remove the right-hand footpeg/brake pedal bracket assembly as described under *Rear Brake Pedal Removal/Installation* in Chapter Twelve.
6. Remove the pinch bolt securing the shift lever (A, **Figure 157**) and pull the shift lever off the shaft. If the splined boss is tight on the shaft, spread the slot open with a screwdriver.
7. Remove the screws securing the drive sprocket cover (B, **Figure 157**) and remove the cover.
8A. On XT600 models, to remove the lower oil hose from the oil tank, perform the following:
  a. Remove the screws securing the lower oil hose fitting (A, **Figure 152**) to the oil tank.
  b. Carefully lower the oil hose down and away from the oil tank.
  c. Remove the oil strainer.
  d. Place the loose end of the hose in a re-closable plastic bag. Close the end of the bag around the hose to prevent the entry of foreign matter and to catch any residual oil that may drain out of the hose.

8B. On TT600 models, to remove the lower oil hose from the oil tank, perform the following:
  a. Unscrew the fitting securing the lower oil hose fitting (E, **Figure 150**) to the oil tank.
  b. Carefully lower the oil hose down and away from the oil tank.
  c. Place the loose end of the hose in a re-closable plastic bag. Close the end of the bag around the hose to prevent the entry of foreign matter and to catch any residual oil that may drain out of the hose.

9. The lower oil hose may still be filled with oil. Either place a small container under the fitting or a

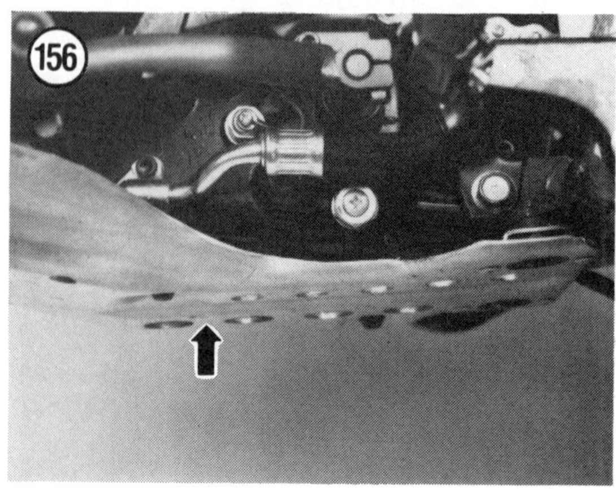

disposable rag to catch the oil when the fitting is removed.

10A. On XT600 models, remove the bolts (A, **Figure 158**) securing the lower oil hose (B, **Figure 158**) to the side of the crankcase.

10B. On TT600 models, remove the bolts securing the lower oil hose (F, **Figure 150**) to the side of the crankcase.

11. Move the hose out of the way and drain out the residual oil.

12. Remove the O-ring seal (**Figure 153**) from the lower fitting.

13. Place the end of the hose in a re-closable plastic bag. Close the end of the bag around the hose to prevent the entry of foreign matter and to catch any residual oil that may drain out of the hose.

14. Remove the lower oil hose from the frame.

15. Install by reversing these removal steps. Note the following.

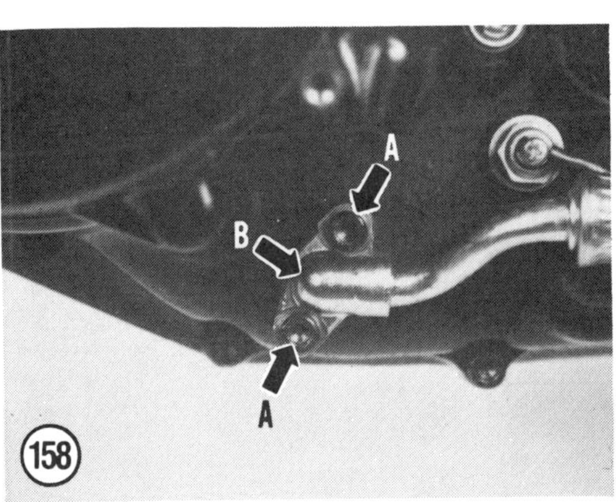

16. Inspect the O-ring for hardness or deterioration, replace if necessary. Reinstall the O-ring seal into the lower fitting.

17. Refill the oil tank and engine with the correct type and quantity of oil as described under *Engine Oil and Filter Change* in Chapter Three.

18. Start the engine and check for oil leaks. If necessary, tighten the drain bolt or screws.

19. Turn the engine off and check the oil level, correct if necessary.

EXTERNAL SHIFT MECHANISM

The external shift mechanism is located on the same side of the crankcase as the clutch assembly and can be removed with the engine in the frame. To remove the shift shaft, change shaft, shift drum and shift forks, it is necessary to remove the engine and split the crankcases as described in Chapter Five.

6

Removal

Refer to **Figure 159** and **Figure 160** for this procedure.

1. Remove the clutch assembly as described in this chapter.
2. Removed the kickstarter assembly as described in this chapter.
3. Remove the circlip (**Figure 161**) and remove the oil pump idle gear (**Figure 162**).
4. Remove the E-clip (**Figure 163**) securing the shift lever assembly.
5. Slide the shift lever/return spring assembly (**Figure 164**) and the washer (**Figure 165**) off of the shift shaft.
6. Remove the shoulder bolt (A, **Figure 166**) securing the stopper arm (B, **Figure 166**).
7. Remove the stopper arm, collar and the spring.

Inspection

1. Check the shift lever assembly (**Figure 167**). Check the engagement arms on the lever for wear or damage. Damage or severe wear with the engagements will cause shifting problems.
2. Check the return spring (**Figure 168**) on the shift lever assembly. Replace the return spring if it shows signs of fatigue or if it is cracked.

EXTERNAL SHIFT MECHANISM

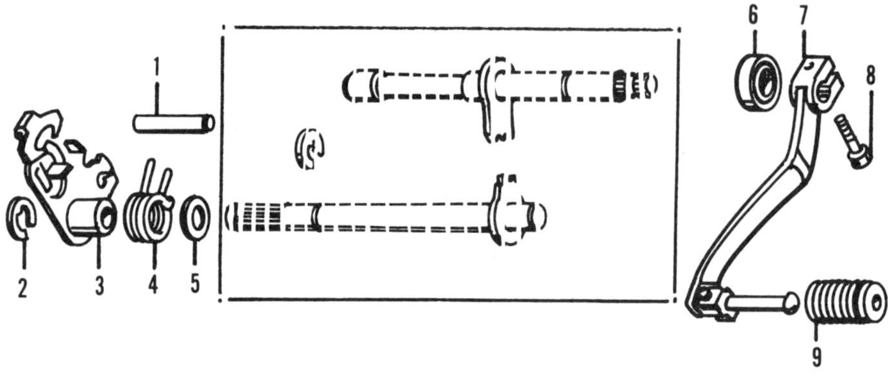

1. Dowel pin
2. Circlip
3. Shift lever assembly
4. Return spring
5. Washer
6. Oil seal
7. Gearshift lever
8. Bolt
9. Rubber pad

EXTERNAL SHIFT MECHANISM

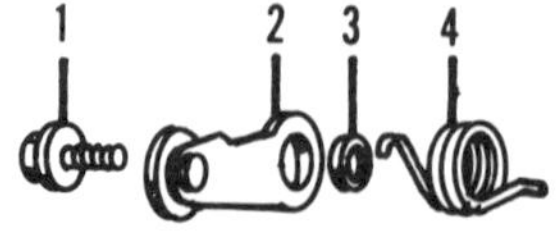

1. Bolt
2. Stopper arm
3. Collar
4. Spring

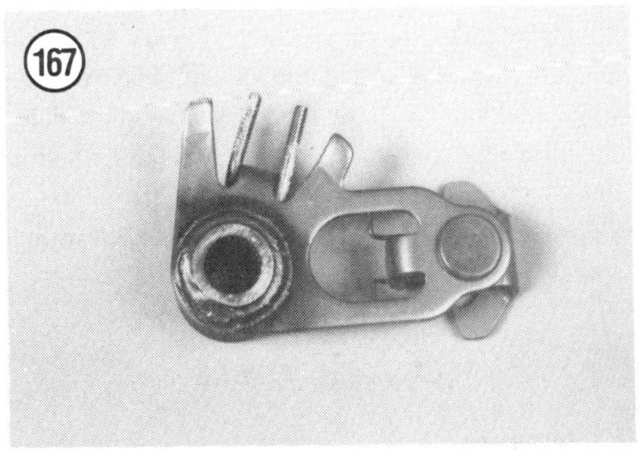

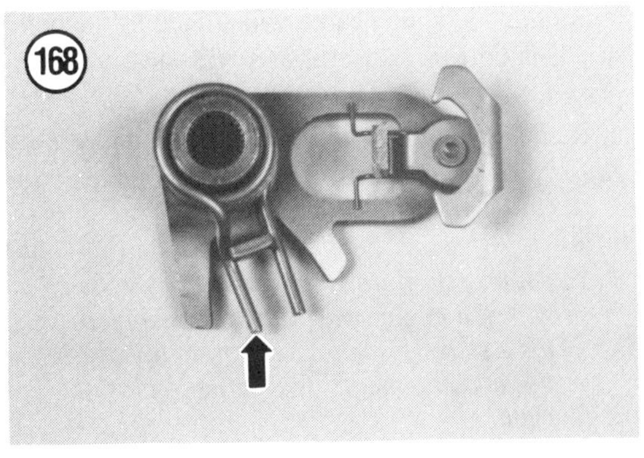

6

3. Check the roller (**Figure 169**) on the stopper lever. It must rotate freely with no signs of binding.

Installation

Refer to **Figure 159** and **Figure 160** for this procedure.

1. Install the spring, stopper arm and collar (A, **Figure 170**) onto the raised boss.
2. Install the shoulder bolt (B, **Figure 170**) securing the stopper arm. Do not tighten the bolt at this time.
3. Hook the spring onto the stopper arm (B, **Figure 166**).
4. Move the stopper arm up and onto the shift drum cam (C, **Figure 166**).
5. Tighten the shoulder bolt securely.
6. Slide the washer (**Figure 165**) onto the shift shaft.
7. Align the index mark on the shift lever assembly with the index mark on the shift shaft and install the shift lever onto the shift shaft (**Figure 171**).
8. Make sure the return spring is properly indexed onto the raised pin (**Figure 172**).
9. Install the E-clip (**Figure 163**) securing the shift lever assembly. Make sure the E-clip is properly seated on the shaft.
10. Install the oil pump idle gear (**Figure 162**) onto the oil pump and install the circlip (**Figure 161**). Make sure the circlip is properly seated on the shaft.
11. Install the kickstarter assembly as described in this chapter.
12. Install the clutch assembly as described in this chapter.

CLUTCH CABLE

Replacement

In time, the clutch cable will stretch to the point that it is no longer useful and will have to be replaced.

1. Remove the fuel tank as described under *Fuel Tank Removal/Installation* in Chapter Eight.

NOTE
Some of the following figures are shown with the engine partially disassembled for clarity. It is not necessary to remove these components for cable replacement.

2. Pull the protective boot (A, **Figure 173**) away from the clutch lever.
3. Loosen the locknut (B, **Figure 173**) and adjusting barrel (C, **Figure 173**).

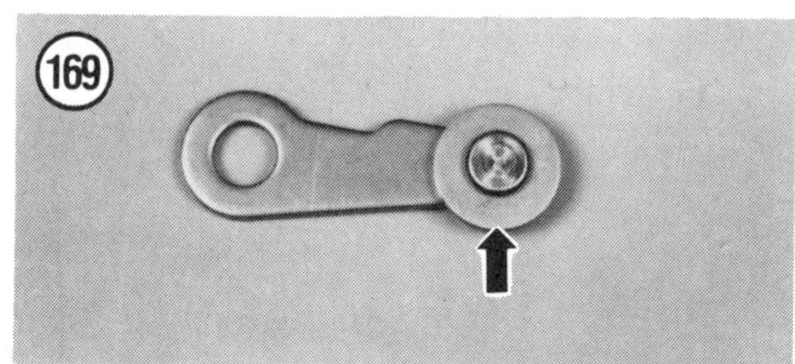
169

170

171

172

4. Slip the cable end out of the hand lever.
5. Loosen the locknuts (A, **Figure 174**) at the cable receptacle on the alternator cover.
6. Disconnect the clutch cable (B, **Figure 174**) from the push lever (C, **Figure 174**) on the left-hand side of the engine.

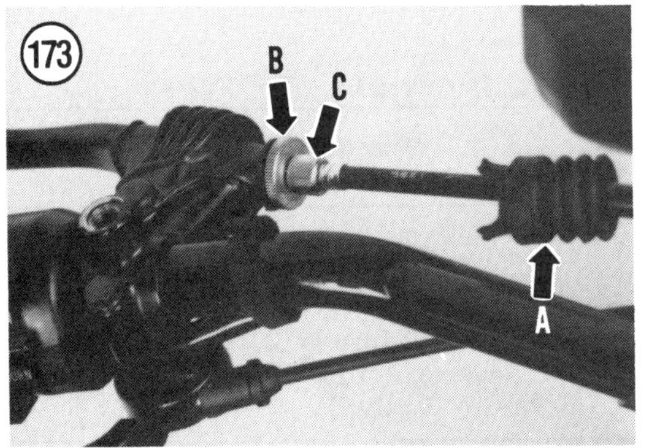

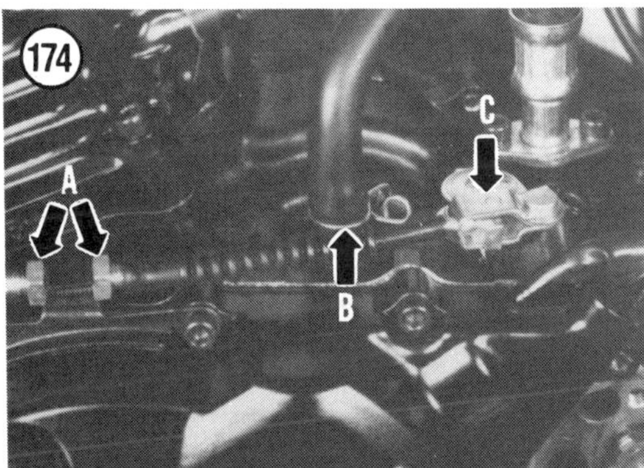

NOTE

Prior to removing the cable, make a drawing (or take a Polaroid picture) of the cable routing through the frame. It is very easy to forget its routing after it has been removed. Replace the cable exactly as it was, avoiding any sharp turns.

7. Unhook the cable straps holding the clutch cable to the handlebar.
8. Pull the cable out of the retaining clip (**Figure 175**) on the frame down tube on the left-hand side.
9. Remove the cable and replace it with a new one.
10. Install by reversing these removal steps. Note the following.
11. Make sure it is correctly routed with no sharp turns.
12. Adjust the clutch cable as described in Chapter Three.

6

Tables are on the following page.

Table 1 GENERAL CLUTCH SPECIFICATIONS

Clutch type	Wet, multiple-disc
Clutch release method	Cam push type
Number of clutch plates	
Friction	
Small inner diameter	2
Large inner diameter	6
Steel plates	7

Table 2 CLUTCH SERVICE SPECIFICATIONS

Item	Specification mm (in.)	Wear limit mm (in.)
Friction plate thickness		
Small inner diameter	2.72-2.88 (0.107-0.113)	2.60 (0.102)
Large inner diameter	2.90-3.10 (0.114-0.122)	2.80 (0.110)
Metal clutch plate thickness	1.2 (0.047)	—
Warp limit	—	0.20 (0.008)
Clutch spring free length	34.6 (1.362)	32.6 (1.284)
Push rod bend limit	—	0.5 (0.02)

Table 3 TIGHTENING TORQUES

Item	N•m	ft.-lb.
Clutch nut	70	51
Adjust nut on pushrod No. 1	8	5.8
Primary drive gear nut	110	81
Balancer shaft driven gear nut		
XT600	60	44
TT600	90	66
Camshaft chain rear guide bolts	8	5.8
Oil tank drain bolt	18	13

Table 4 KICKSTARTER SERVICE SPECIFICATIONS

Item	Specification	Wear limit
Ratchet spring free length	17.2 mm (0.677 in.)	15.0 mm (0.59 in.)

Table 5 OIL PUMP SERVICE SPECIFICATIONS

Item	Specification mm (in.)	Wear limit mm (in.)
Oil pump*		
Inner tip-to-outer rotor clearance	0.15 (0.006)	— —
Housing and outer rotor clearance	0.03-0.09 (0.0012-0.0035)	0.15 (0.006)

* Specifications are for both the scavenger and feed set of rotors.

CHAPTER SEVEN

TRANSMISSION AND INTERNAL SHIFT MECHANISM

7

The transmission is a 5-speed unit. To gain access to the transmission and internal shift mechanism, it is necessary to remove the engine and split the crankcase as described in Chapter Five. Once the crankcase has been split, removal of the transmission and shift drum and forks is a simple task of pulling the assemblies up and out of the crankcase.

Transmission ratios are listed in **Table 1** located at the end of the chapter.

NOTE

If disassembling a used, well run-in engine for the first time by yourself, pay particular attention to any additional shims that may have been added by a previous owner. These may have been added to take up the tolerance of worn components and must be reinstalled in the same position since the shims have developed a wear pattern. If new parts are going to be installed, these shims may be eliminated. This is something you will have to determine upon reassembly.

TRANSMISSION OPERATION

The basic transmission has 5 pairs of constantly meshed gears on the mainshaft (A, **Figure 1**) and countershaft (B, **Figure 1**). Each pair of meshed gears gives one gear ratio. In each pair, one of the gears is locked to its shaft and always turns with it. The other gear is not locked to its shaft and can spin freely on it. Next to each free spinning gear is a third gear which is splined to the same shaft, always turning with it. This third gear can slide from side-to-side along the shaft splines. The side of the sliding gear and the free spinning gear have mating "dogs" (**Figure 2**) and "slots" (**Figure 3**). When the sliding gear moves up against the free spinning gear, the 2 gears are locked together, locking the free spinning gear to its shaft. Since both meshed mainshaft and countershaft gears are now locked to their shafts, power is transmitted at that gear ratio.

Shift Drum and Forks

Each sliding gear has a deep groove machined around its outside (**Figure 4**). The curved shift fork arm rides in this groove, controlling the side-to-side sliding of the gear and therefore the selection of different gear ratios. Each shift fork slides back and forth on a shift fork shaft (**Figure 5**). Each shift fork has a peg (**Figure 6**) that rides in a groove (**Figure 7**) machined in the shift drum. When the shift linkage rotates the shift drum, the zigzag grooves move the shift forks thus sliding the gears back and forth to shift from gear-to-gear.

TRANSMISSION TROUBLESHOOTING

Refer to Chapter Two.

TRANSMISSION OVERHAUL

Removal/Installation

Remove and install the transmission and internal shift mechanism as described under *Crankcase Disassembly* and *Crankcase Assembly* in Chapter Five.

Transmission Service Notes

1. A divided container such as a 3 dozen egg flat can be used to help maintain correct alignment and position of the parts as they are removed from the transmission shafts.
2. The circlips are a tight fit on the transmission shafts. Circlips are relatively inexpensive and should all be replaced every time the transmission is disassembled.
3. Circlips will turn and fold over, making removal and installation difficult. To ease circlip removal and installation, open the circlip with a pair of circlip pliers while at the same time holding the back of the circlip with a pair of pliers.

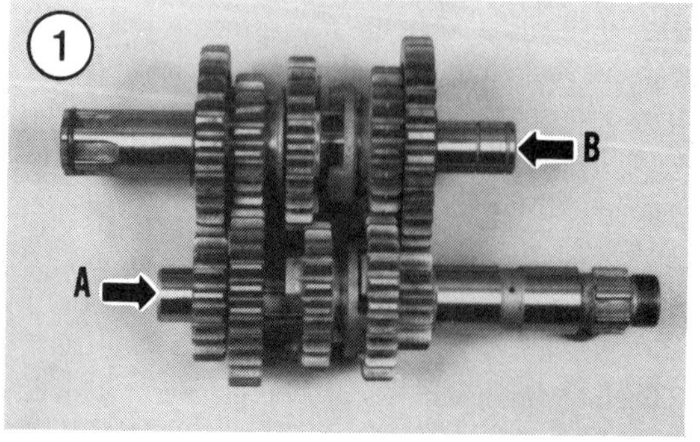

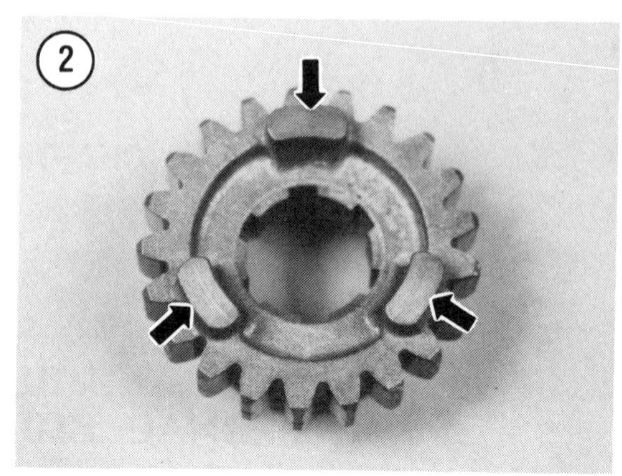

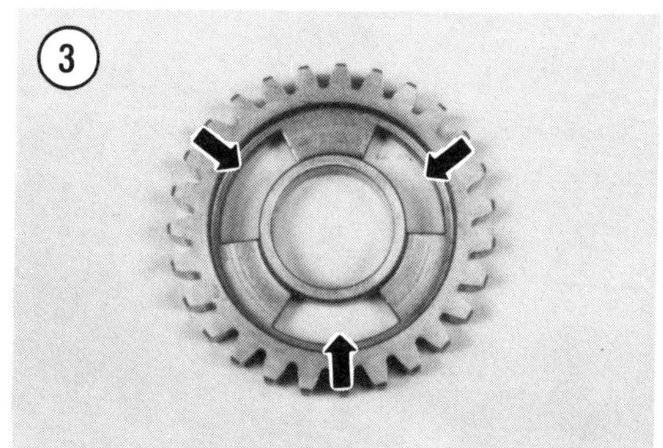

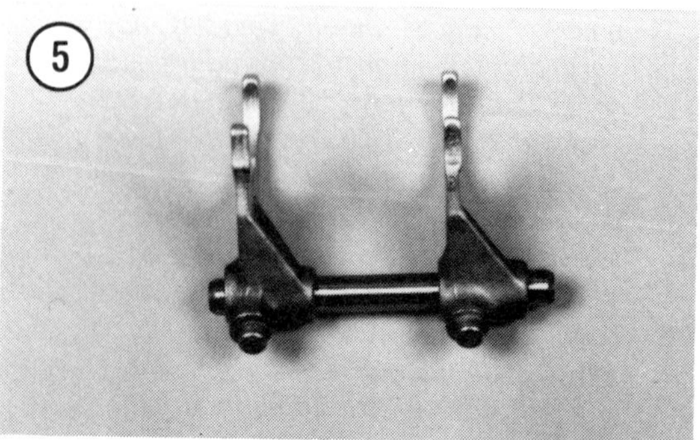

6

7

8

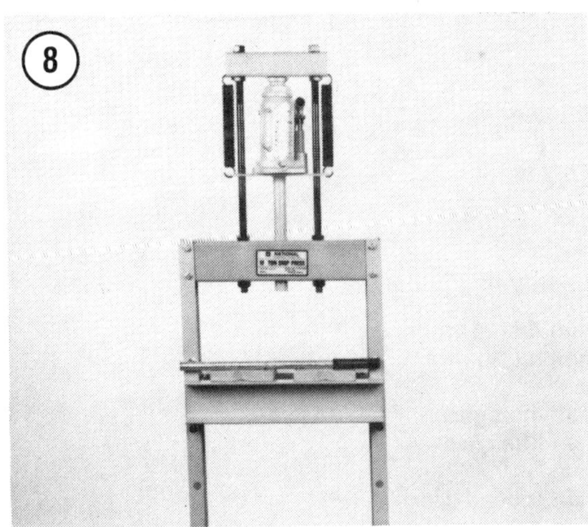

9

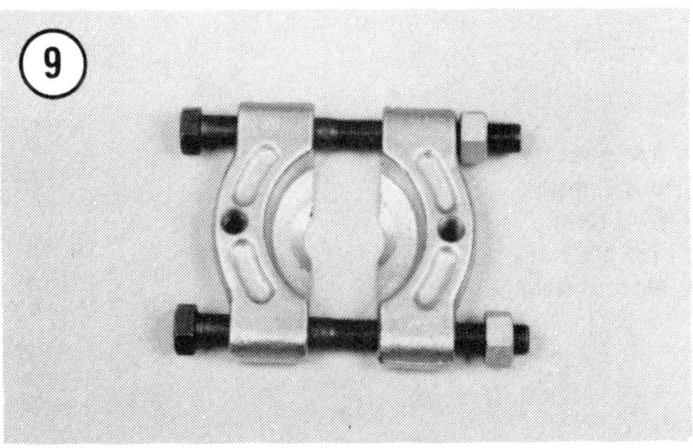

Mainshaft Disassembly/Assembly

A hydraulic press (**Figure 8**) and a bearing splitter (**Figure 9**) are required to disassemble and reassemble the mainshaft. If you do not have access to a press, have the mainshaft rebuilt by a Yamaha dealer or machine shop.

Refer to **Figure 10** for this procedure.

Yamaha does not provide specific dimensions for the overall length of the transmission mainshaft nor the clearance between the second and fifth gears. If your transmission was not operating correctly prior to disassembly, refer to a Yamaha service department for advice.

NOTE

A helpful "tool" that should be used for transmission disassembly is a large egg flat (the type restaurants get their eggs in). See ***Figure 11****. As you remove a part from the shaft, set it in one of the depressions in the same position from which it was removed. This is an easy way to remember the correct relationship of all parts.*

1. Place the assembled shaft into a large can or plastic bucket and thoroughly clean with solvent and a stiff brush. Dry with compressed air or let sit on rags to drip dry.

CAUTION

*When measuring the width of the mainshaft, be sure to place one end of the vernier caliper on the machined surface of the second gear shoulder (****A, Figure 12****). Do* ***not*** *place the vernier caliper on the end of the transmission mainshaft (****B, Figure 12****) since it is not a machined surface and may not provide a consistent measuring point.*

2. Measure the width of the installed gears on the mainshaft with a vernier caliper from one side of the second gear shoulder (A, **Figure 13**) to the other side of the first gear (B, **Figure 13**); record this measurement. This information will be used when reassembling the mainshaft.

3. Use a flat feeler gauge and measure the clearance between the mainshaft second and fifth gears (C, **Figure 13**); record each measurement. This infor-

(10)

TRANSMISSION

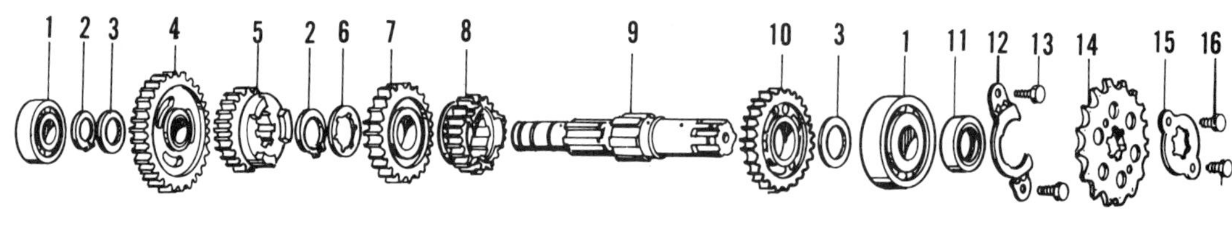

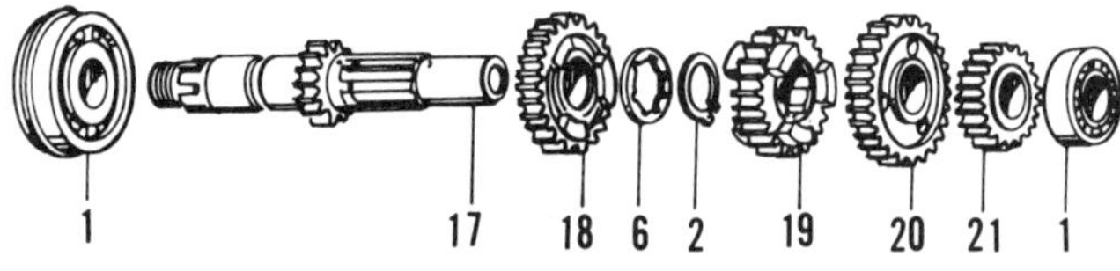

1. Bearing
2. Circlip
3. Spacer
4. Countershaft first gear
5. Countershaft fourth gear
6. Splined washer
7. Countershaft third gear
8. Countershaft fifth gear
9. Countershaft
10. Countershaft second gear
11. Oil seal
12. Seal retainer
13. Bolt
14. Drive sprocket
15. Lockplate
16. Bolt
17. Mainshaft/first gear
18. Mainshaft fourth gear
19. Mainshaft third gear
20. Mainshaft fifth gear
21. Mainshaft second gear

mation will be used when reassembling the mainshaft.

NOTE
When using a press and bearing splitter to disassemble and assemble the mainshaft, follow the manufacturer's instructions and guidelines when using their equipment. It is recommended to wear safety glasses when using press equipment.

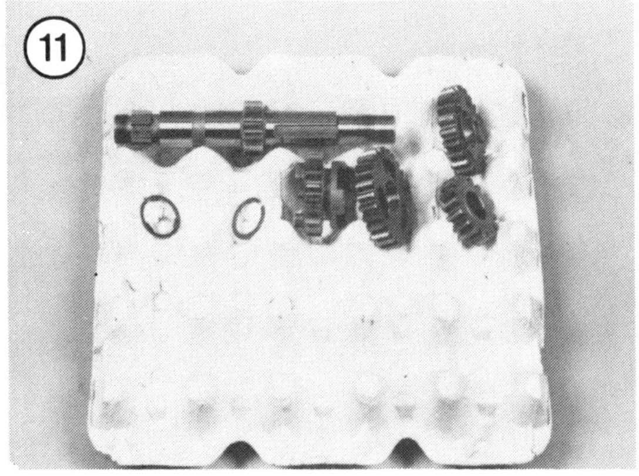
11

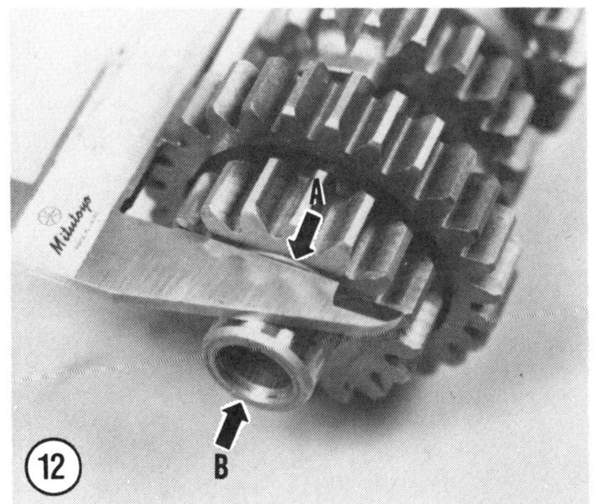

12

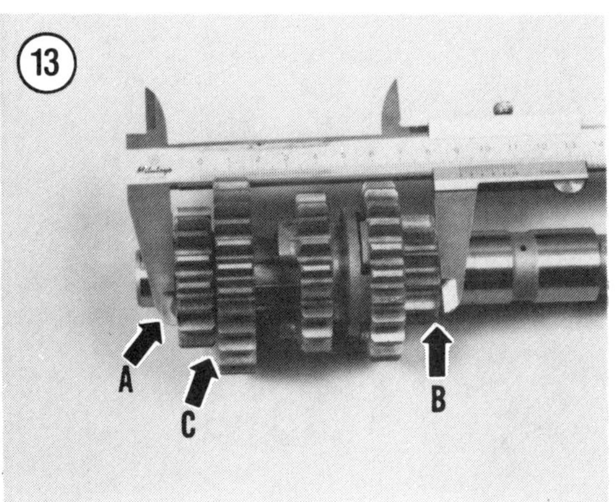

13

4. Press off mainshaft second gear as follows:

CAUTION
Do not position the bearing splitter under the second gear. The approach angle on the bearing splitter is usually too shallow and may damage the backside of the second gear. There is more room between the fifth gear and the third gear and there is less chance of damaging the gears by placing the bearing splitter in this location.

a. Install a bearing splitter below the mainshaft fifth gear (A, **Figure 14**). Then tighten the bearing splitter and install the mainshaft onto the press plate.
b. Place a 1/2 inch socket extension (B, **Figure 14**) between the end of the shaft and the press.
c. Apply pressure and press off the mainshaft second gear (C, **Figure 14**). Make sure to place your hand or another support underneath the transmission assembly to catch the assembly as the second gear is pressed off.
d. Remove the mainshaft second gear and fifth gear (D, **Figure 14**).
e. Relieve the press pressure and remove the transmission shaft from the press.

5. Slide off the third gear.
6. Remove the circlip and slide off the splined washer.

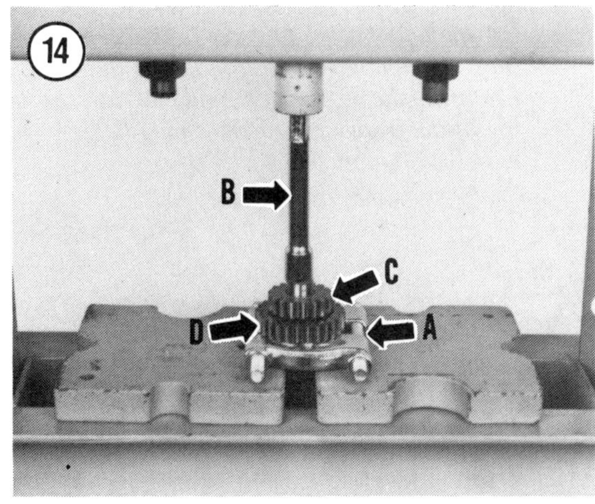

14

7. Slide off the fourth gear.

8. The mainshaft first gear (**Figure 15**) is part of the mainshaft assembly.

9. Inspect the mainshaft parts as described under *Transmission Inspection* in this chapter.

10. Slide on the fourth gear (**Figure 16**) with the dog side going on last.

11. Install the splined washer (**Figure 17**).

12. Install a *new* circlip (**Figure 18**) into the groove.

13. Slide on the third gear with the shift fork groove (**Figure 19**) side going on first and slide the gear on (**Figure 20**).

14. Slide on the fifth gear (**Figure 21**) with the flat side going on last. The side with the engagement slots for the dogs going on first.

NOTE

Pressing the second gear onto the shaft can be frustrating. The second gear may not press on smoothly and may tend to "jump" as it travels down the mainshaft. The second gear must be pressed on until there is a specified clearance between the second and fifth gears and also the overall length must be correct. There is no shoulder on the mainshaft for the second gear to bottom out on. When the second gear approaches the fifth gear it may "jump" and make contact with the fifth gear eliminating the required clearance between the two gears. If this happens and the clearance has been eliminated, or is less than specified, the second gear must be pressed back off of the mainshaft and then pressed back on again. The ease or difficulty of this procedure is based on the manufacturing tolerance between these two parts. The recommended heating of the second gear and the cooling of the transmission shaft may help ease installation.

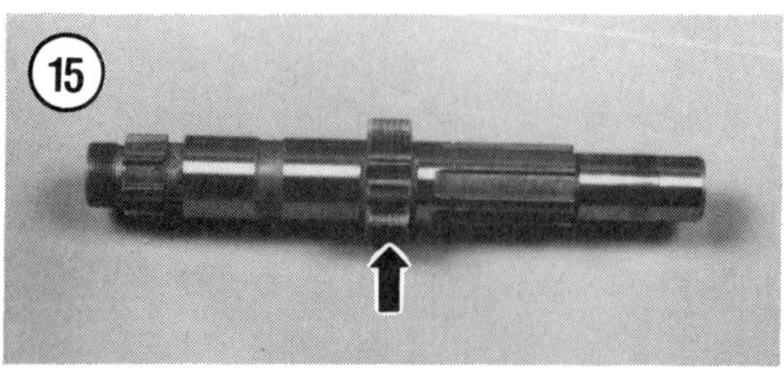
15

16

17

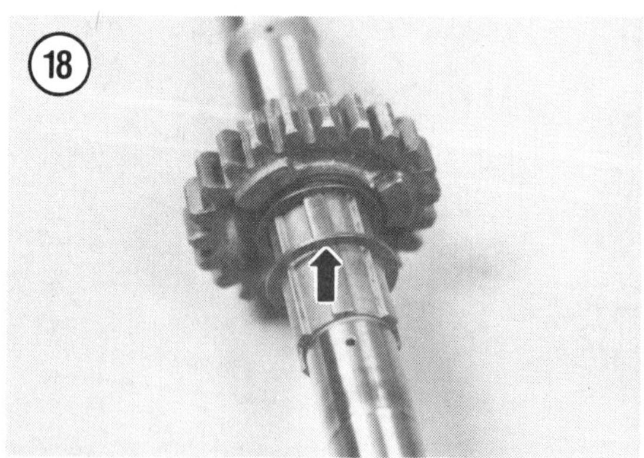
18

19

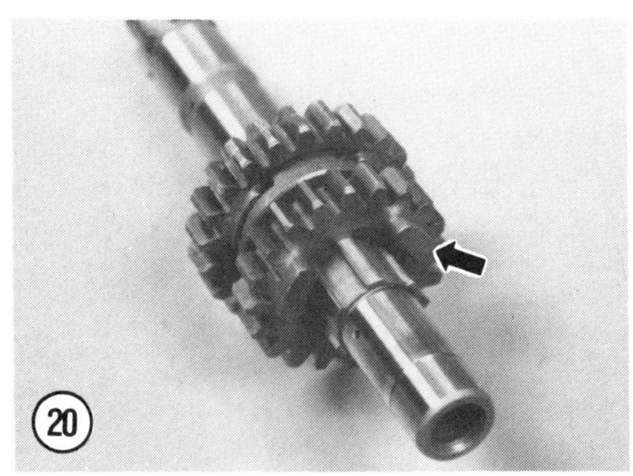

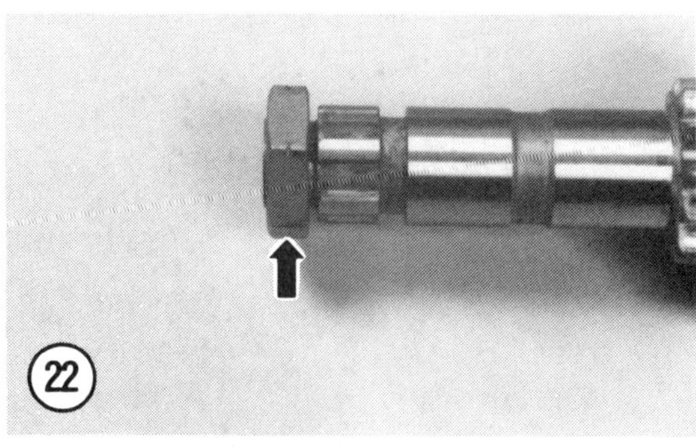

15. Press the second gear onto the mainshaft as follows:
   a. Install the clutch nut (**Figure 22**) onto the end of the mainshaft. Screw the nut on only far enough so the end of the mainshaft does not protrude past the end of the nut. The press pressure is to be applied to the face of the nut and not onto the end of the mainshaft where the threaded end could be damaged.
   b. Place the transmission shaft assembly in the freezer for about one-half hour. This will slightly reduce the outer diameter of the shaft where the second gear is going to be pressed on.
   c. Place the second gear on a hot plate or in a shop oven and heat it to a temperature of about 212° F (100° C). An easy way to check to see that it is at the proper temperature is to drop tiny drops of water on the gear; if they sizzle and evaporate immediately, the temperature is correct. This will slightly increase the inside diameter of the transmission shaft hole in the gear.
   d. Apply a light coat of assembly oil or molybdenum disulfide grease to the outer surface of the transmission shaft.

WARNING

Use heavy gloves to handle the second gear—remember that it is hot.

   e. Position the second gear with the large shoulder going on first—facing toward the fifth gear.
   f. Partially install the second gear (**Figure 23**) onto the end of the transmission shaft.
   g. Place the transmission shaft assembly onto the press plates (A, **Figure 24**).

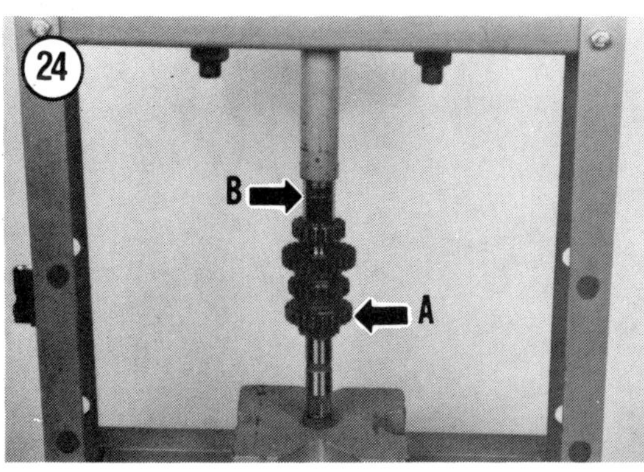

h. Place a suitable size socket (B, **Figure 24**) onto the second gear. The inside diameter of the socket must be large enough so that it doesn't contact the end of the mainshaft.

i. Apply a small amount of press pressure.

j. Carefully press the second gear onto the mainshaft.

k. Place the correct thickness flat feeler gauge (**Figure 25**) between the second and the fifth gears. The correct gauge thickness was determined prior to disassembly in Step 3.

l. While pressing the gear into place, periodically stop and check the clearance between the two gears. Continue to press the second gear on until the clearance is correct. As previously noted, if the gear "jumps" and takes up all of the clearance; the second gear must be pressed back off and this procedure repeated until the clearance is correct.

m. Relieve the press pressure and remove the transmission shaft from the press.

n. Measure the assembled length of the gears with a vernier caliper (**Figure 13**). Refer to the measurements taken before disassembly in Step 2.

o. Assembly is complete when the assembled gear length is correct and the clearance between the second and fifth gears are the same as that recorded during disassembly in Step 2.

16. After assembly is complete, refer to **Figure 26** for the correct placement of all gears.

Countershaft Disassembly/Assembly

Refer to **Figure 10** for this procedure.

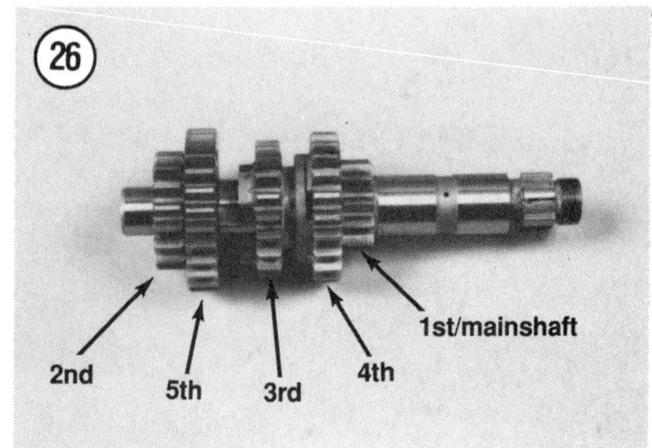

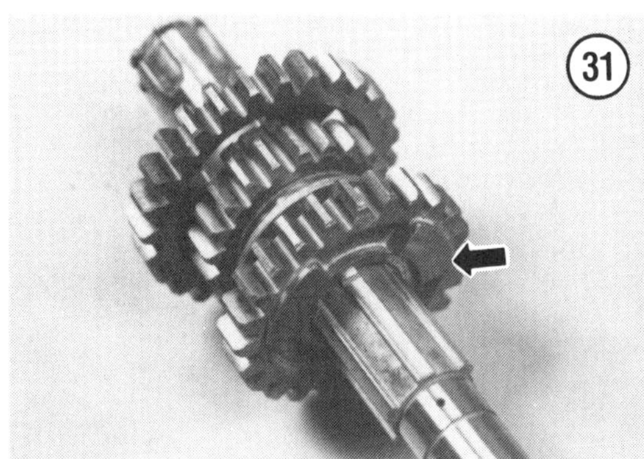

1. Place the assembled shaft into a large can or plastic bucket and thoroughly clean with solvent and a stiff brush. Dry with compressed air or let it sit on rags to drip dry.
2. Remove the circlip and slide off the flat washer.
3. Slide off the first gear.
4. Slide off the fourth gear.
5. Remove the circlip and slide off the splined washer.
6. Slide off the third gear.
7. Slide off the fifth gear.
8. Slide off the washer and the second gear.
9. Check the countershaft assembly as described under *Transmission Inspection* in this chapter.
10. Install the second gear (**Figure 27**).
11. Install the splined washer (**Figure 28**).
12. Position the fifth gear with the shift fork groove (**Figure 29**) going on last and install the gear (**Figure 30**).
13. Slide on third gear so that the dog engagement receptacles side (**Figure 31**) goes on last and install the gear.
14. Slide on splined washer (**Figure 32**).
15. Install the *new* circlip (**Figure 33**).
16. Position the fourth gear with the shift fork groove (**Figure 34**) going on first and install the gear (**Figure 35**).
17. Position the first gear with the flush side (**Figure 36**) going on last and install the gear.
18. Install the flat washer (**Figure 37**).
19. Install a *new* circlip (**Figure 38**) in the groove next to the washer.
20. After assembly is complete, refer to **Figure 39** for the correct placement of all gears. Make sure all

7

circlips are seated correctly in the countershaft grooves.

NOTE
*After both transmission shafts have been assembled, mesh the 2 assemblies together in the correct position (**Figure 40**). Check that all gears meet correctly. This is your last check prior to installing the assemblies into the crankcase to make sure they are correctly assembled.*

Transmission Inspection

1. Check each gear for excessive wear, burrs, pitting, or chipped or missing teeth (A, **Figure 41**).
2. Make sure the lugs (dogs) (**Figure 42**) on the gears are in good condition.
3. Make sure the slots (A, **Figure 43**) on the gears are in good condition.
4. Check each sliding gear groove (**Figure 44**) for wear, cracks or other damage.
5. Check each stationary gear bore (B, **Figure 43**) for scoring, cracks or other damage.

35

36

37

38

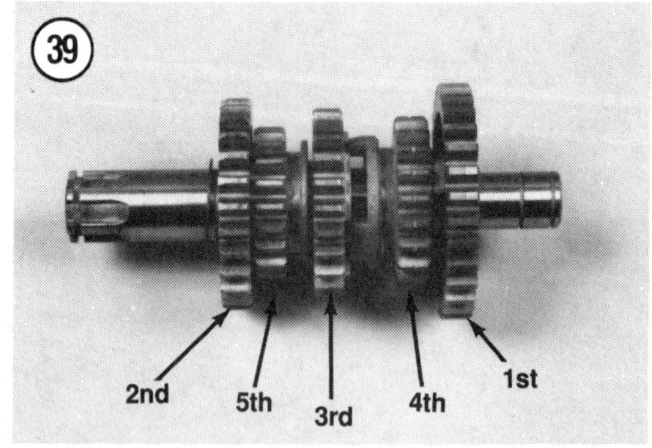

39

40

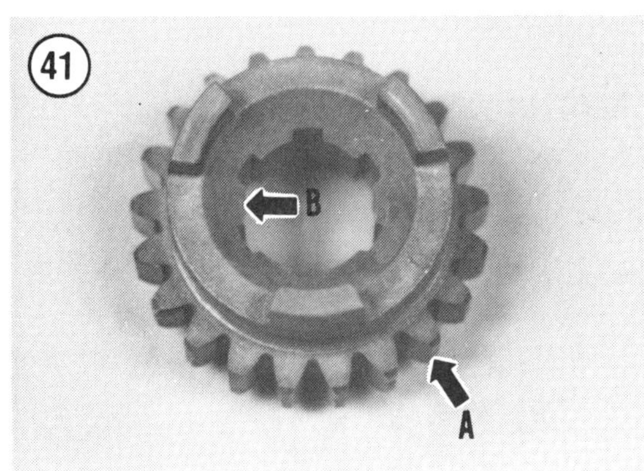

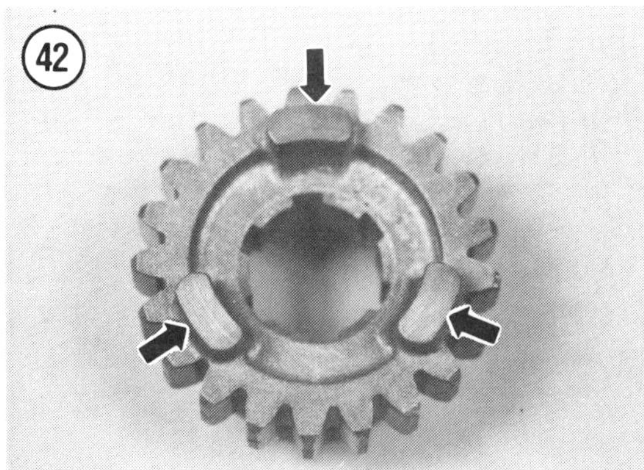

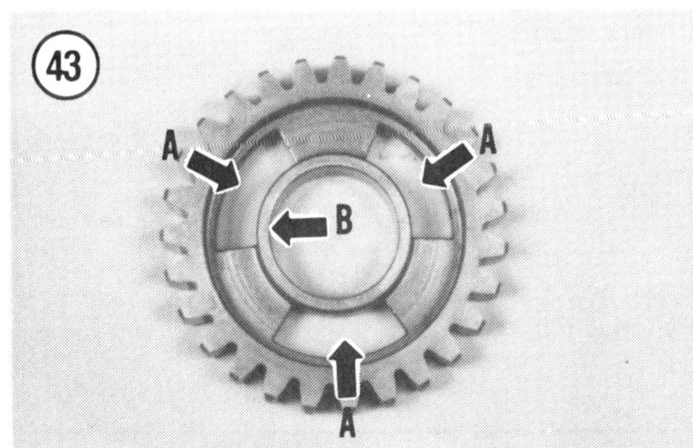

6. Check each sliding gear shaft splines (B, **Figure 41**) for scoring, cracks or other damage.

7. Make sure that all gears slide or turn on their respective shafts smoothly. If any gear movement is noisy or rough, replace the gear and/or shaft as required.

NOTE

Defective gears should be replaced, and it is a good idea to replace the mating gear even though it may not show as much wear or damage.

8. Check the splines of the mainshaft (A, **Figure 45**) and countershaft (A, **Figure 46**) for wear, cracks or other damage.

9. Check the mainshaft first gear (B, **Figure 45**). If the gear is damaged, replace the mainshaft assembly.

10. Check the circlip groove(s) of the mainshaft (C, **Figure 45**) and countershaft (B, **Figure 46**) for wear or other damage.

11. Place each transmission shaft on V-blocks and check runout with a dial indicator. If runout exceeds 0.08 mm (0.0031 in.), replace the transmission shaft.

12. Replace all circlips during reassembly. In addition, check the washers for burn marks, scoring or cracks. Replace if necessary.

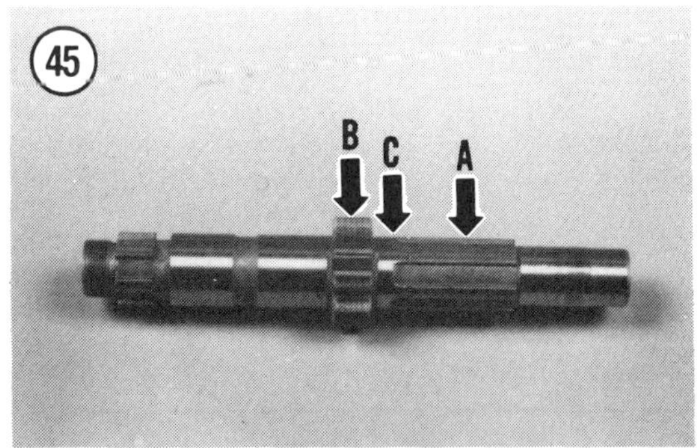

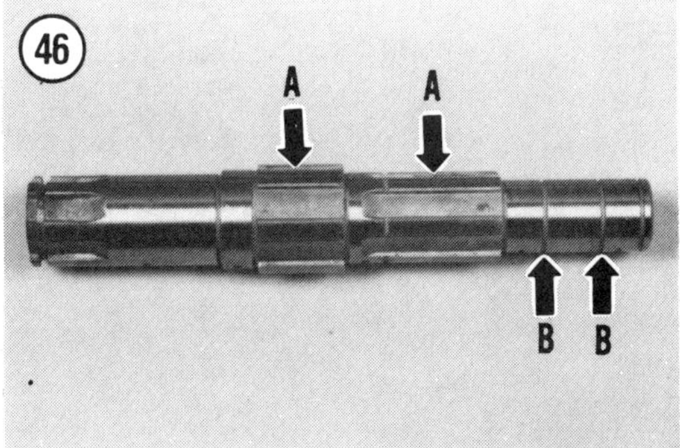

7

(47)

INTERNAL SHIFT MECHANISM

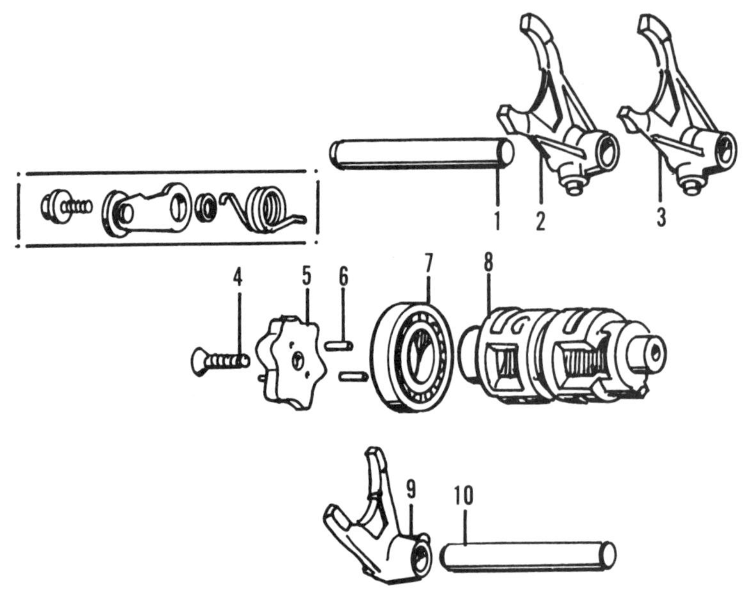

1. No. 2 shift fork shaft
2. Shift fork No. 3
3. Shift fork No. 1
4. Torx bolt
5. Segment
6. Locating pins
7. Bearing
8. Shift drum
9. Shift fork No. 2
10. No. 1 shift fork shaft

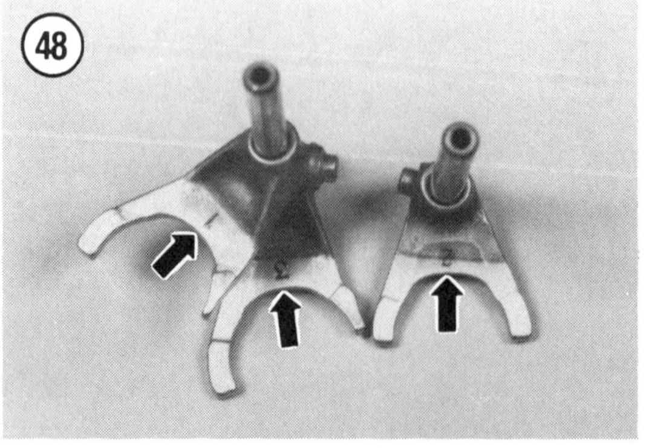

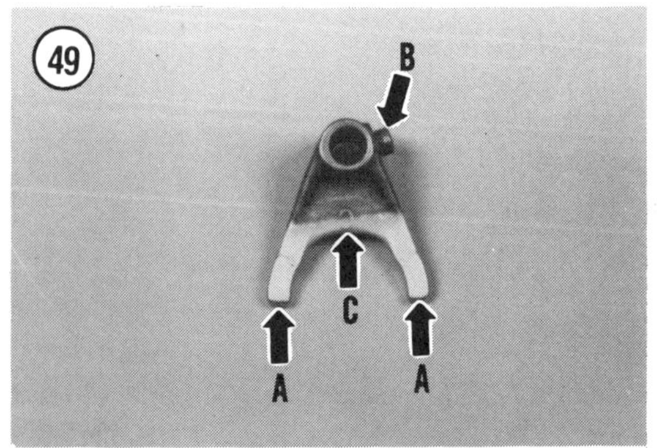

50

51

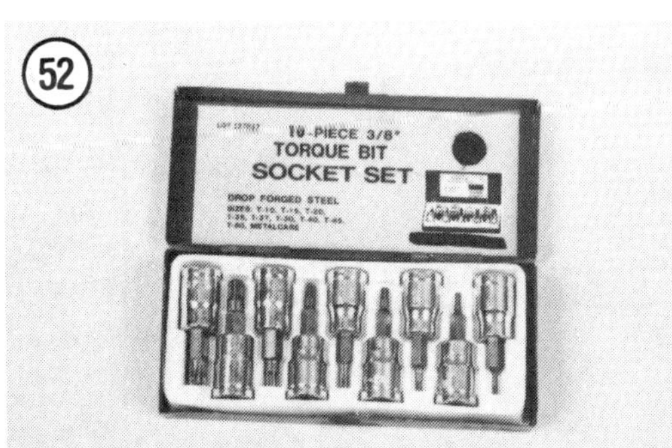

52

53

INTERNAL SHIFT MECHANISM

Removal/Installation

Remove and install the transmission and internal shift mechanism as described under *Crankcase Disassembly* and *Crankcase Assembly* in Chapter Five.

Shift Fork Inspection

Refer to **Figure 47** for this procedure.

1. Inspect each shift fork (**Figure 48**) for signs of wear or cracking.
2. Examine the shift forks at the points where they contact the slider gear (A, **Figure 49**). This surface should be smooth with no signs of wear or damage.
3. Make sure the forks slide smoothly on their respective shafts (**Figure 50**).
4. Make sure the shafts are not bent. This can be checked by removing the shift forks from the shaft and rolling the shaft on a piece of plate glass (**Figure 51**). Any clicking noise detected indicates that the shaft is bent and should be replaced.
5. Check each shift fork peg (B, **Figure 49**) for wear or damage.
6. Check for any arc-shaped wear or burn marks on the shift forks (C, **Figure 49**). This indicates that the shift fork has come in contact with the gear. The fork fingers have become excessively worn and the fork must be replaced.

Shift Drum Disassembly/Inspection/Reassembly

Refer to **Figure 47** for this procedure.

NOTE
*An impact driver with a T-30 Torx bit (**Figure 52**) will be necessary to loosen the shift drum screw in Step 1.*

1. Inspect the ramps on the segment (**Figure 53**) for wear or roughness. If segment removal is necessary, perform the following:
   a. Using an impact driver, loosen and remove the Torx screw (A, **Figure 54**).
   b. Remove the segment (B, **Figure 54**) and the locating pins behind it.
2. Check the grooves in the shift drum (**Figure 55**) for wear or roughness.

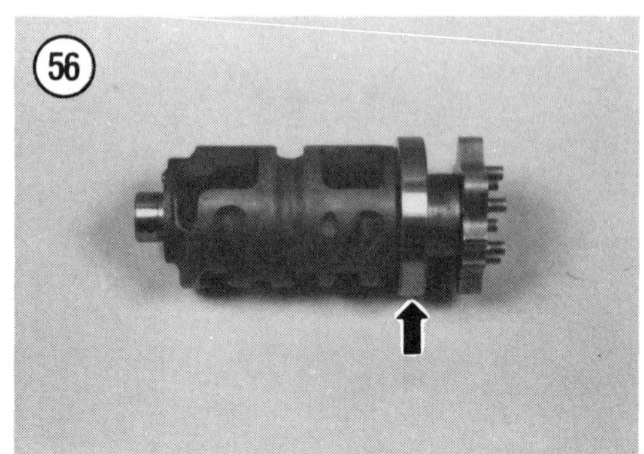

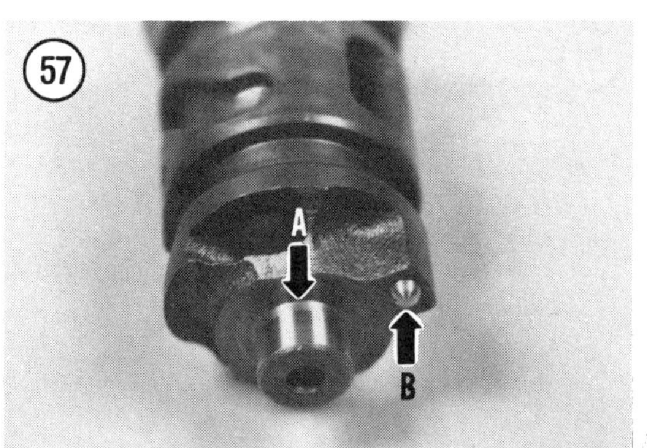

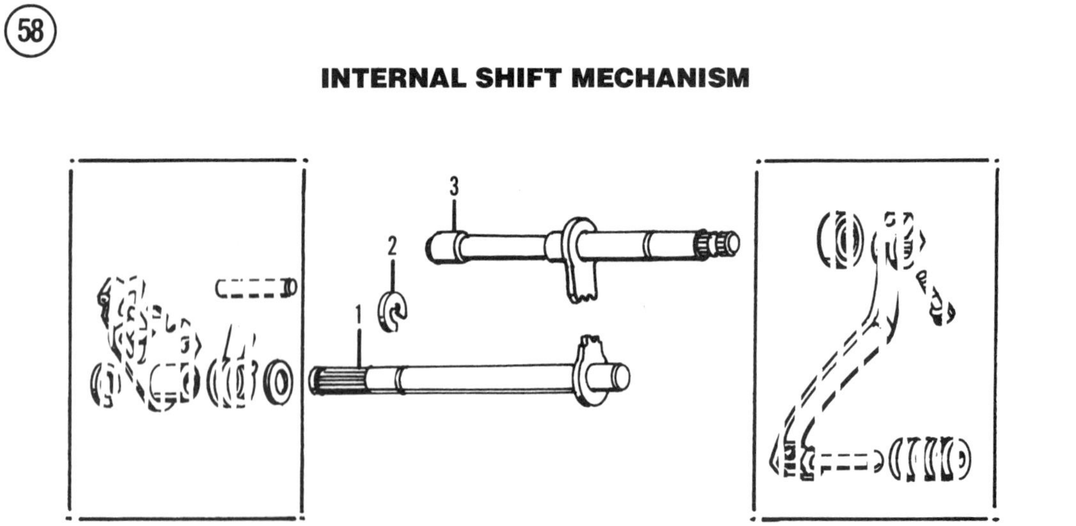

58

INTERNAL SHIFT MECHANISM

3

2

1

1. Shift shaft
2. E-clip
3. Change shaft

3. Check the bearing (**Figure 56**) for roughness or damage. If necessary, replace the bearing by pressing it off of the shift drum with a press. Reverse to install the bearing.

4. Oil the bearing with clean engine oil.

5. Check the bearing surface (A, **Figure 57**) on the opposite end for wear or damage.

6. On XT600 models, check the neutral switch detent (B, **Figure 57**) for wear or damage.

7. If the segment was removed, perform the following:

   a. Install the segment.
   b. Apply Loctite 242 (blue) to the Torx screw threads and install the screw. Tighten the screw securely.

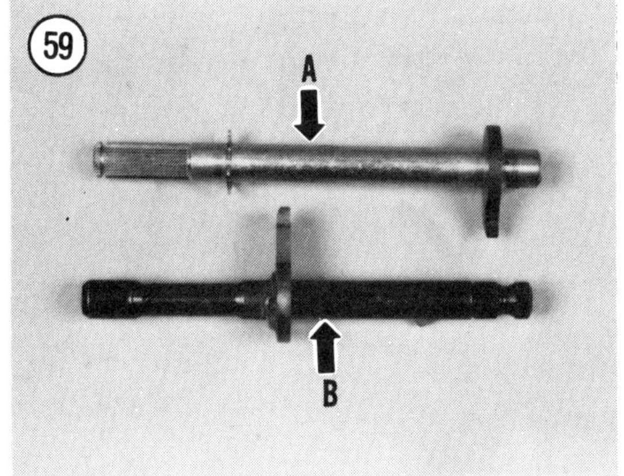

Shift Shaft and Change Shaft Inspection

Refer to **Figure 58** for this procedure.

1. Make sure that the shift shaft (A, **Figure 59**) or the change shaft (B, **Figure 59**) is not bent.

2. Place each shaft on V-blocks and check runout with a dial indicator. If runout exceeds 0.16 mm (0.0062 in.), replace the bent shaft.

3. Inspect the splines (**Figure 60**) for wear or damage. Replace the shaft(s) if necessary.

4. Check the engagement gear teeth (**Figure 61**) for wear or damage. Replace the shaft(s) if necessary.

7

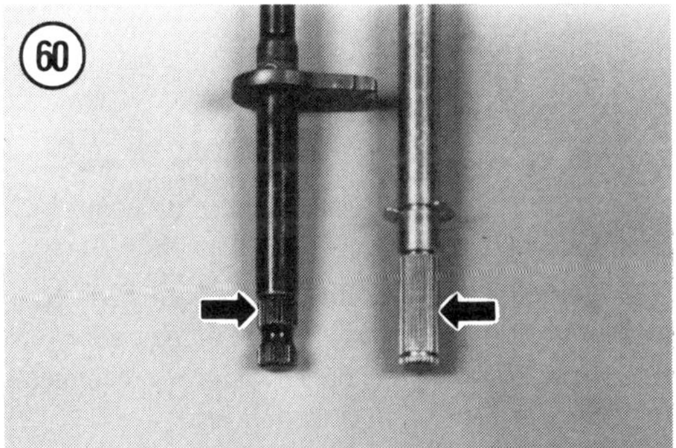

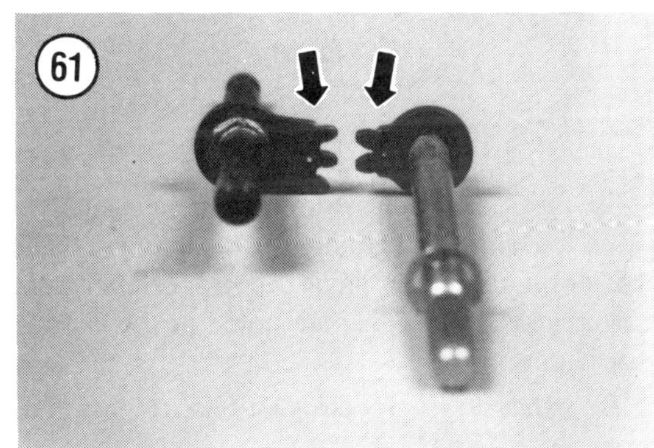

Table 1 TRANSMISSION RATIOS

Primary reduction ratio	74:31 (2.387)
Secondary reduction ratio	
XT600	42:15 (2.800)
TT600	50:14 (3.571)
Gear ratios	
1st	30:13 (2.307)
2nd	27:17 (1.588)
3rd	24:20 (1.200)
4th	21:22 (0.954)
5th	21:27 (0.777)

CHAPTER EIGHT

FUEL, EXHAUST AND EMISSION CONTROL SYSTEMS

The fuel system consists of the fuel tank, shutoff valve, a dual Teikei carburetor assembly and foam type air filter. There are slight differences among the various models and they are noted in the various procedures.

The exhaust system consists of an exhaust pipe assembly and a muffler.

All XT600 models originally sold in California are equipped with an evaporative emission control system and all U.S. models are equipped with a crankcase ventilation control system.

This chapter includes service procedures for all parts of the fuel, exhaust and emission control systems.

Carburetor specifications are listed in **Table 1**. **Tables 1-2** are at the end of the chapter.

FUEL/EMISSION CONTROL DECALS (XT600)

A vehicle emission control information decal (A, **Figure 1**) is fixed to the backside of the left-hand side cover. This decal lists all emission control related tune-up information.

On models sold in California, an emission hose routing label (B, **Figure 1**) is fixed to the back of the side cover. Refer to this decal whenever reconnecting one of the emission control hoses.

CARBURETOR SERVICE

Carburetor Identification

Refer to **Table 1** for carburetor specifications for all models.

All models use a dual throttle cable setup. One cable is a "pull" cable and the other is a "push" cable. The throttle cables are labeled 1 and 2. The No. 1 is the "pull" cable and is attached to the top portion of the throttle cable bracket on the carburetor assembly. The No. 2 is the "push" cable and is attached to the lower portion of the throttle cable bracket on the carburetor assembly.

Removal/Installation

1. Place wood block(s) under the engine to support the bike securely.

2. Remove the seat as described under *Seat Removal/Installation* in Chapter Thirteen.

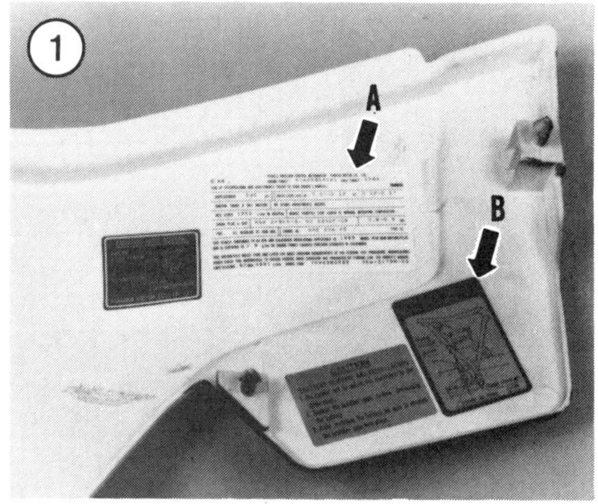

3. Remove the fuel tank as described in this chapter.

4. To drain the carburetor assembly prior to removal, perform the following:

   a. Place a drain pan under the drain tube coming from the carburetor.
   b. Open the drain screw (**Figure 2**) and allow the gasoline to drain out of the float bowl.
   c. Close the drain screw.
   d. Dispose of the drained gasoline properly and safely.

NOTE

The throttle cables are labeled, No. 1 and No. 2. If the labels are no longer visible; label the throttle cables at the throttle wheel prior to removal. The No. 1 cable is attached to the top portion of the throttle cable bracket and the No. 2 is attached to the lower portion of the throttle cable bracket.

5. Locate the 2 throttle cables at the point where they attach to the carburetor assembly and perform the following:

   a. Loosen the No. 1 "pull" throttle cable adjuster locknuts (A, **Figure 3**) and turn the adjuster (B, **Figure 3**) to achieve the maximum amount of cable slack.
   b. Loosen the No. 2 throttle "push" cable adjuster locknuts (A, **Figure 4**) and turn the adjuster (B, **Figure 4**) to achieve the maximum amount of cable slack.
   c. Disconnect both throttle cables from the throttle wheel on the carburetor assembly. Refer to **Figure 5** and **Figure 6**.

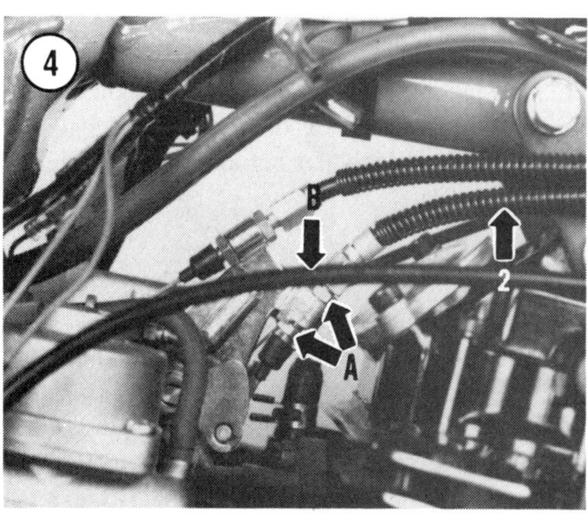

6. On XT600 models, loosen the cable clamp screw (A, **Figure 7**) and disconnect the choke cable (B, **Figure 7**) from the carburetor assembly.

7. On California models, remove the charcoal canister as described in this chapter.

8. Loosen the clamping screws (A, **Figure 8**) on the rear rubber inlet boots. Slide the clamps away from the carburetor.

9. Remove both rubber inlet boots (B, **Figure 8**) from the carburetor and air filter air box.

10. Make sure all overflow and drain tubes (**Figure 9**) are free of the frame.

11. Loosen the clamping screws (**Figure 10**) on the intake manifolds. Slide the clamps away from the carburetor.

12. Carefully work the carburetor assembly free from the intake manifolds and remove it from the right-hand side (**Figure 11**).

13. Take the carburetor assembly to a workbench for disassembly and cleaning. If the carburetor assembly is not going to be disassembled, place it in a clean reclosable plastic bag and close the bag to prevent it from getting dirty.

14. Stuff clean shop rags into the intake manifolds (**Figure 12**) on the cylinder head to prevent dirt and other debris from entering the cylinder head.

15. Install by reversing these removal steps. Note the following.

16. Apply a light coat of rubber lubricant such as Armor All around the ends of the intake manifolds and the rubber inlet boots to make carburetor installation easier.

17. Make sure the carburetor assembly is properly positioned and tighten all clamp screws evenly and securely.

18. Adjust the throttle cables as described under *Throttle Cable Adjustment* in Chapter Three.

19. Connect the fuel line and turn the shutoff valve to the ON position. Check for fuel leaks. If any occur, correct the problem before starting the engine.

Disassembly

Refer to **Figure 13** for this procedure.

All models use a dual carburetor assembly, one primary and one secondary. During this procedure, the carburetor assemblies will be referred to as either primary or secondary.

1. Remove the overflow and drain tubes (**Figure 14**).

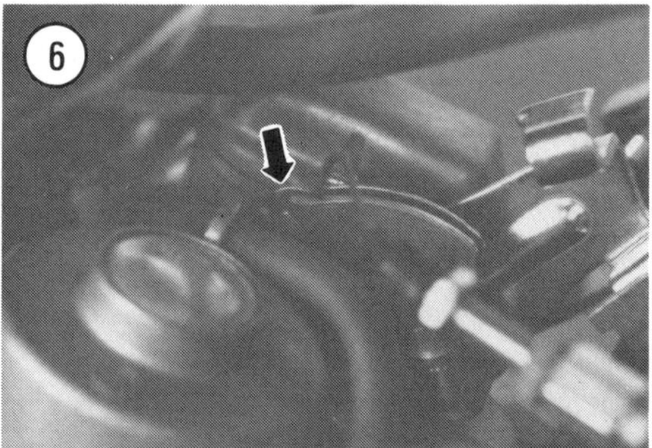

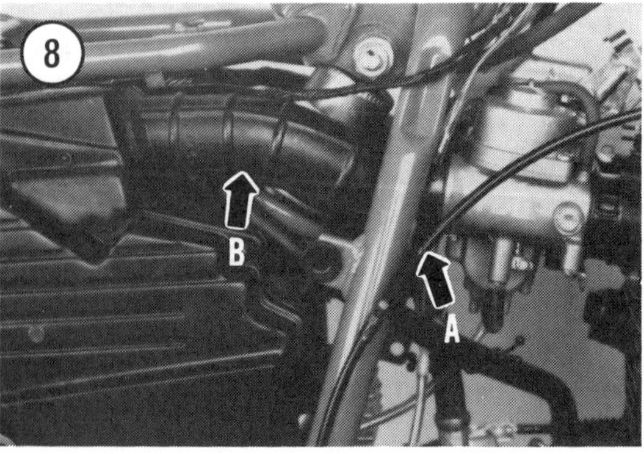

9

10

11

12

NOTE

Steps 2-10 describes primary carburetor disassembly.

2. Perform the following to remove the coasting enricher:
   a. Remove the 2 screws and remove the coasting enricher cover (**Figure 15**).
   b. Remove the spring (**Figure 16**).
   c. Remove the diaphragm (**Figure 17**).
3. Remove the secondary throttle valve as follows:
   a. Remove the screws securing the cap and remove the cap (**Figure 18**).
   b. Remove the connecting arm screw (**Figure 19**).
   c. Remove the screws securing the throttle valve assembly and needle set assembly (**Figure 20**).
   d. Pull up on the connecting rod assembly and remove the throttle valve assembly from the bore in the carburetor body.
   e. Remove the jet needle and spring (A, **Figure 21**) from the throttle valve (B, **Figure 21**).
4. Disconnect the fuel line (**Figure 22**) running from the primary carburetor assembly to the secondary carburetor assembly.
5. Remove the screws securing the float bowl (A, **Figure 23**) and remove the float bowl. Note the location of the overflow and drain tube clips (B, **Figure 23**). They must be reinstalled in the same location during assembly.
6. Remove the float pin (**Figure 24**) and remove the float and fuel valve assembly (**Figure 25**).
7. Remove the main jet (**Figure 26**) and the main jet nozzle (**Figure 27**).
8. Remove the pilot jet (**Figure 28**).
9. Remove the O-ring (**Figure 29**).
10. Remove the screw (A, **Figure 30**) securing the fuel valve seat (B, **Figure 30**) and remove the fuel valve seat.

NOTE

Steps 11-15 describes secondary carburetor disassembly.

11. Remove the main jet (**Figure 31**).
12. Disconnect the vent tube (**Figure 32**) from both carburetor assemblies.
13. Remove the screws securing the cover (**Figure 33**) and remove the cover.
14. Remove the spring (**Figure 34**).

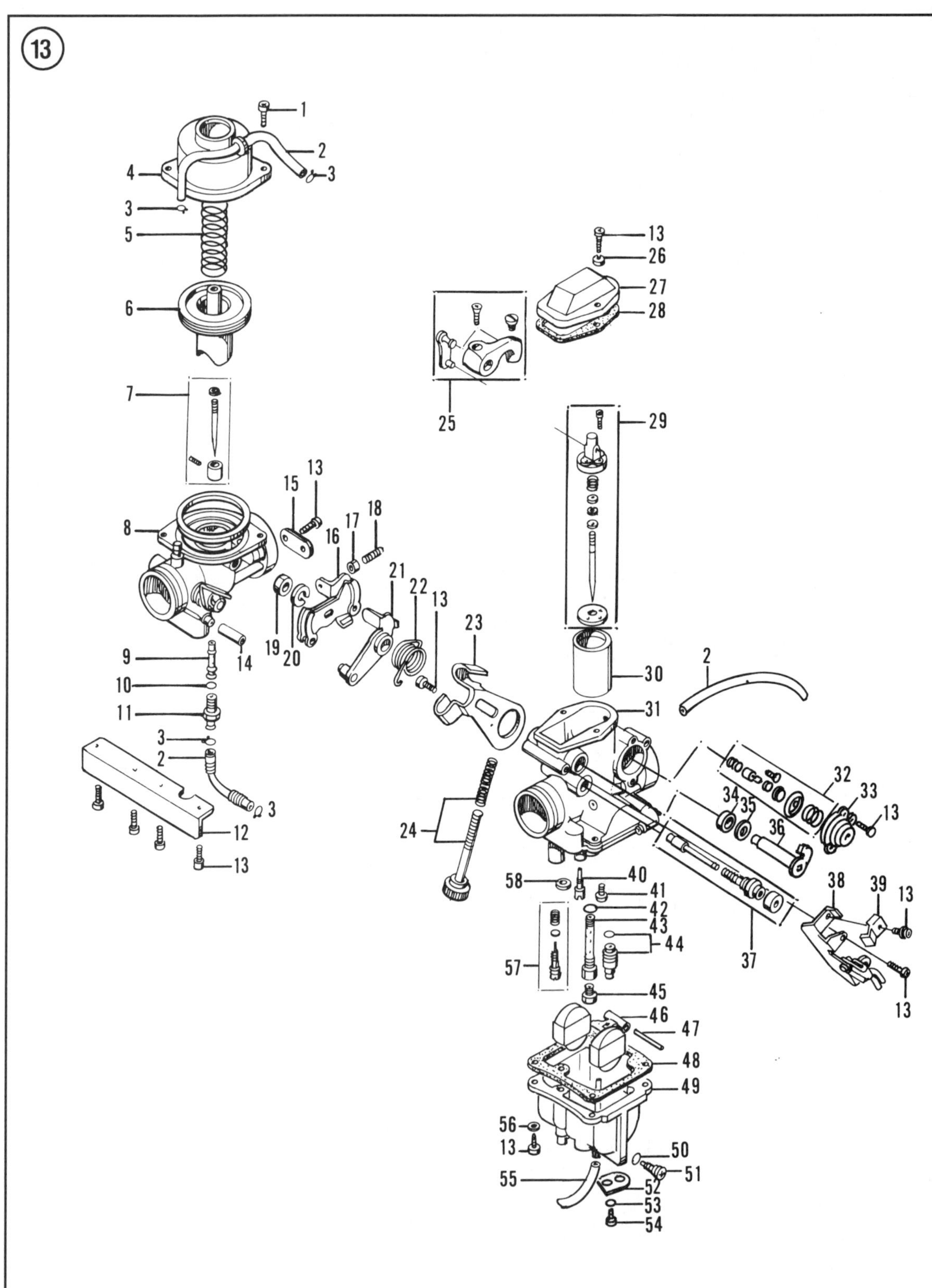
13

CARBURETOR

1. Screw
2. Hose
3. Hose clamp
4. Cap
5. Spring
6. Throttle valve
7. Jet needle assembly
8. Secondary carburetor body
9. Main jet nozzle
10. O-ring
11. Main jet
12. Front bracket
13. Screw
14. Hose
15. Plate
16. Throttle lever
17. Locknut
18. Adjust screw
19. Nut
20. Lockwasher
21. Throttle lever
22. Spring
23. Throttle cable bracket
24. Throttle adjust screw
25. Connecting arm assembly
26. Lockwasher
27. Cap
28. Gasket
29. Jet needle assembly
30. Throttle arm
31. Primary carburetor housing
32. Coasting richer diaphragm set
33. Cover
34. Seal
35. Washer
36. Throttle shaft
37. Choke assembly
38. Choke lever (XT600)
39. Clip
40. Pilot jet
41. Screw
42. O-ring seal
43. Main jet nozzle
44. Needle valve set
45. Main jet
46. Float
47. Float pivot pin
48. Gasket
49. Float bowl
50. Gasket
51. Drain screw
52. Plate
53. Washer
54. Screw
55. Drain tube
56. Washer
57. Pilot screw set
58. Gasket

14

15

16

17

8

18

19

20

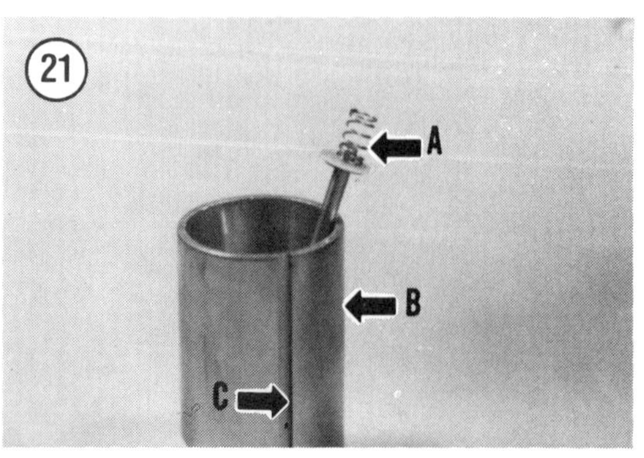
21
A
B
C

22

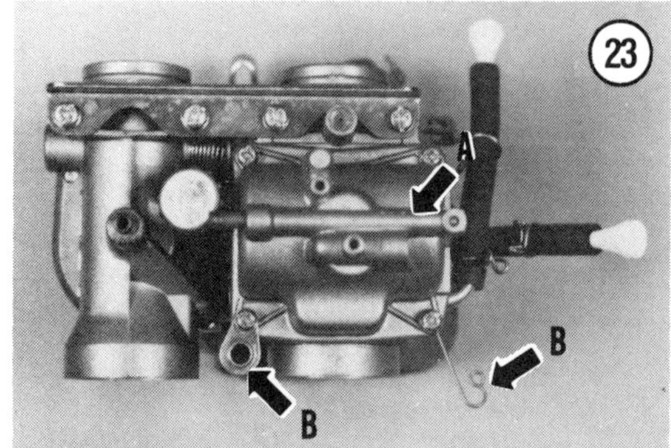
23
A
B
B

24

25

26

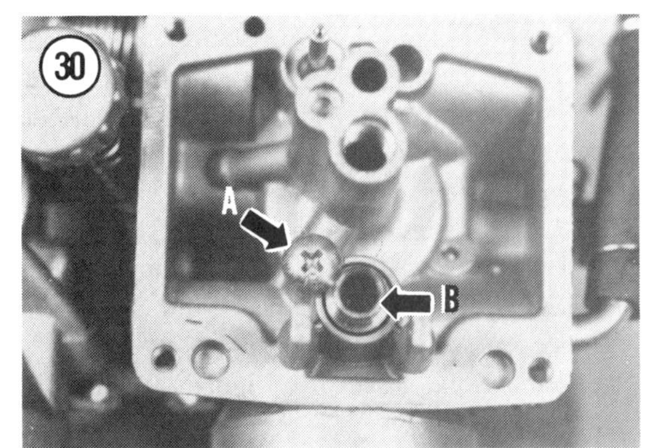
30
A
B

27

31

28

32

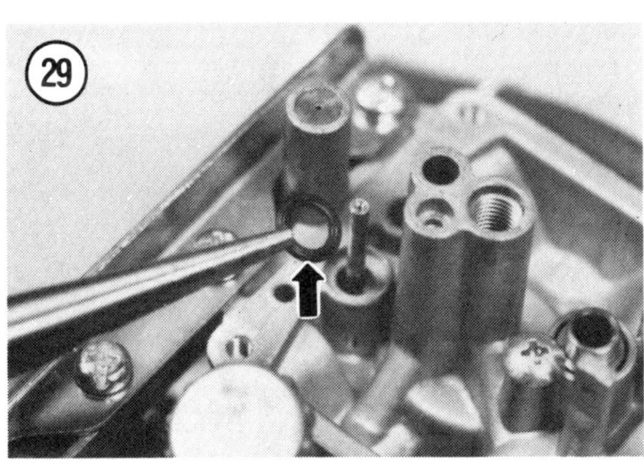
29

33

15. Remove the throttle valve assembly (**Figure 35**).
16. Remove the set screw (**Figure 36**) from the side of the throttle valve and separate the slide/jet needle assembly (**Figure 37**).
17. On all models, the pilot air screw is fixed in a blind housing (**Figure 38**) and removal is not recommended as the housing plug must be removed.
18. Unscrew the throttle adjust screw and spring (**Figure 39**).
19. Remove the gasket (A, **Figure 40**) from the secondary carburetor.

NOTE
The following steps are not usually required for routine carburetor cleaning. They may require removal at some time if one of them malfunctions or is damaged.

20. If necessary, remove the screw (A, **Figure 41**) securing the coasting richer plunger assembly (B, **Figure 41**) and remove the plunger assembly and spring.
21. If necessary, remove the nut and lockwasher (A, **Figure 42**) and remove the throttle cable bracket (B, **Figure 42**) and throttle lever and return spring (C, **Figure 42**).
22. If necessary, remove the screws securing the choke cable bracket (A, **Figure 43**) and remove the bracket and the choke assembly (B, **Figure 43**).
23. Clean and inspect the carburetor assembly components as described in this chapter.

Cleaning/Inspection

WARNING
Carburetor cleaner is extremely caustic and can cause permanent eye damage.

34

35

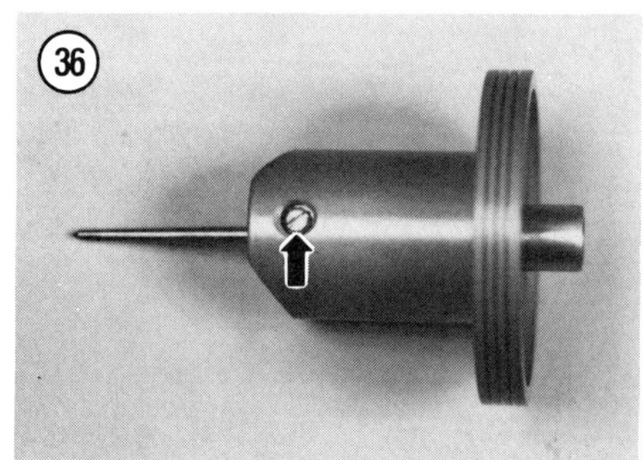
36

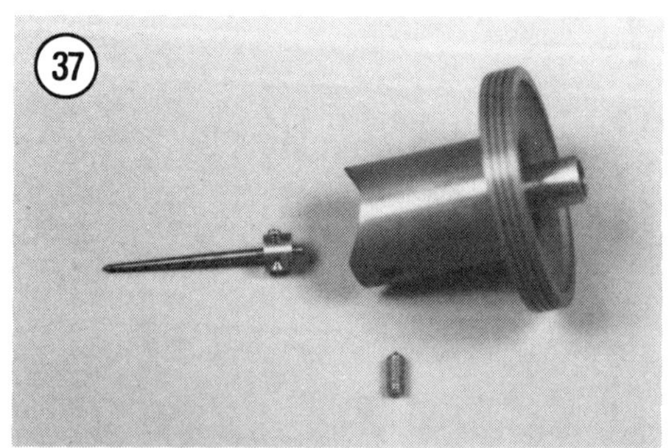
37

38

Always wear eye protection when using any type of carburetor cleaner.

Carburetors are best cleaned by completely disassembling them and cleaning the fuel and air orifices with an aerosol carburetor cleaner. Never use a wire to clean out jets or orifices; such a process could enlarge the passage which would adversely affect the air-to-fuel ratio.

Motorcycle carburetors have much smaller air and fuel passages than automotive carburetors. For this reason, soaking the carburetor parts in an automotive type carburetor cleaner is not recommended. The exterior of nearly all motorcycle carburetors is usually coated with a corrosion-protective clear coating. These caustic liquid cleaners will remove the protective coatings from the outside of the carburetor body. The dissolved coating could plug one or more of the air or fuel passages within the carburetor plus the exterior appearance of the carburetors will be damaged. Also, if the cleaner was used previously, there will be sediment held in suspension within the solution. These could also plug a passage.

Clean the carburetor parts in a good grade of fresh solvent and thoroughly dry with compressed air. Many good aerosol carburetor cleaners (i.e., Zep Choke and Carburetor Cleaner) can help remove any residue not removed with the solvent. Thoroughly rinse off all parts with clean water and dry with compressed air. If you do not have access to compressed air, place the cleaned parts on a piece of newspaper and allow to dry.

1. Clean all parts, except rubber or plastic parts, in a good grade of aerosol carburetor cleaner or cleaning solvent.

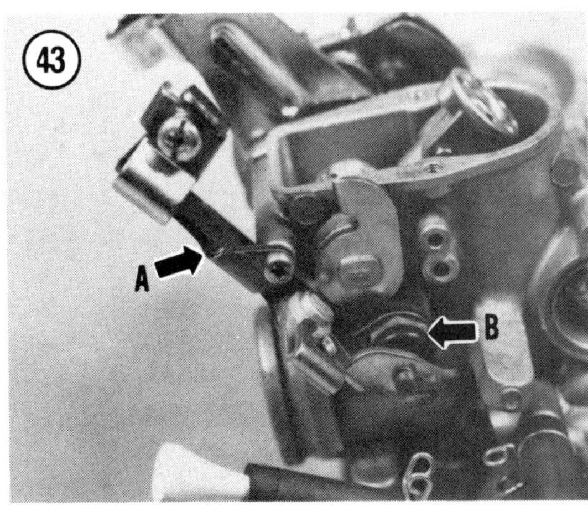

8

NOTE
A special carburetor cleaner is ***not*** *usually necessary to clean a carburetor unless it is very dirty or corroded. A good grade of parts cleaning solvent will usually clean most carburetors sufficiently.*

CAUTION
Do not put non-metallic parts such as floats, gaskets and O-rings in special carburetor cleaner as these components will be damaged. Clean these components in common solvent or kerosene.

2. Remove all parts from the cleaner and wash thoroughly in soap and water. Rinse with clean water and dry thoroughly.

CAUTION
If compressed air is not available, allow the parts to air dry or use a clean lint-free cloth. Do not use paper towels to dry carburetor parts, as small paper particles may plug openings in the carburetor body or jets.

3. Blow out the jets with compressed air. *Do not* use a piece of wire to clean them as minor gouges in the

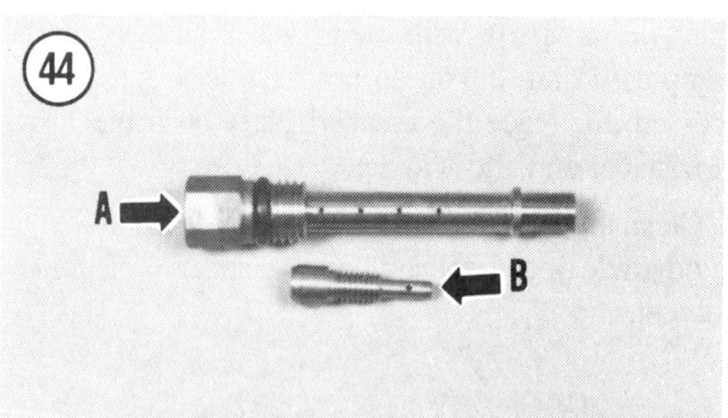

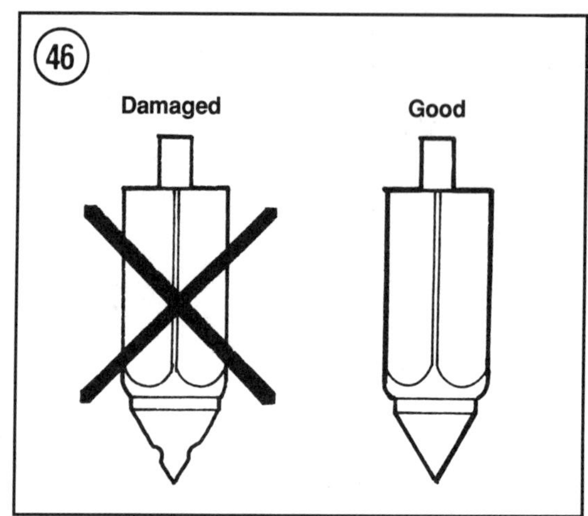

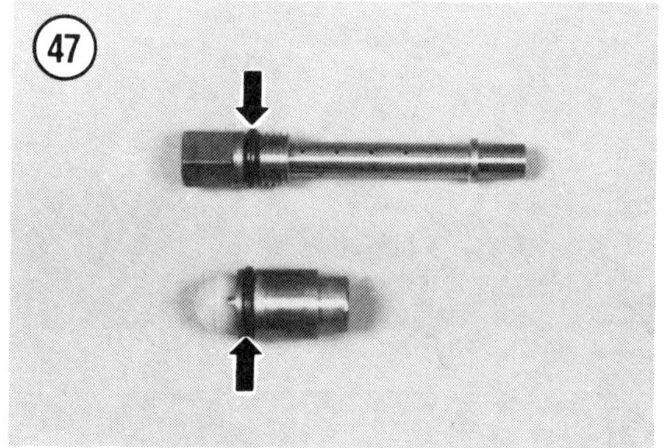

50

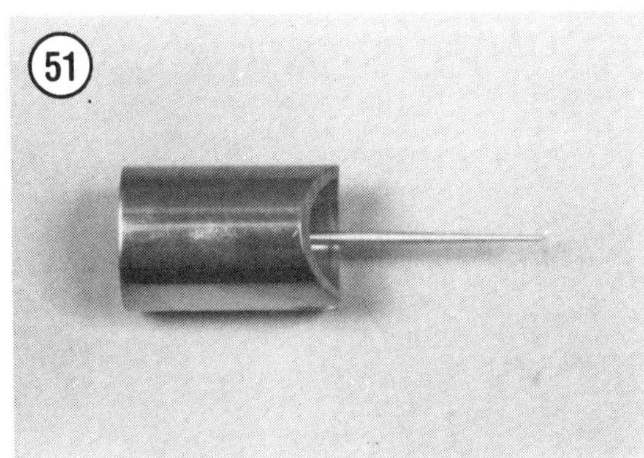
51

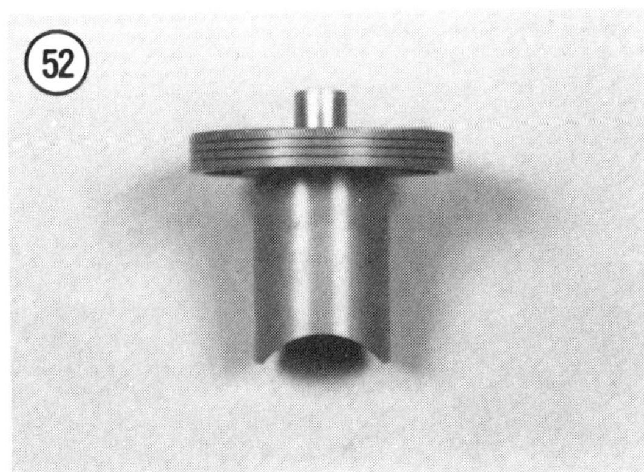
52

53

jet can alter flow rate and upset the fuel:air mixture. If compressed air is not available, use a piece of straw from a broom to clean the jets.

4. Make sure the small openings in the main jet nozzle (A, **Figure 44**) and pilot set screw (B, **Figure 44**) are clean and open.

5. Be sure to clean out the float bowl overflow tube (**Figure 45**) from both ends.

6. Inspect the tip of the float valve (**Figure 46**) for wear or damage. Replace the valve and seat as a set.

7. O-ring seals tend to become hardened after prolonged use and heat and therefore lose their ability to seal properly. Inspect all O-rings and replace if necessary. Refer to **Figure 47** and **Figure 48**.

8. Remove the O-ring gasket (**Figure 49**) from the float bowl and install a new gasket.

9. Check the floats (**Figure 50**) for leaks. Fill the float bowl with water and try to push the floats down. There should be no signs of bubbles. Replace the floats if they leak.

10. Check the throttle valve for scratches or other damage that would allow it to stick open during engine operation. Refer to **Figure 51** for the primary carburetor or **Figure 52** for the secondary carburetor.

11. Check the coating enricher diaphragm (**Figure 53**) for tears, splitting or other damage. Replace if necessary.

12. Check the primary carburetor throttle valve (A, **Figure 54**) operation by operating the throttle valve linkage (B, **Figure 54**). The valve and shaft should turn smoothly. If the shaft is tight or damaged, replace the primary carburetor assembly as the valve is not available as a replacement item. Make sure the screws (C, **Figure 54**) securing the butterfly are tight. Tighten securely if necessary.

54

8

13. Blow out all jets and passages in the carburetor bodies with compressed air. Refer to **Figure 55**, **Figure 56** and **Figure 57**. Clean out if they are plugged in any way.
14. Inspect the float pivot pin posts (**Figure 58**) for cracks or damage. If any damage is noted, replace the carburetor assembly.
15. Inspect the inner surface of the secondary carburetor cap (**Figure 59**) for wear or damage. Replace if necessary.

Assembly

Refer to **Figure 13** for this procedure.
1. If removed, install the choke cable bracket (A, **Figure 43**) and the choke assembly (B, **Figure 43**). Install the screws and tighten securely.
2. If removed, install the throttle cable bracket (B, **Figure 42**) and throttle lever and return spring (C, **Figure 42**). Install the nut and lockwasher (A, **Figure 42**) and tighten securely.
3. If removed, install the coasting richer plunger assembly (B, **Figure 41**) and spring. Install the screw (A, **Figure 41**) and tighten securely.
4. Install a new gasket (A, **Figure 40**) onto the secondary carburetor.
5. Install the throttle adjust screw and spring (**Figure 39**).

NOTE
Steps 6-11 describes secondary carburetor assembly.

6. Reassemble the slide as follows:
   a. Install the small spring (**Figure 60**) into the jet needle holder.

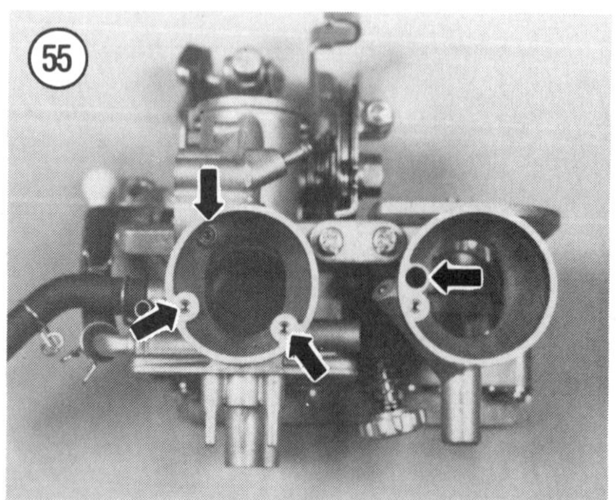

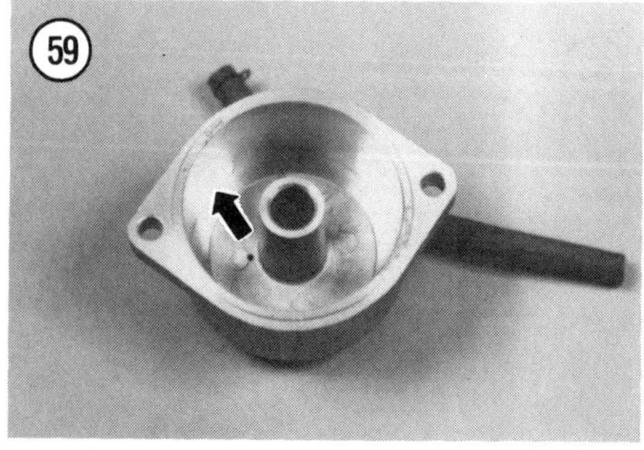

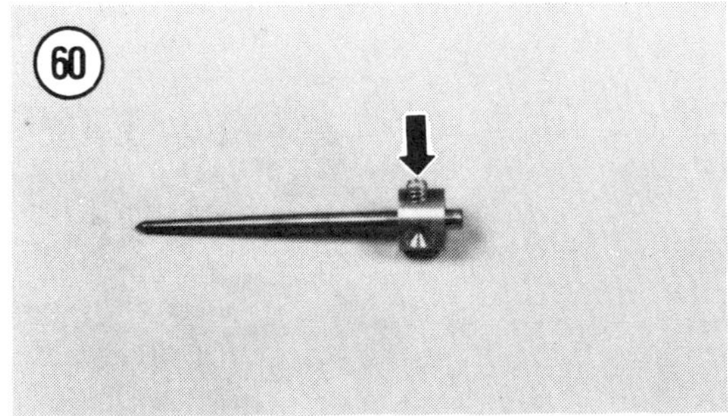

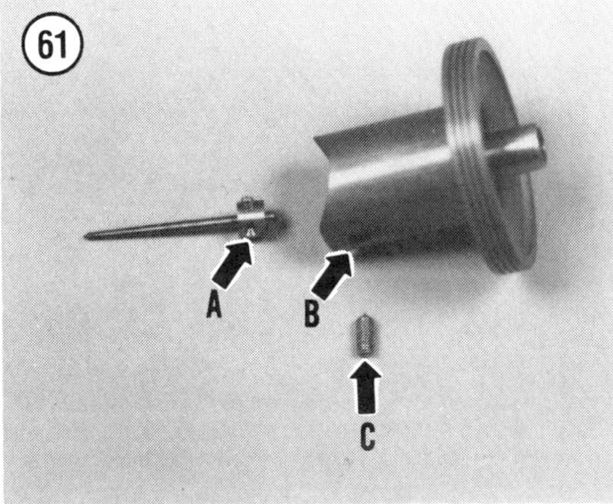

b. Align the set screw relief (A, **Figure 61**) in the jet needle holder with the set screw hole (B, **Figure 61**) in the slide.
c. Insert the jet needle into the throttle valve and install the set screw (C, **Figure 61**).
d. Tighten the set screw (**Figure 36**) securely.

7. Align the groove in the side of the throttle valve with the locating pin (B, **Figure 40**) in the carburetor body bore and install the throttle valve.
8. Install the spring (**Figure 34**).
9. Install the cover (**Figure 33**) and the screws securing the cover. Tighten the screws securely.
10. Connect the vent tube (**Figure 32**) onto both carburetor assemblies.
11. Install the main jet (**Figure 31**).

NOTE
Steps 12-23 describes primary carburetor assembly.

12. Make sure the O-ring seal (**Figure 62**) is in place on the fuel valve seat and install the fuel valve seat (B, **Figure 30**). Install the screw (A, **Figure 30**) and tighten securely.
13. Install a new O-ring (**Figure 29**).
14. Install the pilot jet (**Figure 28**) and tighten securely.
15. Install the main jet nozzle (**Figure 63**) and the main jet (**Figure 26**).
16. Install the float and fuel valve assembly (**Figure 50**) into position (**Figure 25**).
17. Install the float pin (**Figure 24**) from the left-hand side and push it in until it stops. The float pin will not come out through the right-hand side but will stop within it.
18. Make sure the new O-ring seal gasket (**Figure 49**) is in place and install the float bowl (A, **Figure 23**).
19. Position the overflow and drain tube clips (B, **Figure 23**) in the correct location and install the screws. Tighten the screws securely.
20. Connect the fuel line (**Figure 22**) running from the primary carburetor to the secondary carburetor.
21. Install the secondary throttle valve as follows:

a. If removed, install the jet needle and spring (A, **Figure 21**) into the throttle valve (B, **Figure 21**).
b. Install the screws (**Figure 64**) into the holes in the connecting arm cap.
c. Align the groove (C, **Figure 21**) in the side of the throttle valve with the locating pin (**Figure**

8

65) in the carburetor body bore and install the throttle valve.

d. Insert your finger into the carburetor inlet and hold the throttle valve in the UP position (A, **Figure 66**).

e. Insert a thin drift or scribe (B, **Figure 66**) into one of the screw holes in the connecting arm cap and the matching hole in the throttle valve. This will correctly align the 2 parts and make installation of the small screw in the next step easier.

f. Install the screw in the other hole and tighten only gently with a screwdriver (**Figure 67**). Do not tighten all the way to allow alignment of the other screw hole.

g. Remove the thin drift or scribe (B, **Figure 66**).

h. Install the remaining screw (**Figure 20**) securing the throttle valve assembly and needle set assembly. Tighten both screws securely.

i. Install the connecting arm screw (**Figure 19**) and tighten securely.

22. Install a new gasket (**Figure 68**) in the cap and install the cap (**Figure 18**) onto the carburetor body. Tighten the screws securely.

23. Perform the following to install the coasting enricher:

a. Install the diaphragm (A, **Figure 69**) and align the tab with the air channel (B, **Figure 69**).

b. Install the spring (**Figure 16**).

c. Install the coasting enricher cover (**Figure 15**) and screws. Tighten the screws securely.

24. Install the overflow and drain tubes (**Figure 14**).

25. Check the float height and adjust if necessary. Refer to *Float Adjustment* in this chapter.

26. After the carburetor has been installed on the bike, adjust the idle speed. Refer to Chapter Three.

Carburetor Body Separation/Assembly

NOTE

An impact driver with a Phillips bit (described in Chapter One) will be necessary to loosen the front and rear bracket screws. Attempting to loosen the screws with a Phillips screwdriver may ruin the screw heads.

1. Loosen the screws (A, **Figure 70**) holding the front bracket to the carburetor assemblies. Remove the front bracket (B, **Figure 70**).

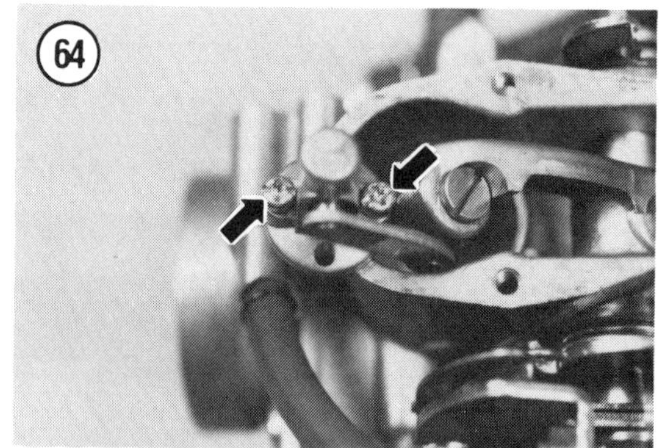

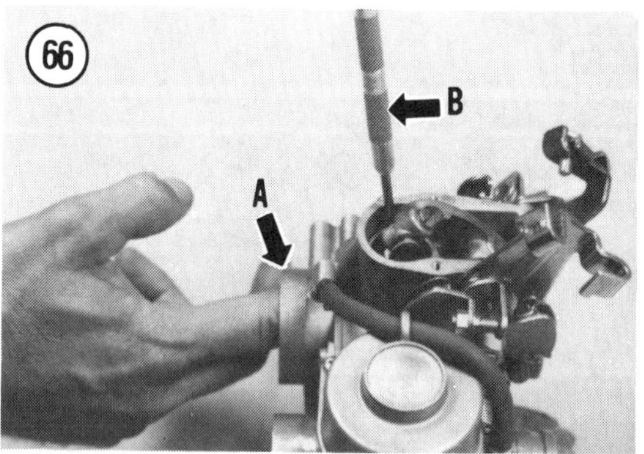

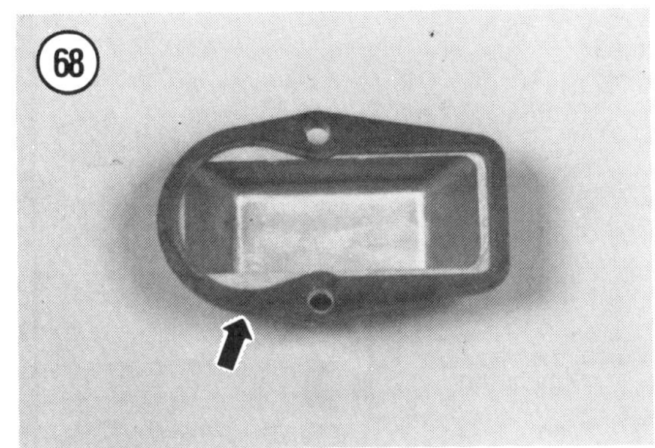
68

69

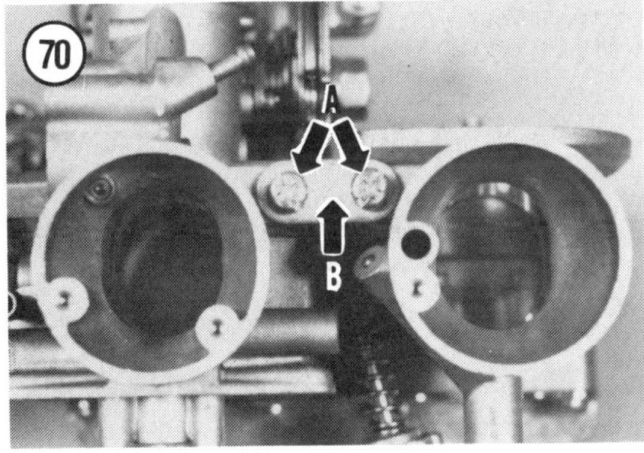

70

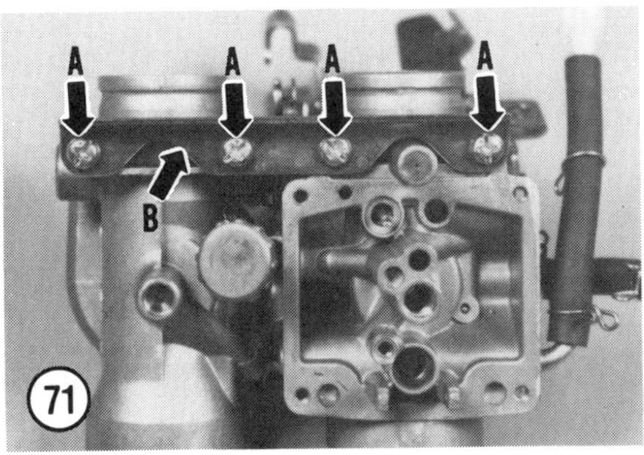

71

2. Loosen the screws (A, **Figure 71**) holding the lower bracket to the carburetor assemblies. Remove the lower bracket (B, **Figure 71**).

NOTE
The primary and secondary carburetor assemblies are held together with a rubber balance tube, a vacuum tube and a fuel tube.

3. Pull the carburetor assemblies straight apart and separate the 2 assemblies.
4. Place both carburetor assemblies on a surface plate like a thick piece of plate glass. This will align the inlet throats of both carburetor assemblies, then connect them at the 3 tube connections.
5. Make sure the roller on the secondary carburetor engages the arm bracket on the primary carburetor.
6. Push the two assemblies together until they are connected correctly.
7. Install the front bracket (B, **Figure 70**). Install the front bracket screws finger tight.
8. Install the lower bracket (B, **Figure 71**) and screws.
9. Push down on both carburetor assemblies to make sure they are properly aligned and tighten all bracket screws securely.
10. Before installing the carburetor assembly onto the bike, perform the *Carburetor Synchronization* procedures described in this chapter.

CARBURETOR ADJUSTMENTS

Float/Arm Height Adjustment

The fuel level in the primary carburetor float bowl is critical to proper performance. The fuel flow rate from the bowl up to the carburetor bore depends not only on the vacuum in the throttle bore and the size of the jets, but also upon the fuel level. Yamaha gives a specification of actual *fuel level*, measured from the top edge of the float bowl with the carburetor held level.

The measurement is more useful than a simple float height measurement because actual fuel level can vary from bike to bike, even when their floats are set at the same height. However, fuel level inspection requires a special fuel gauge tube that screws into the bottom of the carburetor. You can get the proper fitting at a Yamaha dealer (part No. YM-01312).

The fuel level is adjusted by bending the float arm tang (**Figure 72**).

Fuel Level Inspection

1. Place a jack underneath the engine and raise the engine so that the carburetor assembly is level.
2. Turn the fuel valve OFF
3. Remove the overflow tube from the bottom of the float bowl and install the Yamaha fuel gauge tube (A, **Figure 73**).
4. Hold the tube up and loosen the drain screw (B, **Figure 73**). This will allow fuel to enter the fuel gauge tube.
5. Start the engine and allow it to idle for a few minutes then turn it off. This will obtain the correct fuel level within the float bowl.
6. Hold the clear tube against the carburetor body. Measure the distance from the fuel level in the tube to the carburetor body lower surface at the float bowl line "dimension A" (**Figure 73**). The correct level is 6-8 mm (0.24-0.32 in.).

NOTE
Take your readings just after the fuel level has risen to its maximum in the tube. If you raise the tube (and the fuel drops in the tube) you'll probably get a faulty level reading. Try it again, forcing the fuel level to rise against surface tension within the tube.

7. If the fuel level is incorrect, adjust the float/arm height setting as described in Step 8. Then recheck the fuel level. Readjust if necessary.
8. Perform the following to adjust the float level:

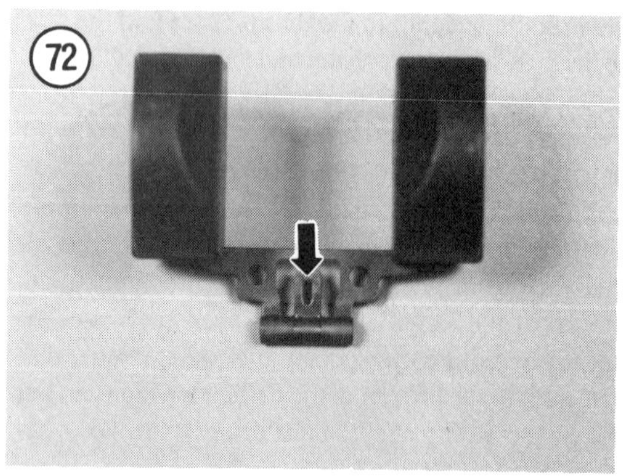

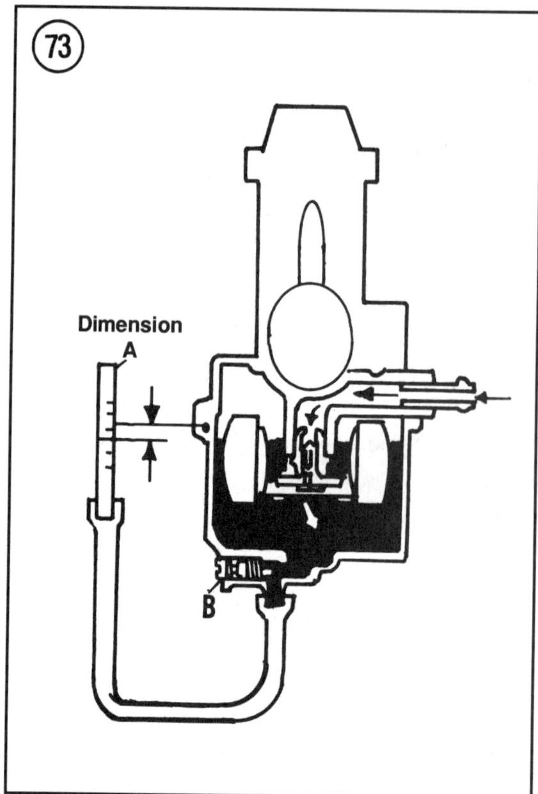

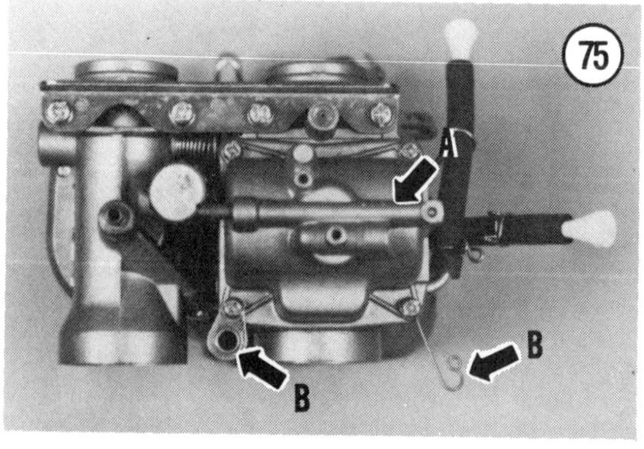

76

77

78

79

a. Tighten the drain screw and disconnect the Yamaha fuel gauge tube.
b. Remove the carburetor as described in this chapter. However, do not disconnect the throttle cables at the carburetor.

WARNING
Before removing the carburetor float bowl in sub-step d, place a clean pan underneath the carburetor to catch any gasoline spilling out of the bowl.

c. Disconnect the fuel line (**Figure 74**) running from the primary carburetor to the secondary carburetor.
d. Remove the screws securing the float bowl (A, **Figure 75**) and remove the float bowl. Note the location of the overflow and drain tube clips (B, **Figure 75**). They must be reinstalled in the same location during assembly.
e. Remove the float pin (**Figure 76**) and remove the float and fuel valve assembly (**Figure 77**).
f. Slip the fuel valve assembly off of the float arm (**Figure 78**).
g. Adjust the float by *carefully* bending the tang (**Figure 72**) with a screwdriver.
h. Reverse to install the float assembly. Make sure the O-ring seal (**Figure 79**) is installed in the groove in the float bowl.
i. Install overflow and drain tube clips (B, **Figure 75**) in their correct locations.

9. After installing the carburetor, reverse Steps 1-7 and recheck the fuel level. Repeat 8 as required to adjust the float.
10. When the fuel level is correct, disconnect the Yamaha fuel gauge tube and reconnect the overflow tube to the bottom of the float bowl.

Carburetor Full-Open Adjustment (Models So Equipped)

1. Remove the carburetor assembly as described in this chapter. However, do not disconnect the throttle cables at the carburetors. Use the throttle grip to open or close the throttle lever in the following steps.
2. Rotate the throttle lever to the wide-open position.
3. Measure the throttle valve distance (Dimension A) indicated in **Figure 80**. The correct distance is 0-0.1 mm (0-0.04 in.).
4. If necessary, loosen the adjuster locknut (A, **Figure 80**) and turn the adjuster (B, **Figure 80**) to

8

position the throttle valve. Tighten the locknut and recheck the adjustment.

5. Release the throttle lever.

6. Install the carburetor assembly as described in this chapter.

Carburetor Synchronization

1. Remove the carburetor assembly as described in this chapter. However, do not disconnect the throttle cables at the carburetors. Use the throttle grip to open or close the throttle lever in the following steps.

NOTE

***Figure 81** is shown with the carburetor partially disassembled. It is not necessary to disassemble the carburetor for this adjustment.*

2. Loosen the adjuster locknut (A, **Figure 81**).

3. Raise the primary throttle valve so that the height distance (dimension A) is 5 mm (0.20 in.) as shown in **Figure 82**.

4. Then turn the adjuster (B, **Figure 81**) in or out until the secondary throttle shaft just contacts the secondary throttle push lever. Tighten the locknut (A).

5. Recheck the adjustment.

6. Open the primary throttle valve all the way. Then check that the secondary throttle valve is in a horizontal position. Dimension A is equal to dimension B (**Figure 83**). If not, repeat Steps 2-4.

7. Install the carburetor assembly as described in this chapter.

Idle Speed Adjustment

Refer to Chapter Three.

Pilot Air Screw Adjustment

The pilot air screw is located in the primary carburetor. On 1986-on models, the pilot air screw is fixed in a blind housing (**Figure 84**) and removal is not recommended as the housing plug must be removed. On 1985 models, the pilot screw can be removed. If you are going to remove the screw, count the number of turns required to lightly seat the screw, then turn the screw counterclockwise and remove it and the spring. Refer to *Carburetor Removal/Installation* in this chapter.

High Altitude Adjustment (Main Jet Replacement)

If the bike is going to be ridden for any sustained period of time in high elevations (above 5,000 ft./1,500 m), the main jet should be changed to a one-step smaller jet. Never change the jet by more than one size at a time without test riding the bike and running a spark plug test. Refer to *Reading Spark Plugs* in Chapter Three.

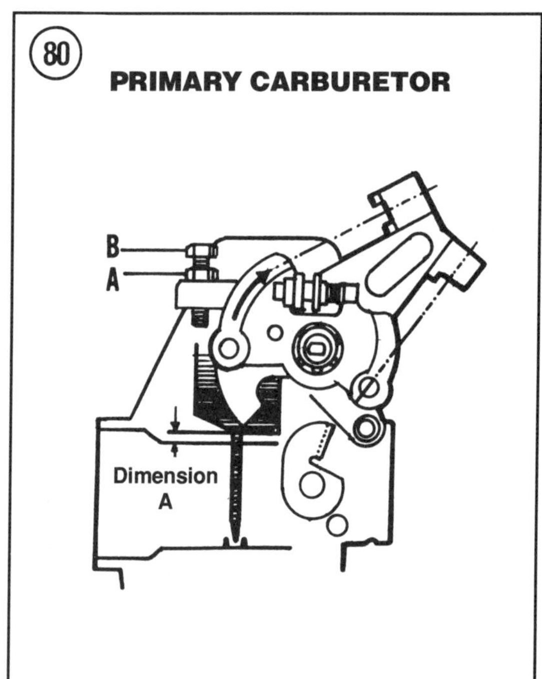

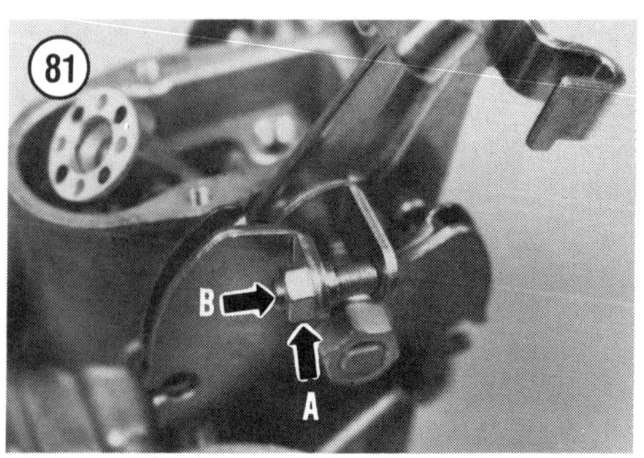

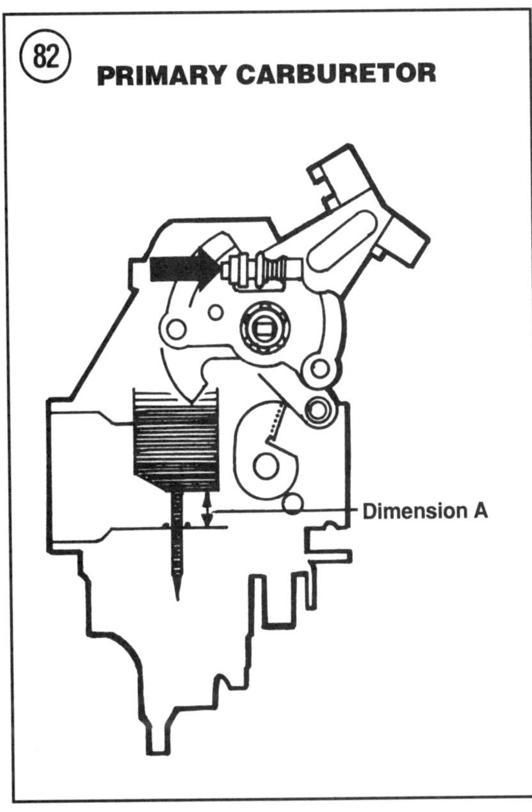

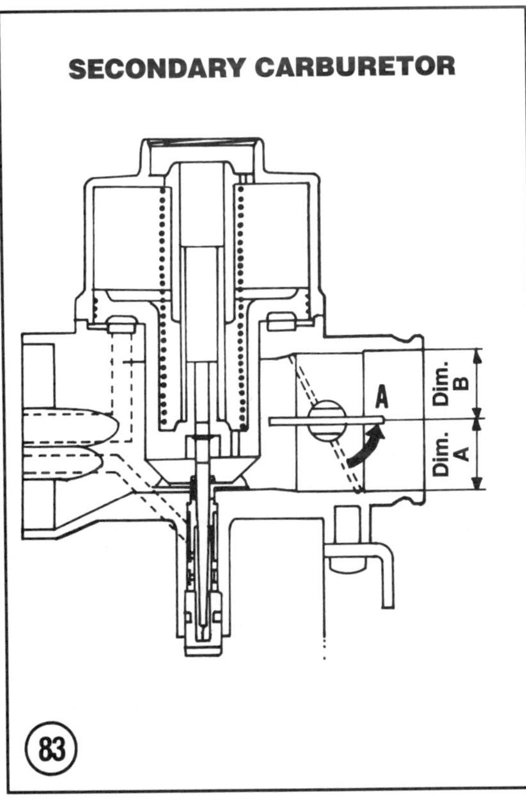

The carburetor is set with the standard jet for normal sea level conditions. But if the bike is run at higher altitudes or under heavy load—deep sand or mud—the main jet should be replaced or it will run too rich and carbon up quickly.

CAUTION

If the bike has been rejetted for high altitude operation (smaller jet), it must be changed back to the standard main jet if ridden at altitudes below 5,000 ft. (1,500 m). Engine overheating and piston seizure will occur if the engine runs too lean with the smaller jet.

Refer to **Table 1**, at the end of this chapter, for standard main jet sizes. Yamaha does not offer high altitude jets, but they are available from some aftermarket manufacturers.

1. Remove the carburetor assembly as described in this chapter.
2. To replace the main jet in the primary carburetor, perform the following:
   a. Disconnect the fuel line (**Figure 74**) running from the primary carburetor to the secondary carburetor.
   b. Remove the screws securing the float bowl (A, **Figure 75**) and remove the float bowl. Note the location of the overflow and drain tube clips (B, **Figure 75**). They must be reinstalled in the same location during assembly.
   c. Remove the main jet (**Figure 76**) and replace it with a different one. Remember, change only one jet size at a time.
3. To replace the main jet in the secondary carburetor, perform the following:
   a. Disconnect the fuel line (**Figure 74**) from the secondary carburetor.

8

b. Remove the main jet (**Figure 85**) and replace it with a different one. Remember, change only one jet size at a time.

4. Install all items removed and install the carburetor assembly as described in this chapter.

THROTTLE CABLE REPLACEMENT

1. Remove the fuel tank as described in this chapter.

NOTE
The throttle cables are labeled, No. 1 and No. 2. If the labels are no longer visible; label the throttle cables at the throttle wheel prior to removal. The No. 1 cable is attached to the top portion of the throttle cable bracket and the No. 2 cable is attached to the lower portion of the throttle cable bracket.

2. Locate the 2 throttle cables at the point where they attach to the carburetor assembly and perform the following:

a. Loosen the No. 1 "pull" throttle cable adjuster locknuts (A, **Figure 86**) and turn the adjuster (B, **Figure 86**) to achieve the maximum amount of cable slack.

b. Loosen the No. 2 throttle "push" cable adjuster locknuts (A, **Figure 87**) and turn the adjuster (B, **Figure 87**) to achieve the maximum amount of cable slack.

c. Disconnect both throttle cables from the throttle wheel on the carburetor assembly. Refer to **Figure 88** and **Figure 89**.

3A. On XT600 models, perform the following:

a. Remove the screws (A, **Figure 90**) holding the switch housings together.

b. Separate the switch housing (B, **Figure 90**).

c. Disconnect the throttle cables (C, **Figure 90**) from the switch housing.

3B. On TT600 models, perform the following:

a. Remove the screws holding the throttle housing together.

b. Separate the throttle housing.

c. Disconnect the throttle cables from the switch housings.

NOTE
The piece of string attached in the next steps will be used to pull the new throttle cables back through the frame so they will be routed in exactly the same position as the old cables.

4. Tie a piece of heavy string or cord (approximately 3 ft./1 meter long) to the carburetor end of the throttle cables. Wrap this end with masking or duct

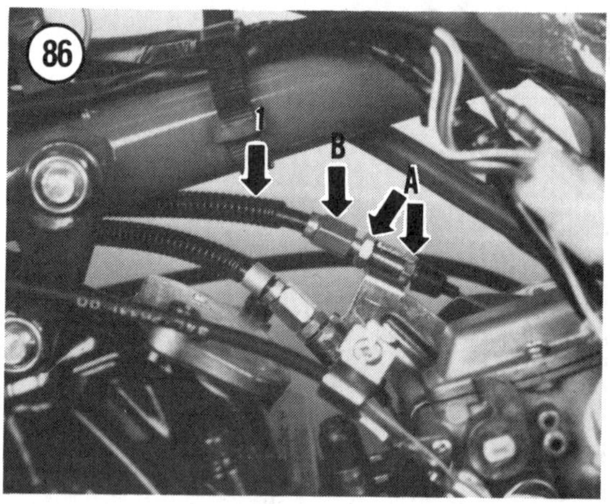

tape. Do not use a lot of tape as it must be pulled through the frame during removal. Tie the other end of the string to the engine or frame.

5. At the throttle grip end of the cable, carefully pull the cables and attached string out through the frame.

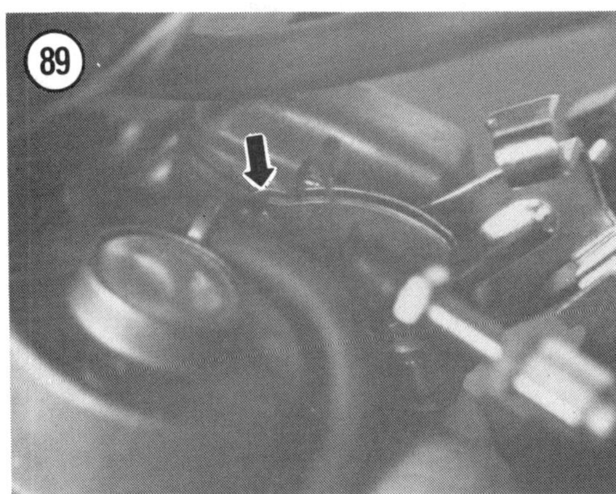

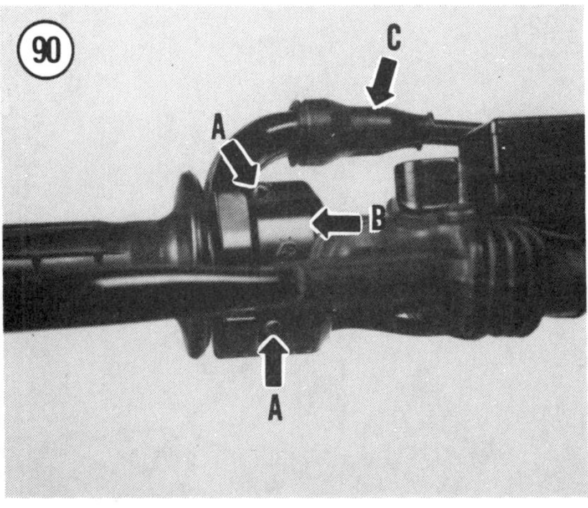

Make sure the attached string follows the same path as the cables through the frame.

6. Remove the tape and untie the string from the old cables.

7. Lubricate the new cables as described under *Control Cables* in Chapter Three.

8. Tie the string to the carburetor end of the new throttle cables and wrap them with tape.

9. Carefully pull the string back through the frame routing the new cables through the same path as the old cables.

10. Remove the tape and untie the string from the cables and the frame.

11. Connect the new throttle cables by reversing Steps 2-5. Note the following.

12. Operate the throttle grip and make sure the throttle cables and linkage are operating correctly, with no binding. If operation is incorrect or there is binding, carefully check that the cables are attached correctly and there are no tight bends in the cables.

13. Install the fuel tank as described in this chapter.

14. Adjust the throttle cables as described under *Throttle Cable Adjustment* in Chapter Three.

15. Test ride the bike slowly at first and make sure the throttle is operating correctly.

8

CHOKE CABLE REPLACEMENT (XT600)

NOTE

On the TT600 models, the choke assembly is operated by a knob on the carburetor and is not controlled by a cable.

1. Remove the fuel tank as described in this chapter.

2. Loosen the cable clamp screw (A, **Figure 91**) and unhook the cable from the clamp.

3. Unhook the cable end from the choke lever (B, **Figure 91**) on the carburetor.

4. On the left-hand end of the handlebar, perform the following:
   a. Remove the screw and washer (A, **Figure 92**) securing the choke lever assembly together.
   b. Separate the choke lever assembly and unhook the choke cable (B, **Figure 92**) from the lever assembly.

NOTE

The piece of string attached in the next step will be used to pull the new upper choke cable back through the frame so it will be routed in the same position as the old cable.

5. Tie a piece of heavy string or cord (approximately 3 ft./1 m long) to the carburetor end of the choke cable. Wrap this end with masking or duct tape. Do not use an excessive amount of tape as it must be pulled through the frame during removal. Tie the other end of the string to the carburetor or frame.
6. At the choke lever end of the cable, carefully pull the cable and attached string out through the frame and steering stem area. Make sure it follows the same path that the old cable does through the frame.
7. Remove the tape and untie the string from the old cable.
8. Lubricate the new cable as described under *Control Cables* in Chapter Three.
9. Tie the string to the carburetor end of the new choke cable and wrap it with tape.
10. Carefully pull the string back through the frame routing the new cable through the same path as the old cable.
11. Remove the tape and untie the string from the cable and the frame.
12. Connect the choke cable by reversing Steps 2-4 and note the following.
13. Operate the choke lever and make sure the choke linkage is operating correctly, with no binding. If operation is incorrect or there is binding, carefully check that the cable is attached correctly and there are no tight bends in the cable.

FUEL TANK

Removal/Installation (XT600)

Refer to **Figure 93** for 49-state fuel tanks or **Figure 94** for California fuel tanks for this procedure.

1. Place the bike on its sidestand.
2. Remove the seat as described in Chapter Thirteen.
3. Remove screws and washers (A, **Figure 95**) securing the front air ducts (B, **Figure 95**) and remove the air duct on each side.
4. Turn the fuel shutoff valve to the OFF position (A, **Figure 96**) and remove the fuel line (B, **Figure 96**) from the shutoff valve.
5. Insert a golf tee (A, **Figure 97**) into the end of the fuel line to prevent the dribbling of fuel.
6. On California models, disconnect the fuel tank roll-over valve vent line (C, **Figure 96**) from the charcoal filter.
7. Insert a golf tee (B, **Figure 97**) into the vent line to prevent the entry of foreign matter.
8. Remove the bolt (**Figure 98**) securing the fuel tank at the rear.
9. Pull the fuel tank toward the rear and remove the fuel tank.
10. Install by reversing these removal steps. Note the following.
11. Check the fuel hose for leaks.

NOTE
Motorcycle fuel tanks are relatively maintenance free. However, a major cause of fuel tank leakage occurs when the fuel tank is not mounted securely and it vibrates during riding. When installing the tank, make sure that the

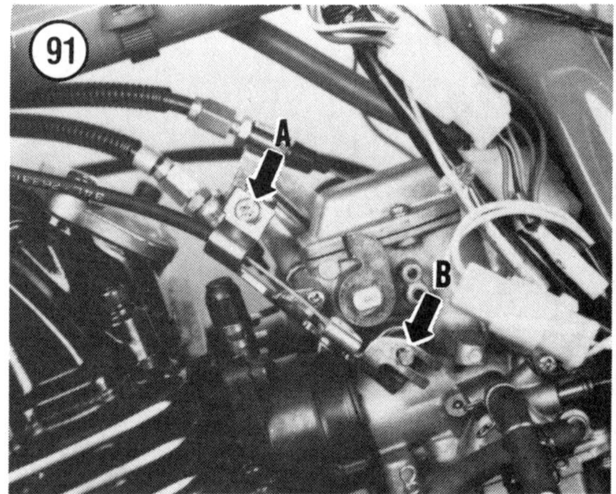

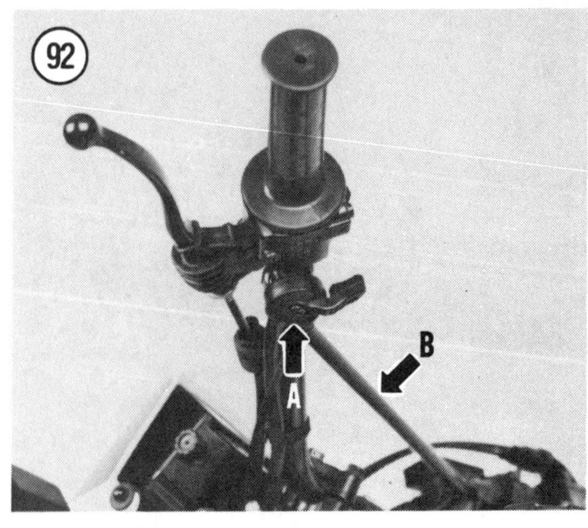

93

FUEL TANK—49-STATE (XT600)

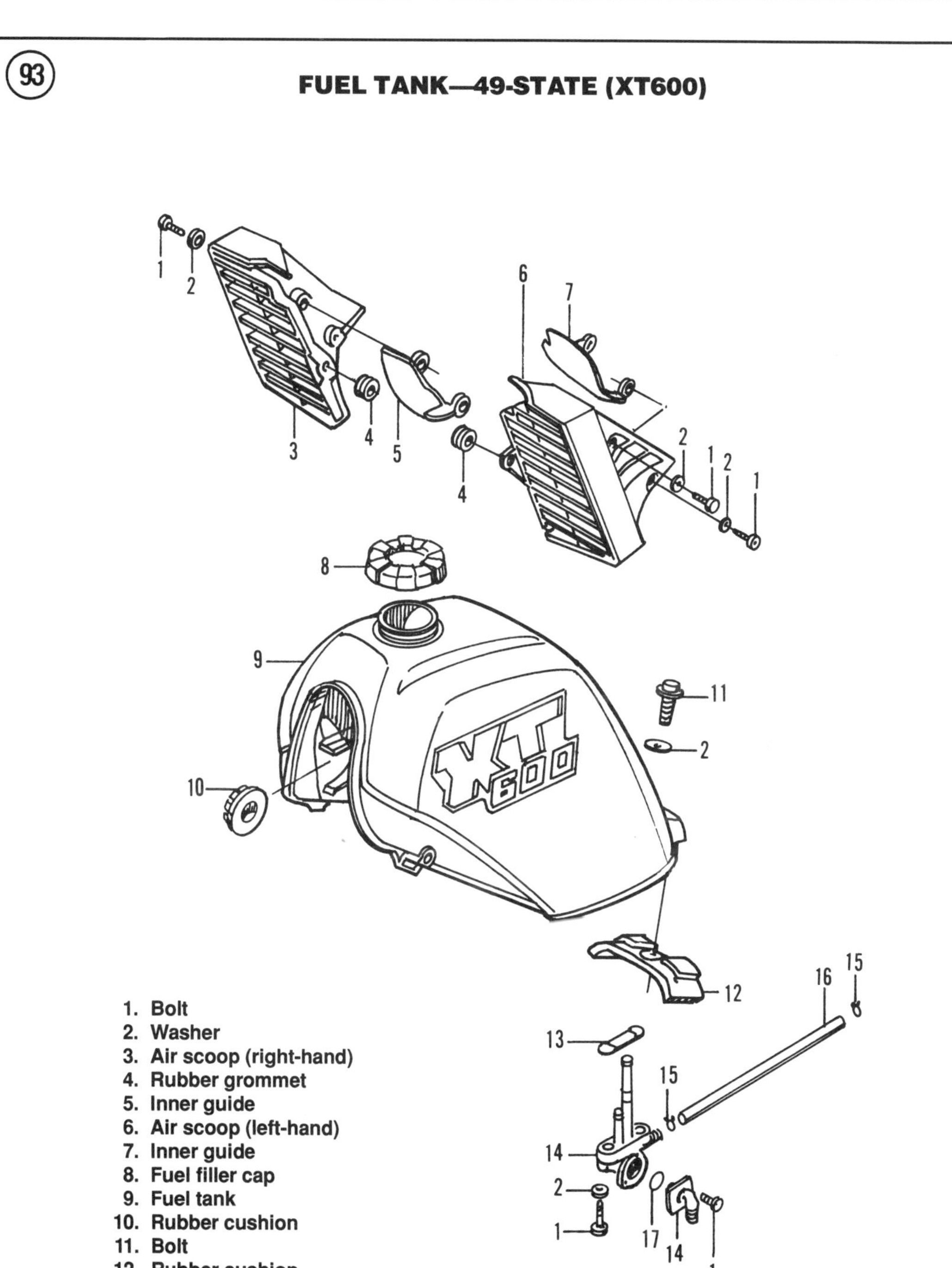

1. Bolt
2. Washer
3. Air scoop (right-hand)
4. Rubber grommet
5. Inner guide
6. Air scoop (left-hand)
7. Inner guide
8. Fuel filler cap
9. Fuel tank
10. Rubber cushion
11. Bolt
12. Rubber cushion
13. Gasket
14. Fuel shutoff valve
15. Hose clamp
16. Hose
17. O-ring seal

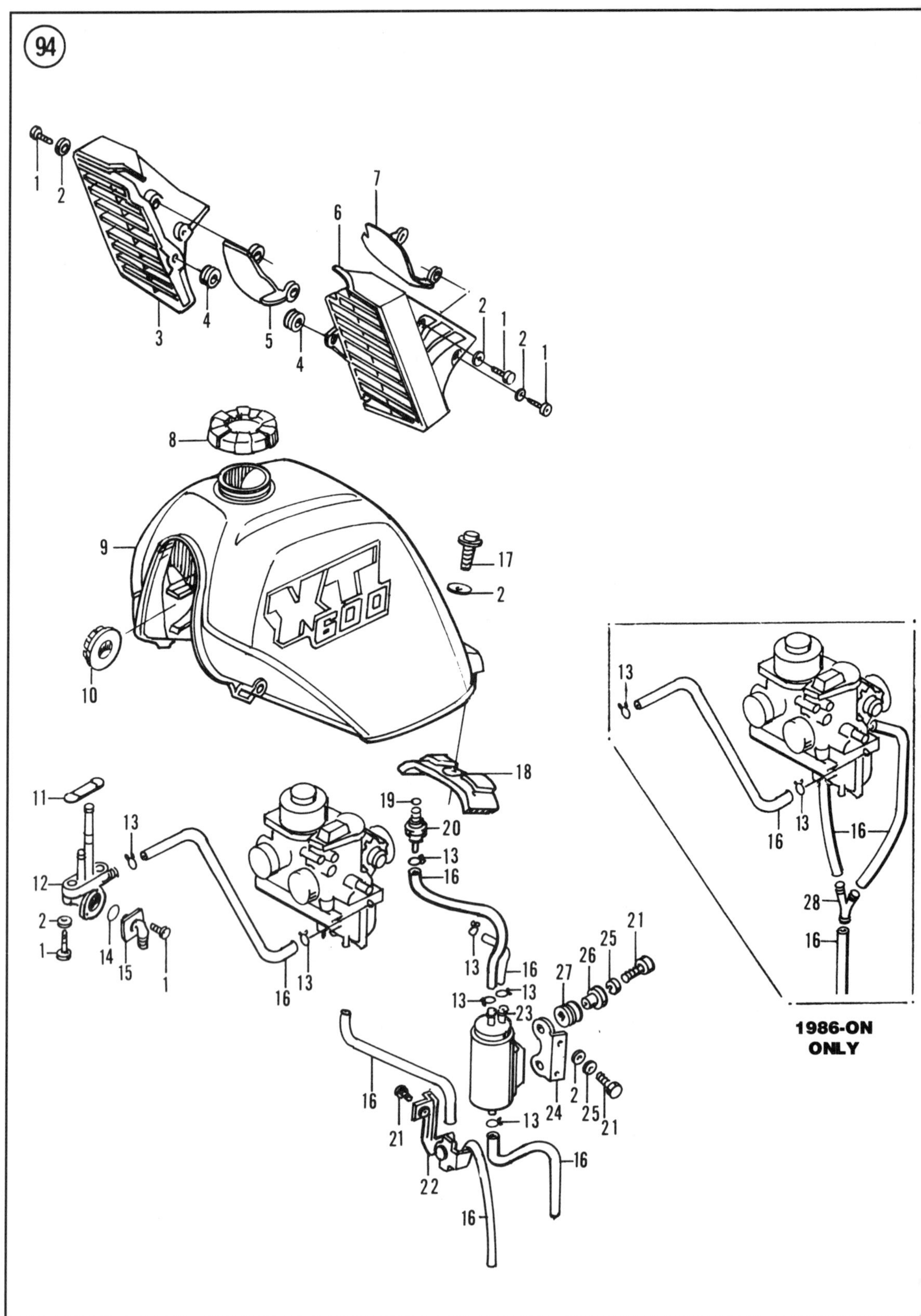
94
1
2
3
4
5
4
6
7
2
1
2
1
8
9
10
17
2
18
11
12
13
19
20
13
16
2
1
14
15
1
16
13
13
16
13
13
23
27
26
25
21
16
21
22
16
24
2
25
21
13
16
16
13
13
16
16
28
16
1986-ON
ONLY

FUEL TANK—CALIFORNIA (XT600)

1. Bolt
2. Washer
3. Air scoop (right-hand)
4. Rubber grommet
5. Inner guide
6. Air scoop (left-hand)
7. Inner guide
8. Fuel filler cap
9. Fuel tank
10. Rubber cushion
11. Gasket
12. Fuel shutoff valve
13. Hose clamp
14. O-ring seal
15. Fuel shutoff valve
16. Hose
17. Bolt
18. Rubber cushion
19. O-ring seal
20. Roll over valve
21. Bolt
22. Bracket
23. Charcoal canister
24. Mounting bracket
25. Lockwasher
26. Collar
27. Rubber bushing
28. Y-fitting

*rubber dampers at the front (**Figure 99**) and rear (**Figure 100**) of the tank are in position and that the tank is mounted securely at the front and back with the proper fasteners.*

Removal/Installation (TT600)

Refer to **Figure 101** for this procedure.

1. Place the bike on its sidestand.

2. Remove the seat as described in Chapter Thirteen.

3. Turn the fuel shutoff valve to the OFF position and remove the fuel line to the carburetor.

4. Remove the bolt and washer (**Figure 102**) on each side securing the fuel tank at the front. Don't lose the metal collar within the rubber damper mount on the frame.

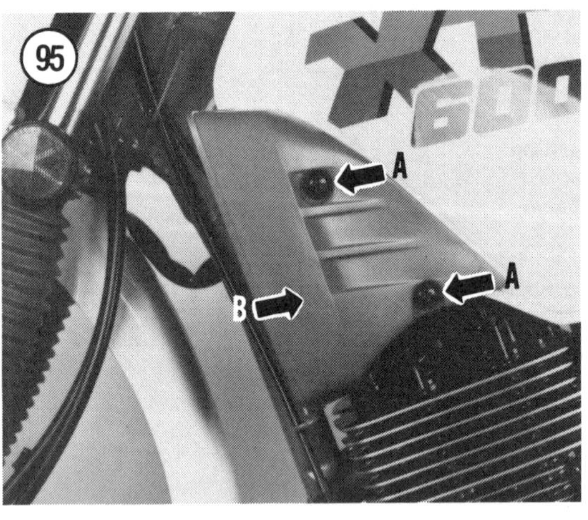

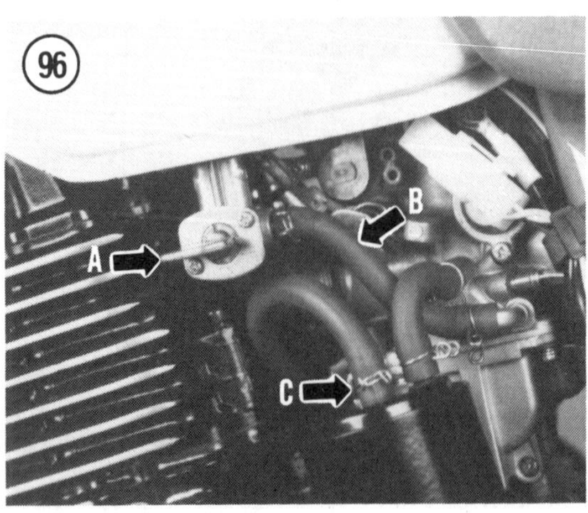

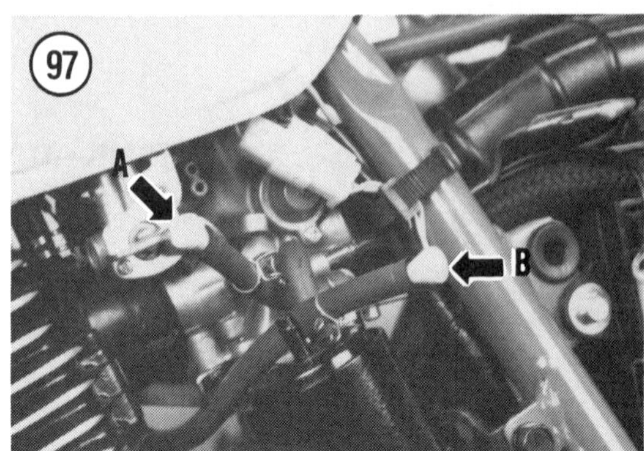

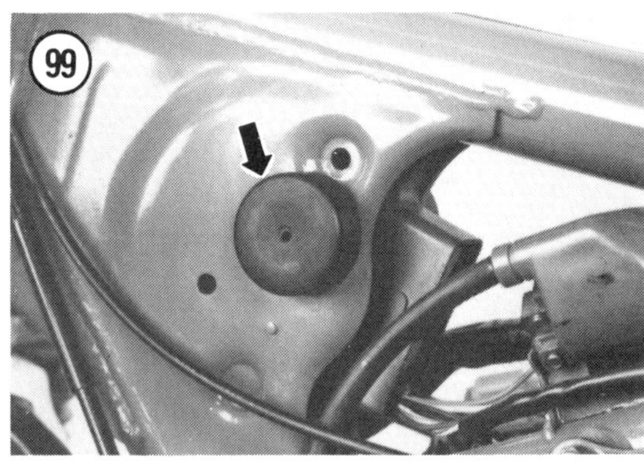

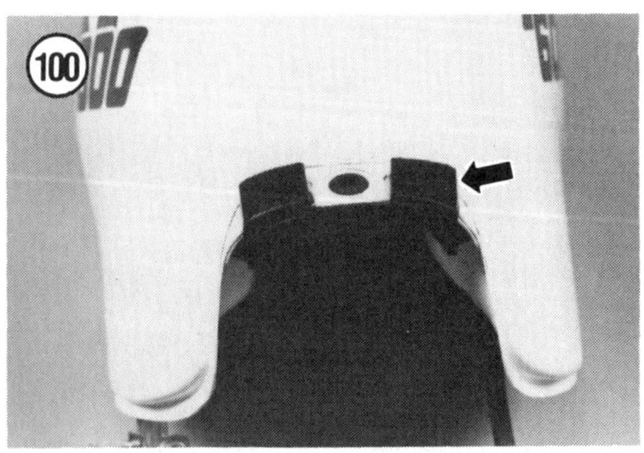

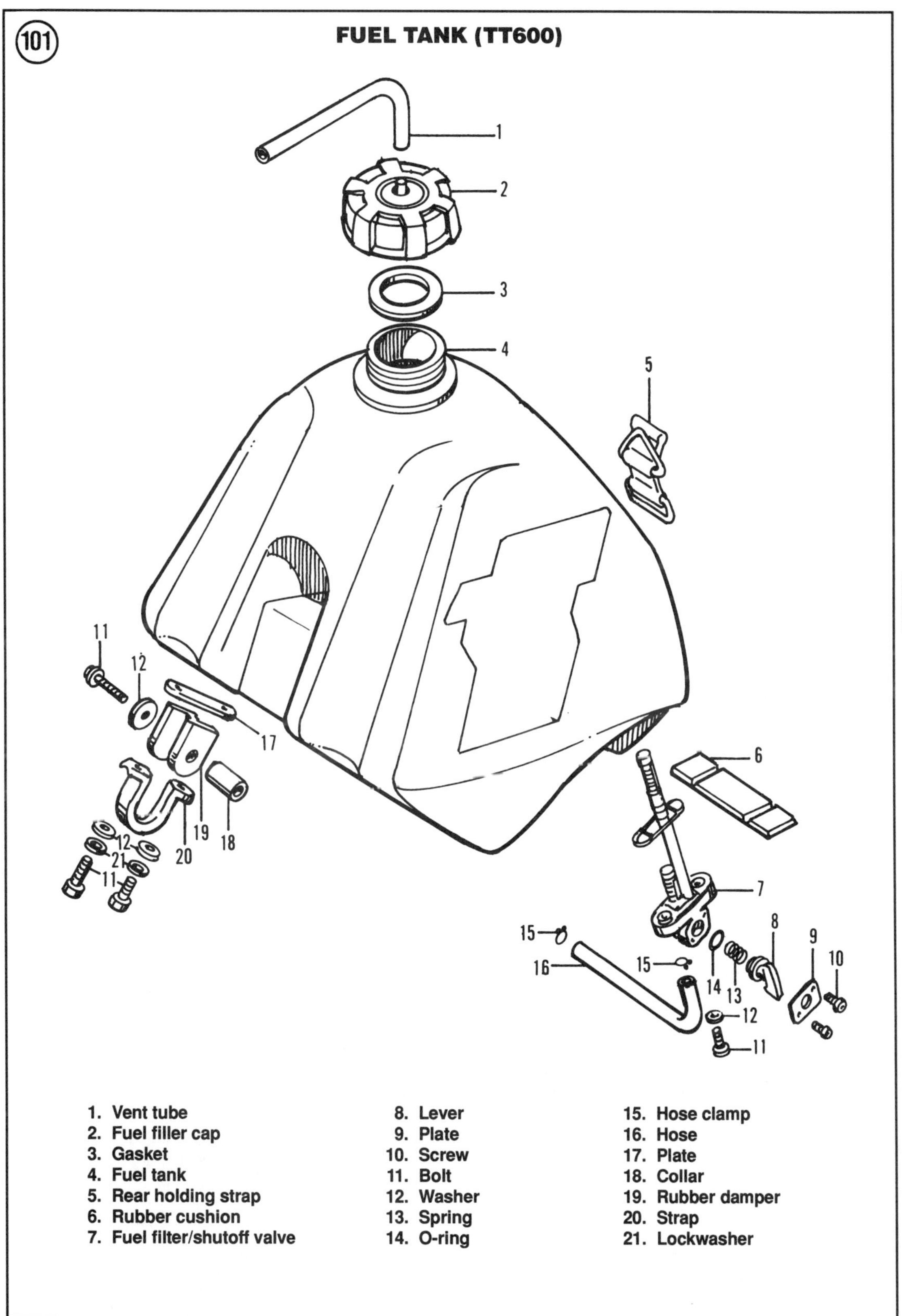

FUEL TANK (TT600)

1. Vent tube
2. Fuel filler cap
3. Gasket
4. Fuel tank
5. Rear holding strap
6. Rubber cushion
7. Fuel filter/shutoff valve
8. Lever
9. Plate
10. Screw
11. Bolt
12. Washer
13. Spring
14. O-ring
15. Hose clamp
16. Hose
17. Plate
18. Collar
19. Rubber damper
20. Strap
21. Lockwasher

8

5. Lift up and unhook the rubber strap (**Figure 103**) securing the fuel tank at the rear.
6. Pull the fuel tank toward the rear and remove the fuel tank.
7. Install by reversing these removal steps. Note the following.
8. Check the fuel hose for leaks.

NOTE
Motorcycle fuel tanks are relatively maintenance free. However, a major cause of fuel tank leakage occurs when the fuel tank is not mounted securely and it vibrates during riding. When installing the tank, make sure that the rubber dampers at the front and rear of the tank are in position and that the tank is mounted securely at the front and back with the proper fasteners.

9. Make sure the metal collar is in place within the rubber damper mount on the frame.

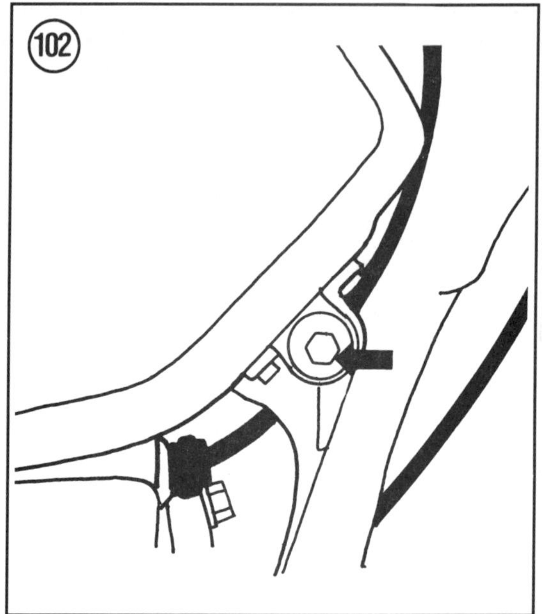

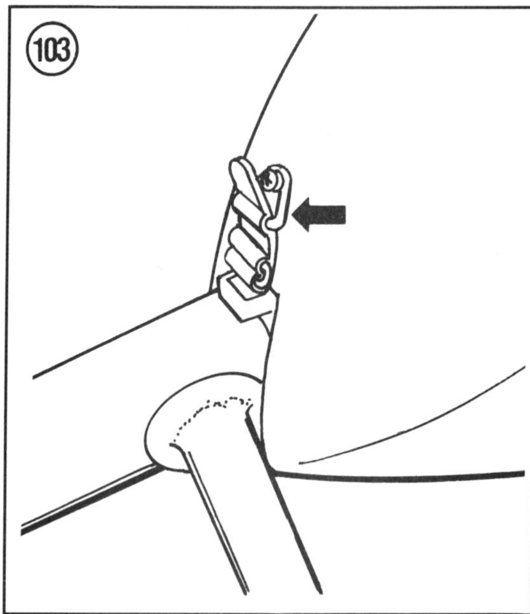

FUEL SHUTOFF VALVE

Removal/Installation

Refer to **Figure 93** for 49-state (XT600), or **Figure 94** for California (XT600) or **Figure 101** for all TT600 models for this procedure.

1. Remove the fuel tank as described in this chapter.
2. Drain the fuel into a safety approved sealable gasoline storage canister.
3. Lay the fuel tank on a blanket or several shop cloths to protect the painted finish.
4. Remove the screws and washers holding the fuel shutoff valve (**Figure 104**) to the bottom of the fuel tank. Remove the fuel valve.
5. Remove the screws and disassemble the valve.
6. Clean all parts in solvent with a medium-soft toothbrush, then dry.
7. Check the small O-ring within the valve and the O-ring gasket; replace if they are starting to deteriorate or get hard. Make sure the spring is not broken or getting soft; replace if necessary.
8. Reassemble the valve and install it on the tank.
9. Don't forget the O-ring gasket between the valve and the fuel tank.
10. Pour a small amount of fuel into the tank and check for leaks. Do not install the fuel tank if it leaks; correct the problem first.

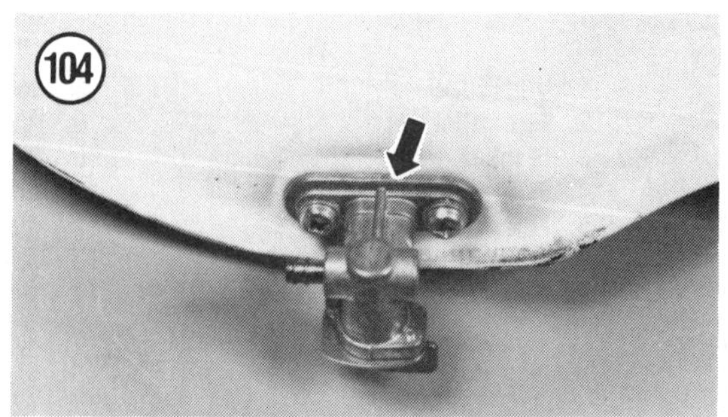

EXHAUST SYSTEM

Removal/Installation

Refer to **Figure 105** for this procedure.

1. Remove the seat as described in Chapter Thirteen.
2. Remove the frame's side cover on each side.
3. Remove the fuel tank as described in this chapter.
4. Place the bike on its sidestand.

5. Loosen the exhaust pipe nuts (**Figure 106**) at the cylinder head. Only 2 nuts are visible, there are a total of 4 nuts, loosen all nuts.

6. Remove the exhaust pipe-to-muffler clamp bolt (**Figure 107**).

105

EXHAUST SYSTEM

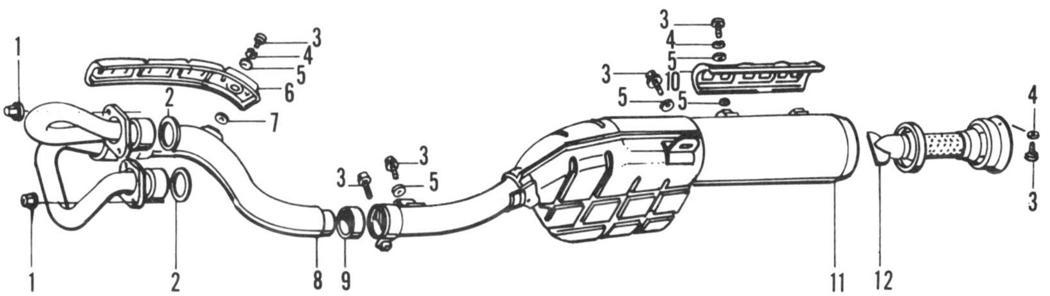

1. Nut
2. Gasket
3. Bolt
4. Lockwasher
5. Washer
6. Heat shield
7. Washer
8. Exhaust pipe
9. Gasket
10. Heat shield
11. Muffler
12. Spark arrester

7. Remove the muffler front (A, **Figure 108**) and rear (B, **Figure 108**) mounting bolts and washers.

8. Pull the muffler toward the rear and out of the exhaust pipe.

9. Remove the muffler (C, **Figure 108**) from the frame.

10. Remove the exhaust pipe nuts (**Figure 106**) at the cylinder head and remove the exhaust pipe assembly (**Figure 109**).

11. Inspect the front (**Figure 110**) and rear (**Figure 111**) heat shields for damage. If necessary, remove the screws, lockwashers and washers securing the heat shields and replace the shields. Tighten the screws securely.

12. Install by reversing the removal steps. Note the following.

13. Install new exhaust pipe gaskets at the cylinder head.

14. Install a new gasket (**Figure 112**) at the rear of the exhaust pipe assembly.

15. Install the exhaust pipe and muffler loosely until the complete exhaust system is installed. Then tighten the bolts starting with the exhaust pipe bolts at the cylinder head and work toward the muffler. See **Table 2** for tightening torques.

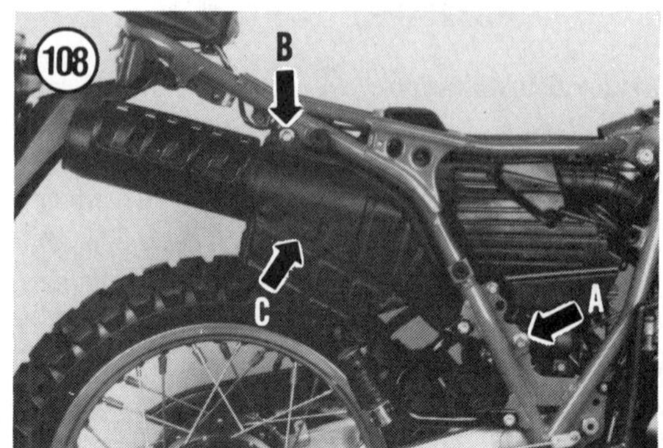

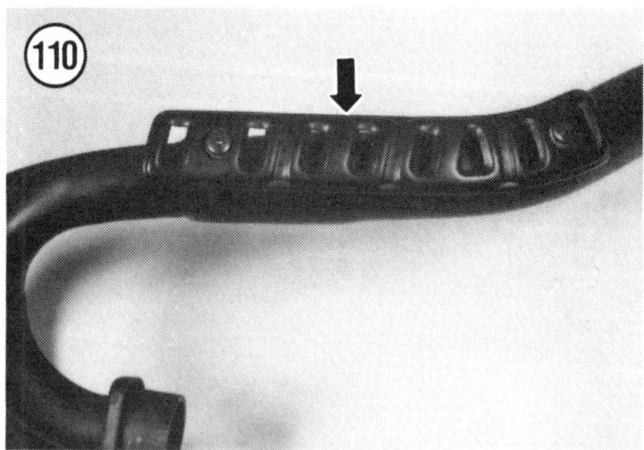

Carbon Removal

The spark arrester (**Figure 113**) mounted in the muffler should be cleaned at specified intervals. Refer to Chapter Three for the specified time interval and the complete procedure.

EXHAUST SYSTEM REPAIR

A dent in the exhaust pipe will alter the system's flow characteristics and degrade performance. Minor damage can be easily repaired if you have welding equipment, some simple body tools, and a bodyman's slide hammer.

Small Dents

1. Drill a small hole in the center of the dent. Screw the end of the slide hammer into the hole.

2. Heat the area around the dent evenly with a torch.

3. When the dent is heated to a uniform orange-red color, operate the slide hammer to raise the dent.

4. When the dent is removed, unscrew the slide hammer and weld the drilled hole closed.

Large Dents

Large dents that are not crimped can be removed with heat and a slide hammer as previously described. However, several holes must be drilled along the center of the dent so that it can be pulled out evenly.

If the dent is sharply crimped along the edges, the affected section should be cut out with a hacksaw, straightened with a body dolly and hammer and welded back into place.

Before cutting the exhaust pipe apart, scribe alignment marks over the area where the cuts will be made to aid correct alignment when the section is rewelded back onto the exhaust pipe.

After the welding is completed, wire brush and clean up all welds. Paint the entire pipe with a high-temperature paint to prevent rusting.

112

113

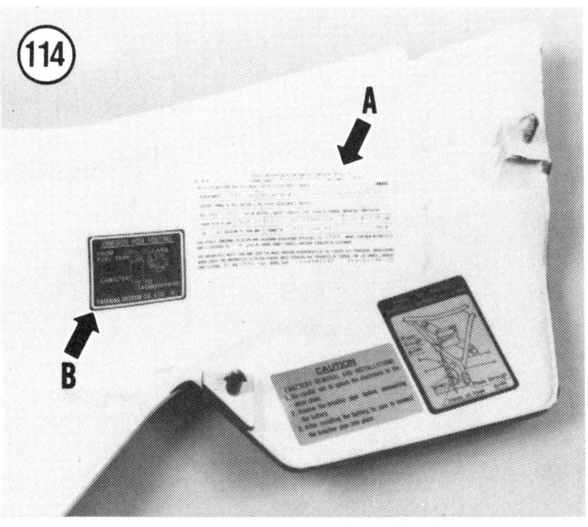

114

EVAPORATION EMISSION CONTROL SYSTEM (XT600 CALIFORNIA MODELS)

All XT600 models originally sold in California are equipped with an evaporative emission control system to reduce the amount of fuel vapors released into the atmosphere. The system consists of a charcoal canister, unvented fuel filler cap, roll-over valve, assorted vacuum lines and a modified carburetor and fuel tank.

A vehicle emission control information decal (A, **Figure 114**) is fixed to the backside of the left-hand side cover. This decal lists all emission control related tune-up information.

On models sold in California, an emission hose routing label (B, **Figure 114**) is fixed to the back of the side cover. Refer to this decal whenever reconnecting one of the emission control hoses.

During engine operation, fuel vapors formed in the fuel tank exit the tank through a roll-over valve and enter the charcoal canister through a connecting hose. The vapors are stored in the charcoal canister until the bike is ridden at a high speed. At which time, the vapors are passed through a hose to the carburetor and mixed and burned with the incoming fresh air. During low-speed engine operation or when the bike is parked, the fuel vapors remain stored in the charcoal canister.

The roll-over valve is installed in the bottom of the fuel tank. Air and fuel vapor passage through the valve is controlled by an internal weight. During normal riding (or when the fuel tank is properly positioned), the weight is at the bottom of the valve. In this position, the breather passage is open to allow the fuel vapors to flow to the charcoal canister where they are stored. If the bike is accidentally turned over on its side, the weight moves to block off the passage. In this position, it is impossible for fuel vapors to flow to the charcoal canister. The roll-over valve also prevents fuel from flowing to the carburetor under these conditions, since the fuel filler cap is not vented.

Service to the emission control system is limited to replacement of damaged parts. No attempt should be made to modify or remove the emission control system.

Parts Replacement

When purchasing replacement parts (e.g., carburetor, fuel tank, fuel tank cap, etc.), always make sure the parts are for California emission controlled bikes. Parts sold for non-emission controlled bikes will not work with the emission control system. Order all emission or fuel system related components with your engine serial number located on the upper right-hand crankcase (**Figure 115**).

Charcoal Canister Removal/Installation

1. Remove the frame's left-hand side cover.
2. Disconnect the carburetor hose (A, **Figure 116**) from the carburetor canister.
3. Disconnect the roll-over valve hose (leading from the fuel tank) (B, **Figure 116**) from the canister.
4. Insert a golf tee (A, **Figure 117**) into the end of both hoses to prevent the entry of foreign matter.
5. Remove the bolts (B, **Figure 117**) securing the canister (C, **Figure 117**) to the frame. Remove the charcoal canister.

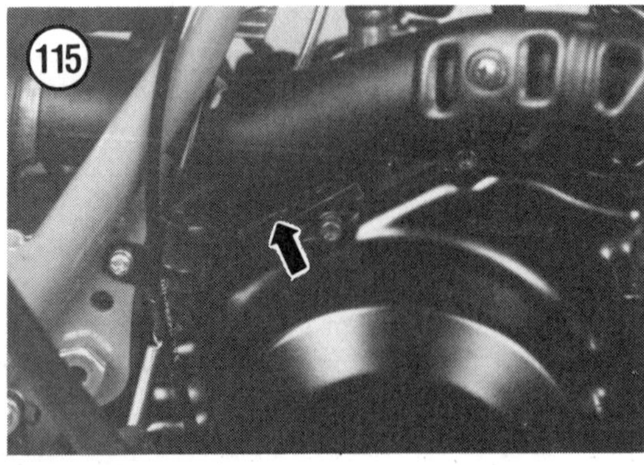

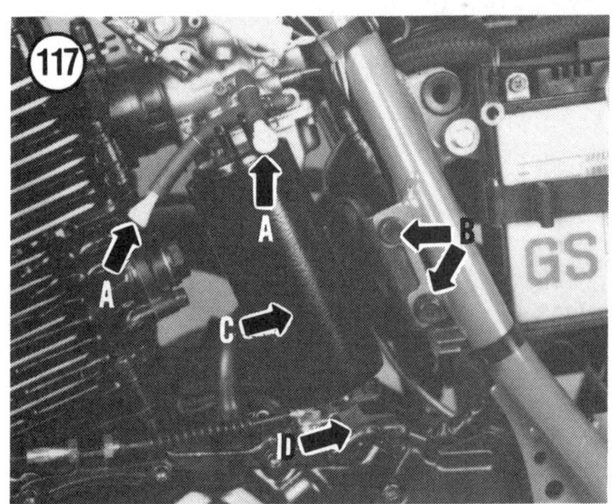

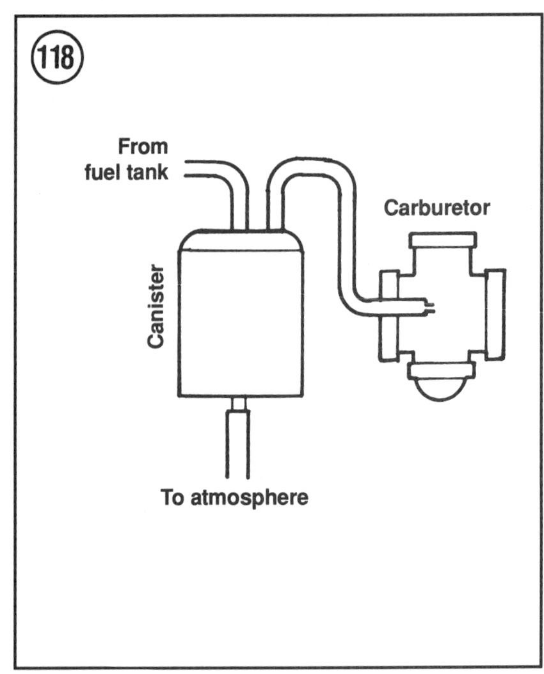

6. Install by reversing these removal steps. Note the following.
7. Refer to **Figure 118** for correct hose connections and routing.
8. Make sure the bottom vent hose (D, **Figure 117**) is not kinked or blocked.

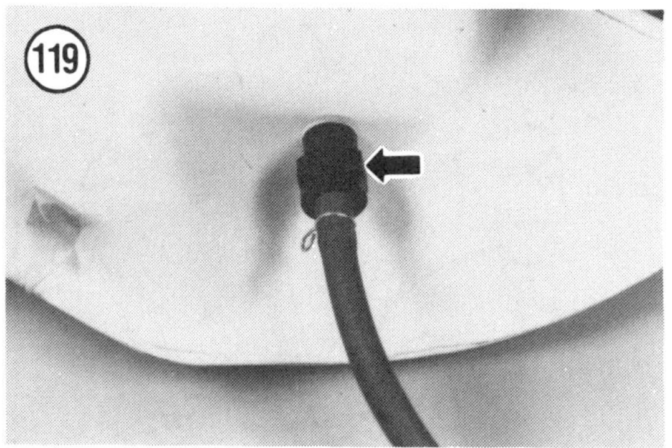
119

121

122

Roll-over Valve Removal/Installation

1. Remove the fuel tank as described in this chapter.
2. Drain the fuel tank of all gasoline. Store the gasoline in a safety approved sealable gasoline storage canister.
3. Unscrew the roll-over valve (**Figure 119**) from the bottom of the fuel tank.
4. Install by reversing these removal steps. Note the following.
5. Partially fill the fuel tank with fuel and check for fuel leakage.

CRANKCASE VENTILATION CONTROL SYSTEM

To comply with air pollution standards, the XT600 is equipped with a crankcase ventilation control system. The system draws blowby gases from crankcase and recirculates them into the fuel/air mixture and thus into the engine to be burned.

Refer to **Figure 120** for this procedure.

1. Remove the seat as described in Chapter Thirteen.
2. Remove both frame side covers.
3. Check the hose (**Figure 121**) for deterioration and replace as necessary.
4. Make sure the hose clamps are tight, replace if necessary. Refer to **Figure 122** for the crankcase fitting and **Figure 123** for the air filter air box connection.

123

Figure 120 and tables are on the following pages.

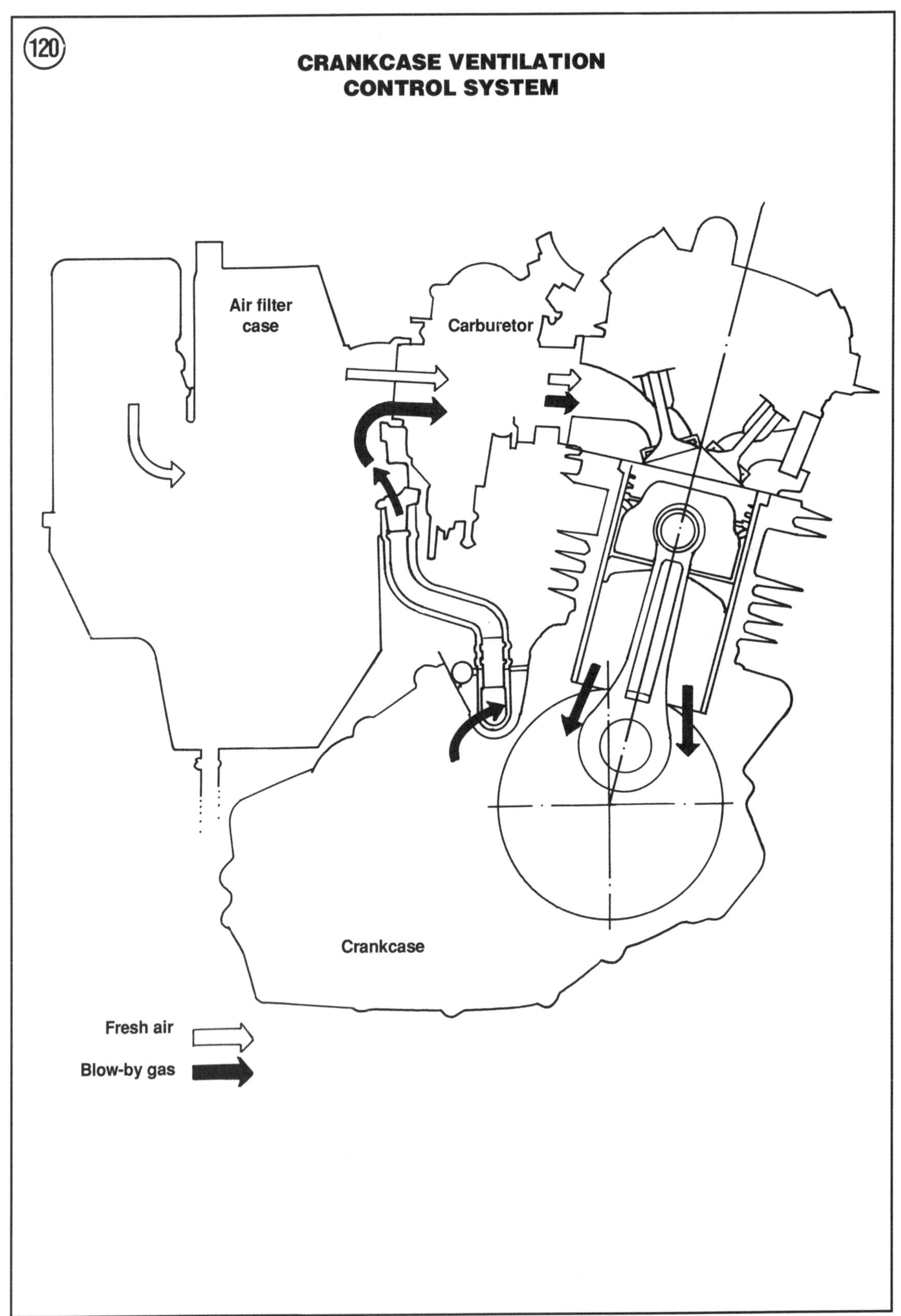
120
CRANKCASE VENTILATION
CONTROL SYSTEM
Air filter
case
Carburetor
Crankcase
Fresh air
Blow-by gas

Table 1 CARBURETOR SPECIFICATIONS

XT600 Models		
Carburetor type		Y27PV/TEIKEI/1
I.D. mark		
49-state models		49N 00
California models		49R 00
Fuel level		6-8 mm (0.24- 0.32 in.)
Float height		25-27 mm (0.98-1.06 in.)
Item	**Primary carb.**	**Secondary carb.**
Main jet	125	130
Main air jet	0.8	1.0
Jet needle no.	5C38	4A72
Pilot jet	46	—
Pilot air jet	1.0	—
Pilot screw turns out	preset	—
Starter jet	0.64	0.62
Valve seat	2.5	—
TT600 (1983-1984)		
Carburetor type		Y27PV/TEIKEI KIKAKI/1
I.D. mark		34K 00
Fuel level		6-7 mm (0.24-0.28 in.)
Float height		23.5-28.5 mm (0.92-1.12 in.)
Item	**Primary carb.**	**Secondary carb.**
Main jet	135	135
Main air jet	0.8	0.8
Jet needle/clip position	5C37-3/5	4A70-3/5
Needle jet	2.60	2.60
Pilot jet	48	—
Pilot air jet	0.5	—
Pilot screw turns out	preset	—
Valve seat	2.5	—
TT600 (1985-1986)		
Carburetor type		Y27PV/TEIKEI KIKAKI/1
I.D. mark		55U 00
Fuel level		6-7 mm (0.24-0.28 in.)
Float height		23.5-28.5 mm (0.92-1.12 in.)
Item	**Primary carb.**	**Secondary carb.**
Main jet	135	135
Main air jet	0.8	0.9
Jet needle/clip position	5C3B-3/5	4A71-3/5
Needle jet	2.60	2.60
Pilot jet	46	—
Pilot air jet	0.7	—
Pilot screw turns out	preset	—
Valve seat	2.5	—

8

Table 2 EXHAUST SYSTEM TIGHTENING TORQUES

Item	N•m	ft.-lb.
Exhaust pipe-to-cylinder head nut	10	7.2
Exhaust pipe-to-muffler clamp bolt	20	14
Muffler mount bolt	20	14
Heat shield screw	7	5.1
Spark arrester screw	7	5.1

CHAPTER NINE

ELECTRICAL SYSTEM

This chapter contains operating principles and service procedures for all electrical and ignition components.

The electrical systems include:

a. Charging system.
b. Ignition system.
c. Lighting system.
d. Switches.

Refer to Chapter Three for routine ignition system maintenance. Electrical system specifications are found in **Tables 1-4** at the end of the chapter.

ELECTRICAL TROUBLESHOOTING

This section describes the basics of electrical troubleshooting, how to use test equipment and the basic test procedures with the various pieces of test equipment.

Electrical troubleshooting can be very time consuming and frustrating without proper knowledge and a suitable plan. Refer to the wiring diagrams at the end of the book and the individual system diagrams included with the charging system, ignition system and lighting system sections in this chapter. Wiring diagrams will help you determine how the circuit should work by tracing the current paths from the power source through the circuit components to ground.

As with all troubleshooting procedures, analyze typical symptoms in a systematic procedure. Never assume anything and don't overlook the obvious, such as an electrical connector that has separated. Test the simplest and most obvious cause first and try to make tests at easily accessible points on the bike.

Preliminary Checks and Precautions

Prior to starting any electrical troubleshooting procedure, perform the following:

a. On XT600 models, check the circuit breaker (**Figure 1**) located above the battery. If it has tripped, reset it as described in this chapter.
b. Inspect the battery. Make sure it is fully charged, the electrolyte level is correct and that the battery leads are clean and securely attached to the battery terminals. Refer to *Battery* in Chapter Three.
c. Disconnect each electrical connector in the suspect circuit and check that there are no bent

metal pins on the male side of the electrical connector (**Figure 2**). A bent pin will not connect to its mating receptacle in the female end of the connector, causing an open circuit.

d. Check each female end of the connector. Make sure that the metal connector on the end of each wire (**Figure 3**) is pushed all the way into the plastic connector. If not, carefully push them in with a narrow-blade screwdriver.

e. Check all electrical wires where they enter the individual metal connector in both the male and female plastic connector.

f. Make sure all electrical connectors within the connector are clean and free of corrosion. Clean, if necessary, and pack the connectors with a dielectric grease compound.

g. After all is checked out, push the connectors together and make sure they are fully engaged and locked together (**Figure 4**).

h. Never pull on the electrical wires when disconnecting an electrical connector—pull only on the connector plastic housing.

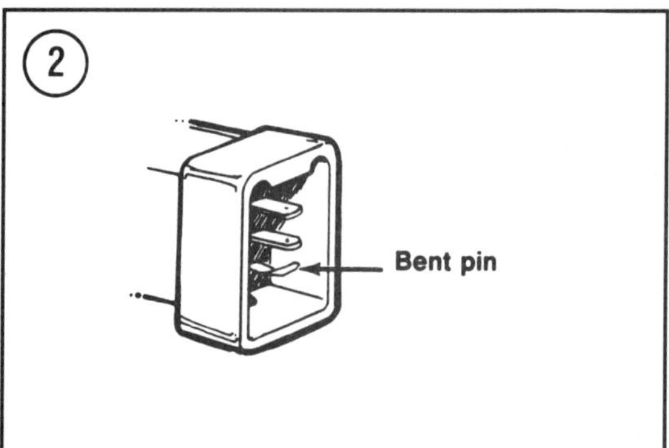

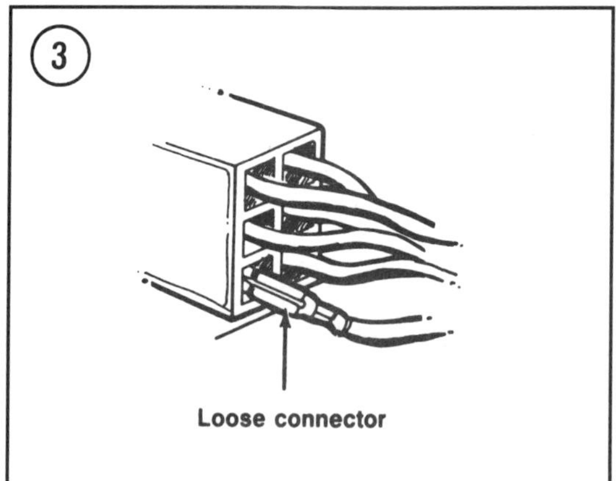

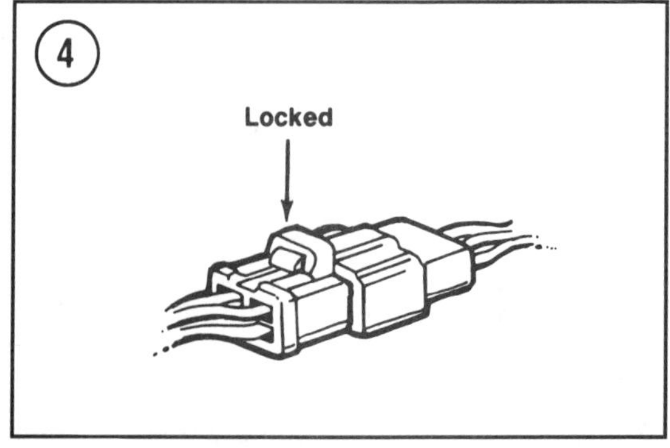

CHARGING SYSTEM (XT600)

The charging system consists of the battery, alternator and a solid state rectifier/voltage regulator as shown in **Figure 5**.

The alternator generates an alternating current (AC) which the rectifier converts to direct current (DC). The regulator maintains the voltage to the battery and load (lights, ignition, etc.) at a constant level regardless of variations in engine speed and load. Refer to Chapter Three for battery service.

Charging System Output Test

Whenever the charging system is suspected of trouble, make sure the battery is fully charged before going any further. Clean and test the battery as described in Chapter Three. If the battery is in good condition, test the charging system as follows.

1. Remove the left-hand side cover (**Figure 6**).

2. Disconnect the battery positive (+) lead from the battery.

3. Connect an ammeter between the battery positive (+) lead (A, **Figure 7**) and the non-fuse breaker positive (+) terminal (B, **Figure 7**).

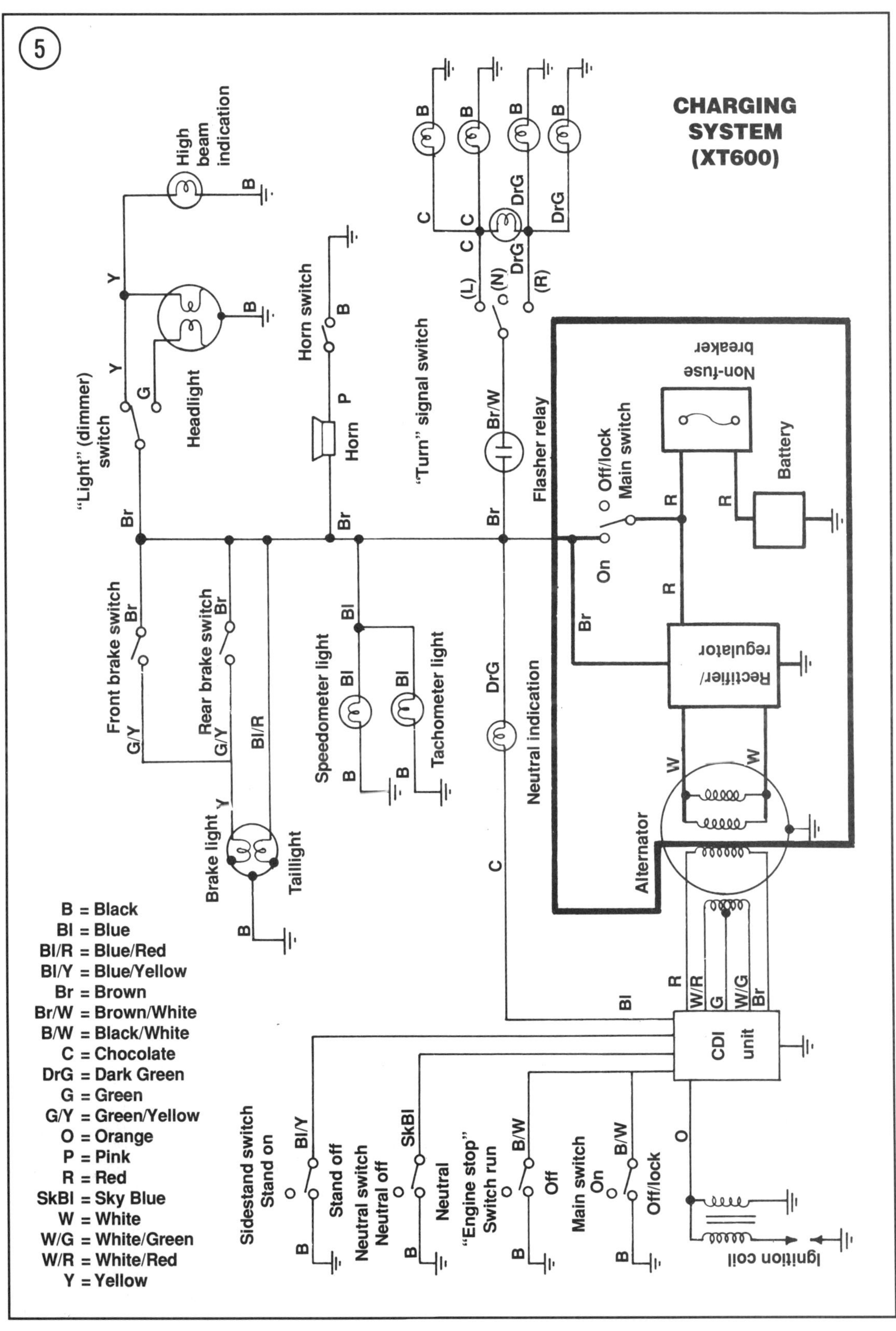
5
CHARGING
SYSTEM
(XT600)
High beam indication
Headlight
"Light" (dimmer) switch
Horn switch
Horn
"Turn" signal switch
Flasher relay
Off/lock
Main switch
On
Non-fuse breaker
Battery
Rectifier/ regulator
Front brake switch
Rear brake switch
Speedometer light
Tachometer light
Neutral indication
Brake light
Taillight
Alternator
CDI unit
Sidestand switch
Stand on
Stand off
Neutral switch
Neutral off
Neutral
"Engine stop" Switch run
Off
Main switch
On
Off/lock
Ignition coil
B = Black
Bl = Blue
Bl/R = Blue/Red
Bl/Y = Blue/Yellow
Br = Brown
Br/W = Brown/White
B/W = Black/White
C = Chocolate
DrG = Dark Green
G = Green
G/Y = Green/Yellow
O = Orange
P = Pink
R = Red
SkBl = Sky Blue
W = White
W/G = White/Green
W/R = White/Red
Y = Yellow

CAUTION
Never disconnect the leads from the battery while the engine is running. Shut the engine OFF, then disconnect the battery leads.

4. Start the engine and perform the following:
   a. Let the engine idle at 1,500 rpm. The ammeter should read 6.3 amps or more for the charging system to be operating correctly.
   b. Increase engine speed to 5,000 rpm. The ammeter should read 10 amps or less for the charging system to be operating correctly.
   c. If the amperage is not within specifications, check the charging coil resistance as described under *Charge Coil Testing* in this chapter.

NOTE
Yamaha does not provide testing information for the voltage regulator/rectifier.

5. If the charge coil tests indicate the charge coil is operating correctly and if the connectors and all wiring are okay, the rectifier/regulator unit is damaged. Replace the rectifier/regulator and retest.

Charge Coil Testing

It is not necessary to remove the stator assembly to perform the following tests. It is shown removed in the following procedures for clarity.

In order to get accurate resistance measurements, the stator assembly and coil must be approximately 68° F (20° C).

1. Remove the seat as described under *Seat Removal/Installation* in Chapter Thirteen.

2. Remove the fuel tank as described under *Fuel Tank Removal/Installation* in Chapter Eight.

3. Disconnect the alternator electrical connector (**Figure 8**). The connector contains 2 wires (2 white).

4. Connect an ohmmeter between the 2 white wire connector terminals. Test the connector on the stator coil side.

5. If the value is not within the specified range listed in **Table 1**, check the electrical wires to and within the connector. If they are okay, replace the alternator stator assembly as outlined in this chapter.

CHARGING SYSTEM (TT600)

The charging system on the TT600 models is used for the lighting system. The charging system performance test is described in the lighting system section of this chapter. Refer to *Lighting System (TT600)* for testing information.

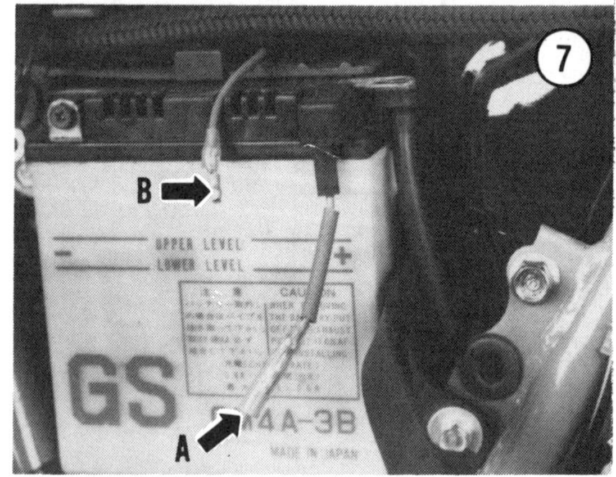

ALTERNATOR

The alternator is a form of electrical generator in which a magnetized field called a rotor revolves around a set of stationary coils called a stator. As the rotor revolves, alternating current is induced in the stator. The current is then rectified to direct current and used to operate the electrical accessories on the motorcycle and to charge the battery. The rotor is a permanent magnet.

Stator Assembly Removal/Installation

Refer to **Figure 9** for this procedure.

1. Remove the seat as described under *Seat Removal/Installation* in Chapter Thirteen.
2. Remove the fuel tank as described under *Fuel Tank Removal/Installation* in Chapter Eight.
3. Remove the frame's left-hand side cover (**Figure 6**).

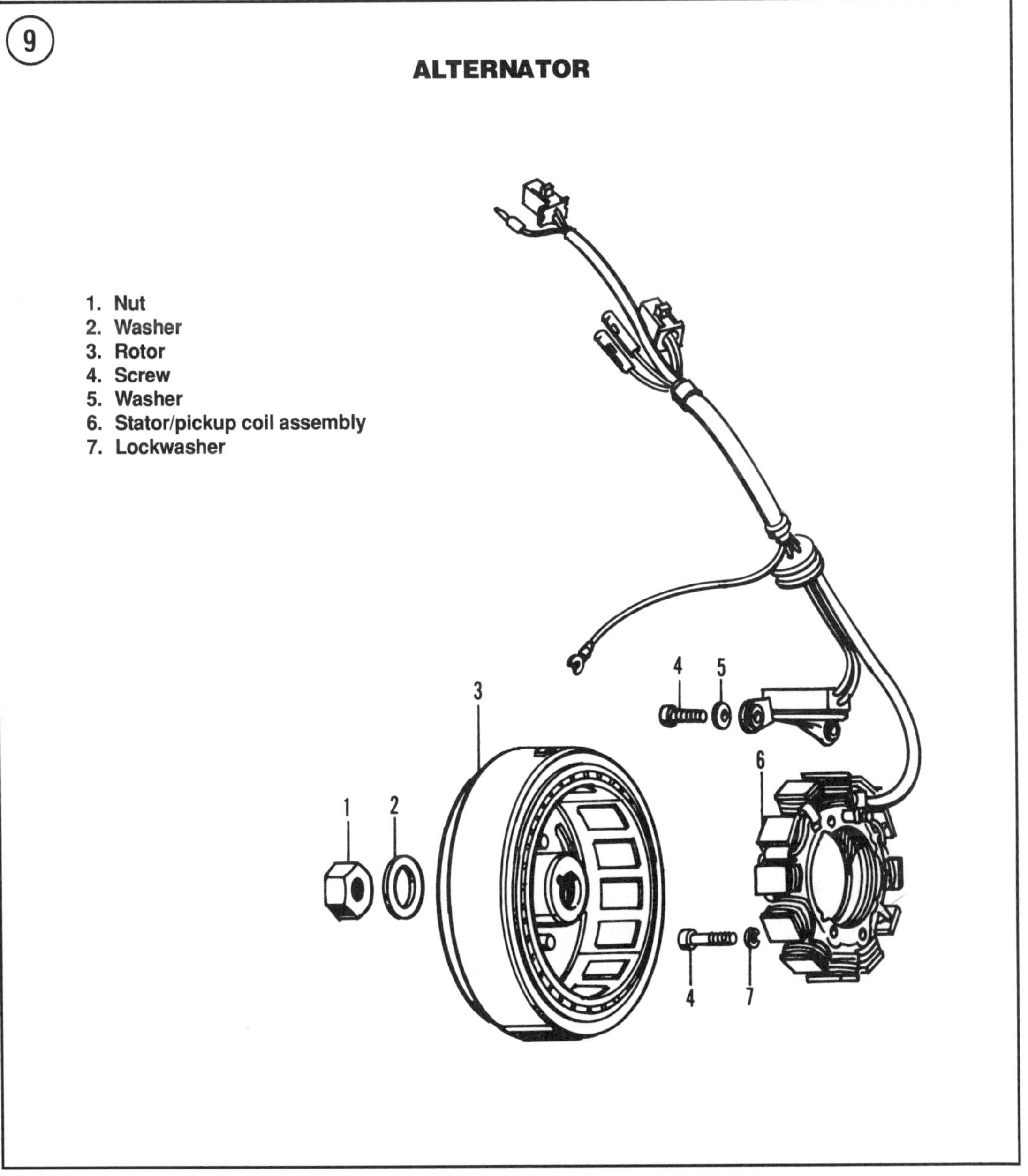

9

4. Disconnect the battery negative (–) electrical terminal connector (**Figure 10**).

5. Drain the engine oil as described under *Engine Oil and Filter Change* in Chapter Three.

6A. On XT600 models, remove the bolts securing the engine skid plate (A, **Figure 11**) and remove the skid plate.

6B. On TT600 models, remove the bolts securing the engine guard and remove the guard.

7. Remove the right-hand footpeg/brake pedal bracket assembly as described under *Rear Brake Pedal Removal/Installation* in Chapter Twelve.

8. Remove the pinch bolt securing the shift lever (B, **Figure 11**) and pull the shift lever off the shaft. If the splined boss is tight on the shaft, spread the slot open with a screwdriver.

9. Remove the screws securing the drive sprocket cover (C, **Figure 11**) and remove the cover.

10. Disconnect the following alternator electrical connectors (A, **Figure 12**):

a. Two pin connector: 2 white wires.
b. Three pin connector: 2 white/green, 1 green wires.

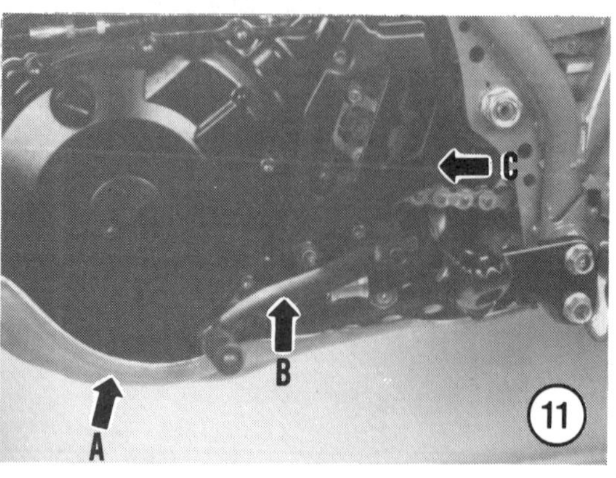

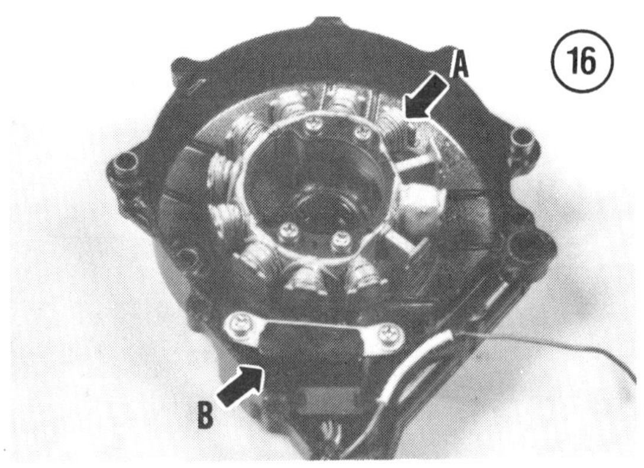

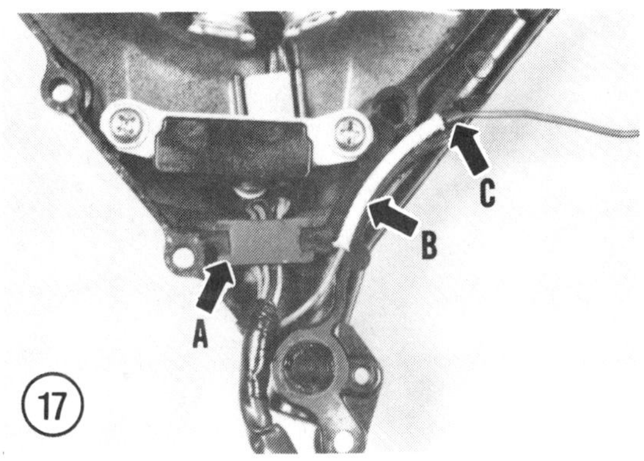

c. Single connector: 1 red wire.

d. Single connector: 1 brown wire.

11. Remove the tie wrap (B, **Figure 12**) securing the alternator electrical harness to the frame down tube.

NOTE

The following steps are shown with additional components removed from the engine. It is not necessary to remove any components other than what is specified in this procedure.

12. Remove the screw securing the neutral switch wire (**Figure 13**) to the switch.

13. Remove the screws securing the left-hand crankcase cover (**Figure 14**) and remove the cover and gasket. Don't lose the locating dowels or the O-ring seal.

14. Inspect the left-hand crankcase cover (**Figure 15**) for cracks or damage. Replace if necessary.

15. Remove the screws and washers securing the stator assembly (A, **Figure 16**).

16. Remove the screws and washers securing the pickup coil assembly (B, **Figure 16**).

17. Carefully pull the electrical harness out along with the rubber grommet (A, **Figure 17**) from the left-hand crankcase cover.

18. Install by reversing these removal steps. Note the following.

19. Be sure to route the neutral switch wire in the groove (B, **Figure 17**) and out the opening (C, **Figure 17**) in the left-hand crankcase cover.

20. Install new O-ring seals (**Figure 18**) in the crankcase.

21. Make sure the locating dowels (**Figure 19**) are in place and install a new gasket (**Figure 20**).

22. Check that the neutral switch wire (**Figure 21**) is located properly where the left-hand crankcase cover attaches to the crankcase.

23. Make sure all electrical connectors are free of corrosion and are tight.

24. Route the electrical wires in the original frame location.

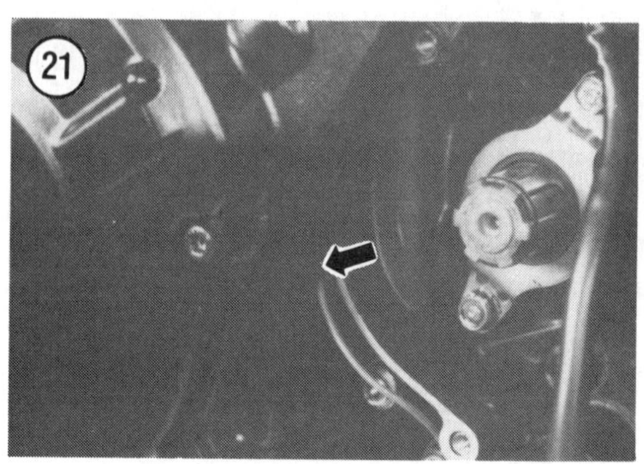

Rotor Removal

Refer to **Figure 9** for this procedure.

1. Perform Steps 1-14 of *Alternator Stator Removal/Installation* in this chapter.

2. Shift the transmission into 5th gear and have an assistant apply the rear brake. This will prevent the rotor from turning in the next step.

3. Loosen the alternator rotor nut (**Figure 22**).

4. Remove the nut and washer.

CAUTION

Don't try to remove the rotor without a puller; any attempt to do so will ultimately lead to some form of damage to the engine and/or rotor. Aftermarket pullers are available from most motorcycle dealers or mail order houses. If you can't buy or borrow one, have a dealer or service shop remove the rotor for you.

5. Attach a Yamaha flywheel puller (XT600 models/part No. YU-90105) or (TT600 models/part No. YU-33270), or a universal accessory puller (A, **Figure 23**) to the rotor.

6. Gradually tighten the center bolt (B, **Figure 23**) until the rotor disengages from the crankshaft.

NOTE

If the rotor is difficult to remove, strike the puller's center bolt with a hammer a few times. This will usually break the rotor loose.

CAUTION

If normal rotor removal attempts fail, do not force the puller as the threads may be stripped out of the rotor causing expensive damage or the end of the crankshaft may be damaged. Take it to a dealer or service shop and have them remove it.

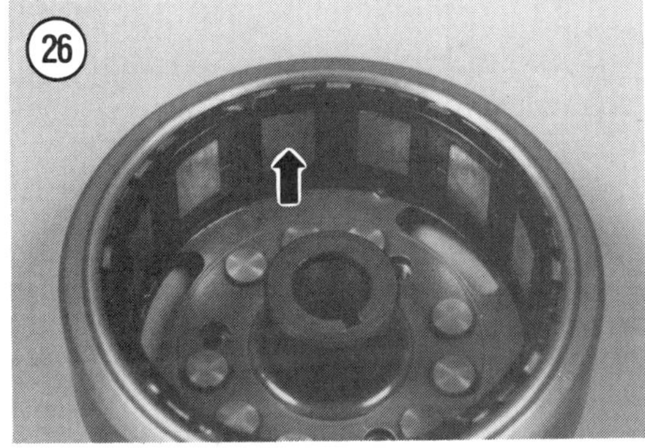

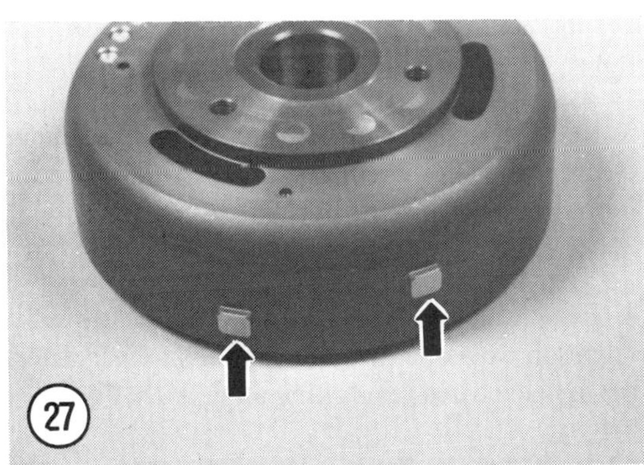

7. Remove the rotor and puller. Remove the puller from the rotor.
8. If necessary, remove the Woodruff key (**Figure 24**) from the crankshaft.
9. Check the Woodruff key and the keyway (**Figure 25**) in the rotor for damage.
10. While the rotor is off, check the stator mounting screws (A, **Figure 16**) and the pulse generator screws (B, **Figure 16**) for tightness. If necessary, tighten securely.
11. Inspect the inside of the rotor (**Figure 26**) for small bolts, washers or other metal "trash" that may have been picked up by the magnets. These small metal bits can cause severe damage to the magneto stator plate components.
12. Check the ignition pickup tabs (**Figure 27**) for damage.
13. Install by reversing these removal steps. Note the following.
14. Make sure the Woodruff key (**Figure 24**) is in place on the crankshaft. Align the keyway in the rotor with the key when installing the rotor (**Figure 28**).
15. Install the washer and rotor nut. Tighten the nut to the torque specification in **Table 2**.

9

VOLTAGE REGULATOR/RECTIFIER (XT600)

Removal/Installation

1. Remove the seat as described under *Seat Removal/Installation* in Chapter Thirteen.
2. Remove the fuel tank as described under *Fuel Tank Removal/Installation* in Chapter Eight.
3. Remove the frame's left-hand side cover.
4. Disconnect the battery negative (–) electrical terminal connector (**Figure 10**).
5. Disconnect the following voltage regulator/rectifier electrical connectors:
   a. Two pin connector: 2 white wires.
   b. Three pin connector: 1 red, 1 black, 1 brown wires.
6. Remove the screw and washers securing the voltage regulator/rectifier (**Figure 29**) to the frame and remove the voltage regulator/rectifier.
7. Install by reversing these removal steps. Note the following.
8. Make sure all electrical connectors are free of corrosion and are tight.

9. Tighten the mounting screws securely.

Testing

Yamaha does not provide testing information for the voltage regulator/rectifier.

VOLTAGE REGULATOR (TT600)

Removal/Installation

1. Remove the seat as described under *Seat Removal/Installation* in Chapter Thirteen.
2. Remove the frame's left-hand side cover.
3. Disconnect the single wire (yellow/white) electrical connector (yellow/white) to the voltage regulator.
4. Remove the screws securing the voltage regulator to the top of the air filter air box and remove the voltage regulator.
5. Install by reversing these removal steps. Note the following.
6. Make sure all electrical connectors are free of corrosion and are tight.
7. Tighten the mounting screws securely.

Testing

Yamaha does not provide testing information for the voltage regulator.

IGNITION SYSTEM (XT600)

The XT600 model is equipped with a capacitor discharge ignition (CDI) system which is a solid-state system that uses no breaker points. Refer to **Figure 30**.

Alternating current from the alternator is rectified to direct current and is used to charge the capacitor. As the piston approaches the firing position, a pulse from the pickup coil is used to trigger the silicone controlled rectifier. The rectifier in turn allows the capacitor to discharge quickly into the primary circuit of the ignition coil, where the voltage is stepped up in the secondary circuit to a value sufficient to fire the spark plug.

An ignition control system is installed on all XT600 models that consists of a neutral indicator light, neutral switch, engine stop switch and a sidestand switch. When the ignition switch and the engine stop switch are ON, the ignition will produce a spark for starting only if the following conditions exist:

a. The sidestand is up (the sidestand switch is ON). The engine will start if the transmission is in gear and the clutch lever is pulled in.

b. The transmission is in neutral (the neutral switch is ON).

Precautions

Certain measures must be taken to protect the capacitor discharge system.

1. Never connect the battery backwards. If the battery polarity is wrong, damage will occur to the voltage regulator, alternator and ignition unit.

2. Do not disconnect the battery while the engine is running. A voltage surge will occur which will damage the voltage regulator and possibly burn out the lights.

3. Keep all connections between the various units clean, free of corrosion and tight. Be sure that the wiring connectors are pushed together firmly to make a good electrical connection.

4. Each solid state unit is mounted on a rubber vibration isolator. Always be sure that the isolators are in place when reinstalling all units.

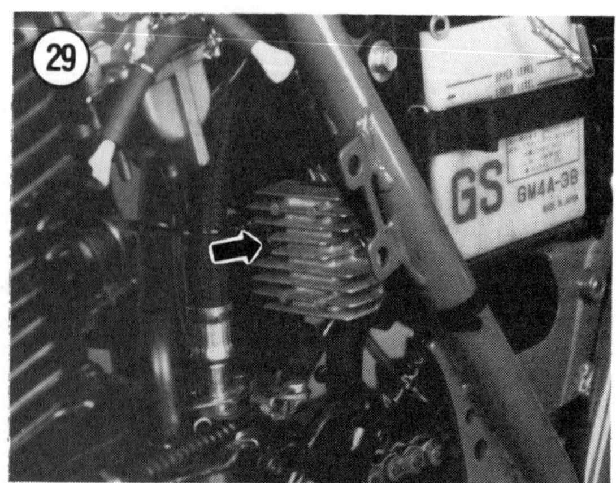

30
IGNITION SYSTEM (XT600)
"Light" (dimmer) switch
Front brake switch
Rear brake switch
Headlight
High beam indication
Brake light
Taillight
Horn switch
Horn
Speedometer light
Tachometer light
"Turn" signal switch
Flasher relay
Neutral indication
On
Off/lock
Main switch
Alternator
Rectifier/ regulator
Non-fuse breaker
Battery
CDI unit
Ignition coil
Sidestand switch
Stand on
Stand off
Neutral switch
Neutral off
Neutral
"Engine stop"
Switch run
Off
Main switch
On
Off/lock
B = Black
Bl = Blue
Bl/R = Blue/Red
Bl/Y = Blue/Yellow
Br = Brown
Br/W = Brown/White
B/W = Black/White
C = Chocolate
DrG = Dark Green
G = Green
G/Y = Green/Yellow
O = Orange
P = Pink
R = Red
SkBl = Sky Blue
W = White
W/G = White/Green
W/R = White/Red
Y = Yellow

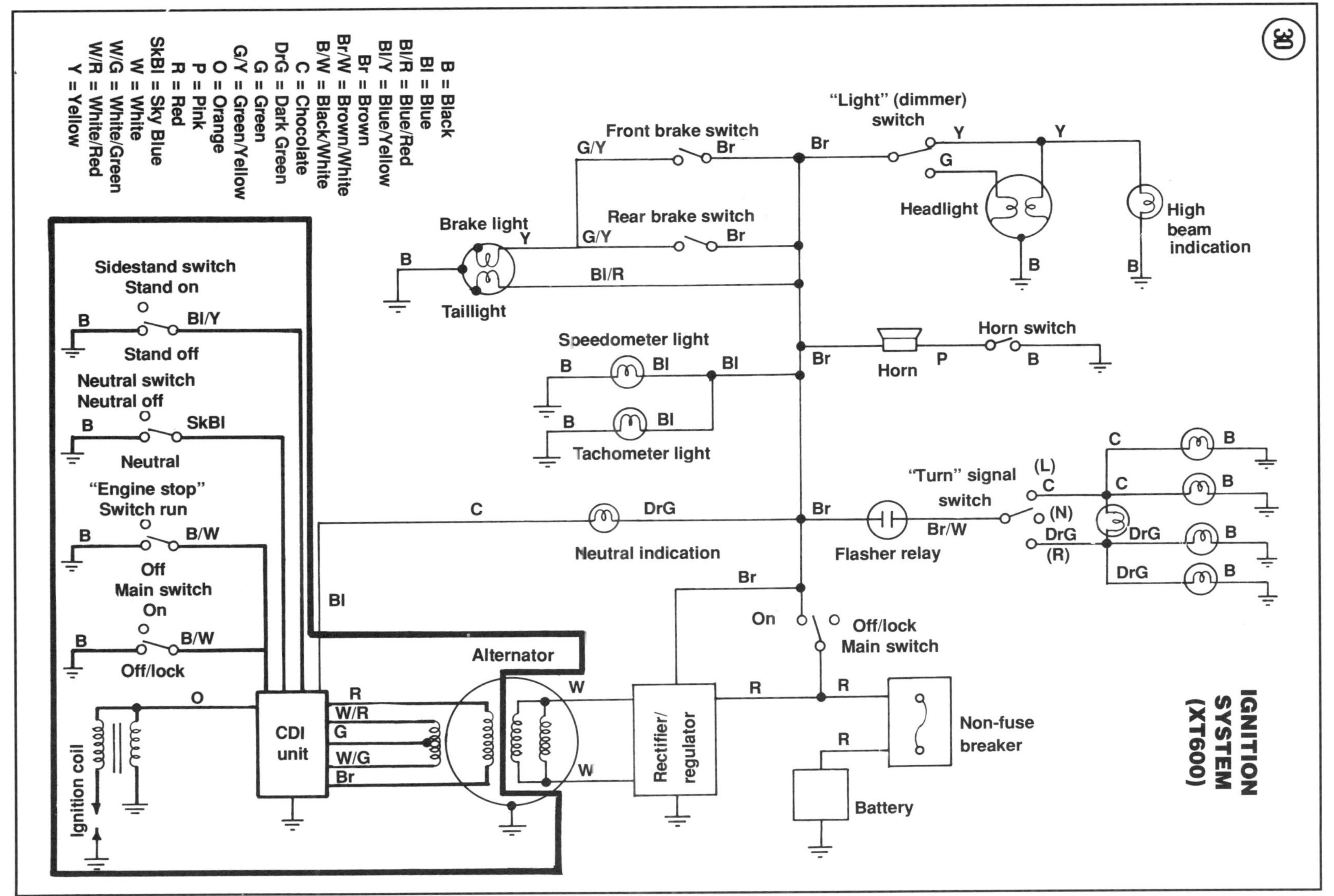

9

Pickup Coil and Source Coil

The pickup and source coils cannot be replaced separately since both are an integral part of the stator assembly. If either coil is defective, replace the alternator stator assembly as described in this chapter.

Pickup Coil Testing

It is not necessary to remove the stator assembly to perform the following tests. To get accurate resistance measurements, the stator assembly and coil must be approximately 68° F (20° C).

1. Remove the seat as described under *Seat Removal/Installation* in Chapter Thirteen.
2. Remove the fuel tank as described under *Fuel Tank Removal/Installation* in Chapter Eight.
3. Remove the frame's left-hand side cover.
4. Disconnect the battery negative (–) electrical terminal connector (**Figure 10**).
5. Disconnect the pickup coil 3-pin electrical connector (1 white/red, 1 white/green, 1 green) (A, **Figure 31**).
6. Connect an ohmmeter set at R × 100 and check resistance between the white/red and the white/green wire connector terminals. Test the connector on the pickup coil side.
7. If there is continuity (specified resistance listed in **Table 3**), the coil is good. If there is no continuity or the resistance is much less or more than specified, check the electrical wires to and within the connector. If they are okay, replace the alternator stator assembly as described in this chapter. The pickup coil cannot be replaced separately since the pickup coil is an integral part of the stator assembly.
8. Reconnect the electrical connector and the battery negative connector.
9. Install the frame's left-hand side cover, fuel tank and the seat.

Source Coil Testing

It is not necessary to remove the stator assembly to perform the following tests. To get accurate resistance measurements, the stator assembly and coil must be approximately 68° F (20° C).

1. Remove the seat as described under *Seat Removal/Installation* in Chapter Thirteen.
2. Remove the fuel tank as described under *Fuel Tank Removal/Installation* in Chapter Eight.
3. Remove the frame's left-hand side cover.
4. Disconnect the battery negative (–) electrical terminal connector (**Figure 10**).
5. Disconnect the source coil 2 individual electrical connectors, 1 red and 1 brown (B, **Figure 31**).
6. Connect an ohmmeter set at R × 100 and check resistance between the red and the brown wire connector. Test the connector on the source coil side.
7. If there is continuity (specified resistance listed in **Table 3**), the coil is good. If there is no continuity or the resistance is much less or more than specified, check the electrical wires to and within the connector. If they are okay, replace the alternator stator assembly as described in this chapter. The source coil cannot be replaced separately since the source coil is an integral part of the stator assembly.
8. Reconnect the electrical connectors and the battery negative connector.
9. Install the frame's left-hand side cover, fuel tank and the seat.

CDI Unit Removal/Installation

1. Remove the seat as described under *Seat Removal/Installation* in Chapter Thirteen.
2. Remove the fuel tank as described under *Fuel Tank Removal/Installation* in Chapter Eight.
3. Remove the frame's left-hand side cover.

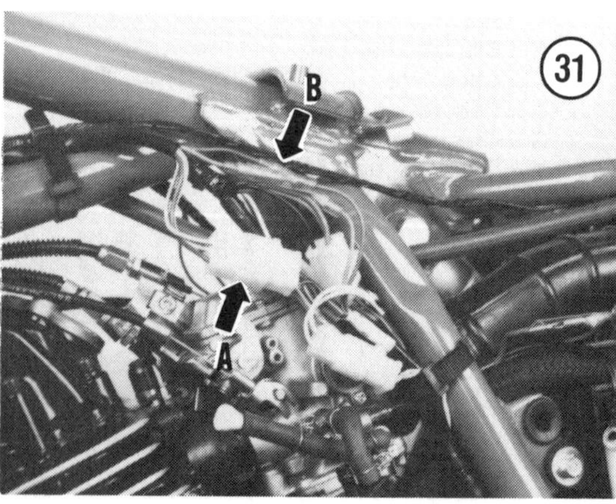

4. Disconnect the battery negative (–) electrical terminal connector (**Figure 10**).

5. Disconnect all electrical connectors from the CDI unit. Refer to **Figure 32** and A, **Figure 33**.

6. Remove the nuts (B, **Figure 33** securing the CDI unit to the mounting bracket and remove the CDI unit (C, **Figure 33**).

7. Install by reversing these removal steps. Note the following.

8. Before connecting the electrical wire connectors at the CDI unit, make sure the connectors are clean of any corrosion, dirt or moisture.

9. Make sure all electrical connectors are tight.

Testing

The CDI unit should be tested by a Yamaha mechanic familiar with capacitor discharge ignition testing. Improper testing of a good unit can damage it.

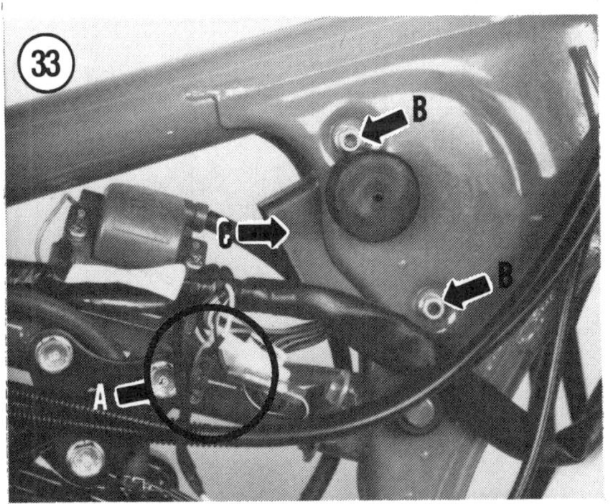

IGNITION SYSTEM (TT600)

The TT600 model is equipped with a capacitor discharge ignition (CDI) system which is a solid-state system that uses no breaker points. Refer to **Figure 34**.

Alternating current from the alternator is rectified to direct current and is used to charge the capacitor. As the piston approaches the firing position, a pulse from the pickup coil is used to trigger the silicone controlled rectifier. The rectifier in turn allows the capacitor to discharge quickly into the primary circuit of the ignition coil, where the voltage is stepped up in the secondary circuit to a value sufficient to fire the spark plug.

Precautions

Certain measures must be taken to protect the capacitor discharge system.

1. Never disconnect any of the electrical connections while the engine is running.

2. Keep all connections between the various units clean and tight. Be sure that the wiring connectors are pushed together firmly to help keep out moisture.

3. Each solid state unit is mounted on a rubber vibration isolator. Always be sure that the isolators are in place when replacing any units.

Pickup Coil Removal/Installation

The pickup coil cannot be replaced separately since it is an integral part of the stator assembly. If the coil is defective, replace the alternator stator assembly as described in this chapter.

Source Coil Removal/Installation

The source coil cannot be replaced separately since it is an integral part of the stator assembly. If the coil is defective, replace the alternator stator assembly as described in this chapter.

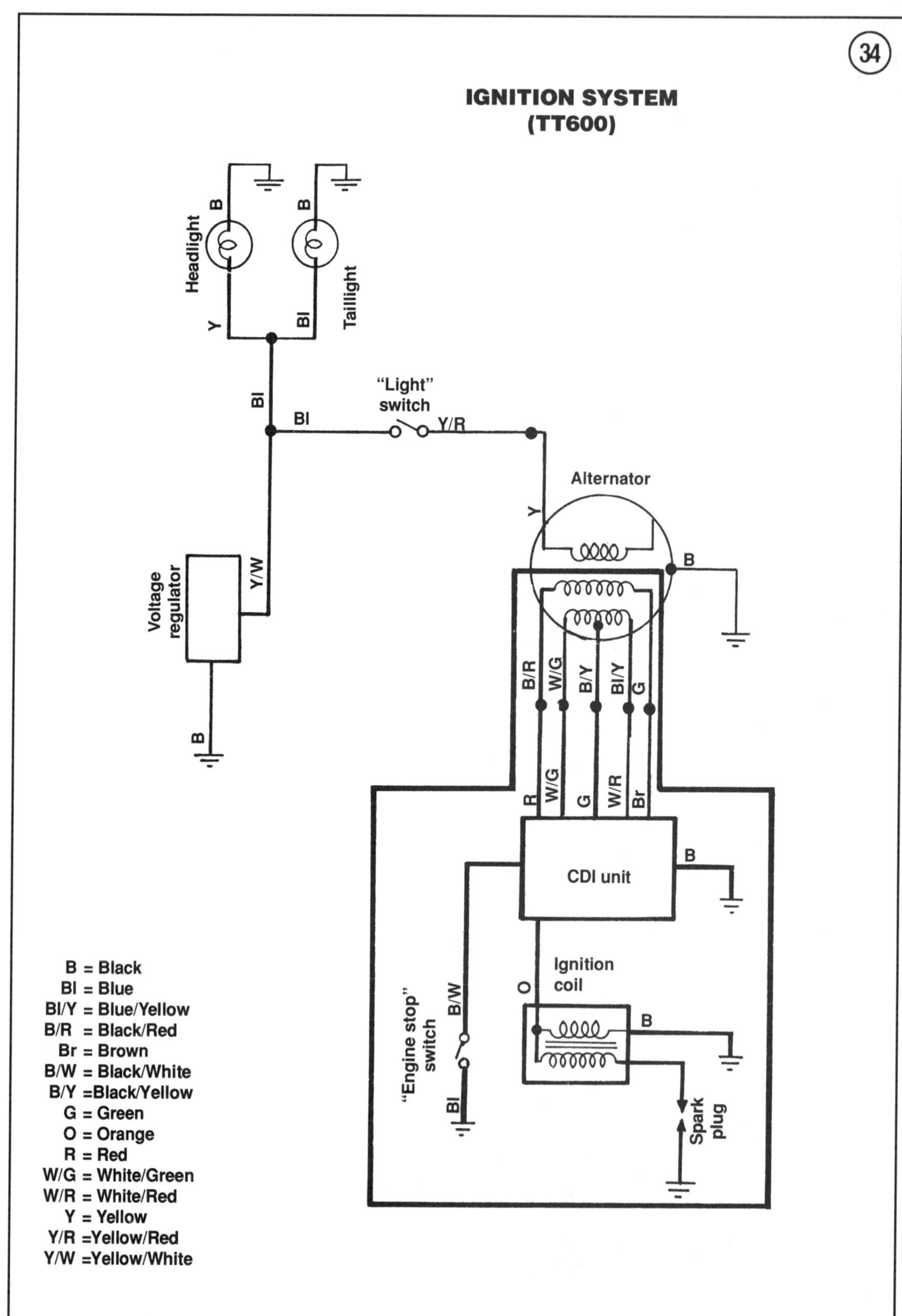
34
IGNITION SYSTEM
(TT600)
Headlight
Taillight
B
B
Y
Bl
Bl
Bl
"Light"
switch
Y/R
Alternator
Y
B
Voltage
regulator
Y/W
B
B/R
W/G
B/Y
Bl/Y
G
R
W/G
G
W/R
Br
CDI unit
B
Ignition
coil
O
B/W
"Engine stop"
switch
Bl
B
Spark
plug
B = Black
Bl = Blue
Bl/Y = Blue/Yellow
B/R = Black/Red
Br = Brown
B/W = Black/White
B/Y =Black/Yellow
G = Green
O = Orange
R = Red
W/G = White/Green
W/R = White/Red
Y = Yellow
Y/R =Yellow/Red
Y/W =Yellow/White

Pickup Coil Testing (1983-1984)

It is not necessary to remove the stator plate to perform the following tests.

To get accurate resistance measurements, the stator assembly and coil must be 68° F (20° C).

1. Remove the seat as described under *Seat Removal/Installation* in Chapter Thirteen.
2. Remove the fuel tank as described under *Fuel Tank Removal/Installation* in Chapter Eight.
3. Disconnect the pickup/source coil connector. It has 3 wires (white/green, white/red and green).
4. Use an ohmmeter set at R × 10 and check resistance between the green and white/green wires. If there is continuity (specified resistance listed in **Table 1**), the coil is good. If there is no continuity or the resistance is much less or more than specified, the coil is bad and must be replaced.
5. Use an ohmmeter set at R × 10 and check resistance between the green and white/red wires. If there is continuity (specified resistance listed in **Table 1**), the coil is good. If there is no continuity or the resistance is much less or more than specified, the coil is bad and must be replaced.
6. Make sure the connector is free of any corrosion, dirt or moisture.
7. Reconnect the connector and make sure it is tight.
8. Install the fuel tank and seat.

Pickup Coil Testing (1985-1986)

It is not necessary to remove the stator plate to perform the following tests.

To get accurate resistance measurements, the stator assembly and coil must be 68° F (20° C).

1. Remove the seat as described under *Seat Removal/Installation* in Chapter Thirteen.
2. Remove the fuel tank as described under *Fuel Tank Removal/Installation* in Chapter Eight.
3. Disconnect the pickup/source coil connector. It has 3 wires (blue/yellow, green/white and black/yellow).
4. Use an ohmmeter set at R × 10 and check resistance between the black/yellow and blue/yellow wires. If there is continuity (specified resistance listed in **Table 1**), the coil is good. If there is no continuity or the resistance is much less or more than specified, the coil is bad and must be replaced.
5. Use an ohmmeter set at R × 10 and check resistance between the black/yellow and green/white wires. If there is continuity (specified resistance listed in **Table 1**), the coil is good. If there is no continuity or the resistance is much less or more than specified, the coil is bad and must be replaced.
6. Make sure the connector is free of any corrosion, dirt or moisture.
7. Reconnect the connector and make sure it is tight.
8. Install the fuel tank and seat.

Source Coil Testing (1983-1984)

It is not necessary to remove the stator plate to perform the following tests.

To get accurate resistance measurements, the stator assembly and coil must be 68° F (20° C).

1. Remove the seat as described under *Seat Removal/Installation* in Chapter Thirteen.
2. Remove the fuel tank as described under *Fuel Tank Removal/Installation* in Chapter Eight.
3. Disconnect the pickup/source coil electrical connectors. One wire is brown and the other is red.
4. Use an ohmmeter set at R × 100 and check resistance between the brown and red wires. If there is continuity (specified resistance listed in **Table 1**), the coil is good. If there is no continuity or the resistance is much less or more than specified, the coil is bad and must be replaced.
5. Make sure the connectors are free of any corrosion, dirt or moisture.
6. Reconnect the connectors and make sure they are tight.
7. Install the fuel tank and seat.

Source Coil Testing (1985-1986)

It is not necessary to remove the stator plate to perform the following tests.

To get accurate resistance measurements, the stator assembly and coil must be 68° F (20° C).

1. Remove the seat as described under *Seat Removal/Installation* in Chapter Thirteen.

2. Remove the fuel tank as described under *Fuel Tank Removal/Installation* in Chapter Eight.
3. Disconnect the pickup/source coil electrical connectors. One wire is black/red and the other is green.
4. Use an ohmmeter set at R × 100 and check resistance between the black/red and green wires. If there is continuity (specified resistance listed in **Table 1**) the coil is good. If there is no continuity or the resistance is much less or more than specified, the coil is bad and must be replaced.
5. Make sure the connectors are free of any corrosion, dirt or moisture.
6. Reconnect the connectors and make sure they are tight.
7. Install the fuel tank and seat.

CDI Unit Removal/Installation

1. Remove the seat as described under *Seat Removal/Installation* in Chapter Thirteen.
2. Remove the fuel tank as described under *Fuel Tank Removal/Installation* in Chapter Eight.
3. Disconnect the electrical connectors from the CDI unit. It has 8 wires (black/white, orange, black, red, white/green, green, white/red and brown).
4. Unhook the rubber retaining strap and remove the CDI unit.
5. Make sure all connectors are free of any corrosion, dirt or moisture.
6. Reconnect the connectors and make sure they are tight.
7. Install the fuel tank and seat.

Testing

The CDI unit should be tested by a Yamaha mechanic familiar with capacitor discharge ignition testing. Improper testing of a good unit can damage it.

IGNITION COIL

Removal/Installation

1. Remove the seat as described under *Seat Removal/Installation* in Chapter Thirteen.
2. Remove the fuel tank as described under *Fuel Tank Removal/Installation* in Chapter Eight.
3. Remove the frame's left-hand side cover.
4. Disconnect the battery negative (–) electrical terminal connector (**Figure 10**).
5. Disconnect the spark plug lead (A, **Figure 35**) from the spark plug.
6. Disconnect the coil primary electrical wire (B, **Figure 35**) at the electrical connector on the ignition coil.
7. Remove the screws (C, **Figure 35**) securing the ignition coil and remove the coil from the frame.
8. Install by reversing these removal steps. Note the following.
9. Make sure to correctly connect the primary electrical wires to the coil and the spark plug leads to the spark plug.
10. Make sure the ground wire (**Figure 36**) is attached to one of the ignition coil mounting lugs.
11. Make sure all electrical connectors are free of corrosion and are tight.

Dynamic Test

Disconnect the high voltage lead from the spark plug. Remove the spark plug from the cylinder head.

Connect a new or known good spark plug to the high voltage lead and place the spark plug base on a good ground like the engine cylinder head. Position the spark plug so you can see the electrodes.

WARNING
If it is necessary to hold the high voltage lead, do so with an insulated pair of pliers. The high voltage generated could produce serious or fatal shocks.

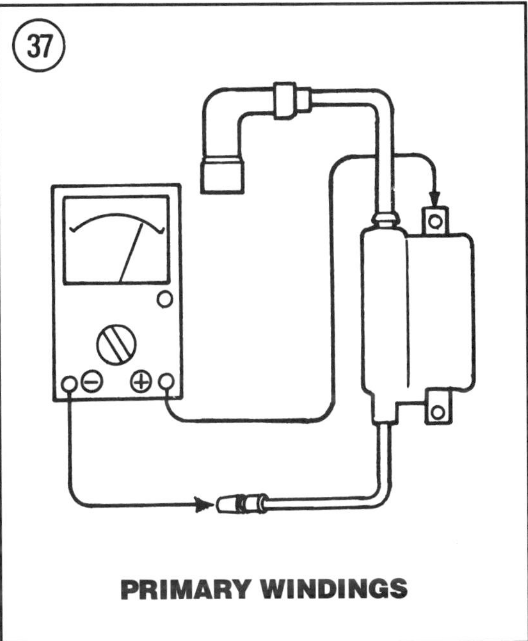

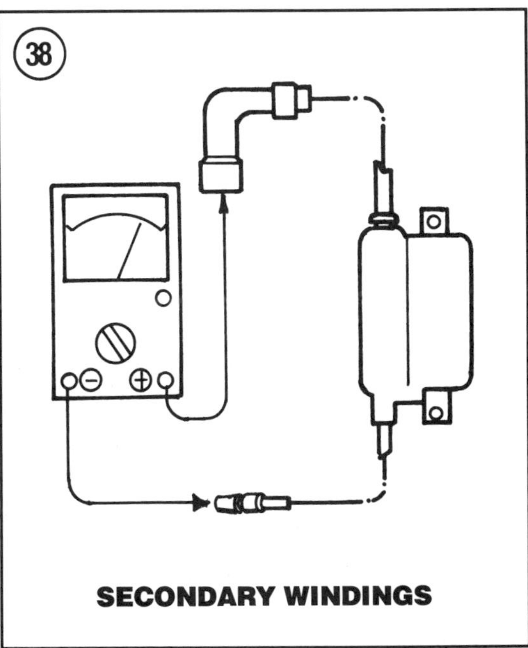

Use the kickstarter and turn the engine over a couple of times. If a fat blue spark occurs, the coil is in good condition; if not, it must be replaced. Make sure that you are using a known good spark plug for this test. If the spark plug used is defective, the test results will be incorrect.

Reinstall the spark plug in the cylinder head and reconnect the spark plug lead.

Resistance Testing

The ignition coil is a form of transformer which develops the high voltage required to jump the spark plug gap. The only maintenance required is that of keeping the electrical connections clean and tight and occasionally checking to see that the coil is mounted securely.

If the coil condition is doubtful, there are several checks which may be made. Disconnect all ignition coil wires before testing.

NOTE
In order to get accurate resistance measurements, the coil must be approximately 68° F (20° C).

1. Disconnect the spark plug lead (A, **Figure 35**) from the spark plug.
2. Disconnect the coil primary electrical wire (B, **Figure 35**) at the electrical connector on the ignition coil.
3. Measure the coil primary resistance using an ohmmeter set at R × 1. Measure between the primary terminal (orange wire) and ground (**Figure 37**). Resistance is specified in **Table 3**.
4. Measure the secondary resistance using an ohmmeter set at R × 100. Measure between the secondary lead (spark plug lead) and the orange coil wire (**Figure 38**). Resistance is specified in **Table 3**.

NOTE
If the coil test readings are marginal, prior to replacing the coil, have the coil tested by a Yamaha dealer using a spark

9

gap tester. This test is a better indication of the coils performance.

5. If the coil resistance does not meet either of these specifications, the coil must be replaced.
6. Replace the coil if the spark plug lead shows visible damage.

SPARK PLUG

The spark plug recommended by the factory is usually the most suitable for your machine. If riding conditions are mild, it may be advisable to go to a spark plug one step hotter than normal. Unusually

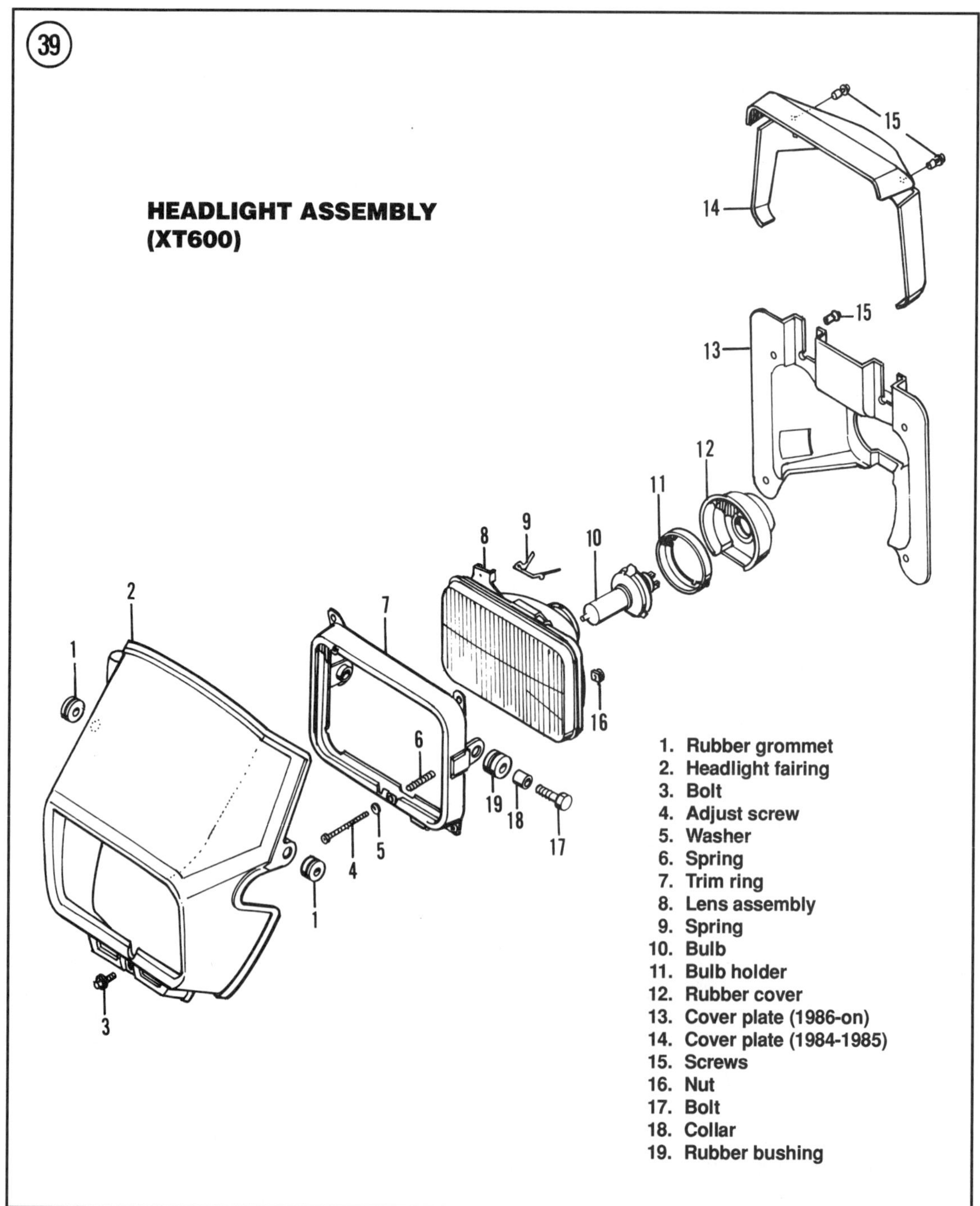

severe riding conditions may require slightly colder plugs. See Chapter Two and Chapter Three for details.

LIGHTING SYSTEM (XT600)

The lighting system consists of a headlight, taillight, turn signals and indicator bulbs.

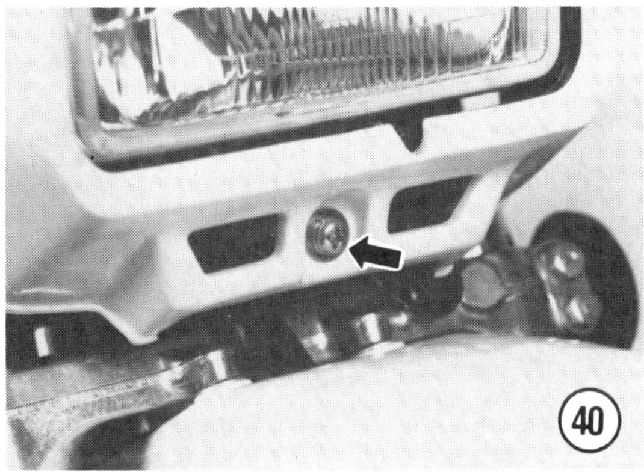
40

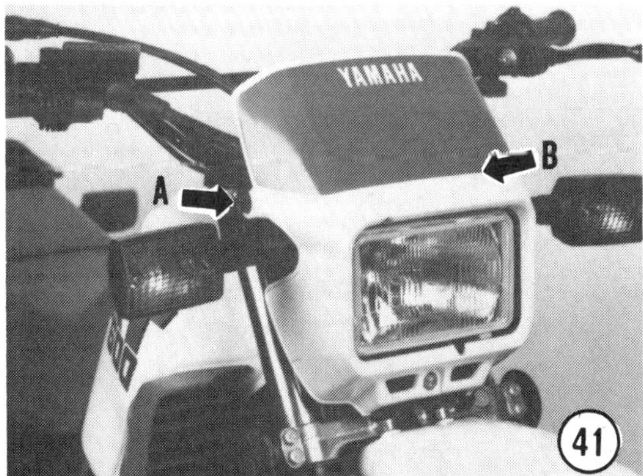

41

42

Always use the correct wattage bulb. A larger wattage bulb will give a dim light and a smaller wattage bulb will burn out prematurely. **Table 4** lists bulb sizes.

Headlight Bulb Replacement

Refer to **Figure 39** for this procedure.

1. Remove the screw (**Figure 40**) securing the lower portion of the headlight fairing.
2. Pivot the lower portion of the fairing up and unhook it from the rubber mounts (A, **Figure 41**) on each side at each upper rear corner. Remove the fairing (B, **Figure 41**).
3. Remove the bolt (**Figure 42**) on each side securing the headlight housing to the mounting bracket. Within the headlight trim ring, don't lose the metal collar in the rubber bushing.
4. Rest the headlight assembly on the front fender.
5. Disconnect the electrical connector (**Figure 43**) from the bulb.
6. Remove the rubber cover (**Figure 44**).

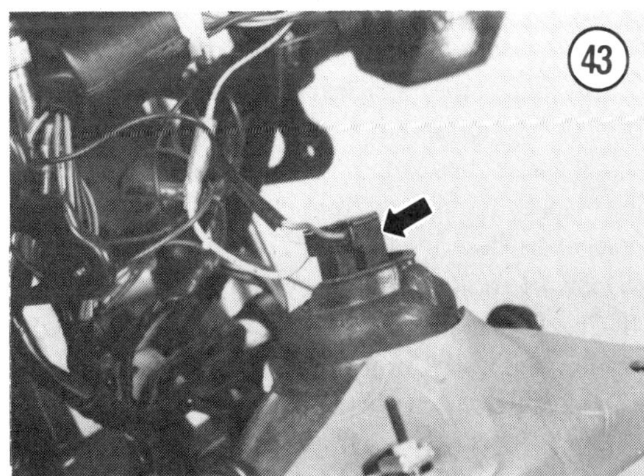
43

44

9

7. Then turn the outer ring bulb holder (**Figure 45**) *counterclockwise* and remove it from the lens assembly.

8. Remove the bulb (**Figure 46**) from the socket.

CAUTION

Do not touch the bulb glass with your fingers because oil on your skin will transfer to the glass. Any traces of oil on the quartz halogen bulb will drastically reduce the life of the bulb. Clean any traces of oil from the bulb with a cloth moistened in alcohol or lacquer thinner.

9. Install by reversing these removal steps. Note the following.

10. Adjust the headlight as described in this chapter.

Headlight Mounting Bracket Removal/Installation

1. Remove the headlight assembly as described under *Headlight Bulb Replacement* in this chapter.

2. Remove the meter housing (A, **Figure 47**) as described under *Indicator Bulb Replacement and Meter Housing Removal/Installation* in this chapter.

3. Disconnect the electrical connectors going to the front turn signal assemblies (B, **Figure 47**). The turn signal assemblies can remain attached to the mounting bracket or removed from the headlight mounting bracket as described under *Turn Signal Assembly Removal/Installation* in this chapter.

4. Check the electrical wires in the area of the headlight housing bracket. Some may have to be disconnected in order to remove the bracket.

5. Remove the bolts securing the headlight housing bracket (C, **Figure 47**).

6. Carefully work the electrical wires out through the headlight housing bracket and remove the bracket.

7. Install by reversing these removal steps. Note the following.

8. Make sure all electrical connectors are free of corrosion and are tight.

9. Adjust the headlight as described in this chapter.

Headlight Beam Adjustment

The headlight beam can be set for vertical and horizontal adjustments.

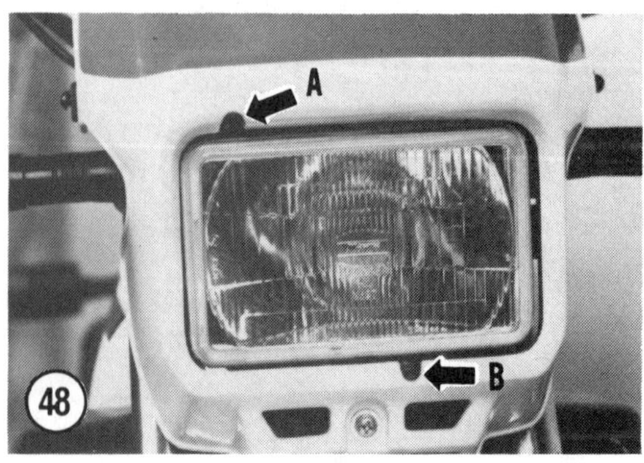

1. Park the bike on level ground. Block the kickstand to level the bike.

2. *Horizontal adjustment*: Turn the adjusting screw (A, **Figure 48**) *clockwise* to adjust the beam to the right. Turn the adjusting screw *counterclockwise* to adjust the beam to the left.

3. *Vertical adjustment*: Turn the adjusting screw (B, **Figure 48**) *clockwise* to raise the beam. Turn the adjusting screw *counterclockwise* to lower the beam.

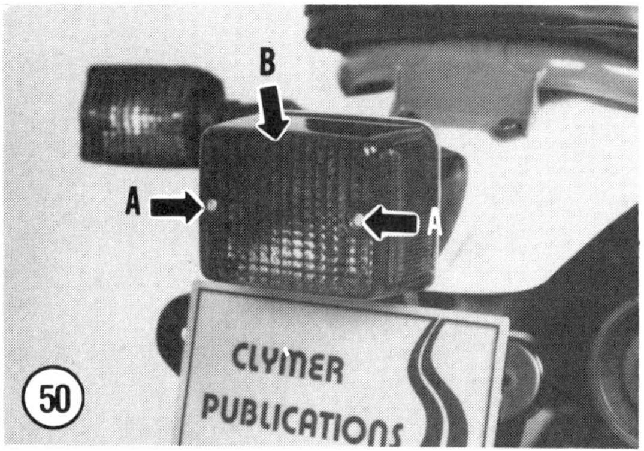

50

Taillight/Brake Light Bulb Replacement

Refer to **Figure 49** for this procedure.

1. Remove the screws (A, **Figure 50**) securing the lens and remove the lens (B, **Figure 50**).
2. Wash the lens with a mild detergent and wipe dry.
3. Inspect the lens gasket and replace it if damaged or deteriorated.
4. Turn the bulb counterclockwise and remove it.

49

TAILLIGHT/BRAKE LIGHT (XT600)

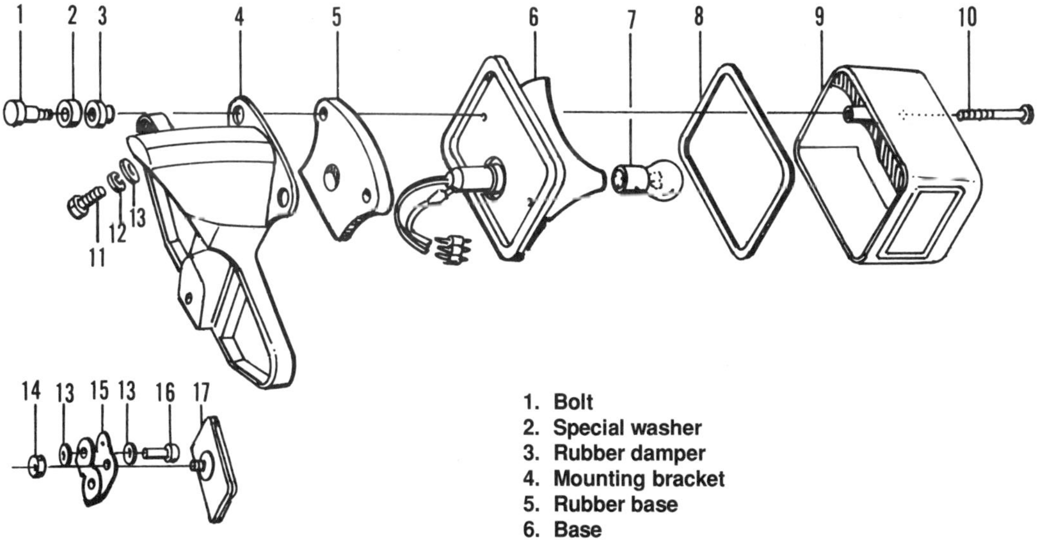

1. Bolt
2. Special washer
3. Rubber damper
4. Mounting bracket
5. Rubber base
6. Base
7. Bulb
8. Gasket
9. Lens
10. Screw
11. Bolt
12. Lockwasher
13. Washer
14. Nut
15. Reflector bracket
16. Blind rivet
17. Reflex reflector

5. Install by reversing these removal steps. Note the following.
6. When installing the lens, do not overtighten the screws as the lens may crack.

Taillight/Brake Light Assembly Removal/Installation

Refer to **Figure 49** for this procedure.
1. Remove the seat as described in Chapter Thirteen.
2. Disconnect the electrical connector to the taillight assembly —it has 2 wires (yellow and blue/red).
3. From under the rear fender, remove the bolts, lockwashers and washers securing the assembly to the rear fender and remove the assembly.
4. Install by reversing these removal steps. Note the following.
5. Make sure the electrical connector is free of corrosion and is tight.

Turn Signal Light Replacement

Refer to **Figure 51** for this procedure.
1. Remove the screws (A, **Figure 52**) securing the lens and remove the lens (B, **Figure 52**).
2. Wash out the inside of the lens with a mild detergent.
3. Inspect the lens gasket and replace it if damaged or deteriorated.
4. Turn the bulb counterclockwise and remove it.
5. Install by reversing these removal steps. Note the following.
6. When installing the lens, do not overtighten the screws as the lens may crack.

Turn Signal Assembly Removal/Installation

Refer to **Figure 51** for this procedure.
1A. To remove the rear turn signal assembly, perform the following:
   a. Remove the seat as described under *Seat Removal/Installation* in Chapter Thirteen.
   b. Disconnect the electrical connector to the turn signal assembly.
   c. Pull the rubber boot (A, **Figure 53**) off of mounting nut.
   d. Remove the nut (B, **Figure 53**) securing the turn signal assembly to the frame tab.

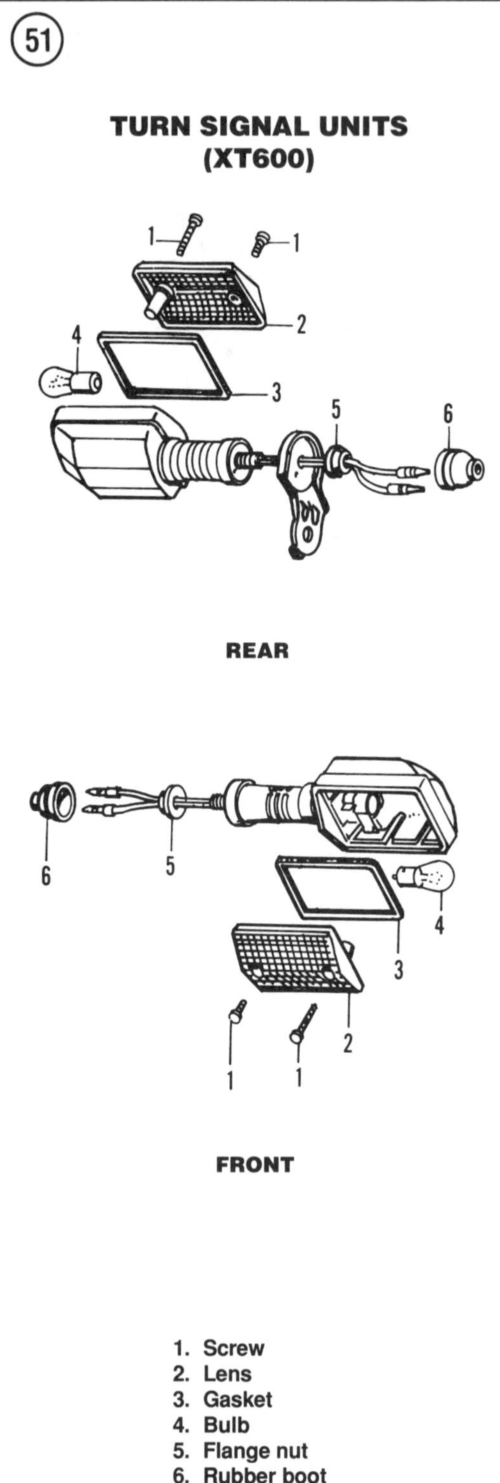

1B. To remove the front turn signal assembly, perform the following:

a. Remove the headlight assembly as described under *Headlight Bulb Replacement* in this chapter.
b. Disconnect the electrical connectors (A, **Figure 54**) to the turn signal assembly.

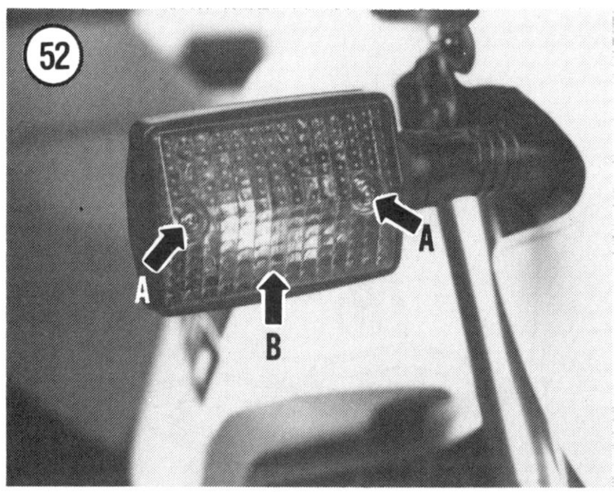

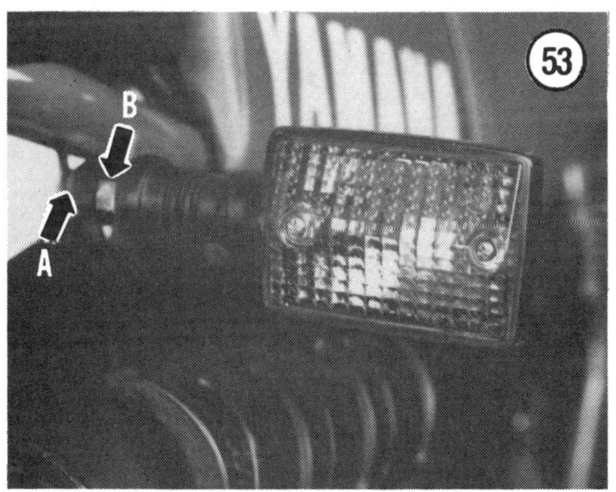

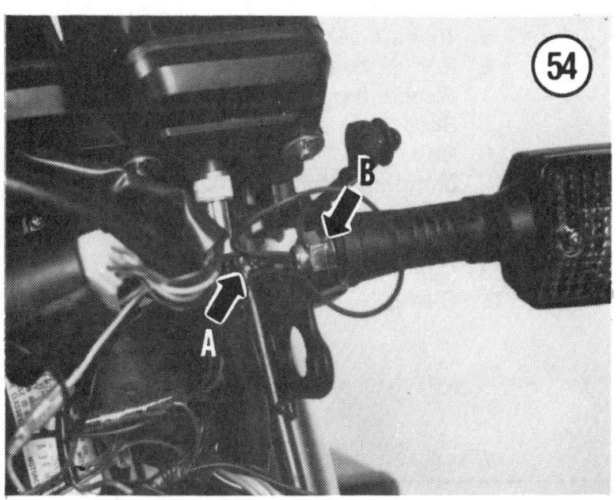

c. Remove the nut (B, **Figure 54**) securing the turn signal assembly to the headlight mounting bracket.

2. Carefully pull the turn signal assembly and electrical wires out of the mounting tab or bracket.
3. Install by reversing these removal steps. Note the following.
4. Make sure the electrical connector is free of corrosion and is tight.

Indicator Bulb Replacement, Meter Housing and Bracket Removal/Installation

Refer to **Figure 55** for this procedure.

1. Remove the headlight assembly as described under *Headlight Bulb Replacement* in this chapter.
2. Disconnect the speedometer and/or tachometer cable(s) at the base of the meter housing(s) (A, **Figure 56**).
3. Remove the cotter pins and washers (B, **Figure 56**) at the bottom of the meter(s).
4. Remove the meter(s) from the mounting bracket.
5. Carefully pull the bulb socket out of the back side of the meter housing. Remove and replace the bulb(s).
6. If necessary, disconnect the electrical connectors from the meter housing and remove the meter housing.
7. If necessary, remove the bolts securing the meter housing mounting bracket and remove it from the upper fork bridge.
8. Install by reversing these removal steps. Note the following.
9. If disconnected, make sure the electrical connectors are free of corrosion and are tight.

9

Headlight Test

If the headlight does not come on when the ignition switch is turned to the ON position, perform the following test.

1. First check the condition of the battery as described under *Battery* in Chapter Three. The battery must be fully charged and the electrical cables must be tight and free from corrosion in order for the lighting system to function properly.
2. Check that the circuit breaker (**Figure 57**) has not tripped. If it has tripped, push the red button down

and recheck to see if the headlight is on, if not proceed to Step 3.

3. Check that the headlight bulb or the high beam indicator bulb is not blown. Refer to *Headlight Bulb Replacement* and *Indicator Bulb Replacement* in this chapter. If the bulbs are okay, leave the headlight housing off and proceed to Step 4.

4. Disconnect the headlight dimmer switch connector. Trace the wire harness from the headlight dimmer switch to the wire junction at the front of the bike.

5. Connect a 0-20 DC voltmeter to the brown terminal on the wire harness connector.

6. Turn the ignition switch to ON. The voltmeter should read 12 volts. Turn the ignition switch OFF. Interpret results as follows:

  a. *Voltage correct*: If the voltage is correct, check the wiring from the connector to the bulb socket. Check the connectors for damaged, loose or dirty connectors then proceed to Step 8.
  b. *Less than 12 volts*: Check the ignition switch as described in this chapter. If the switch is okay, recheck the battery charge as described in Chapter Three.

7. Reconnect the dimmer switch brown terminal to the wire harness connector.

8. Check for battery voltage at the headlight. Connect a 0-20 DC voltmeter to the yellow terminal on the wire harness connector.

9. Turn the ignition switch to ON. The voltmeter should read 12 volts. Turn the ignition switch OFF. Interpret results as follows:

  a. *Voltage correct*: If the voltage is correct, check the wiring from the connector to the dimmer switch. Check the connectors for damaged, loose or dirty connectors.
  b. *Less than 12 volts*: Check the headlight dimmer switch as described in this chapter.

10. Connect all electrical connectors and install the headlight housing after locating and repairing the electrical problem.

11. Make sure the electrical connector is free of corrosion and is tight.

Taillight Troubleshooting

If the taillight does not operate correctly, perform the following voltage test.

(55)

METERS (XT600)

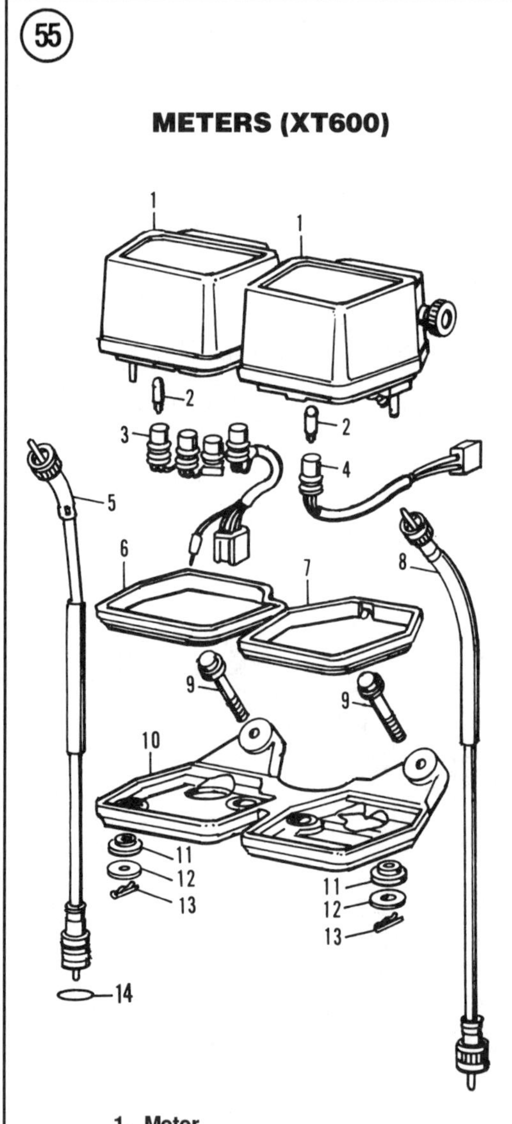

1. Meter
2. Bulb
3. Bulb socket
4. Bulb socket
5. Tachometer drive cable
6. Rubber base
7. Rubber base
8. Speedometer drive cable
9. Bolt
10. Mounting bracket
11. Rubber bushing
12. Washer
13. Clip
14. O-ring

1. First check the condition of the battery as described under *Battery* in Chapter Three. The battery must be fully charged and the electrical cables must be tight and free from corrosion in order for the lighting system to function properly.

2. Check that the circuit breaker (**Figure 57**) has not tripped. If it has tripped, push the red button down and recheck to see if the taillight is on, if not proceed to Step 3.

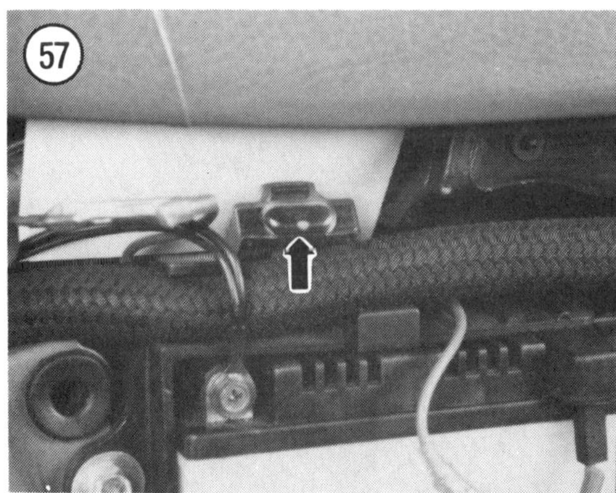

3. Remove the frame's left-hand side cover (**Figure 58**).

4. Remove the seat as described under *Seat Removal/Installation* in Chapter Thirteen.

5. Disconnect the taillight blue/red electrical connector.

6. Connect a 0-20 DC voltmeter as follows:
   a. Connect the red voltmeter lead to the blue/red connector terminal.
   b. Connect the black voltmeter lead to a good ground.

7. Turn the ignition switch to ON. The voltmeter should read 12 volts. Turn the ignition switch OFF. Interpret results as follows:
   a. *Voltage correct*: If the voltage is correct, check the wiring from the connector to the bulb socket.
   b. *Less than 12 volts*: Check the ignition switch as described in this chapter. If the switch is okay, check the battery charge as described in Chapter Three.

8. Connect the electrical connector and make sure the electrical connector is free of corrosion and is tight.

9. Install the seat and left-hand side cover.

9

Flasher Light and Indicator Light Troubleshooting

If the flasher light or its indicator light do not operate correctly, perform the following voltage check.

1. First check the condition of the battery as described under *Battery* in Chapter Three. The battery must be fully charged and the electrical cables must be tight and free from corrosion in order for the lighting system to function properly.

2. Check that the circuit breaker (**Figure 57**) has not tripped. If it has tripped, push the red button down and recheck to see if the flasher and indicator light work properly, if not proceed to Step 3.

3. Remove the screws (A, **Figure 52**) securing the lens and remove the lens (B, **Figure 52**).

4. Remove and check the bulb. Replace the bulb if blown. Also check that the indicator light bulb in the tachometer housing is not blown. Refer to *Turn Signal Light Replacement* in this section. If the bulbs

are okay, leave the headlight housing off and proceed to Step 5.

5. Remove the seat as described under *Seat Removal/Installation* in Chapter Thirteen.

6. Remove the fuel tank as described under *Fuel Tank Removal/Installation* in Chapter Eight.

7. Disconnect the flasher relay electrical connector from the relay.

8. Connect a 0-20 DC voltmeter as follows:
   a. Connect the red voltmeter lead to the brown connector terminal.
   b. Connect the black voltmeter lead to a good ground.

9. Turn the ignition switch to ON. The voltmeter should read 12 volts. Turn the ignition switch OFF. Interpret results as follows:
   a. *Less than 12 volts*: Check the ignition switch as described in this chapter. If the switch is okay, check the battery charge as described in Chapter Three.
   b. *Voltage correct*: Perform Step 10.

10. If the voltage tested correctly in Step 9, perform the following:
   a. Connect a jumper wire across the brown to brown/white flasher relay connector terminals.
   b. Turn the ignition switch to ON. Then turn the turn signal switch on the left-hand handlebar to "L" or "R." The turn signal lights should operate correctly.
   c. If the turn signal operated correctly in sub-step b, check all connections in the flasher and indicator light circuit. If these are okay, replace the flasher relay. If the turn signal did not operate correctly in sub-step b, replace the turn signal switch as described under *Switches* in this chapter.

12. Connect the electrical connectors and make sure the electrical connectors are free of corrosion and are tight.

13. Install the seat and fuel tank.

Flasher Relay Replacement

1. Remove the headlight assembly as described under *Headlight Bulb Replacement* in this chapter.

2. Disconnect the electrical connector from the flasher relay (**Figure 59**).

3. Pull the relay out of its mounting position and replace it.

4. Install by reversing these removal steps. Note the following.

5. Make sure all electrical connectors are free of corrosion and are tight.

Brake Light Troubleshooting

If the brake light does not operate correctly, perform the following.

1. Remove the screws (A, **Figure 50**) securing the lens and remove the lens (B, **Figure 50**).

2. Replace the bulb if blown. If the bulb is okay, reinstall it and perform the following.

3. If you are going to test the rear brake light switch, perform the following:
   a. Remove the seat as described under *Seat Removal/Installation* in Chapter Thirteen.
   b. Remove the fuel tank as described under *Fuel Tank Removal/Installation* in Chapter Eight.

4. Disconnect the front (**Figure 60**) or rear (**Figure 61**) brake light switch electrical connectors.

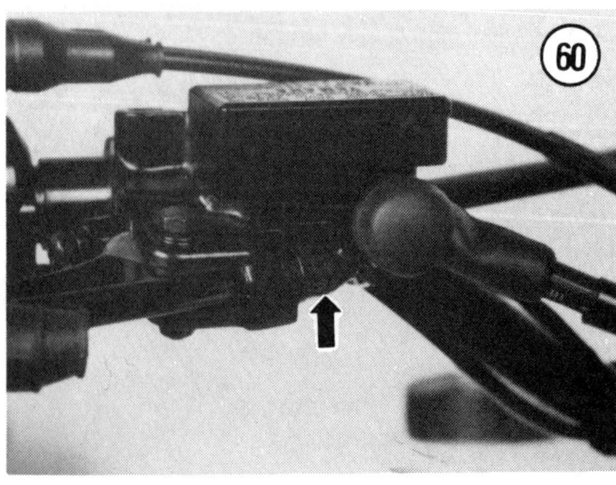

5. Connect a jumper cable between the brake light switch connectors on the wiring harness side of the connector. This bypasses the switch.

6. Turn the ignition switch to ON. The front or rear brake light should operate. Interpret results as follows:

   a. *Brake light on*: Check all wiring and connectors in the brake light circuit. If these are okay, replace the brake switch as described under *Switches* in this chapter.

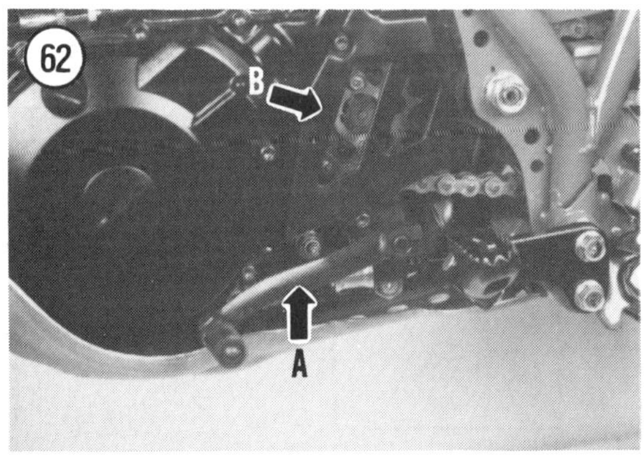

   b. *Brake light off*: Check the ignition switch as described in this chapter. If the switch is okay, check the battery charge as described in Chapter Three.

7. Remove the jumper cable and reconnect the brake light switch connectors.
8. Connect the electrical connectors and make sure the electrical connectors are free of corrosion and are tight.
9. Install the fuel tank and seat.

Neutral Indicator Light Troubleshooting

If the neutral indicator light in the tachometer housing does not come on when the ignition switch is turned to ON and the transmission is in neutral, perform the following voltage test.

1. Check that the neutral indicator light bulb in the tachometer housing is not blown. Refer to *Indicator Bulb Replacement* in this chapter. If the bulb is okay, proceed to Step 2.
2. Remove the pinch bolt securing the shift lever (A, **Figure 62**) and pull the shift lever off the shaft. If the splined boss is tight on the shaft, spread the slot open with a screwdriver.
3. Remove the screws securing the drive sprocket cover (B, **Figure 62**) and remove the cover.
4. Disconnect the screw securing the electrical connector (**Figure 63**) from the neutral switch on the crankcase.
5. Connect a 0-20 DC voltmeter as follows:
   a. Connect the red voltmeter lead to the sky blue electrical connector.
   b. Connect the black voltmeter lead to a good ground.
6. Turn the ignition switch to ON. The voltmeter should read 12 volts. Turn the ignition switch OFF. Interpret results as follows:
   a. *Less than 12 volts*: Check the ignition switch as described in this chapter. If the switch is okay, check the battery charge as described in Chapter Three.
   b. *Voltage correct*: Proceed to Step 7.
7. Touch the electrical connector to a bare (not covered with black paint) portion of the crankcase. The light should come on.
8. Turn the ignition switch to ON and shift the transmission into NEUTRAL. Observe the neutral indicator light. Interpret results as follows:

9

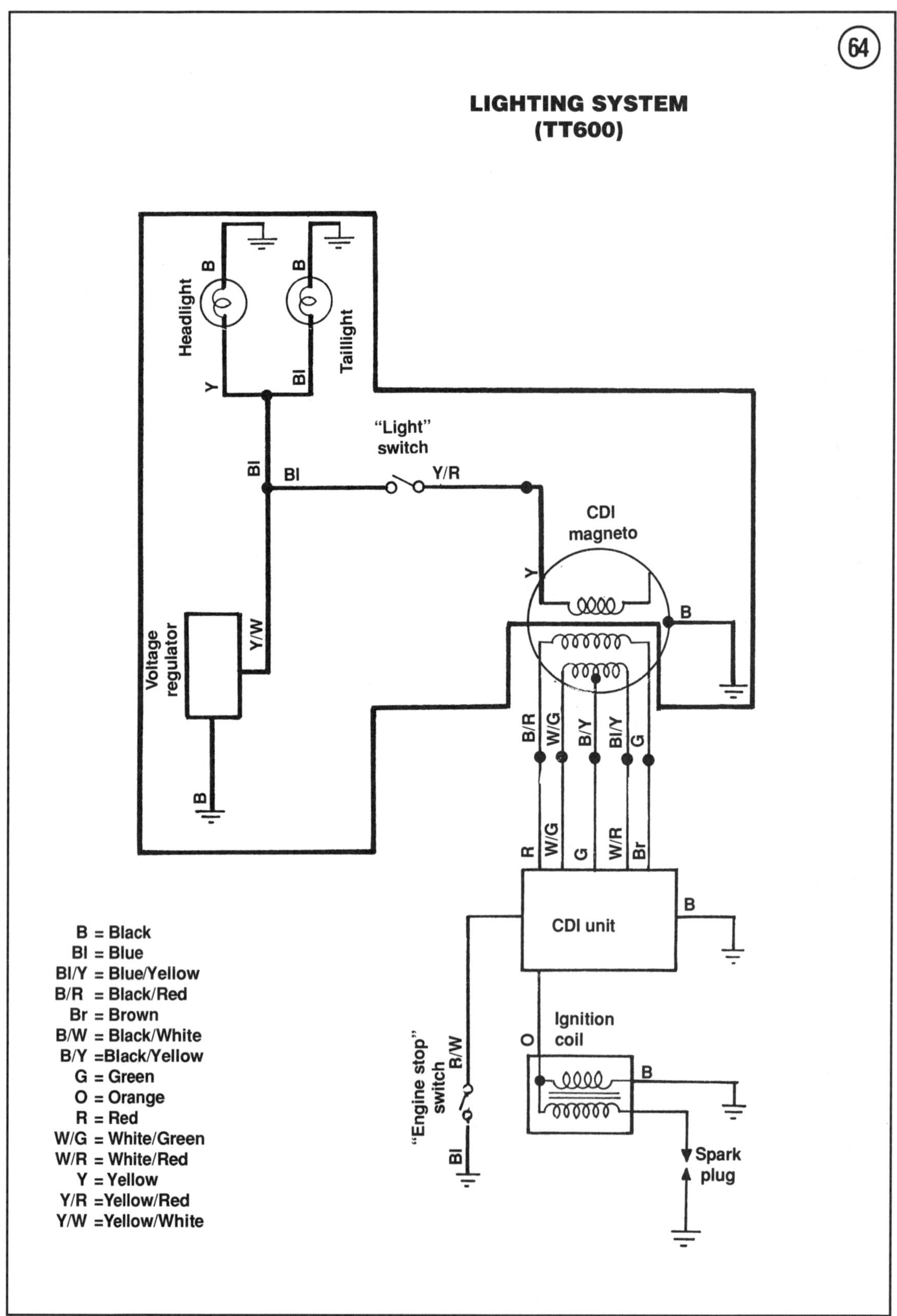
64
LIGHTING SYSTEM
(TT600)
Headlight
Taillight
B
B
Y
Bl
Bl
Bl
"Light"
switch
Y/R
CDI
magneto
Y
B
Voltage
regulator
Y/W
B
B/R
W/G
B/Y
Bl/Y
G
R
W/G
G
W/R
Br
CDI unit
B
"Engine stop"
switch
B/W
Bl
O
Ignition
coil
B
Spark
plug
B = Black
Bl = Blue
Bl/Y = Blue/Yellow
B/R = Black/Red
Br = Brown
B/W = Black/White
B/Y = Black/Yellow
G = Green
O = Orange
R = Red
W/G = White/Green
W/R = White/Red
Y = Yellow
Y/R = Yellow/Red
Y/W = Yellow/White

a. *Neutral light on*: Replace the neutral switch as described under *Switches* in this chapter.

b. *Neutral light off*: Check all wiring in the neutral light circuit.

9. Reconnect the electrical wire to the neutral switch and make sure the electrical connector is free of corrosion and is tight.

10. Install the drive sprocket cover and bolts.

11. Install the gearshift lever and bolt. Tighten the bolt securely.

LIGHTING SYSTEM (TT600)

The TT600 lighting circuit is shown in **Figure 64**. When replacing bulbs, always use the correct wattage bulb. A larger wattage bulb will give a dim light and a small wattage bulb will burn out prematurely. **Table 4** lists bulb sizes.

Headlight Bulb Replacement

Refer to **Figure 65** for this procedure.

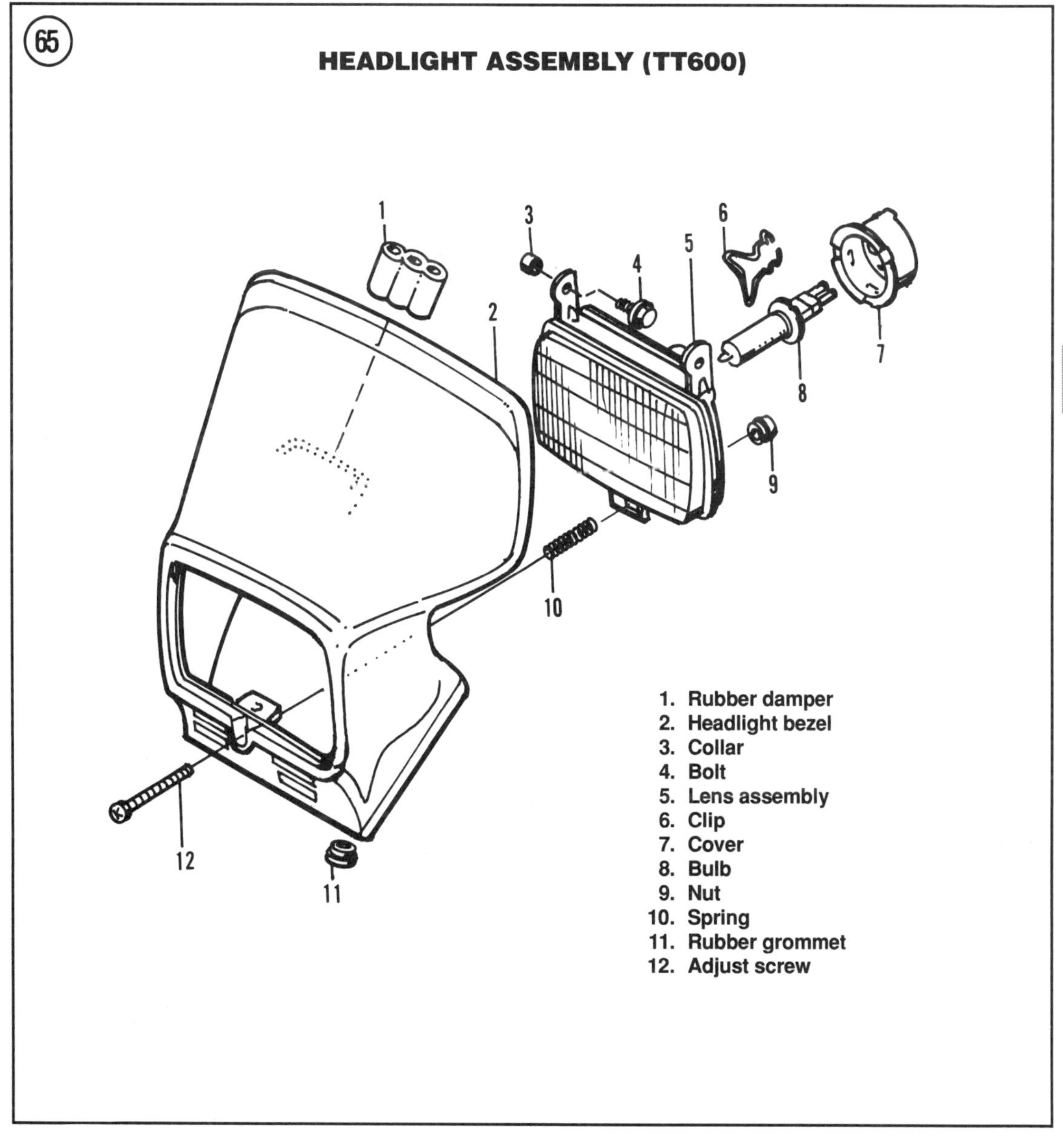

1. Lift the headlight fairing assembly (A, **Figure 66**) up, unhook it and remove it.
2. Disconnect the electrical connector from the bulb.
3. Remove the rubber cover (**Figure 67**).
4. Then unhook the bulb holder (A, **Figure 68**).

CAUTION
Do not touch the bulb glass with your fingers because oil on your skin will transfer to the glass. Any traces of oil on the quartz halogen bulb will drastically reduce the life of the bulb. Clean any traces of oil from the bulb with a cloth moistened in alcohol or lacquer thinner.

5. Remove the bulb (B, **Figure 68**) and replace with a new bulb.
6. Install by reversing these removal steps.

Headlight Beam Adjustment

The headlight beam can only be set for vertical adjustment.

1. Park the bike on level ground. Block the kickstand to level the bike.
2. Turn the adjusting screw (B, **Figure 66**) *clockwise* to raise the beam or *counterclockwise* to lower the beam.

Taillight Bulb Replacement

Refer to **Figure 69** for this procedure.

1. Remove the screws (A, **Figure 70**) securing the lens (B, **Figure 70**) and remove the lens.
2. Wash the lens with a mild detergent and wipe dry.
3. Inspect the lens gasket and replace it if damaged or deteriorated.
4. Turn the bulb (**Figure 71**) *counterclockwise* and remove it.
5. Install by reversing these removal steps. Note the following.
6. When installing the lens, do not overtighten the screws as the lens may crack.

A.C. Lighting Circuit Output Test

1. Remove the headlight housing as described under *Headlight Bulb Replacement* in this section.
2. Connect a portable tachometer following the manufacturer's instructions.
3. Connect the red voltmeter lead to the headlight blue connector terminal and the black voltmeter lead to the black headlight connector terminal.
4. Switch the voltmeter to the AC20V scale.
5. Start the engine and warm up to normal operating temperature.

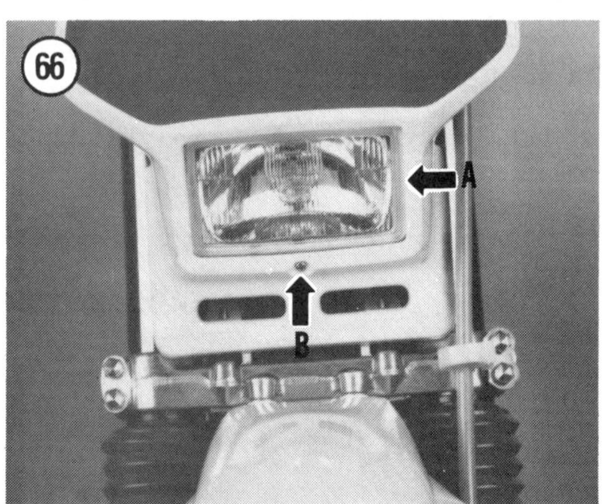

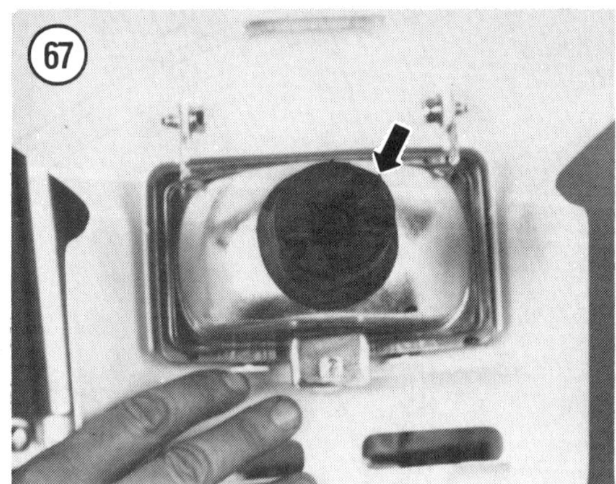

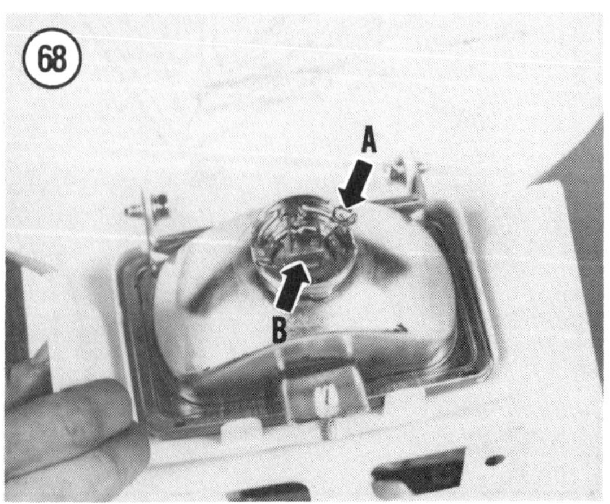

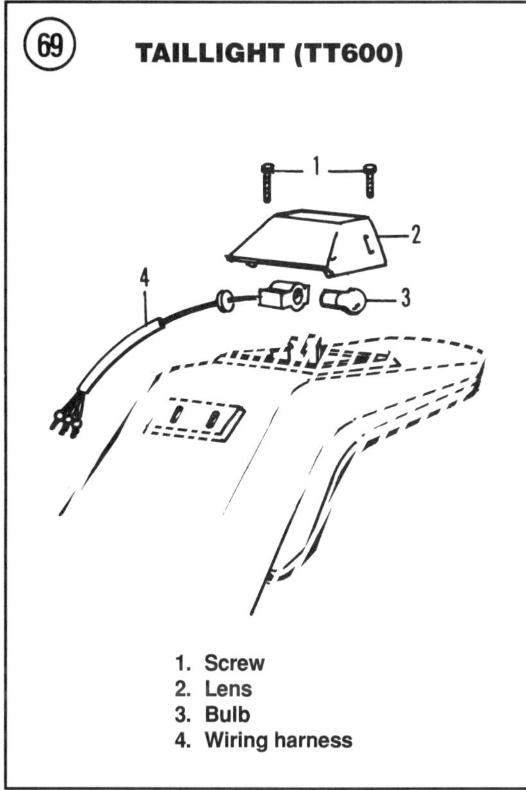

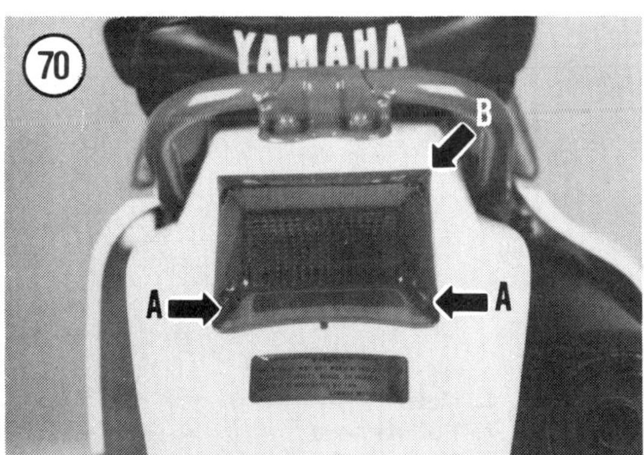

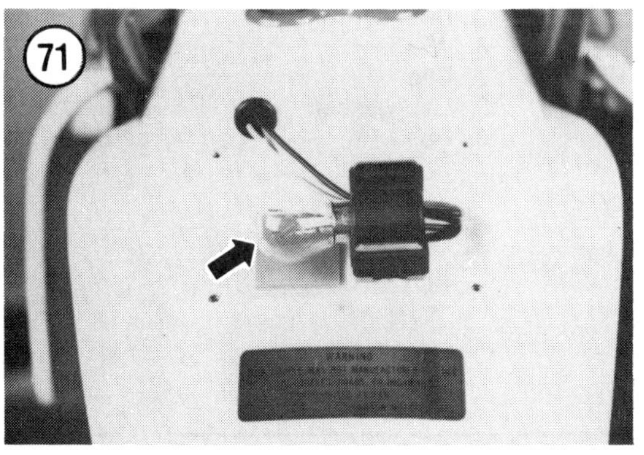

6. Gradually increase engine speed to 3,500 rpm. At 3,000 rpm, note the voltmeter reading and then turn the engine off. If the voltage is not 11.5 volts or higher, perform the *Lighting Coil Resistance Check* in this section. If the voltage was 11.5 volts or higher, the lighting system is operating correctly.

CAUTION
Do not run the engine in neutral above 6,000 rpm for more than 1-2 seconds.

7. Gradually increase engine speed to 8,000 rpm. At 8,000 rpm, note the voltmeter reading and then turn the engine off. If the voltage is not 19.6 volts or higher, perform the *Lighting Coil Resistance Check* in this section. If the voltage was 19.6 volts or higher, the lighting system is operating correctly.

8. Disconnect the voltmeter and tachometer.

9. Install the headlight housing as described in this chapter.

Lighting Coil Resistance Check

1. Remove the seat as described under *Seat Removal/Installation* in Chapter Thirteen.

2. Remove the fuel tank as described under *Fuel Tank Removal/Installation* in Chapter Eight.

3. Disconnect the black and yellow leads at the CDI unit.

4. Connect an ohmmeter between the yellow and black connector leads. Set the ohmmeter on the R × 1 scale. Replace the lighting coil if the reading is not within specifications listed in **Table 1**. Refer to *Alternator* in this chapter.

5. Remove the ohmmeter and reconnect the electrical connector.

6. Install the fuel tank and seat.

Meter Housing and Bracket Removal/Installation

Refer to **Figure 72** for this procedure.

1. Remove the headlight assembly as described under *Headlight Bulb Replacement* in this chapter.

2. Disconnect the speedometer cable (A, **Figure 73**) at the base of the meter housing.

3. Remove the cotter pins and washers (B, **Figure 73**) at the bottom of the meter.

4. Remove the meter from the mounting bracket.

5. If necessary, remove the bolts securing the meter housing (C, **Figure 73**) mounting bracket and remove it from the upper fork bridge.
6. Install by reversing these removal steps.

SWITCHES

Switches can be tested with an ohmmeter that is described in Chapter One or with a homemade test light (**Figure 74**). To test a switch, disconnect the electrical connector for that specific switch. The following figures show the continuity diagram for each specific switch and indicates which terminals should show continuity when the switch is in a given position.

If you suspect a faulty switch, perform the following test.

1. Disconnect the switch electrical connector from the main wiring harness.
2. Refer to the following illustrations:
   a. **Figure 75**: main ignition switch.
   b. **Figure 76**: engine stop switch.
   c. **Figure 77**: headlight dimmer switch (XT600).
   d. **Figure 78**: headlight switch (TT600).
   e. **Figure 79**: turn signal switch.
   f. **Figure 80**: horn switch.
3. To check continuity of the switch, use an ohmmeter and perform the following:
   a. Connect the ohmmeter test leads to the indicated color wires in the switch side of the electrical connector and check for continuity (indicated resistance) in all switch positions.
   b. Also check for continuity (indicated resistance) of all related electrical wires.
   c. If the switch fails any portion of this test, replace the switch as described in this chapter.
4. When testing switches, perform the following:
   a. First check the circuit breaker as described in this chapter. Reset it if necessary.
   b. Check the battery as described under *Battery* in Chapter Three. Bring the battery to the correct state of charge, if required.

CAUTION
Do not attempt to start the engine with the battery negative cable disconnected or you will damage the wiring.

   c. When replacing handlebar switch assemblies, make sure the cables are routed correctly so

72

METER (TT600)

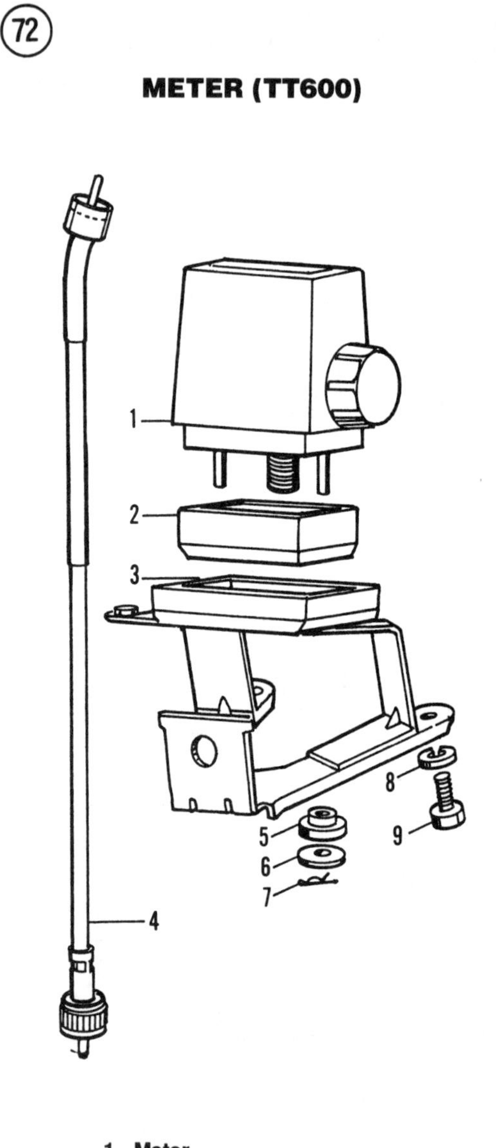

1. Meter
2. Rubber base
3. Mounting bracket
4. Speedometer drive cable
5. Rubber grommet
6. Washer
7. Clip
8. Lockwasher
9. Bolt

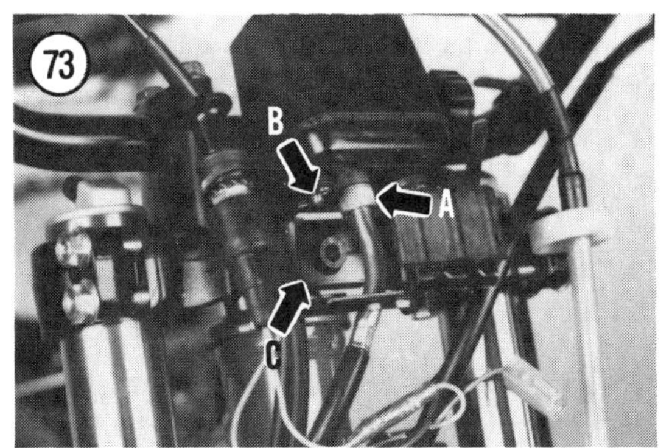

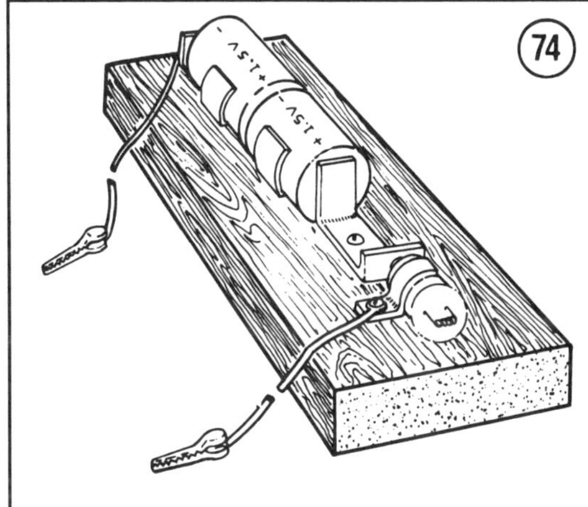

MAIN IGNITION SWITCH

Switch position	Lead color				
	B/W	B	B	Br	Bl/R
On			●	●	●
Off	●	●			
Lock	●	●			
P (parking)	●	●	●		●

ENGINE STOP SWITCH

Switch position	Lead color	
	B/W	B
Run		
Off	●	●

HEADLIGHT DIMMER SWITCH (XT600)

Switch position	Lead color		
	Y	Br	G
Hi	●	●	
Lo		●	●

78

HEADLIGHT SWITCH (TT600)

Switch position	Lead color	
	Y/R	Bl
Pull	●	●
Off		

TURN SIGNAL SWITCH

Switch position	Lead color		
	DrG	Br/W	CH
R	●	●	
N			
L		●	●

80

HORN SWITCH

Switch position	Lead color	
	Y/R	Bl
Push	●	●
Off		

9

that they are not crimped when the handlebar is turned from side-to-side.

d. When separating 2 connectors, pull on the connector housings and not the wires.

e. After locating a defective circuit, check the connectors to make sure they are clean and properly connected. Check all wires going into a connector housing to make sure each wire is properly positioned and that the wire end is not loose.

f. To properly connect connectors, push them together until they click into place.

Left Handlebar Switch Replacement (XT600)

1. The left handlebar switch housing is equipped with the following switches:
   a. Dimmer switch.
   b. Turn signal switch.
   c. Horn button switch.

2. Remove the headlight housing as described under *Headlight Bulb Replacement* in this chapter.
3. Disconnect the switch connectors (**Figure 81**).
4. Remove the screws holding the switch housings together (A, **Figure 82**).
5. Remove the tie wraps (B, **Figure 82**) from the handlebar and remove the switch assembly.
6. Install by reversing these removal steps. Note the following.
7. Make sure the electrical connectors are free of corrosion and are tight.

Right Handlebar Switch Replacement (XT600)

The engine stop switch is mounted in the right-hand switch housing.

1. Remove the headlight housing as described under *Headlight Bulb Replacement* in this chapter.
2. Disconnect the engine stop switch connectors (**Figure 81**).
3. Remove the screws (A, **Figure 83**) holding the switch housings together.
4. Separate the switch housing (B, **Figure 83**).
5. Disconnect the throttle cables (C, **Figure 83**) from the switch housings.
6. Remove the switch.
7. Install by reversing these removal steps. Note the following.
8. Make sure the electrical connectors are free of corrosion and are tight.
9. Adjust the throttle cables as described under *Throttle Cable Adjustment* in Chapter Three.

Engine Kill Switch (TT600)

1. Remove the fuel tank as described under *Fuel Tank Removal/Installation* in Chapter Eight.

81

82

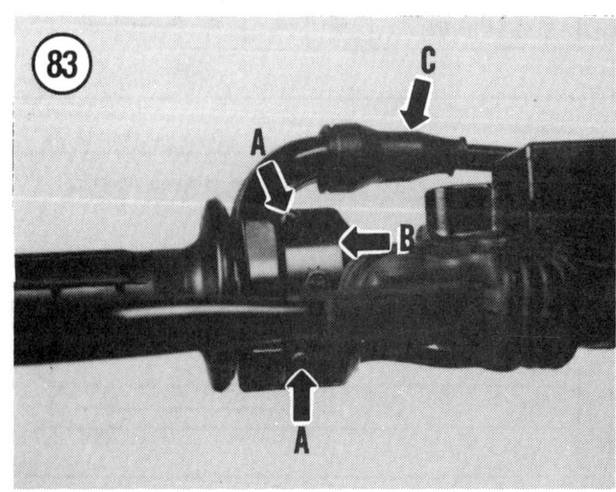

83

2. Disconnect the kill switch connectors at the CDI unit.

3. Remove the screw holding the switch to the left-hand handlebar.

4. Remove the switch (**Figure 84**).

5. Install by reversing these removal steps. Note the following.

6. Make sure the electrical connectors are free of corrosion and are tight.

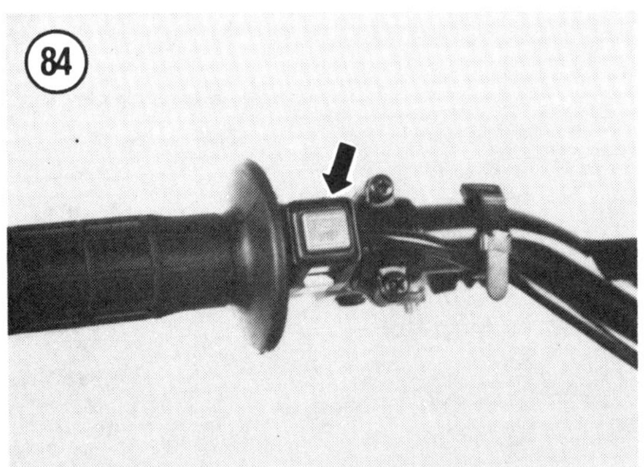

84

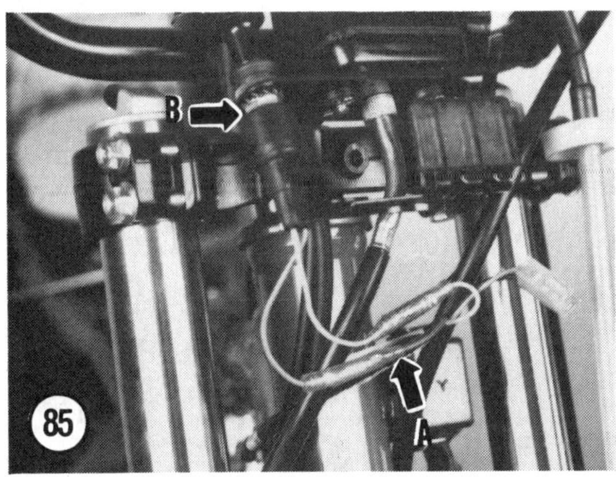

85

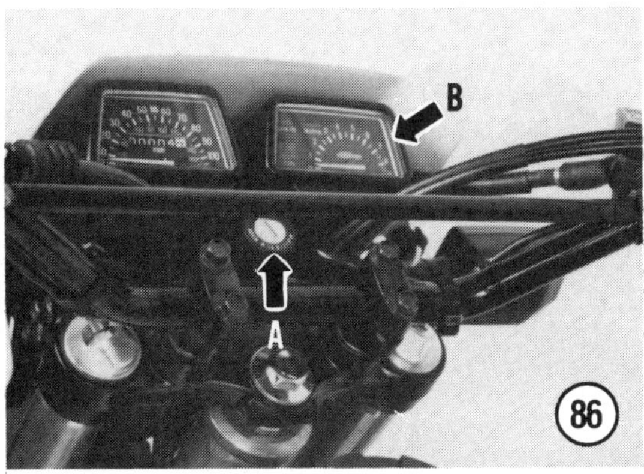

86

Light Switch (TT600)

1. Remove the headlight housing as described under *Headlight Bulb Replacement* in this chapter.

2. Disconnect the electrical wires (A, **Figure 85**) from the light switch.

3. Remove the light switch (B, **Figure 85**).

4. Install by reversing these removal steps. Note the following.

5. Make sure the electrical connectors are free of corrosion and are tight.

Ignition Switch Replacement (XT600)

The ignition switch (A, **Figure 86**) is bolted to the upper steering stem between the speedometer and tachometer drive units.

1. Remove the headlight housing as described under *Headlight Bulb Replacement* in this chapter.

2. Remove the tachometer and speedometer meters (B, **Figure 86**) as described under *Indicator Bulb Replacement and Meter Housing Removal/Installation* in this chapter.

3. Disconnect the ignition switch electrical connectors (**Figure 81**).

4. Remove the bolts securing the ignition switch (A, **Figure 86**) to the upper steering stem. Remove the ignition switch.

5. Install by reversing these removal steps. Note the following.

6. Make sure the electrical connectors are free of corrosion and are tight.

Sidestand Switch Replacement (XT600)

The sidestand switch is mounted on the left-hand side of the bike above the sidestand.

1. Place wood blocks under the engine to support the bike securely.

2. Remove the frame left-hand side cover (**Figure 58**).

3. Remove the seat as described under *Seat Removal/Installation* in Chapter Thirteen.

4. Disconnect the sidestand switch electrical connectors underneath the seat. It has 2 wires (sky blue and black).

5. Unhook the switch's electrical wire from the clips (**Figure 87**) on the frame down tube.
6. Remove the screws (A, **Figure 88**) holding the sidestand switch (B, **Figure 88**) to the frame.
7. Remove the sidestand switch.
8. Install by reversing these removal steps. Note the following.
9. Make sure the electrical connectors are free of corrosion and are tight.
10. Be sure to hook the switch's electrical wire into the clips (**Figure 87**) on the frame down tube.

Neutral Switch Replacement (XT600)

The neutral switch is mounted in the left-hand crankcase near the shift lever.

1. Remove the pinch bolt securing the shift lever (A, **Figure 62**) and pull the shift lever off the shaft. If the splined boss is tight on the shaft, spread the slot open with a screwdriver.
2. Remove the screws securing the drive sprocket cover (B, **Figure 62**) and remove the cover.
3. Disconnect the screw securing the electrical connector (A, **Figure 89**) from the neutral switch on the crankcase.
4. Place a drain pan underneath the neutral switch as some engine oil will drain out when the switch is removed.
5. Unscrew the neutral switch (B, **Figure 89**) and remove it.
6. Install by reversing these removal steps. Note the following.
7. Make sure the electrical connectors are free of corrosion and are tight.
8. Refill the engine oil as required as described under *Engine Oil and Filter Change* in Chapter Three.

Front Brake Switch Replacement (XT600)

The front brake switch is mounted on the master cylinder housing.

1. Remove the headlight housing as described under *Headlight Bulb Replacement* in this chapter.
2. Disconnect the front brake switch electrical connectors. It has 2 wires (brown and green/yellow).
3. Insert a thin flat-bladed screwdriver (A, **Figure 90**) into the slot in the base of the master cylinder

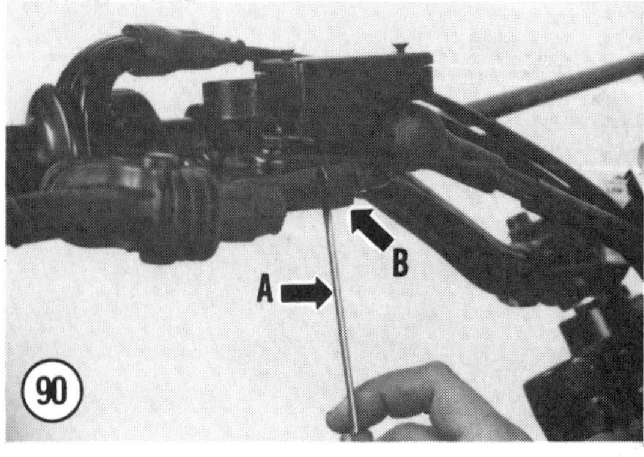

housing and depress the locking tab on the switch housing.

CAUTION
Do not try to pull the switch out of the master cylinder receptacle without completely depressing the locking tab as it will be broken off.

4. Carefully pull the switch assembly (B, **Figure 90**) out of the receptacle in the master cylinder housing.
5. Install by reversing these removal steps. Note the following.
6. Make sure the electrical connectors are free of corrosion and are tight.
7. Be sure to push the switch into the receptacle in the master cylinder housing until you hear the locking tabs "click" into their respective locking slots.

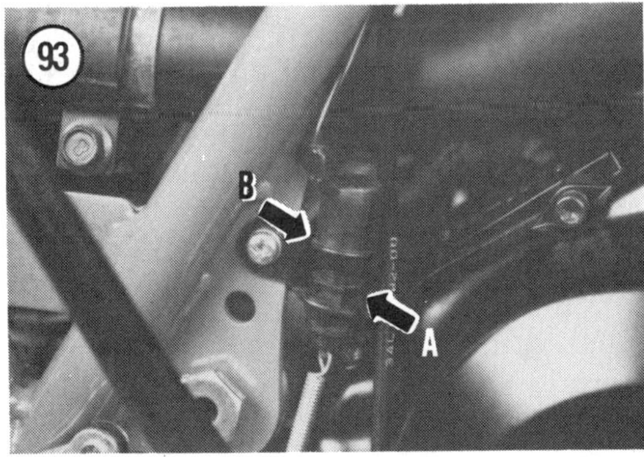

Rear Brake Switch Replacement (XT600)

The rear brake switch is mounted on the right-hand side of the bike.

1. Remove the seat as described under *Seat Removal/Installation* in Chapter Thirteen.
2. Remove the frame right-hand side cover.
3. Disconnect the rear brake switch electrical connectors on the frame down tube (**Figure 91**). It has 2 wires (green/yellow and brown).
4. Disconnect the rear brake switch spring (**Figure 92**) from the brake pedal.
5. Loosen the rear brake switch locknut (A, **Figure 93**) and remove the switch (B, **Figure 93**).
6. Install by reversing these removal steps. Note the following.
7. Make sure the electrical connectors are free of corrosion and are tight.
8. Adjust the brake switch as described under *Rear Brake Light Adjustment* in Chapter Three.

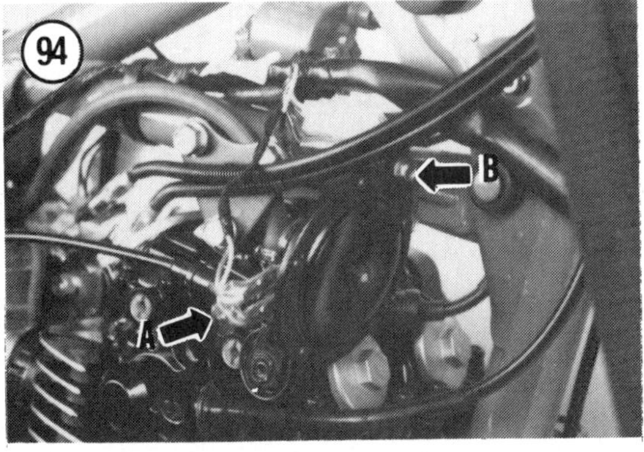

HORN (XT600)

Removal/Installation

1. Remove the fuel tank as described under *Fuel Tank Removal/Installation* in Chapter Eight.
2. Disconnect the electrical connectors (A, **Figure 94**) at the horn.

9

3. Remove the bolt (B, **Figure 94**) securing the horn frame and remove the horn.
4. Install by reversing these removal steps. Note the following.
5. Make sure the electrical connectors are free of corrosion and are tight.

Testing

If the horn does not sound when the horn button is depressed, perform the following.
1. Check the horn button switch as described under *Switches* in this chapter. If the horn button switch is okay, perform Step 2.
2. Perform a voltage check as follows:
   a. Connect a red voltmeter lead to the brown wire at the horn. Connect the black voltmeter lead to a good engine ground.
   b. Turn the ignition switch to ON. Depress the horn button and read the voltmeter. It should show 12 volts. Turn the ignition switch to OFF.
3. Disconnect the pink and brown wires at the horn (A, **Figure 94**).
4. Connect an ohmmeter red lead to the horn brown lead. Connect the ohmmeter black lead to the horn pink lead. Set the ohmmeter on the R × 1 scale. It show a resistance of 1.23-1.25 ohms. If the resistance values are not as specified, replace the horn.

CIRCUIT BREAKER (XT600)

A 10 amp circuit breaker (**Figure 95**) is mounted behind the left-hand side cover above the battery. If a short circuit should occur in the electrical system, the breaker will shut off the current flow in the system. If the circuit breaker shuts the current off, turn off the ignition switch. Then wait 30 seconds and push in the breaker button. If the circuit breaker shuts off the current again, there is a problem in the electrical system. Refer to troubleshooting in Chapter Two and to the procedures listed in this chapter.

WIRING DIAGRAMS

Wiring diagrams are located at the end of this book.

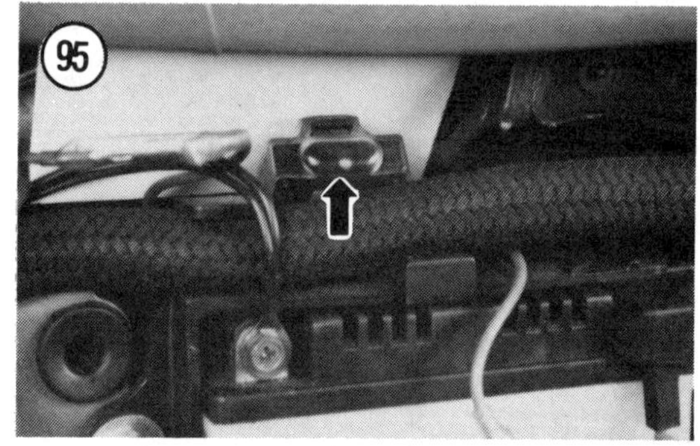

Table 1 CHARGING SYSTEM TEST SPECIFICATIONS

Item	Specification
Charging system (XT600)	
Type	Flywheel alternator
Battery	
Type or model	GM4A-3B or FB4L-B
Capacity	12 volts; 4 amp hours
Charging system	
1,500 rpm	6.3A or more
5,000 rpm	10A or less
Charging coil resistance	
White-to-white connectors	0.2-0.6 ohms*
Charging system (TT600)	
Type	Flywheel alternator
Lighting voltage	
3,000 rpm	11.5 volts or more
8,000 rpm	19.6 volts or less
Lighting coil resistance	
Yellow-to-black connectors	0.2-0.4 ohms*

* All tests should be made at an ambient temperature of 68° F (20° C).

Table 2 TIGHTENING TORQUES

	N•m	ft.-lb.
Alternator rotor nut	90	66
Stator plate screws	7	5.1

Table 3 IGNITION SYSTEM TEST SPECIFICATIONS

Item	Specification
XT600	
Pickup coil resistance	
White/red-to-white/green connectors	90-129 ohms*
Source coil resistance	
Red-to-brown wire connectors	160-240 ohms*
Ignition coil	
Primary resistance	0.27-0.33 ohms
Secondary resistance	3.44-5.16 K ohms
TT600	
Pickup coil resistance	
1983-1984	
Green-to-white/red connectors	90-120 ohms*
1985-1986	
Black/yellow-to-blue/yellow connectors	90-120 ohms*
Source coil resistance	
1983-1984	
Red-to-brown wire connectors	110-170 ohms*
1985-1986	
Black/red and green	110-170 ohms*
Ignition coil	
Primary resistance	0.48-0.51 ohms
Secondary resistance	4.80-7.20 K ohms

* All tests should be made with the component at 68° F (20° C).

Table 4 REPLACEMENT BULBS

	XT600	TT600
Headlight	60W/55W (12V)	55W (12V)
Taillight	—	8W (12V)
Taillight/brake light	27W/8W (12V)	—
Flasher light	27W (12V)	—
License plate light	8W (12V)	—
Meter lights	3.4W (12V)	—

CHAPTER TEN

FRONT SUSPENSION AND STEERING

This chapter describes repair and maintenance on the front wheel, forks, and steering components.

Front suspension specifications are listed in **Table 1**. Tightening torques are listed in **Table 2**. **Tables 1-4** are at the end of the chapter.

FRONT WHEEL (XT600)

Removal

CAUTION

*Care must be taken when removing, handling and installing a wheel with a disc brake rotor. The disc rotor is relative thin in order to dissipate heat and to minimize unsprung weight. The rotor is designed to withstand tremendous rotational loads but can be damaged when subjected to side impact loads. If the rotor is knocked out of true by a side impact, a pulsation will be felt in the front brake lever when braking. The rotor is too thin to be trued and must be replaced with a new one. Protect the rotor when transporting a wheel to a dealer or tire specialist for tire service. Do **not** place a wheel in a car trunk or pickup bed without protecting the rotor from side impact damage.*

1. Support the motorcycle with the front wheel off the ground.

NOTE

The front wheel can be removed with the brake caliper still attached to the front fork slider.

2. Unscrew the speedometer cable collar (A, **Figure 1**) from the speedometer drive unit on the front wheel.

3. Remove the front axle nut cotter pin (B, **Figure 1**).

4. Loosen and remove the front axle nut (C, **Figure 1**) and washer.

5. Loosen the front axle holder nuts (A, **Figure 2**).

6. Insert a screwdriver or drift into the hole in the end of the front axle.

7. Slide the axle out (B, **Figure 2**) from the right-hand side. Don't loose the collar and dust cover on the right-hand side of the hub.

NOTE

After removing the front wheel in Step 8, insert a piece of wood or hose in the caliper between the brake pads. That way, if the brake lever is accidentally squeezed, the piston will not be forced out of the brake caliper cylinder. If the brake lever is squeezed and the piston comes out, the caliper might have to be disassembled to reseat the piston and the system will have to be bled.

8. Pull the wheel forward and remove it.

CAUTION

Do not set the wheel down on the disc surface as it may get scratched or warped. Set the tire sidewalls on 2 wood blocks as shown in ***Figure 3****.*

9. Install the washer and axle nut on the axle to prevent their accidental loss when servicing the wheel.

10. Inspect the wheel spokes and hub as described in this chapter.

Installation

1. Clean the axle and axle spacers in solvent and thoroughly dry. Make sure all axle contact surfaces are clean and free of dirt and old grease prior to installation. If these surfaces are not cleaned, the axle may be difficult to install.

2. Apply a light coat of grease to the axle and to the front hub bearings and grease seals.

3. Make sure the dust cover and collar are installed on the right-hand side of the hub (**Figure 4**).

4. When installing the speedometer housing, align the slots in the speedometer housing (**Figure 5**) with the raised tabs (**Figure 6**) in the front hub. Push the housing down until it's completely seated.

5. Remove the piece of wood or hose from the caliper.

6. Correctly position the front wheel between the front forks and carefully insert the disc between the brake pads and install the wheel. Don't damage the leading edges of the brake pads.

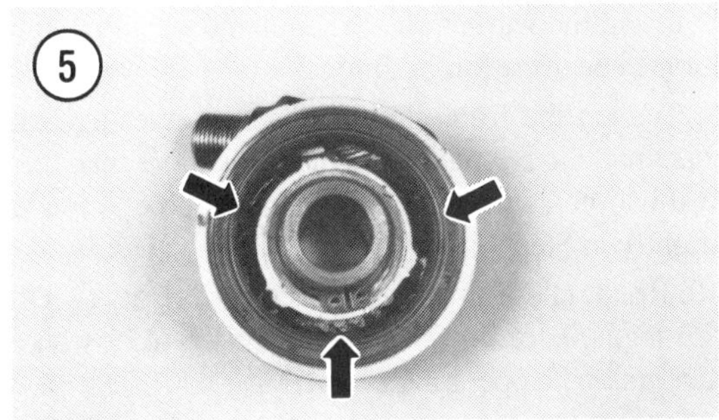
5

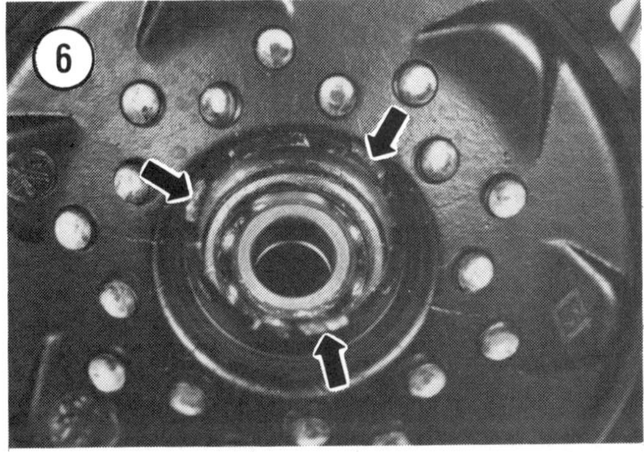
6

7

8

7. Make sure to align the slot in the speedometer drive unit with the tab on the left-hand fork tube.

8. If the front axle holder was removed, install it as follows:

a. Install the front axle holder with the UP arrow (**Figure 7**) facing up.
b. Install the lockwasher and nuts.

9. Tighten the front axle holder nuts finger-tight at this time. Do not tighten the nuts any more than this at this time as the front axle must be able to move slightly in Step 15.

10. Install the axle nut (C, **Figure 1**) and tighten to the torque specification in **Table 3**.

11. Secure the axle nut with a *new* cotter pin (B, **Figure 1**). Bend the end of the cotter pin over to lock it.

12. Rotate the front wheel and apply the brake. Do this a couple of times to make sure the front wheel and brake are operating correctly.

13. Slowly rotate the front wheel while inserting the speedometer cable into the speedometer housing. Screw the cable collar onto the housing and tighten securely.

14. Remove the wood block(s) from under the engine.

15. Sit on the seat, apply the front brake and push down on the handlebars several times. This will center the front axle within the front forks.

16. Place the bike on the sidestand.

WARNING
*In the following step, the front axle holder nuts must be tightened in the specific manner and to the specified torque value. After installation, there must be a slight gap at the bottom (**A, Figure 8**), with **no gap** (**B, Figure 8**) at the top. If done incorrectly, the studs may fail, resulting in the loss of control of the bike when riding.*

17. Tighten the front axle holder nuts to the torque specification in **Table 3**. Tighten the upper nuts first, then the lower nuts. There must be a gap (A, **Figure 8**) at the lower portion of the front axle holder.

FRONT WHEEL (TT600)

Removal (1983-1984)

1. Support the motorcycle with the front wheel off the ground.
2. Unscrew the speedometer cable collar from the speedometer drive unit on the right-hand side of the front wheel.
3. Remove the screws securing the front brake cable guide at the base of the left-hand fork slider.
4. Loosen then remove the front axle nut and washer.
5. Loosen the front axle holder nut on the right-hand side.
6. Slide the axle out from the right-hand side. Don't lose the collar and dust cover on the right-hand side of the hub.
7. Pull the wheel forward and pull the drum brake panel straight out of the hub.
8. Remove the front wheel.
9. Remove the speedometer drive unit from the right-hand side of the hub.
10. Install the washer and axle nut on the axle to prevent their accidental loss when servicing the wheel.
11. Inspect the wheel spokes and hub as described in this chapter.

Installation (1983-1984)

1. Clean the axle in solvent and thoroughly dry. Make sure all axle contact surfaces are clean and free of dirt and old grease prior to installation. If these surfaces are not cleaned, the axle may be difficult to install.
2. Apply a light coat of grease to the axle and to the front hub bearings and grease seals.
3. When installing the speedometer housing, align the raised tabs in the speedometer housing with the slots in the front hub. Push the housing down until it's completely seated.
4. Move the front wheel into position and install the drum brake panel into the front hub. Push it in until it bottoms out.
5. Correctly position the front wheel between the front forks and install the wheel.
6. Make sure to align the slot in the speedometer drive unit with the tab on the left-hand fork tube.
7. Install the front axle from the right-hand side.
8. Install the washer and axle nut and tighten to the torque specification in **Table 3**.
9. Tighten the front axle holder nut finger-tight at this time. Do not tighten the nuts any more than this at this time as the front axle must be able to move slightly in Step 13.
10. Rotate the front wheel and apply the brake. Do this a couple of times to make sure the front wheel and brake are operating correctly.
11. Slowly rotate the front wheel while inserting the speedometer cable into the speedometer housing. Screw the cable collar onto the housing and tighten securely.
12. Remove the wood block(s) from under the engine.
13. Sit on the seat, apply the front brake and push down on the handlebars several times. This will center the front axle within the front forks.
14. Place the bike on the sidestand.

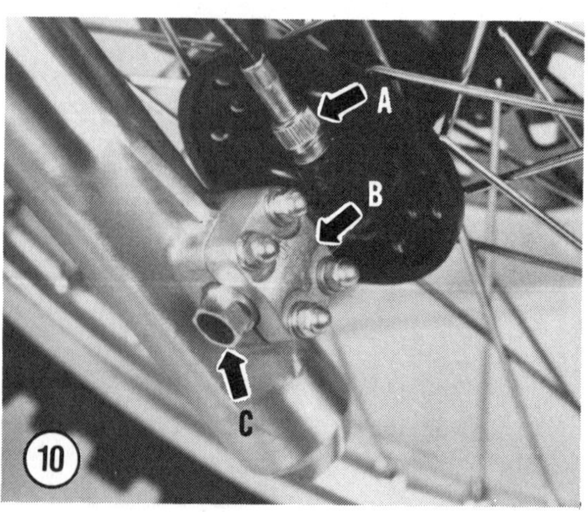

15. Tighten the front axle holder nut to the torque specification in **Table 3**.

Removal (1985-1986)

CAUTION
*Care must be taken when removing, handling and installing a wheel with a disc brake rotor. The disc rotor is relatively thin in order to dissipate heat and to minimize unsprung weight. The rotor is designed to withstand tremendous rotational loads but can be damaged when subjected to side impact loads. If the rotor is knocked out of true by a side impact, a pulsation will be felt in the front brake lever when braking. The rotor is too thin to be trued and must be replaced with a new one. Protect the rotor when transporting a wheel to a dealer or tire specialist for tire service. Do **not** place a wheel in a car trunk or pickup bed without protecting the rotor from side impact damage.*

1. Support the motorcycle with the front wheel off the ground.

NOTE
The front wheel can be removed with the brake caliper still attached to the front fork slider.

2. Remove the front axle nut cotter pin (A, **Figure 9**).
3. Loosen and remove the front axle nut (B, **Figure 9**) and washer.

4. Remove the screws securing the brake disc dust cover (C, **Figure 9**) and remove the dust cover.
5. Unscrew the speedometer cable (A, **Figure 10**) from the speedometer drive unit on the front wheel.
6. Loosen the front axle holder (B, **Figure 10**) nuts.
7. Insert a screwdriver or drift into the hole in the end of the front axle and slide the axle out (C, **Figure 10**) from the right-hand side.
8. Don't loose the collar and dust cover on the left-hand side of the hub.

NOTE
After removing the front wheel in Step 9, insert a piece of wood or hose in the caliper between the brake pads. That way, if the brake lever is accidentally squeezed, the piston will not be forced out of the brake caliper cylinder. If the brake lever is squeezed and the piston comes out, the caliper might have to be disassembled to reseat the piston and the system will have to be bled.

9. Pull the wheel forward and remove it.

CAUTION
*Do not set the wheel down on the disc surface as it may get scratched or warped. Set the tire sidewalls on 2 wood blocks as shown in **Figure 3**.*

10. Remove the speedometer housing from the front hub.
11. Install the washer and axle nut on the axle to prevent their accidental loss when servicing the wheel.
12. Inspect the wheel spokes and hub as described in this chapter.

Installation (1985-1986)

1. Clean the axle and axle spacers in solvent and thoroughly dry. Make sure all axle contact surfaces are clean and free of dirt and old grease prior to installation. If these surfaces are not cleaned, the axle may be difficult to install.
2. Apply a light coat of grease to the axle and to the front hub bearings and grease seals.
3. Make sure the dust cover and collar (**Figure 11**) are installed on the left-hand side of the hub.
4. When installing the speedometer housing, align the slots (A, **Figure 12**) in the speedometer housing

with the raised tabs (B, **Figure 12**) in the front hub. Push the housing down until it's completely seated (**Figure 13**).

5. Remove the piece of wood or hose from the caliper.

6. If the front axle holder was removed, install it as follows:

   a. Install the front axle holder (**Figure 14**) with the UP arrow facing up.
   b. Install the lockwasher and nuts.

7. Correctly position the front wheel between the front forks and carefully insert the disc between the brake pads and install the wheel. Don't damage the leading edges of the brake pads.

8. Make sure to align the slot in the speedometer drive unit with the tab on the left-hand fork tube.

9. Install the front axle from the right-hand side.

10. Install the axle nut (B, **Figure 9**) and tighten to the torque specification in **Table 3**.

11. Secure the axle nut with a *new* cotter pin (A, **Figure 9**). Bend the end of the cotter pin over to lock it.

12. Tighten the front axle holder nuts finger-tight at this time. Do not tighten the nuts any more than this at this time as the front axle must be able to move slightly in Step 16.

13. Rotate the front wheel and apply the brake. Do this a couple of times to make sure the front wheel and brake are operating correctly.

14. Slowly rotate the front wheel while inserting the speedometer cable into the speedometer housing. Screw the cable collar onto the housing and tighten securely.

15. Remove the wood block(s) from under the engine.

16. Sit on the seat, apply the front brake and push down on the handlebars several times. This will center the front axle within the front forks.

17. Place the bike on the sidestand.

WARNING

*In the following step, the front axle holder nuts must be tightened in the specific manner and to the specified torque value. After installation, there must be a slight gap at the bottom (**A, Figure 15**), with **no gap (B, Figure 15)** at the top. If done incorrectly, the studs may fail, resulting in the loss of control of the bike when riding.*

18. Tighten the front axle holder nuts to the torque specification in **Table 3**. Tighten the upper nuts first, then the lower nuts. There must be a gap (A, **Figure 15**) at the lower portion of the front axle holder.

19. Install brake disc dust cover (C, **Figure 9**).

WHEEL SPOKE SERVICE

Spoke Inspection

Spokes loosen with use and should be checked periodically. The "tuning fork" method for checking

12

13

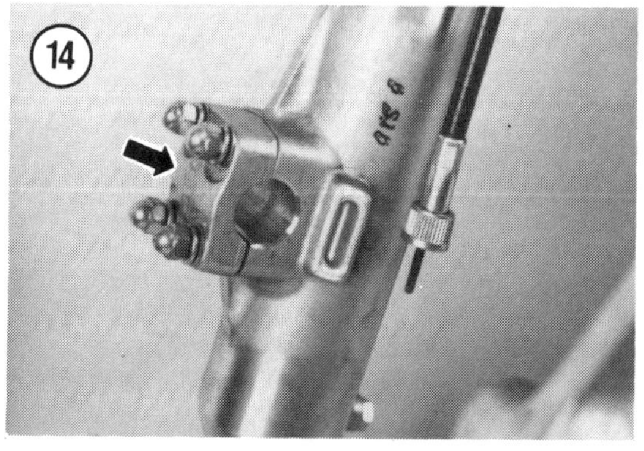

14

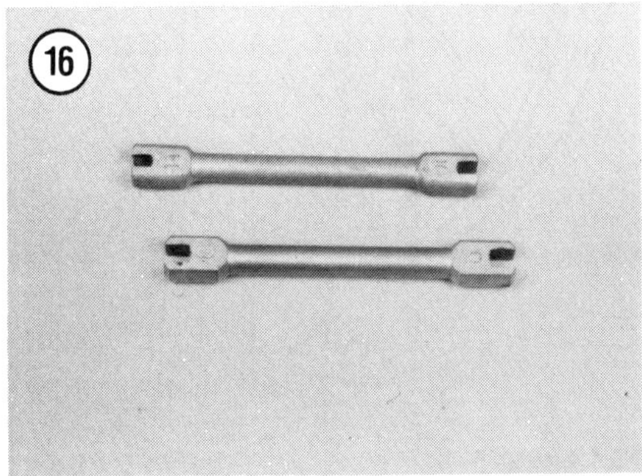

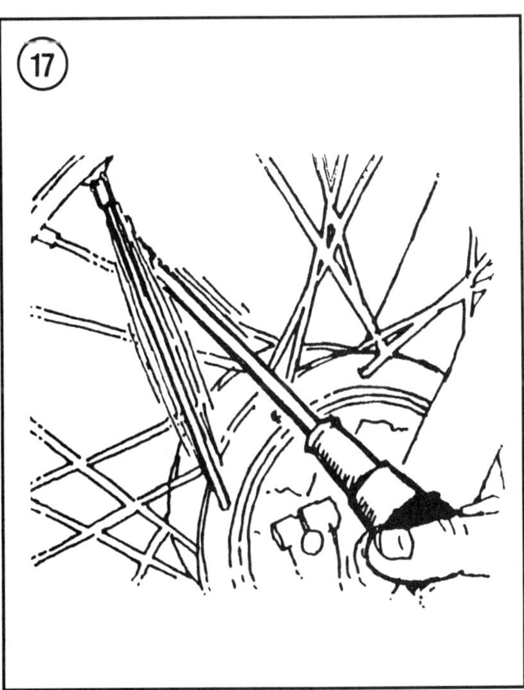

spoke tightness is simple and works well. Tap each spoke with a spoke wrench (**Figure 16**) or the shank of a screwdriver (**Figure 17**) and listen for a tone. A tightened spoke will emit a clear, ringing tone and a loose spoke will sound flat. All the spokes in a correctly tightened wheel will emit tones of similar pitch but not necessarily the same precise tone.

Bent, stripped or broken spokes should be replaced as soon as they are detected, as they can cause the destruction of an expensive hub.

NOTE

If you are riding and one or more of the spokes should break, tie the broken spoke(s) to an adjacent spoke with wire, tape or string until you can ride home and replace it. This will prevent the broken spoke from dangling loose and eventually causing component damage.

Spoke Replacement

1. Unscrew the nipple from the spoke and depress the nipple into the rim far enough to free the end of the spoke, taking care not to push the nipple all the way in.
2. Remove the damaged spoke from the hub and use it to match a new spoke of identical length. If necessary, trim the new spoke to match the original and dress the end of the thread with a thread die.
3. Install the new spoke in the rim and hub and screw on the nipple; tighten it until the spoke's tone is similar to the tone of the other spokes in the wheel.
4. Periodically check the new spoke; it will stretch and must be retightened several times before it takes its final set.

Spoke Adjustment

1. Draw the high point of the rim toward the centerline of the wheel by loosening the spokes in the area of the high point and tightening the spokes on the side opposite the high point. See **Figure 18**.
2. Rotate the wheel and check runout. Continue adjusting until the runout is within specification. Be patient and thorough, adjusting the position of the rim a little at a time. If you loosen 2 spokes at the high point 1/2 turn, loosen the adjacent spokes 1/4 turn. Tighten the spokes on the opposite side in equivalent amounts.

Wheel Runout

Wheel rim runout is the amount of "wobble" a wheel shows as it rotates. You can check runout with the wheels on the bike by simply supporting the wheel off the ground and turning the wheel slowly while you hold a pointer solidly against a fork leg. Just make sure any wobble you observe isn't caused by your own hand.

Off the motorcycle, runout can be checked with the wheel installed on a truing stand (**Figure 19**).

NOTE
A discarded rear swing arm mounted in a vise makes an ideal wheel truing stand.

The maximum allowable lateral (side-to-side) and radial (up and down) play is listed in **Table 1**. Tighten or replace any bent or loose spokes. Always use the correct size spoke wrench (**Figure 16**) or you may damage the spoke nipple.

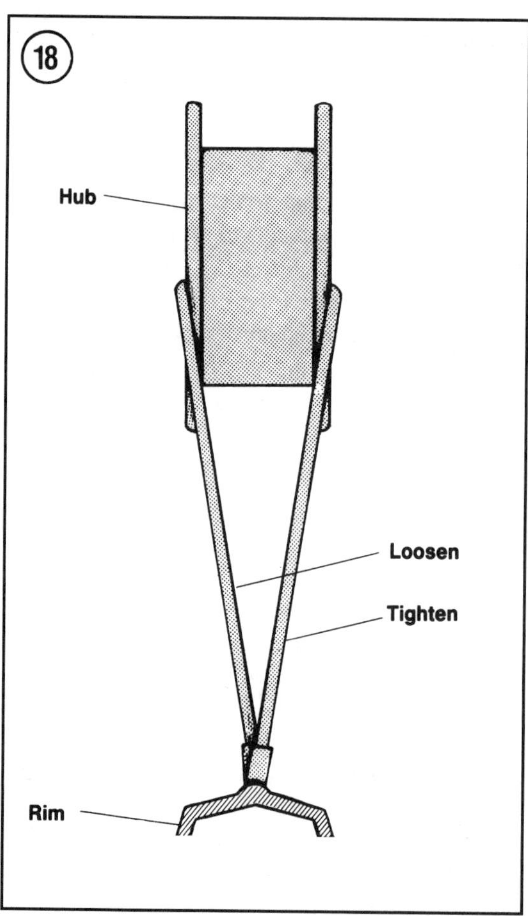

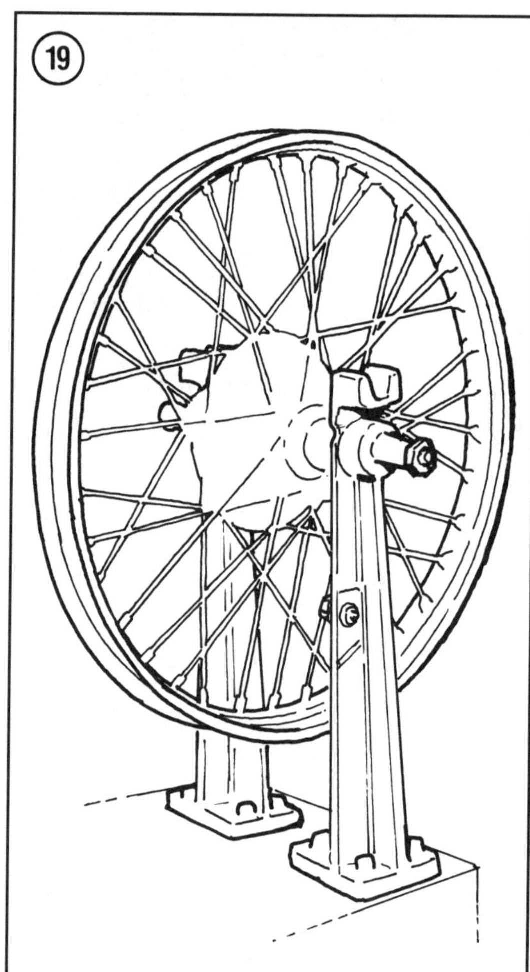

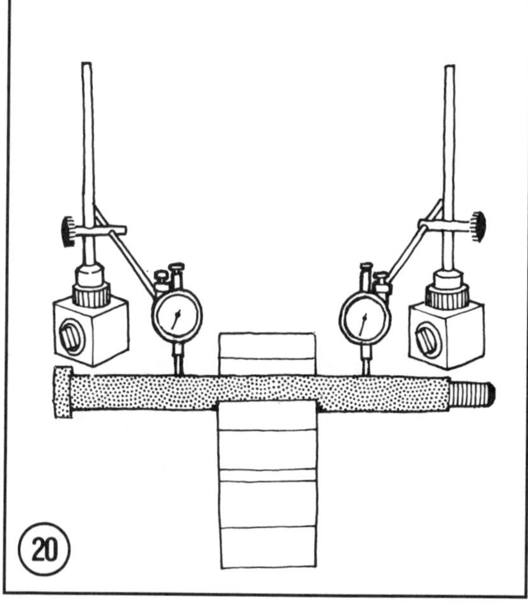

FRONT HUB

Inspection

1. Visually check the front axle surface for cracks, deep scoring or excessive wear. Check axle runout with a set of V-blocks and dial indicator (**Figure 20**).

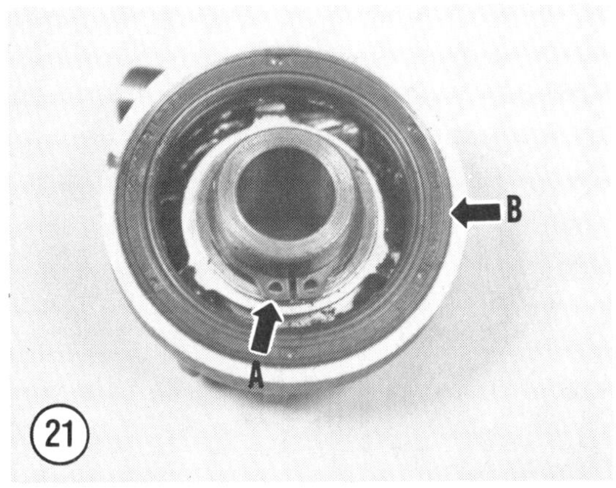

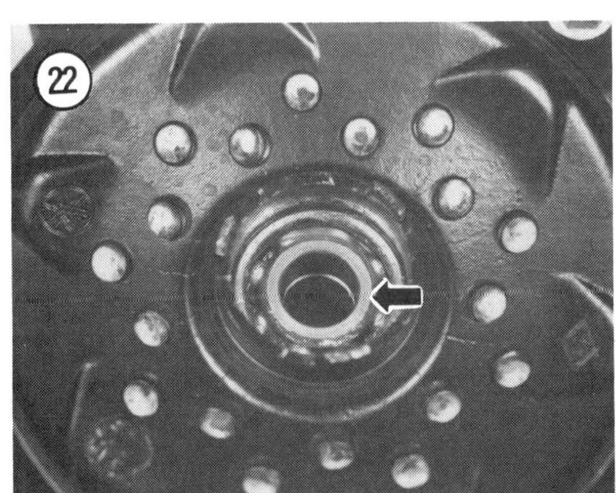

The maximum allowable bend is listed in **Table 1**. If you do not have access to the special tools, roll the axle on a flat surface and visually check the runout. Replace a bent axle. Do not attempt to straighten it.

2. Check the speedometer drive assembly for damage. Make sure the circlip (A, **Figure 21**) is correctly seated.

3. Check the oil seal (B, **Figure 21**) for signs of wear, cracks or other damage. A damaged oil seal will allow bearing contamination. Replace the oil seal as described in this section.

4. Turn the inner bearing race (**Figure 22**) by hand and check for any sign of roughness or damage. Replace the bearings (as a set) as described in this section.

5. Check the front brake disc bolts (A, **Figure 23**) for tightness. If loose, tighten the bolts securely.

6. Check the brake disc surface (B, **Figure 23**) for oil residue. Clean with lacquer thinner before reinstalling the front wheel.

Inspection/Disassembly

Refer to the following illustrations for this procedure:

a. **Figure 24**: 1983-1984 TT600 drum brake.
b. **Figure 25**: 1985-1986 TT600 disc brake.
c. **Figure 26**: XT600 disc brake.

CAUTION
Do not remove the wheel bearings for inspection purposes as they will be damaged during the removal process. Remove wheel bearings only if they are to be replaced.

1. Remove the front wheel as described in this chapter.

2. Remove the speedometer drive unit (**Figure 27**) from the left-hand side of the wheel.

3. Remove the collar and dust cover (**Figure 28**) from the right-hand side of the wheel.

4. Remove the oil seal (A, **Figure 29**) by carefully prying it out of the right-hand side of the hub with a long flat-bladed screwdriver (A, **Figure 30**). Lift the screwdriver and work it around the seal every few degrees until it pops out of the hub. Prop a piece of wood or rag (B, **Figure 30**) underneath the screwdriver to prevent damaging the hub.

(24)

FRONT WHEEL
(1983-1984 TT600 DRUM BRAKE)

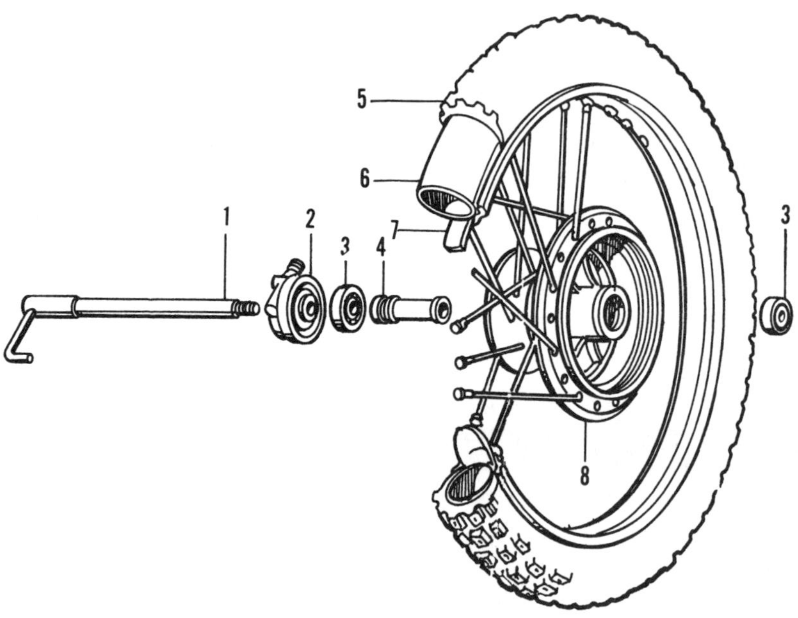

1. Axle
2. Speedometer drive assembly
3. Bearing
4. Middle spacer
5. Tire
6. Inner tube
7. Band
8. Hub

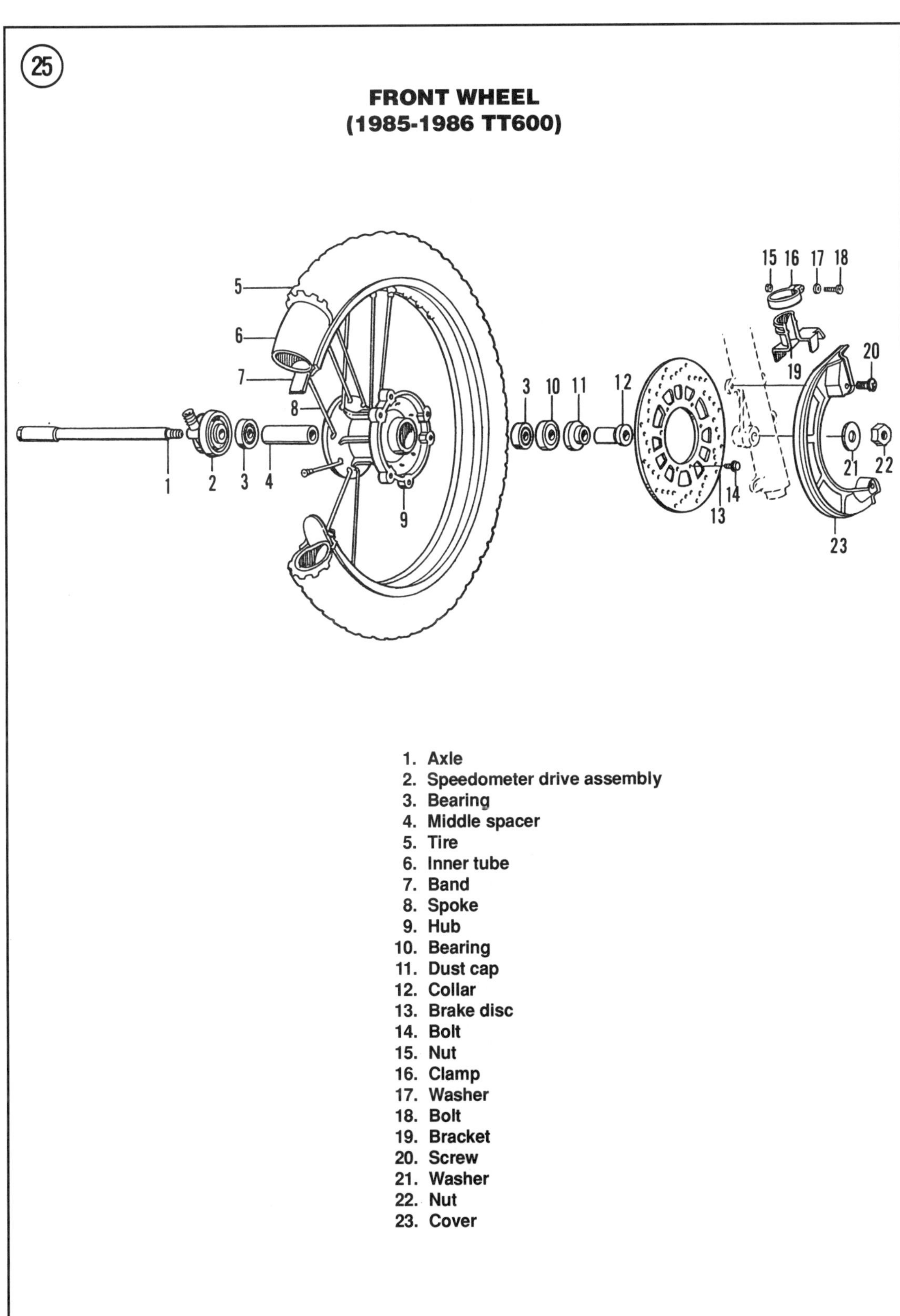
25
FRONT WHEEL
(1985-1986 TT600)
1. Axle
2. Speedometer drive assembly
3. Bearing
4. Middle spacer
5. Tire
6. Inner tube
7. Band
8. Spoke
9. Hub
10. Bearing
11. Dust cap
12. Collar
13. Brake disc
14. Bolt
15. Nut
16. Clamp
17. Washer
18. Bolt
19. Bracket
20. Screw
21. Washer
22. Nut
23. Cover

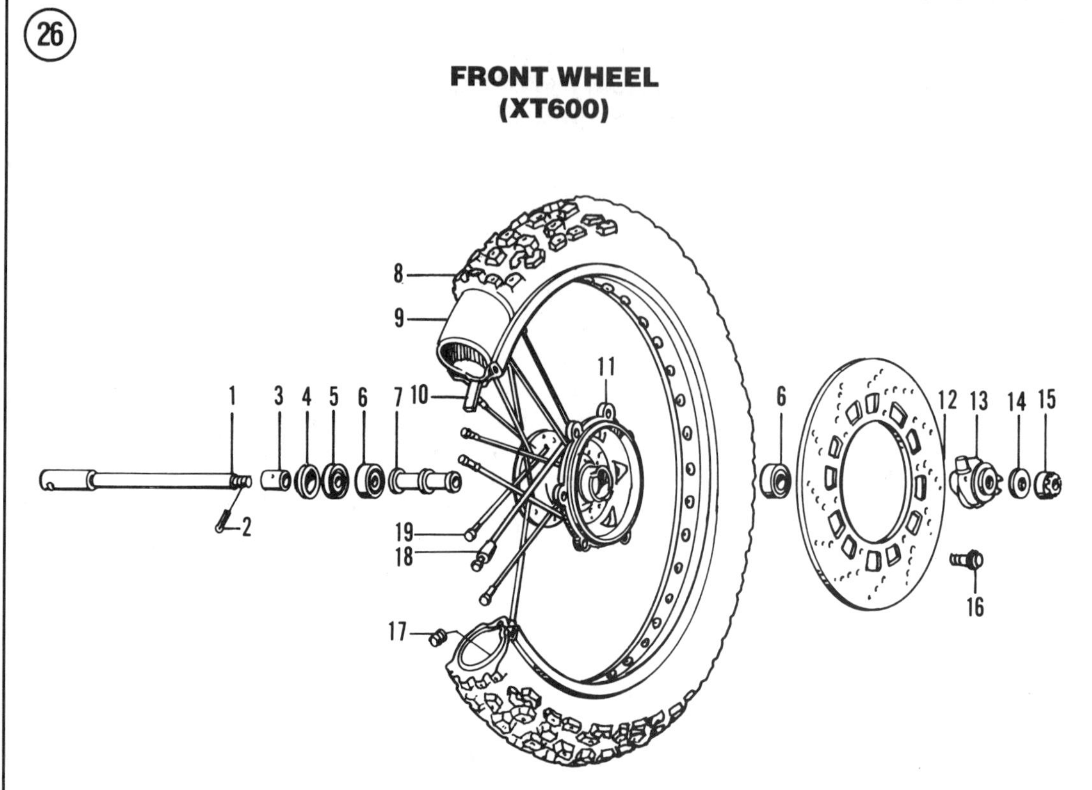

1. Axle
2. Cotter pin
3. Collar
4. Dust cover
5. Grease seal
6. Bearing
7. Middle spacer
8. Tire
9. Inner tube
10. Band
11. Hub
12. Brake disc
13. Speedometer drive assembly
14. Washer
15. Nut
16. Bolt
17. Rubber plug
18. Balance weight
19. Spoke

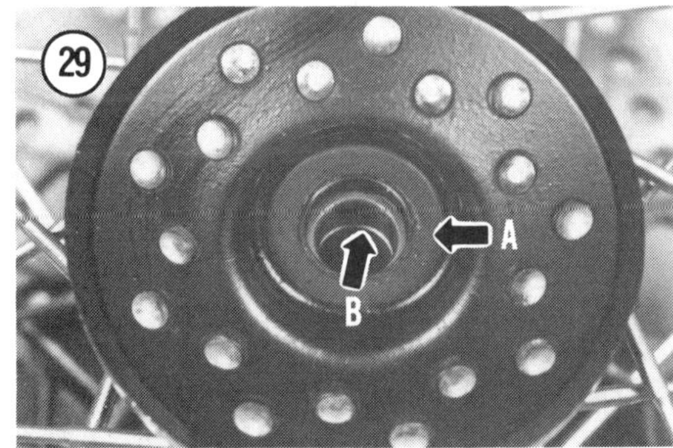

NOTE
When replacing the bearings, be sure to take your old bearings along to ensure a perfect matchup.

5. Turn the inner race (B, **Figure 29**) of each bearing by hand. Make sure bearings turn smoothly and check for any signs of roughness or damage. Replace the bearings as a complete set if they are noisy or have excessive play.
6. On non-sealed bearings, check the rollers or balls for evidence of wear, pitting or excessive heat (bluish tint). Replace the bearings if necessary.
7. To remove the left- (**Figure 31**) and right-hand bearings and spacer, perform the following:
   a. Insert a soft aluminum or brass drift into one side of the hub.
   b. Push the middle spacer over to one side and place the drift on the inner race of the lower bearing (**Figure 32**).

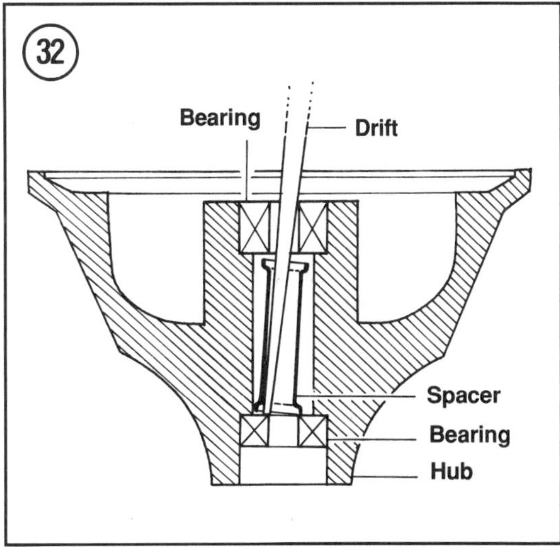

c. Tap the bearing out of the hub with a hammer, working around the perimeter of the inner race.
d. Remove the middle spacer.
e. Repeat for the opposite bearing.

8. Thoroughly clean out the inside of the hub with solvent and dry with compressed air or a shop cloth.

Assembly

1. Blow any dirt or foreign matter out of the hub prior to installing the bearings.

NOTE
Fully sealed bearings are available from many good bearing specialty shops. Fully sealed bearings provide better protection from dirt and moisture that may get into the hub.

2. Pack non-sealed bearings with good-quality bearing grease. Work the grease in between the balls thoroughly. Turn the bearing by hand a couple of times to make sure the grease is distributed evenly inside the bearing.
3. Place the new wheel bearing outer races in a freezer if possible. Chilling them will slightly reduce their overall diameter. This will make installation easier.
4. Pack the wheel hub and middle spacer with multipurpose grease.

NOTE
If a bearing has only one sealed side, install the bearing with the sealed side facing out.

CAUTION
*When installing the bearings in the following procedures, tap the bearings squarely into place and tap on the outer race only. Use a socket (**Figure 33**) that matches the outer race diameter. Do not tap on the inner race or the bearing will be damaged. Be sure that the bearings are completely seated.*

5. Install one of the bearings. It doesn't matter which bearing is installed first.
6. Install the middle spacer.
7. Install the opposite bearing.
8. Lubricate the new oil seal with multipurpose grease and tap it squarely into the hub with a suitable

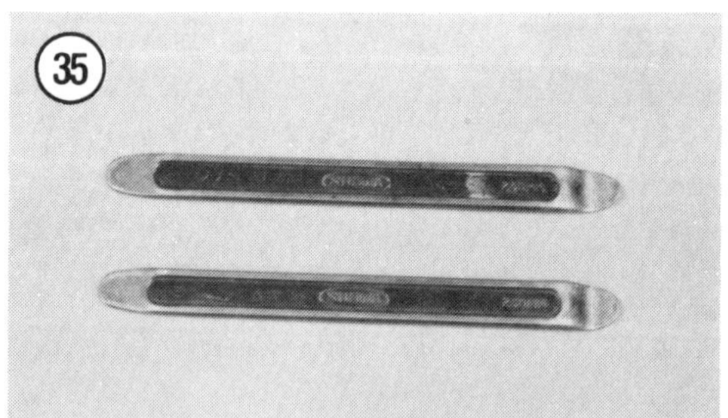

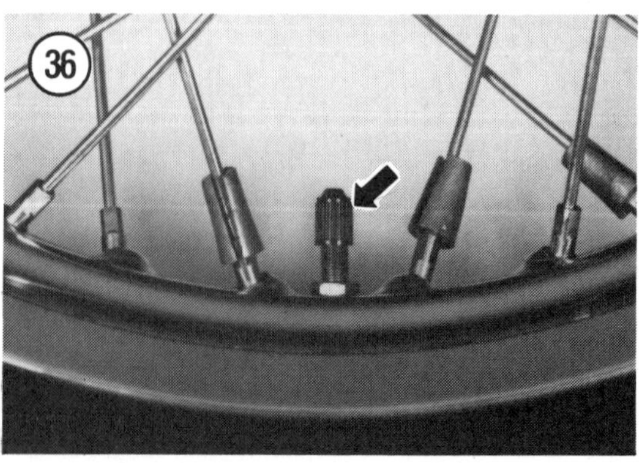

size socket placed on the outside portion of the seal. Install the oil seal (A, **Figure 29**) until it is at least flush with the hub.

9. Install the collar and dust cover (**Figure 28**) into the right-hand side of the wheel.

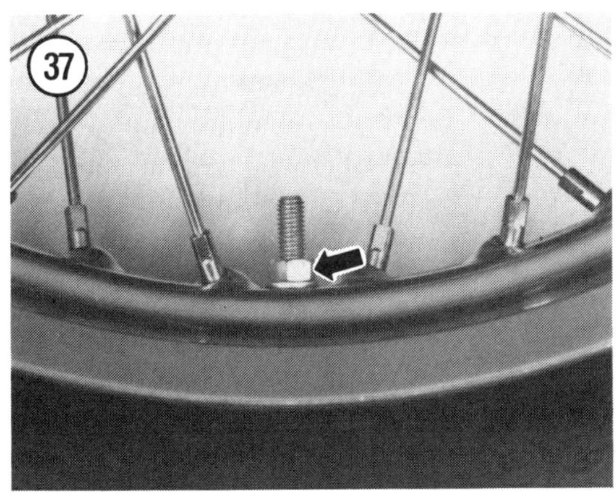

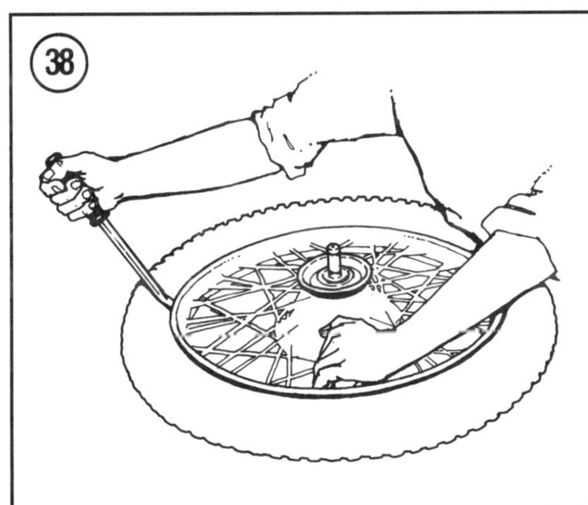

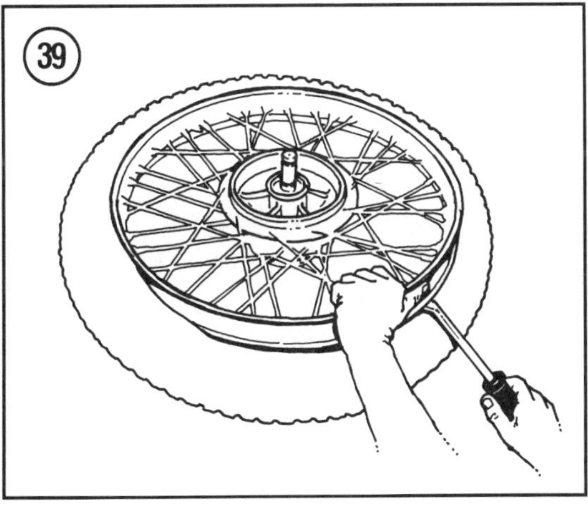

10. When installing the speedometer housing, align the slots in the speedometer housing (A, **Figure 34**) with the raised tabs (B, **Figure 34**) in the front hub. Push the housing down until it's completely seated.
11. Install the front wheel as described in this chapter.

TIRE CHANGING

Removal

Use only quality tire irons (**Figure 35**) without sharp edges. If necessary, file the ends of the tire irons to remove rough edges. Do not use screwdrivers or other sharp objects as these tools will probably puncture the tube.

1. Remove the valve cap (**Figure 36**), nut and core and deflate the tire.
2. Loosen the rim locknuts (**Figure 37**).
3. Press the entire bead on both sides of the tire into the center of the rim.
4. Lubricate the beads with soapy water.
5. Insert the tire iron under the bead next to the valve (**Figure 38**). Force the bead on the opposite side of tire into the center of the rim and pry the bead over the rim with the tire iron.
6. Insert a second tire iron next to the first to hold the bead over the rim. Then work around the tire with the first tire iron, prying the bead over the rim. Be careful not to pinch the inner tube with the tire irons.
7. Remove the valve from the hole in the rim and remove the tube from the tire.

NOTE
Step 8 is required only if it is necessary to completely remove the tire from the rim, such as for tire replacement.

8. Stand the tire upright. Insert the tire iron between the second bead and the side of the rim that the first bead was pried over (**Figure 39**). Force the bead on the opposite side from the tire iron into the center of the rim. Pry the second bead off of the rim, working around as with the first.

Installation

1. Carefully check the tire for any damage, especially inside. On the front tire, carefully check the sidewall as it is very vulnerable to damage from rocks.

2. Check that the spoke ends do not protrude through the nipples into the center of the rim to puncture the tube. File off any protruding spoke ends.

NOTE
If you are having trouble with water and dirt entering the wheel, remove and discard the rubber rim band. Then wrap the rim center with 2 separate revolutions of duct tape. Punch holes through the tape at the rim lock and valve stem mounting areas.

3. Install the rim lock if removed.

4. If you are using the rubber rim band, be sure the band is in place with the rough side toward the rim. Align the holes in the band with the holes in the rim.

5. Liberally sprinkle the inside tire casing with talcum powder. The powder reduces chafing between the tire and tube and minimizes tube pinching.

NOTE
*Before installing a tire, check the sidewall for a weight identification mark. This is usually a round circle like the one shown in **A, Figure 40**. When installing the tire, align the weight mark with either the valve stem hole (B, **Figure 40**) or the rim lock hole in the rim.*

6. If the tire was removed or a new tire is being installed, perform the following:
   a. Install the tire so that it revolves in the proper direction. Some tire manufacturer's mark their tires with an arrow and "Direction" on the side wall (**Figure 41**).
   b. Lubricate one bead with soapy water.

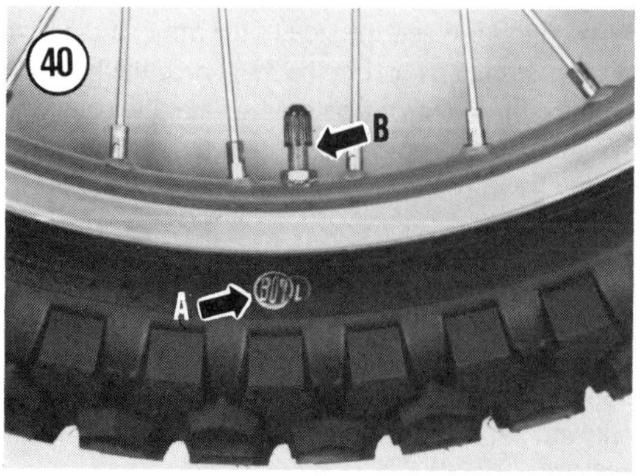

   c. Align the tire with the rim and push the tire onto the rim (**Figure 42**). Work around the tire in both directions (**Figure 43**).

7. Install the core into the tube valve. Put the tube in the tire and insert the valve stem through the hole in the rim. Inflate just enough to round it out. Too much

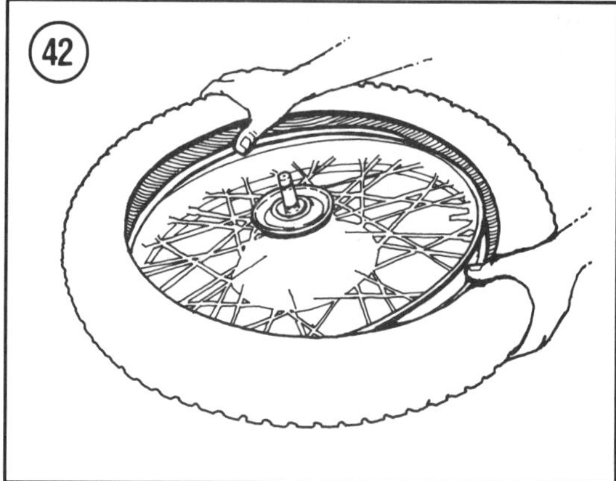

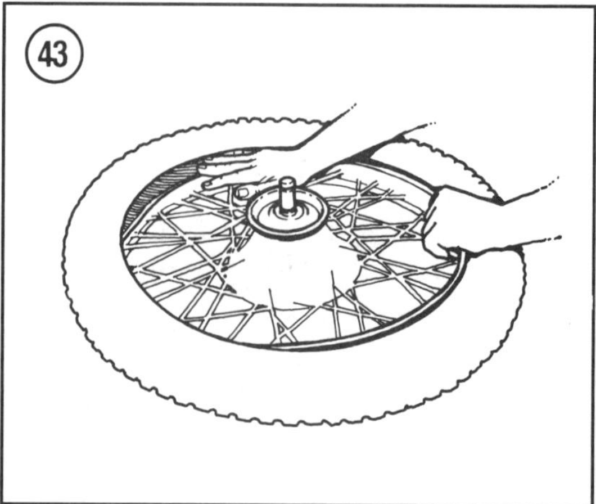

air will make installing it in the tire difficult, and too little will increase the chances of pinching the tube with the tire irons.

8. Lubricate the upper tire bead and rim with soapy water.

9. Press the upper bead into the rim opposite the valve. Pry the bead into the rim on both sides of the initial point with your hands and work around the rim to the valve. If the tire wants to pull up on one side, either use a tire iron or one of your knees to hold the tire in place. The last few inches are usually the toughest to install and is also where most pinched tubes occur. If you can, continue to push the tire into the rim with your hands. Re-lubricate the bead if necessary. If the tire bead wants to pull out from under the rim, use both of your knees to hold the tire in place. If necessary, use a tire iron for the last few inches (**Figure 44**).

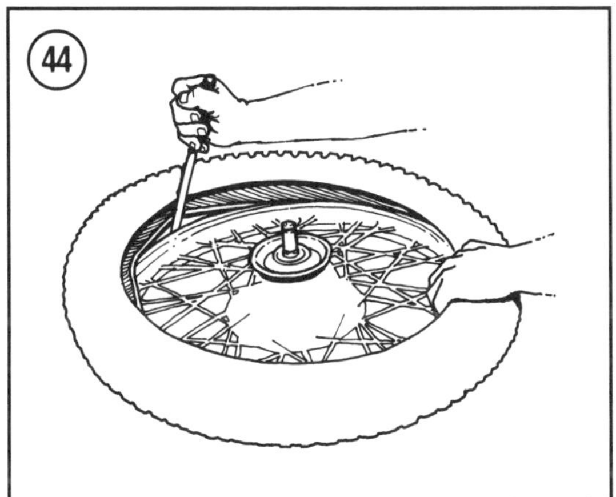

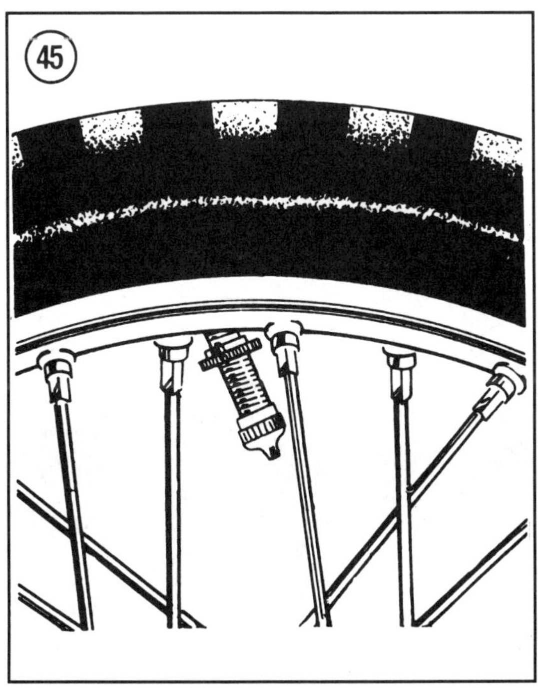

10. Wiggle the valve to be sure the tube is not trapped under the bead. Set the valve squarely in its hole before screwing on the valve nut.

NOTE
Make sure the valve stem is not cocked in the rim as shown in ***Figure 45****.*

11. Check the bead on both sides of the tire for an even fit around the rim. Inflate the tire to approximately 25-30 psi to insure the tire bead is seated properly on the rim. If the tire is hard to seat, re-lubricate both sides of the tire and re-inflate.

12. Tighten the rim locknut securely (**Figure 37**).

13. Bleed the tire back down to between 10 and 14 psi. Never tighten the valve stem nut against the rim. It should always be installed finger-tight, near the valve stem cap rather than flush against the rim.

14. Inflate the tire to the recommended inflation pressure listed in **Table 4**.

TIRE REPAIRS

Every rider eventually experiences trouble with a tire or tube. Repairs and replacement are fairly simple, and every rider should know how to patch a tube.

Patching a motorcycle tube is only a *temporary fix*, especially on a dual-purpose bike that is ridden a lot in the dirt. The tire flexes too much and the patch could rub right off.

NOTE
If you do a lot of off-road riding, install a stronger heavy-duty tube. This type of tube lasts longer and is not as easy to puncture.

Tire Repair Kits

Tire repair kits can be purchased from motorcycle dealers and some auto supply stores. When buying, specify that the kit you want is for motorcycles.

There are 2 types of tire repair kits:

a. Hot patch.
b. Cold patch.

Hot patches are stronger because they actually vulcanize to the tube, becoming part of it. However, they are far too bulky to carry for trail repairs, and the strength is unnecessary for a temporary repair.

Cold patches are not vulcanized to the tube; they are simply glued to it. Though not as strong as hot patches, cold patches are still very durable. Cold patch kits are less bulky than hot and more easily applied while on the road or trail. A cold patch kit contains everything necessary and tucks easily in with your emergency tool kit.

Tube Inspection

1. Remove the tube as described under *Tire Changing* in this chapter.

2. Install the valve core into the valve stem (**Figure 46**) and inflate the tube slightly. Do not overinflate.

3. Immerse the tube in water a section at a time (**Figure 47**). Look carefully for bubbles indicating a hole. Mark each hole and continue checking until you are certain that all holes are discovered and marked. Also make sure that the valve core is not leaking. Tighten it if necessary.

NOTE
If you do not have enough water to immerse sections of the tube, try running your hand over the tube slowly and very close to the surface. If your hand is damp, it works even better. If you suspect a hole anywhere, apply some saliva to the area to verify it.

4. Apply a cold patch using the techniques described under *Cold Patch Repair*, following.

5. Dust the patch area with talcum powder to prevent it from sticking to the tire.

6. Carefully check the inside of the tire casing for small rocks, sand or twigs which may have damaged the tube. If the inside of the tire is split, apply a patch to the area to prevent it from pinching and damaging the tube again.

7. Check the inside of the rim. Make sure the rubber rim band is in place, with no spoke ends protruding, which could puncture the tube.

8. Deflate the tube prior to installing the tire.

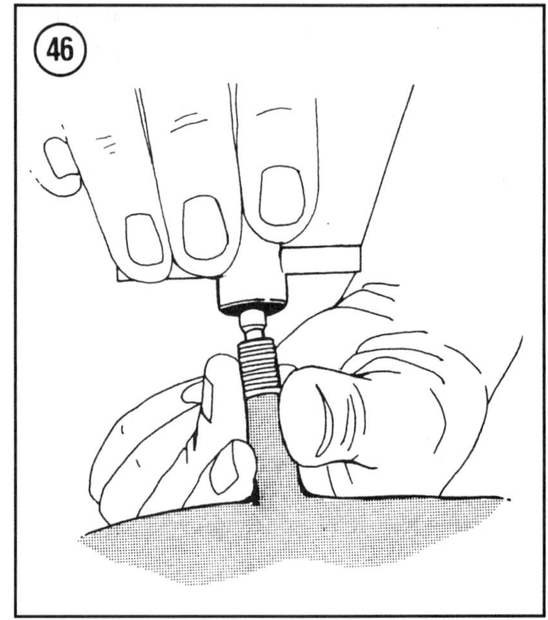

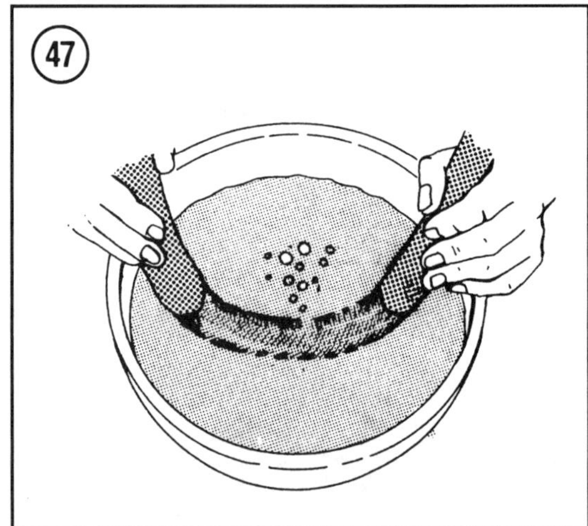

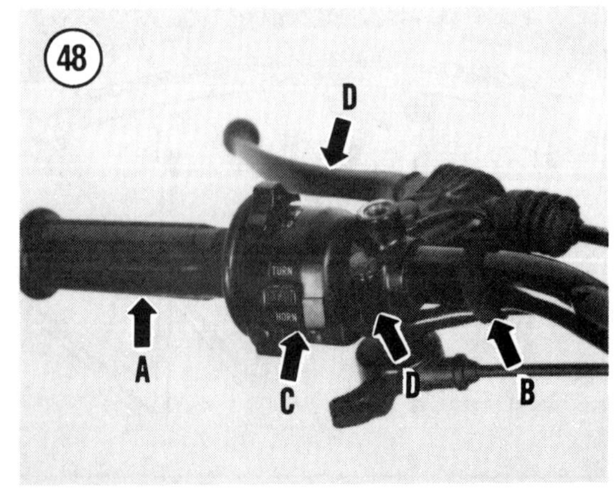

Cold Patch Repairs

1. Remove the tube from the tire as previously described.
2. Using a cap from the tire repair kit or a pocket knife, roughen an area around the hole slightly larger than the patch. Do not scrape too vigorously or you may cause additional damage.
3. Apply a small amount of the special cement from the kit to the puncture and spread it evenly with your finger.
4. Allow the cement to dry until tacky—usually 30 seconds or so is sufficient.
5. Remove the backing from the patch.

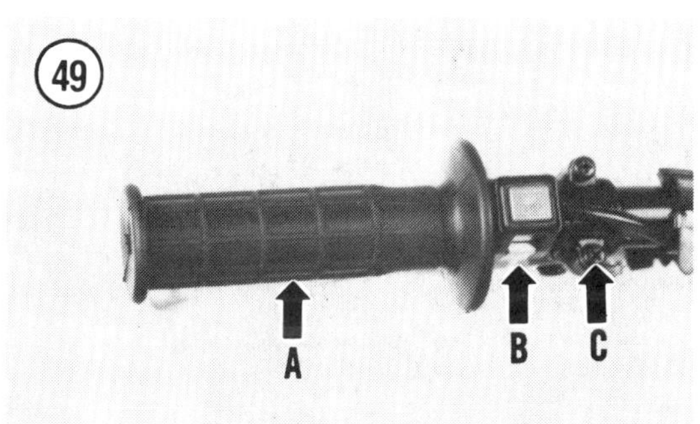

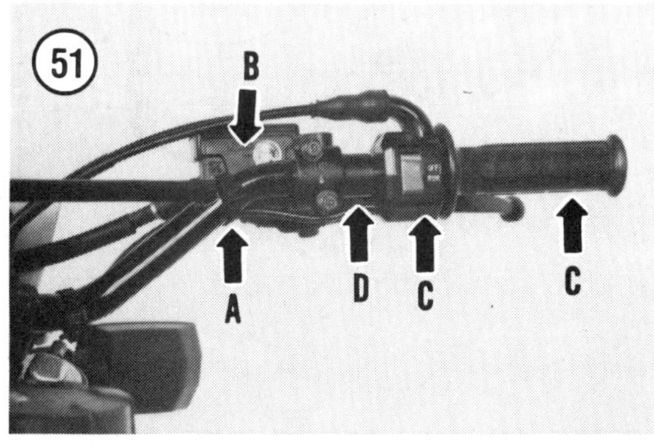

CAUTION
Do not touch the newly exposed rubber with your fingers or the patch will not stick firmly.

6. Center the patch over the hole. Hold the patch firmly in place for about 30 seconds to allow the cement to set.
7. Dust the patched area with talcum powder to prevent sticking.
8. Install the tube as previously described.

HANDLEBAR

Removal/Installation

1. On XT600 models, remove the rear view mirror from each side.

2A. On XT600 models, from the left-hand side of the handlebar, perform the following:
   a. Remove the left-hand side hand grip (A, **Figure 48**).
   b. Remove the electrical cable strap (B, **Figure 48**).
   c. Remove the screws securing the left-hand switch (C, **Figure 48**) and remove the switch.
   d. Loosen the bolt clamping the clutch lever and choke lever assembly (D, **Figure 48**).
   e. Slide the assembly off of the handlebar and carefully lay it over the front fender. Be careful not to kink the clutch cable.

2B. On TT600 models, from the left-hand side of the handlebar, perform the following:
   a. Remove the left-hand side hand grip (A, **Figure 49**).
   b. Remove the electrical cable strap.
   c. Remove the screws securing the engine kill switch (B, **Figure 49**) and remove the switch.
   d. Loosen the bolt clamping the clutch lever assembly (C, **Figure 49**).
   e. Carefully lay the clutch lever assembly and cable over the front fender. Be careful not to kink the clutch cable.

3A. On XT600 models, from the right-hand side of the handlebar, perform the following:
   a. Loosen the screws securing the right-hand switch assembly (**Figure 50**).
   b. Remove the electrical cable strap (A, **Figure 51**).

10

c. Remove the bolts securing the master cylinder (B, **Figure 51**) to the handlebar and remove the master cylinder. Support the master cylinder with a Bungee cord so that it does not hang by its brake hose.

3B. On TT600 models, from the right-hand side of the handlebar, perform the following:

a. Remove the screws holding the throttle housing together.
b. Separate the throttle housing.
c. Disconnect the throttle cables from the switch housings.

4A. On 1983-1984 TT600 models, perform the following:

a. Remove the bolts and washers securing the front drum brake lever to the handlebar and remove the brake lever assembly.
b. Carefully lay the front brake lever and cable over the front fender.

4B. On 1985-1986 TT600 models, perform the following:

a. Remove the bolts securing the master cylinder to the handlebar and remove the master cylinder.
b. Support the master cylinder with a Bungee cord so that it does not hang by its hose.

5. Remove the bolts (**Figure 52**) securing the handlebar holders and remove the holders.

NOTE

Carefully lay the throttle assembly and cables over the front fender, or back over the frame, so the cables do not get crimped or damaged.

6. Move the handlebar toward the left and slide the throttle assembly and right-hand switch assembly (C, **Figure 51**) off the handlebar.
7. Remove the handlebar and slide the spacer (D, **Figure 51**) off the handlebar.
8. Install by reversing these removal steps. Note the following.
9. To maintain a good grip in the handlebar and to prevent them from slipping down, clean the knurled section of the handlebar with solvent. It should be kept rough so it will be held securely by the holders. The holders should also be kept clean and free of any metal that may have been gouged loose by handlebar slippage.
10. Install the handlebar holders with the punch mark (**Figure 53**) toward the front of the bike.
11. Tighten the front bolts first and then the rear bolts (**Figure 52**) securing the handlebar. There must be a gap at the rear (**Figure 54**). Tighten to the torque specification listed in **Table 3**.
12. On disc brake models, perform the following:

a. Be sure to install the spacer (A, **Figure 55**) between the right-hand switch assembly and the master cylinder assembly.
b. Install the master cylinder clamp so that the "UP" arrow (B, **Figure 55**) faces up.

13. Apply a light coat of light machine oil to the throttle grip area on the handlebar prior to installation.

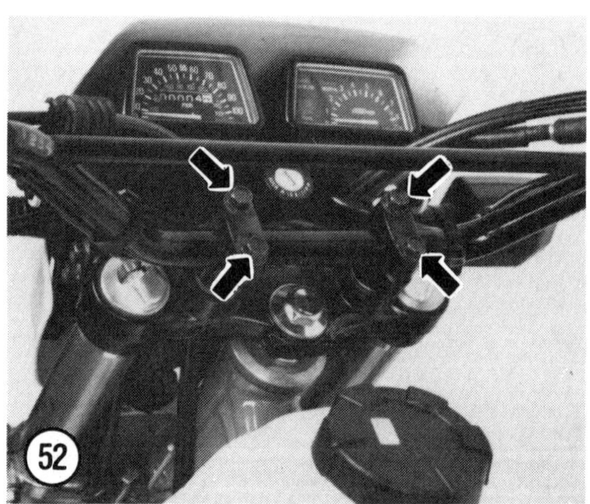

52

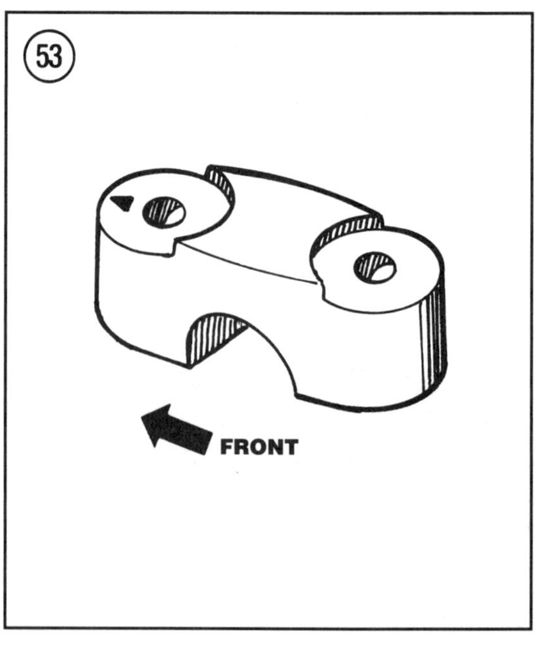

53

WARNING
After installation is completed, make sure the brake lever does not come in contact with the throttle grip assembly when it is pulled on fully.

WARNING
Make sure the front brake and clutch operate properly before riding the bike.

14. Adjust the throttle cables as described under *Throttle Cable Adjustment* in Chapter Three.

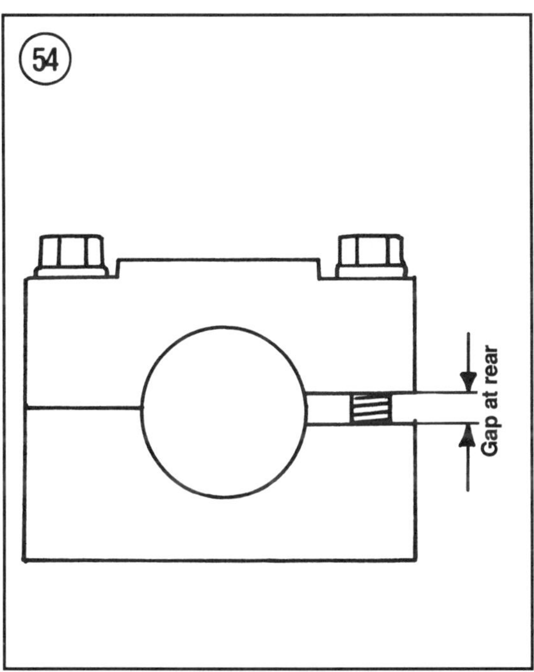

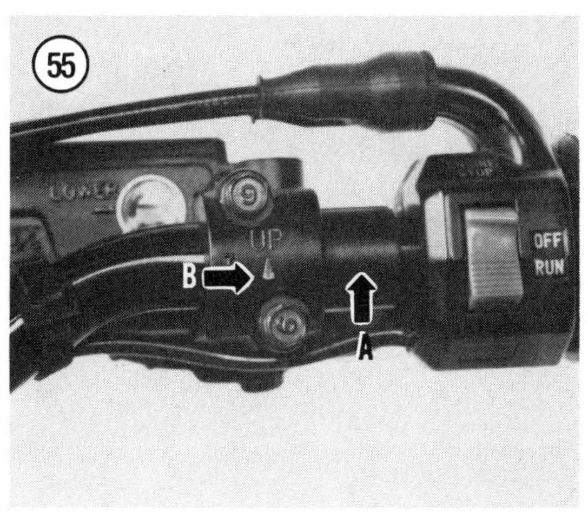

STEERING HEAD

The steering head on these models uses tapered roller bearings at both top and bottom pivot locations. Refer to **Figure 56** for this procedure.

Disassembly

1. Remove the front wheel as described in this chapter.
2. Remove the front fender as described in Chapter Thirteen.
3. Remove the headlight assembly as described under *Headlight Mounting Bracket Removal/Installation* in Chapter Nine.
4. Remove the meter housing assembly as described under *Indicator Bulb Replacement and Meter Housing Removal/Installation* in Chapter Nine.
5. Remove the handlebar (A, **Figure 57**) as described in this chapter.
6A. On XT600 models, perform the following:
   a. Loosen but do not remove the steering stem bolt (B, **Figure 57**).
   b. Remove the front forks as described in this chapter.
   c. Remove the steering stem bolt.
   d. Remove the upper fork bridge (C, **Figure 57**).

NOTE
After the steering stem adjusting nut is removed in Step 6A e, the steering stem must be held in place or it will fall out of the frame head tube.

   e. Have an assistant hold onto the steering stem and remove the steering stem adjusting nut (D, **Figure 57**). Use a large drift and hammer or a spanner wrench and remove the steering stem nut.
   f. Remove the bearing cover (E, **Figure 57**).
6B. On TT600 models, perform the following:
   a. Loosen but do not remove the steering stem nut (A, **Figure 58**).
   b. Remove the front forks as described in this chapter.
   c. Remove the steering stem nut.
   d. Remove the upper fork bridge (B, **Figure 58**).

NOTE
After the steering stem adjusting nut is removed in Step 6B e, the steering stem

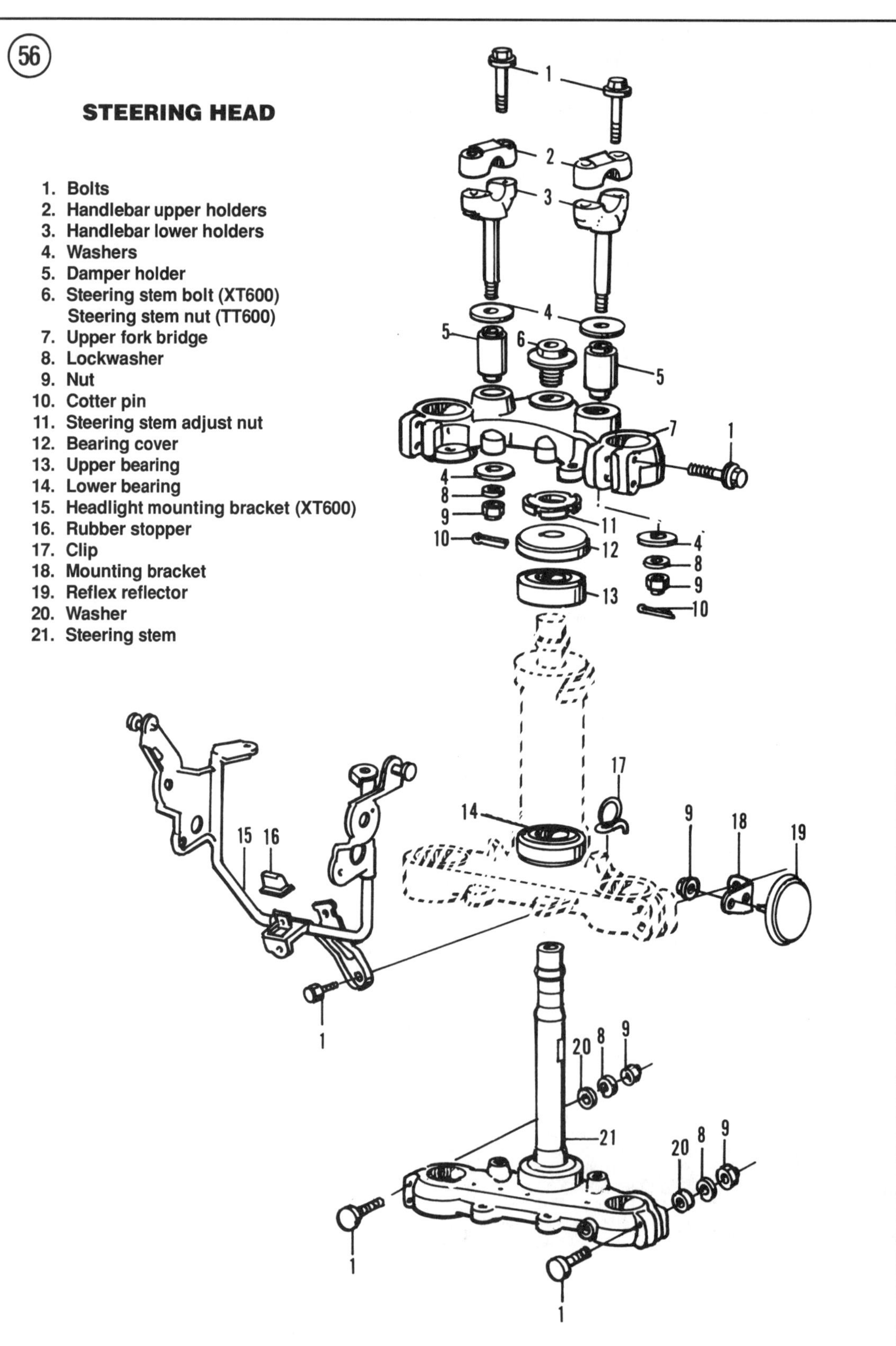
56
STEERING HEAD
1. Bolts
2. Handlebar upper holders
3. Handlebar lower holders
4. Washers
5. Damper holder
6. Steering stem bolt (XT600)
Steering stem nut (TT600)
7. Upper fork bridge
8. Lockwasher
9. Nut
10. Cotter pin
11. Steering stem adjust nut
12. Bearing cover
13. Upper bearing
14. Lower bearing
15. Headlight mounting bracket (XT600)
16. Rubber stopper
17. Clip
18. Mounting bracket
19. Reflex reflector
20. Washer
21. Steering stem

must be held in place or it will fall out of the frame head tube.

e. Have an assistant hold onto the steering stem and remove the steering stem adjusting nut (C, **Figure 58**). Use a large drift and hammer or a spanner wrench and remove the steering stem nut.

f. Remove the bearing cover (D, **Figure 58**).

7. Carefully tap the steering stem down and out of the steering stem bearings in the frame head tube.

8. Don't worry about catching any loose steel balls as the steering stem is equipped with assembled roller bearings.

9. Remove the upper roller bearing from the top of the steering head portion of the frame tube.

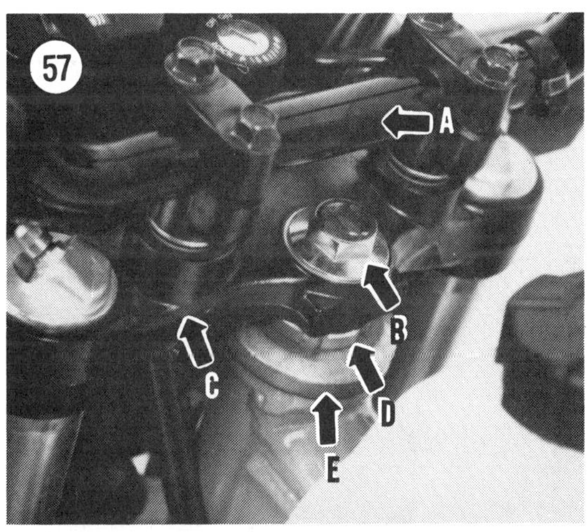

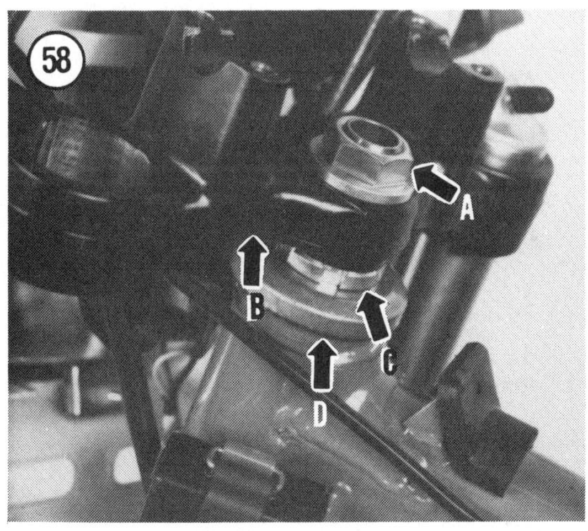

Inspection

1. Clean the bearing races in the steering head, the steering stem races and the tapered roller bearings with solvent.
2. Check the welds around the steering head for cracks and fractures. If any are found, have them repaired by a competent frame shop or welding service.
3. Check the races for pitting or galling and corrosion. If any of these conditions exist, replace the races as described under *Bearing Race Replacement* in this chapter.
4. Check the steering stem bolt (XT600) or nut (TT600), steering stem adjust nut and the upper bearing cover for cracks or damage. Replace if necessary.
5. Check the steering stem for cracks and damage.
6. Check the tapered roller bearings for pitting, scratches or discoloration indicating wear or corrosion. If necessary, replace the lower bearing as follows:
   a. Install a bearing puller onto the steering stem and bearing.
   b. Pull the bearing off of the steering stem.
   c. Clean the steering stem thoroughly in solvent.
   d. Slide a new bearing onto the steering stem until it stops.
   e. Align the bearing with the machined portion of the shaft and slide a long hollow pipe over the steering stem until it seats against the inner bearing race. Drive the bearing onto the shaft until it bottoms out.
7. Check the upper and lower fork bridges for cracks or damage, especially where the fork tubes mount.

Headset Race Replacement

To remove an upper or lower headset race, insert a hardwood stick or soft punch into the frame's head tube and carefully tap the race out from the inside. After it is started, tap around the race so that neither the race nor the head tube is damaged.

To install the headset race, tap it in slowly with a block of wood or suitable size socket or piece of pipe (**Figure 59**). Make sure they are squarely seated in the race bores before tapping them in. Tap them in until they are flush with the steering head.

Steering Head Assembly

Refer to **Figure 56** for this procedure.

1. Make sure the steering head races and stem lower bearing are properly seated.

2. Apply a coat of bearing grease to both tapered roller bearings. Carefully work the grease into the rollers.

3. Install the steering stem into the head tube and hold it firmly in place.

4. Install the upper bearing into the steering head race. Push the bearing down to seat it in the race.

5. Install the bearing cover (E, **Figure 57**).

6A. On XT600 models, install and tighten the steering stem adjusting nut as follows:

a. Install the steering stem adjusting nut. To prevent from over tightening the adjusting nut, use the Yamaha ring nut wrench (part No. YU-33975) and a torque wrench.
b. Engage the ring nut wrench with the adjusting nut. Attach a torque wrench onto the end of the ring nut wrench so that both wrenches form a right angle.
c. Tighten the adjust nut to the torque specification listed in **Table 3**. If you do not have the ring nut wrench, tighten the adjust nut with a spanner wrench (**Figure 60**) securely.
d. After the steering stem is tightened, check the bearing play. The adjusting nut should be just tight enough to remove play, both horizontal and vertical yet loose enough so that the assembly will turn to both lock positions under its own weight after an assist.

6B. On TT600 models, install and tighten the steering stem adjusting nut as follows:

a. Install the steering stem adjusting nut.
b. The adjust nut should be tightened to an initial torque of 30 N•m (22 ft.-lb.) to seat the bearings. To prevent from over tightening the adjust nut, use the Yamaha ring nut wrench (part No. YU-33975) and a torque wrench. Engage the ring nut wrench with the adjust nut. Attach a torque wrench onto the end of the ring nut wrench so that both wrenches form a right angle.
c. Tighten the adjust nut to 30 N•m (22 ft.-lb.). If you do not have the ring nut wrench, tighten the adjust nut with a spanner wrench (**Figure 60**) securely.
d. Loosen the adjust nut one turn, rotate the steering stem from side-to-side several times. Then tighten the adjusting nut to approximately 10 N•m (7.2 ft.-lb.).
e. Check the bearing play. The adjusting nut should be just tight enough to remove play, both horizontal and vertical yet loose enough so that the assembly will turn to both lock positions under its own weight after an assist.

7. Install the upper fork bridge (C, **Figure 57**).

8A. On XT600 models, install the steering bolt (B, **Figure 57**) only finger-tight at this time.

8B. On TT600 models, install the steering nut (A, **Figure 58**) only finger-tight at this time.

9. Slide both fork tubes into position as described in this chapter and tighten *only the lower pinch bolts* to the torque specification in **Table 3**. This is necessary to properly align the upper and lower fork bridges in relation to the front forks.

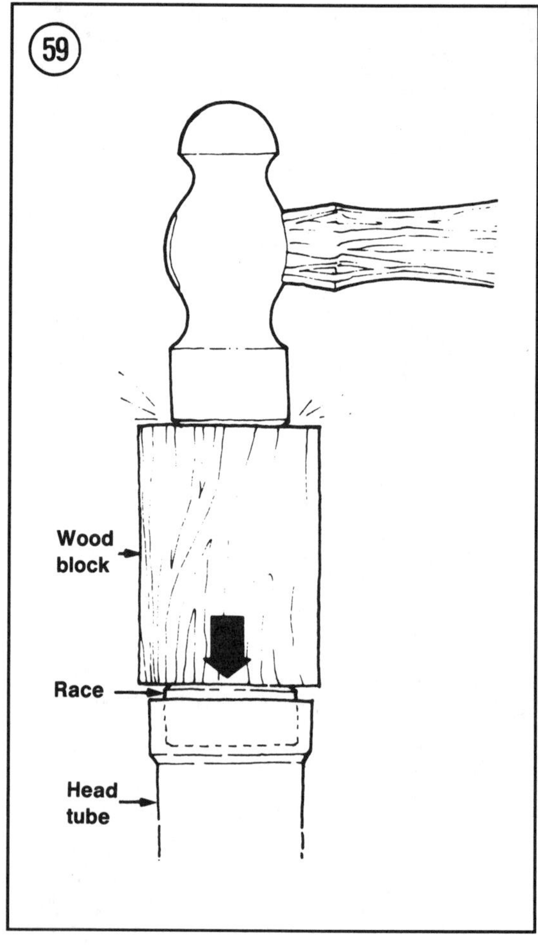

10. Have an assistant hold onto the front fork assemblies and tighten the steering stem bolt to the torque specification in **Table 3**.
11. Tighten the upper fork pinch bolts to the torque specification in **Table 3**.
12. Install the handlebar as described in this chapter.
13. Install the meter housing assembly as described under *Indicator Bulb Replacement and Meter Housing Removal/Installation* in Chapter Nine.
14. Install the headlight assembly as described under *Headlight Mounting Bracket Removal/Installation* in Chapter Nine.
15. Install the front fender as described in Chapter Thirteen.
16. Install the front wheel as described in this chapter.
17. After a few hours of riding, the bearings have had a chance to seat; readjust the free play in the steering stem with the steering stem adjusting nut.

Steering Adjustment

1. Raise the front wheel off the ground. Support the motorcycle securely under the engine.

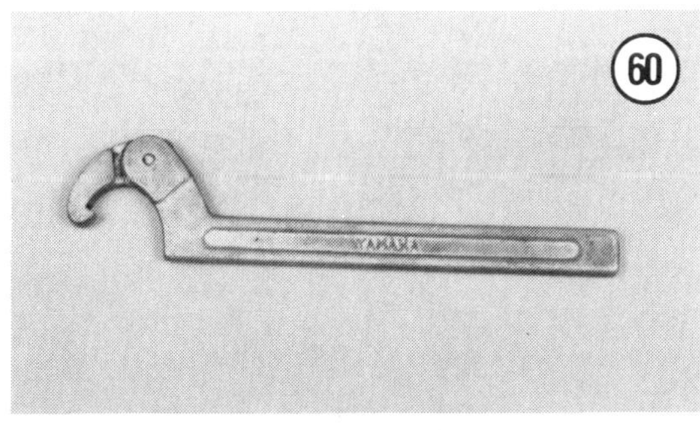

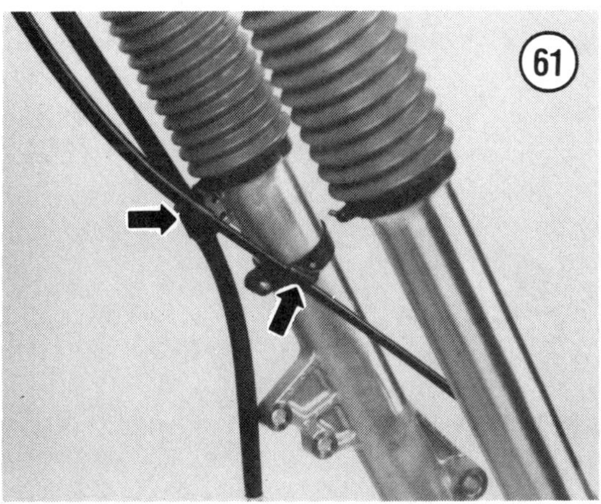

2. Loosen the lower fork tube pinch bolts.
3. Loosen the steering stem bolt (XT600) or nut (TT600).
4. Turn the steering stem adjusting nut with a spanner wrench or punch until you just feel the steering play taken up.
5. Tighten all steering bolts to the torque specifications in **Table 3**.
6. Recheck the steering play.
7. Tighten all bolts to the torque specifications in **Table 3**.

FRONT FORK (XT600)

The Yamaha front forks are spring-controlled and hydraulically damped. The damping rate is determined by the viscosity (weight) of the oil used, and the spring rate can be altered by varying the amount of oil used and by air pressurization of the forks. Before suspecting major trouble with the front forks, drain the fork oil and refill with the proper type and quantity. If you still have trouble, such as poor damping, tendency to bottom out or top out, or leakage around the rubber seals, then follow the service procedures in this section.

To simplify fork service and to prevent the mixing of parts, the fork legs should be removed, serviced and reinstalled individually.

Each front fork leg consists of the fork tube (inner tube), slider (outer tube), fork spring, damper rod with its damper components and bushings.

If the front forks are going to be removed without disassembly, perform the *Removal/Installation* procedure in this chapter. If the front forks require disassembly, refer to *Disassembly* in this chapter.

Removal/Installation

1. Remove the front wheel as described in this chapter.
2. Remove the front brake caliper as described under *Front Brake Caliper Removal/Installation* in Chapter Twelve.
3. Loosen the clamps securing the front brake hose and the speedometer cable to the left-hand fork slider (**Figure 61**).

4. Remove the air valve cap (**Figure 62**) from both fork tubes.

WARNING
Always bleed off all air pressure; failure to do so may cause personal injury when disassembling the fork assembly.

WARNING
Release the air pressure gradually. If released too fast, fork oil will spurt out with the air. Protect your eyes and clothing accordingly.

5. Depress the air valve and release *all* fork air pressure.

6A. If the fork assembly is going to be disassembled, perform the following:

a. Loosen the upper (A, **Figure 63**) fork bridge pinch bolts.
b. Loosen the fork cap bolt (B, **Figure 63**).

6B. If the fork assembly is just going to be removed, loosen the upper and lower fork bridge pinch bolts (**Figure 64**).

7. Twist the upper fork tube and slide the fork tube out of the upper and lower fork bridge (**Figure 65**).

8. Repeat for the opposite side.

9. Install by reversing these removal steps. Note the following.

10. Position the fork tube as follows:

a. Make sure the top surface of the fork tube is flush with the upper fork bridge (**Figure 66**).
b. Position the air valve so it is at a 45° angle from straight ahead (**Figure 67**). This is necessary for easy access to the air valve for pressurization.

11A. If the fork was disassembled for service, perform the following:

a. Tighten the *lower* fork bridge pinch bolts sufficiently to hold the fork tube from turning while tightening the top cap bolt.
b. Tighten the top cap bolt to the torque specification in **Table 3**.
c. Tighten the upper and lower fork bridge pinch bolts to the torque specification in **Table 3**.

11B. If the fork assemblies were not disassembled, tighten the upper and lower fork bridge pinch bolts to the torque specification in **Table 3**.

12. Position the front brake hose and the speedometer cable into their respective clamps on the left-hand fork slider (**Figure 61**) and tighten the clamps securely.

62

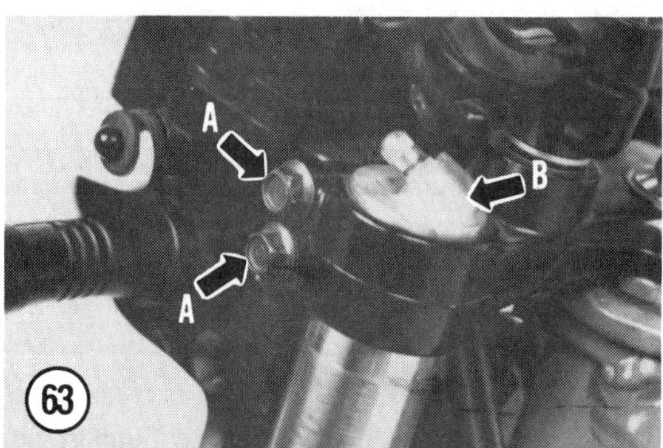

63

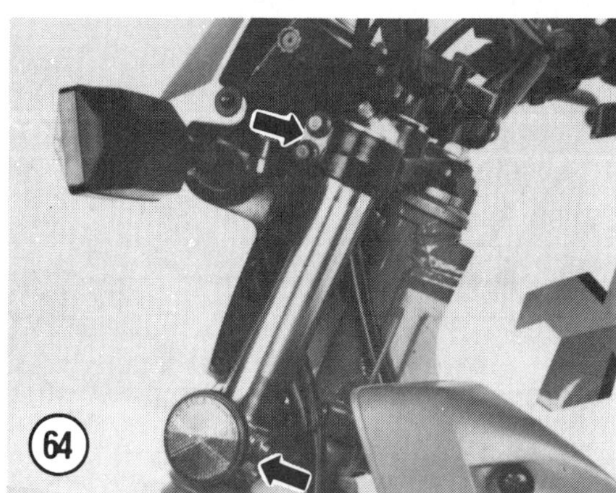

64

65

13. Install the front wheel as described in this chapter.
14. Install the front brake caliper as described under *Front Brake Caliper Removal/Installation* in Chapter Twelve.

WARNING
*After installing the front brake caliper, squeeze the front brake lever. If the brake lever feels spongy, bleed the brake as described under **Bleeding the System** in Chapter Twelve.*

15. Place wood blocks under the engine so the front wheel is off the ground.

WARNING
During the next step, never use any type of compressed gas as an explosion may be lethal. Never heat the fork assembly with a torch or place it near an open flame or extreme heat, as this will also result in an explosion.

CAUTION
Never exceed the maximum air pressure of 98.1 kPa (14.2 psi) as damage may occur to internal components of the fork assembly.

NOTE
The maximum allowable difference in air pressure between the 2 fork assemblies is 9.81 kPa (1.4 psi). If the pressure differential is greater, the handling characteristics will be affected.

16. Inflate the forks to within the specifications listed in **Table 1**. Do not use compressed air; use only a small hand-operated air pump (**Figure 68**).
17. Remove the wood blocks from under the engine, apply the front brake lever and pump the forks several times. Recheck the air pressure and readjust if necessary.

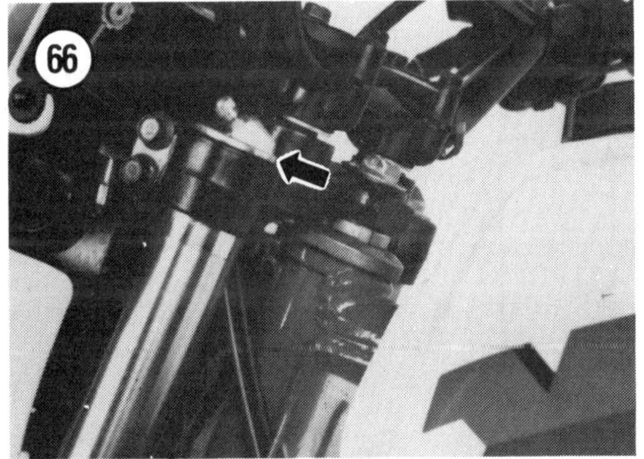
66

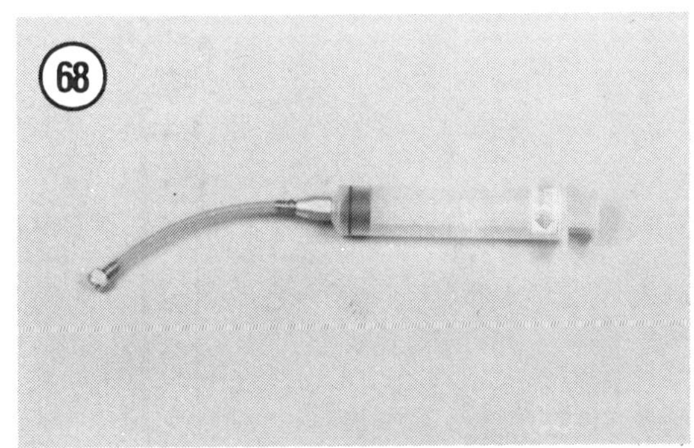
68

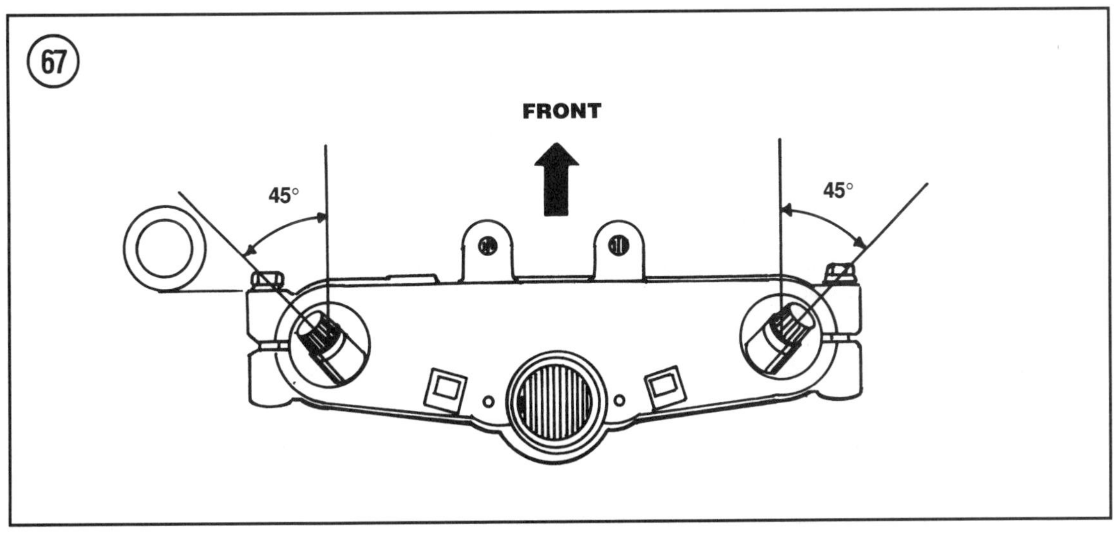
67

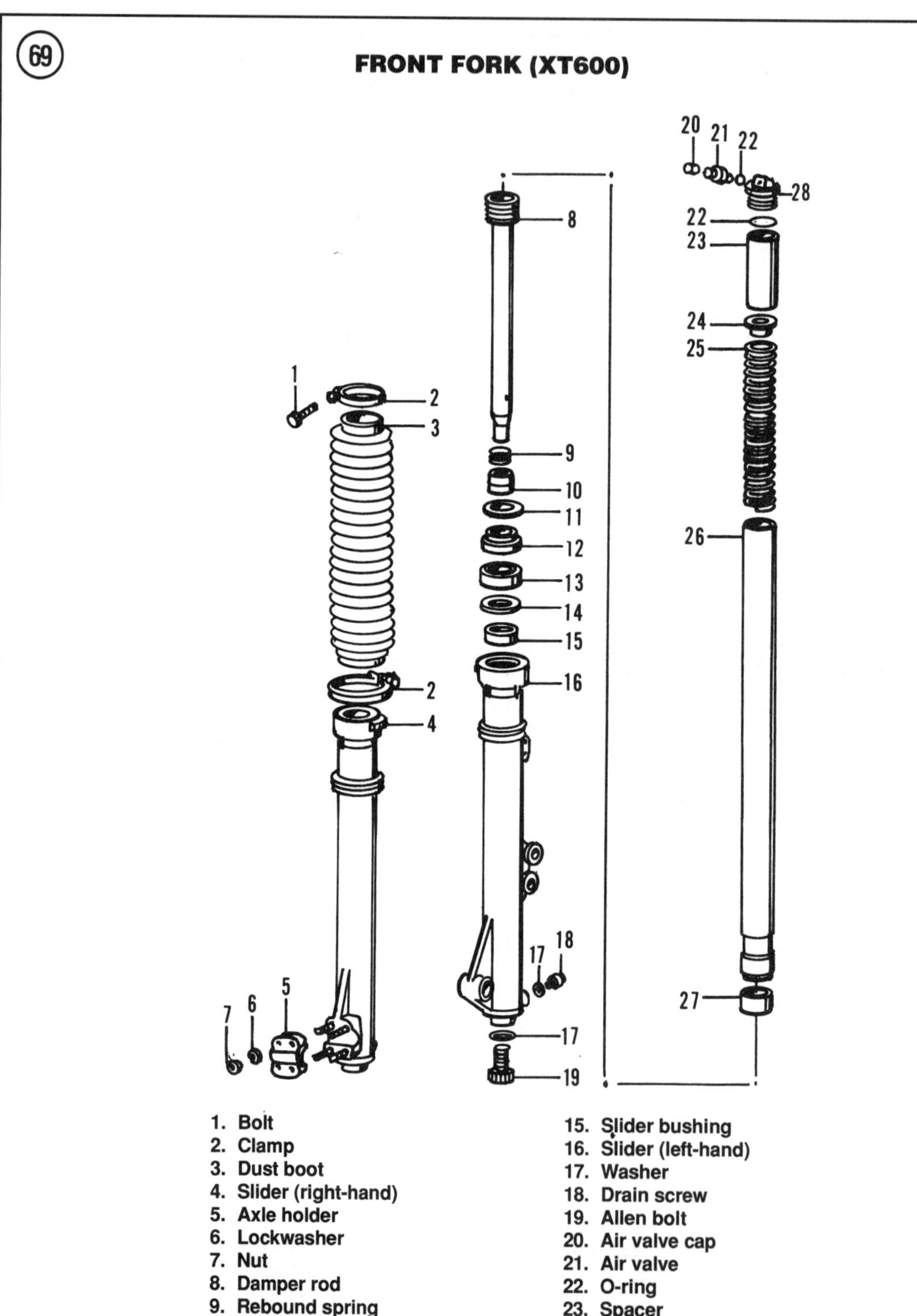

1. Bolt
2. Clamp
3. Dust boot
4. Slider (right-hand)
5. Axle holder
6. Lockwasher
7. Nut
8. Damper rod
9. Rebound spring
10. Oil lock piece
11. Clip
12. Dust seal
13. Oil seal
14. Washer
15. Slider bushing
16. Slider (left-hand)
17. Washer
18. Drain screw
19. Allen bolt
20. Air valve cap
21. Air valve
22. O-ring
23. Spacer
24. Upper spring seat
25. Spring
26. Fork tube
27. Fork tube bushing
28. Top cap bolt

Disassembly

Refer to **Figure 69** for this procedure.

Fork tube disassembly is easier if Steps 1-4 of this procedure is performed while the fork tubes are mounted on the bike.

NOTE
If you recycle your old engine oil, ***never*** *add used fork oil to the old engine oil. Most oil retailers that accepts old oil for recycling may not accept the oil if other fluids (fork oil, brake fluid or any other type of petroleum based fluids) have been combined with it.*

1. Remove the air valve cap (**Figure 62**) from both fork tubes.

WARNING
Always bleed off all air pressure; failure to do so may cause personal injury when disassembling the fork assembly.

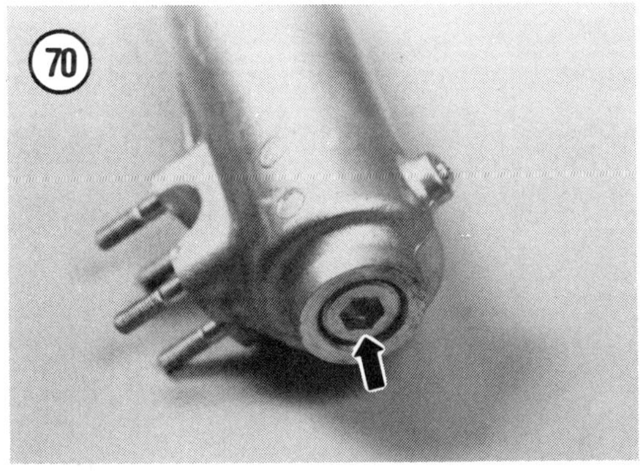
70

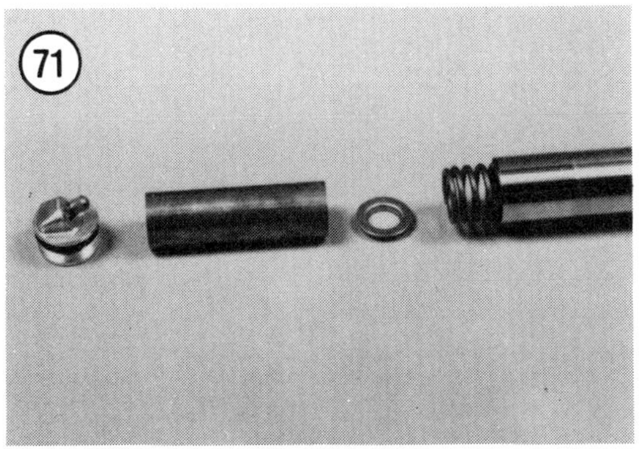
71

WARNING
Release the air pressure gradually. If released too fast, fork oil will spurt out with the air. Protect your eyes and clothing accordingly.

2. Depress the air valve and release *all* fork air pressure.

NOTE
The fork slider bottom Allen bolt is secured with a locking agent and is hard to remove. If a heavy duty air powered impact wrench is available, try that first. If necessary, you may be able to keep the damper rod inside from turning with the fork spring, spring seat, spacer and fork cap installed, and at the same time having an assistant compress the fork while you try to loosen the bottom bolt. If these methods are not successful, you will have to remove the fork assembly and use special Yamaha tools as described later in this procedure.

3. To loosen the fork slider bottom Allen bolt with the fork assembly still installed on the bike, perform the following:
   a. Have an assistant sit on the bike and push down on the handlebar to compress the fork spring.

   NOTE
   In the following step, loosen but do not remove the fork tube Allen bolt as the fork oil will drain out. When the bolt is loosened, some fork oil may drip out. If this happens, tighten the bolt by hand to stop the dripping.

   b. First try to loosen the bottom bolt with an Allen wrench and socket wrench. If the bolt will not loosen, proceed to Step 3c.
   c. Use a heavy duty air powered impact wrench and loosen the fork slider bottom bolt.
4. Remove the forks as described in this chapter.
5. Remove the fork slider bottom Allen bolt (**Figure 70**).
6. Remove the fork cap bolt, spacer and spring seat (**Figure 71**).
7. Remove the fork spring.
8. Turn the fork assembly upside down and drain out the fork oil.

9. If you were unable to previously loosen the slider bottom Allen bolt, perform the following:

a. Install the damper rod holder (part No. YM-01327) onto the long T-handle (part No. YM-01301). You can substitute the long T-handle with a short socket wrench and a very long 3/8 in. drive extension.
b. Insert the damper rod holder into the hex fitting on top of the damper rod and hold the damper rod steady with the T-handle.
c. Loosen the fork slider bottom bolt (**Figure 70**) and remove the Allen bolt and gasket.

10. Loosen the clamps on the dust boot and slide boot (**Figure 72**) up and off of the fork tube.

11. Remove the clip (A, **Figure 73**) securing the dust seal and oil seal (B, **Figure 73**) into the slider.

12. There is an interference fit between the bushing in the fork slider and the bushing on the fork tube. In order to remove the slider from the fork tube, pull hard on the slider using quick in-and-out strokes. Doing this will withdraw the dust seal, oil seal, plate washer and slider bushing.

13. Separate the slider from the fork tube.

14. Remove the oil lock piece from the end of the damper rod.

15. Slide the damper rod and spring out of the fork tube.

16. Slide off the dust seal, oil seal, washer and slide bushing off of the fork tube.

Inspection

1. Thoroughly clean all parts in solvent and dry them.

2. Check both fork tubes for wear or scratches.

3. Check the fork tube for straightness. If the fork tube is slightly bent, it may be straightened with a hydraulic press. If the fork tube is bent to the point

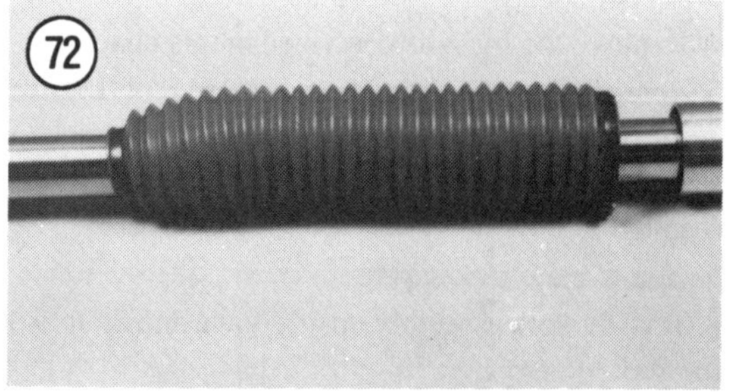

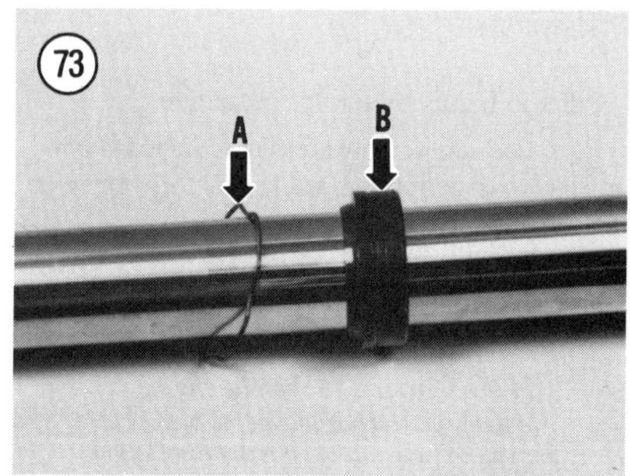

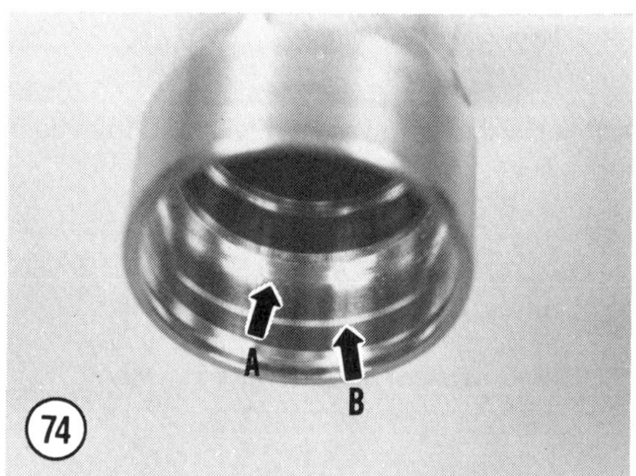

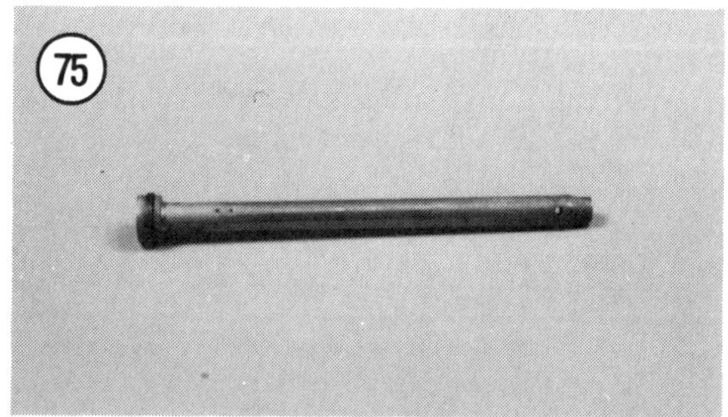

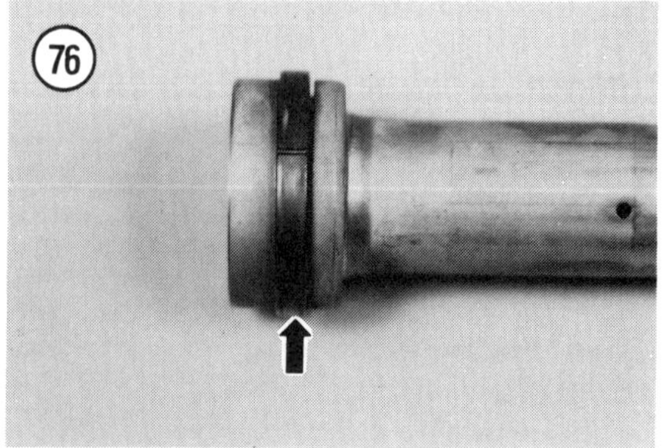

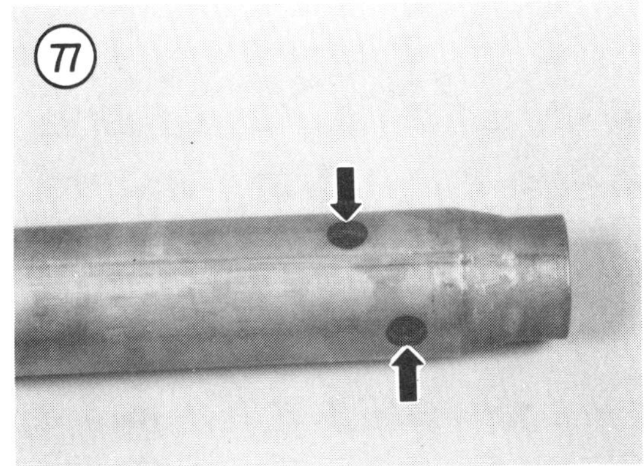

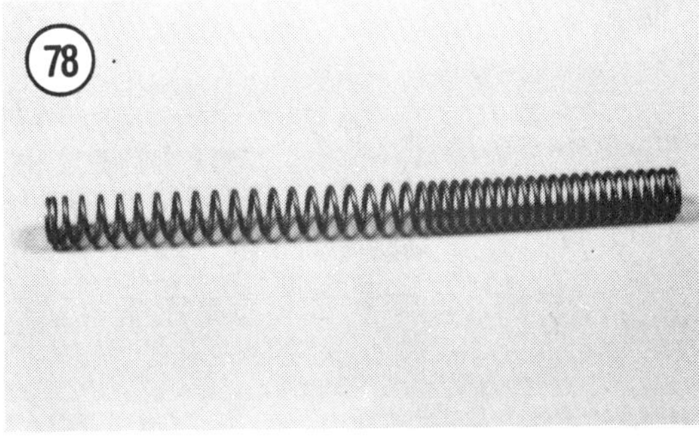

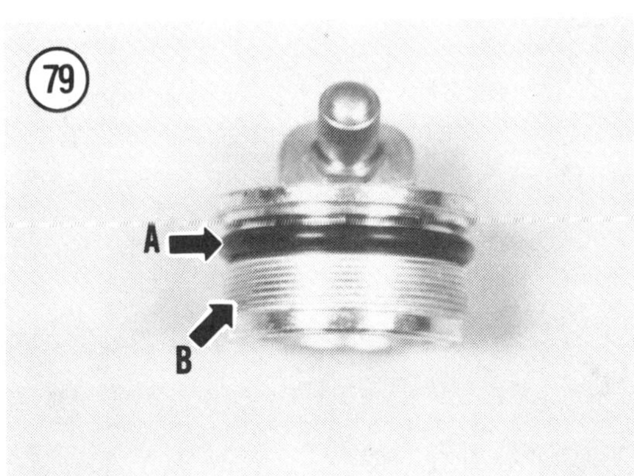

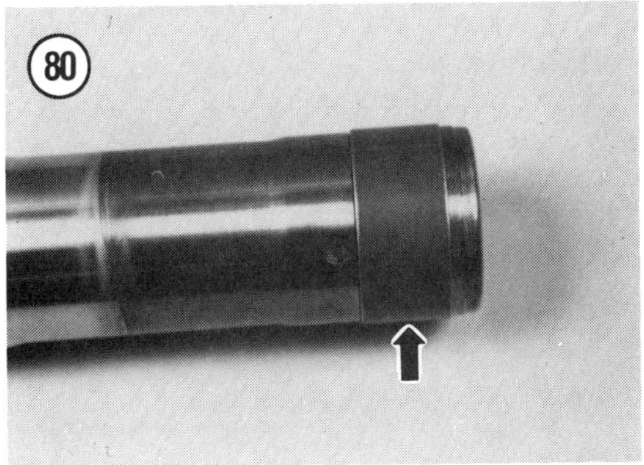

that it has creased or the chrome has flaked, the fork tube must be replaced.

4. Check the oil seal area in the slider (A, **Figure 74**) for dents or other damage that would allow oil leakage. Check the clip groove (B, **Figure 74**) in the slider for cracks or other damage. Replace the slider if necessary.

5. Check the damper rod (**Figure 75**) for straightness by rolling it on a flat surface. Replace the rod if bent or otherwise damaged.

6. Check the damper rod piston ring (**Figure 76**) for damage.

7. Make sure the oil passages (**Figure 77**) in the damper rod are open and free of dirt or foreign matter. Clean out if necessary with solvent and blow dry with compressed air.

NOTE

If an aftermarket fork spring has been installed, the un-compressed length may differ from the stock Yamaha fork spring. Refer to manufacturer's literature for spring length.

8. Measure the un-compressed length of the stock Yamaha fork spring (**Figure 78**) with a tape measure and compare to specifications in **Table 1**. Replace the fork spring if it has sagged to the service limit or less.

9. Replace the fork cap bolt O-ring (A, **Figure 79**) if deformed or damaged.

10. Inspect the fork cap bolt threads (B, **Figure 79**) for wear or damage. Clean them up with the proper size tap or replace the fork cap bolt if necessary.

11. Check the fork tube Allen bolt washer for damage that would allow oil leakage; replace if necessary.

12. Inspect the fork tube bushing (**Figure 80**) and slider bushing (A, **Figure 81**). If the Teflon coating

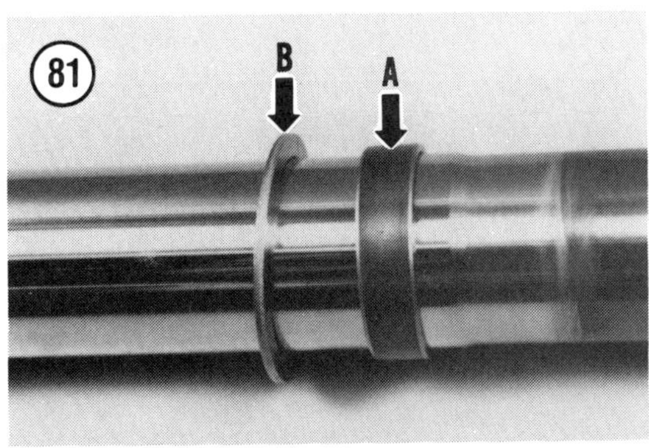

10

is worn off so that the copper base material is showing on approximately 3/4 of the total surface, the bushing must be replaced.

13. Check the oil seal (**Figure 82**) and dust seal for tears or other damage that would allow oil leakage. Replace both seals if necessary.

14. Inspect the threads on the front axle holder studs (**Figure 83**) for wear or damage. Clean them up with the proper size tap or replace the fork slider if necessary. The studs are not available separately from Yamaha.

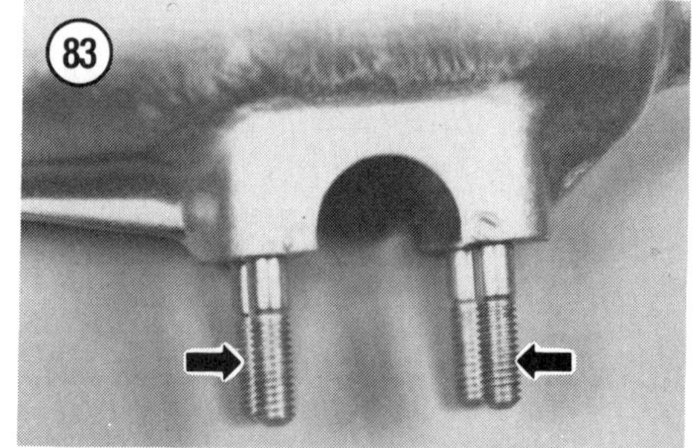

Assembly

Refer to **Figure 69** for this procedure.

1. Slide the spring (**Figure 84**) onto the damper rod and insert the damper rod and spring into the fork tube (**Figure 85**).

2. Slide the oil lock piece (**Figure 86**) onto the end of the damper rod.

3. Install the fork tube assembly into the fork slider (**Figure 87**). Push the fork tube down until the damper rod bottoms out on the slider.

4. Position the fork spring with the closer wound coils toward the top and insert the fork spring (**Figure 88**) into the fork tube.

5. Temporarily install the spring seat, spacer and fork cap bolt (**Figure 71**) into the fork tube. Tighten the fork cap bolt by hand until it seats. Do not tighten with a wrench as it will be removed to add fork oil later in this procedure.

6. Make sure the gasket (A, **Figure 89**) is on the Allen bolt (B, **Figure 89**).

7. Apply blue Loctite 242 to the threads on the Allen bolt. Install the Allen bolt (**Figure 70**) and tighten to the torque specification listed in **Table 3**.

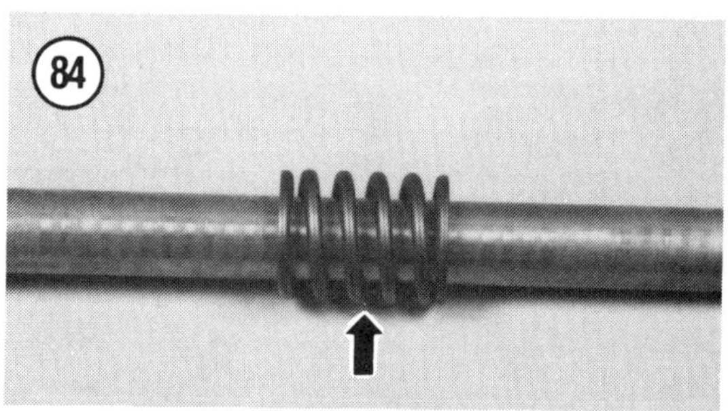

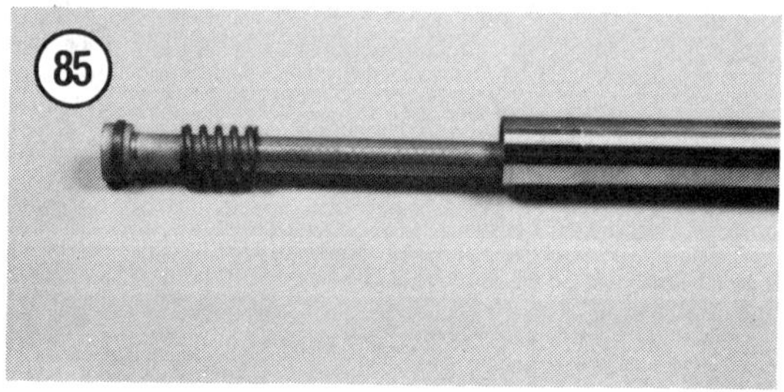

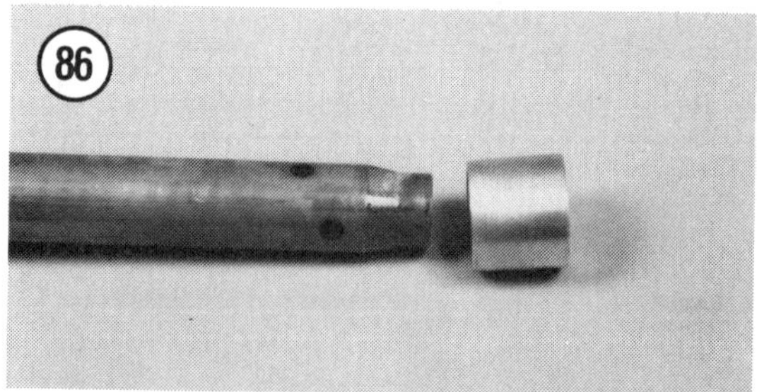

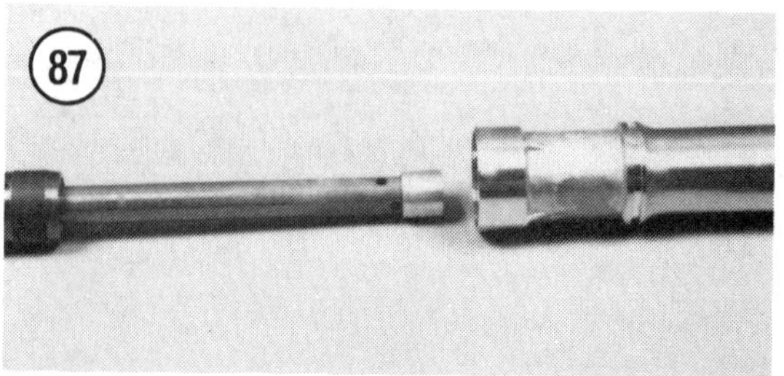

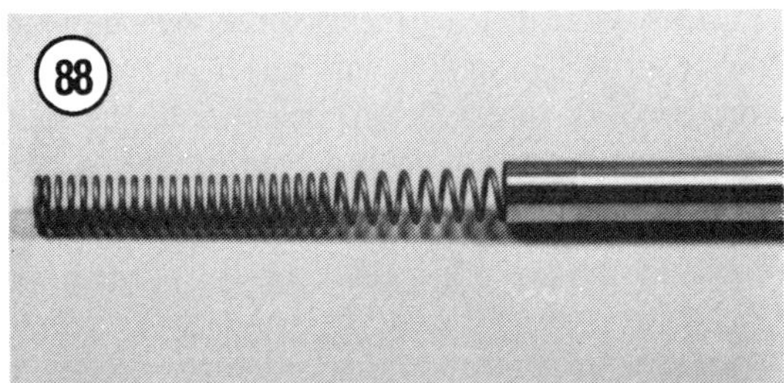

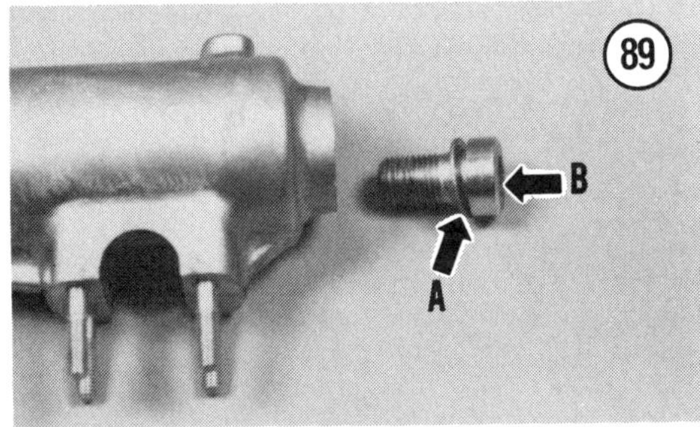

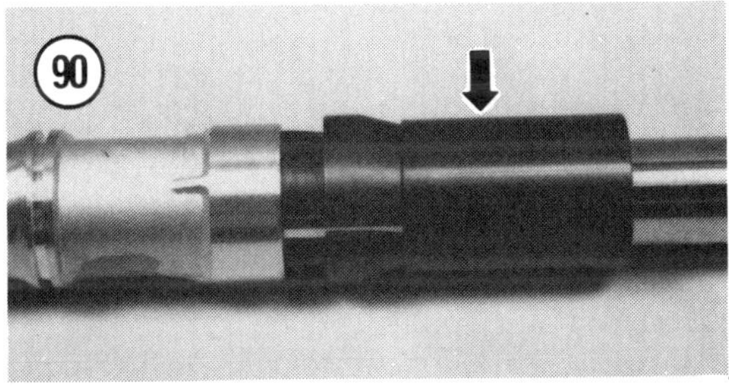

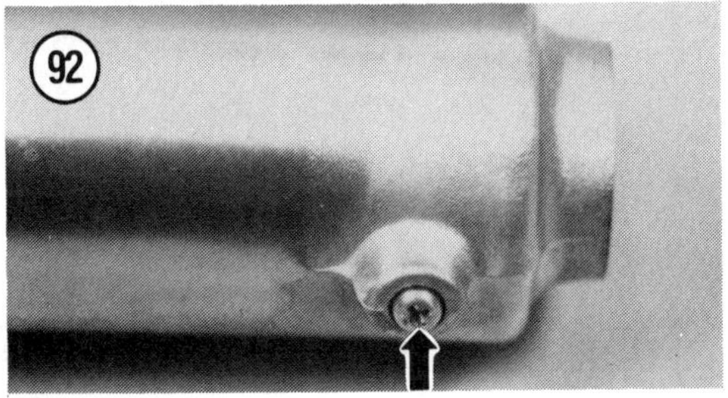

8. Slide the slider bushing (A, **Figure 81**) and washer (B, **Figure 81**) over the fork tube.

NOTE

Some type of fork seal driver is required to install the guide bushing, oil seal and dust seal. Yamaha sells a fork seal driver set (part No. YM-08020). The adjustable fork seal driver shown in ***Figure 90*** *is made by Suzuki and can be used on almost all Japanese fork assemblies (including Japanese "Showa" forks equipped on some late model Harleys).*

NOTE

If you do not have a special tool, the guide bushing and oil seals can be installed with a piece of pipe or other piece of tubing that fits over the fork tube. If both ends of the pipe are threaded, wrap one end with duct tape to prevent the threads from damaging the interior of the slider.

9. Tap the slider bushing into the slider until it bottoms.
10. Move the washer down the fork tube until it rests against the bushing.
11. Position the oil seal with the marking facing upward and slide down onto the fork tube.
12. Slide the dust seal onto the fork tube and rest it on top of the oil seal.
13. Drive the oil and dust seals (B, **Figure 73**) into the slider with the fork seal driver (**Figure 90**). Drive the seals into the slider until they rest against the washer and are below the clip groove in the slider.

NOTE

Make sure the groove in the slider can be seen above the dust seal. If not, the bushing, oil seal and dust seal will have to be driven farther into the slider.

14. Slide the clip (A, **Figure 73**) down the fork tube and seat it in the slider groove. Make sure the clip is completely seated in the groove.
15. Install the dust boot onto the fork tube.
16. Make sure the drain screw O-ring seal (**Figure 91**) is in the receptacle in the fork slider.
17. Install the drain screw (**Figure 92**) and tighten securely.
18. Remove the fork cap bolt, spacer and spring seat.
19. Remove the fork spring.

20. Fill the fork tube with the correct quantity and weight fork oil as described in Chapter Three.
21. Hold the fork assembly upright.
22. Position the fork spring with the closer wound coils toward the top and insert the fork spring (**Figure 88**) into the fork tube.
23. Install the spring seat, spacer and fork cap bolt (**Figure 71**) into the fork tube. Tighten the fork cap bolt by hand securely. Do not tighten with a wrench as it will be tightened after the fork assembly is installed on the bike.
24. Install the fork tubes onto the motorcycle as described in this chapter.

FRONT FORK (TT600)

The Yamaha front fork is spring-controlled and hydraulically damped. The damping rate is determined by the viscosity (weight) of the oil used, and the spring rate can be altered by varying the amount of oil used and by air pressurization of the fork. Before suspecting major trouble with the front fork, drain the fork oil and refill with the proper type and quantity. If you still have trouble, such as poor damping, tendency to bottom out or top out, or leakage around the rubber seals, then follow the service procedures in this section.

To simplify fork service and to prevent the mixing of parts, the legs should be removed, serviced and reinstalled individually.

Each front fork leg consists of the fork tube (inner tube), slider (outer tube), fork spring, damper rod with its damper components and bushings.

If the front fork is going to be removed without disassembly, perform the *Removal/Installation* procedure in this chapter. If the front fork requires disassembly, refer to *Disassembly* in this chapter.

Removal/Installation

1. On 1985-1986 models, disconnect the front brake hose at the left-hand fork tube.
2. Disconnect the speedometer cable at the right-hand fork tube (**Figure 93**).
3. Remove the front wheel as described in this chapter.
4. On 1985-1986 models, remove the front brake caliper as described under *Front Brake Caliper Removal/Installation* in Chapter Twelve.
5. Measure the distance the fork tube extends above the upper fork bridge. Record this measurement so that the fork tubes can be installed to the same height.

6. Remove the air valve cap (A, **Figure 94**) from both fork tubes.

93

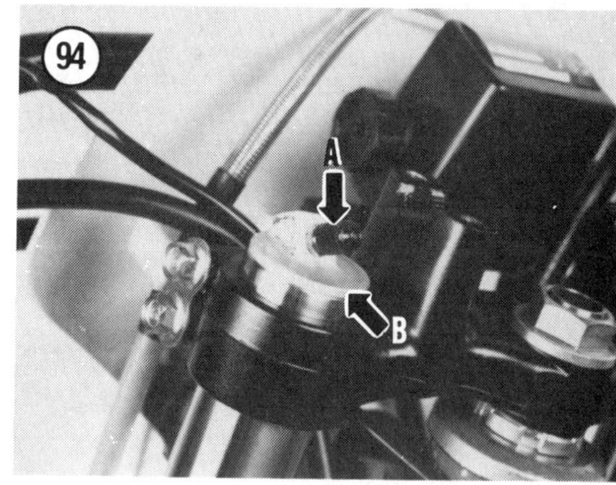
94

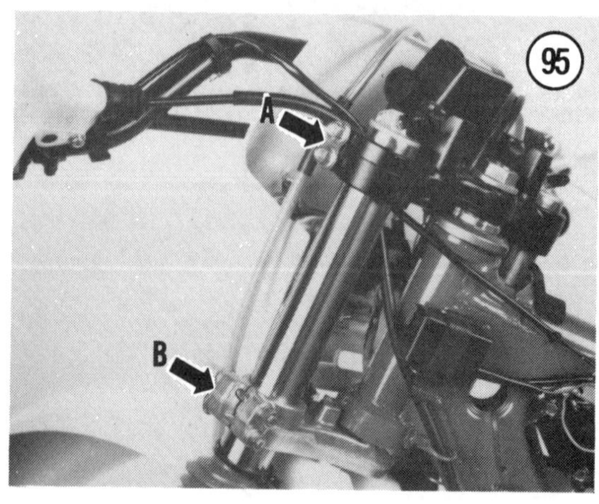
95

WARNING
Always bleed off all air pressure; failure to do so may cause personal injury when disassembling the fork assembly.

WARNING
Release the air pressure gradually. If released too fast, fork oil will spurt out with the air. Protect your eyes and clothing accordingly.

7. Depress the air valve to release all fork air pressure.

8A. If the fork assembly is going to be disassembled, perform the following:

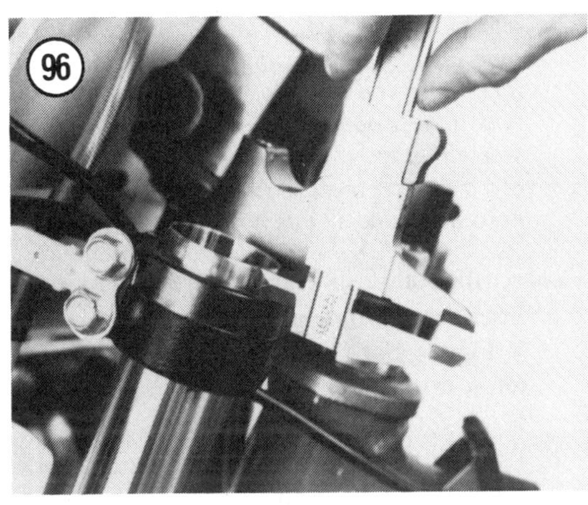

96

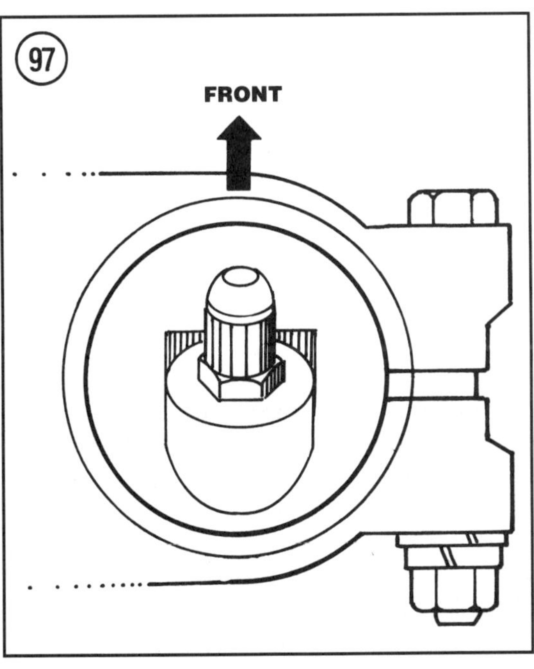

97

a. Loosen the upper (A, **Figure 95**) fork bridge pinch bolts.
b. Loosen the fork cap bolt (B, **Figure 94**).

8B. If the fork assembly is just going to be removed, loosen the upper (A, **Figure 95**) and lower (B, **Figure 95**) fork bridge pinch bolts.

9. Twist the upper fork tube and slide the fork tube out of the steering stem.

10. Repeat for the opposite side.

11. Install by reversing these removal steps. Note the following.

12. Position the fork tube as follows:

a. Make sure the top surface of the fork tube is positioned so that the distance from the upper fork bridge to the top of the fork tube (**Figure 96**) is the same as that recorded during removal.
b. Position the air valve so it is pointed straight ahead (**Figure 97**). This is necessary for easy access to the air valve for pressurization.

13A. If the fork was disassembled for service, perform the following:

a. Tighten the *lower* fork bridge pinch bolts sufficiently to hold the fork tube from turning while tightening the top cap bolt.
b. Tighten the top cap bolt to the torque specification in **Table 3**.
c. Tighten the upper and lower fork bridge pinch bolts to the torque specification in **Table 3**.

13B. If the fork assemblies were not disassembled, tighten the upper and lower fork bridge pinch bolts to the torque specification in **Table 3**.

14. Install the front wheel as described in this chapter.

WARNING
*After installing the front brake caliper, squeeze the front brake lever. If the brake lever feels spongy, bleed the brake as described under **Bleeding the System** in Chapter Twelve.*

15. On 1985-1986 models, install the front brake caliper as described under *Front Brake Caliper Removal/Installation* in Chapter Twelve.

WARNING
During the next step, never use any type of compressed gas as an explosion may be lethal. Never heat the fork assembly with a torch or place it near an open

flame or extreme heat, as this will also result in an explosion.

CAUTION
Never exceed the maximum air pressure of 118.1 kPa (17.0 psi) as damage may occur to internal components of the fork assembly.

NOTE
The maximum allowable difference in air pressure between the 2 fork assemblies is 9.81 kPa (1.4 psi). If the pressure differential is greater, the handling characteristics will be affected.

16. Inflate the forks to within the specifications listed in **Table 1**. Do not use compressed air; use only a small hand-operated air pump (**Figure 68**).

17. Remove the wood blocks from under the engine, apply the front brake lever and pump the forks several times. Recheck the air pressure and readjust if necessary.

Disassembly

Refer to the following illustrations for this procedure:

a. **Figure 98**: 1983-1984 TT600.
b. **Figure 99**: 1985-1986 TT600.

Fork tube disassembly is easier if some of the procedures are performed while the fork tubes are mounted on the bike.

NOTE
*If you recycle your old engine oil, **never** add used fork oil to the old engine oil. Most oil retailers that accepts old oil for recycling may not accept the oil if other fluids (fork oil, brake fluid or any other type of petroleum based fluids) have been combined with it.*

1. Perform Steps 1-4 described under front fork *Removal/Installation.*

2. Remove the air valve cap (A, **Figure 94**) from both fork tubes.

WARNING
Always bleed off all air pressure; failure to do so may cause personal injury when disassembling the fork assembly.

WARNING
Release the air pressure gradually. If released too fast, fork oil will spurt out with the air. Protect your eyes and clothing accordingly.

3. Depress the air valve to release all fork air pressure.

NOTE
The fork slider bottom Allen bolt is secured with a locking agent and is hard to remove. If a heavy duty air powered impact wrench is available, try that first. If necessary, you may be able to keep the damper rod inside from turning with the fork spring, spring seat, spacer and fork cap installed, and at the same time having an assistant compress the fork while you try to loosen the bottom bolt. If these methods are not successful, you will have to remove the fork assembly and use special Yamaha tools as described later in this procedure.

4. Loosen the bottom fork tube Allen bolt as follows:
   a. Insert the axle through the fork tubes as shown in **Figure 100**. This will hold the lower fork tubes in position while loosening the Allen bolt.
   b. Place a drain pan under the fork slider in case some fork oil drains out during the next step.
   c. Loosen but do not remove the fork tube Allen bolt (**Figure 101**).

NOTE
*If these methods are not successful, you will have to remove the fork assembly and keep the damper rod from turning with a special tool. Yamaha sells a long T-handle (part No. YM-01326) and adapter (part No. YM-01300-1). See **Figure 102**. You can substitute the long T-handle with a short T-handle and a long 3/8 in. socket drive extension.*

5. Loosen the top fork tube pinch bolts (**Figure 95**).

6. Loosen and remove the fork cap (B, **Figure 94**).

7. Remove the spacer and the spring seat (**Figure 103**).

8. Remove the fork spring (**Figure 104**).

9. Remove the Allen bolt and gasket from the bottom of the slider (**Figure 101**).

10. Slide the fork boot away from the slider.

(98)

FRONT FORK (TT600—1983-1984)

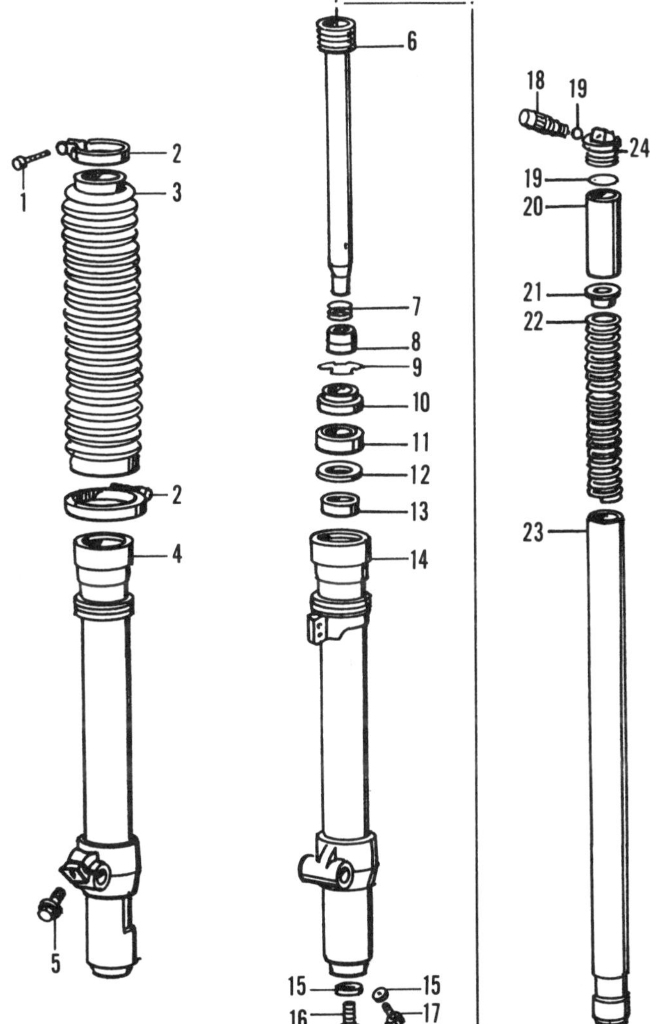

1. Bolt
2. Clamp
3. Dust boot
4. Slider (right-hand)
5. Bolt
6. Damper rod
7. Rebound spring
8. Oil lock piece
9. Clip
10. Dust seal
11. Oil seal
12. Washer
13. Slider bushing
14. Slider (left-hand)
15. Washer
16. Allen bolt
17. Drain screw
18. Air valve
19. O-ring
20. Spacer
21. Upper spring seat
22. Spring
23. Fork tube
24. Top cap bolt

(99)

FRONT FORK (TT600—1985-1986)

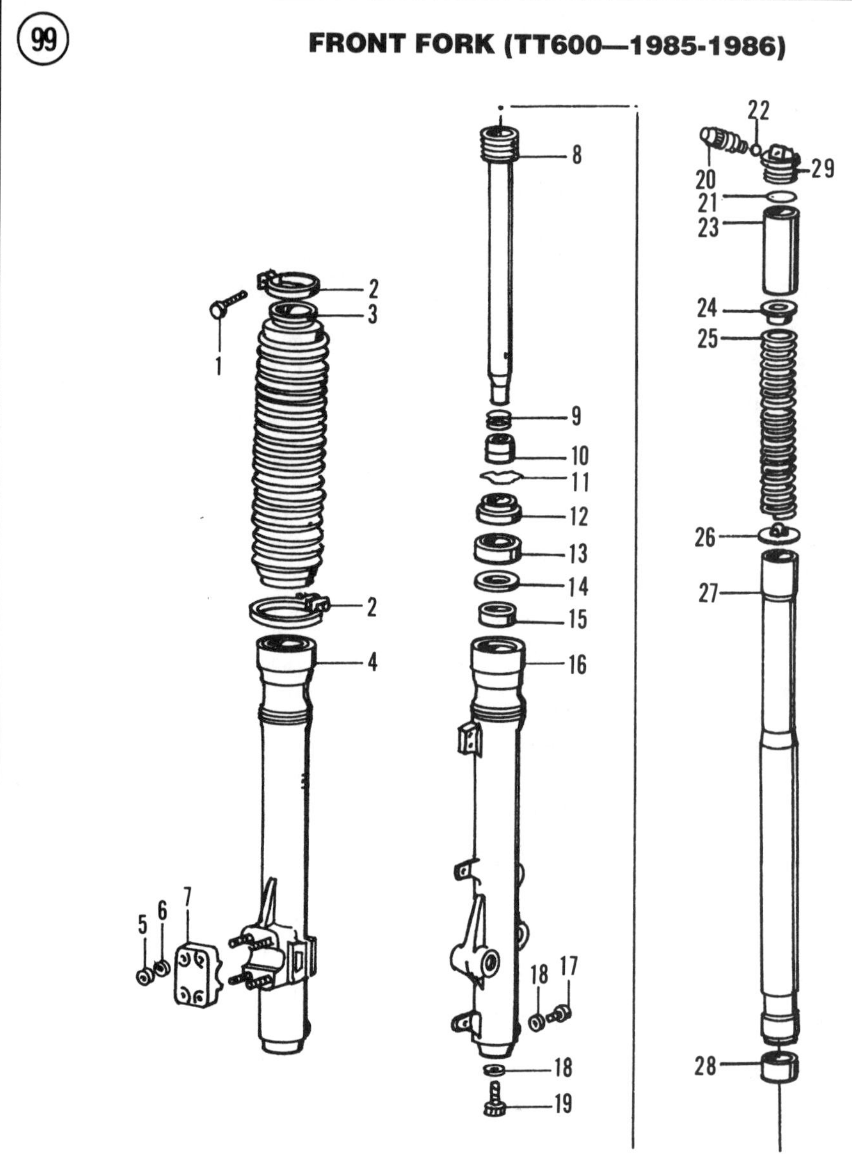

1. Bolt
2. Clamp
3. Dust boot
4. Slider (right-hand)
5. Nut
6. Lockwasher
7. Axle holder
8. Damper rod
9. Rebound spring
10. Oil lock piece
11. Clip
12. Dust seal
13. Oil seal
14. Washer
15. Slider bushing
16. Slider (left-hand)
17. Drain screw
18. Washer
19. Allen bolt
20. Air valve
21. O-ring
22. O-ring
23. Spacer
24. Upper spring seat
25. Spring
26. Lower spring seat
27. Fork tube
28. Fork tube bushing
29. Top cap bolt

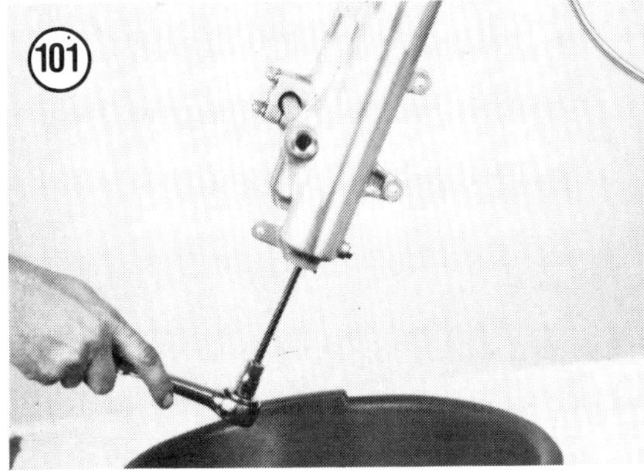

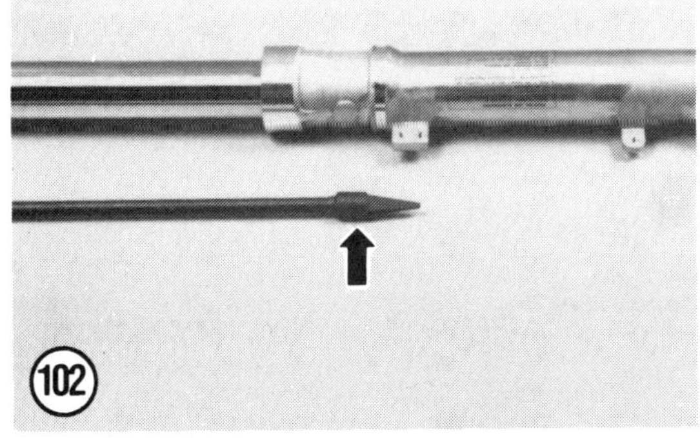

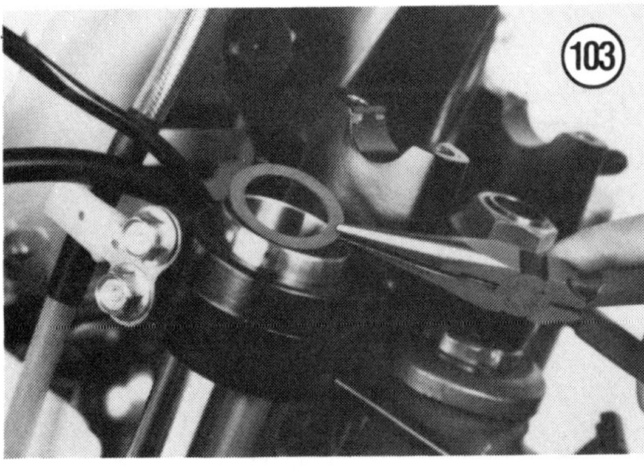

11. Carefully pry the dust seal (**Figure 105**) out of the slider.

12. Remove the clip (**Figure 106**) from the groove in the slider.

13. There is an interference fit between the bushing in the fork slider and the bushing on the fork tube.

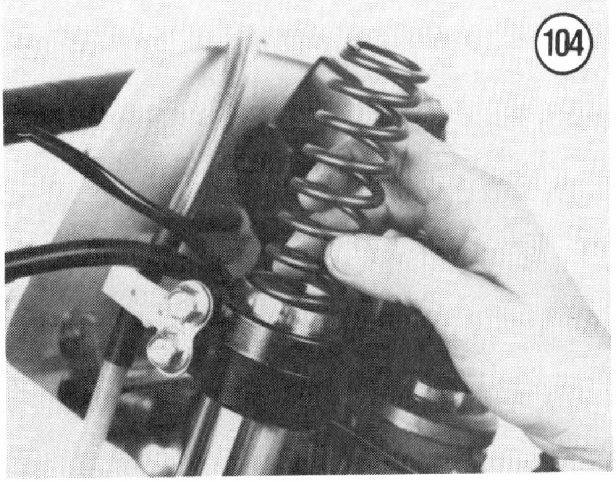

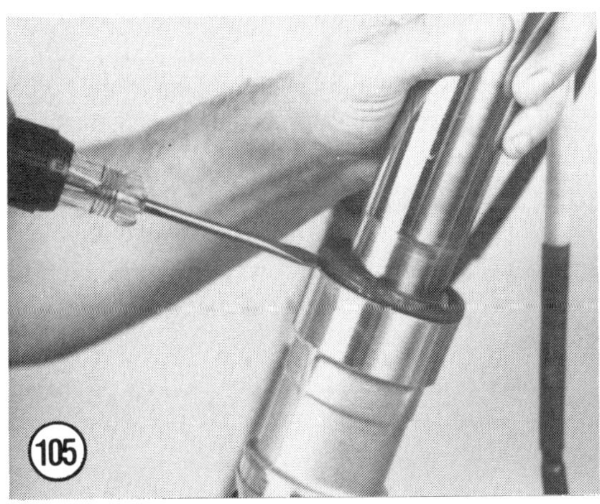

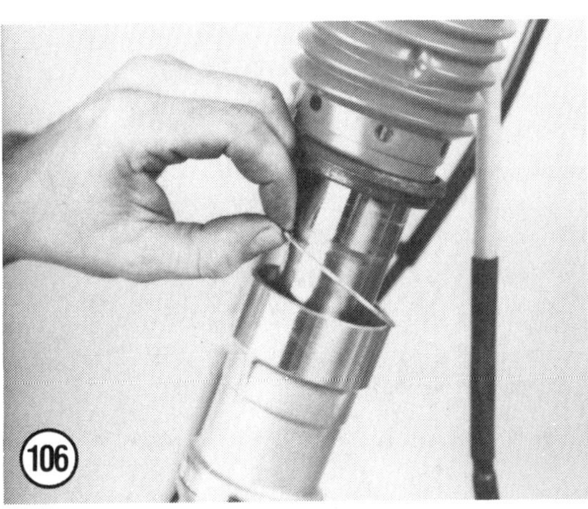

In order to remove the slider from the fork tube, pull hard on the slider using quick in-and-out strokes (**Figure 107**). Doing this will withdraw the dust seal, oil seal, plate washer and guide bushing (**Figure 108**).

14. If it hasn't already fallen off, remove the oil lock piece (**Figure 109**) from the end of the damper rod.

15. Loosen the upper (A, **Figure 95**) and lower (B, **Figure 95**) fork bridge pinch bolts.

16. Remove the fork tube assembly.

17. Slide the damper rod and spring out of the fork tube (**Figure 110**).

18. Slide the dust seal, oil seal, washer and slider bushing off of the fork tube.

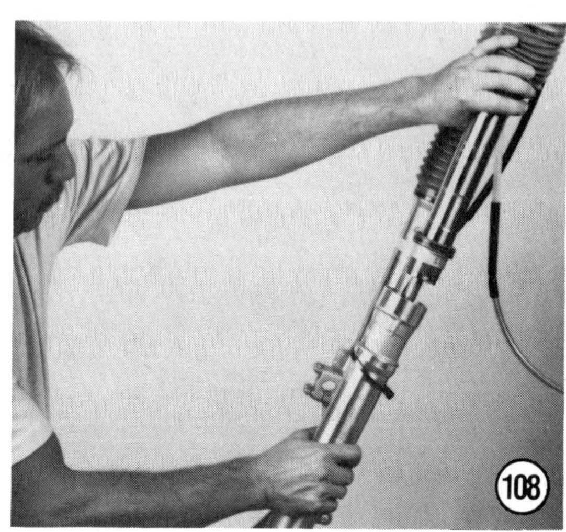

Inspection

1. Thoroughly clean all parts in solvent and dry them.

2. Check both fork tubes for wear or scratches.

3. Check the fork tube for straightness. If the fork tube is slightly bent, it may be straightened with a hydraulic press. If the fork tube is bent to the point that it has creased or the chrome has flaked, the fork tube must be replaced.

4. Check the oil seal area (A, **Figure 111**) in the slider for dents or other damage that would allow oil leakage. Check the clip groove (B, **Figure 111**) in the slider for cracks or other damage. Replace the slider if necessary.

5. Check the damper rod (**Figure 112**) for straightness by rolling it on a flat surface. Replace the rod if bent or otherwise damaged.

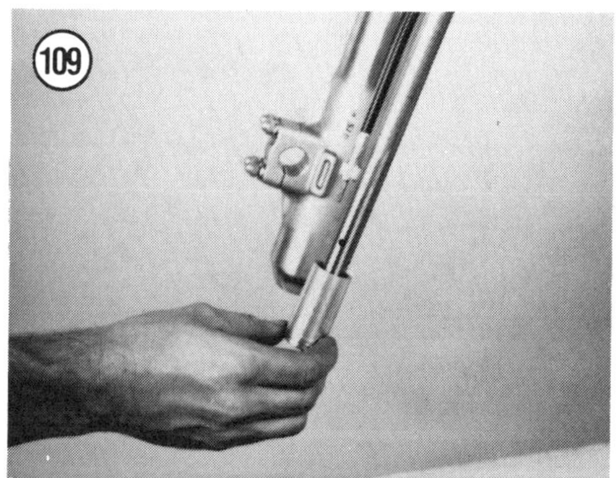

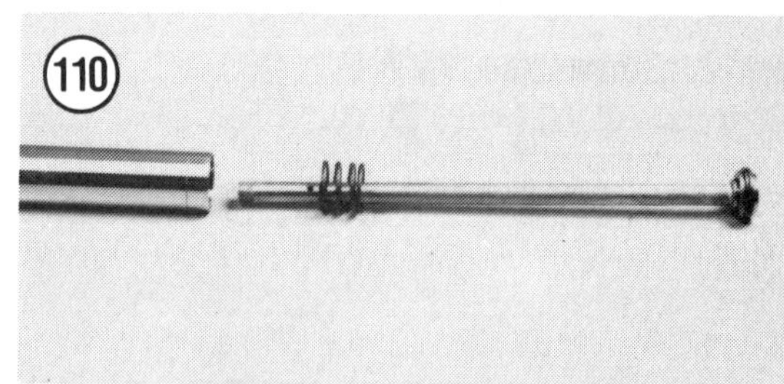

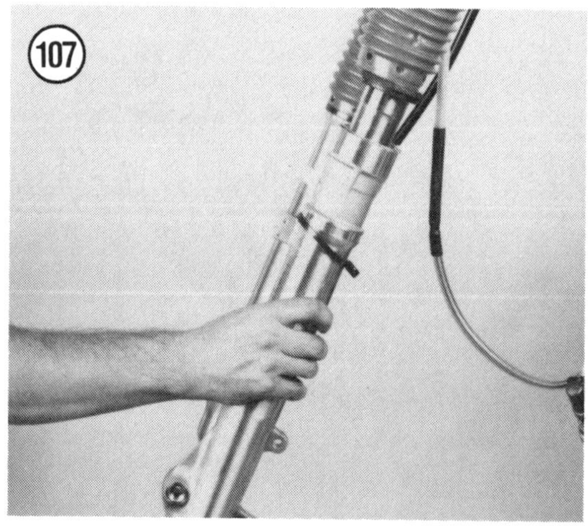

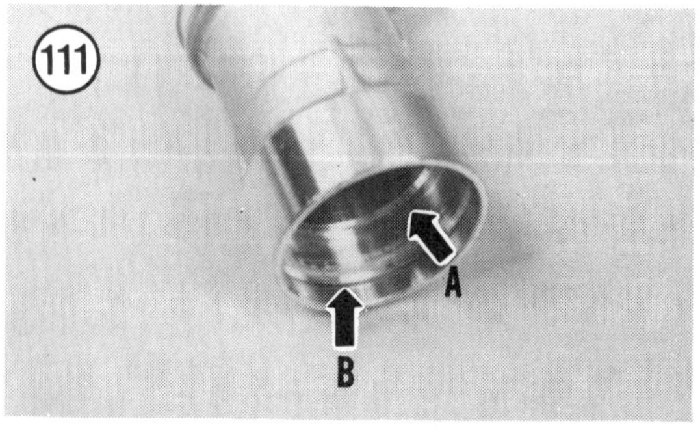

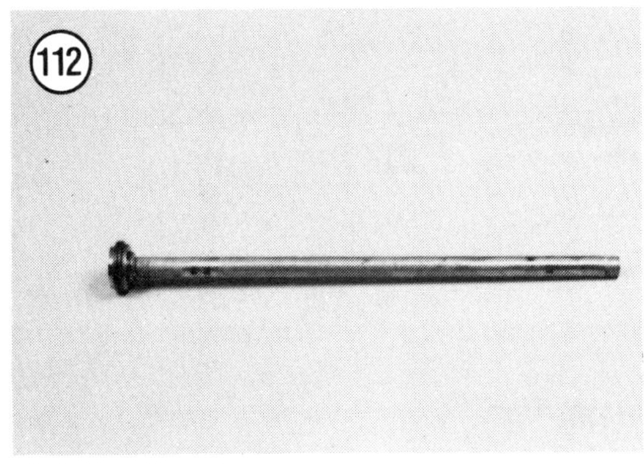

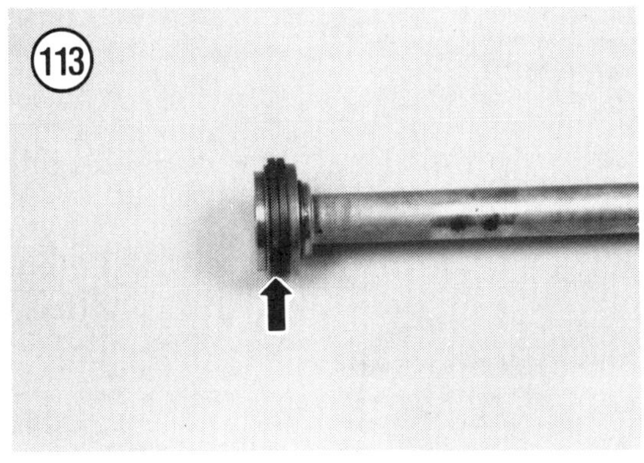

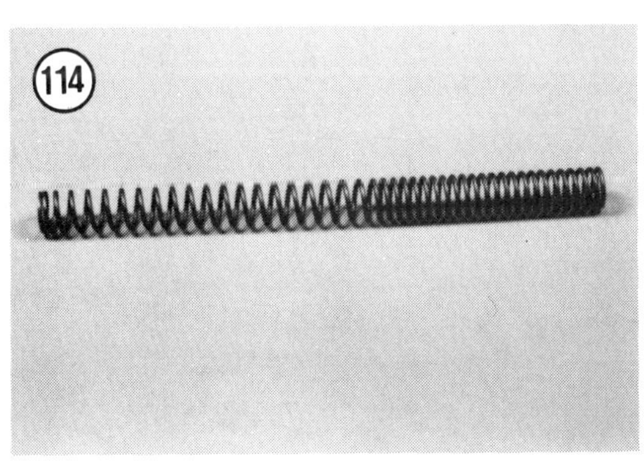

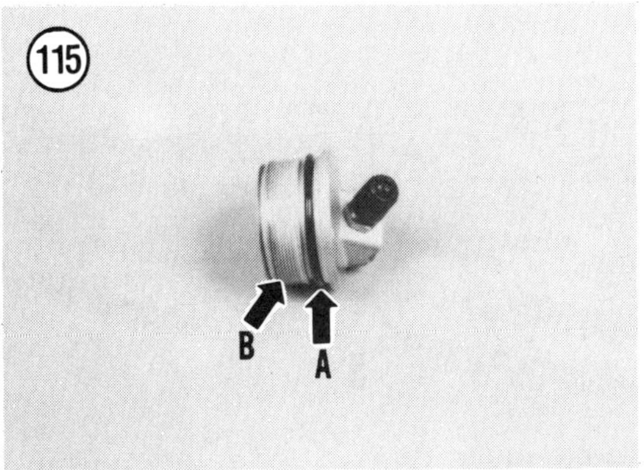

6. Check the damper rod piston rings (**Figure 113**) for damage.
7. Make sure the oil passages in the damper rod are open and free of dirt or foreign matter. Clean out if necessary with solvent and blow dry with compressed air.

NOTE

If an aftermarket fork spring has been installed, the un-compressed length may differ from the stock Yamaha fork spring. Refer to manufacturer's literature for spring length.

8. Measure the un-compressed length of the stock Yamaha fork springs (**Figure 114**) with a tape measure and compare to specifications in **Table 2**. Replace the fork spring(s) if too short.
9. Replace the fork cap bolt O-ring (A, **Figure 115**) if deformed or damaged.
10. Inspect the fork cap bolt threads (B, **Figure 115**) for wear or damage. Clean them up with the proper size tap or replace the fork cap bolt if necessary.
11. Check the fork tube Allen bolt washer for damage that would allow oil leakage; replace if necessary.
12. Inspect the fork tube bushing (**Figure 116**) and slider bushing. If the Teflon coating is worn off so that the copper base material is showing on approximately 3/4 of the total surface, the bushing must be replaced.
13. Check the oil seal and dust seal for tears or other damage that would allow oil leakage. Replace both seals if necessary.
14. On 1985-1986 models, inspect the threads on the front axle holder studs for wear or damage. Clean them up with the proper size tap or replace the fork slider if necessary. The studs are not available separately from Yamaha.

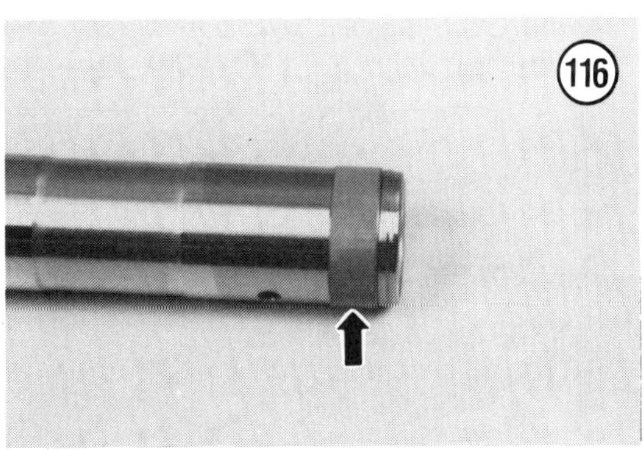

Assembly

Refer to the following illustrations for this procedure:

a. **Figure 98**: 1983-1984 TT600.
b. **Figure 99**: 1985-1986 TT600.

1. Slide the spring (**Figure 117**) onto the damper rod.
2. Insert the damper rod and spring into the fork tube (**Figure 110**).
3. Install the oil lock piece (**Figure 118**) onto the end of the damper rod.
4. Insert the damper rod/fork tube into the slider (**Figure 119**).
5. Position the fork spring with the closer wound coils toward the top and insert the fork spring into the fork tube.
6. Install the fork tube assembly into the fork slider. Push the fork tube down until the damper rod bottoms out on the slider.
7. Temporarily install the spring seat, spacer and fork cap bolt into the fork tube. Tighten the fork cap bolt by hand until it seats. Do not tighten with a wrench as it will be removed to add fork oil later in this procedure.
8. Make sure the gasket (A, **Figure 120**) is on the Allen bolt (B, **Figure 120**).
9. Apply blue Loctite 242 to the threads on the Allen bolt. Install the Allen bolt and tighten to the torque specification listed in **Table 3**.

NOTE
*Refer to **Figure 121** for the correct positioning of the parts that are to be installed from Step 10 through Step 16.*

10. Slide the slider bushing (**Figure 122**) and washer (**Figure 123**) over the fork tube.

NOTE
Some type of fork seal driver is required to install the guide bushing, oil seal and dust seal. Yamaha sells a fork seal driver set (part No. YM-08020). The

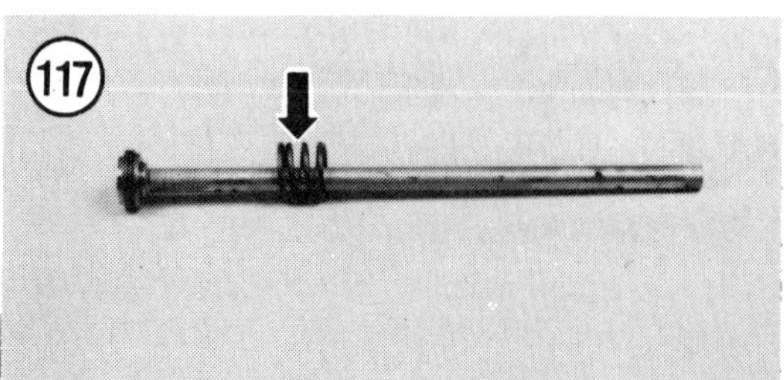
117

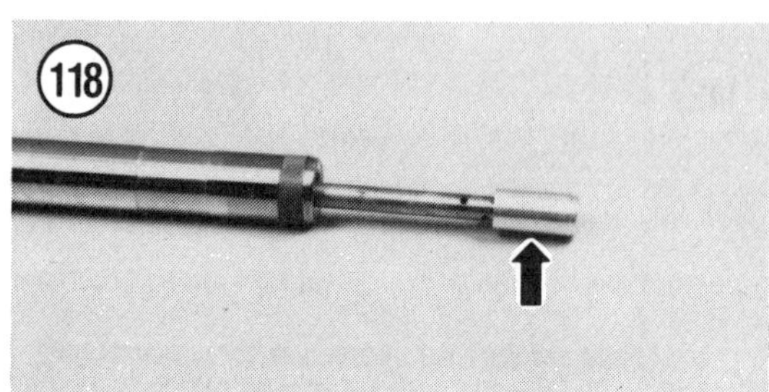
118

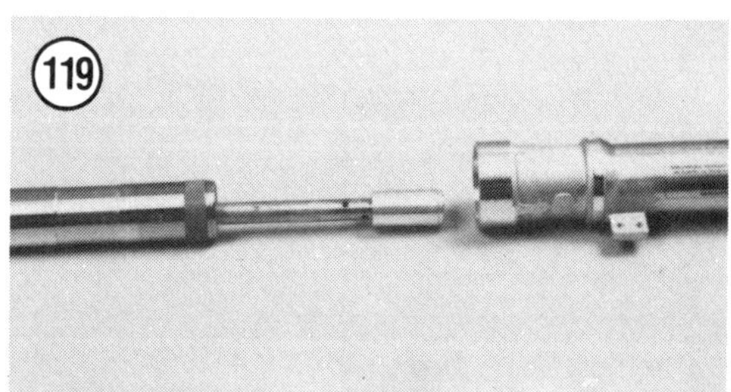
119

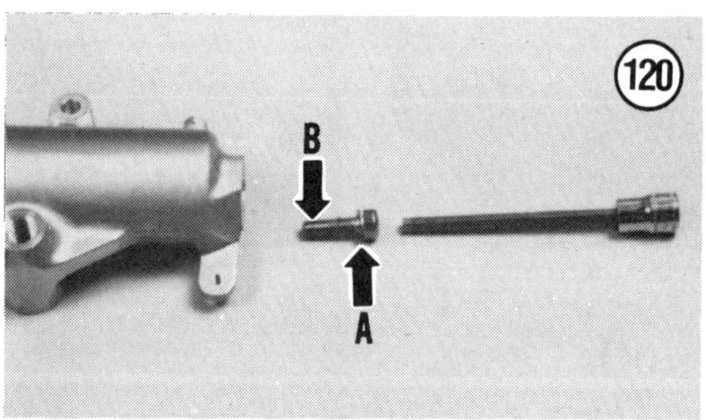

120

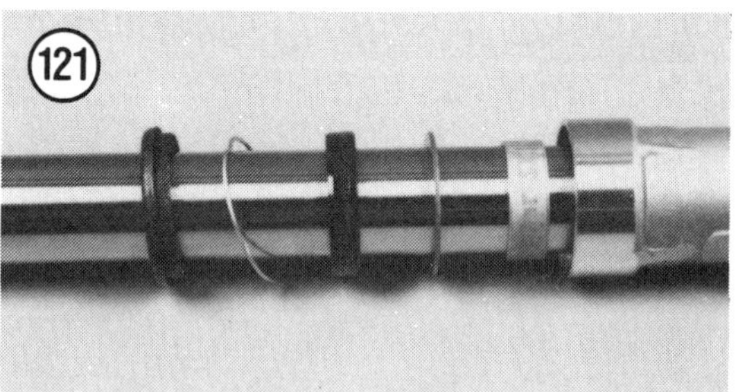
121

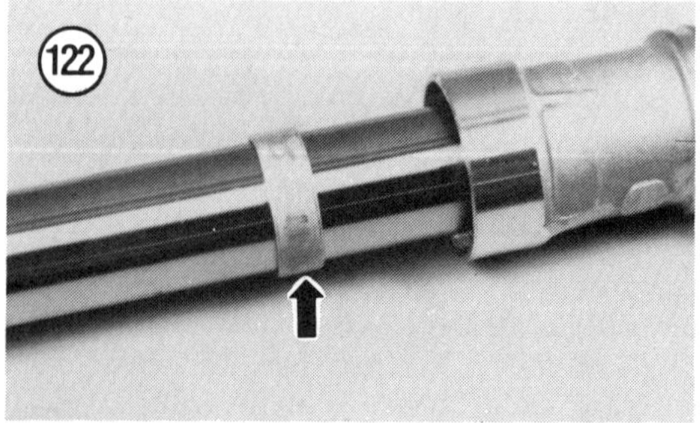
122

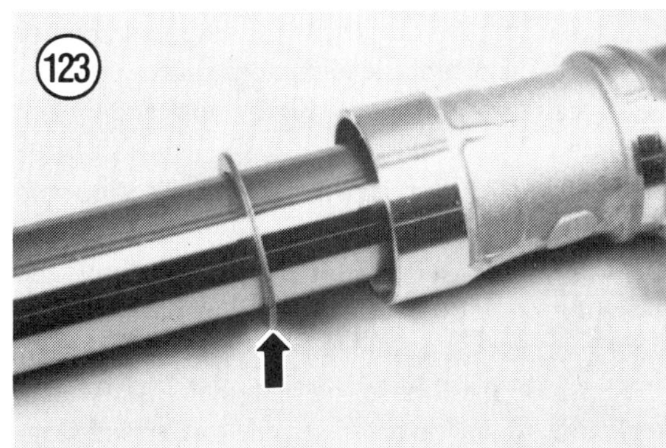
123

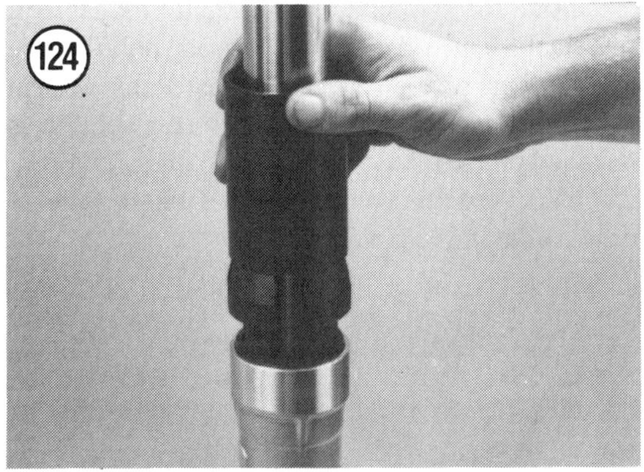
124

125

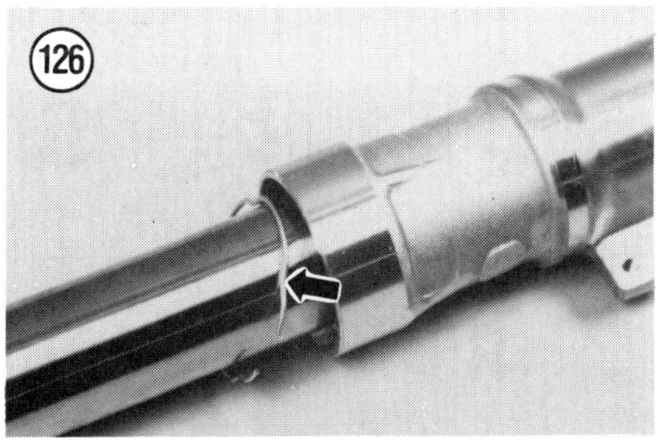
126

*adjustable fork seal driver shown in **Figure 124** is made by Suzuki and can be used on almost all Japanese fork assemblies (including Japanese "Showa" forks equipped on some late model Harleys).*

NOTE

If you do not have a special tool, the guide bushing and oil seals can be installed with a piece of pipe or other piece of tubing that fits over the fork tube. If both ends of the pipe are threaded, wrap one end with duct tape to prevent the threads from damaging the interior of the slider.

11. Using the special tool or piece of pipe, tap the slider bushing into the slider until it bottoms.
12. Position the oil seal with the marking facing upward and slide the oil seal down onto the fork tube (**Figure 125**).
13. Using the special tool or piece of pipe, drive the seal into the slider (**Figure 124**) until it rests against the washer and is below the clip groove in the slider.

NOTE

Make sure the groove in the slider can be seen above the oil seal. If not, the bushing and oil seal will have to driven farther into the slider.

14. Slide the clip (**Figure 126**) down the fork tube and seat it in the slider groove. Make sure the clip is completely seated in the groove (**Figure 127**).
15. Slide the dust seal down the fork tube (**Figure 128**) and press the dust seal down into the slider (**Figure 129**).
16. Install the dust boot (**Figure 130**) onto the fork tube.

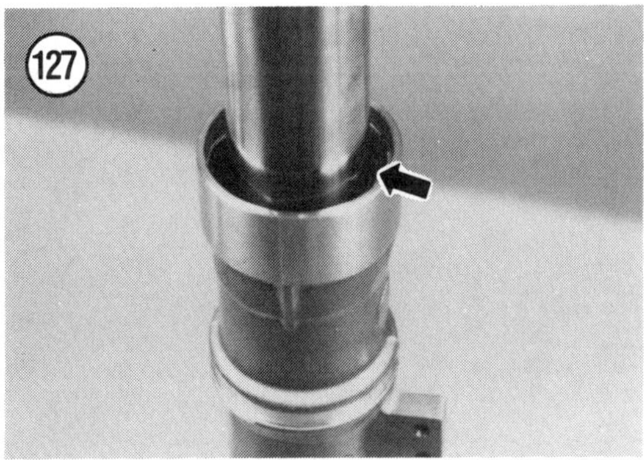
127

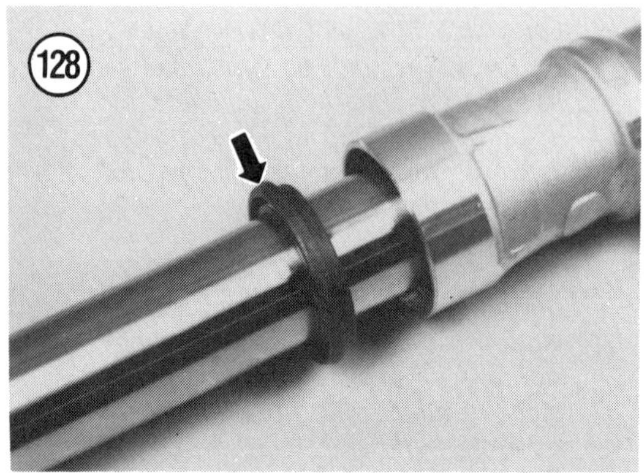
128

129

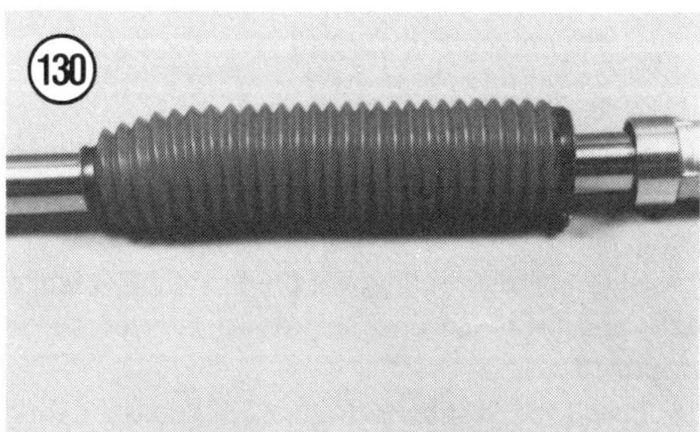
130

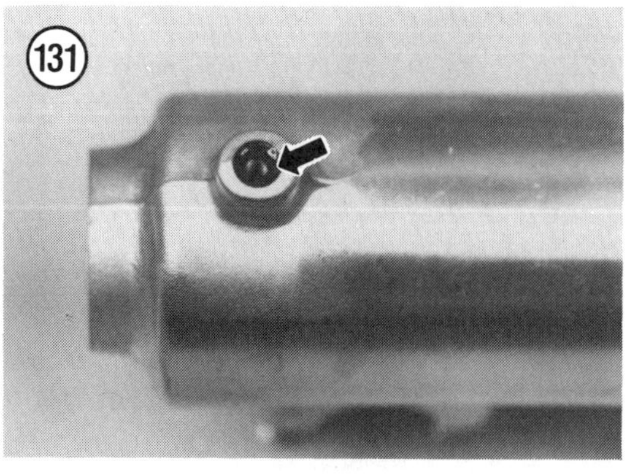
131

17. Make sure the drain screw O-ring seal (**Figure 131**) is in the receptacle in the fork slider.
18. Install the drain screw (**Figure 132**) and tighten securely.
19. Remove the fork cap bolt, spacer and spring seat.
20. Remove the fork spring.
21. Fill the fork tube with the correct quantity and weight fork oil as described in Chapter Three.
22. Hold the fork assembly upright.
23. Position the fork spring with the closer wound coils toward the top and insert the fork spring (**Figure 133**) into the fork tube.
24. Install the spring seat, spacer and fork cap bolt into the fork tube. Tighten the fork cap bolt (**Figure 134**) by hand securely. Do not tighten with a wrench as it will be tightened after the fork assembly is installed on the bike.
25. Install the fork tubes onto the motorcycle as described in this chapter.

132

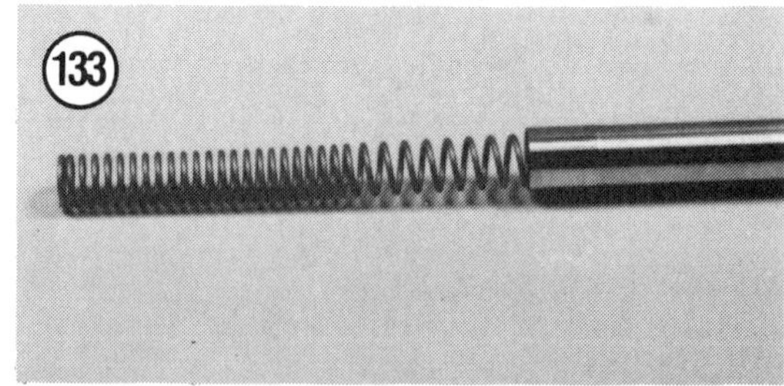
133

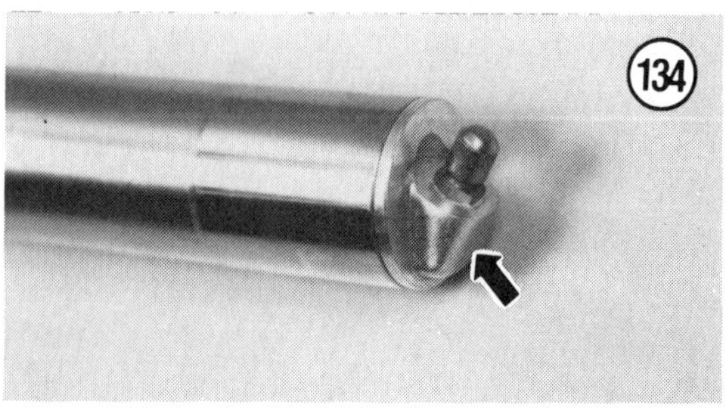
134

Table 1 FRONT SUSPENSION SPECIFICATIONS—XT600

Chassis	
Frame type	Diamond
Caster	28°
Trail	107 mm (4.60 in.)
Front wheel	
Travel	255 mm (10.0 in.)
Rim size	1.60 × 21
Rim runout	
Radial (up and down)	2.0 mm (0.08 in.)
Lateral (side-to-side)	2.0 mm (0.08 in.)
Front axle bend	0.25 mm (0.01 in.)
Front fork spring length	
Standard	465.5 mm (18.33 in.)
Wear limit	460.5 mm (18.13 in.)
Front fork oil	
Capacity	483 cc (16.33 oz.)
Oil level	147 mm (5.79 in.)
Oil grade	10 wt.
Front fork air capacity	
Standard	5.7 psi (39.2 kPa)
Maximum	14.2 psi (98.1 kPa)

Table 2 FRONT SUSPENSION SPECIFICATIONS—TT600

Chassis	
Frame type	Diamond
Caster	28°
Trail	118 mm (4.65 in.)
Front wheel	
Travel	300 mm (11.8 in.)
Rim size	1.60 × 21
Rim runout	
Radial (up and down)	2.0 mm (0.08 in.)
Lateral (side-to-side)	2.0 mm (0.08 in.)
Front axle bend	0.25 mm (0.01 in.)
Front fork spring length	
Standard	519 mm (20.4 in.)
Wear limit	514 mm (20.2 in.)
Front fork oil	
Capacity	589 cc (19.9 oz.)
Oil level	140 mm (5.5 in.)
Oil grade	10 wt.
Front fork air capacity	
Standard	0 psi (0 kPa)
Maximum	17 psi (118 kPa)

Table 3 FRONT SUSPENSION TIGHTENING TORQUES

XT600	N•m	ft.-lb.
Front axle nut	100	73
Front fork pinch bolts	23	17
Steering stem bolt	95	70
Steering adjust nut	38	27
Handlebar holder bolts	23	17
Valve stem locknut	1.5	1.1
Wheel spoke tension	3	2.2
Front fork		
Top cap bolt	23	17
Bottom Allen bolt*	20	14

(continued)

10

Table 3 FRONT SUSPENSION TIGHTENING TORQUES (continued)

TT600	N•m	ft.-lb.
Front axle nut	58	42
Axle holder nut or bolt	20	14
Front fork pinch bolts	23	17
Steering stem nut	95	70
Steering adjust nut		
Initial	30	22
Final	10	7.2
Handlebar holder bolts	23	17
Valve stem locknut	1.5	1.1
Wheel spoke tension	3	2.2
Front fork		
Top cap bolt	23	17
Bottom Allen bolt*	55	40

* Apply locking agent to bolt threads.

Table 4 TIRE INFLATION PRESSURE (COLD)

	Front tire	Rear tire
XT600		
Size	3.00-S21-4PR	4.60-S18-4PR
Tire pressure		
0-198 lb. (0-90 kg)	22 psi (147 kPa)	22 psi (147 kPa)
Maximum load	22 psi (147 kPa)	26 psi (177 kPa)
High speed riding	22 psi (147 kPa)	22 psi (147 kPa)
Off-road riding	14 psi (98.1 kPa)	14 psi (98.1 kPa)
TT600		
Size	100/80-21-4PR	140/80-18-4PR
Tire pressure	14 psi (98.1 kPa)	14 psi (98.1 kPa)

CHAPTER ELEVEN

REAR SUSPENSION

This chapter contains repair and replacement procedures for the rear wheel and hub and rear suspension components. Service to the rear suspension consists of periodically checking bolt tightness, replacing swing arm bushings, and checking the condition of the spring/gas shock unit.

Rear suspension specifications are listed in **Table 1. Tables 1-6** are found at the end of the chapter.

REAR WHEEL (XT600)

Removal

1. Support the bike so that the rear wheel is off of the ground.
2. Unscrew the rear brake adjusting nut (**Figure 1**) completely from the brake rod.
3. Withdraw the brake rod from the brake lever and pivot it out of the way. Reinstall the adjusting nut to avoid misplacing it.
4. Remove the axle nut cotter pin (A, **Figure 2**).
5. Loosen and remove the axle nut (B, **Figure 2**).
6. Remove the right-hand chain adjuster.
7. Push the wheel forward to provide as much chain slack as possible. Then turn the rear wheel and slip the drive chain off of the sprocket.
8. Remove the axle and chain adjuster from the left-hand side.
9. Pull the wheel back as required to disconnect the brake panel from the tab welded to the swing arm and remove the rear wheel.
10. Install the axle adjusters, axle spacers and axle nut on the axle to prevent their accidental loss when servicing the wheel.
11. Inspect the wheel spokes as described under *Wheel Spoke Service* in Chapter Ten.
12. Inspect the hub as described in this chapter.

Installation

1. Clean the axle, axle spacers and chain adjusters in solvent and thoroughly dry. Make sure all axle contact surfaces are clean and free of dirt and old grease prior to installation. If these surfaces are not cleaned, the axle may be difficult to install.
2. Apply a light coat of grease to the axle and to the rear hub bearings and grease seals.

3. Make sure the axle spacers are installed on each side of the hub.

4. Position the rear wheel into the rear of the swing arm and push it forward.

5. Engage the drive chain onto the driven sprocket.

6. Make sure to align the groove in the brake panel (**Figure 3**) with the tab welded to the swing arm.

7. Install the axle adjuster onto the rear axle and install the rear axle from the left-hand side.

8. Install the other axle adjuster and the rear axle nut.

9. If the drive chain was disconnected, install the clip (**Figure 4**) on the drive chain master link and install it so that the closed end of the clip is facing the direction of chain travel (**Figure 5**).

10. Adjust the drive chain as described under *Drive Chain Adjustment* in Chapter Three.

11. Tighten the axle nut (B, **Figure 2**) to the torque specification in **Table 2**.

12. Secure the axle nut with a *new* cotter pin (A, **Figure 2**). Bend the end of the cotter pin over to lock it.

13. After the wheel is completely installed, rotate it several times to make sure it rotates smoothly. Apply the brakes several times to make sure it operates correctly.

14. Adjust the rear brake as described under *Rear Brake Pedal Adjustment* in Chapter Three.

REAR WHEEL (TT600)

Removal

1. Support the bike so that the rear wheel is off of the ground.

2. Unscrew the rear brake adjusting nut completely from the brake rod (**Figure 6**).

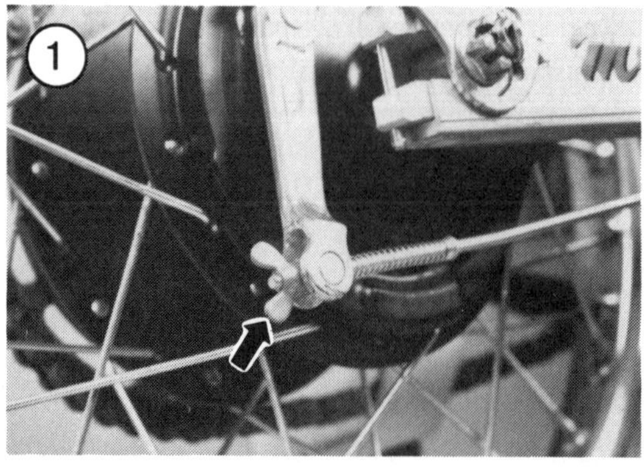

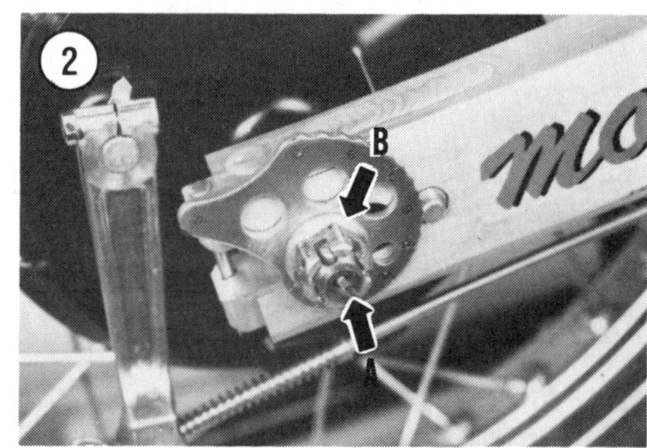

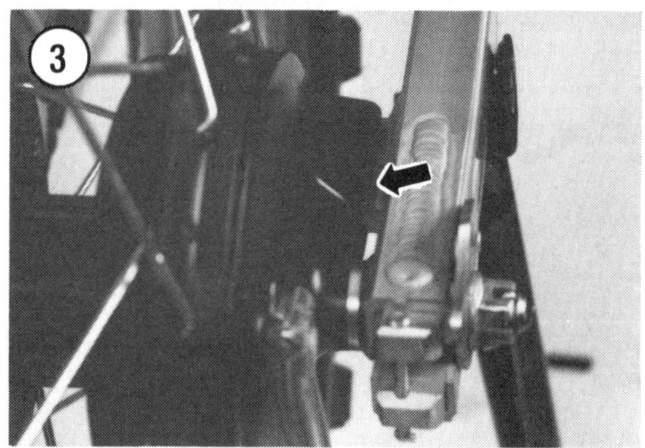

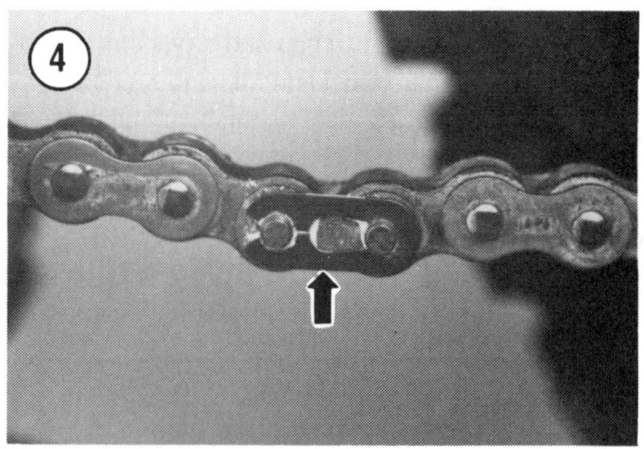

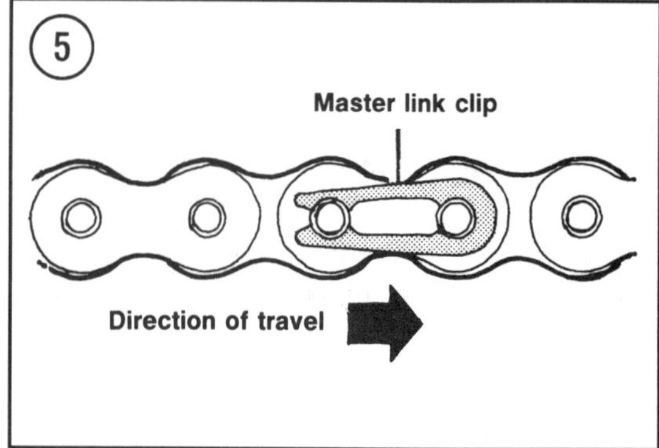

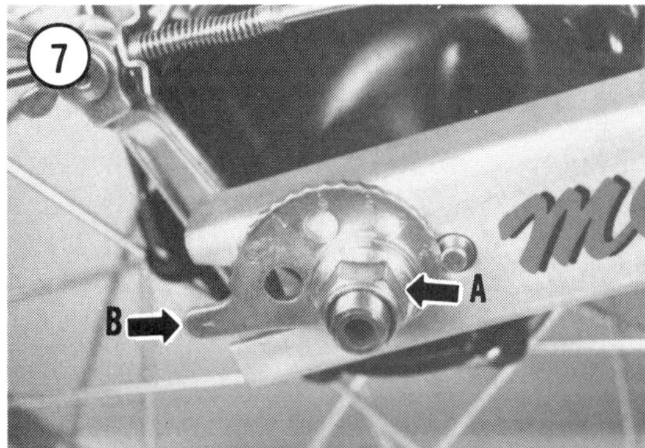

3. Depress the brake pedal and withdraw the brake rod from the brake lever and pivot it out of the way. Reinstall the adjusting nut to avoid misplacing it.

NOTE
The rear wheel can be removed by one of two methods. Refer to Step 4A or Step 4B.

4A. To remove the rear wheel without removing the axle, perform the following:

a. Loosen the rear axle nut (A, **Figure 7**).
b. Push the wheel forward to provide as much chain slack as possible.
c. Then turn the rear wheel and slip the drive chain off of the sprocket.
d. Remove the axle bolts from the end of the swing arm (**Figure 8**).
e. Pull the wheel to the back and remove it from the swing arm.

4B. To remove the rear wheel by removing the rear axle, perform the following:

a. Loosen and remove the rear axle nut (A, **Figure 7**).
b. Remove the right-hand chain adjuster (B, **Figure 7**).
c. Push the wheel forward to provide as much chain slack as possible.
d. Then turn the rear wheel and slip the drive chain off of the sprocket.
e. Remove the axle and chain adjuster from the left-hand side.
f. Pull the wheel back as required to disconnect the brake panel from the tab welded to the swing arm and remove the rear wheel.
g. Remove the axle spacer (**Figure 9**) from the left-hand side.
h. Remove the brake panel (A, **Figure 10**) from the right-hand side.

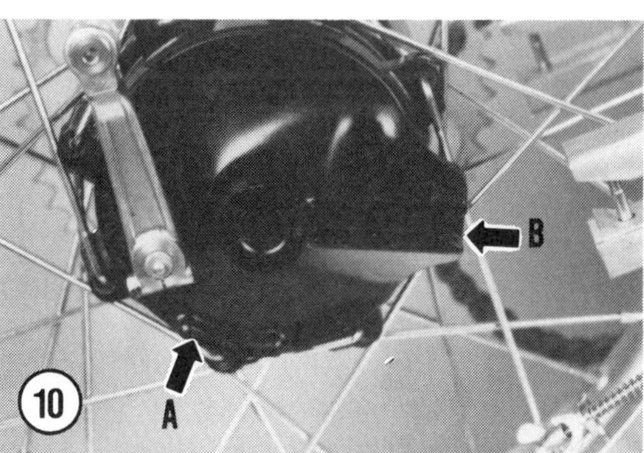

Installation

1. Clean the axle, axle spacers and chain adjusters in solvent and thoroughly dry. Make sure all axle contact surfaces are clean and free of dirt and old grease prior to installation. If these surfaces are not cleaned, the axle may be difficult to install.
2. Apply a light coat of grease to the axle and to the rear hub bearings and grease seals.
3. Make sure the axle spacer is installed on the left-hand side of the hub.
4. Position the rear wheel into the rear of the swing arm and push it forward.
5. Engage the drive chain onto the driven sprocket.
6. Make sure to align the groove in the brake panel (B, **Figure 10**) with the tab welded to the swing arm.

7A. To install the rear wheel with the axle installed in the wheel, perform the following:

a. Move the wheel into position in the swing arm.
b. Install the axle bolts into the end of the swing arm (**Figure 8**).
c. Then turn the rear wheel and feed the drive chain onto the sprocket.
d. Pull the wheel toward the rear.
e. Temporarily tighten the rear axle nut (A, **Figure 7**).

7B. To install the rear wheel with the rear axle removed, perform the following:

a. Install the brake panel (A, **Figure 10**) into the right-hand side.
b. Install the axle spacer (**Figure 9**) into the left-hand side.
c. Move the wheel into position in the swing arm.
d. Move the wheel on and align the brake panel groove with the tab welded to the swing arm. This alignment is necessary for proper brake operation.
e. Install the drive chain adjuster onto the left-hand side and install the axle from the left-hand side.
f. Then turn the rear wheel and feed the drive chain onto the sprocket.
g. Install the right-hand chain adjuster (B, **Figure 7**).
h. Install the rear axle nut (A, **Figure 7**).
i. Pull the wheel toward the rear.
j. Temporarily tighten the rear axle nut.

8. If the drive chain was disconnected, install the clip (**Figure 4**) on the drive chain master link and install it so that the closed end of the clip is facing the direction of chain travel (**Figure 5**).
9. Adjust the drive chain as described under *Drive Chain Adjustment* in Chapter Three.
10. Tighten the axle nut to the torque specification in **Table 3**.
11. After the wheel is completely installed, rotate it several times to make sure it rotates smoothly. Apply the brakes several times to make sure it operates correctly.
12. Adjust the rear brake as described under *Rear Brake Pedal Adjustment* in Chapter Three.

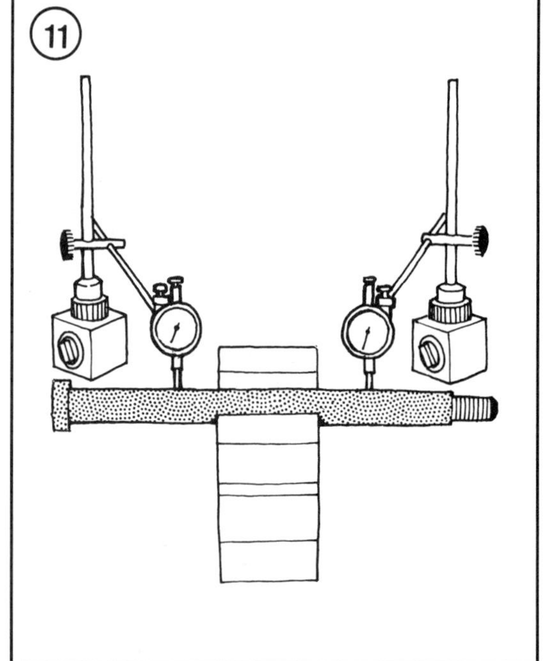

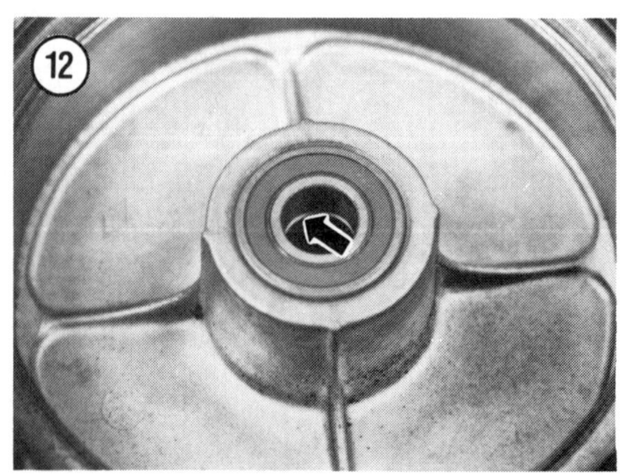

WHEEL SPOKE SERVICE

Wheel spoke service is covered in Chapter Ten.

REAR HUB

Inspection

1. Visually check the rear axle surface for cracks, deep scoring or excessive wear. Check axle runout with a set of V-blocks and dial indicator (**Figure 11**).

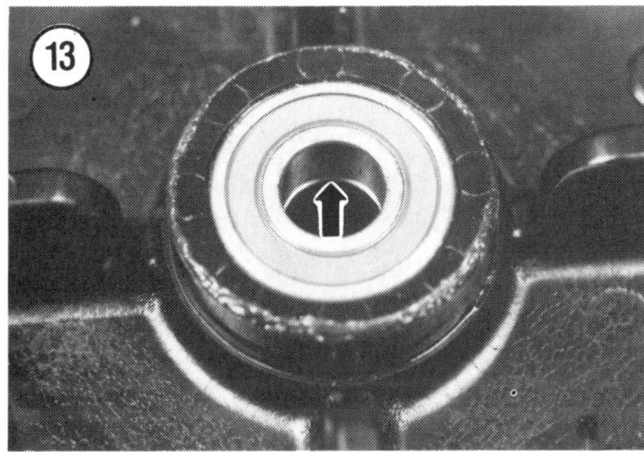
13

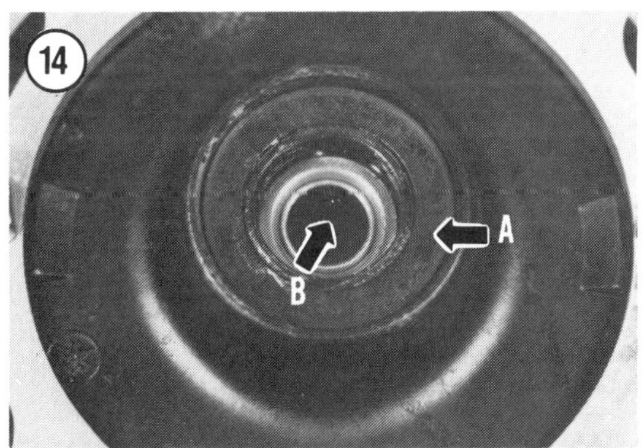

14

15

The maximum allowable bend is listed in **Table 1**. If you do not have access to the special tools, roll the axle on a flat surface and visually check the runout. Replace a bent axle. Do not attempt to straighten it.

2. If not already removed, pull the rear brake assembly straight out of the rear hub.
3. In the rear hub, turn the inner bearing race by hand and check for any sign of roughness or damage. Refer to **Figure 12** for the right-hand side and **Figure 13** for the left-hand side of the rear hub. Replace the bearings (as a set) as described in this section.
4. In the driven flange, perform the following:
   a. Check the oil seal (A, **Figure 14**) for signs of wear, cracks or other damage. A damaged oil seal will allow bearing contamination. Replace the oil seal as described in this section.
   b. Turn the inner bearing race (B, **Figure 14**) by hand and check for any sign of roughness or damage. Replace the bearing as described in this section.
5. Check the driven sprocket nuts (**Figure 15**) for tightness. If loose, tighten the nuts to the torque specification listed in **Table 2**.

Inspection/Disassembly

Refer to **Figure 16** for XT600 models or **Figure 17** for TT600 models for this procedure.

CAUTION

Do not remove the wheel bearings for inspection purposes as they will be damaged during the removal process. Remove wheel bearings only if they are to be replaced.

1. Remove the rear wheel as described in this chapter.
2. If not already removed, pull the rear brake assembly straight out of the rear hub.
3. On XT600 models, remove the driven flange from the rear wheel as described in this chapter.

4A. On XT600 models, to remove the oil seal in the driven flange assembly, perform the following:
   a. Remove the oil seal (A, **Figure 14**) by carefully prying it out of the left-hand side of the driven flange with a long screwdriver.
   b. Lift the screwdriver and work it around the seal every few degrees until it pops out of the driven flange.

(16)

REAR WHEEL (XT600)

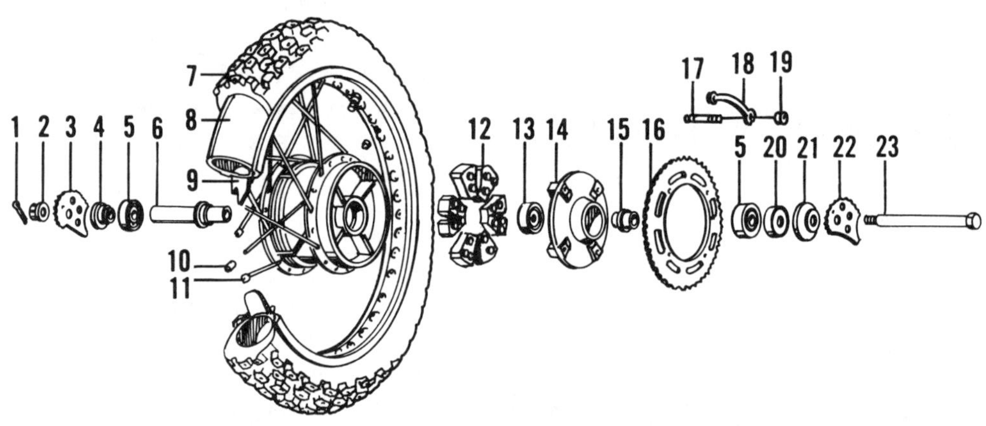

1. Cotter pin
2. Axle nut
3. Chain adjuster
4. Right-hand spacer
5. Bearing
6. Middle spacer
7. Tire
8. Inner tube
9. Band
10. Balance weight
11. Spoke
12. Rubber dampers
13. Bearing
14. Driven flange
15. Spacer
16. Rear driven sprocket
17. Threaded stud
18. Lockwasher
19. Nut
20. Oil seal
21. Left-hand spacer
22. Chain adjuster
23. Axle

(17)

REAR WHEEL (TT600)

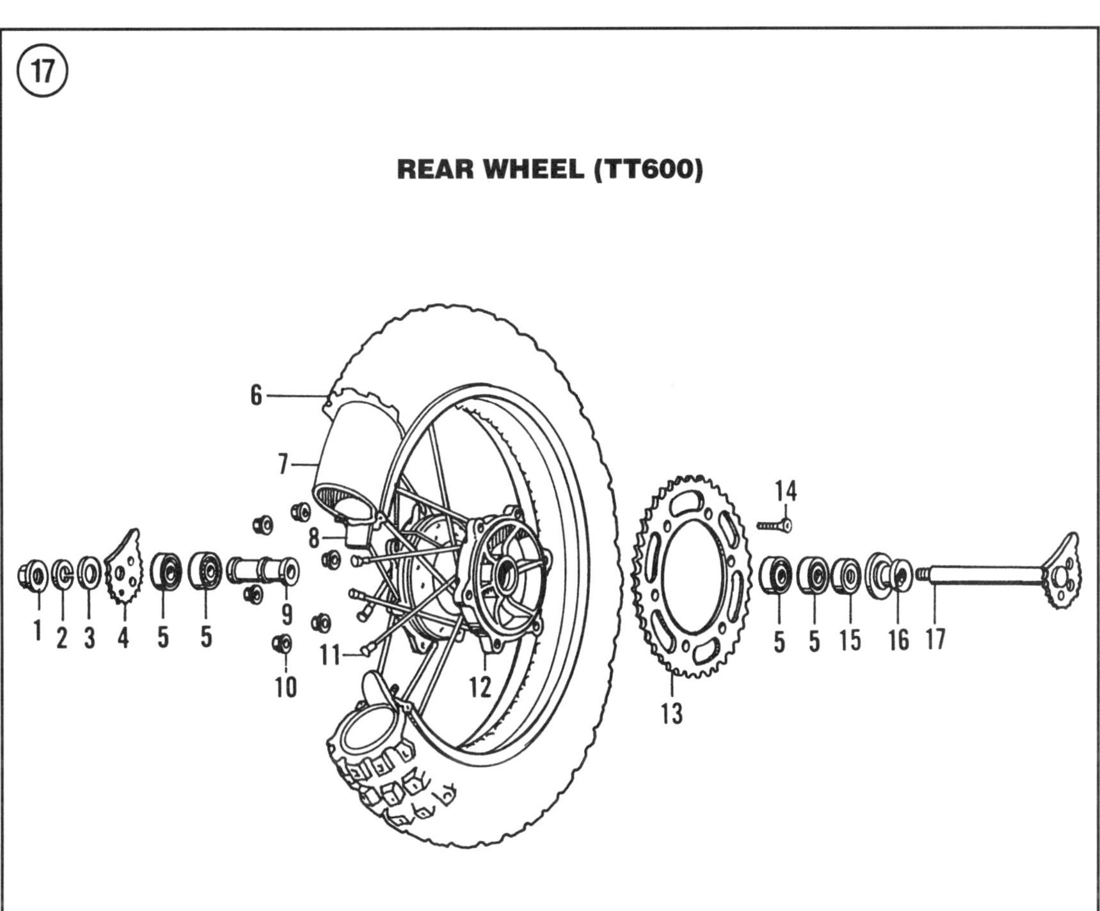

1. Nut
2. Lockwasher
3. Washer
4. Chain adjuster
5. Bearing
6. Tire
7. Inner tube
8. Band
9. Middle spacer
10. Nut
11. Spoke
12. Hub
13. Rear driven sprocket
14. Bolt
15. Oil seal
16. Left-hand spacer
17. Axle (with attached chain adjuster)

c. Prop a piece of wood or rag underneath the screwdriver to prevent damaging the driven flange.

4B. On TT600 models, to remove the oil seal in the hub, perform the following:

a. Remove the oil seal by carefully prying it out of the rear hub with a long screwdriver.
b. Lift the screwdriver and work it around the seal every few degrees until it pops out of the driven flange.
c. Prop a piece of wood or rag underneath the screwdriver to prevent damaging the driven flange.

NOTE
When replacing the bearings, be sure to take your old bearings along to ensure a perfect matchup.

5. Turn the inner race of each bearing by hand. Make sure bearings turn smoothly and check for any signs of roughness or damage. Replace the hub bearings as a complete set if they are noisy or have excessive play.

6. On non-sealed bearings, check the rollers or balls for evidence of wear, pitting or excessive heat (bluish tint). Replace the bearings if necessary.

7. To remove the left- and right-hand hub bearings and spacer, perform the following:

a. Insert a soft aluminum or brass drift into one side of the hub.
b. Push the middle spacer over to one side and place the drift on the inner race of the lower bearing (**Figure 18**).
c. Tap the bearing out of the hub with a hammer, working around the perimeter of the inner race.
d. Remove the middle spacer.
e. Repeat for the opposite bearing.

8. Thoroughly clean out the inside of the hub with solvent and dry with compressed air or a shop cloth.

9. On XT600 models, to remove the driven flange bearing, perform the following:

a. Remove the collar (**Figure 19**) from the inner surface of the driven flange.
b. Place the driven flange on soft wood blocks with the inside surface facing up.
c. Insert a soft aluminum or brass drift into the inside surface of the driven flange.
d. Tap the bearing out of the driven flange with a hammer, working around the perimeter of the inner race.

10. Thoroughly clean out the inside of the driven flange with solvent and dry with compressed air or a shop cloth.

Assembly

1. Blow any dirt or foreign matter out of the hub and driven flange prior to installing the bearings.

NOTE
Fully sealed bearings are available from many good bearing specialty shops. Fully sealed bearings provide better protection from dirt and moisture that may get into the hub.

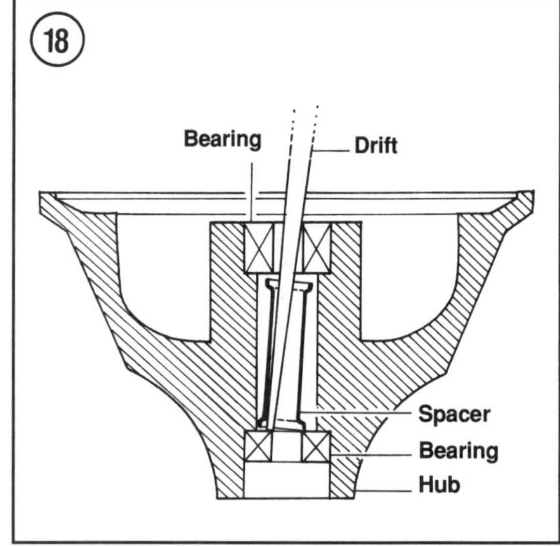

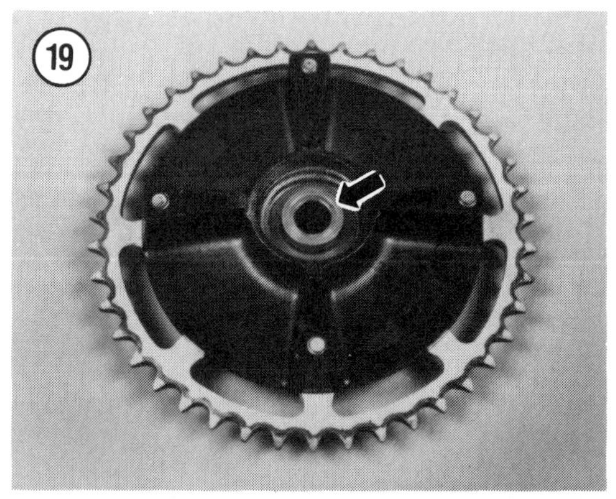

2. Pack non-sealed bearings with good-quality bearing grease. Work the grease in between the balls thoroughly. Turn the bearing by hand a couple of times to make sure the grease is distributed evenly inside the bearing.
3. Place the new wheel bearing outer races in a freezer if possible. Chilling them will slightly reduce their overall diameter. This will make installation easier.
4. On the rear hub, perform the following:
   a. Pack the wheel hub and middle spacer with multipurpose grease.

NOTE
If a bearing has only one sealed side, install the bearing with the sealed side facing out.

CAUTION
*When installing the bearings in the following procedures, tap the bearings squarely into place and tap on the outer race only. Use a socket (**Figure 20**) that matches the outer race diameter. Do not tap on the inner race or the bearing will be damaged. Be sure that the bearings are completely seated.*

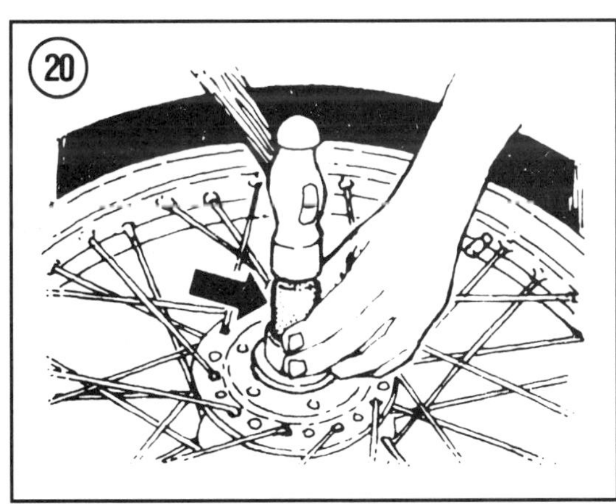

   b. Install one of the bearings. It doesn't matter which bearing is installed first.
   c. Install the middle spacer.
   d. Install the opposite bearing.
5. On XT600 models, on the driven flange, perform the following:

NOTE
If a bearing has only one sealed side, install the bearing with the sealed side facing out.

CAUTION
*When installing the bearing in the following procedures, tap the bearings squarely into place and tap on the outer race only. Use a socket (**Figure 20**) that matches the outer race diameter. Do not tap on the inner race or the bearing will be damaged. Be sure that the bearing is completely seated.*

   a. Place the driven flange on soft wood blocks with the outside surface facing up.
   b. Install the bearing.
   c. Lubricate the new oil seal with multipurpose grease and tap it squarely into the driven flange with a suitable size socket placed on the outside portion of the seal. Install the oil seal (A, **Figure 14**) until it bottoms out on the bearing.
   d. Install the collar (**Figure 19**) into the inner surface of the driven flange.
6. Install the driven flange into the rear wheel as described in this chapter.
7. Install the rear brake assembly into the rear hub.
8. Install the rear wheel as described in this chapter.

DRIVEN FLANGE (XT600)

Removal/Inspection/Installation

Refer to **Figure 16** for this procedure.

1. Remove the rear wheel as described in this chapter.
2. Pull the driven flange (**Figure 21**) out of the rear wheel.

3. Remove the collar (**Figure 19**) from the inner surface of the driven flange.
4. Remove the rubber dampers (**Figure 22**) from the hub.
5. Inspect the rubber dampers (**Figure 23**) for wear, damage or deterioration. Replace as a set of 4 if any require replacement.
6. Inspect the ribs (**Figure 24**) in the rear hub where the rubber dampers mount onto for wear, cracks or damage. If any of the ribs are damaged, replace the rear wheel.
7. Inspect the ribs (**Figure 25**) in the driven flange, where the rubber dampers seat, for wear, cracks or damage. If any of the ribs are damaged, replace the driven flange.
8. Check the oil seal (A, **Figure 14**) for wear or damage.
9. Turn the inner bearing race (B, **Figure 14**) by hand and check for any signs of roughness or damage. Replace the bearing as described under *Rear Hub* in this chapter.
10. Install by reversing these removal steps.

SPROCKETS

This procedure describes service to the front drive and the rear driven sprockets.

Front Drive Sprocket Removal/Installation

1. Remove the pinch bolt securing the shift lever (A, **Figure 26**) and pull the shift lever off the shaft. If the splined boss is tight on the shaft, spread the slot open with a screwdriver.

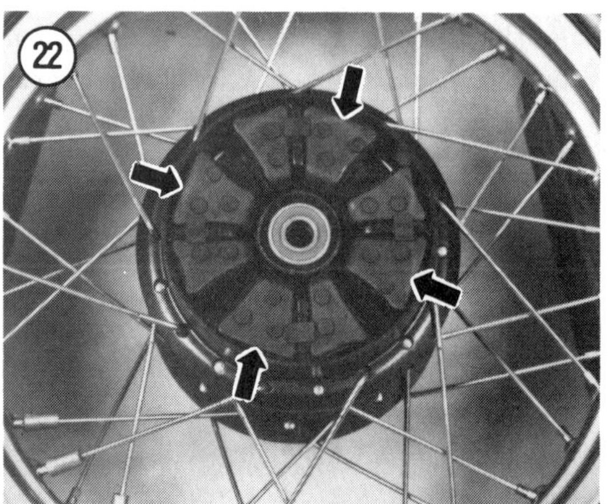

2. Remove the screws securing the drive sprocket cover (B, **Figure 26**) and remove the cover.
3. Remove the 2 sprocket lockplate mounting bolts (**Figure 27**).
4. Turn the sprocket lockplate (**Figure 28**) in either direction until it clears the groove in the splines and slide it off of the countershaft.

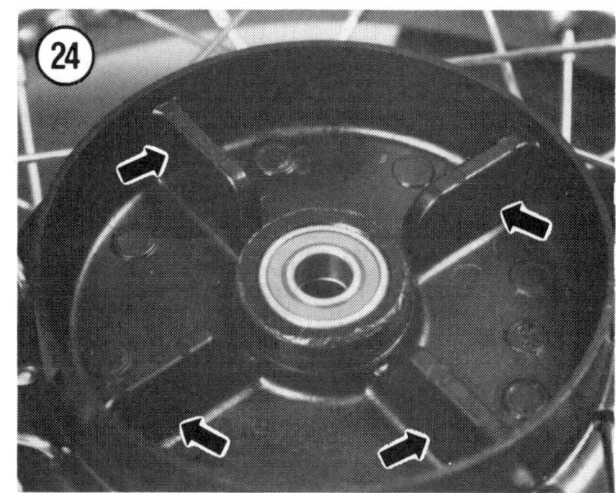

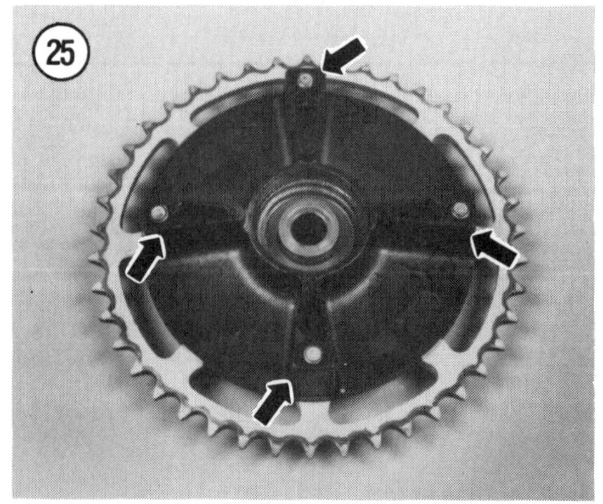

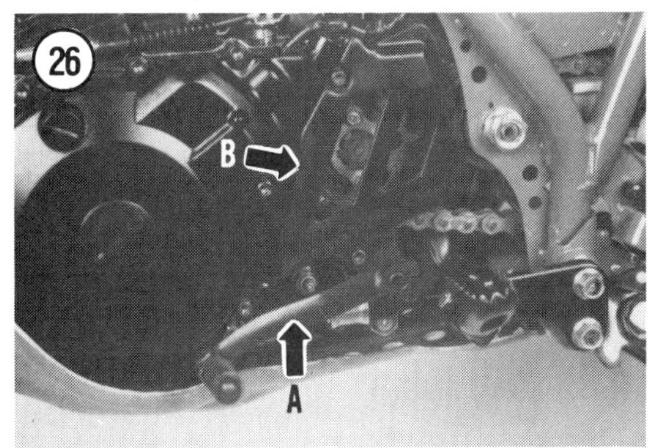

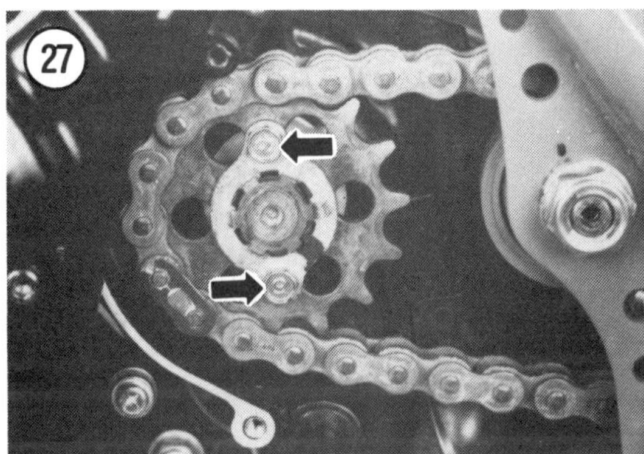

5. Slide the drive sprocket and drive chain (**Figure 29**) off of the transmission countershaft.

NOTE
If the drive chain is tight, loosen the rear axle nut and loosen the chain adjusters.

NOTE
*If the drive sprocket requires replacement, the drive chain is probably worn also and may need replacement. Refer to **Drive Chain Inspection** in Chapter Three. Also inspect the driven sprocket as described in this chapter.*

6. Inspect the sprocket teeth. If they are visibly worn (**Figure 30**), replace the sprocket.

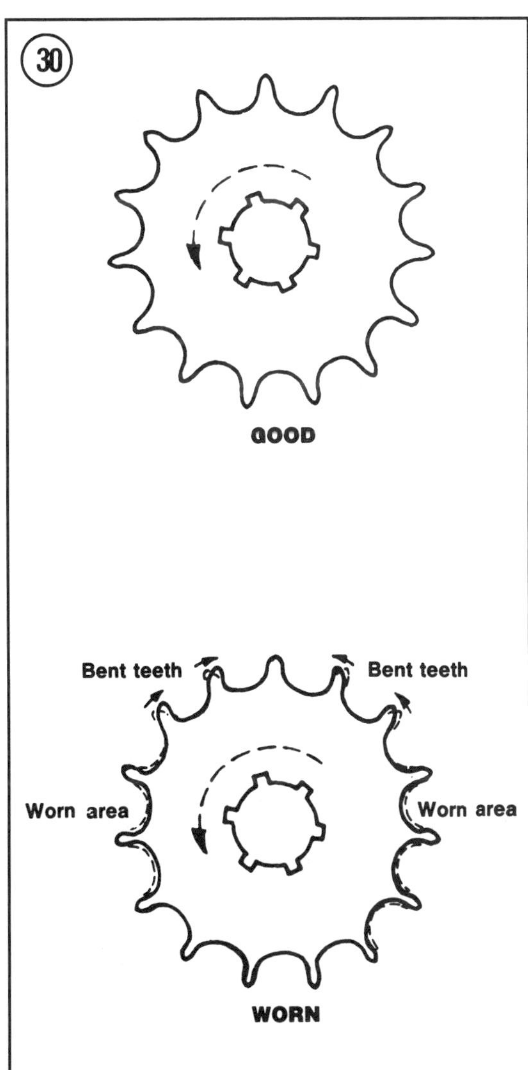

11

7. Install by reversing these removal steps. Note the following.
8. Make sure to align the holes in the lockplate with the holes in the sprocket. Then install the lockplate mounting bolts (**Figure 27**) and tighten to the torque specification listed in **Table 2**.
9. If the rear wheel axle nut was loosened, adjust the drive chain as described under *Drive Chain Adjustment* in Chapter Three.
10. Tighten the axle nut to the torque specification in **Table 2** (XT600) or **Table 3** (TT600).
11. On XT600 models, secure the axle nut with a *new* cotter pin. Bend the end of the cotter pin over to lock it.
12. Adjust the rear brake as described under *Rear Brake Pedal Adjustment* in Chapter Three.

Rear Driven Sprocket Removal/Installation

Refer to **Figure 16** or **Figure 17** for this procedure.
1. Remove the rear wheel as described in this chapter.

NOTE
If the driven sprocket requires replacement, the drive chain is probably worn also and may need replacement. Refer to ***Drive Chain Inspection*** *in Chapter Three. Also inspect the drive sprocket as described in this chapter.*

2. Inspect the sprocket teeth (**Figure 31**) for wear or damage. If they are visibly worn (**Figure 30**), replace the sprocket.
3A. On XT600 models, perform the following:
   a. Pry the lockwasher tabs (A, **Figure 32**) away from the sprocket nuts.
   b. Loosen, then remove the nuts (B, **Figure 32**) holding the sprocket to the driven flange.
   c. Remove the sprocket (C, **Figure 32**).
3B. On TT600 models, perform the following:
   a. Loosen, then remove the Allen bolts holding the sprocket to the rear hub.
   b. Remove the sprocket from the rear hub.
4. Check all of the sprocket fasteners for damage. Replace if necessary. Replace the lockwashers if the locking tabs are starting to break.
5. Install by reversing these removal steps. Note the following.
6. Tighten the bolts or nuts to the torque specification in **Table 2** (XT600) or **Table 3** (TT600).
7. On XT600 models, bend the lockwasher tabs up against the sprocket nuts to lock them.
8. Install the rear wheel as described in this chapter.

DRIVE CHAIN

Removal/Installation

1. Shift the transmission into NEUTRAL.

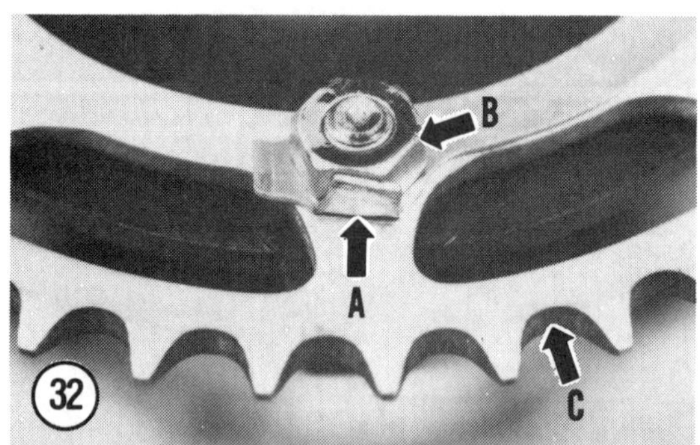

2. Remove the pinch bolt securing the shift lever (A, **Figure 26**) and pull the shift lever off the shaft. If the splined boss is tight on the shaft, spread the slot open with a screwdriver.

3. Remove the screws securing the drive sprocket cover (B, **Figure 26**) and remove the cover.

4. Place wood block(s) under the frame or a stand under the swing arm (**Figure 33**) so the rear wheel is off the ground.

5. Turn the rear wheel and drive chain until the master link is accessible.

6. Remove the master link clip and remove the master link.

34

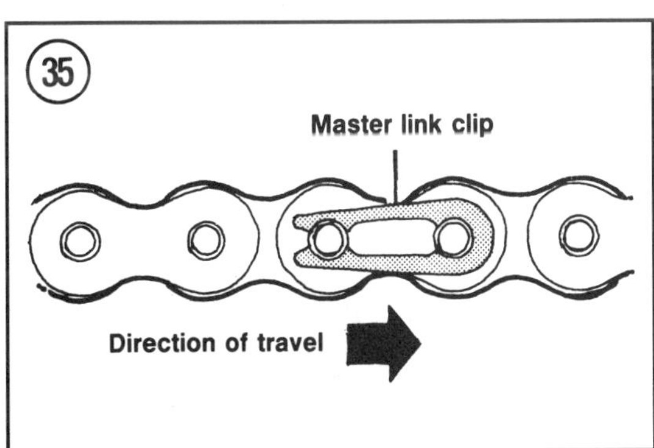

35

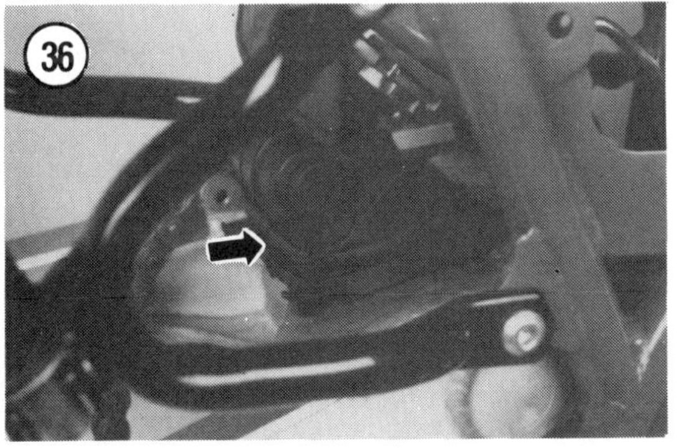

36

7. Slowly rotate the rear wheel and pull the drive chain off the drive sprocket.

8. Install by reversing these removal steps. Note the following.

9. Be sure to feed the drive chain through the guide (**Figure 34**) on the swing arm.

10. Install the clip on the master link so that the closed end of the clip is facing the direction of chain travel (**Figure 35**).

Service and Inspection

For service and inspection of the drive chain, refer to *Periodic Lubrication* and *Periodic Maintenance* in Chapter Three.

TIRE CHANGING AND TIRE REPAIR

Tire changing and repair is covered in Chapter Ten.

MONOCROSS REAR SUSPENSION

All models use a single rear shock absorber/spring unit. The single shock controls swing arm movement through a compound linkage system with bearings at both ends of a vertical connecting rod and a relay arm.

The single shock/spring unit eliminates the requirement for periodic inspection for equal damping and spring tension between dual shocks. However, several suspension bushings carry a great load in the Monocross system and frequent lubrication and wear inspections are necessary to preserve good handling and prevent premature component wear.

SHOCK ABSORBER

Removal/Installation (XT600)

1. Remove the rear wheel as described in this chapter.

2. Remove the seat as described in Chapter Thirteen.

3. Remove both frame side covers.

4. Unhook and pull the rubber boot (**Figure 36**) up and off of the boot support on the swing arm.

5. Remove the upper pivot bolt nut and washer (A, **Figure 37**).
6. Remove the cotter pin and washer (**Figure 38**) from the lower pivot pin.
7. Withdraw the lower pivot pin and the upper pivot bolt and remove the shock absorber (B, **Figure 37**) out through the bottom.
8. Replace the pivot washers if worn or damaged.
9. Install by reversing these removal steps. Note the following.
10. Apply a lithium base grease to all pivot bolts.
11. Tighten the upper pivot bolt nut to the torque specification in **Table 2.**
12. Make sure the thrust bushings (**Figure 39**) are in place on each side of the lower mount prior to installing the shock absorber.
13. Be sure to correctly install the rubber boot onto the swing arm receptacle. If not installed correctly, dirt and water will get into the lower pivot area and wear out the parts prematurely.

Removal/Installation (TT600)

1. Remove the rear wheel as described in this chapter.
2. Remove the seat as described in Chapter Thirteen.
3. Remove both frame side covers.
4. Remove the upper pivot bolt nut and washer.
5. Remove the bolts securing the air filter air box. It is not necessary to remove the air box. It must just be loose in order to remove the remote reservoir and hose around it.
6. Loosen the clamping bolt securing the remote reservoir to the frame and carefully pull the reservoir out of the clamp.
7. Remove the lower pivot bolt nut and washers.
8. Carefully remove the remote reservoir and connecting hose out through the frame and from behind the air box.
9. Replace the pivot washers if worn or damaged.
10. Install by reversing these removal steps. Note the following.
11. Apply a lithium base grease to all pivot bolts.
12. Tighten the upper and lower pivot bolt nuts to the torque specification in **Table 3**.
13. Make sure the thrust bushings are in place on each side of the lower mount prior to installing the shock absorber.

Inspection (All Models)

Refer to **Figure 40** for XT600 models or **Figure 41** for TT600 models for this procedure.

NOTE
This procedure is shown on a XT600 unit. Where differences occur between the two models they are identified.

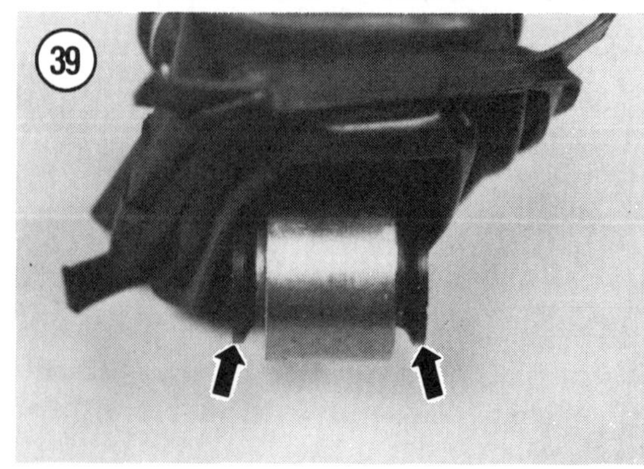

SHOCK ABSORBER (XT600)

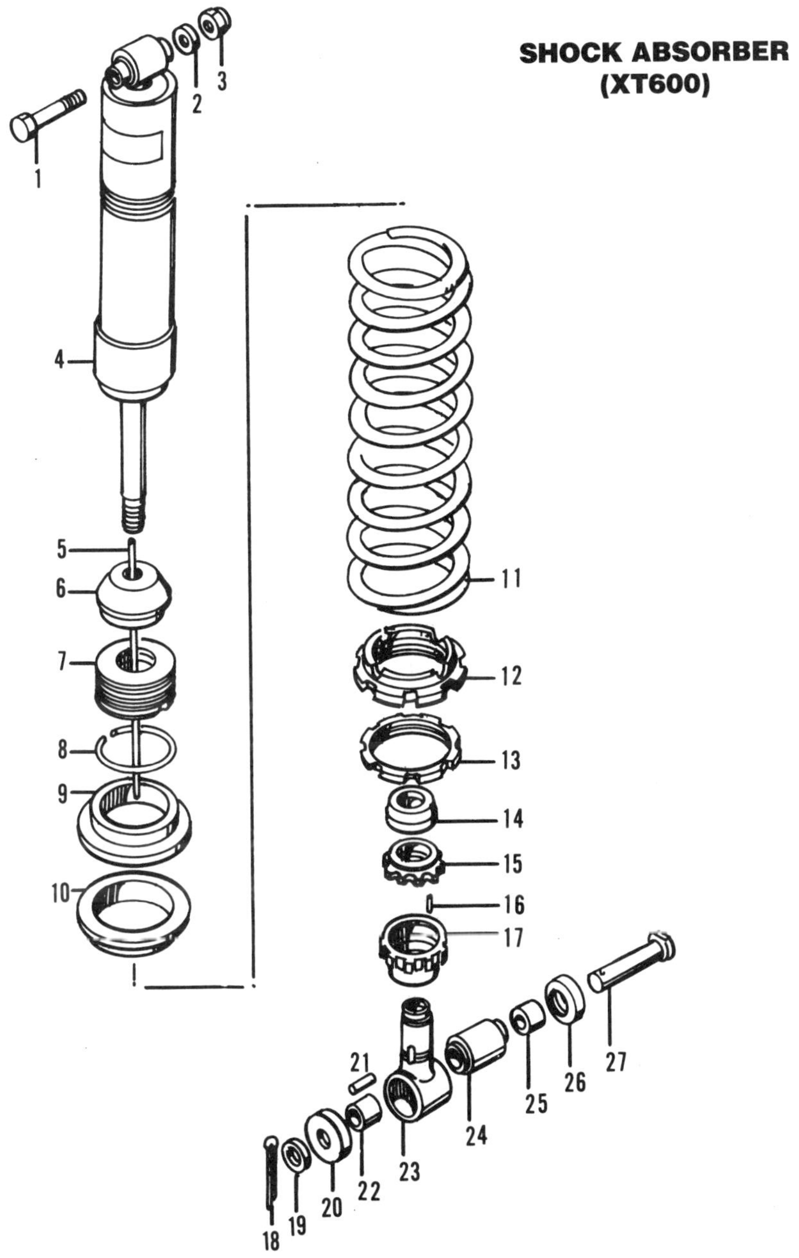

1. Upper pivot bolt
2. Washer
3. Nut
4. Damper unit
5. Pushrod
6. Rubber stopper
7. Collar
8. Clip
9. Spring seat
10. Spring guide
11. Spring
12. Spring adjuster
13. Locknut
14. Cover
15. Damping adjusting nut
16. Pin
17. Cover
18. Cotter pin
19. Washer
20. Thrust bushing
21. Pin
22. Bushing
23. Lower bracket
24. Rubber bushing
25. Bushing
26. Thrust bushing
27. Lower pivot pin

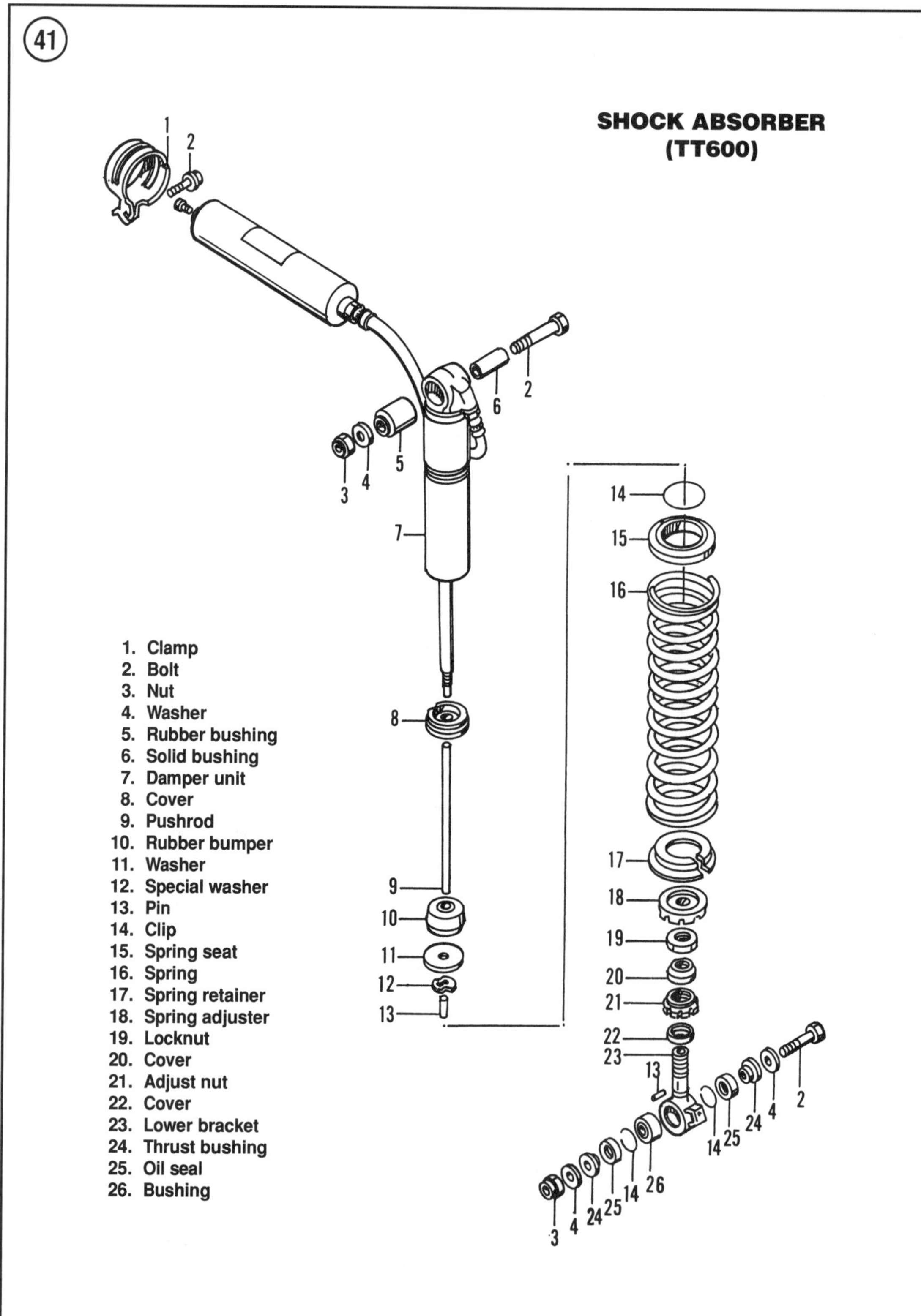
41
SHOCK ABSORBER
(TT600)
1. Clamp
2. Bolt
3. Nut
4. Washer
5. Rubber bushing
6. Solid bushing
7. Damper unit
8. Cover
9. Pushrod
10. Rubber bumper
11. Washer
12. Special washer
13. Pin
14. Clip
15. Spring seat
16. Spring
17. Spring retainer
18. Spring adjuster
19. Locknut
20. Cover
21. Adjust nut
22. Cover
23. Lower bracket
24. Thrust bushing
25. Oil seal
26. Bushing

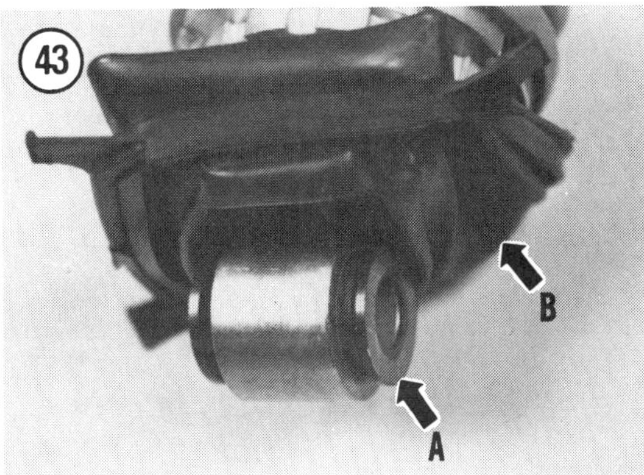

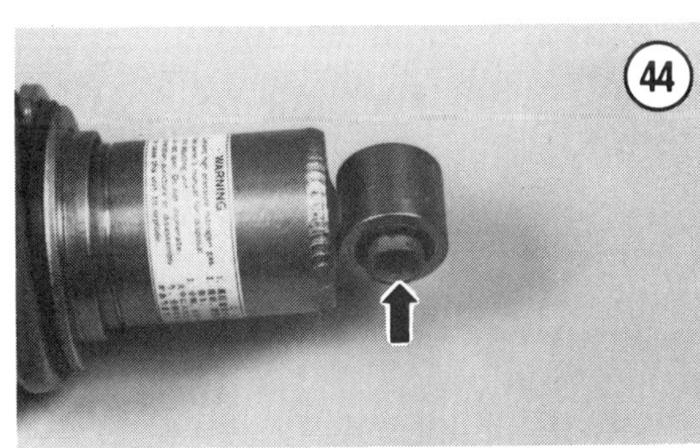

WARNING

*The damper unit contains highly pressurized nitrogen gas. Do not attempt to open the damper unit or place it near an open flame or high heat source. Read the warning label **(Figure 42)** at the top of the damper unit for care and instructions for the proper safe handling of the unit. If the damper unit has to be replaced, return the old damper unit to a Yamaha dealer so they can properly dispose of the unit.*

1. Remove the thrust bushing (A, **Figure 43**) from each side of the lower mount.

2. On XT600 models, remove the rubber boot (B, **Figure 43**) from the shock absorber.

3A. On XT600 models, inspect the upper (**Figure 44**) and lower (**Figure 45**) rubber mounting bushings of the shock absorber where it attaches to the frame and relay. If the lower bushing is damaged, replace it. The upper bushing cannot be replaced. If damaged, the damper unit must be replaced.

3B. On TT600 models, perform the following:

a. Remove the oil seal from each side of the lower mounting point.
b. Inspect the upper rubber mounting bushing and the lower bushing of the shock absorber where it attaches to the frame and relay arm. If either bushing is damaged, replace the damper unit assembly since the bushings cannot be replaced separately.

4. Clean the mounting bushings with solvent. Thoroughly dry and apply molybdenum disulfide grease to the mounting bushings.

5. Check the damper unit for leakage. If it is leaking, replace the damper unit.

6. Make sure the damper rod (A, **Figure 46**) is straight and that the rubber bumper (B, **Figure 46**)

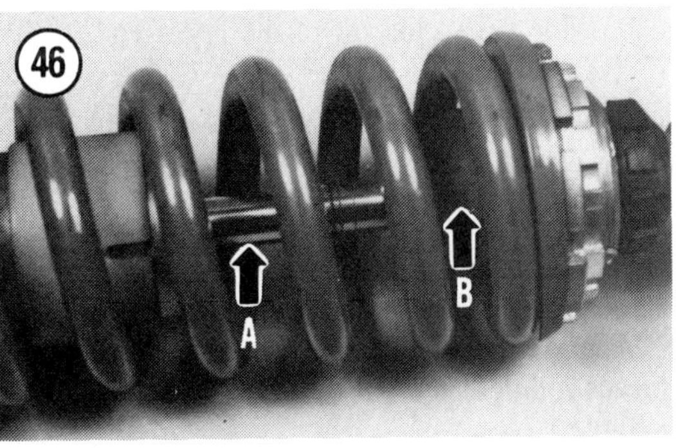

is not damaged or worn. If either is faulty, replace the damper unit or rubber bumper.

7. On XT600 models, inspect the rubber boot (**Figure 47**). If the rubber boot is torn or deteriorated, replace with a new one.

Spring Removal (All Models)

Refer to **Figure 40** for XT600 models or **Figure 41** for TT600 models for this procedure.

NOTE
This procedure is shown on a XT600 unit. Where differences occur between the two models they are identified.

1. Remove the rear shock absorber as described in this chapter.

2. If you are satisfied with the handling of the bike and want to maintain the same spring preload, measure the shock spring length (**Figure 48**) with a tape measure and record the measurement.

3. Using the spanner wrench provided in your bike's tool kit, slowly loosen the spring adjuster locknut (A, **Figure 49**).

4. Loosen the spring adjuster (B, **Figure 49**) to relieve the spring pressure.

5A. On XT600 models, perform the following:

a. From the upper end of the shock absorber, remove the clip, then remove the spring seat (A, **Figure 50**) and guide (B, **Figure 50**).

b. Slide the spring off of the upper end of the shock absorber unit.

5B. On TT600 models, perform the following:

a. From the lower end of the shock absorber, remove the spring retainers.

b. Slide the spring off of the lower end of the shock absorber unit.

6. Install by reversing these removal steps. Note the following.

7. Install and adjust the spring to the length measurement recorded in Step 2. Refer to **Table 4** for spring preload length measurements.

8. Apply Loctite No. 242 (blue) to the locknut threads and tighten to the torque specification listed in **Table 2**.

Spring Preload Adjustment

1. Remove the rear shock absorber as described in this chapter.

2A. On XT600 models, perform the following:

a. Using the spanner wrench provided in your bike's tool kit, slowly loosen the spring locknut (A, **Figure 49**).

b. Turn the spring adjuster (B, **Figure 49**) to obtain the desired spring preload within the minimum and maximum limits specified in **Table 4**.

2B. On TT600 models, perform the following:

a. Using a wrench, slowly loosen the spring locknut (A, **Figure 51**).

47

48

49

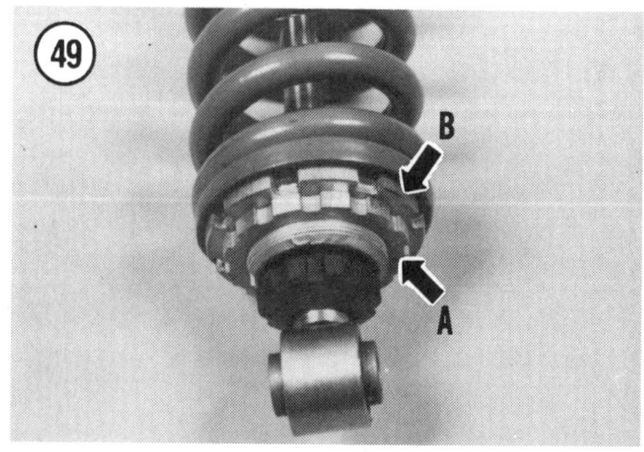

b. Using the spanner wrench provided in your bike's tool kit, turn the spring adjuster (B, **Figure 51**) to obtain the desired spring preload within the minimum and maximum limits specified in **Table 4**.

3A. On XT600 models, apply Loctite No. 242 (blue) to the locknut threads and tighten to the torque specification listed in **Table 2**.

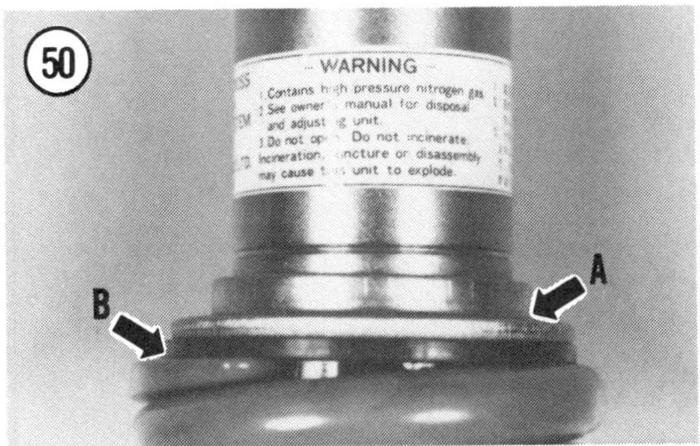

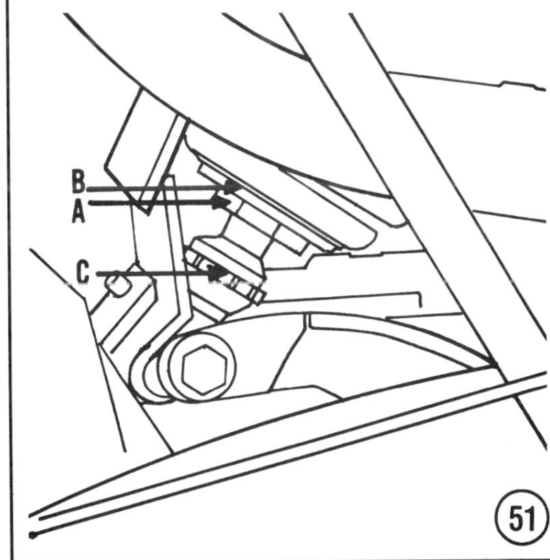

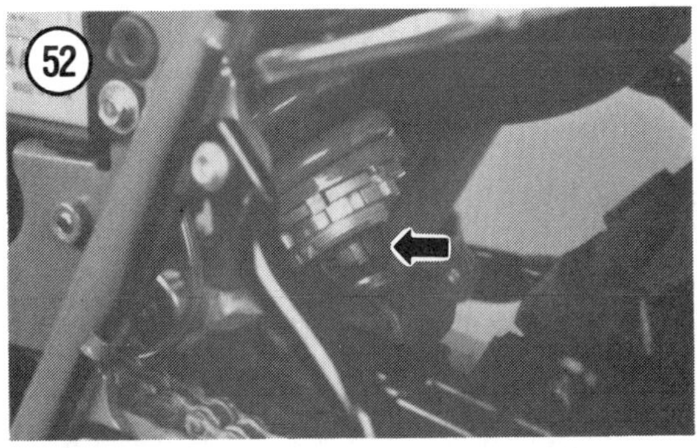

3B. On TT600 models, tighten the locknut securely.

Rebound Damping Adjustment

1. Rebound damping adjustment is made by turning the rebound adjuster ring at the shock's rear mount bracket. Refer to **Figure 52** for XT600 models or C, **Figure 51** for TT600 models.

2. To make rebound damping stiffer, turn the adjuster *clockwise* as viewed from the right-hand side of the bike. Turn the adjuster *counterclockwise* to soften rebound damping. Always turn the adjuster ring by hand.

NOTE
When turning the adjuster, make sure it clicks into position. Otherwise, the adjuster will automatically be set in the stiffest position.

CAUTION
*Do not turn the adjuster more than the maximum number of adjustments provided. See **Table 5 (XT600) or Table 6 (TT600).***

MONOCROSS LINKAGE

The Monocross linkage has a connecting rod mounted on the frame that connects to the relay arm. The relay arm attaches to the swing arm and the shock absorber. The bushings at all these joints must be inspected and lubricated according to the maintenance schedule in Chapter Three and replaced when worn.

NOTE
Grease fittings (zerk fittings) are installed on some models. These can be used to periodically lubricate the bushings. Other models will require disassembly of the linkage for periodic lubrication.

Monocross Linkage Disassembly/Inspection/Lubrication/Assembly

Refer to **Figure 53** for XT600 models or **Figure 54** for TT600 models for this procedure.

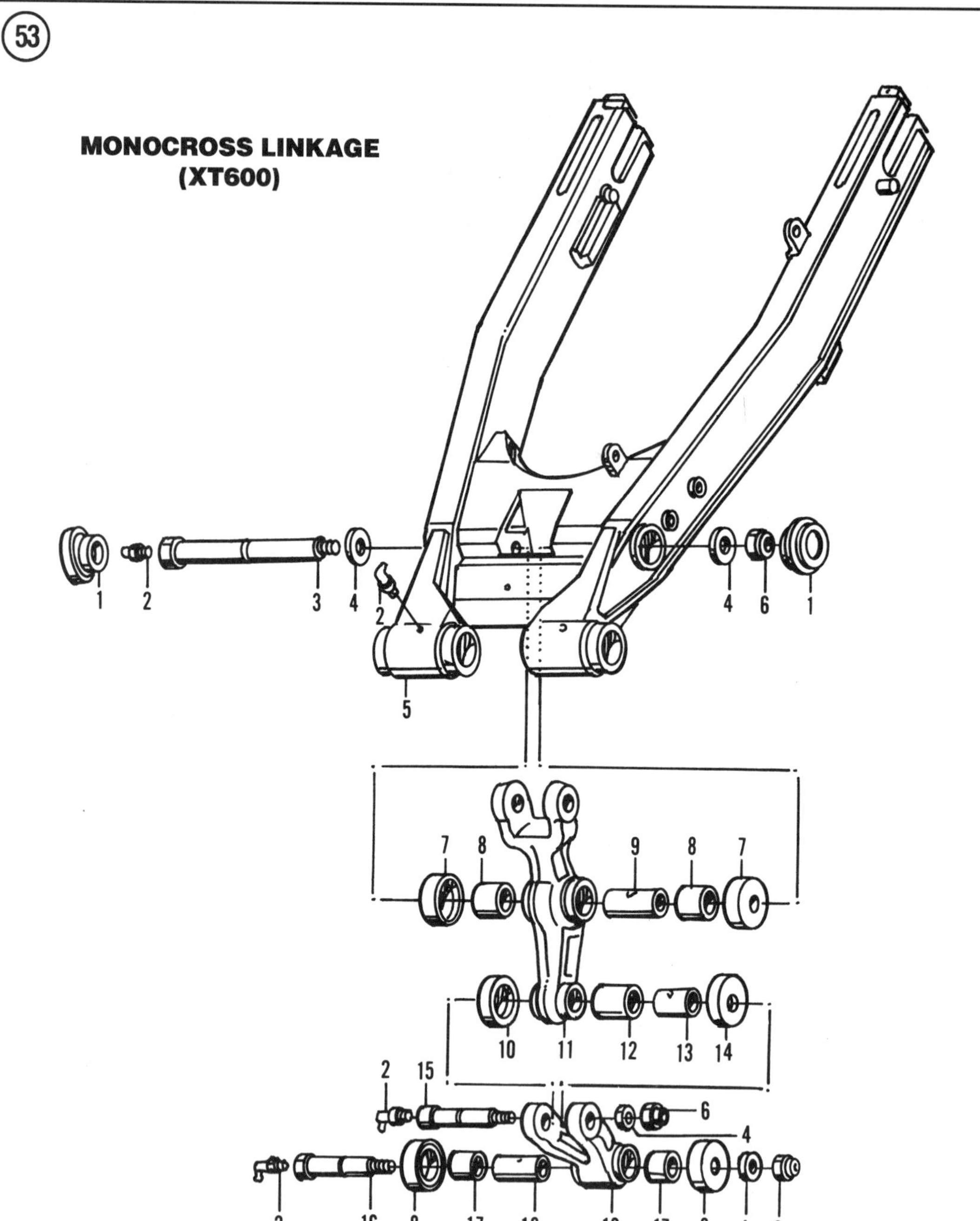

1. Cap
2. Grease nipple
3. Pivot bolt
4. Washer
5. Swing arm
6. Nut
7. Thrust cover
8. Sleeve bushing
9. Solid bushing
10. Thrust cover
11. Relay arm
12. Needle bearing
13. Collar
14. Thrust cover
15. Pivot bolt
16. Pivot bolt
17. Sleeve bushing
18. Connecting rod

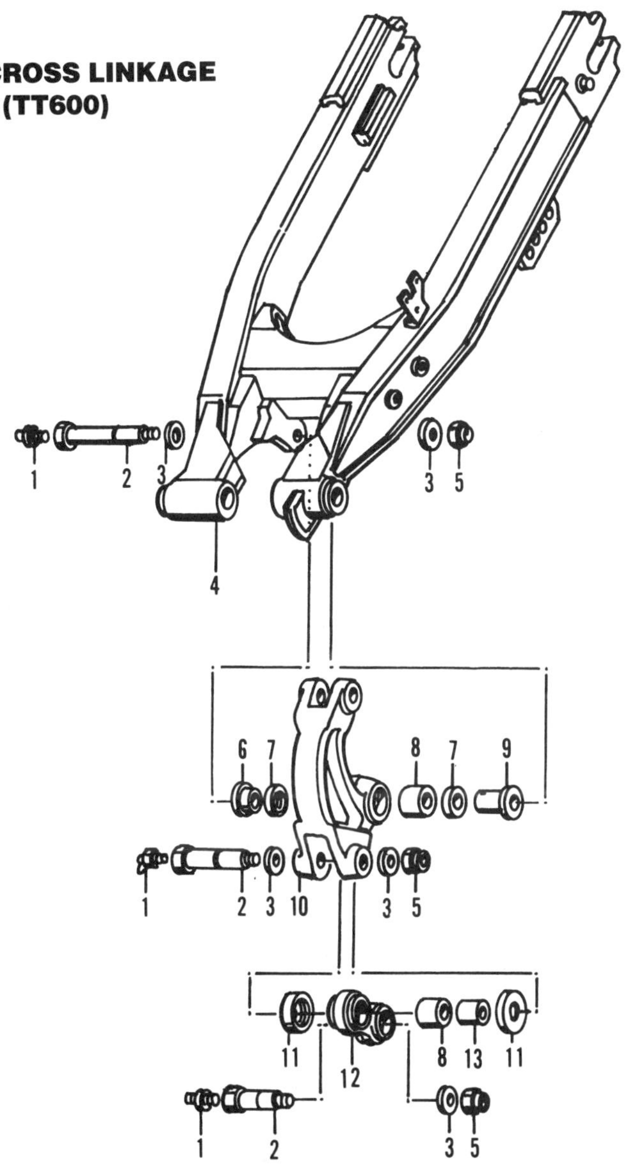

1. Grease nipple
2. Pivot bolt
3. Washer
4. Swing arm
5. Nut
6. Collar
7. Oil seal
8. Needle bearing
9. Collar
10. Relay arm
11. Thrust cover
12. Relay arm
13. Collar

WARNING
*All bolt and nuts used on the Monocross suspension must be replaced with parts of the same type. Do **not** use a replacement part of lesser quality or substitute design, as this may affect the performance of the system or result in failure of the part which will lead to loss of control of the bike. Torque values listed must be used during installation to assure proper retention of these parts.*

1. Remove the rear wheel as described in this chapter.
2. Remove the shock absorber as described in this chapter.
3. Remove the pivot bolt, nut and washer (**Figure 55**) securing the connecting rod to the frame.

NOTE
The following steps are shown with the swing arm removed for clarity. It is not necessary to remove the swing arm in order to remove the Monocross linkage.

4A. On XT600 models, to remove the connecting rod, perform the following:
   a. Remove the bolt, nut and washer (A, **Figure 56**) securing the connecting rod to the relay arm.
   b. Remove the connecting rod (B, **Figure 56**).

4B. On TT600 models, to remove the connecting rod, perform the following:
   a. Remove the bolt, nut and washers (A, **Figure 57**) securing the connecting rod to the relay arm.
   b. Remove the connecting rod (B, **Figure 57**).

5A. On XT600 models, to remove the relay arm, perform the following:
   a. If not already removed, remove the cap from each side of the swing arm.
   b. Remove the bolt, nut and washer (A, **Figure 58**) securing the relay arm to the swing arm.
   c. Remove the relay arm (B, **Figure 58**).

5B. On TT600 models, to remove the relay arm, perform the following:
   a. Remove the bolt, nut and washers (C, **Figure 57**) securing the relay arm to the swing arm.
   b. Remove the relay arm (D, **Figure 57**).

6. Remove the thrust covers from both parts.
7. Clean the assembly in solvent and dry thoroughly. Flush the pivot bolts with solvent.
8. Refer to **Figure 53** for XT600 models or **Figure 54** for TT600 models; remove the bearing collars and various bushings.
9. Inspect the needle bearing in the relay arm on all models and in the connecting rod on TT600 models. Replace the bearing if it shows excessive wear or damage. Bearing replacement requires a press. Refer to *Rear Suspension Bearing Replacement* in this chapter.
10. Inspect the solid and sleeve bushing and the pivot bolts. Replace any bearings that show excessive wear or damage.
11. Lubricate the bearing, all bushings and pivot bolts with lithium base wheel bearing grease.
12. Assemble by reversing these removal steps. Note the following.
13. Tighten all pivot bolts to the torque specifications in **Table 2** (XT600) or **Table 3** (TT600).

SWING ARM

In time, the bearings will wear beyond service limits and must be replaced. The condition of the bearings can greatly affect handling performance and if not replaced they can produce erratic and dangerous handling.

While bearing alignment differs between the 2 models, replacement is the same.

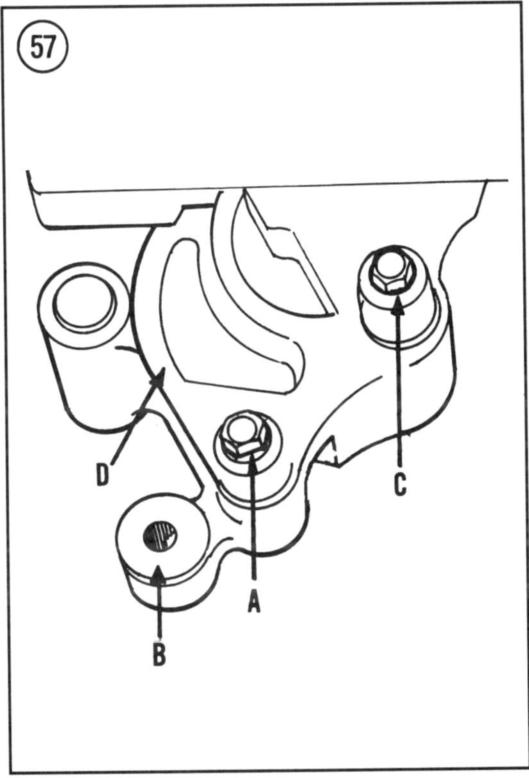

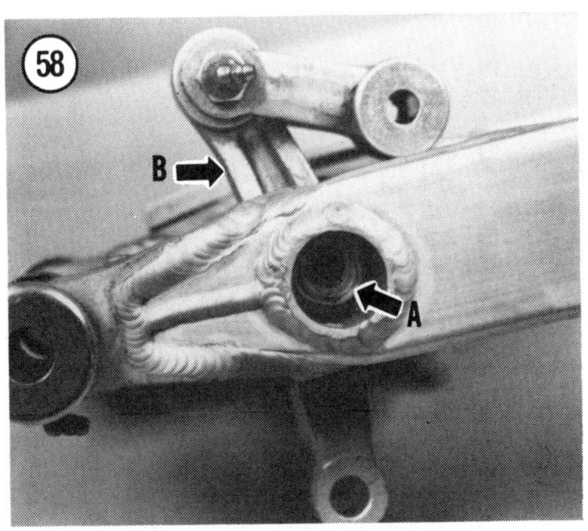

Removal/Installation

Refer to **Figure 59** for XT600 models or **Figure 60** for TT600 models for this procedure.

NOTE
This procedure is shown on a XT600 unit. Where differences occur between the two models they are identified

1. Remove the seat as described under *Seat Removal/Installation* in Chapter Thirteen.
2. Remove both frame side covers.
3. Remove the rear wheel (A, **Figure 61**) as described in this chapter.
4. Remove the bolts and nuts securing the drive chain guide (B, **Figure 61**) and remove it from the swing arm. Let it hang on the drive chain.

5A. On XT600 models, perform the following:

a. Unhook and pull the rubber boot (**Figure 62**) up and off of the boot support on the swing arm.
b. Remove the cotter pin and washer (**Figure 63**) from the shock absorber lower pivot pin.
c. Remove the pivot pin and release the shock absorber from the relay arm.
d. Remove the pivot bolt, nut and washer (**Figure 55**) securing the connecting rod to the frame.

5B. On TT600 models, perform the following:

a. Remove the pivot bolt, nut and washers from the shock absorber lower mount on the relay arm.
b. Disconnect the shock absorber from the relay arm.
c. Remove the pivot bolt, nut and washers securing the connecting rod to the frame.

6. Grasp the swing arm at the rear (**Figure 64**) and try to rock it back and forth, pulling the top and pushing the bottom, then reversing. If you feel any more than a very slight movement of the swing arm, and the pivot bolt is correctly tightened, the needle bearings should be replaced.
7. Remove the swing arm pivot bolt nut (A, **Figure 65**). If you have to knock the pivot bolt out with a rod, take care not to damage the bearings or the end of the pivot bolt. Remove the pivot bolt.

8A. On XT600 models, perform the following:

a. Remove the swing arm from the frame. Don't lose the 3 thrust collars and oil seals (**Figure 66**).

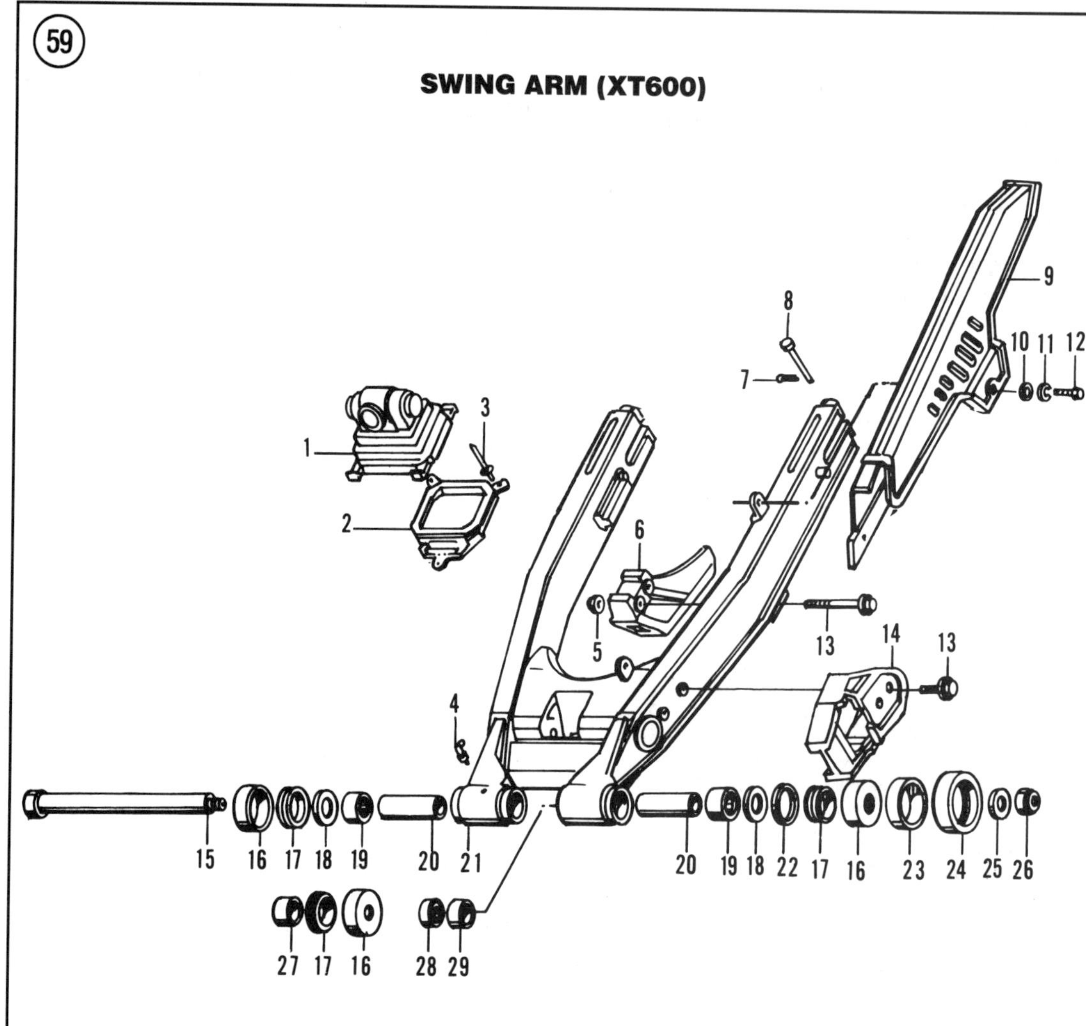

1. Rubber boot
2. Boot support
3. Blind rivet
4. Grease fitting
5. Nut
6. Drive chain guide
7. Cotter pin
8. Pin
9. Drive chain guard
10. Washer
11. Lockwasher
12. Bolt
13. Bolt
14. Drive chain slider
15. Pivot shaft
16. Thrust cover
17. Oil seal
18. Shim
19. Needle bearing
20. Bushing
21. Swing arm
22. Washer
23. Collar
24. Drive chain guard
25. Washer
26. Nut
27. Solid bushing
28. Oil seal
29. Solid bushing

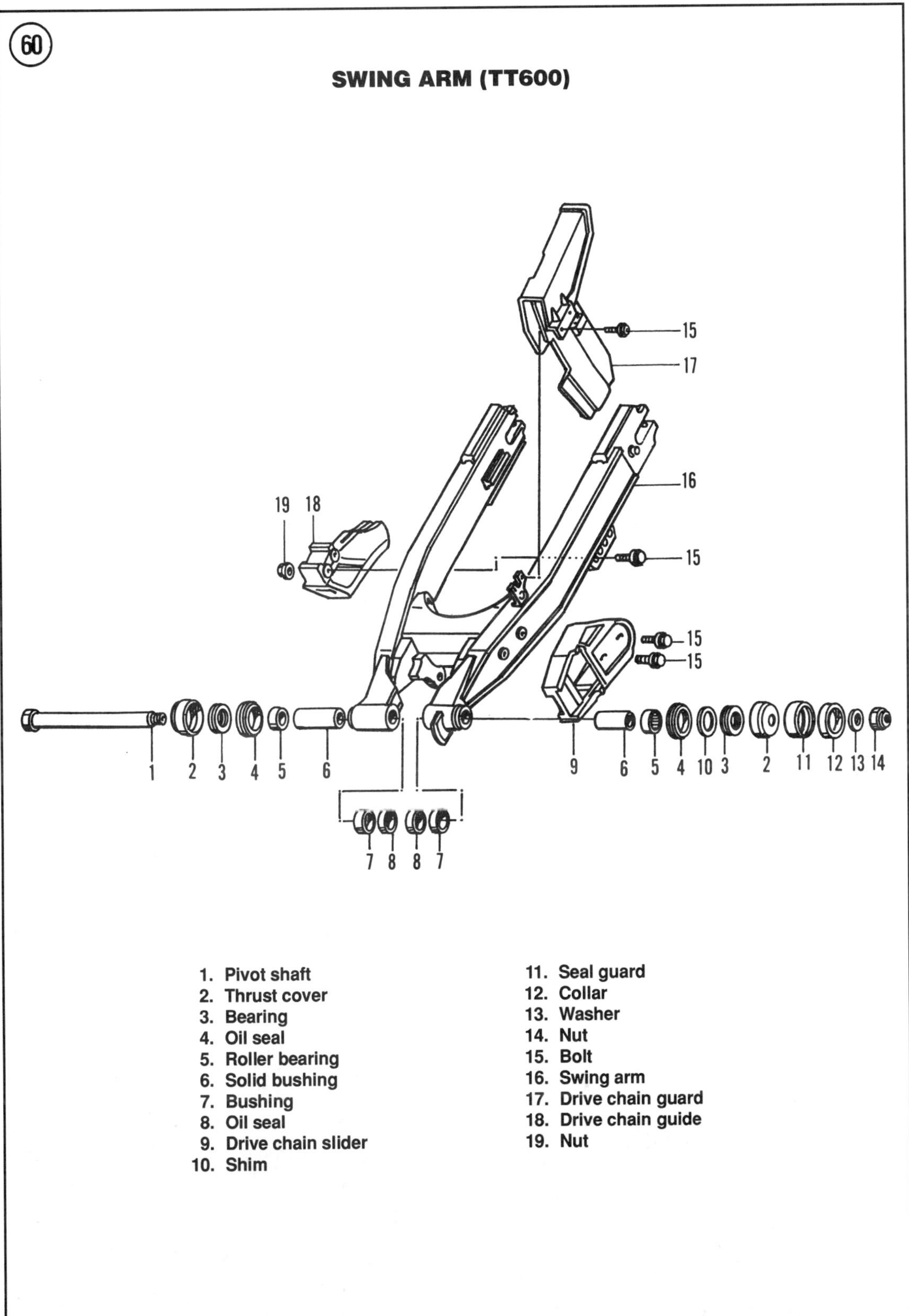

1. Pivot shaft
2. Thrust cover
3. Bearing
4. Oil seal
5. Roller bearing
6. Solid bushing
7. Bushing
8. Oil seal
9. Drive chain slider
10. Shim
11. Seal guard
12. Collar
13. Washer
14. Nut
15. Bolt
16. Swing arm
17. Drive chain guard
18. Drive chain guide
19. Nut

b. If any fall off during removal, immediately reinstall them onto the swing arm to avoid misplacing them.

8B. On TT600 models, perform the following:

a. Remove the swing arm from the frame. Don't lose the 2 thrust collars.

b. If any fall off during removal, immediately reinstall them onto the swing arm to avoid misplacing them.

9. Install by reversing these removal steps. Note the following.

10. Be sure to install the drive chain (A, **Figure 67**) over the swing arm (B, **Figure 67**) prior to installing the pivot bolt.

NOTE

*The swing arm pivot bolt goes through the engine crankcase as well as the frame. When the swing arm pivot bolt was removed, the engine may have moved slightly. If you are unable to insert the pivot bolt through the frame and the engine crankcase, you may have to loosen the engine rear mounting bolt and nut (**B, Figure 65**) to allow for realignment of the engine to the frame and the swing arm.*

11. Tighten the swing arm pivot shaft nut to the torque specification in **Table 2** (XT600) or **Table 3** (TT600).

12. Tighten the relay arm pivot bolt to the torque specification in **Table 2** (XT600) or **Table 3** (TT600).

13. If loosened, tighten the engine rear mounting bolt and nut to the torque specification in **Table 2** (XT600) or **Table 3** (TT600).

14. Adjust the drive chain as described under *Drive Chain Adjustment* in Chapter Three.

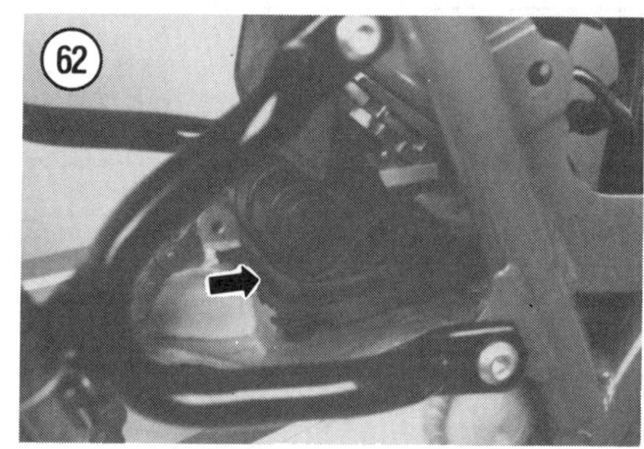

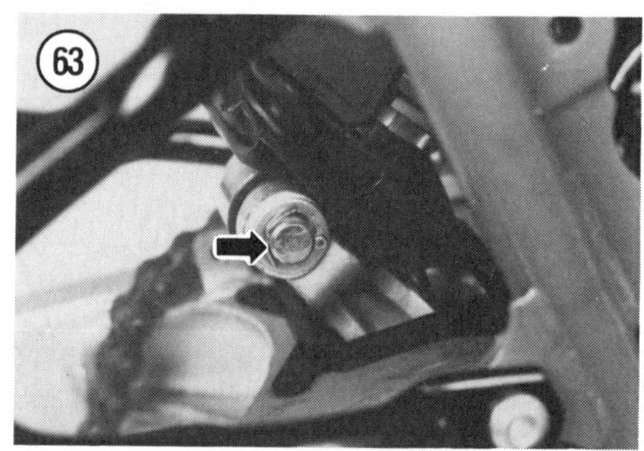

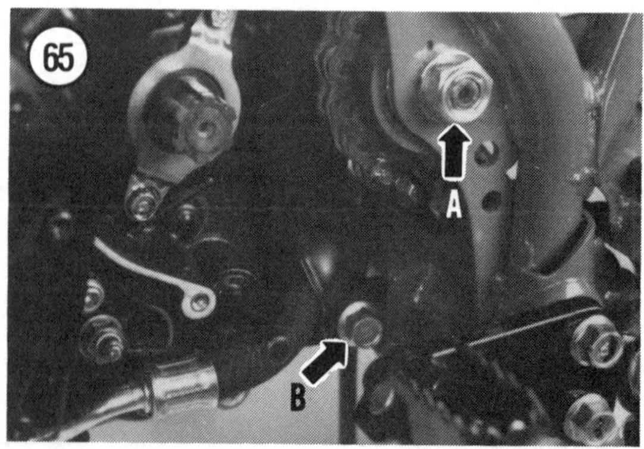

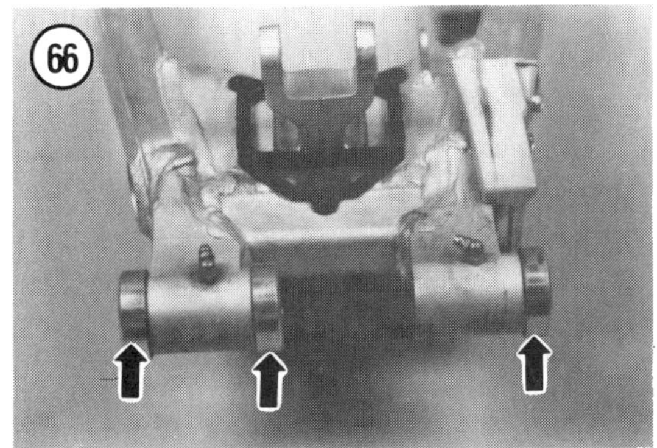

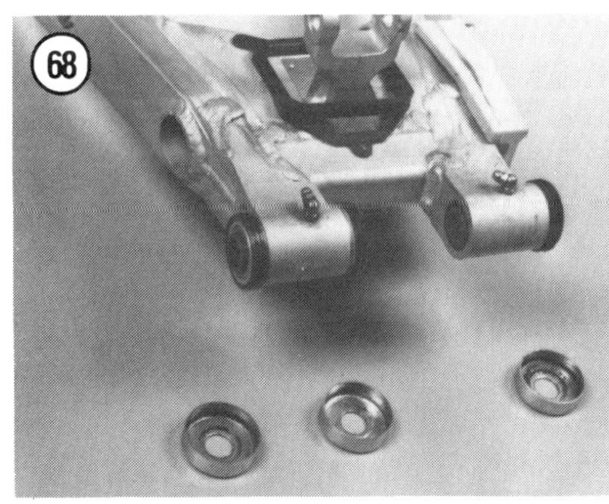

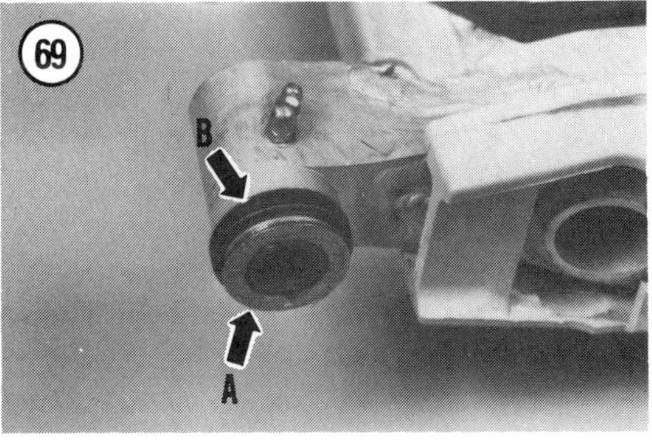

Inspection

NOTE
This procedure is shown on a XT600 unit. Where differences occur between the two models they are identified.

1. Remove the thrust collars (**Figure 68**) from the pivot points. There are 3 thrust collars on the XT600 models or 2 thrust collars on the TT600 models.

2A. On XT600 models, perform the following:

a. Remove the washer (A, **Figure 69**).
b. Inspect the oil seals (B, **Figure 69**) for damage or deterioration.
c. Even if only one seal is damaged, replace all 3 as a set.

2B. On TT600 models, perform the following:

a. Inspect the oil seals for damage or deterioration.
b. Even if only one seal is damaged, replace both as a set.

3. Remove the bushing (**Figure 70**) and inspect the needle bearings. They must rotate freely with no signs of wear or damage from lack of grease or water damage. If necessary, replace them as described in this chapter.

4. Inspect the drive chain slider (**Figure 71**) for wear or damage. If the plastic is worn halfway through,

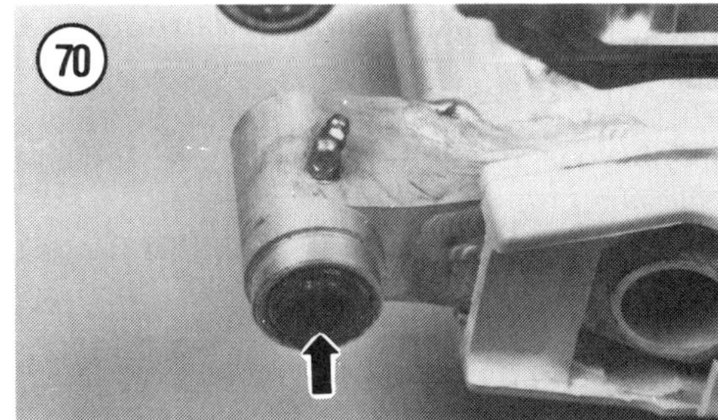

remove the bolts and remove the slider before the drive chain starts to wear into the swing arm.

5. Inspect the drive chain guard on the left-hand side for wear or damage. Replace if necessary.

6. Inspect the rear portion of the swing arm where the rear axle rides. Make sure the pin and cotter pin (**Figure 72**) are secured in place.

7. Inspect the drive chain slider mounting bracket (**Figure 73**) for damage. The bracket cannot be replaced. If damaged, the swing arm must be replaced.

8. Clean the old grease from all parts. After the parts have been cleaned and dry, apply a liberal amount of lithium waterproof wheel bearing grease to the bearings, sleeves and pivot shaft.

9. Make sure the grease fittings are clear and not clogged. Apply grease with a grease gun and note whether grease is flowing out of the swing arm area or not. If the grease does not flow out, remove the grease fitting and thoroughly clean it. Replace the grease fitting if you cannot clean it sufficiently.

10. On XT600 models, inspect the boot support (**Figure 74**) for damage. Replace if necessary.

11. Perform the *Swing Arm Side Clearance Check and Adjustment* as described in this chapter.

12. Install by reversing these removal steps. Note the following.

13. Tighten the swing arm pivot shaft nut to the torque specification in **Table 2** (XT600) or **Table 3** (TT600).

14. Tighten the relay arm pivot bolt to the torque specification in **Table 2** (XT600) or **Table 3** (TT600).

15. Adjust the drive chain as described in Chapter Three.

Swing Arm Side Clearance Check and Adjustment

This procedure describes how to check and adjust swing arm side clearance. A vernier caliper will be required to check side clearance.

Refer to **Figure 75** for this procedure.

1. Remove the swing arm as described in this chapter.

2. Remove the thrust collars from the swing arm pivot points.

3. To measure the overall length of the bushings, perform the following:

   a. Measure the length of the right-hand bushing A1. The standard length is 75.2-75.3 mm (2.961-2.965 in.).

   b. Measure the length of the left-hand bushing A2. The standard length is 68.2-68.3 mm (2.685-2.689 in.).

   c. If either bushing is worn to less than these dimensions, replace the bushing(s) with a new one and re-measure the new bushing(s). Record these measurements (A1 and B1).

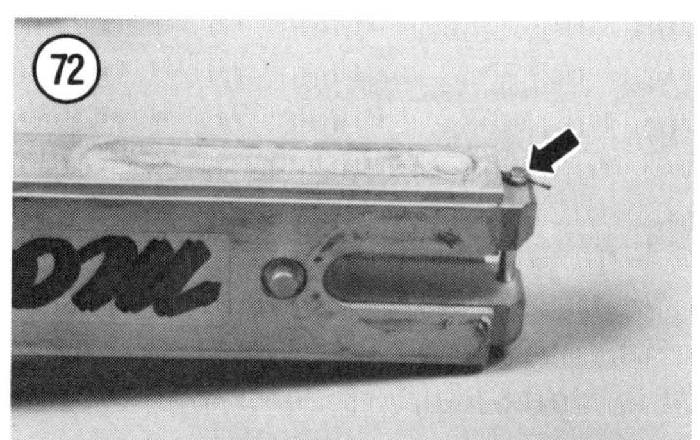
72

73

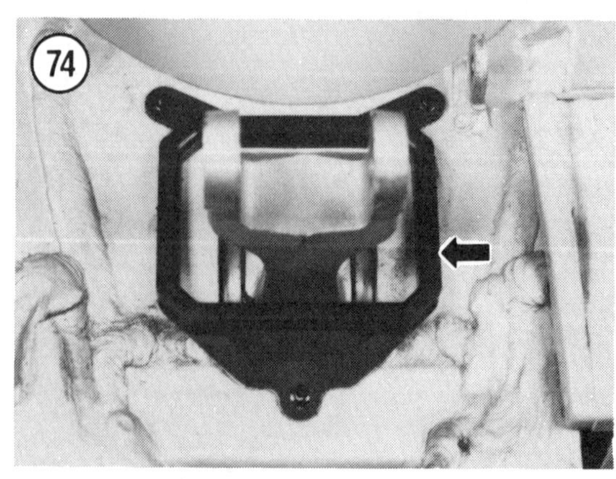
74

4. To measure the overall length from the inside surface of the bushing-to-the shim, perform the following:

   a. Measure the length of the right-hand bushing to the shim B1; record this dimension.
   b. Measure the length of the left-hand bushing to the shim B2; record this dimension.

5. Calculate the swing arm side clearance "C" by subtracting (B1 + B2) from (A1 + A2).

Example

A1 (75.2 mm) + A2 (68.2 mm) = 143.4 mm
B1 (75.0 mm) + B2 (68.0 mm) = 143.0 mm
Subtract B dimensions from A dimensions = C (clearance).

(A1 + A2) = 143.4 mm
− (B1 + B2) = 143.0 mm
Clearance = 0.4 mm

6. The correct swing arm side clearance is 0.1-0.3 mm (0.004-0.012 in.).
7. If the side clearance is incorrect, 1 or 2 adjusting shims will be required. Adjusting shims are available in one thickness only: 0.3 mm (0.012 in.).
8. If only one shim is required, install it on the left-hand side. If 2 shims are required, install 1 shim on each side.
9. Install the 2 (TT600) or 3 (XT600) thrust collars and oil seals (**Figure 66**).
10. Install the swing arm as described in this chapter.

REAR SUSPENSION BEARING REPLACEMENT

Refer to **Figure 76** for this procedure.

1. Remove the swing arm as described in this chapter.
2. Remove the following parts from the swing arm:
   a. Thrust collars.
   b. Oil seals, washers and shims.
   c. Bushings.
3. Secure the swing arm in a vise with soft jaws.

CAUTION
Do not remove the bearings and bushings just for inspection as they are usually damaged during removal.

4. Carefully tap out the bearings and bushings. Use a suitable size drift or socket and extension and carefully drive the bearing or bushing out from the opposite end.

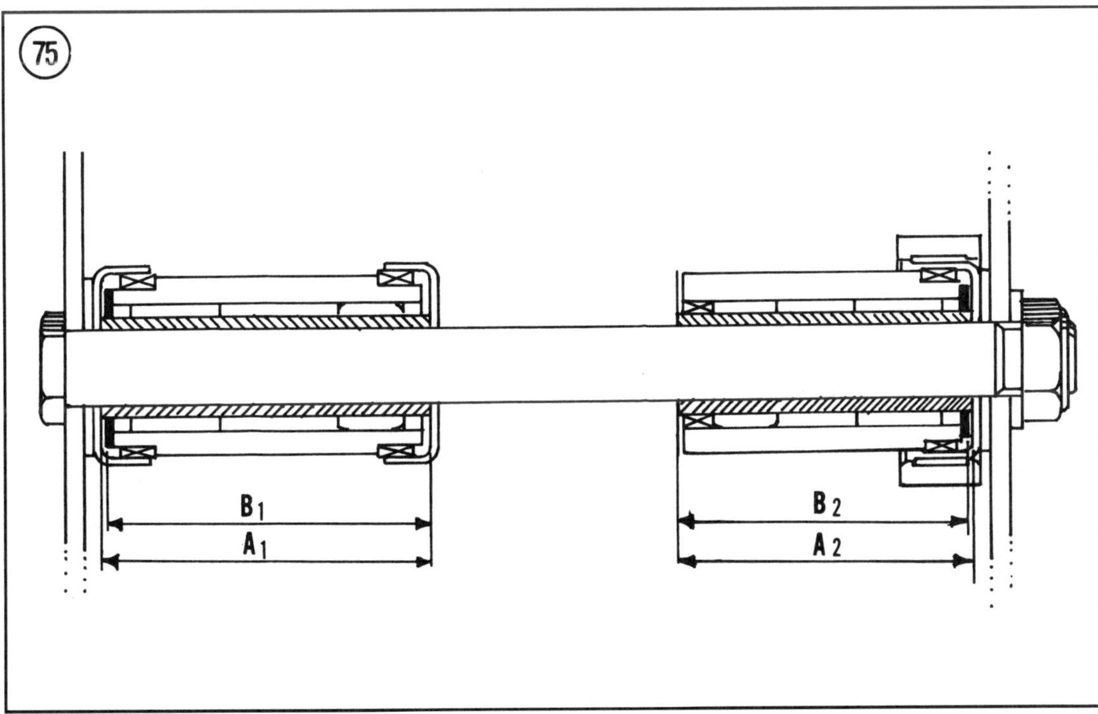

11

5. Clean the swing arm thoroughly in solvent. Check the bearing or bushing mounting areas for cracks, wear or other damage.

NOTE
A press will be required to accurately and safely install the bearings and bushings.

6. Apply a light coat of lithium waterproof wheel bearing grease to all parts before installation.
7. Using a press, install the new bearings and bushings until they are 4 mm (0.16 in.) (Dimension A, **Figure 76**) from the outer edge of the swing arm pivot point.
8. After installing the bearings and bushings, liberally coat them with lithium waterproof wheel bearing grease.
9. Install the following parts into the swing arm:
   a. Bushings.
   b. Oil seals, washers and shims.
   c. Thrust collars.
10. Install the swing arm as described in this chapter.

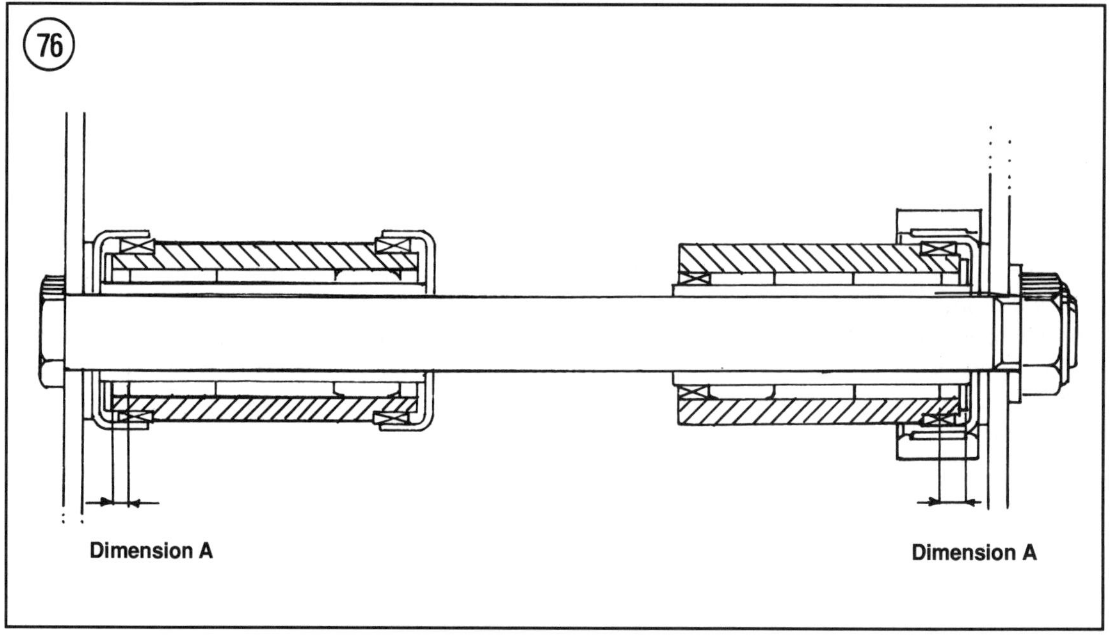

Table 1 REAR SUSPENSION SPECIFICATIONS

Rear wheel	
Travel	
XT600	235 mm (9.3 in.)
TT600	270 mm (10.6 in.)
Rim size	2.15 × 18
Rim runout	
Radial (up and down)	2.0 mm (0.08 in.)
Lateral (side-to-side)	2.0 mm (0.08 in.)
Rear axle runout	0.25 mm (0.01 in.)
Swing arm free play limit	
End play	1.0 mm (0.04 in.)
Side play	
XT600	0.3 mm (0.012 in.)
TT600	0.2 mm (0.008 in.)

Table 2 REAR SUSPENSION TIGHTENING TORQUES—XT600

	N•m	ft.-lb.
Rear axle nut	100	73
Driven sprocket nuts	62	45
Drive sprocket bolts	10	7.2
Swing arm pivot bolt and nut	100	73
Shock absorber		
Upper pivot bolt and nut	50	36
Lower pivot bolt and locknut	70	51
Relay arm		
To frame	50	36
To connecting rod	50	36
Connecting rod-to-swing arm	50	36
Engine rear mounting bolt and nut	50	36

Table 3 REAR SUSPENSION TIGHTENING TORQUES—TT600

	N•m	ft.-lb.
Rear axle nut	105	77
Driven sprocket nuts	30	22
Drive sprocket bolts	10	7.2
Swing arm pivot bolt and nut	85	62
Shock absorber-upper and lower mounting bolts and nuts	32	23
Relay arm		
At swing arm	58	42
At connecting rod	32	23
Connecting rod-to-swing arm	58	42
Engine rear mounting bolt and nut	50	36

Table 4 REAR SHOCK SPRING PRELOAD*

	Standard mm (in.)	Minimum mm (in.)	Maximum mm (in.)
XT600	239 (9.4)	226.5 (8.9)	247.5 (9.7)
TT600	230 (9.1)	216 (8.5)	241 (9.5)

* Turning the spring adjuster 1 complete turn changes the preload by 1 mm (0.04 in.).

Table 5 REAR SHOCK DAMPING ADJUSTER—XT600

	Soft	Standard	Stiff
Shock position	1	2	3-4-5

Table 6 REAR SHOCK DAMPING ADJUSTER—TT600*

Standard Position Turns out	Minimum position Turns out	Maximum position Turns out
10	20	0

* To increase damping, turn the adjuster clockwise. To decrease damping, turn the adjuster counter-clockwise.

CHAPTER TWELVE

BRAKES

The 1983 and 1984 TT600 models are equipped with a drum brake on the front while all other models are equipped with a single disc brake on the front. All models are equipped with a drum brake on the rear.

Disc brake specifications are listed in **Table 1**. Drum brake specifications are listed in **Table 2**. **Tables 1-3** are at the end of this chapter.

FRONT DISC BRAKE

The front disc brake is actuated by hydraulic fluid and controlled by a hand lever on the master cylinder that is mounted on the right-hand side of the handlebar. As the brake pads wear, the brake fluid level drops in the reservoir and automatically adjusts for wear.

When working on hydraulic brake systems, it is necessary that the work area and all tools be absolutely clean. Any tiny particles of foreign matter and grit in the caliper assembly or master cylinder can damage the components.

NOTE

*If you recycle your old engine oil, **never** add used brake fluid to the old engine oil. Most oil retailers that accepts old oil for recycling may not accept the oil if other fluids (fork oil, brake fluid or any other type of petroleum based fluids) have been combined with it.*

Consider the following when servicing the front disc brake.

1. Disc brake components rarely require disassembly, so do not disassemble them unless necessary.

WARNING

Do not intermix silicone based (DOT 5) brake fluid as it can cause brake component damage leading to brake system failure.

2. Use only DOT 3 brake fluid from a sealed container.
3. Do not allow disc brake fluid to contact any plastic, painted or plated surfaces or surface damage will occur.
4. Always keep the master cylinder reservoir and spare cans of brake fluid closed to prevent dust or

moisture from entering. If moisture enters the brake fluid, it would result in brake fluid contamination and brake problems.

5. Use only disc brake fluid (DOT 3) to wash parts. Never clean any internal brake components with solvent or any other petroleum base cleaners.

6. Whenever *any* component has been removed from the brake system, the system is considered "opened" and must be bled to remove air bubbles. Also, if the brake feels "spongy," this usually means there are air bubbles in the system and it must be bled. For safe brake operation, refer to *Brake Bleeding* in this chapter.

CAUTION

Do not use solvents of any kind on the brake system's internal components. Solvents will cause the seals to swell and distort. When disassembling and cleaning brake components (except brake pads) use new DOT 3 brake fluid.

WARNING

*When working on the brake system, do **not** inhale brake dust. It may contain asbestos, which can cause lung injury and cancer. Wear a disposable face mask and wash your hands and forearms thoroughly after completing the work.*

FRONT BRAKE CALIPER (XT600)

Front Brake Pad Replacement

There is no recommended mileage interval for changing the friction pads in the disc brake. Pad wear depends greatly on riding habits and conditions. The pads should be checked for wear every 7,000 km (4,400 miles) or every 7 months and replaced when the lining thickness reaches the minimum thickness listed in **Table 1**.

CAUTION

*Watch the pads more closely when the wear line groove (**A, Figure 1**) approaches the disc. On some pads, the wear line is very close to the metal backing plate. If pad wear happens to be uneven for some reason, the backing plate may come in contact with the disc and cause damage.*

To maintain an even brake pressure on the disc, always replace both pads in the caliper at the same time. Always use brake pads from the same manufacturer in the front caliper—never intermix different brands.

It is not necessary to remove or disassemble the brake caliper assembly to replace the brake pads.

Refer to **Figure 2** for this procedure.

1. Place the bike on a stand so the front wheel clears the ground.

2. The piston must be repositioned within the caliper assembly prior to installing the new *thicker* brake pads. The front master cylinder brake fluid level will rise as the caliper piston is being repositioned in the following steps. Perform the following:

   a. Clean the top of the front master cylinder of all dirt and foreign matter.

   b. Remove the screws (**Figure 3**) securing the top cover and remove the top cover and diaphragm from the master cylinder.

   c. Note the brake fluid level in the reservoir. If it is up to, or close to, the top surface of the

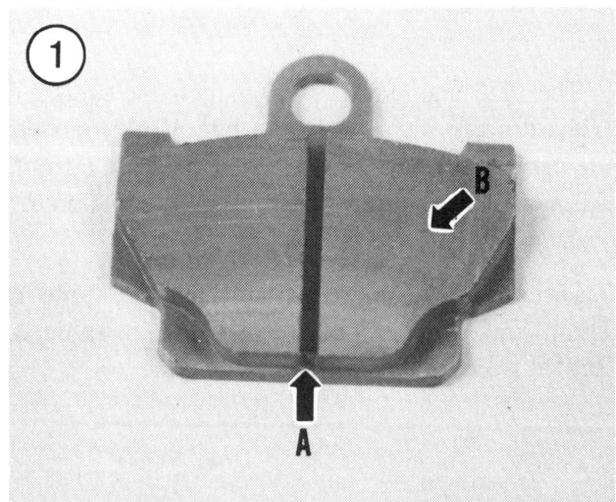

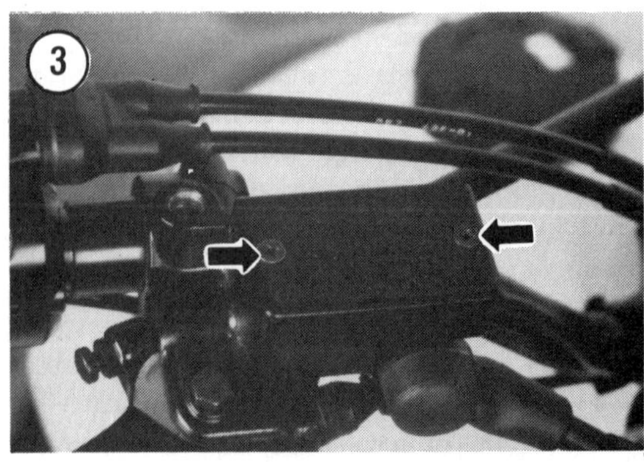

(2)

FRONT BRAKE CALIPER (XT600)

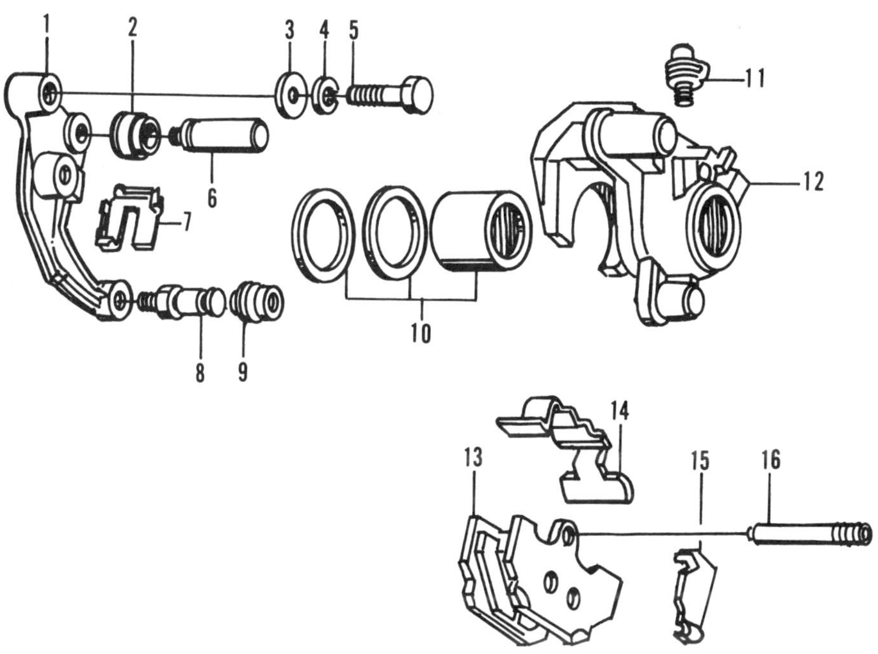

1. Caliper carrier
2. Rubber boot
3. Washer
4. Lockwasher
5. Bolt
6. Carrier pin "B"
7. Spring
8. Carrier pin "A"
9. Rubber boot
10. Piston, dust seal and piston seal assembly
11. Bleed screw and cap
12. Caliper body
13. Brake pads
14. Pad spring
15. Pad shim
16. Pad pin bolt

12

reservoir, siphon off some of the fluid at this time.

d. Push the caliper assembly toward the brake disc until it stops. This will reposition the piston into the caliper cylinder.

e. Constantly check the reservoir to make sure the brake fluid does not overflow. Remove brake fluid, if necessary, prior to it overflowing.

f. The piston should move freely during repositioning. If it doesn't, and there is evidence of sticking in the cylinder, the caliper should be removed and serviced as described in this chapter.

3. To prevent accidental application of the front brake lever, place a spacer between the front brake lever and the hand grip. Hold the spacer in place with a large rubber band, a tie wrap or a piece of tape.

4. Remove the pad pin bolt (**Figure 4**).

CAUTION
Do not scratch or gouge the brake disc with the pliers during the next step.

5. Use a pair of needlenose pliers and carefully pull the brake pads (**Figure 5**) out from the lower portion of the caliper assembly.

6. Check the brake pad friction surface (B, **Figure 1**) for oil and dirt contamination. Also check the friction material for cracking or other damage. Replace the brake pads if the surface is contaminated or damaged.

7. Measure the brake pad friction thickness with a vernier caliper or ruler. Compare to the specifications in **Table 1**. Replace the brake pads if the friction thickness is worn to the service limit or less.

8. Carefully remove any rust or corrosion from the brake disc.

9. Install the shim (**Figure 6**) onto the outboard pad.

10. Make sure the friction material faces against the brake disc.

11. Carefully push the new brake pads up into the caliper assembly. Make sure the upper tab on the brake pads is indexed properly in the caliper assembly.

12. Align the bolt hole in both brake pads with the bolt hole in the caliper bracket and install the pad pin.

13. Lightly coat the pad pin bolt with a lithium base grease.

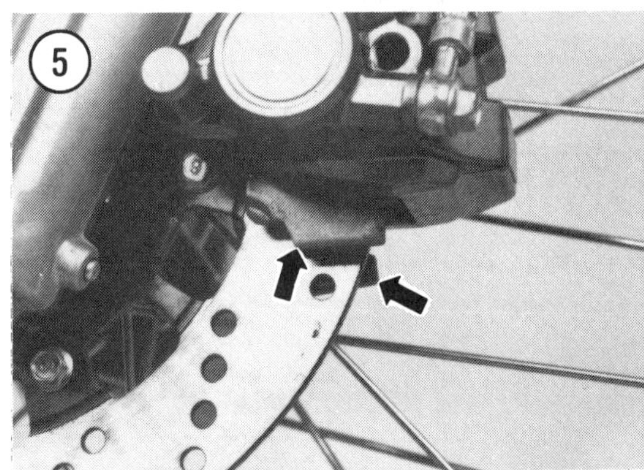

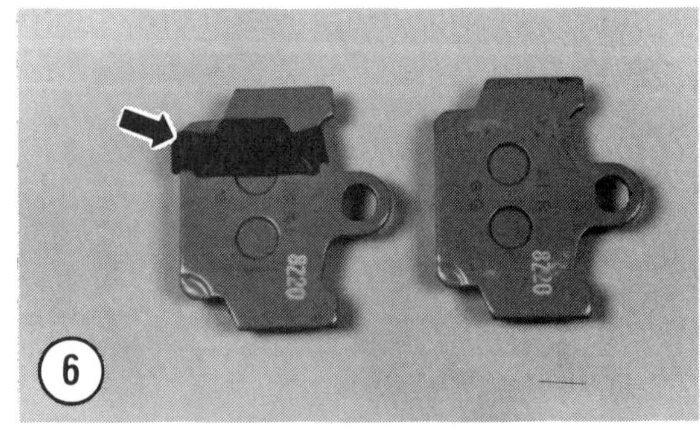

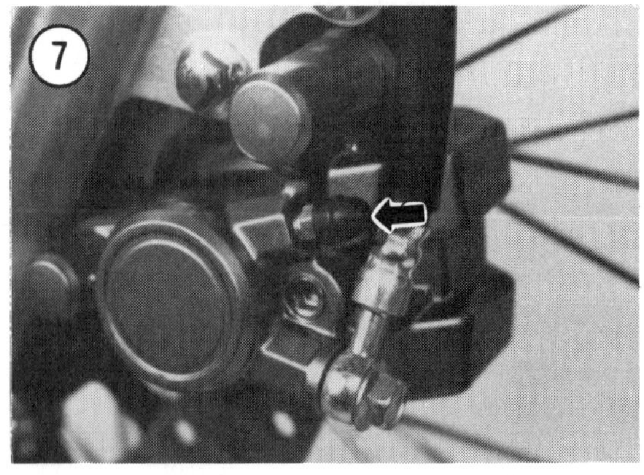

14. Install the pad pin bolt (**Figure 4**) and tighten to the torque specification in **Table 3**.

15. Spin the front wheel and activate the brake lever as many times as required to refill the cylinder in the caliper and correctly locate the pads.

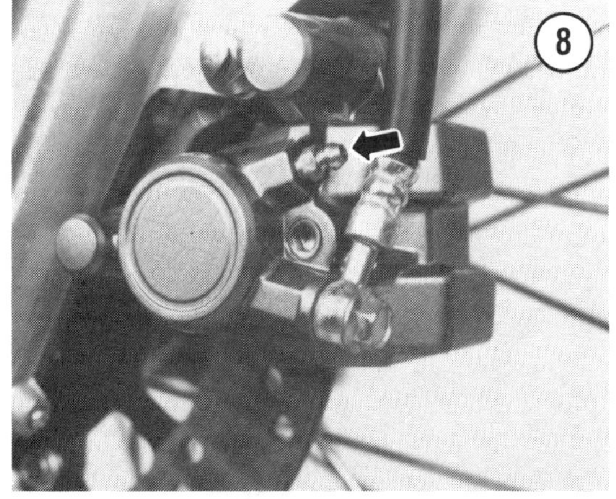
8

9

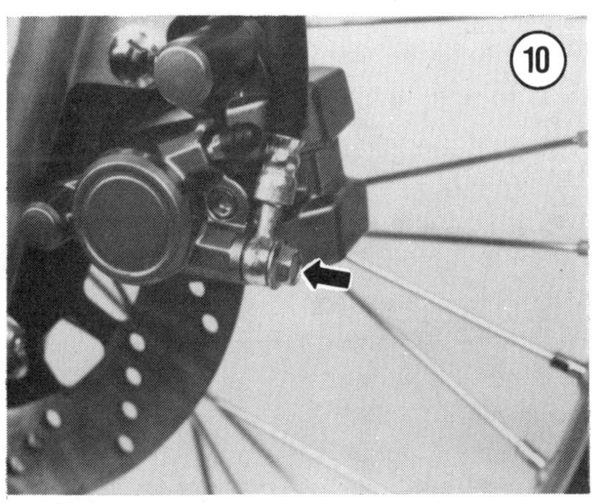
10

WARNING
Use brake fluid clearly marked DOT 3 from a sealed container. Other types may vaporize and cause brake failure. Always use the same brand name; do not intermix as many brands are not compatible. Do not intermix silicone based (DOT 5) brake fluid as it can cause brake component damage leading to brake system failure.

16. Refill the master cylinder reservoir, if necessary, to maintain the correct brake fluid level. Install the diaphragm and top cover and tighten the screws securely.

WARNING
Do not ride the motorcycle until you are sure the brake is operating correctly with full hydraulic advantage. If necessary, bleed the brake system as described in this chapter.

17. Bed the pads in gradually for the first 80 km (50 miles) by using only light pressure as much as possible. Immediate hard application will glaze the new friction pads and greatly reduce the effectiveness of the brake.

Brake Caliper Removal/Installation

Refer to **Figure 2** for this procedure.

1. Place the bike on a stand so the front wheel clears the ground.
2. Remove the cap (**Figure 7**) from the bleed valve.
3. Attach a hose to the bleed valve on the caliper assembly (**Figure 8**).
4. Place the loose end of the hose in a container to catch the brake fluid (**Figure 9**).
5. Open the bleed valve and continue to apply the front brake lever until the brake fluid is pumped out of the system. Dispose of this brake fluid—never reuse brake fluid.
6. Disconnect the hose and tighten the bleed valve.
7. Loosen the brake caliper union bolt (**Figure 10**). Remove the union bolt and sealing washers.
8. Remove the mounting bolts, washers and lockwashers (A, **Figure 11**) securing the caliper assembly to the fork slider.

9. To prevent the entry of moisture and dirt, cap the end of the brake line (B, **Figure 11**) and tie the loose end up to the forks.

10. Slide the caliper assembly (C, **Figure 11**) off of the brake disc and remove the caliper assembly.

11. Install by reversing these removal steps. Note the following.

12. Install the caliper assembly onto the brake disc and front fork. Install the mounting bolts, washers and lockwashers (A, **Figure 11**) and tighten to the torque specification in **Table 3**.

13. Install the brake hose, with a sealing washer on each side of the fitting, onto the caliper. Install the union bolt (**Figure 10**) and tighten to the torque specification in **Table 3**.

14. If removed, install the brake pads as described in this chapter.

15. Bleed the brake as described in this chapter.

WARNING
Do not ride the motorcycle until you are sure the brake is operating properly.

Brake Caliper Disassembly/Inspection/Assembly

Refer to **Figure 2** for this procedure.

WARNING
When working on the brake system, do ***not*** *inhale brake dust. It may contain asbestos, which can cause lung injury and cancer. Wear a disposable face mask and wash your hands and forearms thoroughly after completing the work.*

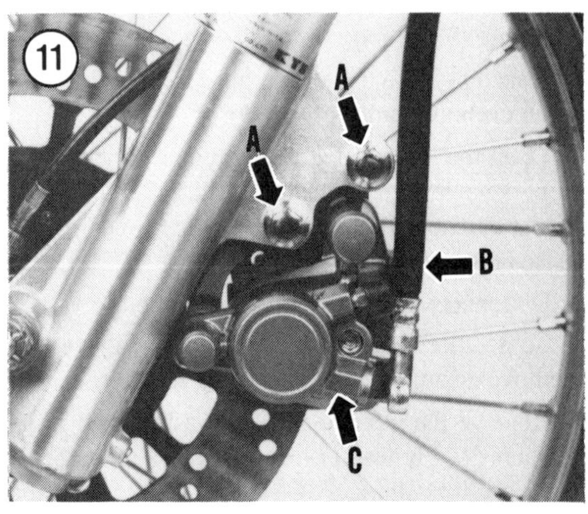

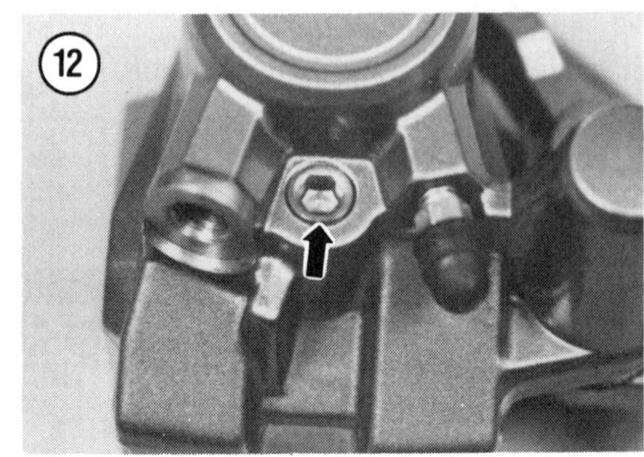

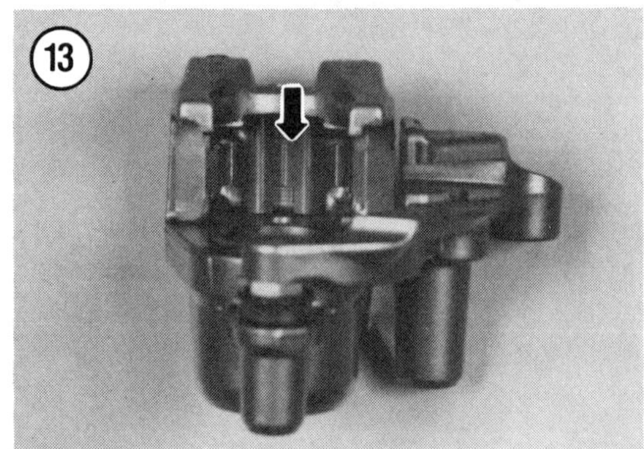

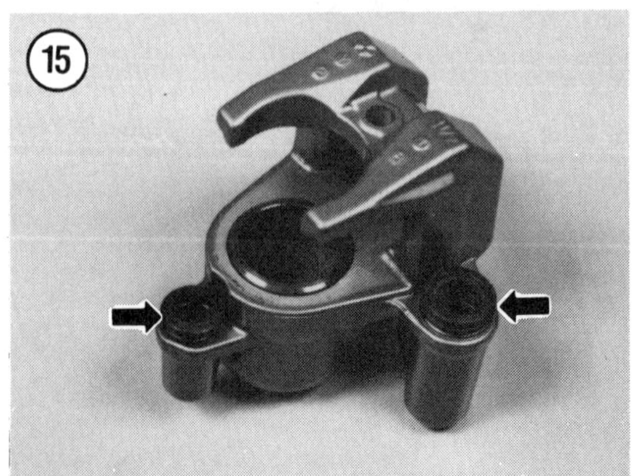

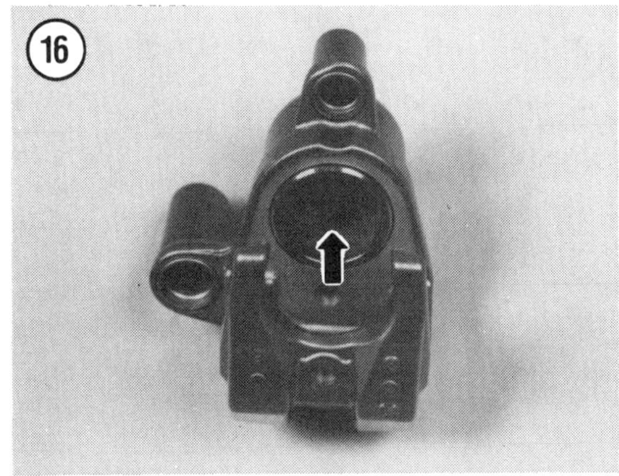
16

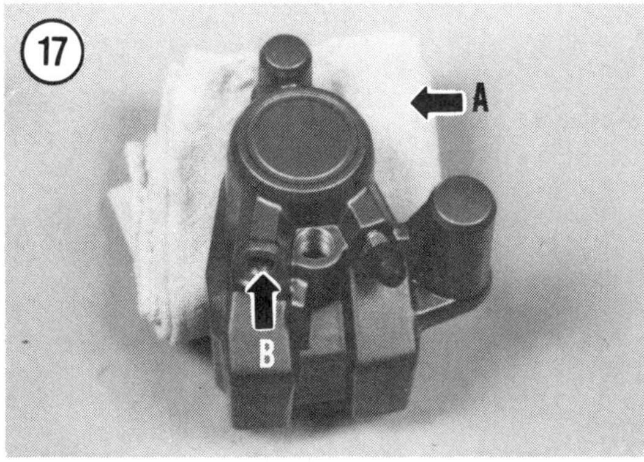

17

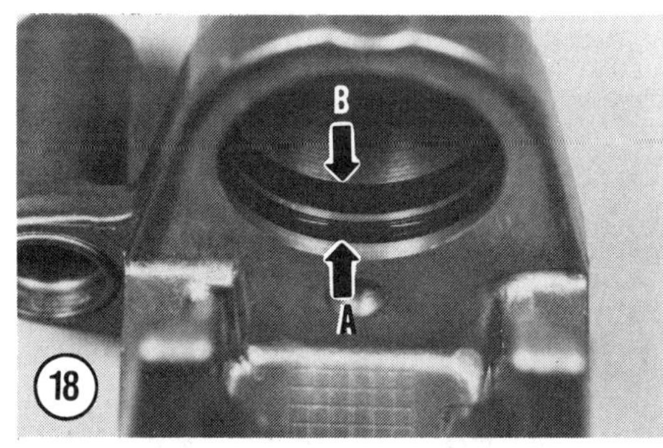

18

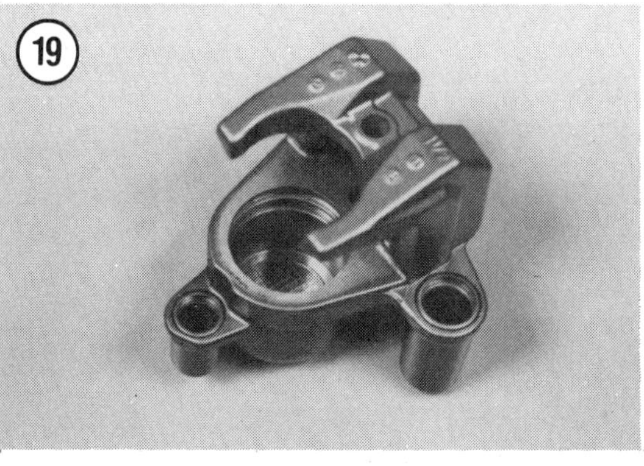
19

1. Remove the caliper assembly as described in this chapter.
2. If the brake pads are still installed, perform the following:
   a. Remove the pad pin bolt (**Figure 12**).
   b. Remove the inboard and outboard brake pads.
3. Remove the brake pad spring (**Figure 13**).
4. Carefully pull the caliper carrier (**Figure 14**) straight up and off of the caliper body.
5. Remove the rubber boots (**Figure 15**) from the caliper body.
6. Withdraw the piston (**Figure 16**) from the caliper body. If you cannot remove the piston easily, perform the following:
   a. Either wrap the caliper body and piston with a heavy cloth or place a shop cloth (A, **Figure 17**) or piece of soft wood over the end of the piston.
   b. Perform this step over and close down to a workbench top. Hold the caliper body with the piston facing away from you.

WARNING
*In the next step, the piston may shoot out of the caliper body like a bullet. Keep your fingers out of the way. Wear shop gloves and apply air pressure gradually. Do **not** use high pressure air nor place the air hose nozzle directly against the hydraulic fluid passageway in the caliper body. Hold the air nozzle away from the inlet allowing some of the air to escape during the procedure.*

   c. Apply the air pressure in short spurts to the hydraulic fluid passageway (B, **Figure 17**) and force the piston out of the caliper body. Use a service station air hose if you don't have an air compressor.
7. Use a piece of plastic or wood and carefully push the dust seal (A, **Figure 18**) and piston seal (B, **Figure 18**) in toward the caliper cylinder and out of their grooves.
8. Remove the dust and piston seals from the caliper body. Discard both seals as they cannot be reused after removal as they will no longer seal effectively.
9. Inspect the caliper body (**Figure 19**) for damage, replace the caliper body if necessary.
10. Inspect the union bolt hole threads (A, **Figure 20**) and the pad pin bolt threads (B, **Figure 20**). If the threads are slightly damaged; clean them up with a proper size thread tap. If the threads are worn or

damaged beyond a "thread clean up," replace the caliper assembly.

11. Remove the bleed screw (**Figure 21**) from the caliper body.

12. Make sure the hole in the bleed screw is clean and open. Apply compressed air to the opening and make sure it is clear. Clean out if necessary with fresh brake fluid.

13. Inspect the hydraulic fluid passageway (A, **Figure 22**) in the base of the cylinder bore. Make sure it is clean and open. Apply compressed air to the opening and make sure it is clear. Clean out if necessary with fresh brake fluid.

14. Inspect the piston seal and dust seal grooves (**Figure 23**) for scoring or other damage. If the grooves are rusty or corroded, replace the caliper assembly.

NOTE

Yamaha does not provide specifications for the piston O.D. If either parts appears to be unserviceable, replace the piston or the caliper assembly.

15. Measure the cylinder inside diameter and compare to the dimension listed in **Table 1**. Replace the caliper assembly if worn to the service limit dimension or greater.

16. Inspect the cylinder wall (B, **Figure 22**) for scratches, scoring or other damage. If it is rusty or corroded, replace the caliper assembly.

17. Inspect the piston wall (**Figure 24**) and end (**Figure 25**) for scratches, scoring or other damage. If it is rusty or corroded, replace the piston.

18. If serviceable, clean the caliper body with rubbing alcohol and rinse with clean DOT 3 brake fluid.

19. Inspect the caliper carrier (**Figure 26**) for damage. If the carrier is damaged, replace the caliper

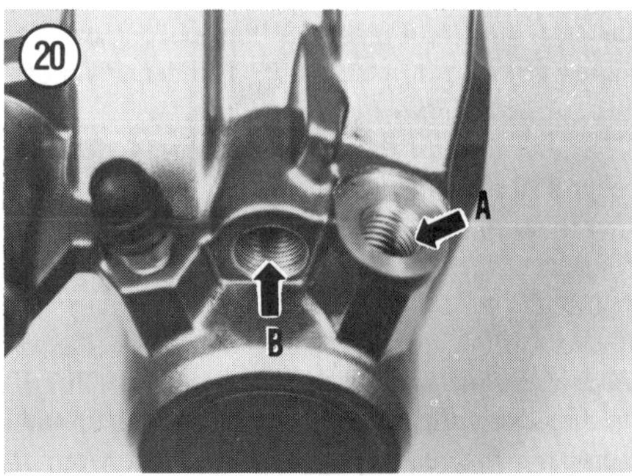

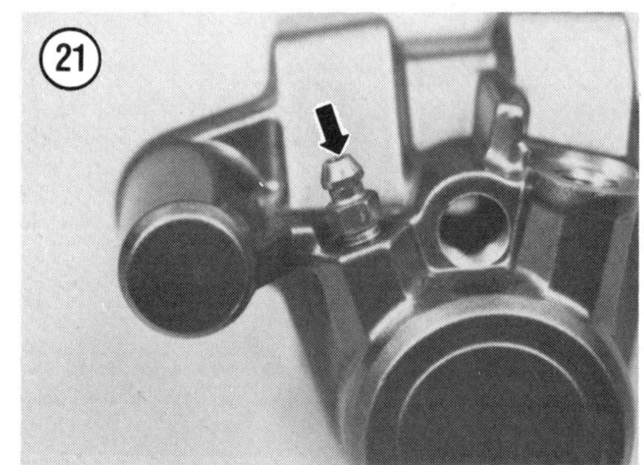

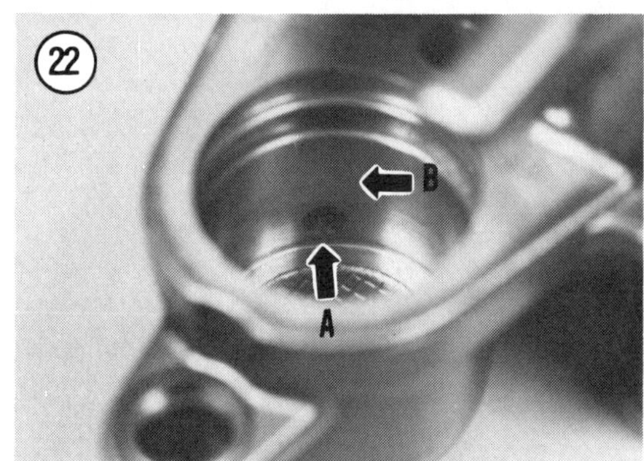

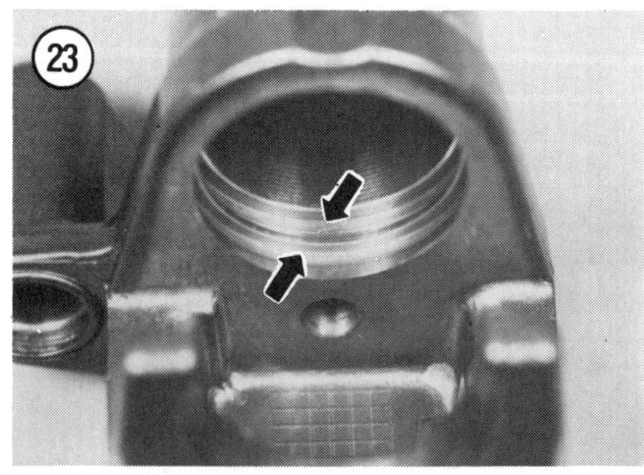

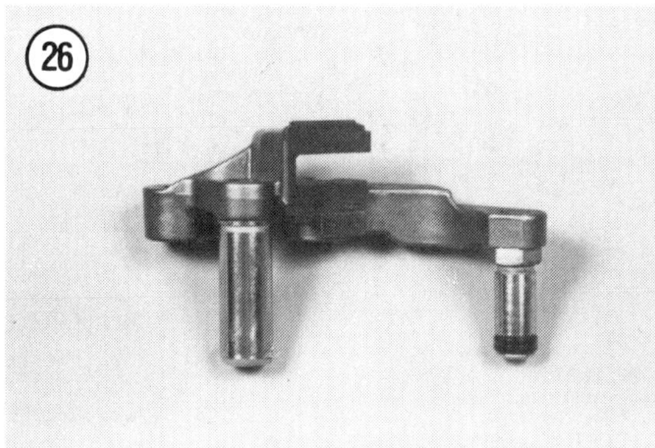

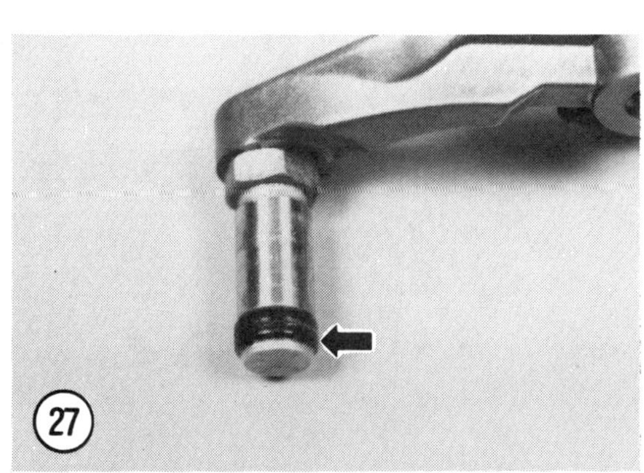

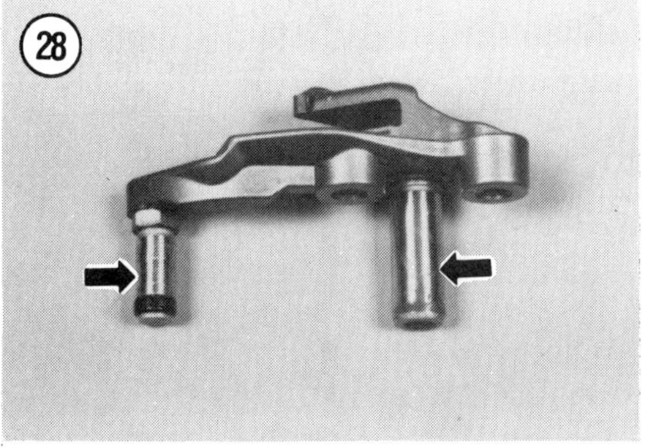

assembly since the carrier cannot be replaced separately.

20. Inspect the rubber seal (**Figure 27**) on the carrier pin A. Replace if necessary.

21. Inspect both carrier pins "A" and "B" (**Figure 28**) for scoring, wear or damage. If damaged, replace the caliper since the carrier and the carrier pins cannot be replaced separately.

NOTE
Never reuse a piston seal or dust seal that has been removed. Very minor damage or age deterioration can make the seal useless.

22. Coat the new dust seal and piston seal with fresh DOT 3 brake fluid.

WARNING
Check that the seal fits squarely in the cylinder bore groove. If the seal is not installed properly, the caliper assembly will leak and braking performance will be reduced.

23. Carefully install the new piston seal (B, **Figure 18**) in the groove in the caliper cylinder. Make sure the seal is properly seated in the groove.

24. Install the new dust seal (A, **Figure 18**) onto the groove in the caliper cylinder.

25. Coat the piston and the caliper cylinder with fresh DOT 3 brake fluid.

26. Position the piston with the sealed end going in first and install the piston into the caliper cylinder (**Figure 29**).

27. Use a suitable size socket and carefully press the piston in until it bottoms out (**Figure 16**).

28. Install the bleed screw and tighten securely.

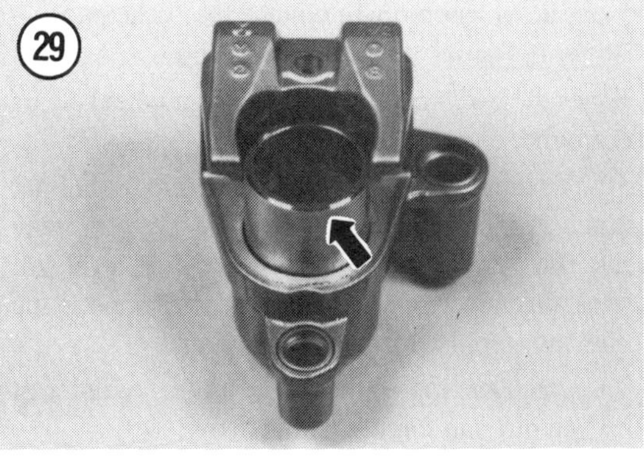

29. Install the rubber boots (**Figure 15**) onto the caliper body.

30. Apply a light coat of a lithium base grease to both carrier pins and to the rubber boots.

31. Carefully push the caliper carrier (**Figure 14**) straight onto the caliper body.

32. Install the brake pad spring (**Figure 13**).

33. Install the outboard brake pad (**Figure 30**) and the inboard brake pad (**Figure 31**).

34. Install the pad pin bolt (**Figure 12**) and tighten to the torque specification listed in **Table 3**.

35. Install the brake caliper assembly as described in this chapter.

FRONT BRAKE CALIPER (TT600)

Front Brake Pad Replacement

There is no recommended time interval for changing the friction pads in the front disc brake. Pad wear depends greatly on riding habits and conditions.

CAUTION

*Watch the pads more closely when the wear line (**A, Figure 32**) approaches the disc. On some pads, the wear line is very close to the metal backing plate. If pad wear happens to be uneven for some reason, the backing plate may come in contact with the disc and cause damage.*

To maintain an even brake pressure on the disc, always replace both pads in the caliper at the same time. Always use brake pads from the same manufacturer in the front caliper—never intermix different brands.

It is not necessary to remove or disassemble the brake caliper assembly to replace the brake pads.

Refer to **Figure 33** for this procedure.

1. Place the bike on a stand so the front wheel clears the ground.

2. The piston must be repositioned within the caliper assembly prior to installing the new *thicker* brake pads. The front master cylinder brake fluid level will rise as the caliper piston is being repositioned in the following step. Perform the following:

   a. Clean the top of the front master cylinder of all dirt and foreign matter.
   b. Remove the screws securing the top cover (**Figure 34**) and remove the top cover and diaphragm from the master cylinder.
   c. Note the brake fluid level in the reservoir. If it is up to, or close to, the top surface of the reservoir, siphon off some of the fluid at this time.

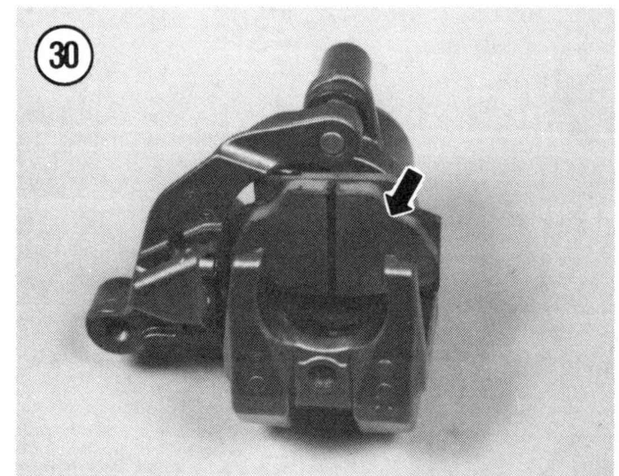

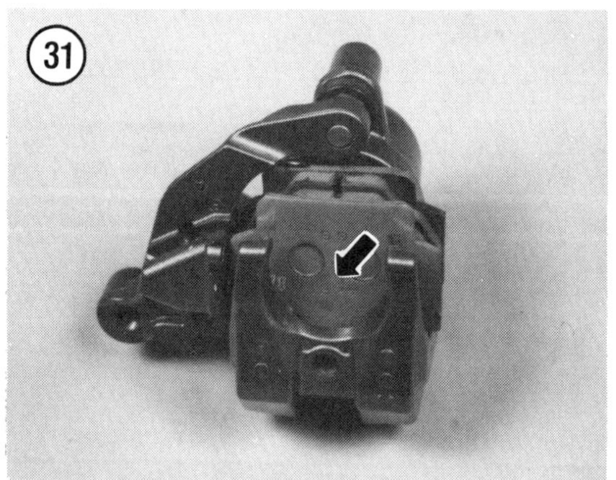

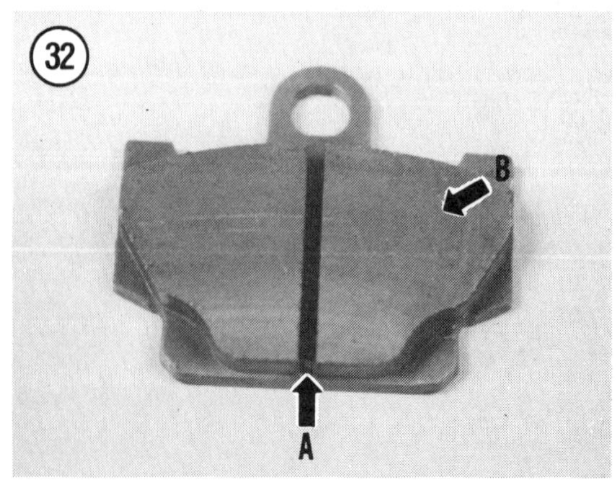

(33)

FRONT BRAKE CALIPER (TT600)

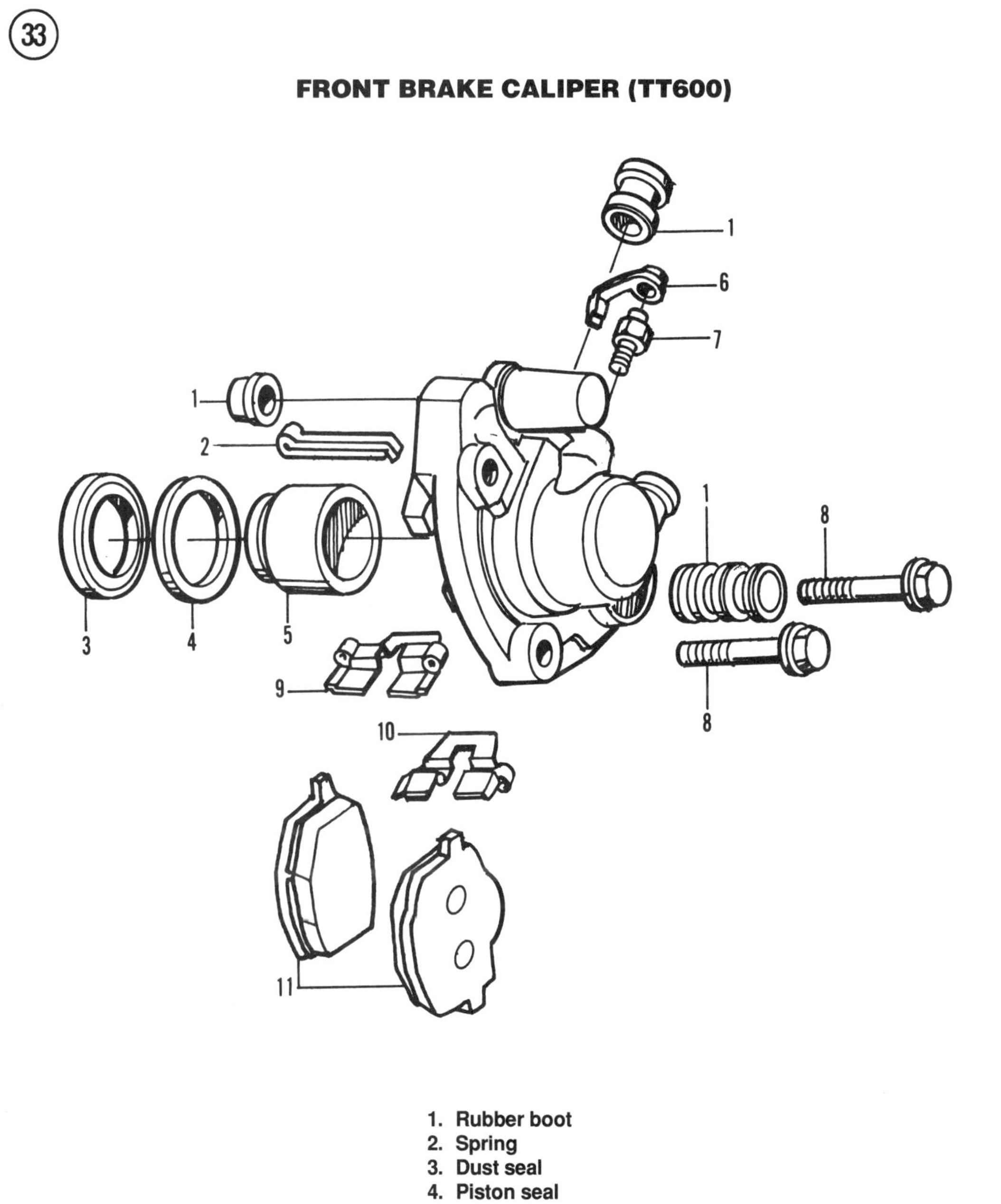

1. Rubber boot
2. Spring
3. Dust seal
4. Piston seal
5. Piston
6. Cap
7. Bleed valve
8. Bolt
9. Spring
10. Spring
11. Brake pads

d. Push the caliper assembly toward the brake disc until it stops. This will reposition the piston into the caliper cylinder.
e. Constantly check the reservoir to make sure the brake fluid does not overflow. Remove brake fluid, if necessary, prior to it overflowing.
f. The piston should move freely during repositioning. If it doesn't, and there is evidence of sticking in the cylinder, the caliper should be removed and serviced as described in this chapter.

3. To prevent accidental application of the front brake lever, place a spacer between the front brake lever and the hand grip. Hold the spacer in place with a large rubber band, a tie wrap or a piece of tape.
4. Remove the brake caliper bolt (**Figure 35**) and pivot the caliper housing up (**Figure 36**) and off of the brake pads.
5. Remove both brake pads (**Figure 37**).
6. Check the condition of the upper and lower pad springs (**Figure 38**). Replace them if cracked or otherwise damaged. Install new pad springs if new brake pads are being installed.
7. Check the brake pad friction surface (B, **Figure 32**) for oil and dirt contamination. Also check the friction material for cracking or other damage. Replace the brake pads if the surface is contaminated or damaged.
8. Measure the brake pad friction thickness (**Figure 39**) with a vernier caliper or ruler. Compare to the specifications in **Table 1**. Replace the brake pads if the friction thickness is too thin.
9. Check the end of the piston assembly in the caliper for signs of fluid leakage or other abnormal conditions. Clean the pad recess with a soft brush. Do not use solvent, wire brush or any hard tool which could damage the cylinder or piston.
10 Carefully remove any rust or corrosion from the brake disc.
11. If removed, install the upper and lower pad springs (**Figure 38**) onto the caliper carrier.
12. Align the pad arms with the caliper bracket and install the inner and outer brake pads (**Figure 37**). Install the brake pads so that the round portion on the back of the pad faces toward the *back* of the bike as shown in **Figure 40**. Make sure the friction material faces against the brake disc.
13. Carefully lower the brake caliper over the brake pads.

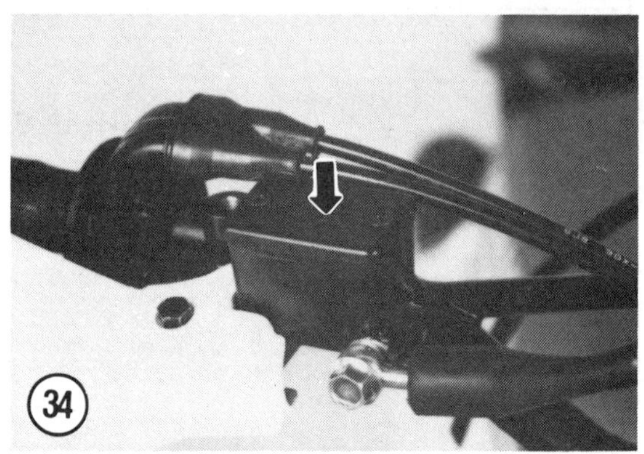
34

35

36

37

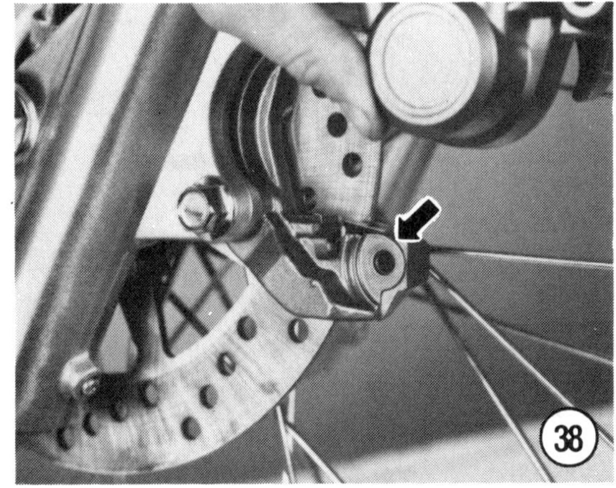
38

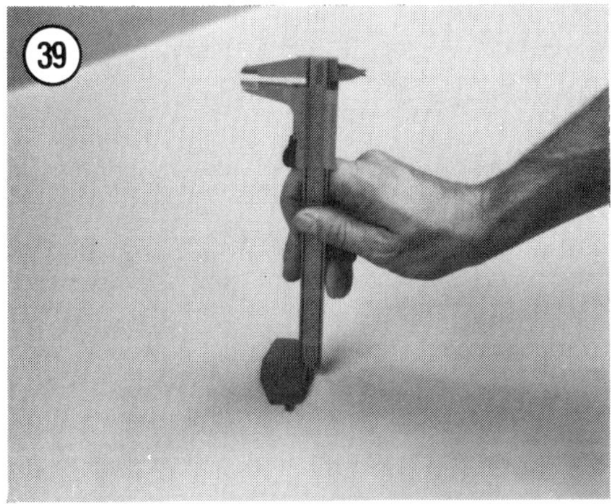
39

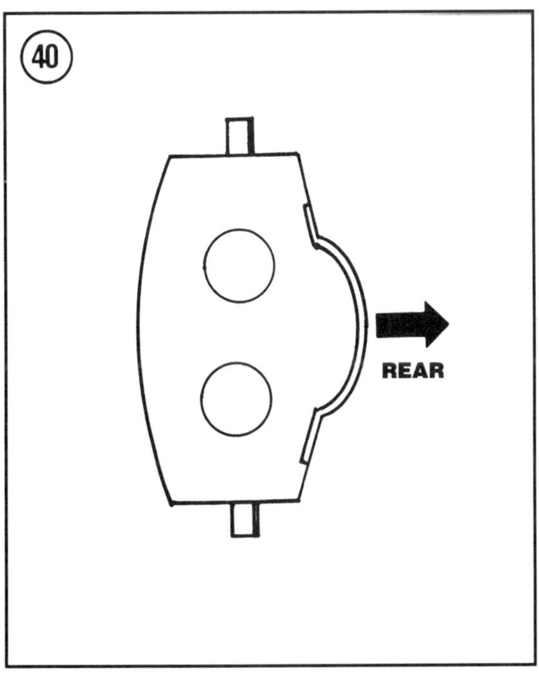

40

14. Lightly coat the caliper retaining bolt with a lithium base grease.

15. Install the retaining bolt (**Figure 35**) and tighten to the torque specification in **Table 3**.

16. Spin the front wheel and activate the brake lever as required to refill the cylinder in the caliper and correctly locate the pads.

WARNING

Use brake fluid clearly marked DOT 3 from a sealed container. Other types may vaporize and cause brake failure. Always use the same brand name; do not intermix as many brands are not compatible. Do not intermix silicone based (DOT 5) brake fluid as it can cause brake component damage leading to brake system failure.

17. Refill the master cylinder reservoir, if necessary, to maintain the correct brake fluid level. Install the diaphragm and top cover (**Figure 36**) and tighten the screws securely.

WARNING

Do not ride the motorcycle until you are sure the brake is operating correctly with full hydraulic advantage. If necessary, bleed the brake system as described in this chapter.

18. Bed the pads in gradually for the first 80 km (50 miles) by using only light pressure as much as possible. Immediate hard application will glaze the new friction pads and greatly reduce the effectiveness of the brake.

Front Caliper Removal/Installation

Refer to **Figure 33** for this procedure.

1. Place the bike on a stand so the front wheel clears the ground.

NOTE

This procedure is shown with the front wheel removed for clarity. It is not necessary to remove it for this procedure.

2. Remove the brake pads as described in this chapter.

3. Remove the cap (**Figure 41**) from the bleed valve.

4. Attach a hose to the bleed valve on the caliper assembly.

5. Place the loose end of the hose in a container to catch the brake fluid.

6. Open the bleed valve and continue to apply the front brake lever until the brake fluid is pumped out of the system. Dispose of this brake fluid—never reuse brake fluid.

7. Disconnect the hose and tighten the bleed valve. Install the cap onto the bleed valve.

8. Loosen the brake caliper union bolt (**Figure 42**). Remove the union bolt and sealing washers (**Figure 43**).

9. Remove the brake pads as described in this chapter.

10. Slide the brake caliper housing (**Figure 44**) off of the mounting bracket.

11. If necessary, remove the bolts (A, **Figure 45**) securing the brake caliper mounting bracket to the fork slider. Remove the mounting bracket (B, **Figure 45**).

12. Install by reversing these removal steps. Note the following.

13. If removed, install the mounting bracket (B, **Figure 45**) and the mounting bolts (A, **Figure 45**). Tighten the bolts to the torque specification in **Table 3**.

14. Apply a light coat of lithium base grease to the mounting bracket pivot rod (C, **Figure 45**).

15. Install the brake hose, with a sealing washer on each side of the fitting, onto the caliper (**Figure 43**). Install the union bolt (**Figure 42**) and tighten to the torque specification in **Table 3**.

41

42

43

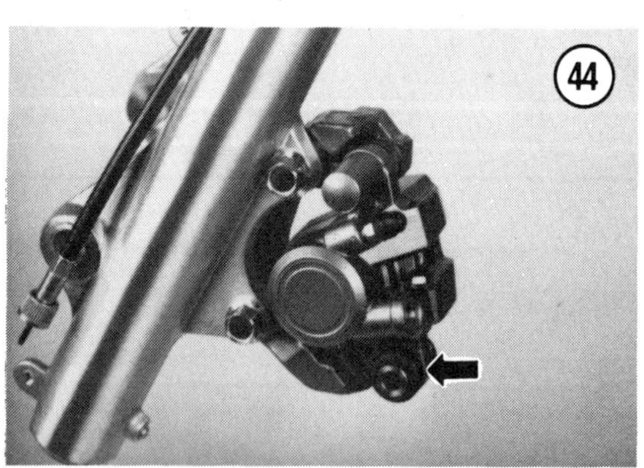
44

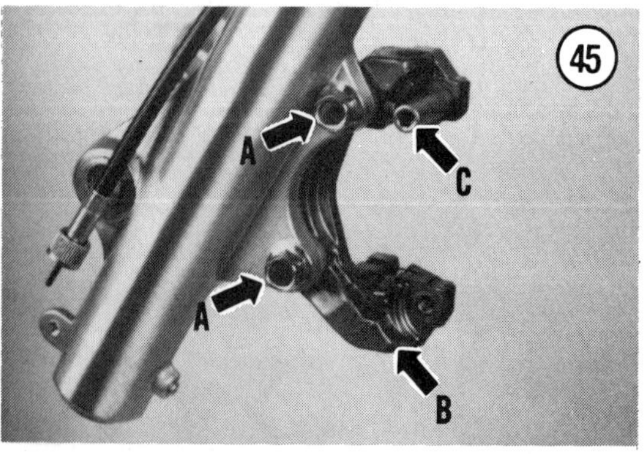

45

46

47

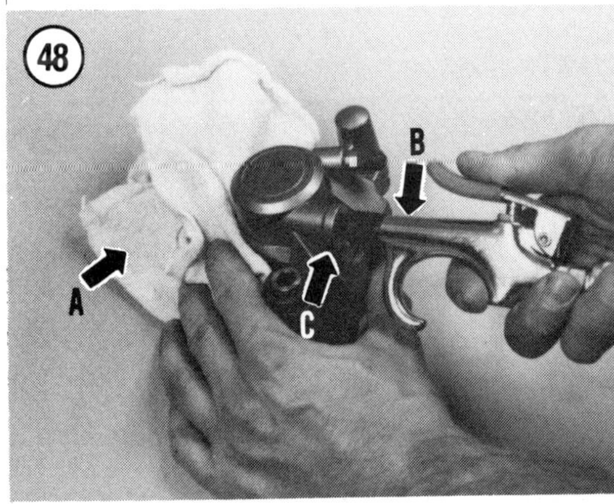

48

49

16. Install the brake pads and tighten the caliper retaining bolt (**Figure 35**) as described in this chapter.

17. Bleed the brake as described in this chapter.

WARNING
Do not ride the motorcycle until you are sure the brake is operating properly.

Front Caliper Disassembly/Inspection/Assembly

Refer to **Figure 33** for this procedure.

1. Remove the caliper assembly as described in this chapter.
2. Carefully pry the clip (**Figure 46**) out of the caliper bore.
3. Withdraw the piston (**Figure 47**) from the caliper body. If you cannot remove the piston easily, perform the following:
   a. Either wrap the caliper body and piston with a heavy cloth or place a shop cloth (A, **Figure 48**) or piece of soft wood over the end of the piston.
   b. Perform this step over and close down to a workbench top. Hold the caliper body with the piston facing away from you.

WARNING
*In the next step, the piston may shoot out of the caliper body like a bullet. Keep your fingers out of the way. Wear shop gloves and apply air pressure gradually. Do **not** use high pressure air nor place the air hose nozzle directly against the hydraulic fluid passageway in the caliper body. Hold the air nozzle (B, **Figure 48**) away from the opening to allow some of the air to escape during the procedure.*

   c. Apply the air pressure in short spurts to the hydraulic fluid passageway (C, **Figure 48**) and force the piston out of the caliper body. Use a service station air hose if you don't have an air compressor.
4. Remove the dust seal (**Figure 49**) from the piston.
5. Use a piece of plastic or wood and carefully push the piston seal (**Figure 50**) in toward the caliper cylinder and out of its groove.

12

6. Discard the piston seal (A, **Figure 51**) and dust seal (B, **Figure 51**) as they cannot be reused after removal as they will no longer seal effectively.

7. Inspect the clip (C, **Figure 51**) for wear or damage, replace if necessary.

8. Inspect the caliper body (**Figure 52**) for damage, replace the caliper body if necessary.

9. Inspect the union bolt hole threads. If the threads are slightly damaged; clean them up with a proper size thread tap. If the threads are worn or damaged beyond a "thread clean up," replace the caliper assembly.

10. Remove the bleed screw from the caliper body.

11. Make sure the hole in the bleed screw is clean and open. Apply compressed air to the opening and make sure it is clear. Clean out if necessary with fresh brake fluid.

12. Inspect the hydraulic fluid passageway in the base of the cylinder bore. Make sure it is clean and open. Apply compressed air to the opening and make sure it is clear. Clean out if necessary with fresh brake fluid.

13. Inspect the piston seal groove in the caliper body for scoring or other damage. If the groove is rusty or corroded, replace the caliper assembly.

14. Inspect the piston seal groove (**Figure 53**) for scoring or other damage. If the groove is rusty or corroded, replace the piston.

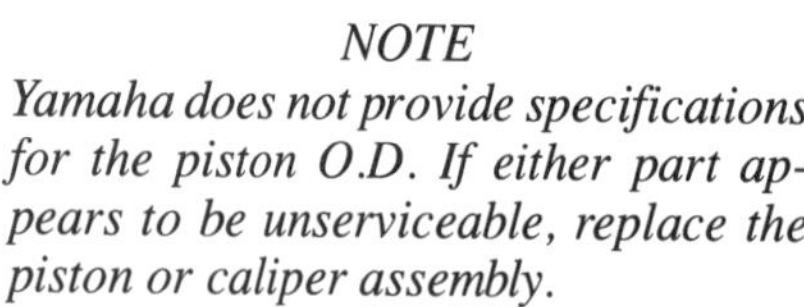

NOTE

Yamaha does not provide specifications for the piston O.D. If either part appears to be unserviceable, replace the piston or caliper assembly.

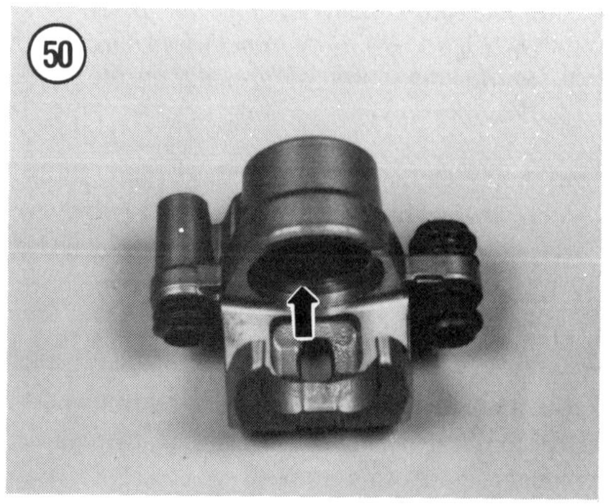

50

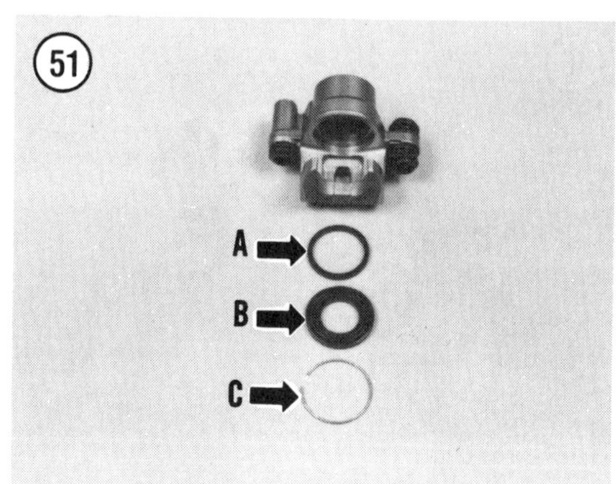

51

52

53

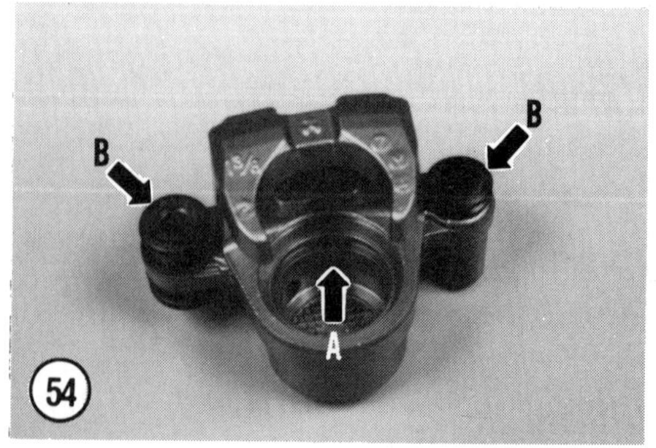

54

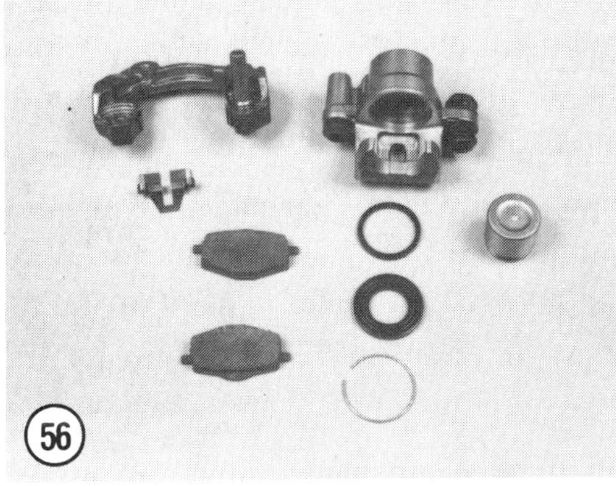

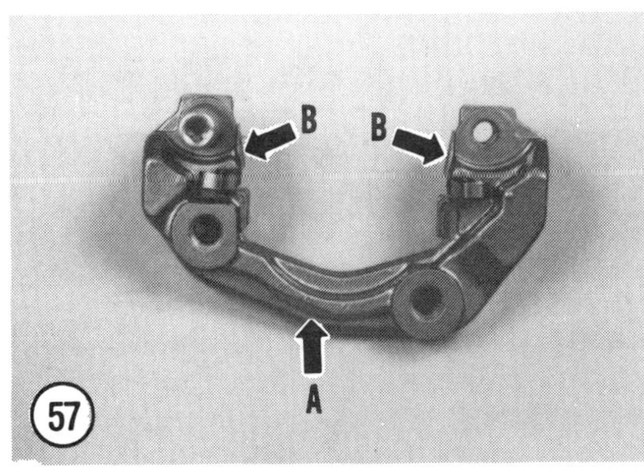

15. Measure the cylinder inside diameter and compare to the dimension listed in **Table 1**. Replace the caliper assembly if worn to the service limit dimension or greater.

16. Inspect the cylinder wall (A, **Figure 54**) for scratches, scoring or other damage. If it is rusty or corroded, replace the caliper assembly.

17. Check the caliper rubber bushings (B, **Figure 54**) for wear or damage. Replace if necessary by pulling them out of the caliper.

18. Inspect the piston wall (**Figure 55**) and end for scratches, scoring or other damage. If it is rusty or corroded, replace the piston.

19. If serviceable, clean all parts (**Figure 56**) except the brake pads with rubbing alcohol and rinse with clean brake fluid.

20. Inspect the caliper bracket (A, **Figure 57**) for damage. If bracket is damaged, replace the caliper assembly since the bracket cannot be replaced separately.

21. Inspect the pad springs (B, **Figure 57**) on the caliper bracket for wear or damage, replace if necessary.

NOTE

Never reuse a piston or dust seal that has been removed. Very minor damage or age deterioration can make the seal useless.

22. Coat the new dust seal and piston seal with fresh DOT 3 brake fluid.

23. Carefully install the new dust seal (**Figure 49**) in the groove in the piston. Make sure the seal is properly seated in the groove.

WARNING

Check that the seal fits squarely in the cylinder bore groove. If the seal is not installed properly, the caliper assembly will leak and braking performance will be reduced.

24. Install the new piston seal (**Figure 50**) into the groove in the caliper assembly.

25. Coat the piston and the caliper cylinder with fresh DOT 3 brake fluid.

26. Position the piston with the sealed end going in first and install the piston into the caliper cylinder.

27. Use a suitable size socket and carefully press the piston in until it bottoms out (**Figure 58**).

28. Fit the lip of the dust seal into the caliper bore groove (**Figure 59**). Work carefully so that you don't damage the dust seal. Make sure the seal fits into the caliper bore completely (**Figure 60**).
29. Install the clip (**Figure 46**) into the caliper bore groove. Make sure the clip completely seats in the groove.
30. Install the bleed screw and tighten securely.
31. Apply a light coat of a lithium base grease to both bracket pins and to the rubber bushings.
32. Install the brake caliper assembly as described in this chapter.

FRONT MASTER CYLINDER (XT600)

Removal/Installation

1. Place the bike on a stand so the front wheel clears the ground.
2. Remove the right-hand rear view mirror.
3. Remove the cap from the bleed valve.
4. Attach a hose to the bleed valve on the caliper assembly.
5. Place the loose end of the hose in a container to catch the brake fluid (**Figure 61**).
6. Open the bleed valve and continue to apply the front brake lever until the brake fluid is pumped out of the master cylinder and the upper portion of the brake hose. Dispose of this brake fluid—never reuse brake fluid. It is not necessary to pump all of the brake fluid out of the system.
7. Disconnect the hose and tighten the bleed valve.
8. Remove the brake switch from the master cylinder housing as described under *Front Brake Switch Replacement* in Chapter Nine.
9. Slide back the rubber boot (**Figure 62**) to gain access to the union bolt.
10. Loosen the brake hose union bolt (**Figure 63**) at the master cylinder. Remove the bolt and sealing washers.
11. Remove the bolts (A, **Figure 64**) holding the master cylinder to the handlebar. Remove the master cylinder (A, **Figure 65**).
12. Place the loose end of the brake hose (B, **Figure 65**) in a reclosable plastic bag to prevent brake fluid from dripping onto other parts. Close the bag onto the hose to keep it in place.
13. Install by reversing these removal steps. Note the following.
14. Mount the master cylinder housing (A, **Figure 65**) onto the handlebar assembly. Install the handlebar clamp so that the arrow faces UP (B, **Figure 64**).
15. Remove the end of the brake hose from the plastic bag and discard the bag properly.
16. Insert the union bolt and the 2 sealing washers through the brake hose. Install the union bolt (**Fig-**

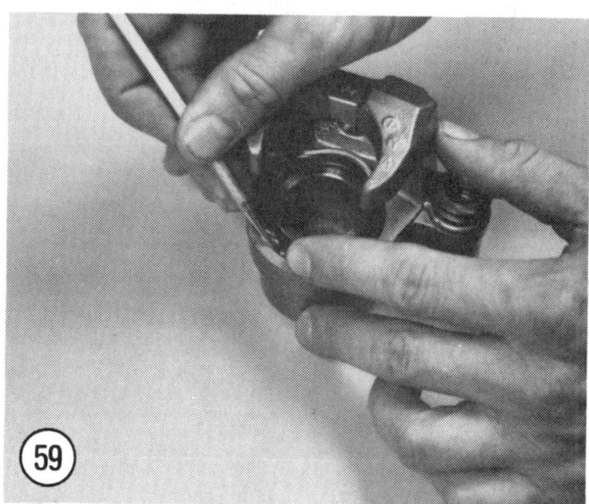

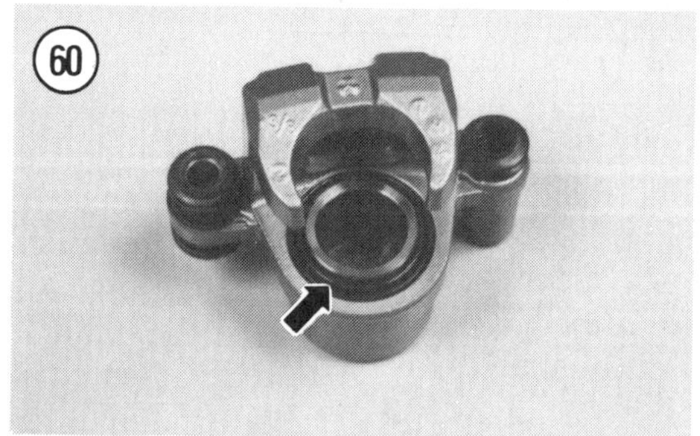

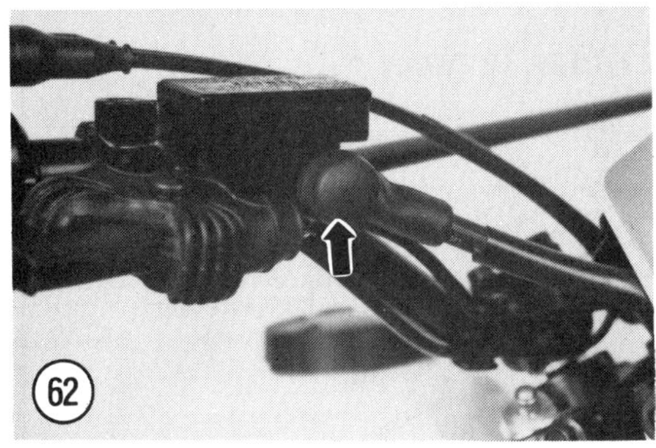

62

63

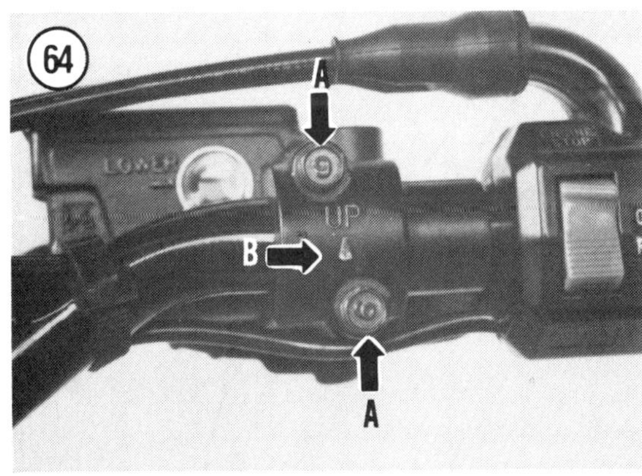

64

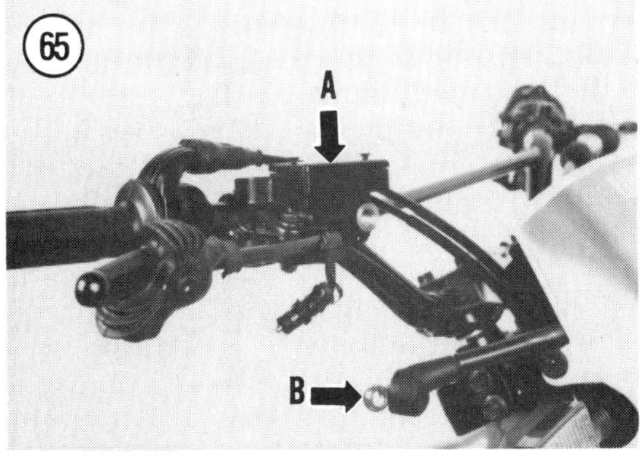

65

ure 63) and tighten to the torque specification in **Table 3**.

17. Slide the rubber boot (**Figure 62**) over the union bolt.

18. Install the brake switch into the master cylinder housing as described under *Front Brake Switch Replacement* in Chapter Nine.

19. Refill the master cylinder and bleed the brake as described in this chapter.

WARNING
Do not ride the bike until the front brake is working properly.

Disassembly

Refer to **Figure 66** for this procedure.

1. Remove the master cylinder as described in this chapter.
2. Remove the screws securing the reservoir cover.
3. Remove the cover (**Figure 67**) and the diaphragm (**Figure 68**). Pour out the remaining brake fluid and discard it. *Never* reuse brake fluid.
4. Remove the brake lever nut and pivot bolt (A, **Figure 69**) and remove the brake lever (B, **Figure 69**) and rubber boot.
5. Remove the spring (**Figure 70**).
6. Remove the rubber boot (**Figure 71**) from the area where the hand lever actuates the internal piston.
7. Using circlip pliers, remove the piston circlip (**Figure 72**).

CAUTION
Do not remove the primary or secondary cup from the piston when removing the piston assembly in Step 8. Removing the cups from the piston will damage them.

8. Carefully withdraw the piston assembly (**Figure 73**) from the reservoir.

Inspection

1. Clean all parts in fresh DOT 3 brake fluid. Place the master cylinder components on a clean lint-free cloth when performing the following inspection procedures.
2. Check the end of the piston (**Figure 74**) for wear caused by the hand lever. Replace the entire piston assembly if any portion of it requires replacement.

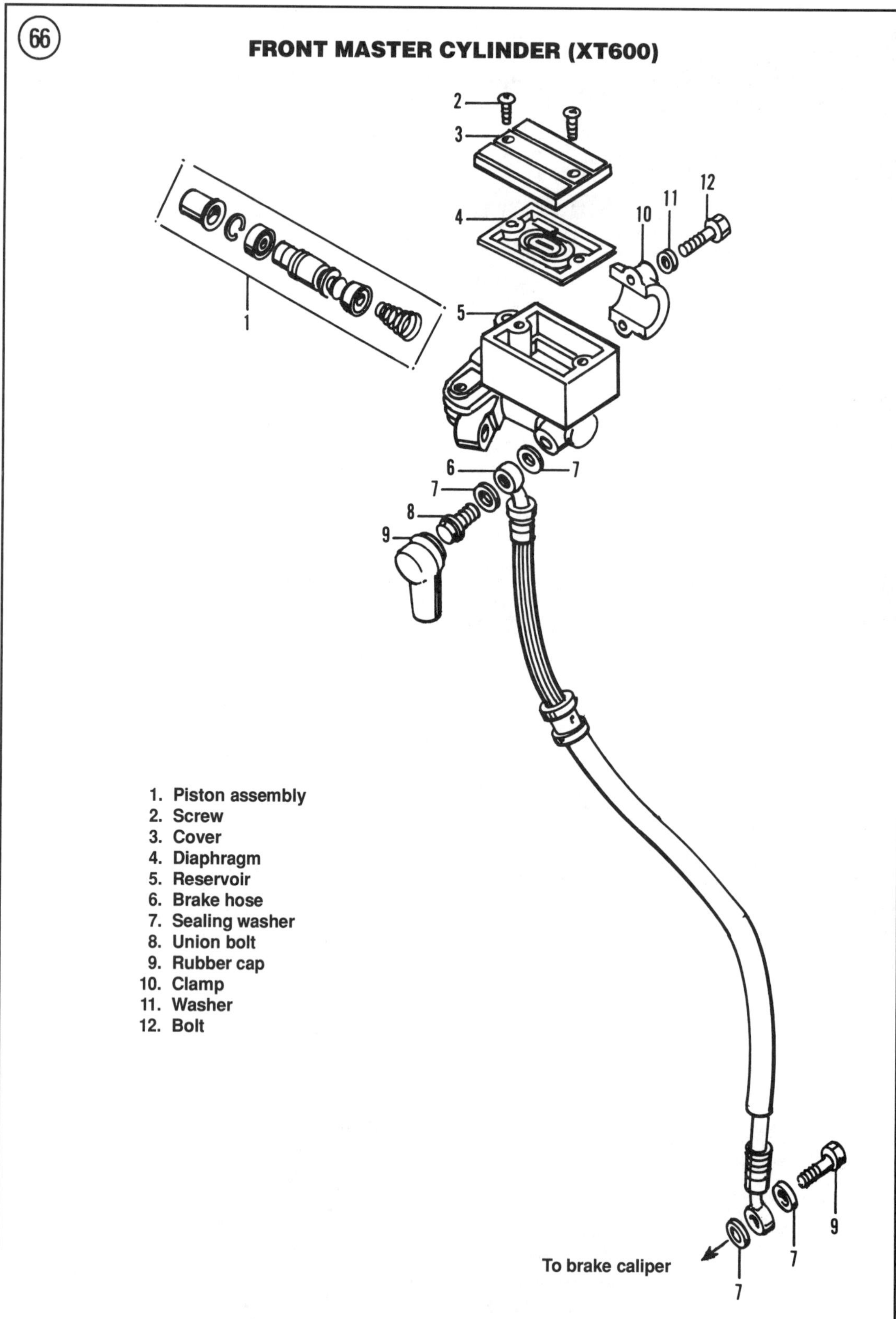
66
FRONT MASTER CYLINDER (XT600)
1
2
3
4
5
6
7
8
9
10
11
12
To brake caliper
1. Piston assembly
2. Screw
3. Cover
4. Diaphragm
5. Reservoir
6. Brake hose
7. Sealing washer
8. Union bolt
9. Rubber cap
10. Clamp
11. Washer
12. Bolt

79

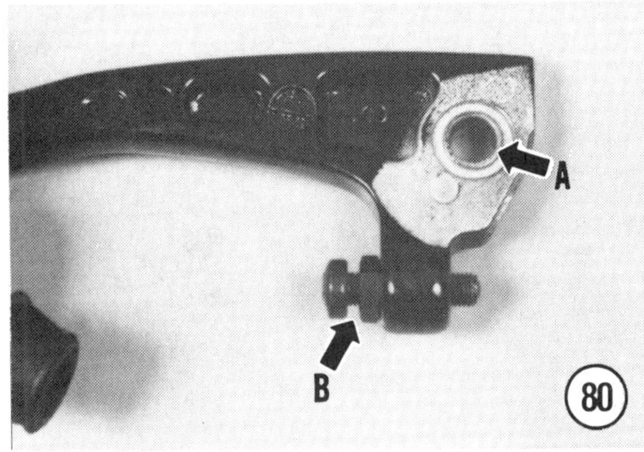

80

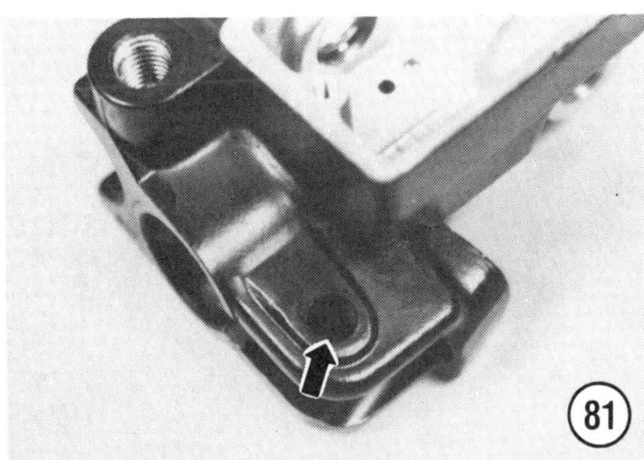
81

82

CAUTION

When installing the piston assembly, do not allow the cups to turn inside out as they will be damaged and allow brake fluid to leak within the cylinder bore.

2. Install the spring onto the end of the piston as shown in (C, **Figure 75**). The small end of the spring should fit onto the piston assembly.
3. Install the piston assembly and spring into the master cylinder bore.
4. Push the piston (**Figure 73**) into the master cylinder.
5. Install the circlip (**Figure 72**) into the master cylinder groove. Make sure the circlip is seated completely in the groove.
6. Install the rubber boot (**Figure 71**). Make sure the boot seats completely in the master cylinder.
7. Install the lever spring (**Figure 70**) into the master cylinder.
8. Install the brake lever (B, **Figure 69**) onto the master cylinder and the pivot bolt (A, **Figure 69**). Secure it with the nut and tighten securely.
9. Install the diaphragm (**Figure 68**) and cover (**Figure 67**). Install but do not tighten the cover screws at this time as fluid will have to be added later.

FRONT MASTER CYLINDER (TT600)

Removal/Installation

1. Place the bike on a stand so the front wheel clears the ground.
2. Remove the cap (**Figure 82**) from the bleed valve.
3. Attach a hose to the bleed valve on the caliper assembly.
4. Place the loose end of the hose in a container to catch the brake fluid.
5. Open the bleed valve and continue to apply the front brake lever until the brake fluid is pumped out of the master cylinder and the upper portion of the brake hose. Dispose of this brake fluid—never reuse brake fluid. It is not necessary to pump all of the brake fluid out of the system.
6. Disconnect the hose and tighten the bleed valve.
7. Remove the right-hand side hand guard (A, **Figure 83**) from the handlebar.
8. Loosen the brake hose union bolt (B, **Figure 83**) at the master cylinder. Remove the bolt and sealing washers.

9. Place the loose end of the brake hose in a reclosable plastic bag to prevent brake fluid from dripping onto other parts. Close the bag onto the hose to keep it in place.

10. Remove the bolts (A, **Figure 84**) securing the master cylinder to the handlebar. Remove the master cylinder (B, **Figure 84**).

11. Install by reversing these removal steps. Note the following.

12. Mount the master cylinder onto the handlebar assembly. Install the handlebar clamp so that the arrow faces UP (**Figure 85**).

13. Remove the end of the brake hose from the plastic bag and discard the bag properly.

14. Insert the union bolt and the sealing washers through the brake hose fitting. Install the union bolt (B, **Figure 83**) and tighten to the torque specification in **Table 3**.

15. Refill the master cylinder and bleed the brake as described in this chapter.

WARNING
Do not ride the bike until the front brake is working properly.

Disassembly

Refer to **Figure 86** for this procedure.

1. Remove the master cylinder as described in this chapter.

2. Remove the screws securing the reservoir cover and remove the cover and the diaphragm. Pour out the remaining brake fluid and discard it. *Never* reuse brake fluid.

3. Remove the brake lever nut and pivot bolt (A, **Figure 87**) and remove the brake lever (B, **Figure 87**).

4. Remove the spring (**Figure 88**).

5. Remove the rubber boot (**Figure 89**) from the area where the hand lever actuates the internal piston.

6. Using circlip pliers, remove the piston circlip (**Figure 90**).

CAUTION
Do not remove the primary or secondary cup from the piston when removing the piston assembly in Step 7. Removing the cups from the piston will damage them.

7. Remove the piston assembly and washer (**Figure 91**).

Inspection

1. Clean all parts (**Figure 92**) in fresh DOT 3 brake fluid. Place the master cylinder components on a clean lint-free cloth when performing the following inspection procedures.

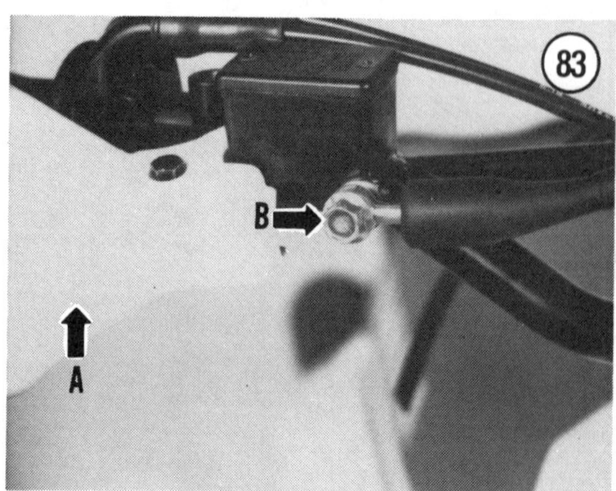

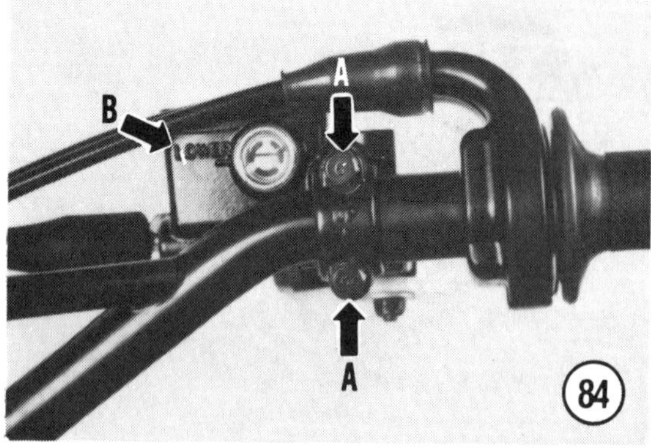

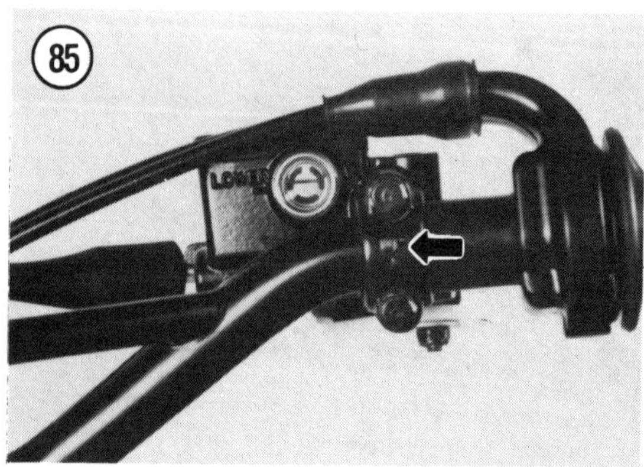

86
FRONT MASTER CYLINDER (TT600)
1
2
3
4
5
6
7
8
9
10
11
12
1. Screws
2. Cover
3. Diaphragm
4. Cap
5. Piston assembly
6. Union bolt
7. Sealing washer
8. Brake hose
9. Reservoir
10. Clamp
11. Washers
12. Bolts
To brake caliper

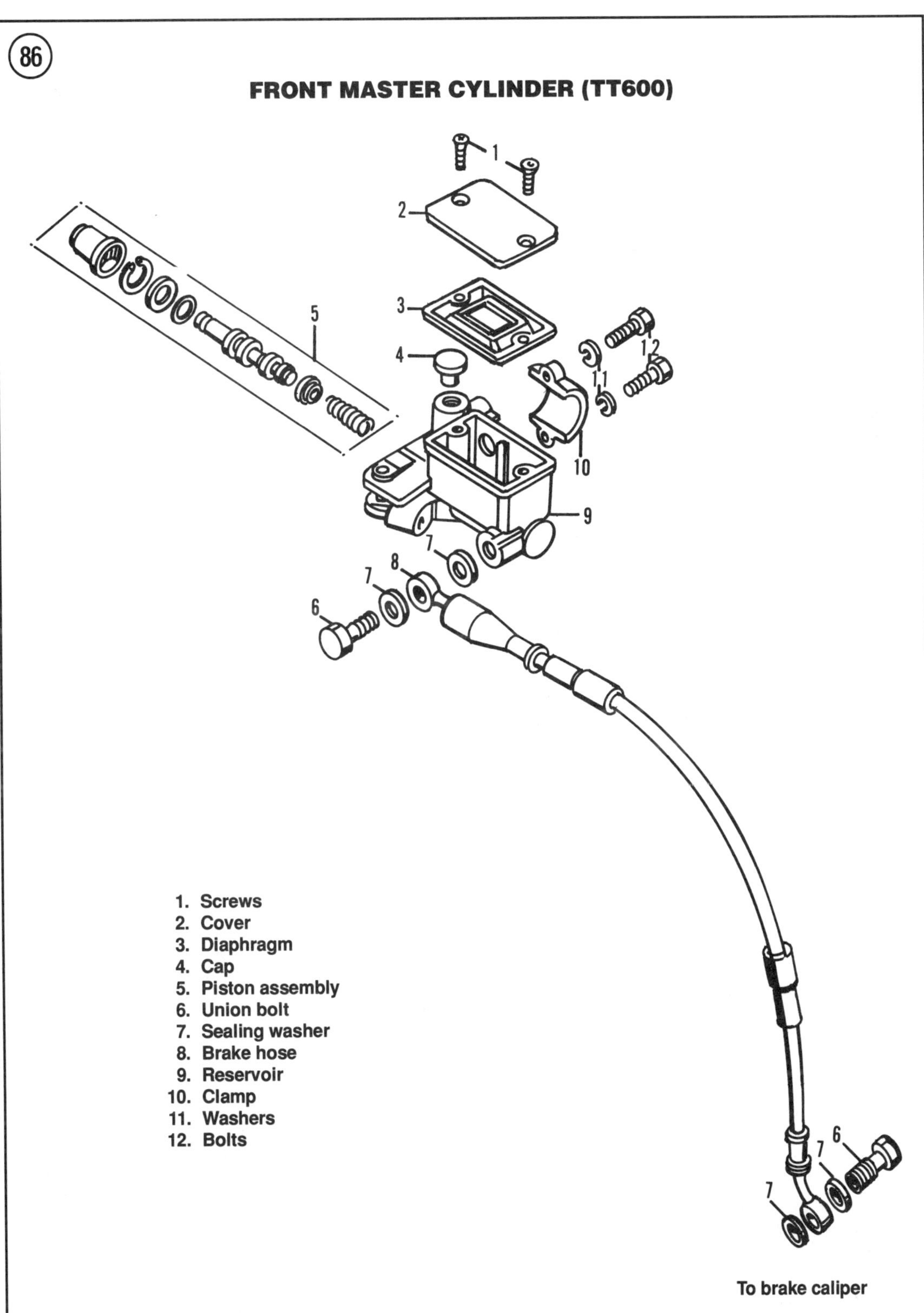

12

2. Check the end of the piston (A, **Figure 93**) for wear caused by the hand lever. Replace the entire piston assembly if any portion of it requires replacement.
3. Check the primary (B, **Figure 93**) and secondary (C, **Figure 93**) cups on the piston for damage, softness or swollen conditions. Replace the piston assembly if any cup is damaged.
4. Check the spring (D, **Figure 93**) for cracks, distortion or other damage; replace if necessary.
5. Check the washer (E, **Figure 93**) for cracks, bending or other damage. Replace if necessary.

NOTE
Yamaha does not provide specifications for the piston O.D. If either the piston

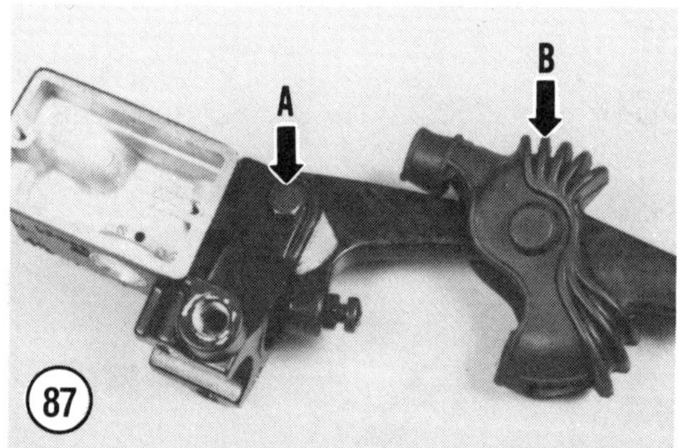

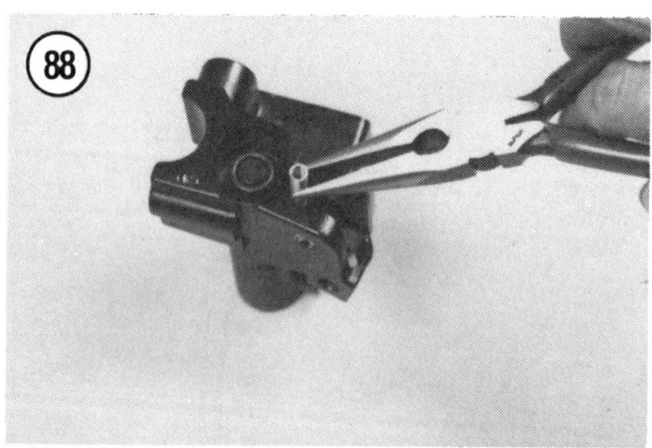

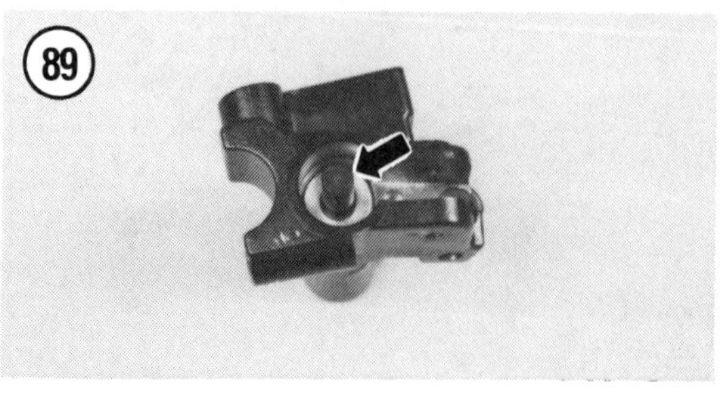

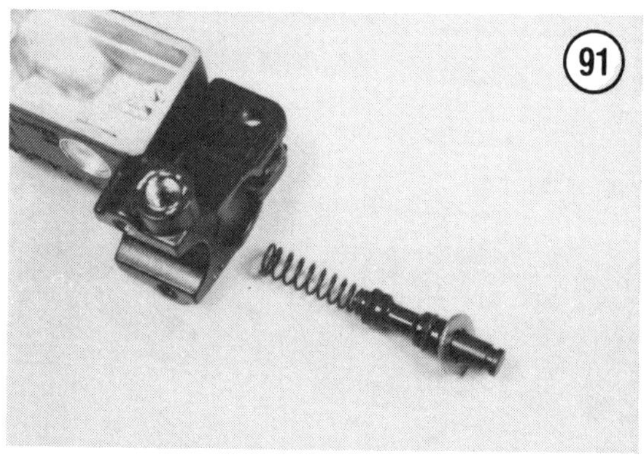

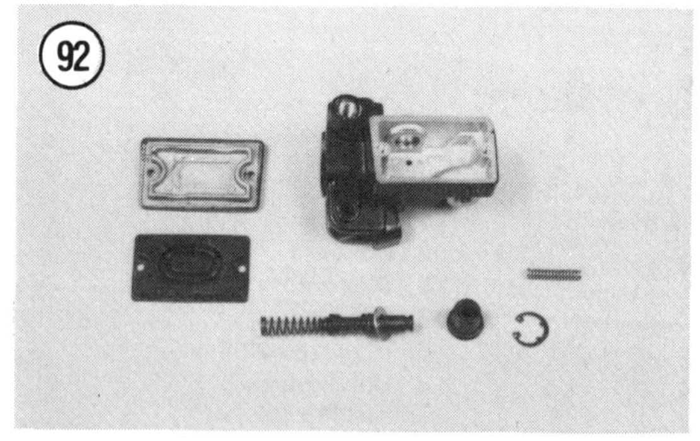

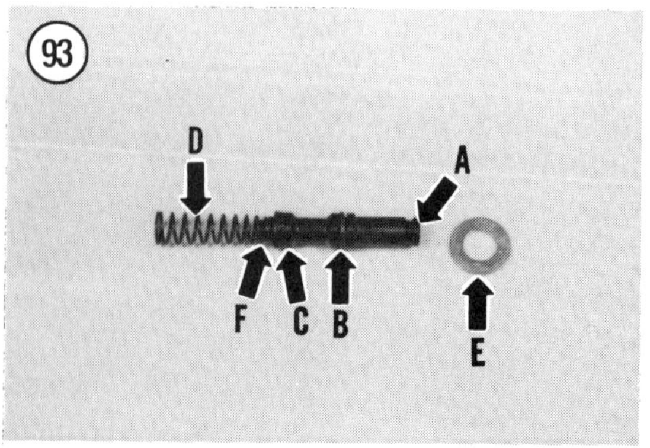

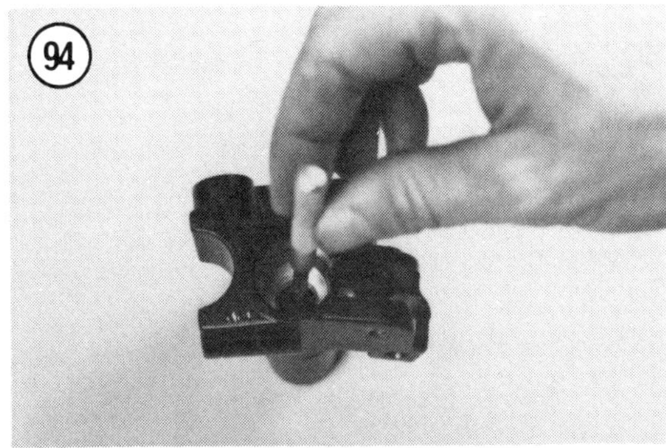

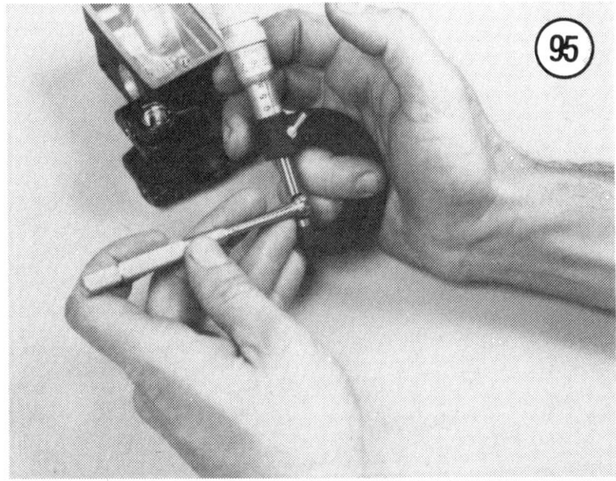

or the master cylinder bore seems to be unserviceable, replace the master cylinder assembly.

6. Measure the cylinder bore with a small hole gauge (**Figure 94**). Then measure the gauge with a micrometer (**Figure 95**) to determine the master cylinder bore diameter. Replace the master cylinder if the bore exceeds the specifications given in **Table 1**.
7. Make sure the passage (**Figure 96**) in the bottom of the brake fluid reservoir are clear. If necessary, clean out with a piece of wire and blow out with compressed air.
8. Check the reservoir cover and diaphragm (**Figure 97**) for damage and deterioration. Replace if necessary.
9. Inspect the threads (**Figure 98**) in the master cylinder body where the brake hose union bolt screws in. Repair the threads if stripped or damaged.
10. Check the circlip groove in the master cylinder bore (**Figure 99**) for cracks, breakage or other damage. Replace the master cylinder if the groove is damaged in anyway.

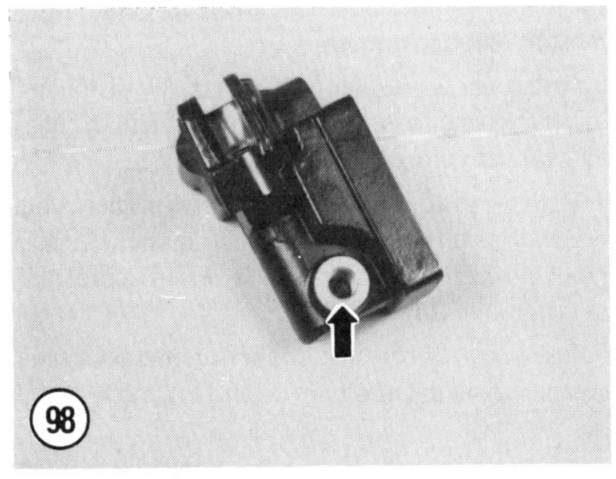

11. Inspect the pivot hole (A, **Figure 100**) in the hand lever. If worn, replace the hand lever.

12. Check the brake lever pivot bolt (B, **Figure 100**) for excessive wear or thread damage; replace the bolt if necessary.

13. Check the brake lever pivot bolt lug in the master cylinder for excessive wear or elongation; replace the master cylinder if necessary.

Assembly

1. Soak the new piston cups in fresh DOT 3 brake fluid for approximately 15 minutes to make them pliable. Coat the inside of the cylinder with fresh DOT 3 brake fluid prior to assembling the parts.

CAUTION

When installing the piston assembly, do not allow the cups to turn inside out as they will be damaged and allow brake fluid to leak within the cylinder bore.

2. Install the spring onto the end of the piston as shown in (F, **Figure 93**). The small end of the spring must fit onto the piston.

3. Install the washer onto the end of the piston and insert the piston assembly (**Figure 91**) into the master cylinder bore.

4. Push the piston (**Figure 89**) into the master cylinder and install the circlip into the master cylinder groove. Make sure the circlip is seated completely in the groove (**Figure 101**).

5. Install the rubber boot. Make sure the boot seats completely in the master cylinder (**Figure 102**).

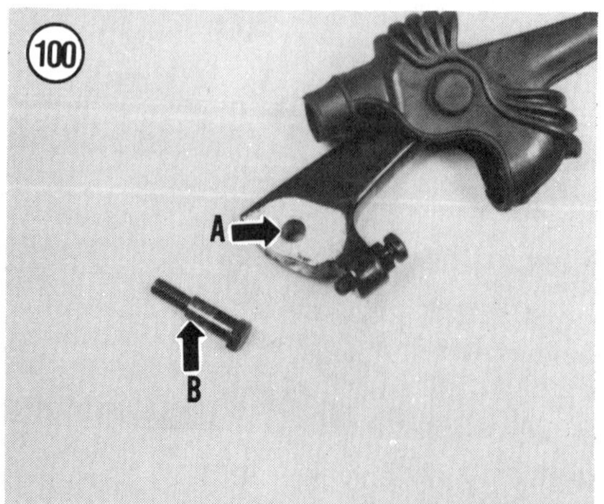

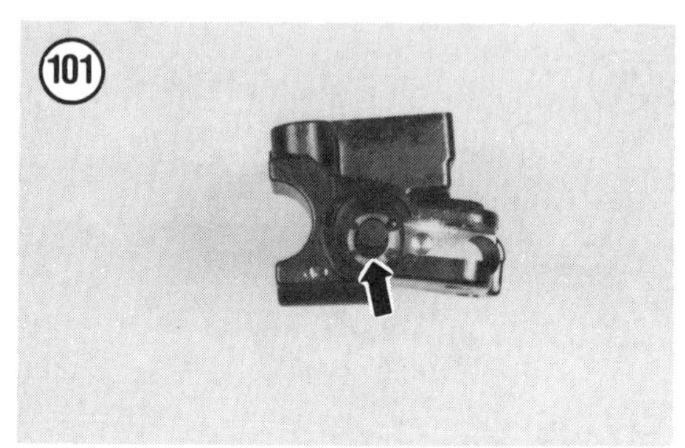

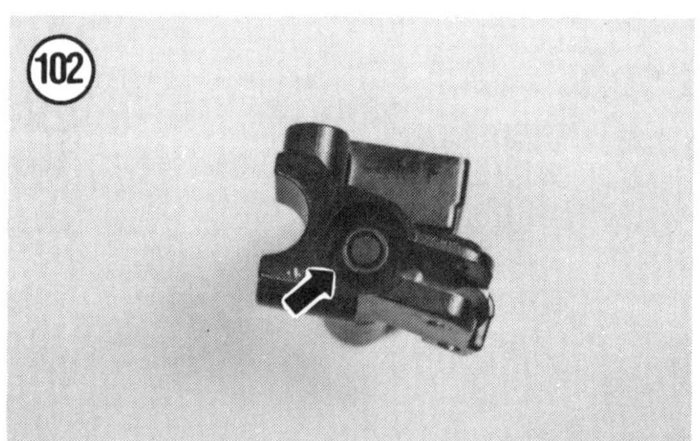

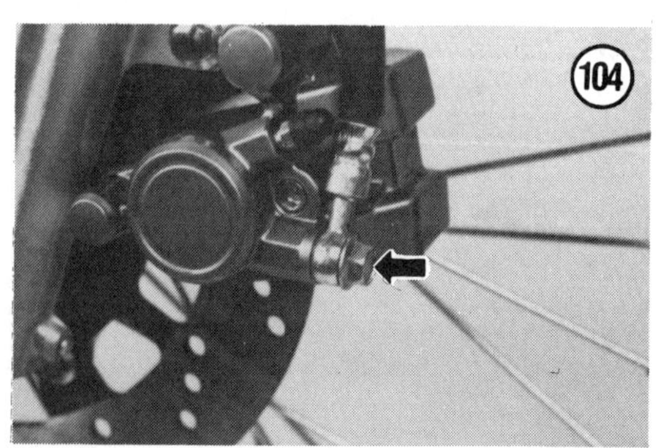

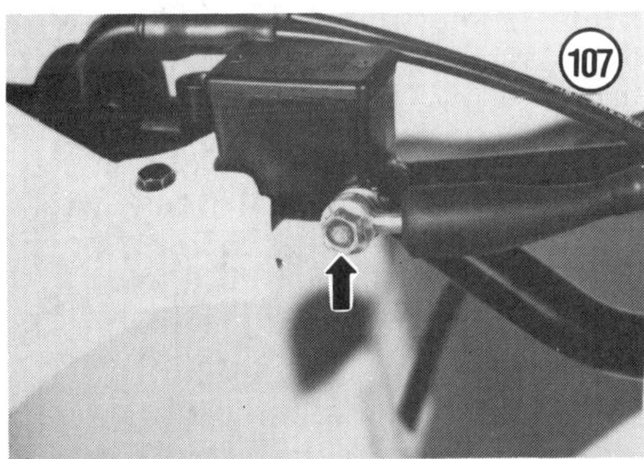

6. Install the spring (**Figure 88**) into the master cylinder.
7. Install the brake lever (B, **Figure 87**) onto the master cylinder. Then install the pivot bolt (A, **Figure 87**) through the brake lever and secure it with the nut. Tighten the nut securely.
8. Install the diaphragm and cover. Install the screws, but do not tighten at this time as fluid will have to be added later.

FRONT BRAKE HOSE REPLACEMENT (ALL MODELS)

The brake hose should be replaced every 4 years or whenever it shows signs of wear or damage.

NOTE
This procedure is shown on a XT600 model. The procedure is the same on TT600 models.

1. Place the bike on a stand so the front wheel clears the ground.
2. Remove the cap from the bleed valve.
3. Attach a hose to the bleed valve on the caliper assembly.
4. Place the loose end of the hose in a container to catch the brake fluid (**Figure 103**).
5. Open the bleed valve and continue to apply the front brake lever until the brake fluid is pumped out of the entire brake system. Dispose of this brake fluid—never reuse brake fluid.
6. Disconnect the hose and tighten the bleed valve.
7. Remove the union bolt and sealing washers (**Figure 104**) at the caliper assembly.
8. On XT600 models, slide back the rubber boot (**Figure 105**).
9. Remove the union bolt and sealing washers from the master cylinder. Refer to **Figure 106** for XT600 models or **Figure 107** for TT600 models.
10. Disconnect the brake hose from the retaining straps on the front fork.
11. Remove the front brake hose (**Figure 108**) from the frame.
12. Install by reversing these removal steps. Note the following.
13. Install new sealing washers and if necessary new union bolts.
14. Tighten the union bolts to torque specification listed in **Table 3**.

15. Refill the master cylinder with fresh brake fluid clearly marked DOT 3. Bleed the brake as described in this chapter.

WARNING
Do not ride the motorcycle until you are sure that the front brake is operating correctly.

FRONT BRAKE DISC

Inspection

It is not necessary to remove the disc from the wheel to inspect it. Small marks on the disc are not important, but radial scratches deep enough to snag a fingernail reduce braking effectiveness and increase brake pad wear. If these grooves are found, the disc should be resurfaced or replaced.

1. Measure the thickness around the disc at several locations with a vernier caliper or a micrometer (**Figure 109**). The disc must be replaced if the thickness at any point meets or is less than the wear limit listed in **Table 1**.
2. Clean the disc of any rust or corrosion and wipe clean with lacquer thinner. Never use an oil based solvent that may leave an oil residue on the disc.

Removal/Installation

1. Remove the front wheel as described under *Front Wheel Removal/Installation* in Chapter Ten.

NOTE
Place a piece of wood or vinyl tube in the caliper in place of the disc. This way, if the brake lever is inadvertently squeezed, the piston will not be forced out of the cylinder. If this does happen, the caliper might have to be disassembled to reseat the piston and the system will have to be bled. By using the wood, bleeding is not necessary when installing the wheel.

2. If not already removed, remove the speedometer drive unit (**Figure 110**) from the hub.
3. Remove the screws (A, **Figure 111**) securing the disc to the wheel.
4. Remove the disc (B, **Figure 111**) from the hub.
5. Install by reversing these removal steps. Note the following.
6. Install the disc onto the front hub so that the holes drilled in the disc face in the direction as shown in **Figure 112**.
7. Tighten the screws securely.

BRAKE BLEEDING

This procedure is necessary only when the brakes feel spongy, there is a leak in the hydraulic system,

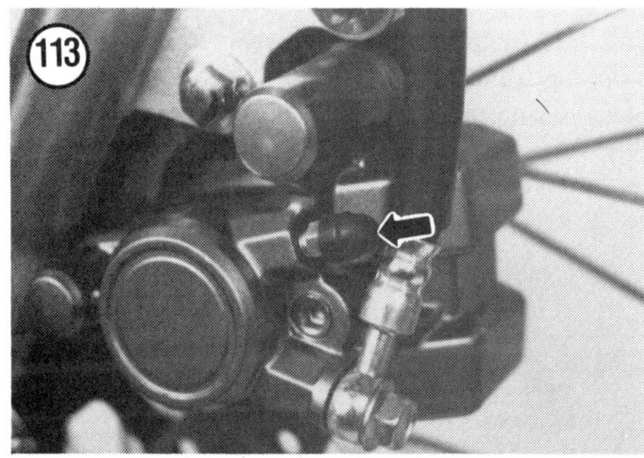

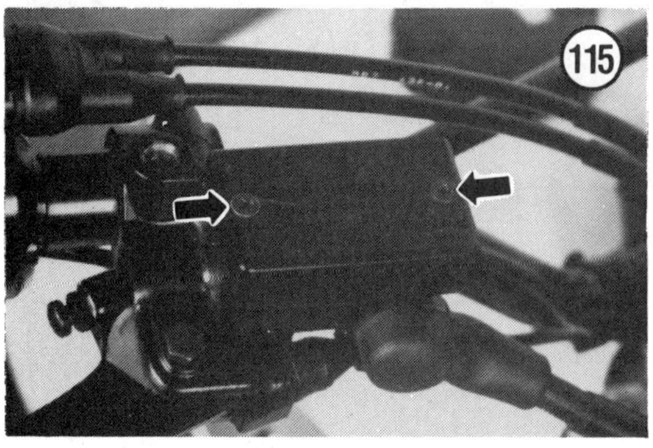

a component has been replaced or the brake fluid has been replaced.

Brake Bleeder Process

This procedure uses a brake bleeder that is available from motorcycle or automotive supply stores or from mail order outlets.

1. Remove the dust cap (**Figure 113**) from the bleed valve on the caliper assembly.
2. Connect the brake bleeder (**Figure 114**) to the bleed valve on the caliper assembly.

CAUTION
Cover the front wheel with a heavy cloth or plastic tarp to protect it from the accidental spilling of brake fluid. Wash any brake fluid off of any plastic, painted or plated surface immediately; as it will destroy the finish. Use soapy water and rinse completely.

3. Clean the top of the master cylinder of all dirt and foreign matter.
4. Remove the screws (**Figure 115**) securing the master cylinder top cover and remove the reservoir top cover and diaphragm.
5. Fill the reservoir almost to the top lip; insert the diaphragm and the cover loosely. Leave the cover in place during this procedure to prevent the entry of dirt.

WARNING
Use brake fluid from a sealed container marked DOT 3 only (specified for disc brakes). Other types may vaporize and cause brake failure. Do not intermix different brands or types as they may not be compatible. Do not intermix a silicone based (DOT 5) brake fluid as it can cause brake component damage leading to brake system failure.

6. Open the bleed valve about one-half turn and pump the brake bleeder.

NOTE
If air is entering the brake bleeder hose from around the bleed valve, apply several layers of Teflon tape to the bleed valve. This should make a good seal between the bleed valve and the brake bleeder hose.

7. As the fluid enters the system and exits into the brake bleeder, the level will drop in the reservoir. Maintain the level to just about the top of the reservoir to prevent air from being drawn into the system.
8. Continue to pump the lever on the brake bleeder until the fluid emerging from the hose is completely free of bubbles.
9. Tap on the brake hoses to help free any bubbles stuck to the walls of the hoses.

NOTE
Do not allow the reservoir to empty during the bleeding operation or more air will enter the system. If this occurs, the entire procedure must be repeated.

10. When the brake fluid is free of bubbles, tighten the bleed valve, remove the brake bleeder tube and install the bleed valve dust cap.
11. If necessary, add fluid to correct the level in the reservoir. It should be to the upper level line.
12. Install the diaphragm and the cover. Install the screws and tighten securely.
13. Test the feel of the brake lever. It should be firm and should offer the same resistance each time it's operated. If it feels spongy, it is likely that there is still air in the system and it must be bled again. When all air has been bled from the system and the fluid level is correct in the reservoir, double-check for leaks and tighten all fittings and connections.

WARNING
Before riding the bike, make certain that the brake is operating correctly by operating the lever several times.

14. Test ride the bike slowly at first to make sure that the front brake assembly is operating properly.

Without a Brake Bleeder

1. Remove the dust cap (**Figure 113**) from the bleed valve on the caliper assembly.
2. Connect a piece of clear tubing (A, **Figure 116**) to the bleed valve on the caliper assembly.

CAUTION
Cover the front wheel with a heavy cloth or plastic tarp to protect it from the accidental spilling of brake fluid. Wash any brake fluid off of any plastic, painted or plated surface immediately; as it will destroy the finish. Use soapy water and rinse completely.

3. Clean the top of the master cylinder of all dirt and foreign matter.
4. Remove the screws (**Figure 115**) securing the master cylinder top cover and remove the reservoir top cover and diaphragm.
5. Place the other end of the tube into a clean container (B, **Figure 116**).
6. Fill the container with enough fresh brake fluid to keep the end submerged.
7. Fill the reservoir almost to the cover lip; insert the diaphragm and the cover loosely. Leave the cover in place during this procedure to prevent the entry of dirt.

WARNING
Use brake fluid from a sealed container marked DOT 3 only (specified for disc brakes). Other types may vaporize and cause brake failure. Do not intermix different brands or types as they may not be compatible. Do not intermix a silicone based (DOT 5) brake fluid as it can cause brake component damage leading to brake system failure.

NOTE
During this procedure, it is very important to check the fluid level in the brake master cylinder reservoir often. If the reservoir runs dry, you'll introduce more air in the system which will require starting over.

8. If the master cylinder was drained, it must be bled first. Remove the union bolt and hose from the master cylinder. Slowly apply the brake lever several times while holding your thumb over the opening in the master cylinder and perform the following:
  a. With the lever applied, slightly release your thumb pressure. Some of the brake fluid and air bubbles will escape.
  b. Apply thumb pressure and pump lever once more.
  c. Repeat this procedure until you can feel resistance at the lever.
9. Quickly reinstall the hose, sealing washers and the union bolt. Refill the master cylinder.
10. Tighten the union bolt and pump the lever again and perform the following:
  a. Loosen the union bolt 1/4 turn. Some brake fluid and air bubbles will escape.
  b. Tighten the union bolt and repeat this procedure until no air bubbles escape.
11. Tighten the union bolts to the torque specification listed in **Table 3**.
12. Slowly apply the brake lever several times as follows:
  a. Pull the lever in and hold it in the applied position.
  b. Open the bleed valve about one-half turn. Allow the lever to travel to its limit.
  c. When this limit is reached, tighten the bleed valve.
13. As the fluid enters the system, the level will drop in the reservoir. Maintain the level to just about the top of the reservoir to prevent air from being drawn into the system.
14. Continue to pump the lever and fill the reservoir until the fluid emerging from the hose is completely free of bubbles.

NOTE
Do not allow the reservoir to empty during the bleeding operation or more air will enter the system. If this occurs, the entire procedure must be repeated.

15. Hold the lever in, tighten the bleed valve, remove the bleed tube and install the bleed valve dust cap.
16. If necessary, add fluid to correct the level in the reservoir.
17. Install the diaphragm and cover and tighten the screws securely.
18. Test the feel of the brake lever. It should be firm and should offer the same resistance each time it's operated. If it feels spongy, it is likely that there is still air in the system and it must be bled again. When all air has been bled from the system and the fluid level is correct in the reservoir, double-check for leaks and tighten all fittings and connections.

WARNING
Before riding the bike, make certain that the brakes are operating correctly. Spin the front wheel and apply the lever several times. The wheel must come to a complete stop each time.

19. Test ride the bike slowly at first to make sure that the brakes are operating properly.

FRONT DRUM BRAKE

The 1983-1984 TT600 models are equipped with a front drum brake. Applying the front brake lever pulls the brake cable which in turn rotates the camshafts. This forces the brake shoes out into contact with the brake drum.

Lever free play must be maintained to minimize brake drag and premature brake wear, and maximize braking effectiveness. Refer to *Front Drum Brake Lever Adjustment* in Chapter Three, for complete adjustment procedures.

Glaze buildup on the brake shoes reduces braking effectiveness. The brake shoes should be removed and cleaned regularly to assure maximum brake shoe contact.

Disassembly

12

Refer to **Figure 117** for this procedure.
1. Remove the front wheel as described under *Front Wheel Removal/Installation* in Chapter Ten.
2. Pull the brake panel up and out of the wheel.
3. Prior to removing the brake shoes from the brake panel, measure the outside diameter of the brake shoe assembly in 3 different locations 120° apart. Refer to dimension listed in **Table 2**. If worn to the service limit or less, replace the brake shoes as an assembly.

NOTE
Mark each brake shoe for position before removing them in Step 3.

FRONT DRUM BRAKE (TT600—1983-1984)

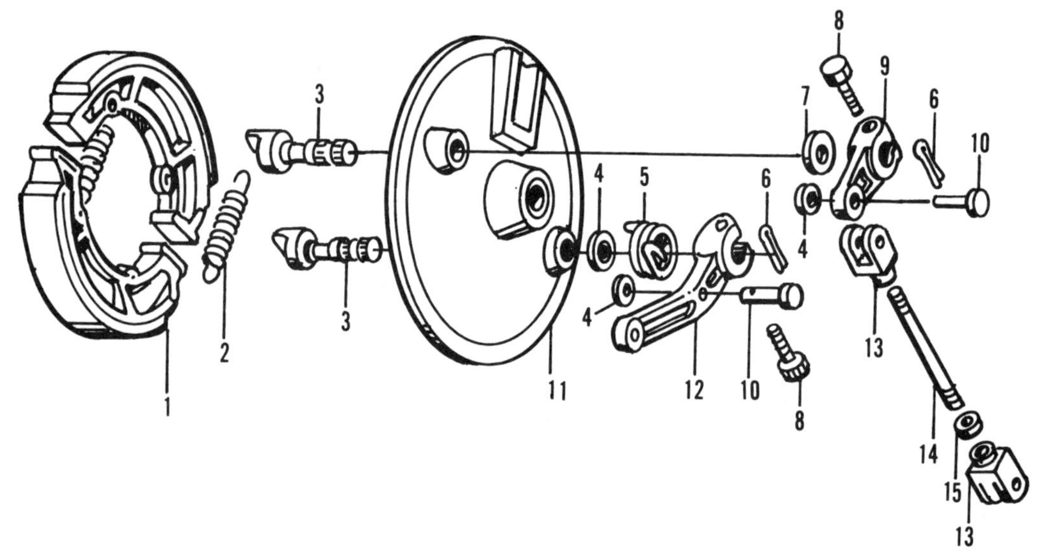

1. Brake shoes
2. Spring
3. Camshaft
4. Gasket
5. Spring
6. Cotter pin
7. Washer
8. Bolt
9. Upper brake lever
10. Pin
11. Brake panel
12. Lower brake lever
13. Yoke
14. Adjuster rod
15. Locknut

NOTE
Place a clean shop rag on the brake linings to protect them from oil and grease during removal.

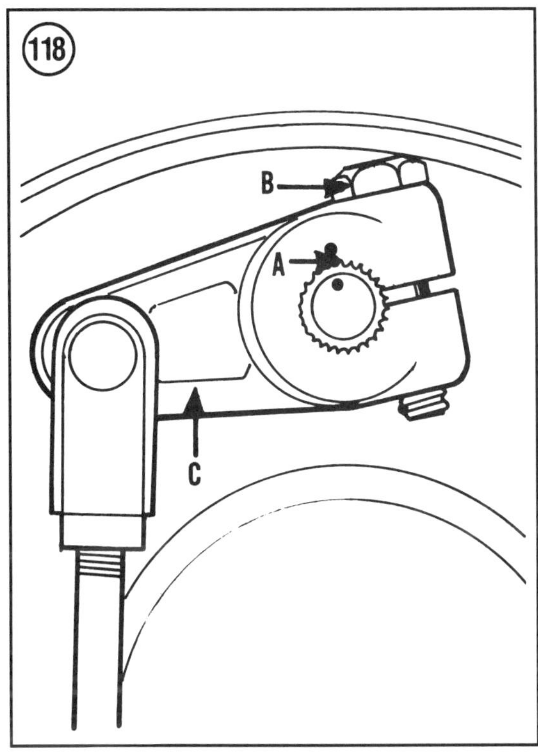

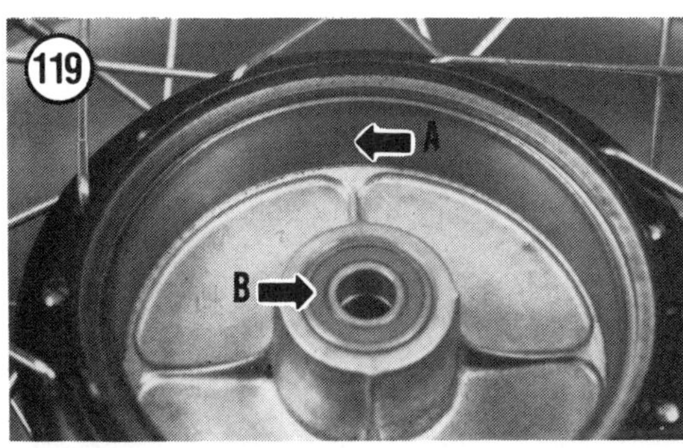

4. Remove the brake shoe assembly, including the return springs, from the brake panel. Pull both brake shoes from the panel.
5. Remove the return springs and separate the shoes.

NOTE
It is not necessary to remove the camshafts in order to replace the brake linings. If the camshafts operate easily with no binding and the brake is adjusted properly, do not remove the camshafts. This will eliminate having to adjust them after installation.

6. To remove the camshafts, perform the following:
   a. Mark the position of each brake lever (A, **Figure 118**) as it is installed on the camshaft so it can be reinstalled in the same position.
   b. Loosen the bolt (B, **Figure 118**) securing the brake lever to the cam.
   c. Repeat Step 6a and Step 6b for the other brake lever.
   d. Remove the brake lever (C, **Figure 118**) assembly from both camshafts.
   e. Remove both camshafts from the backside of the brake panel.

Inspection

1. Thoroughly clean and dry all parts except the linings.
2. Check the contact surface of the brake drum (A, **Figure 119**) for scoring. If there are deep grooves or the drum surface is severely damaged, the wheel hub/drum assembly will have to be replaced. This type of wear can be avoided to a great extent if the brakes are disassembled and thoroughly cleaned after the bike has been ridden in mud or deep sand.

NOTE
If oil or grease is on the drum surface, clean it off with a clean rag soaked in lacquer thinner—do not use any solvent that may leave an oily residue.

3. Check the wheel bearing (B, **Figure 119**) on the brake drum side for damage that would allow grease to enter the brake drum and contaminate the drum and brake shoes. If the bearing is leaking, replace it as described under *Rear Hub* in Chapter Eleven.
4. Use a vernier caliper (**Figure 120**) and measure the inside diameter of the drum for out-of-round or

excessive wear. Refer to **Table 2** for brake specifications.

5. Inspect the linings (**Figure 121**) for imbedded foreign material. Normal glaze buildup can be removed with a course grade sandpaper. Check for traces of oil or grease. If the linings are contaminated, they must be replaced.

NOTE
Do not include the thickness of the aluminum backing shoe when measuring the brake lining thickness.

6. Measure the brake lining thickness with a vernier caliper (**Figure 122**). Replace the linings if worn to the wear limits or less as listed in **Table 2**.
7. Inspect the brake shoe springs for wear or stretching. If the brake shoe springs are stretched, they will not fully retract the brake shoes from the drum, resulting in a power-robbing drag on the drum and premature wear of the linings.
8. Inspect the cam lobe and the pivot pin area on the camshaft (**Figure 123**) for wear and corrosion. Minor roughness can be removed with fine emery cloth.
9. Check both brake camshaft pinch bolts for stripped threads. Replace the bolt(s) if necessary.

Assembly

Refer to **Figure 117** for this procedure.

1. Grease the camshafts with a light coat of wheel bearing grease. Avoid getting any grease on the brake panel where the linings come in contact with it.
2. If the camshafts were removed, perform the following:
   a. Install both camshafts into the backside of the brake panel.
   b. Install the brake lever (C, **Figure 118**) assembly onto both camshafts. Align the punch marks of the camshafts and brake levers made in Step 6a under *Disassembly*.
   c. Tighten the bolts (B, **Figure 118**) securing the brake levers to the camshafts.
3. Hold the brake shoes in a V-formation with the return springs attached and snap them in place on the brake panel. Make sure they are firmly seated on it.
4. If the camshafts were removed or the brake was out of adjustment; adjust the camshaft lever as described in this chapter.
5. Install the brake panel assembly into the brake drum.
6. Install the front wheel as described in Chapter Eleven.
7. Adjust the front brake as described in Chapter Three.

Camshaft Lever Adjustment

On a double leading type of drum brake, both brake shoes must make contact with the brake drum at the same time for maximum braking effectiveness.

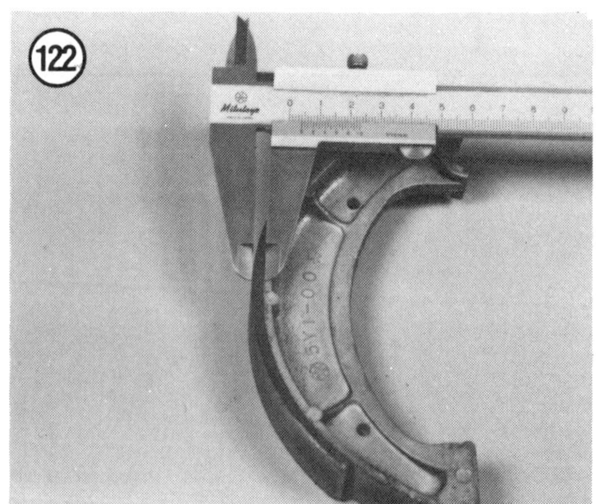

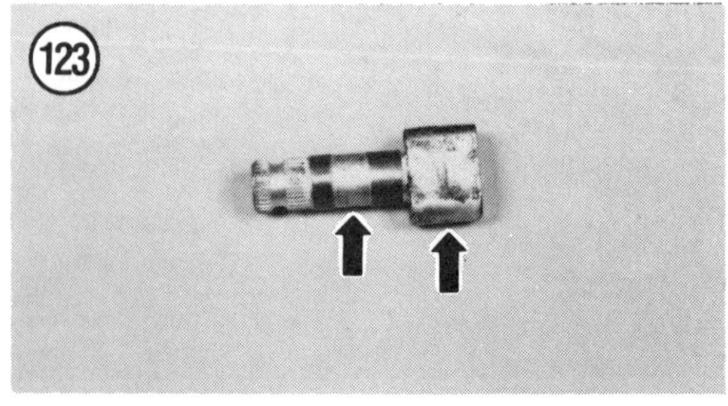

Refer to **Figure 117** for this procedure.

1. Move the adjuster rod to apply the brakes. The camshafts must move brake shoes the same amount (**Figure 124**).

2. If the brake shoes do not move the same amount, proceed to the next step.

3. Loosen the locknut (A, **Figure 125**) on the adjuster rod at the lower brake lever.

4. Rotate the adjuster rod (B, **Figure 125**) in either direction to achieve equal brake shoe movement.

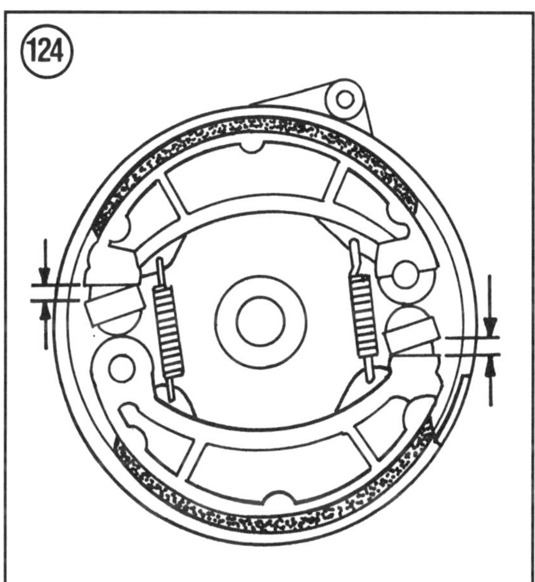

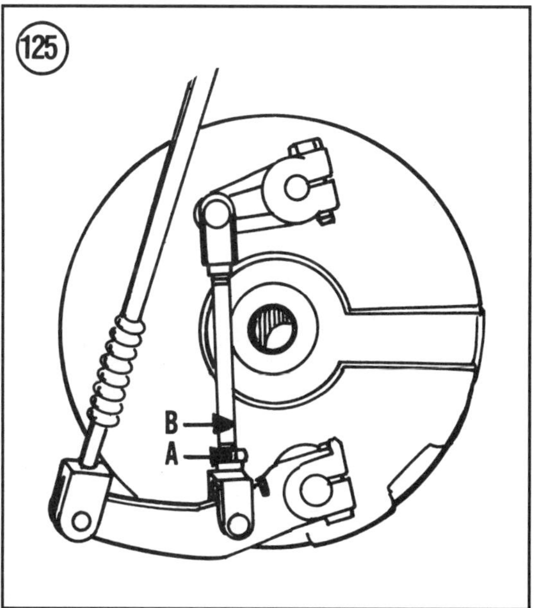

5. Once equal brake shoe movement is achieved, tighten the locknut (A, **Figure 125**).

Front Brake Cable Replacement

In time the front brake cable will stretch to the point that it is no longer useful and will have to be replaced.

1. Pull the protective boot away from the brake lever.

2. Loosen the locknut and turn the adjuster barrel on the brake hand lever all the way toward the hand grip.

3. Slip the cable end out of the end of the hand lever.

4. At the front brake panel, loosen the locknut (A, **Figure 126**) and turn the adjust nut (B, **Figure 126**) to allow the maximum amount of cable slack.

5. Disconnect the brake cable from the end of the lower brake lever (C, **Figure 126**).

6. Remove the brake cable from the receptacle (D, **Figure 126**) on the brake backing plate.

NOTE

Prior to removing the cable, make a drawing (or take a Polaroid picture) of the cable routing through the frame and forks. It is very easy to forget its routing after it has been removed. Replace the cable exactly as it was, avoiding any sharp turns.

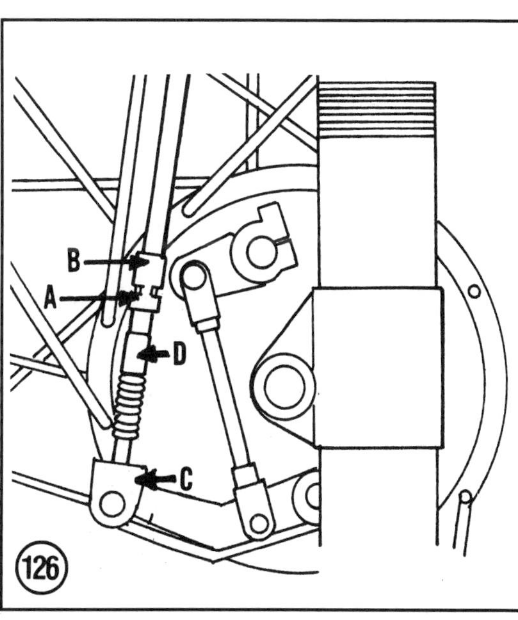

7. Pull the cable out of the cable guides on the upper and lower fork bridges.

8. Remove the cable and replace it with a new one.

9. Install by reversing these removal steps. Note the following.

10. Make sure it is correctly routed with no sharp turns.

11. Operate the brake lever and make sure it moves freely.

12. Adjust the brake free play as described under *Front Brake Lever Free Play Adjustment* in Chapter Three.

REAR DRUM BRAKE

Activating the rear brake pedal pulls the rod which in turn rotates the camshaft. This forces the brake shoes out into contact with the brake drum.

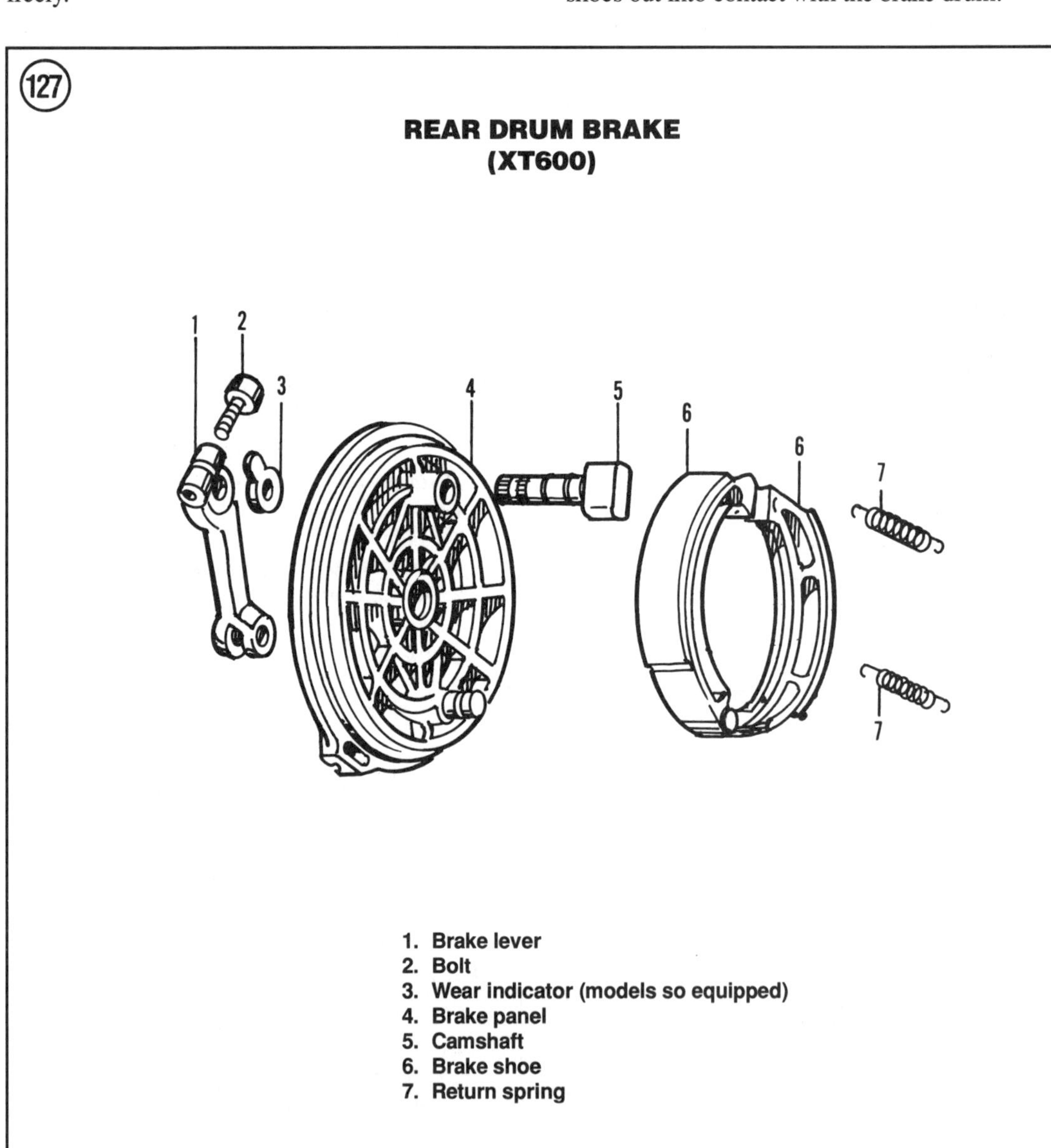

Pedal free play must be maintained to minimize brake drag and premature brake wear and maximize braking effectiveness. Refer to *Rear Brake Pedal Adjustment* in Chapter Three, for complete adjustment procedures.

Glaze buildup on the brake shoes reduces braking effectiveness. The brake shoes should be removed and cleaned regularly to assure maximum brake shoe contact.

Disassembly

Refer to **Figure 127** for XT600 models or **Figure 128** for TT600 models.

1. Remove the rear wheel as described under *Rear Wheel Removal/Installation* in Chapter Eleven.

2. Pull the brake panel straight up and out of the wheel hub.

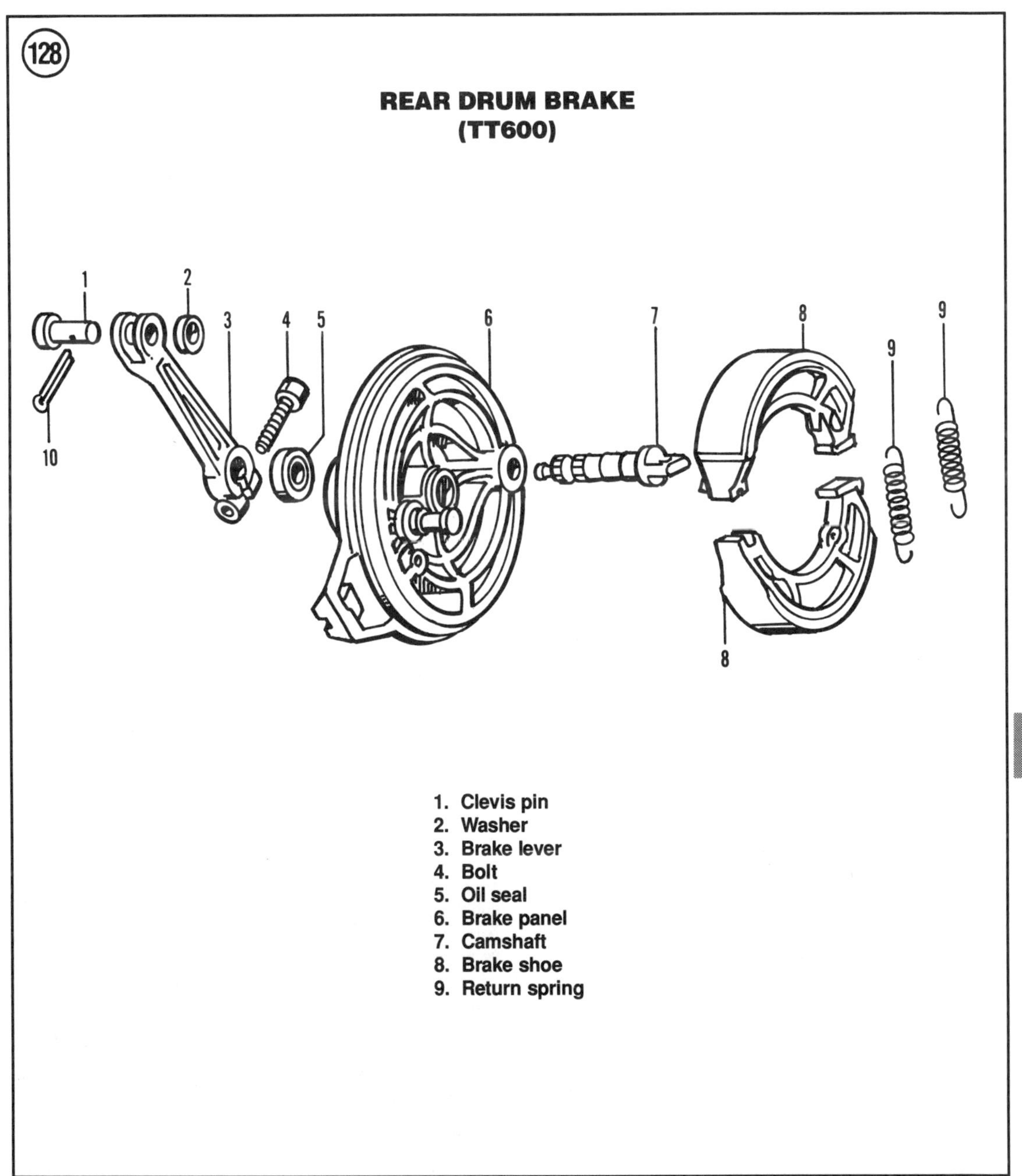

REAR DRUM BRAKE (TT600)

NOTE

Mark each brake shoe for position before removing them in Step 3. In addition, place a clean shop rag on the linings to protect them from oil and grease during removal.

3. Remove the brake shoe assembly, including the return springs, from the brake panel. Pull both brake shoes from the panel (**Figure 129**).
4. Remove the return springs and separate the shoes.
5. Mark the position of the brake lever (**Figure 130**) as it is installed on the camshaft so it can be reinstalled in the same position.
6. Loosen the bolt (A, **Figure 131**) securing the brake lever to the cam. Remove the lever (B, **Figure 131**).
7. On models so equipped, remove the wear indicator (**Figure 132**).
8. Withdraw the camshaft (**Figure 133**).

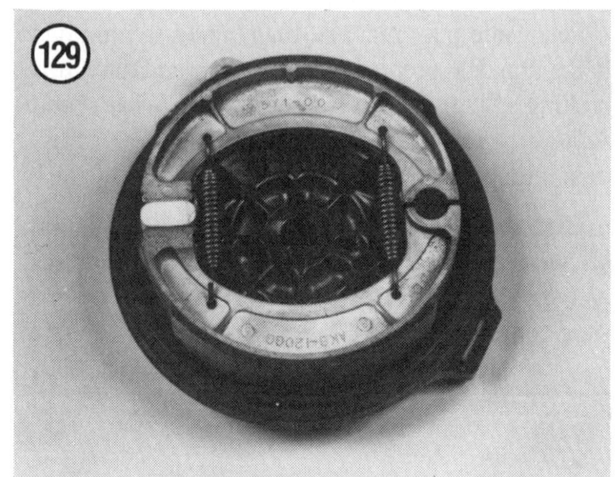

129

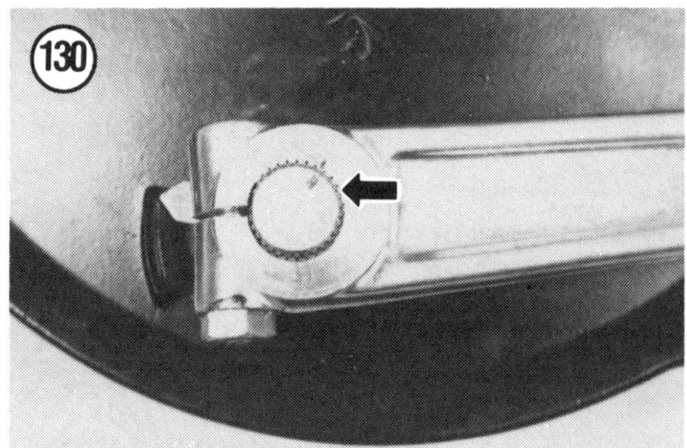

130

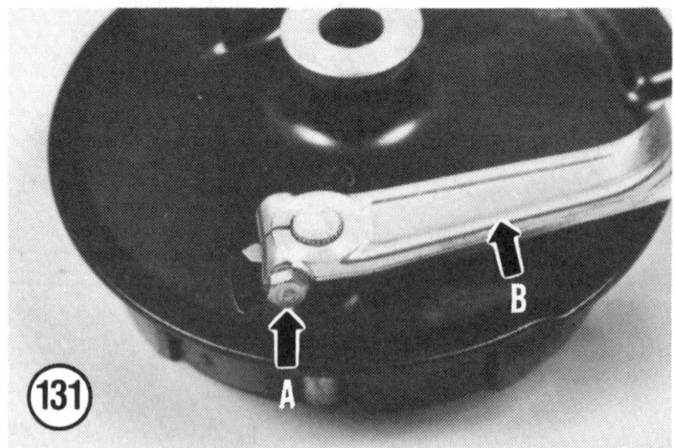

131

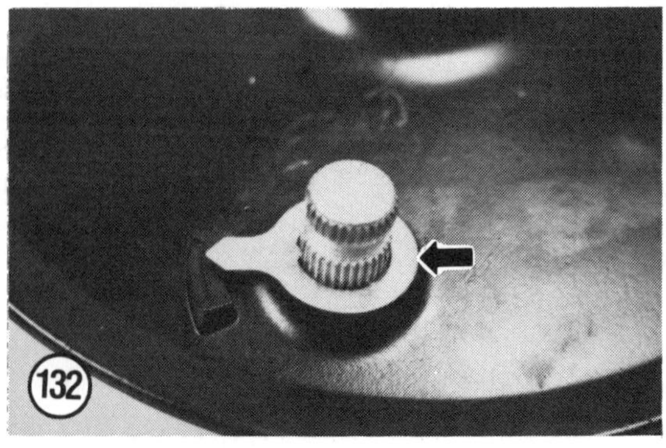

132

Inspection

1. Thoroughly clean and dry all parts except the linings.
2. Check the contact surface of the brake drum (A, **Figure 119**) for scoring. If there are deep grooves or the drum surface is severely damaged, the hub will have to be replaced. This type of wear can be avoided to a great extent if the brakes are disassembled and thoroughly cleaned after the bike has been ridden in mud or deep sand.

NOTE

If oil or grease is on the drum surface, clean it off with a clean rag soaked in lacquer thinner—do not use any solvent that may leave an oily residue.

3. Check the wheel bearing (B, **Figure 119**) on the brake drum side for damage that would allow grease to enter the brake drum and contaminate the drum and brake shoes. Replace the bearing as described under *Rear Hub* in Chapter Eleven.
4. Use a vernier caliper (**Figure 120**) and measure the inside diameter of the drum for out-of-round or excessive wear. Refer to **Table 2** for brake specifications.
5. Inspect the linings (**Figure 121**) for imbedded foreign material. Normal glaze buildup can be removed with a course grade sandpaper. Check for

traces of oil or grease. If the linings are contaminated, they must be replaced.

NOTE
Do not include the thickness of the aluminum backing shoe when measuring the brake lining thickness.

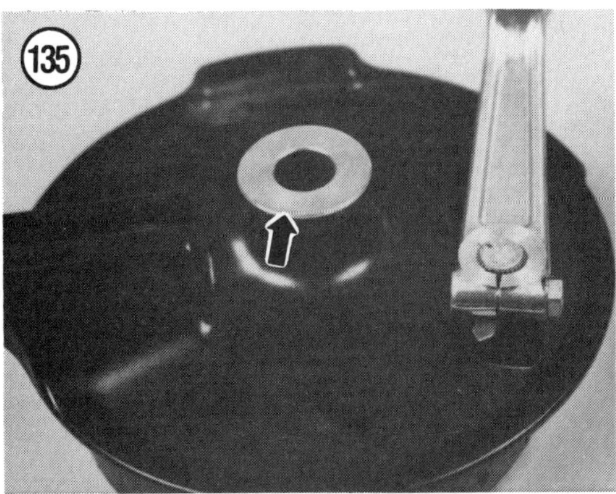

6. Measure the brake lining thickness with a vernier caliper (**Figure 122**). Replace the linings if worn to the wear limits or less as listed in **Table 2**.
7. Inspect the brake shoe springs for wear or stretching. If the brake shoe springs are stretched, they will not fully retract the brake shoes from the drum, resulting in a power-robbing drag on the drum and premature wear of the linings.
8. Inspect the cam lobe and the pivot pin area on the camshaft (**Figure 123**) for wear and corrosion. Minor roughness can be removed with fine emery cloth.
9. Check the brake camshaft pinch bolt for stripped threads. Replace the bolt if necessary.
10. Inspect the brake panel (**Figure 134**) for wear or damage, replace if necessary.
11. On TT600 models, replace the brake panel oil seal if damaged. Pry the seal out with a screwdriver. Install a new seal by driving it into the panel squarely with a suitable size socket.

Assembly

Refer to **Figure 127** for XT600 models or **Figure 128** for TT600 models.

1. Grease the shaft, cam and pivot post with a light coat of wheel bearing grease. Avoid getting any grease on the brake panel where the linings come in contact with it.
2. Insert the camshaft into the brake panel (**Figure 133**).
3. On models so equipped, align the wear indicator with the splines on the camshaft and install the wear indicator (**Figure 132**).
4. Install the brake lever (B, **Figure 131**) onto the brake camshaft. Make sure to align the 2 marks made during disassembly.
5. Install the bolt (A, **Figure 131**) securing the brake lever. Tighten the bolt securely.
6. Hold the brake shoes in a V-formation with the return springs attached and snap them in place on the brake panel. Make sure they are firmly seated on it (**Figure 129**).
7. If removed, install the spacer (**Figure 135**) into the brake panel.
8. Install the brake panel assembly into the brake drum.
9. Install the rear wheel as described in Chapter Eleven.
10. Adjust the rear brake as described under *Rear Brake Pedal Adjustment* in Chapter Three.

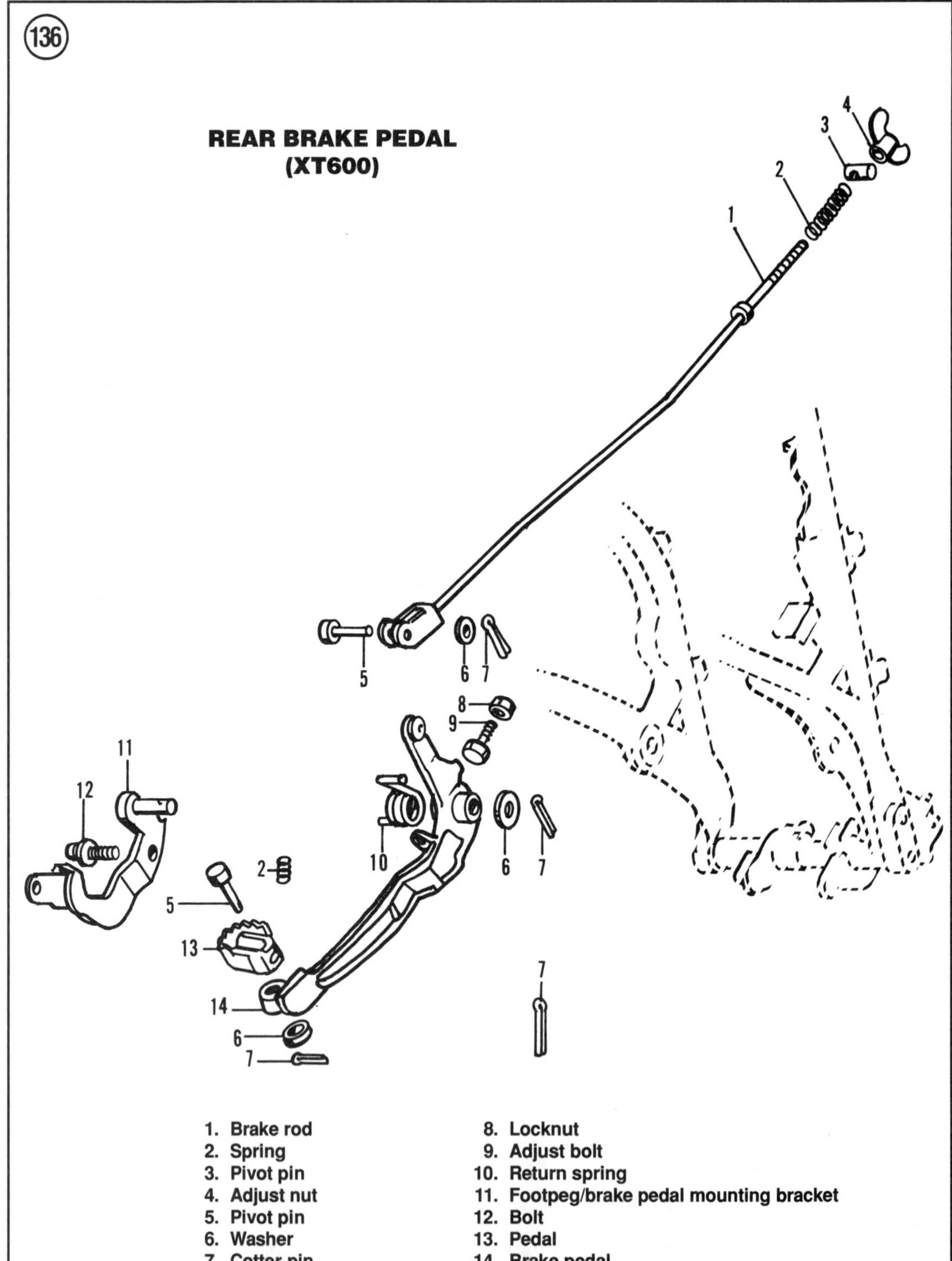

1. Brake rod
2. Spring
3. Pivot pin
4. Adjust nut
5. Pivot pin
6. Washer
7. Cotter pin
8. Locknut
9. Adjust bolt
10. Return spring
11. Footpeg/brake pedal mounting bracket
12. Bolt
13. Pedal
14. Brake pedal

REAR BRAKE PEDAL

Removal/Installation

Refer to **Figure 136** for XT600 models or **Figure 137** for TT600 models.

1. Support the bike on a stand with the rear wheel off of the ground.

2. Unscrew the rear brake adjusting nut completely from the brake rod. Refer to **Figure 138** for XT600 models or **Figure 139** for TT600 models.

3. Withdraw the brake rod from the brake lever and pivot it out of the way. Reinstall the adjusting nut to avoid misplacing it.

4. Remove the bolt securing the kickstarter lever and remove the lever (**Figure 140**).

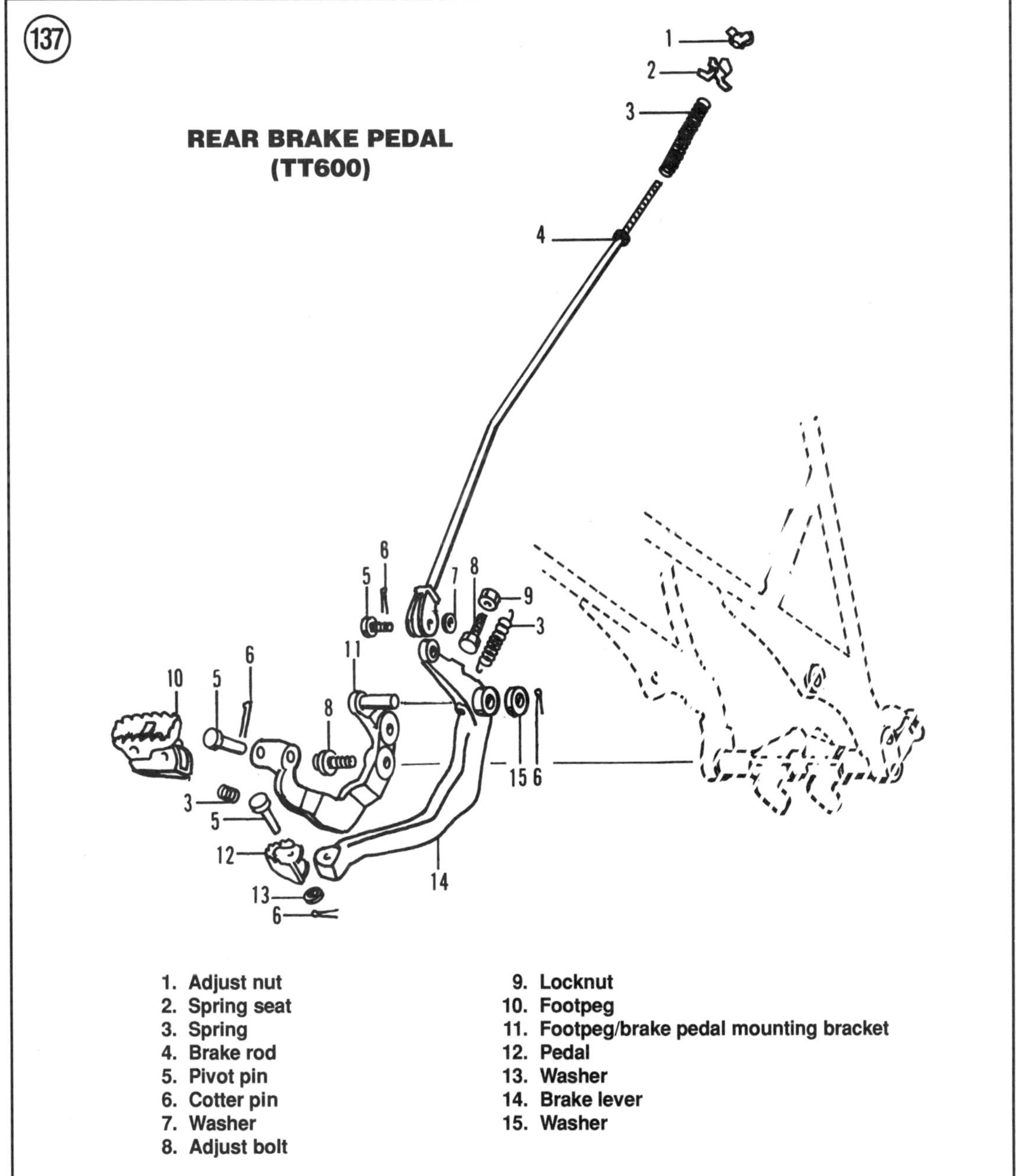

1. Adjust nut
2. Spring seat
3. Spring
4. Brake rod
5. Pivot pin
6. Cotter pin
7. Washer
8. Adjust bolt
9. Locknut
10. Footpeg
11. Footpeg/brake pedal mounting bracket
12. Pedal
13. Washer
14. Brake lever
15. Washer

5. On XT600 models, use needlenose pliers and disconnect the brake light switch spring (A, **Figure 141**) from the brake pedal tab.

6. Remove the bolts (B, **Figure 141**) securing the rear brake pedal and the footpeg assembly to the frame.

7. Remove the rear brake pedal and footpeg assembly from the frame. Carefully pull the brake rod free from the frame.

8. Install by reversing these removal steps. Note the following.

9. Tighten the rear brake pedal and footpeg assembly mounting bolts to the torque specification listed in **Table 3**.

10. Adjust the rear brake as described under *Rear Brake Pedal Adjustment* in Chapter Three.

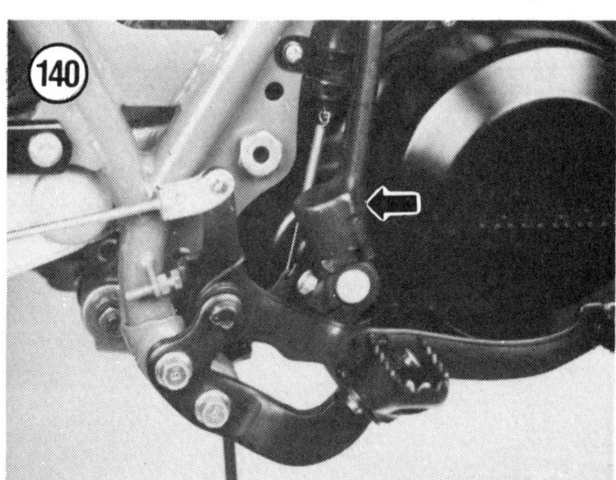

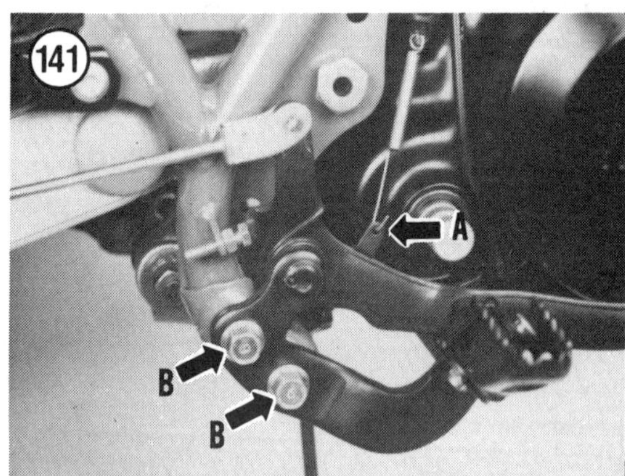

Table 1 DISC BRAKE SERVICE SPECIFICATIONS

Item	Specifications mm (in.)	Wear limit mm (in.)
Brake disc		
Outside diameter		
XT600	267 (10.5)	—
TT600	230 (9.06)	—
Thickness		
XT600	4.0 (0.16)	*
TT600	3.0 (0.12)	2.5 (0.10)
Brake pad thickness		
XT600	6.8 (0.27)	0.8 (0.03)
TT600	6.0 (0.24)	0.8 (0.03)
Master cylinder inside diameter	11.0 (0.4)	—
Brake caliper inside diameter		
XT600	38.1 (1.50)	—
TT600	34.9 (1.37)	—

* Information not provided by Yamaha.

Table 2 DRUM BRAKE SERVICE SPECIFICATIONS

Item	Specifications mm (in.)	Wear limit mm (in.)
Front drum brake		
Brake shoe outer diameter	129 (5.08)	125 (4.92)
Brake lining thickness	4 (0.16)	2 (0.08)
Brake drum inside diameter	130 (5.12)	131 (5.16)
Rear drum brake		
Brake drum inside diameter		
XT600	150 (5.91)	151 (5.94)
TT600	130 (5.12)	131 (5.16)
Brake lining thickness	4 (0.16)	2 (0.08)
Brake shoe spring free length		
XT600	58.0 (2.28)	—
TT600	*	*

* Information not provided by Yamaha.

Table 3 BRAKE TIGHTENING TORQUES

Item	N•m	ft.-lb.
Front caliper (XT600)		
Mounting bolts	35	25
Pad pin bolt	23	17
Front caliper (TT600)		
Retaining bolt	18	13
Bracket mounting bolts	30	22
Brake hose union bolts	26	19
Brake pedal/foot peg assembly mounting bolts	45	32

CHAPTER THIRTEEN

FRAME AND BODY

This chapter includes replacement procedures for components attached to the frame that are not covered in the rest of the book.

This chapter also describes procedures for completely stripping and repainting the frame.

KICKSTAND (SIDESTAND)

Removal/Installation

Refer to **Figure 1** for XT600 models or **Figure 2** for TT600 models for this procedure.

1. Place the bike on a support with the rear wheel off the ground.

2. Raise the kickstand.

3A. On XT600 models, perform the following:

a. Disconnect the return spring (A, **Figure 3**) from the link plate with Vise grip pliers.

b. Remove the pivot bolt (B, **Figure 3**) and nut and remove the kickstand (C, **Figure 3**) from the frame. Don't lose the link plate.

3B. On TT600 models, perform the following:

a. Disconnect the return spring from the frame with Vise grip pliers.

b. Remove the pivot bolt and nut and remove the kickstand from the frame.

4. Install by reversing these removal steps. Note the following.

5. On XT600 models, be sure to install the link plate and spring as shown in A, **Figure 3**.

6. Apply a light coat of multipurpose grease to all pivot surfaces prior to installation.

7. Tighten the bolt and nut securely.

FOOTPEGS

Front Right-hand Footpeg Removal/Installation

Refer to **Figure 1** for XT600 models or **Figure 2** for TT600 models for this procedure.

1. Support the bike on a stand with the rear wheel off of the ground.

2. To remove only the footpeg from the footpeg bracket, perform the following:

a. Remove the cotter pin from the pivot pin.

b. Remove the footpeg and spring from the bracket.

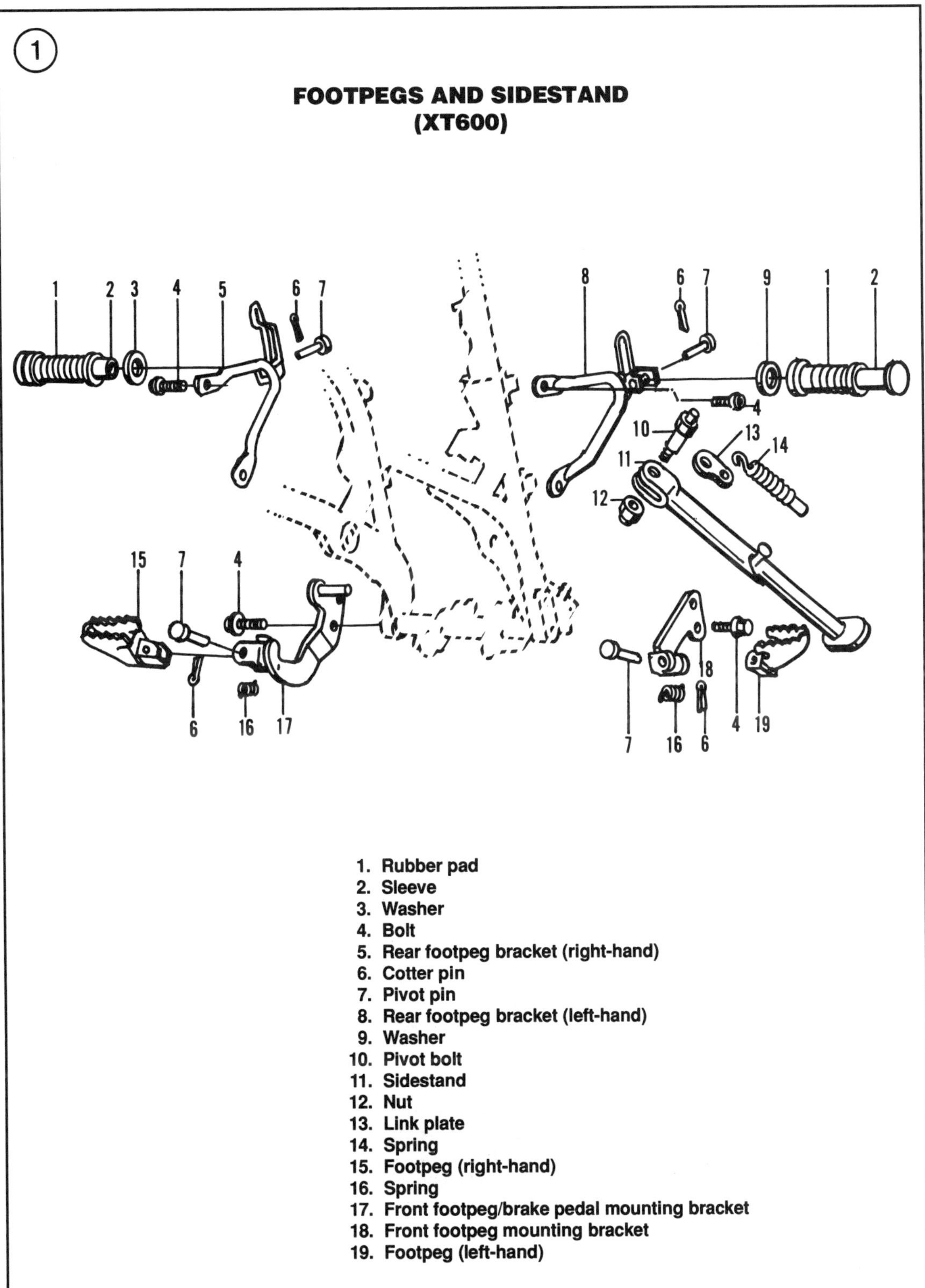
1
FOOTPEGS AND SIDESTAND
(XT600)
1. Rubber pad
2. Sleeve
3. Washer
4. Bolt
5. Rear footpeg bracket (right-hand)
6. Cotter pin
7. Pivot pin
8. Rear footpeg bracket (left-hand)
9. Washer
10. Pivot bolt
11. Sidestand
12. Nut
13. Link plate
14. Spring
15. Footpeg (right-hand)
16. Spring
17. Front footpeg/brake pedal mounting bracket
18. Front footpeg mounting bracket
19. Footpeg (left-hand)

FOOTPEGS AND SIDESTAND (TT600)

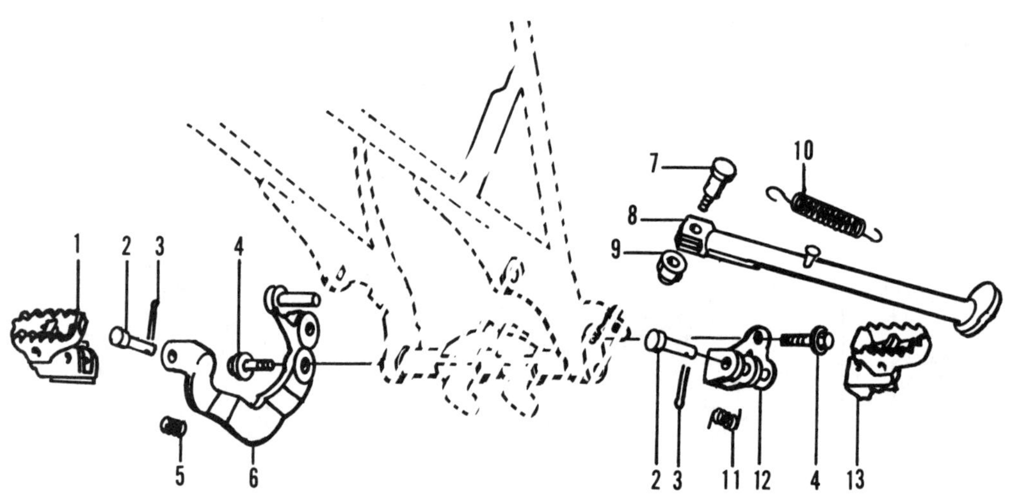

1. Footpeg (right-hand)
2. Pivot pin
3. Cotter pin
4. Bolt
5. Spring
6. Front footpeg/brake pedal mounting bracket
7. Bolt
8. Sidestand
9. Nut
10. Return spring
11. Spring
12. Front footpeg mounting bracket
13. Footpeg (left-hand)

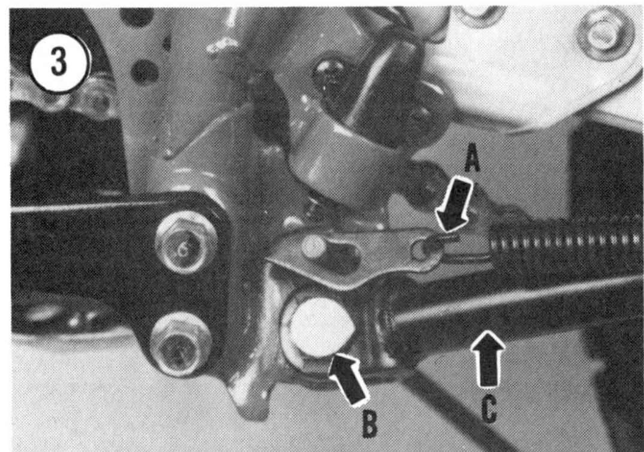

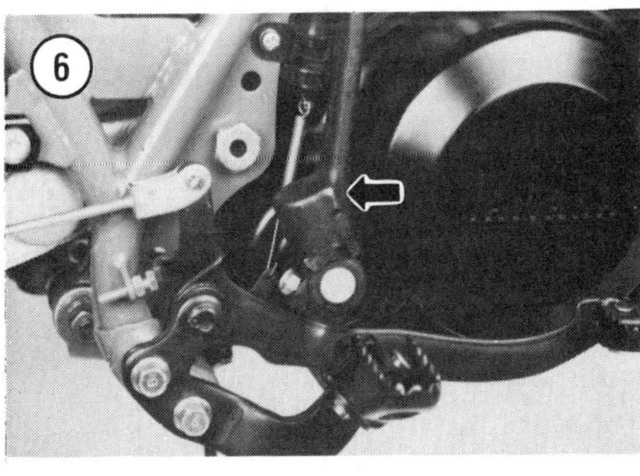

3. To remove the footpeg and bracket assembly, perform the following:

   a. Unscrew the rear brake adjusting nut completely from the brake rod. Refer to **Figure 4** for XT600 models or **Figure 5** for TT600 models.
   b. Withdraw the brake rod from the brake lever and pivot it out of the way. Reinstall the adjusting nut to avoid misplacing it.
   c. Remove the bolt securing the kickstarter lever and remove the lever (**Figure 6**).
   d. Use needlenose pliers and disconnect the brake light switch spring (A, **Figure 7**) from the brake pedal tab.
   e. Remove the bolts (B, **Figure 7**) securing the rear brake pedal and footpeg assembly to the frame.
   f. Remove the rear brake pedal and footpeg assembly from the frame. Carefully pull the brake rod free from the frame.

4. To separate the footpeg bracket from the brake pedal assembly, perform the following:

   a. Remove the cotter pin and washer on the backside of the footpeg bracket.
   b. Remove the footpeg bracket and spring from the brake pedal assembly.

5. Install by reversing these removal steps. Note the following.

6. Lubricate all pivot points prior to installation.

7. Tighten the rear brake pedal and footpeg assembly mounting bolts to the torque specification listed in **Table 1**.

8. Install new cotter pins and bend the ends over completely.

9. Adjust the rear brake as described under *Rear Brake Pedal Adjustment* in Chapter Three.

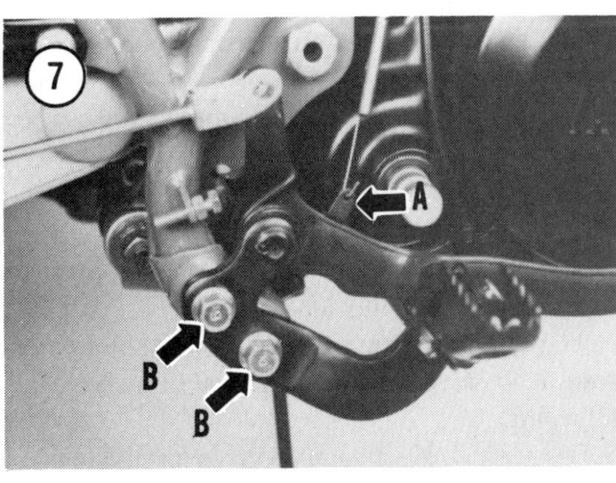

Front Left-hand Footpeg Removal/Installation

Refer to **Figure 1** for XT600 models or **Figure 2** for TT600 models for this procedure.

1. Support the bike on a stand with the rear wheel off of the ground.
2. To remove only the footpeg from the footpeg bracket, perform the following:
   a. Remove the cotter pin from the pivot pin.
   b. Remove the footpeg and spring from the bracket.
3. To remove the footpeg and bracket assembly, perform the following:
   a. Remove the bolts securing the footpeg assembly (**Figure 8**) to the frame.
   b. Remove the footpeg assembly.
4. Install by reversing these removal steps. Note the following.
5. Lubricate all pivot points prior to installation.
6. Tighten the rear brake pedal and footpeg assembly mounting bolts to the torque specification listed in **Table 1**.
7. Install new cotter pins and bend the ends over completely.

Rear Footpegs (XT600) Removal/Installation

Refer to **Figure 1** for this procedure.

NOTE
TT600 models are not equipped with rear footpegs.

1. Support the bike on a stand with the rear wheel off of the ground.
2. To remove only the footpeg from the footpeg bracket, perform the following:
   a. Remove the cotter pin from the pivot pin (A, **Figure 9**).
   b. Remove the footpeg (B, **Figure 9**) and washer from the bracket.
3. To remove the footpeg and bracket assembly, perform the following:
   a. Remove the bolts (C, **Figure 9**) securing the footpeg assembly to the frame.
   b. Remove the footpeg assembly (D, **Figure 9**).
4. Install by reversing these removal steps. Note the following.
5. Lubricate all pivot points prior to installation.

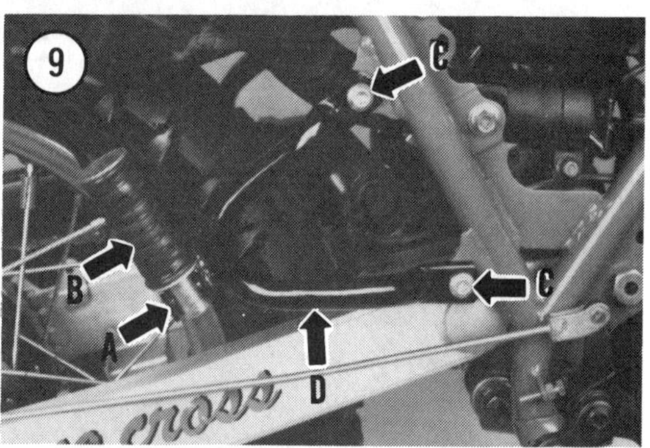

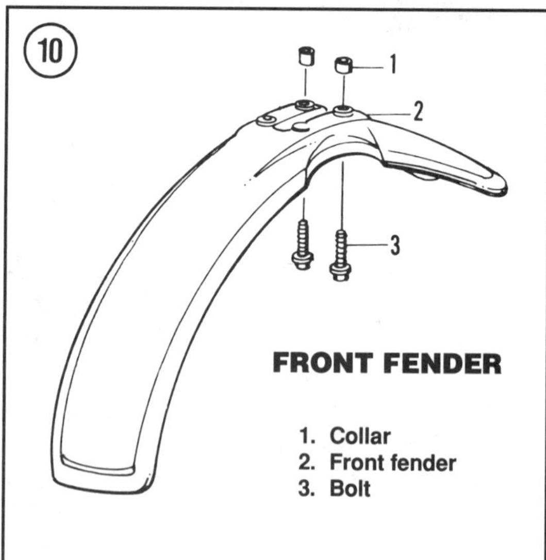

6. Tighten the rear brake pedal and footpeg assembly mounting bolts to the torque specification listed in **Table 1**.

7. Install new cotter pins and bend the ends over completely.

FENDERS

Front Fender Removal/Installation

Refer to **Figure 10** for this procedure.

1. Remove the front wheel as described under *Front Wheel Removal/Installation* in Chapter Ten.

2. Remove the bolts securing the front fender to the lower fork bridge.

3. Remove the front fender (**Figure 11**). Don't lose the metal collars in the mounting holes in the fender.

4. Install by reversing these removal steps. Note the following.

5. Be sure to install the metal collars in the fender mounting holes on each side. If the metal collars are not in place and the bolts are tightened, the fender mounting areas will be damaged and the fender will have to be replaced.

6. Apply a *small* amount of blue Loctite No. 242 to the fender mounting bolts prior to installation.

7. Tighten the bolts securing the fender securely. Don't overtighten the bolts as the fender mounting areas may be damaged even with the metal collars in place.

Rear Fender Removal/Installation

Refer to **Figure 12** for XT600 models or **Figure 13** for TT600 models for this procedure.

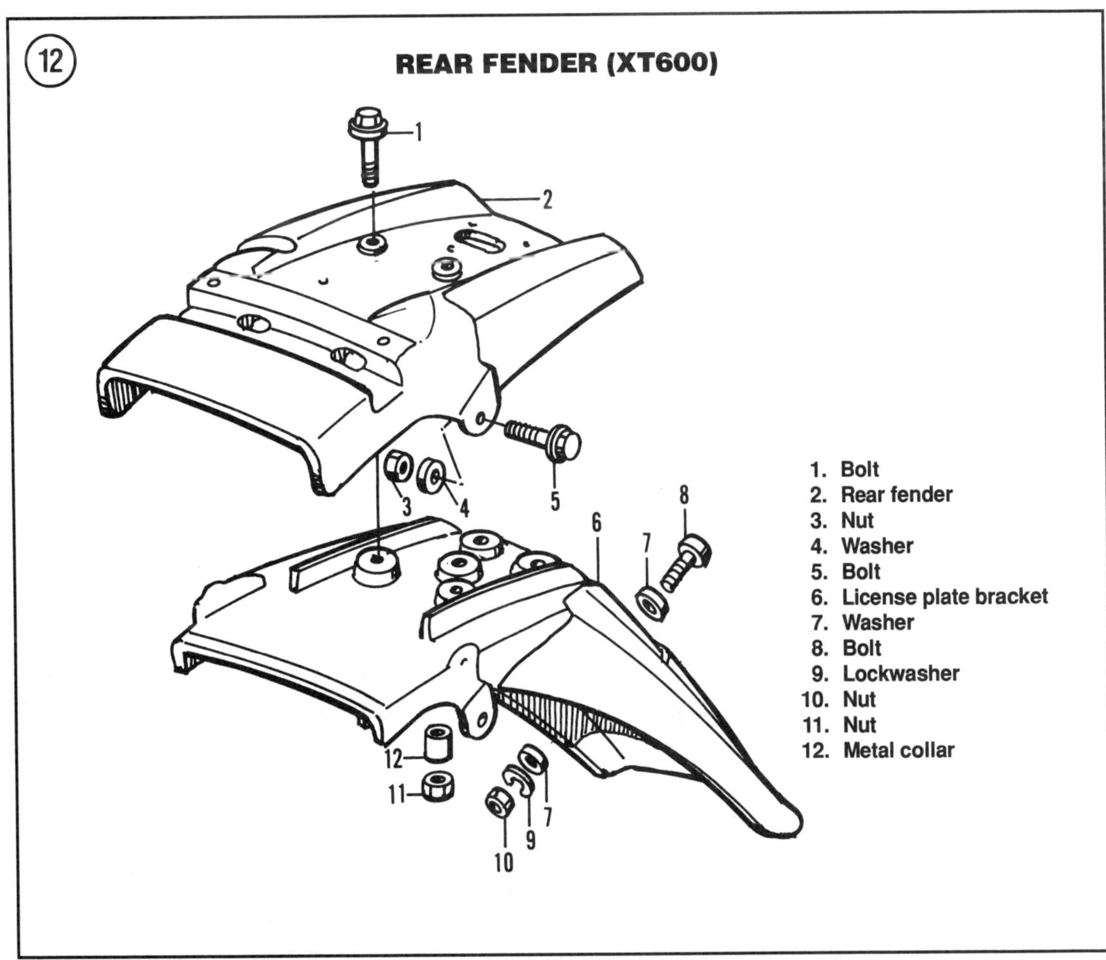

13

1. Remove the rear wheel as described under *Rear Wheel Removal/Installation* in Chapter Eleven.
2. Remove the seat and tool carrier (A, **Figure 14**) as described in this chapter.
3. Disconnect the electrical connector from the taillight assembly (B, **Figure 14**).
4A. On XT600 models, remove the bolts, washers, lockwashers and nuts securing the rear fender assembly (C, **Figure 14**) to the frame.
4B. On TT600 models, remove the bolts, washers and special washers securing the rear fender assembly to the frame.
5. On XT600 models, to remove the license plate bracket from the fender, perform the following:
   a. Remove the bolts and nuts securing the bracket to the rear fender and separate the 3 parts.
   b. Don't lose the metal collars in the license plate bracket mounting holes.
   c. Install by reversing these removal steps. Note the following.
   d. Be sure to install the metal collars in the license plate bracket mounting holes. If the metal collars are not in place and the bolts are tightened, the license plate bracket mounting areas will be damaged and the license plate bracket will have to be replaced.
6. Install by reversing these removal steps. Note the following.
7. Tighten the bolts and nuts securing the fender securely. Don't overtighten the nuts as the fender may be damaged.

SEAT

Removal/Installation

Refer to **Figure 15** for XT600 models or **Figure 16** for TT600 models for this procedure.

1. Place the bike on the sidestand.
2. Remove the frame right- and left-hand side covers (**Figure 17**).
3. Remove the bolts (**Figure 18**) securing the seat to the frame at the rear.
4. Lift up on the rear of the seat (**Figure 19**) and pull it toward the rear to release it from the locking tab on the frame at the front.
5. Remove the seat from the frame.
6. Install by reversing these removal steps. Note the following.
7. Be sure to push and lock the front of the seat into the locking tab at the front and make sure it is properly located. If the seat is not properly secured at the front it could swing to one side when riding the bike, resulting in a possible accident.
8. Make sure the bolts are installed correctly and tightened securely. If they should work loose and fall out, the seat will become loose and unstable resulting in a possible accident.

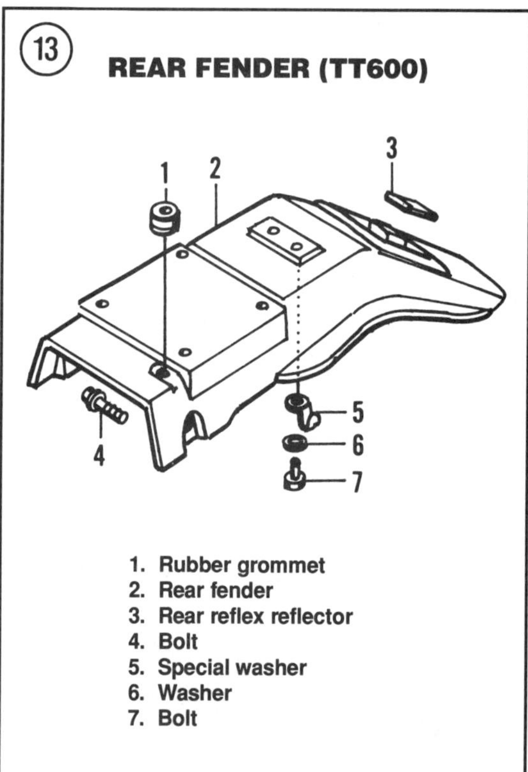

1. Rubber grommet
2. Rear fender
3. Rear reflex reflector
4. Bolt
5. Special washer
6. Washer
7. Bolt

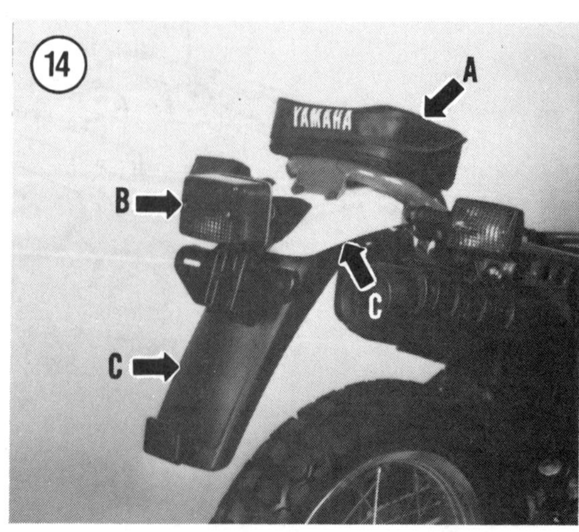

15

SEAT AND TOOL CARRIER (XT600)

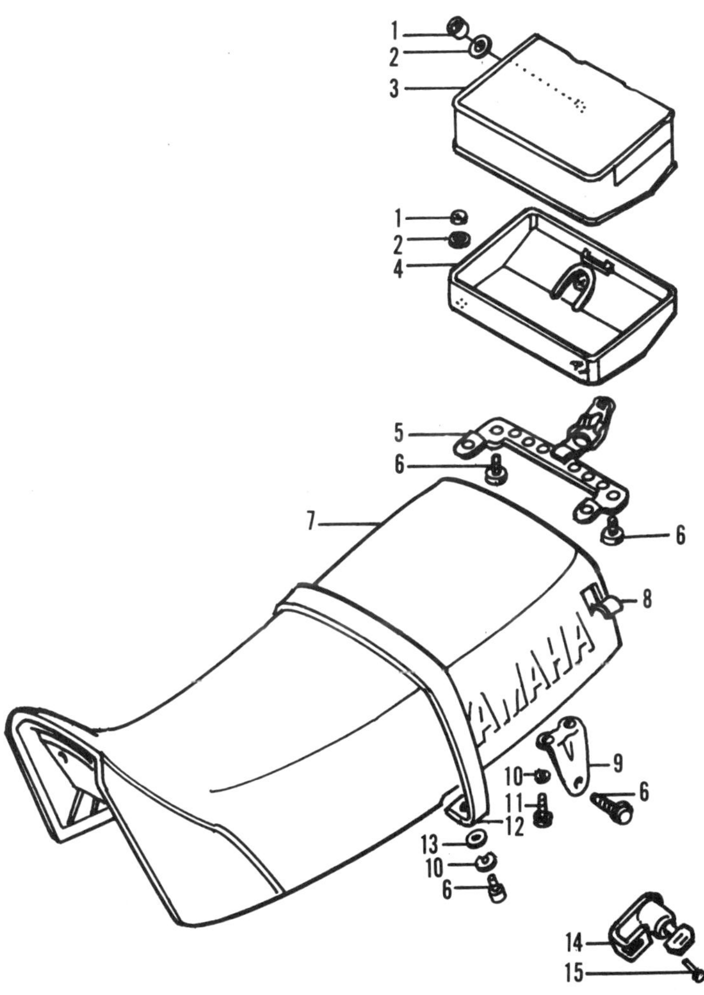

1. Nut
2. Washer
3. Cover
4. Tool carrier
5. Bracket
6. Bolt
7. Seat
8. Seat cover
9. Seat bracket
10. Washer
11. Bolt
12. Seat band
13. Washer
14. Helmet hanger/lock
15. Screw

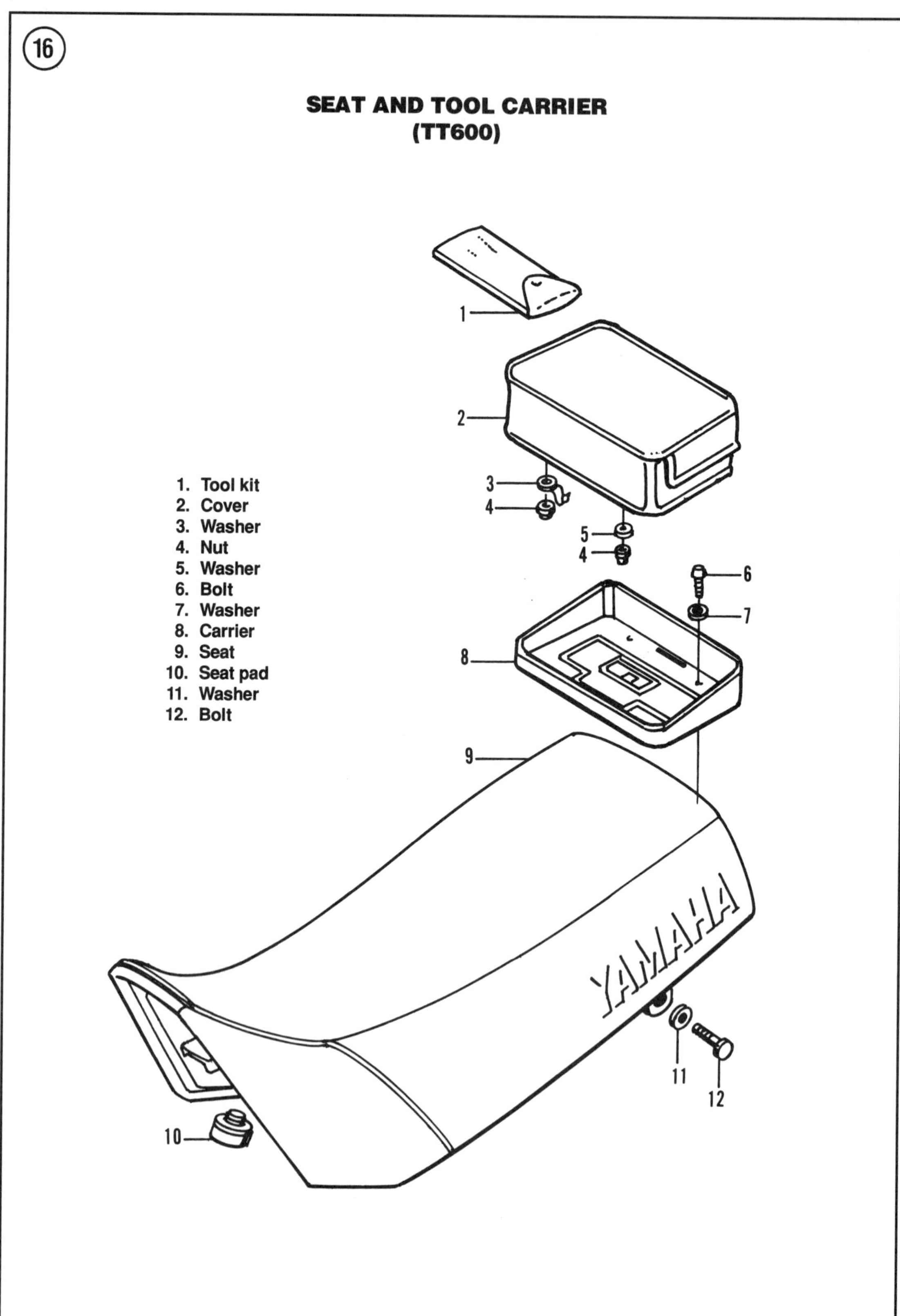
16
SEAT AND TOOL CARRIER
(TT600)
1. Tool kit
2. Cover
3. Washer
4. Nut
5. Washer
6. Bolt
7. Washer
8. Carrier
9. Seat
10. Seat pad
11. Washer
12. Bolt
1
2
3
4
5
4
6
7
8
9
YAMAHA
10
11
12

TOOL BOX

Removal/Installation

Refer to **Figure 15** for XT600 models or **Figure 16** for TT600 models for this procedure.

1. Remove the seat as described in this chapter.
2. Unzip the tool box cover and open it up.

17

18

19

3. Remove the bolts, washers and nuts securing the tool box to the carrier and bracket (XT600) or carrier and frame (TT600).
4. Install by reversing these removal steps. Note the following.
5. Tighten the bolts and nuts securely.

FRAME

The frame does not require routine maintenance. However, it should be inspected immediately after any accident or spill.

Component Removal/Installation

1. Remove both side covers and the seat as described in this chapter.
2. Remove the front and rear fender as described in this chapter.
3. Remove the fuel tank as described in Chapter Eight.
4. On XT600 models, remove the battery as described in Chapter Three.
5. Remove the instrument cluster as described in Chapter Nine.
6. Remove the hydraulic brake system flexible hose as described in Chapter Twelve.
7. Remove the wiring harness from the frame.
8. Remove the front wheel, handlebar, steering head and front forks as described in Chapter Ten.
9. Remove the rear wheel, shock absorber and swing arm as described in Chapter Eleven.
10. Remove the engine and transmission housing as described in Chapter Four.
11. Remove the steering head races from the steering head tube as described in Chapter Ten.
12. Inspect the frame for bends, cracks or other damage, especially around welded joints and areas that are rusted.
13. Assemble by reversing these removal steps.

Stripping and Painting

Remove all components from the frame. Thoroughly strip off all old paint. The best way is to have it sandblasted down to bare metal. If this is not possible, you can use a liquid paint remover and steel wool and a fine, hard wire brush.

CAUTION
Some of the fenders, side covers, frame covers and air box are molded plastic. If your wish to change the color of these parts, consult an automotive paint supplier for the proper procedure. Do not use any liquid paint remover on these components as it will damage the surface. The color is an integral part of some of these components and cannot be removed.

When the frame is down to bare metal, have it inspected for hairline and internal cracks. Magnaflux is the most common and complete process.

Make sure that the primer is compatible with the type of paint you are going to use for the finish color. Spray on one or two coats of primer as smoothly as possible. Let it dry thoroughly and use a fine grade of wet sandpaper (400-600 grit) to remove any flaws. Carefully wipe the surface clean and then spray a couple of coats of the final color. Use either lacquer or enamel base paint and follow the manufacturer's instructions.

A shop specializing in painting will probably do the best job. However, you can do a surprisingly good job with a good grade of spray paint. Spend a few extra dollars and get a good grade of paint as it will make a difference in how well it looks and how long it will stand up. It's a good idea to shake the can and make sure the ball inside the can is loose when you purchase the can of paint. Shake the can as long as is stated on the can. Then immerse the can *upright* in a pot or bucket of *warm* water (not hot—not over 120° F).

WARNING
Higher temperatures could cause the can to burst. ***Do not*** *place the can in direct contact with any flame or heat source.*

Leave the can in the water for several minutes. When thoroughly warmed, shake the can again and spray the frame. Be sure to get into all the crevices where there may be rust problems. Several light mist coats are better than one heavy coat. Spray painting is best done in temperatures of 70-80° F (21-26° C); any temperature above or below this will give you problems.

After the final coat has dried completely, at least 48 hours, any overspray or orange peel may be removed with a *light* application of Dupont rubbing compound (red color) and finished with Dupont polishing compound (white color). Be careful not to rub too hard or you will go through the finish. Finish off with a couple coats of good wax prior to reassembling all the components.

It's a good idea to keep the frame touched up with fresh paint if any minor rust spots, chips or scratches appear.

Table 1 FRAME AND BODY TIGHTENING TORQUES

Item	N•m	ft.-lb.
Brake pedal/footpeg assembly mounting bolts	45	32

INDEX

V

W

WIRING DIAGRAMS

1984-1989 XT600 AND XT600C

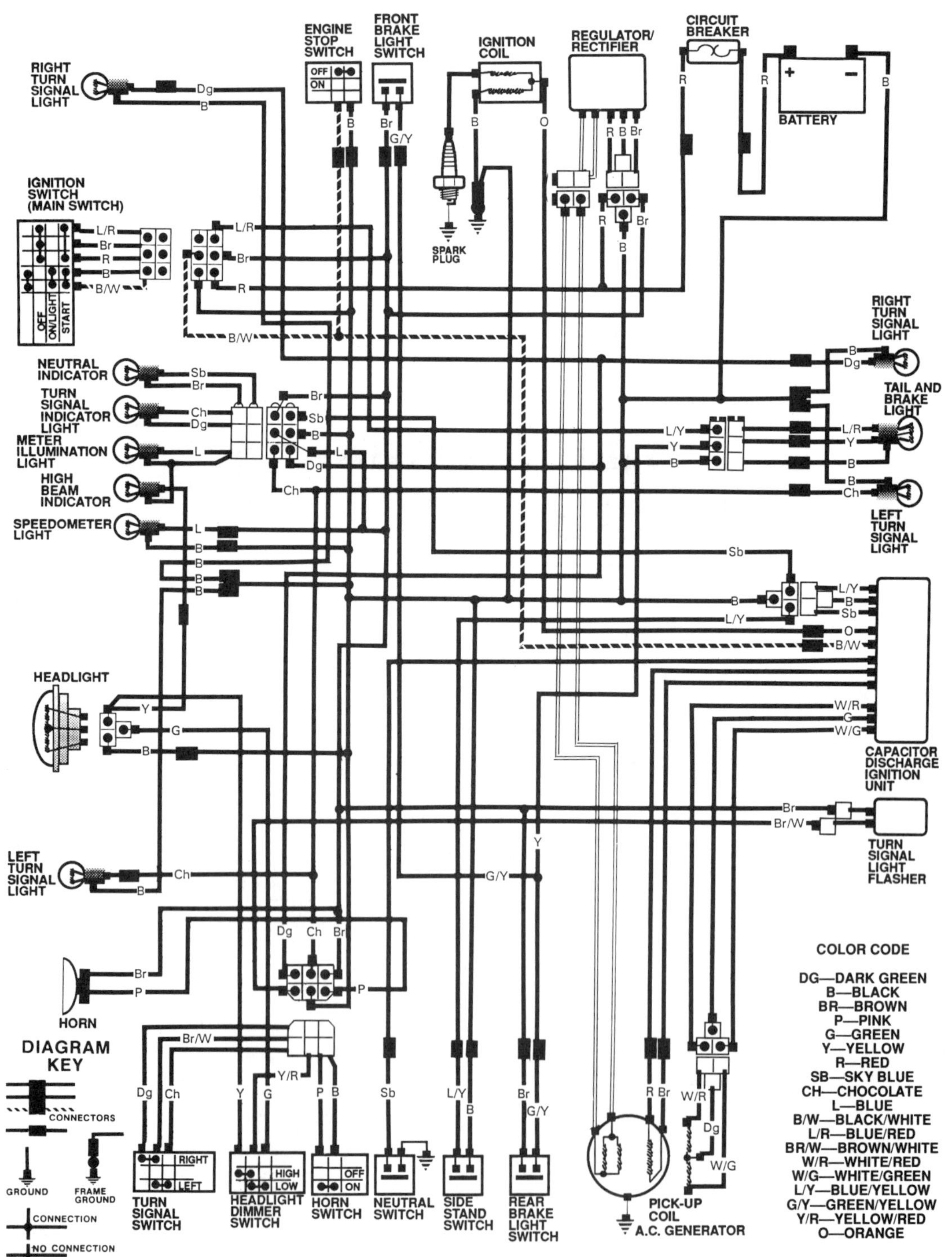

1983-1984 TT600

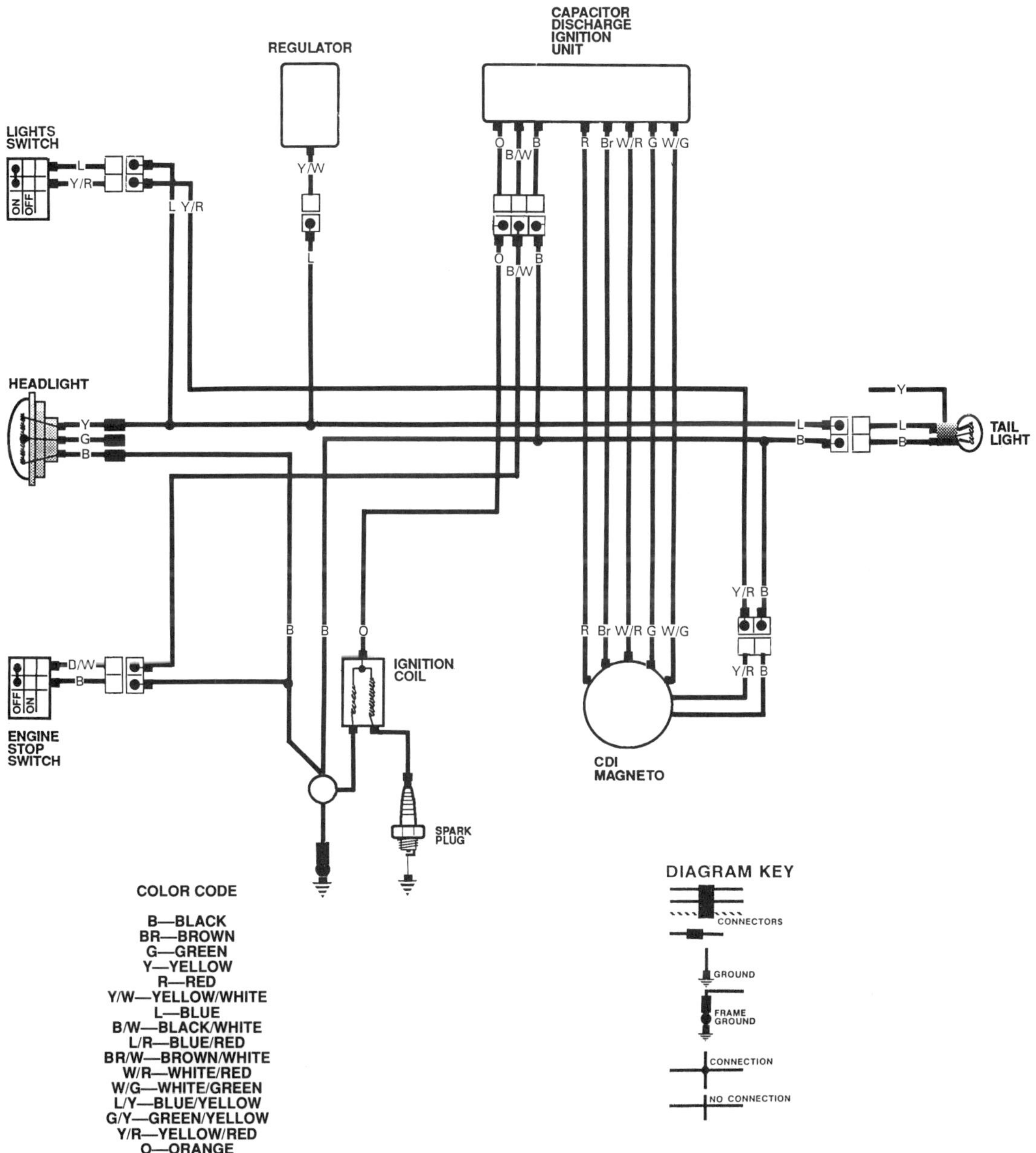

1985-1986 TT600

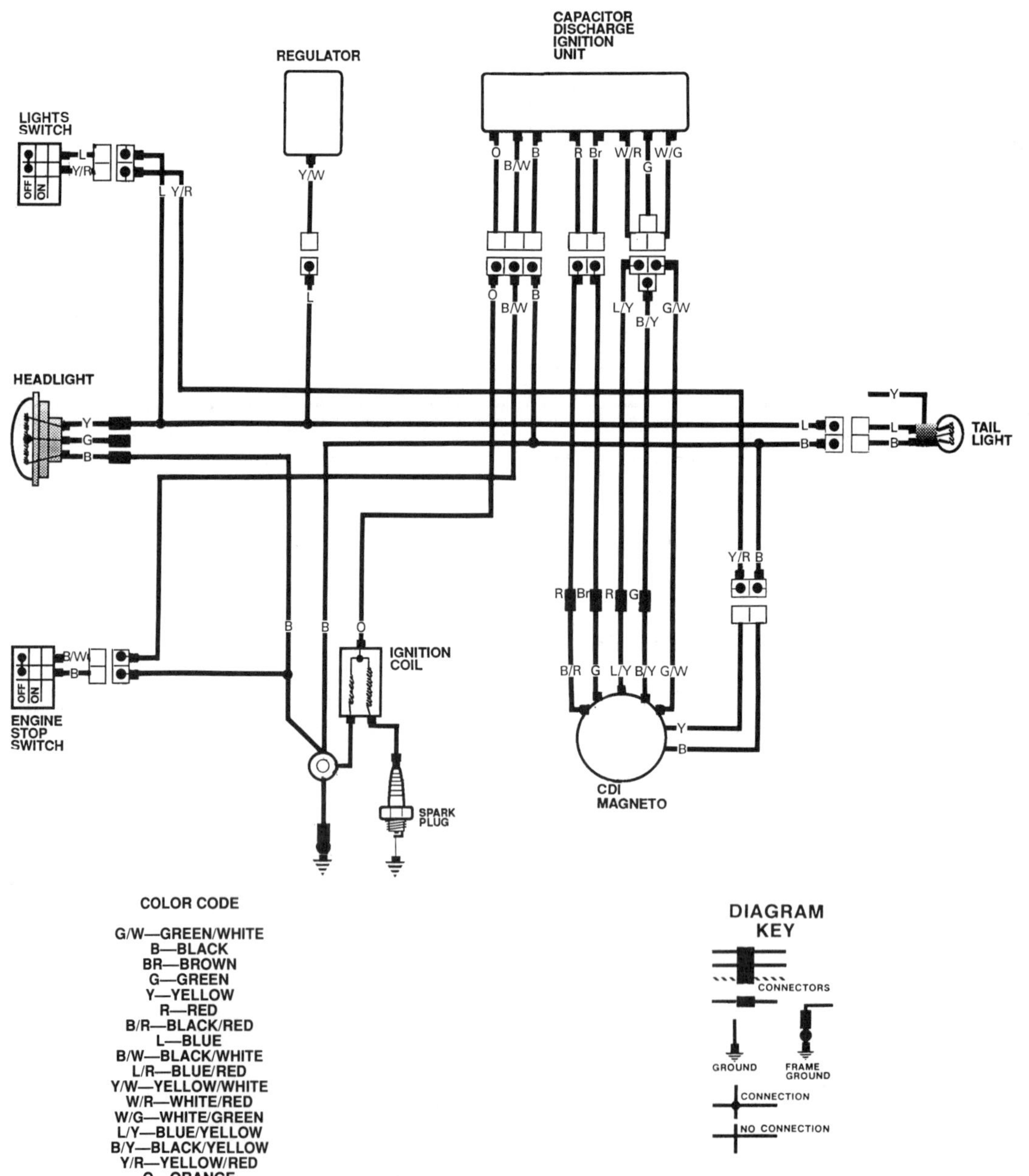

NOTES

NOTES

NOTES

NOTES

NOTES

MAINTENANCE LOG

Service Performed

Oil change (example)					